Handbook of Research on Applications and Implementations of Machine Learning Techniques

Sathiyamoorthi Velayutham
Sona College of Technology, India

A volume in the Advances in Computational
Intelligence and Robotics (ACIR) Book Series

Published in the United States of America by
    IGI Global
    Engineering Science Reference (an imprint of IGI Global)
    701 E. Chocolate Avenue
    Hershey PA, USA 17033
    Tel: 717-533-8845
    Fax: 717-533-8661
    E-mail: cust@igi-global.com
    Web site: http://www.igi-global.com

Library of Congress Cataloging-in-Publication Data

Names: Velayutham, Sathiyamoorthi, 1983- author.
Title: Handbook of research on applications and implementations of machine learning
  techniques / Sathiyamoorthi Velayutham, editor.
Description: Hershey, PA : Engineering Science Reference, [2020] | Includes
  bibliographical references.
Identifiers: LCCN 2019011988| ISBN 9781522599029 (h/c) | ISBN 9781522599043
  (eISBN) | ISBN 9781522599036 (s/c)
Subjects: LCSH: Machine learning--Industrial applications.
Classification: LCC Q325.5 .P73 2020 | DDC 006.3/1--dc23 LC record available at https://lccn.loc.gov/2019011988

This book is published in the IGI Global book series Advances in Computational Intelligence and Robotics (ACIR) (ISSN: 2327-0411; eISSN: 2327-042X)

British Cataloguing in Publication Data
A Cataloguing in Publication record for this book is available from the British Library.

For electronic access to this publication, please contact: eresources@igi-global.com.

Advances in Computational Intelligence and Robotics (ACIR) Book Series

Ivan Giannoccaro
University of Salento, Italy

ISSN:2327-0411
EISSN:2327-042X

MISSION

While intelligence is traditionally a term applied to humans and human cognition, technology has progressed in such a way to allow for the development of intelligent systems able to simulate many human traits. With this new era of simulated and artificial intelligence, much research is needed in order to continue to advance the field and also to evaluate the ethical and societal concerns of the existence of artificial life and machine learning.

The **Advances in Computational Intelligence and Robotics (ACIR) Book Series** encourages scholarly discourse on all topics pertaining to evolutionary computing, artificial life, computational intelligence, machine learning, and robotics. ACIR presents the latest research being conducted on diverse topics in intelligence technologies with the goal of advancing knowledge and applications in this rapidly evolving field.

COVERAGE

- Adaptive and Complex Systems
- Fuzzy Systems
- Artificial Life
- Computational Logic
- Evolutionary computing
- Artificial Intelligence
- Intelligent control
- Machine Learning
- Algorithmic Learning
- Cyborgs

IGI Global is currently accepting manuscripts for publication within this series. To submit a proposal for a volume in this series, please contact our Acquisition Editors at Acquisitions@igi-global.com or visit: http://www.igi-global.com/publish/.

Titles in this Series

For a list of additional titles in this series, please visit: www.igi-global.com/book-series

Edge Computing and Computational Intelligence Paradigms for the IoT
G. Nagarajan (Sathyabama Institute of Science and Technology, India) and R.I. Minu (SRM Institute of Science and Technology, India)
Engineering Science Reference • ©2019 • 347pp • H/C (ISBN: 9781522585558) • US $285.00

Semiotic Perspectives in Evolutionary Psychology, Artificial Intelligence, and the Study of Mind Emerging Research and Opportunities
Marcel Danesi (University of Toronto, Canada)
Information Science Reference • ©2019 • 205pp • H/C (ISBN: 9781522589242) • US $175.00

Handbook of Research on Human-Computer Interfaces and New Modes of Interactivity
Katherine Blashki (Victorian Institute of Technology, Australia) and Pedro Isaías (The University of Queensland, Australia)
Engineering Science Reference • ©2019 • 488pp • H/C (ISBN: 9781522590699) • US $275.00

Machine Learning and Cognitive Science Applications in Cyber Security
Muhammad Salman Khan (University of Manitoba, Canada)
Information Science Reference • ©2019 • 321pp • H/C (ISBN: 9781522581000) • US $235.00

Multi-Criteria Decision-Making Models for Website Evaluation
Kemal Vatansever (Alanya Alaaddin Keykubat University, Turkey) and Yakup Akgül (Alanya Alaaddin Keykubat University, Turkey)
Engineering Science Reference • ©2019 • 254pp • H/C (ISBN: 9781522582380) • US $185.00

Handbook of Research on Deep Learning Innovations and Trends
Aboul Ella Hassanien (Cairo University, Egypt) Ashraf Darwish (Helwan University, Egypt) and Chiranji Lal Chowdhary (VIT University, India)
Engineering Science Reference • ©2019 • 355pp • H/C (ISBN: 9781522578628) • US $295.00

Computational Intelligence in the Internet of Things
Hindriyanto Dwi Purnomo (Satya Wacana Christian University, Indonesia)
Engineering Science Reference • ©2019 • 342pp • H/C (ISBN: 9781522579557) • US $225.00

701 East Chocolate Avenue, Hershey, PA 17033, USA
Tel: 717-533-8845 x100 • Fax: 717-533-8661
E-Mail: cust@igi-global.com • www.igi-global.com

List of Contributors

Table of Contents

Detailed Table of Contents

Chapter 1
Aswathy M. A., VIT University, India
Jagannath Mohan, VIT Chennai, India

As per the latest health ministry registries of 2017-2018, breast cancer among women has ranked number one in India and number two in United States. Despite the fact that breast cancer affects men also, pervasiveness is lower in men than women. This is the reason breast cancer is such a vital concern among ladies. Roughly 80% of cancer malignancies emerge from epithelial cells inside breast tissues. In breast cancer spectrum, ductal carcinoma in situ (DCIS) and invasive ductal carcinoma (IDC) are considered malignant cancers that need treatment and care. This chapter mainly deals with breast cancer and machine learning (ML) applications. All through this chapter, different issues related to breast cancer prognosis and early detection and diagnostic techniques using various ML algorithms are addressed.

Chapter 2
Sangeetha K. N., JSS Academy of Technical Education Bangalore, India
Usha B. Ajay, BMS Institute of Technology and Management, India

The chances of data getting lost while it is being transferred between the sender and receiver is very high these days. Since these data are very sensitive whose security cannot be compromised, there is a need for highly secure systems to transfer the data without compromising the content and the quality. Steganography techniques help us to achieve these objectives. In the present time, various organizations and industries are using cover image arbitrarily. In such cases, it does not provide personalized approach to the whole process of data hiding. Thus, as a result of this limitation, there is motivation to build such an application in which the system selects which image is most suitable for hiding data accordingly. The main algorithm being used here is the regression algorithm which consists of other algorithms like linear regression, decision tree regression. This application also extracts the hidden data from the generated stego image.

Venu K., Kongu Engineering College, India
Natesan Palanisamy, Kongu Engineering College, India
Krishnakumar B., Kongu Engineering College, India
Sasipriyaa N., Kongu Engineering College, India

Early detection of disease in the plant leads to an early treatment and reduction in the economic loss considerably. Recent development has introduced deep learning based convolutional neural network for detecting the diseases in the images accurately using image classification techniques. In the chapter, CNN is supplied with the input image. In each convolutional layer of CNN, features are extracted and are transferred to the next pooling layer. Finally, all the features which are extracted from convolution layers are concatenated and formed as input to the fully-connected layer of state-of-the-art architecture and then output class will be predicted by the model. The model is evaluated for three different datasets such as grape, pepper, and peach leaves. It is observed from the experimental results that the accuracy of the model obtained for grape, pepper, peach datasets are 74%, 69%, 84%, respectively.

Dhayanithi Jaganathan, Sona College of Technology, India
Akilandeswari Jeyapal, Sona College of Technology, India

In recent days, researchers are doing research studies for clustering of data which are heterogeneous in nature. The data generated in many real-world applications like data form IoT environments and big data domains are heterogeneous in nature. Most of the available clustering algorithms deal with data in homogeneous nature, and there are few algorithms discussed in the literature to deal the data with numeric and categorical nature. Applying the clustering algorithm used by homogenous data to the heterogeneous data leads to information loss. This chapter proposes a new genetically-modified k-medoid clustering algorithm (GMODKMD) which takes fused distance matrix as input that adopts from applying individual distance measures for each attribute based on its characteristics. The GMODKMD is a modified algorithm where Davies Boudlin index is applied in the iteration phase. The proposed algorithm is compared with existing techniques based on accuracy. The experimental result shows that the modified algorithm with fused distance matrix outperforms the existing clustering technique.

R. Murugan, National Institute of Technology Silchar, India

The retinal parts segmentation has been recognized as a key component in both ophthalmological and cardiovascular sickness analysis. The parts of retinal pictures, vessels, optic disc, and macula segmentations, will add to the indicative outcome. In any case, the manual segmentation of retinal parts is tedious and dreary work, and it additionally requires proficient aptitudes. This chapter proposes a supervised method to segment blood vessel utilizing deep learning methods. All the more explicitly, the proposed part has connected the completely convolutional network, which is normally used to perform semantic segmentation undertaking with exchange learning. The convolutional neural system has turned out to be an amazing asset for a few computer vision assignments. As of late, restorative picture investigation bunches over the world are rapidly entering this field and applying convolutional neural systems and other deep learning philosophies to a wide assortment of uses, and uncommon outcomes are rising constantly.

Chapter 6

C. Helen Sulochana, St. Xavier's Catholic College of Engineering, India
S. A. Praylin Selva Blessy, Bethlahem Institute of Engineering, India

Brain tumor is a mass of abnormal growth of cells in the brain which disturbs the normal functioning of the brain. MRI is a powerful diagnostic tool providing excellent soft tissue contrast and high spatial resolution. However, imperfections arising in the radio frequency field and scanner-related intensity artifacts in MRI produce intensity inhomogeneity. These intensity variations pose major challenges for subsequent image processing and analysis techniques. To mitigate this effect in the intensity correction process, an enhanced homomorphic unsharp masking (EHUM) method is proposed in this chapter. The main idea of the proposed EHUM method is determination of region of interest, intensity correction based on homomorphic filtering, and linear gray scale mapping followed by cutoff frequency selection of low pass filter used in the filtering process. This method first determines the ROI to overcome the halo effect between foreground and background regions. Then the intensity correction is carried out using homomorphic filtering and linear gray scale mapping.

Chapter 7

Mamata Rath, Birla Global University, India

Electronic commerce associated with highly powerful web technology and mobile communication is currently dominating the business world. Current advancements in machine learning (ML) have also further coordinated to creative business applications and e-commerce administrations to reason about complex system and better solutions. In the course of recent years, the business security and machine-learning networks have created novel strategies for secured business frameworks based on computationally learned models. With the improvement of the internet and digital marketing, every financial platform has been more secured and user friendly for monetary transactions.

Chapter 8

Astha Baranwal, VIT University, India
Bhagyashree R. Bagwe, VIT University, India
Vanitha M, VIT University, India

Diabetes is a disease of the modern world. The modern lifestyle has led to unhealthy eating habits causing type 2 diabetes. Machine learning has gained a lot of popularity in the recent days. It has applications in various fields and has proven to be increasingly effective in the medical field. The purpose of this chapter is to predict the diabetes outcome of a person based on other factors or attributes. Various machine learning algorithms like logistic regression (LR), tuned and not tuned random forest (RF), and multilayer perceptron (MLP) have been used as classifiers for diabetes prediction. This chapter also presents a comparative study of these algorithms based on various performance metrics like accuracy, sensitivity, specificity, and F1 score.

Chapter 9

Sumathi S., St. Joseph's College of Engineering, India
Indumathi S., Jerusalem College of Engineering, India
Rajkumar S., HCL Technologies Ltd., India

Text classification in medical domain could result in an easier way of handling large volumes of medical data. They can be segregated depending on the type of diseases, which can be determined by extracting the decisive key texts from the original document. Due to various nuances present in understanding language in general, a requirement of large volumes of text-based data is required for algorithms to learn patterns properly. The problem with existing systems such as MedScape, MedLinePlus, Wrappin, and MedHunt is that they involve human interaction and high time consumption in handling a large volume of data. By employing automation in this proposed field, the large involvement of manpower could be removed which in turn speeds up the process of classification of the medical documents by which the shortage of medical technicians in third world countries are addressed.

Chapter 10

Logeswaran K., Kongu Engineering College, India
Suresh P., Kongu Engineering College, India
Savitha S., K. S. R. College of Engineering, India
Prasanna Kumar K. R., Kongu Engineering College, India

In recent years, the data analysts are facing many challenges in high utility itemset (HUI) mining from given transactional database using existing traditional techniques. The challenges in utility mining algorithms are exponentially growing search space and the minimum utility threshold appropriate to the given database. To overcome these challenges, evolutionary algorithm-based techniques can be used to mine the HUI from transactional database. However, testing each of the supporting functions in the optimization problem is very inefficient and it increases the time complexity of the algorithm. To overcome this drawback, reinforcement learning-based approach is proposed for improving the efficiency of the algorithm, and the most appropriate fitness function for evaluation can be selected automatically during execution of an algorithm. Furthermore, during the optimization process when distinct functions are skillful, dynamic selection of current optimal function is done.

Chapter 11

Anitha N., Kongu Engineering College, India
Devi Priya R., Kongu Engineering College, India

Prediction of risk during surgical operations is one of the most needed and challenging processes in the healthcare domain. Many researchers use clinical assessment tools to predict perioperative outcomes and postoperative factors in surgical operations. Even though traditional model yields better results, they are not able to achieve promising accuracy due to the enormous growth of data in medical domain. Since the data size grows seamlessly every day, some of the investigators over the past decade use machine learning techniques in their model to predict the risks before and after surgery. Most of the existing systems produced better accuracy by impute missing values in dataset through some common imputation method. However, in order to increase the accuracy level further, two new techniques proposed in this chapter to handle missing values using iterative deepening random forest classifier and identification of surgical risk by using iterative deepening support vector machine. Both of the methods worked well in experimental data set and obtained promising accuracy results.

Chapter 12

Divya Asok, Thiagarajar College of Engineering, India
Chitra P., Thiagarajar College of Engineering, India
Bharathiraja Muthurajan, Indian Institute of Technology Madras, India

In the past years, the usage of internet and quantity of digital data generated by large organizations, firms, and governments have paved the way for the researchers to focus on security issues of private data. This collected data is usually related to a definite necessity. For example, in the medical field, health record systems are used for the exchange of medical data. In addition to services based on users' current location, many potential services rely on users' location history or their spatial-temporal provenance. However, most of the collected data contain data identifying individual which is sensitive. With the increase of machine learning applications around every corner of the society, it could significantly contribute to the preservation of privacy of both individuals and institutions. This chapter gives a wider perspective on the current literature on privacy ML and deep learning techniques, along with the non-cryptographic differential privacy approach for ensuring sensitive data privacy.

Chapter 13

Kannimuthu Subramanian, Karpagam College of Engineering, India
Swathypriyadharsini P., Bannari Amman Institute of Technology, India
Gunavathi C., VIT University, India
Premalatha K., Bannari Amman Institute of Technology, India

Dengue is fast emerging pandemic-prone viral disease in many parts of the world. Dengue flourishes in urban areas, suburbs, and the countryside, but also affects more affluent neighborhoods in tropical and subtropical countries. Dengue is a mosquito-borne viral infection causing a severe flu-like illness and sometimes causing a potentially deadly complication called severe dengue. It is a major public health problem in India. Accurate and timely forecasts of dengue incidence in India are still lacking. In this chapter, the state-of-the-art machine learning algorithms are used to develop an accurate predictive model of dengue. Several machine learning algorithms are used as candidate models to predict dengue incidence. Performance and goodness of fit of the models were assessed, and it is found that the optimized SVR gives minimal RMSE 0.25. The classifiers are applied, and experiment results show that the extreme boost and random forest gives 93.65% accuracy.

Chapter 14

Senbagavalli M., Alliance University Bangalore, India
Sathiyamoorthi V., Sona College of Technology, India
D. Sudaroli Vijayakumar, Alliance University Bangalore, India

Deep learning is an artificial intelligence function that reproduces the mechanisms of the human mind in processing records and evolving shapes to be used in selection construction. The main objective of this chapter is to provide a complete examination of deep learning algorithms and its applications in various fields. Deep learning has detonated in the public alertness, primarily as inspective and analytical products fill our world, in the form of numerous human-centered smart-world systems, with besieged advertisements, natural language supporters and interpreters, and prototype self-driving vehicle systems. Therefore, it provides a broad orientation for those seeking a primer on deep learning algorithms and its various applications, platforms, and uses in a variety of smart-world systems. Also, this survey delivers a precious orientation for new deep learning practitioners, as well as those seeking to innovate in the application of deep learning.

Sathya D., Kumaraguru College of Technology, India
Sudha V., Kumaraguru College of Technology, India
Jagadeesan D., Cherraan's Arts Science College, India

Machine learning is an approach of artificial intelligence (AI) where the machine can automatically learn and improve its performance on experience. It is not explicitly programmed; the data is fed into the generic algorithm and it builds logic based on the data provided. Traditional algorithms have to define new rules or massive rules when the pattern varies or the number of patterns increases, which reduces the accuracy or efficiency of the algorithms. But the machine learning algorithms learn new input patterns capable of handling complex situations while maintaining accuracy and efficiency. Due to its effectual benefits, machine learning algorithms are used in various domains like healthcare, industries, travel, game development, social media services, robotics, and surveillance and information security. In this chapter, the application of machine learning technique in healthcare is discussed in detail.

Bhushan Patil, Mumbai University, India
Manisha Vohra, Mumbai University, India

Neural networks are very useful and are proving to be very beneficial in various fields. Biomedical applications such as breast cancer image classification, differentiating between the malignant and benign type of breast cancer, etc. are now seen to be making use of neural networks rapidly. Neural networks are showing remarkable results of their effectiveness in these biomedical applications and are proving to be immensely profitable. Another field such as agriculture, which is a very crucial field for survival of human life, can be benefitted from neural networks. Likewise, various fields can gain enormous benefits from the usage of neural networks. This chapter shall explain neural networks in detail. Also, the authors shall provide a brief and detailed insight of the contribution of neural networks in different applications, along with its analysis.

Shaila S. G., Dayananda Sagar University, India
Sunanda Rajkumari, Dayananda Sagar University, India
Vadivel Ayyasamy, SRM University AP Amaravati, India

Deep learning is playing vital role with greater success in various applications, such as digital image processing, human-computer interaction, computer vision and natural language processing, robotics, biological applications, etc. Unlike traditional machine learning approaches, deep learning has effective ability of learning and makes better use of data set for feature extraction. Because of its repetitive learning ability, deep learning has become more popular in the present-day research works.

Chapter 18

Arul Murugan R., Sona College of Technology, India
Sathiyamoorthi V., Sona College of Technology, India

Machine learning (ML) is one of the exciting sub-fields of artificial intelligence (AI). The term machine learning is generally stated as the ability to learn without being explicitly programmed. In recent years, machine learning has become one of the thrust areas of research across various business verticals. The technical advancements in the field of big data have provided the ability to gain access over large volumes of diversified data at ease. This massive amount of data can be processed at high speeds in a reasonable amount of time with the help of emerging hardware capabilities. Hence the machine learning algorithms have been the most effective at leveraging all of big data to provide near real-time solutions even for the complex business problems. This chapter aims in giving a solid introduction to various widely adopted machine learning techniques and its applications categorized into supervised, unsupervised, and reinforcement and will serve a simplified guide for the aspiring data and machine learning enthusiasts.

Chapter 19

Shaila S. G., Dayananda Sagar University, India
Vadivel A., SRM University AP, India
Naksha V., Dayananda Sagar University, India

Today, artificial intelligence is a technology which is completely advanced and very fast growingIt has a very strong and significant influence in our daily lives. Artificial intelligence have created tools and techniques linked to various disciplines such as computational logic, the theory of the probability, the theory of the decision, management science, linguistics and philosophy, etc. This technical area is a standout amongst the new fields in science and designing.

Chapter 20

Karthikeyan P., Presidency University Bangalore, India
Karunakaran Velswamy, Karunya Institute of Technology and Sciences, India
Pon Harshavardhanan, VIT Bhopal, India
Rajagopal R., Vel Tech Multi Tech Dr. Rangarajan Dr. Sakunthala Engineering College,
India
JeyaKrishnan V., Saintgits College of Engineering, India
Velliangiri S., CMR Institute of Technology, India

Machine learning is the part of artificial intelligence that makes machines learn without being expressly programmed. Machine learning application built the modern world. Machine learning techniques are mainly classified into three techniques: supervised, unsupervised, and semi-supervised. Machine learning is an interdisciplinary field, which can be joined in different areas including science, business, and research. Supervised techniques are applied in agriculture, email spam, malware filtering, online fraud detection, optical character recognition, natural language processing, and face detection. Unsupervised techniques are applied in market segmentation and sentiment analysis and anomaly detection. Deep learning is being utilized in sound, image, video, time series, and text. This chapter covers applications of various machine learning techniques, social media, agriculture, and task scheduling in a distributed system.

### Chapter 21

Machine learning provides the system to automatically learn without human intervention and improve their performance with the help of previous experience. It can access the data and use it for learning by itself. Even though many algorithms are developed to solve machine learning issues, it is difficult to handle all kinds of inputs data in-order to arrive at accurate decisions. The domain knowledge of statistical science, probability, logic, mathematical optimization, reinforcement learning, and control theory plays a major role in developing machine learning based algorithms. The key consideration in selecting a suitable programming language for implementing machine learning algorithm includes performance, concurrence, application development, learning curve. This chapter deals with few of the top programming languages used for developing machine learning applications. They are Python, R, and Java. Top three programming languages preferred by data scientist are (1) Python more than 57%, (2) R more than 31%, and (3) Java used by 17% of the data scientists.

Preface

The *Handbook of Research on Applications and Implementations of Machine Learning Techniques* provides an overview of recent research and development activities in the field of machine learning systems along with its applications. This book contains 21chapters starting from basic concept level to research and application level.

The main objective of machine learning is used to understand the structure of data and fit the data into a model that can be well understood and utilized by people depending on their needs. Although machine learning is a field within the computer science domain, it differs from traditional computing where human is involved. In traditional computing, techniques are sets of explicitly programmed instructions used by computers to calculate or solve problem whereas machine learning techniques instead allow for computers to train on data inputs and use statistical analysis in order to output values that fall within a specific range. Because of this, machine learning facilitates computers in building models from sample data in order to automate decision-making processes based on data inputs. Any technology user today has benefited from machine learning. Some of the applications are,

- Facial recognition technology allows social media platforms to help users tag and share photos of friends.
- Optical character recognition (OCR) technology converts images of text into movable type.
- Recommendation engines, powered by machine learning, suggest what movies or television shows to watch next based on user preferences.
- Self-driving cars that rely on machine learning to navigate may soon be available to consumers.

Therefore, machine learning is an emerging area in computing field. Because of this, there are some considerations to keep in mind as you work with machine learning methodologies, or analyze the impact of machine learning processes. Therefore, contributions in this book aim to enrich the information system discipline by providing latest research and case studies from all around the world.

All the books published earlier by different authors only address on theoretical study of machine learning in any one application areas or it does not address the practical applications / implementation of various machine learning techniques in various fields like agriculture, medical, Image processing, networking etc. Hence, it is decided to propose a book which not only discusses the research issues in various domains, also solve those problems with help of machine learning. It also provides research insight into machine learning areas. This book also focuses on three categories of users such as beginners, intermediate, sophisticated readers and provides content accordingly. So this is very much useful for students, academicians and research scholars to explore further in their field of study. It is very much opt for readers who seeking learning from examples.

This book, *Handbook of Research on Applications and Implementations of Machine Learning Techniques*, is a reference text. It is a collection of 21 chapters, authored by 55 academics and practitioners from all around the world. The contributions in this book aim to enrich the information system discipline by providing latest research and case studies from around the world. These are organized as follows,

Chapter 1: Machine Learning (ML) is one of the hottest fields in research prospective. ML is acquiring wide level acceptance owing to the variety of real-life applications that can be implemented using different ML techniques. ML is unique in its feature of gathering knowledge from various fields like pattern recognition, data mining, statistics, signal processing etc. Hence, ML is not a new science topic but it is a multidisciplinary research topic. The key objective of this chapter is to present the current researches on the machine learning applications and its novel paradigms towards the detection of breast cancer. This chapter gives an idea of the applications of various machine learning techniques for the computer assisted diagnosis of breast cancer. This chapter comprises of various sections. Section one provides the introduction and background of breast cancer including structure of the breast, information about biopsy and different screening methods. The next section explains the computer assisted analysis of breast cancer using various ML techniques. Finally, this chapter discusses about future scope for the research in this area. This chapter will be informative for researchers, experts and students who are fascinated in the area of machine learning techniques for breast cancer detection.

Chapter 2: Information Security is one of the key areas for protecting information in the case of availability, data integrity, and privacy. The purpose of information security is to protect the information from illegal use and unauthorized access. In order to gain the most benefit from information security it must be applied to the business as a whole. Image steganography provides the solution to attain Information Security. Applying Cognitive method for selecting right image for Hiding Data is one of the challenges which is attained in this chapter.

Chapter 3: Agriculture is one of the most important fields to be concentrated for the welfare of the nation. In order to provide good yield in the field of agriculture, identifying the type of the disease in the leaf plays an important role. There are several algorithms and architectures available for classification. Convolutional Neural Network is widely used architecture for computer vision applications. This architecture is widely used in many applications such as video recognition, medical image analysis, agricultural data and image analysis etc., This chapter will explain the working of convolutional neural network for identifying the type of the disease in the plant leaves.

Chapter 4: In recent days, researchers are doing research studies for clustering of data which are heterogeneous in nature. The data generated in many real world applications like data form IoT environments and big data domains are heterogeneous in nature. Most of the available clustering algorithm is deals with data in homogeneous nature and there are few algorithms discussed in the literature to deal the data with numeric and categorical nature. Applying the clustering algorithm used by homogenous data to the heterogeneous data it leads to information loss. This paper proposes a new Genetically Modified K-Mediod clustering Algorithm (GMODKMD) which takes Fused Distance Matrix as input that adopts from applying individual distance measures for each attributes based on its characteristics. The GMOD-KMD is modified algorithm where Davies Boudlin Index is applied in the iteration phase. The proposed algorithm is compared with existing techniques based on accuracy. The experimental result shows that the modified algorithm with Fused Distance Matrix outperforms the existing clustering technique.

Chapter 5: The retinal parts segmentation has been recognized as a key component in both ophthalmological and cardiovascular sickness analysis. The parts of retinal pictures are vessels, optic disc and macula segmentations will add to the indicative outcome. In any case, the manual segmentation of retinal parts is tedious and dreary work, and it additionally requires proficient aptitudes. This book chapter proposes a supervised method to segment blood vessel utilizing deep learning methods. All the more explicitly, the proposed part has connected the completely convolutional network, which is normally used to perform semantic segmentation undertaking, with exchange learning. The convolutional neural system has turned out to be an amazing asset for a few computer vision assignments. As of late, restorative picture investigation bunches over the world are rapidly entering this field and applying convolutional neural systems and other deep learning philosophies to a wide assortment of uses, and uncommon outcomes are rising constantly.

Chapter 6: Medical imaging includes diverse imaging modalities and methods to image the human body for diagnostic and treatment intentions, and therefore plays a vital role to improve public health. Acquisition of medical image is a challenging task, which may be affected with various noises and intensity inhomogeneity. In order to overcome these issues, it is necessary to preprocess the images. This book chapter aims at providing a novel method for intensity inhomogeneity correction for MRI brain tumor images. This chapter first introduces the need for preprocessing in MR images, then summarizes the existing methods and finally describes the novel method for intensity inhomogeneity correction.

Chapter 7: Electronic commerce associated with highly powerful we b technology and mobile communication is currently dominating the Business world. Current advancements in Machine Learning (ML) have also further coordinated to creative business applications and E-commerce administrations to reason about complex system and better solution. In the course of recent years, the business security and machine-learning networks have created novel strategies for secured business frameworks based on computationally learned models. With the improvement of the Internet and digital marketing every financial platform has been more secured and user friendly for monetary transactions.

Chapter 8: The basis for this research originally stemmed from our passion for machine learning and various data mining techniques. The new unhealthy lifestyle of the modern world is becoming a cause for diseases like type 2 diabetes, blood pressure, etc. These real life problems can be creatively solved by using the predictions made by classifiers built on attribute specific data. These models can predict whether a person with given attributes will have diabetes or not. Once the prediction is acquired, necessary precautions can be taken to avert the disease. Machine learning has proved useful not only in the medical sector but also in the commerce, banking and financial sectors. Python is a user friendly high level language which has been on the rise because of its simplicity and ease of use. Using python and it's libraries for building classifiers and analysis is a recent trend in the field of machine learning.

Chapter 9: Text classification in medical domain could result in shortage of medical technicians in third world countries. Due to various nuances present in understanding language in general, a requirement of large volumes of text based data is required for algorithms to learn patterns properly. Text classification is an easier way of handling large volumes of medical data. They can be segregated depending on the type of diseases, which can be determined by extracting the decisive key texts from the original document. This chapter will explain about the process in classification of text for matching diseases with various kinds of medical documents.

Chapter 10: In Machine learning, the system should be able to arrive at decisions that transform a given situation into a desired situation or goal. Reinforcement learning is a part of machine learning which uses mathematical formalism that captures trial and error learning and that had wide applicability such as autonomous driving, autonomous flying, game playing, etc. The roots of Reinforcement learning are from behavioral psychology. In this chapter, through mathematical approach the learning process has been modeled. The agent is allowed to learn entirely by itself in reinforcement learning. An autonomous agent behaves in an intelligent manner to find optimized fitness function for data mining process. We focus on reinforcement learning for mining High Utility Itemset (HUI) from a given transactional database which is growing exponentially. Through this chapter reader can learn how Reinforcement learning improves the efficiency of traditional evolutionary algorithms. Most appropriate fitness function for evaluation can be selected automatically during execution of an algorithm. Furthermore, during the optimization process when distinct functions are skillful, dynamic selection of current optimal function is done.

Chapter 11: Presents an analysis of machine learning techniques to address the most needful and challenging issues in prediction of risk during surgical operations. Emphasizes the importance of missing values imputation in prediction of risk as well as provide an appropriate novel method to handle missing values to increase model accuracy. The developed model works well with different surgical datasets and produced promising accuracy results.

Chapter 12: In the past years, the usage of internet and quantity of digital data generated by large organizations, firms, and governments have paved way for the researchers to focus on security issues of private data. This collected data is usually related to a definite necessity. For example, in the medical field, health record systems are used for the exchange of medical data. In addition to services based on users' current location, many potential services rely on users' location history or their spatial- temporal provenance. However, most of the collected data contain data identifying individual which is of sensitive nature. This chapter portrait various machine learning and deep learning techniques to preserve the privacy of the sensitive and private data of all individuals. It reviews the current literature on privacy ML and deep learning techniques, along with the non-cryptographic differential privacy approach for ensuring sensitive data privacy.

Chapter 13: Dengue is a major public health problem in India. Some studies have reported that an epidemiological shift in dengue viruses and climate change might be responsible for the observed increase in dengue burden across India. The full life cycle of dengue fever virus involves the role of mosquito as a transmitter (or vector) and humans as the main victim and source of infection. Accurate and timely forecasts of dengue incidence in India are still lacking. The epidemiology of dengue fevers in the Indian subcontinent has been very complex and has substantially changed over almost past six decades in terms of prevalent strains, affected geographical locations and severity of disease. In this work, the state-of-the-art machine learning algorithms are used to develop an accurate predictive model of dengue. In this work, Several machine learning algorithms, including the Support Vector Regression (SVR) algorithm, Step-down Linear Regression(SLR) model, Gradient Boosted Regression Tree (GBRT) algorithm, Negative Binomial Regression (NBM)model, Least Absolute Shrinkage and Selection Operator (LASSO) linear regression model and Generalized Additive Model (GAM)are as candidate models to predict dengue incidence. Performance and goodness of fit of the models were assessed using the root-mean-square error (RMSE) and R-squared measures.

Chapter 14: Deep Learning is an artificial intelligence function that reproduces the mechanisms of the human mind in processing records and evolving shapes to be used in selection construction. The main objective of this chapter is to provide a complete examination of deep learning algorithms and its applications in various fields. Deep learning has detonated in the public alertness, primarily as inspective and analytical products fill our world, in the form of numerous human-centered smart-world systems, with besieged advertisements, natural language supporters and interpreters, and prototype self-driving vehicle systems. Therefore, it provides a broad orientation for those seeking a primer on deep learning algorithms and its various applications, platforms, and uses in a variety of smart-world systems. Also, this survey delivers a precious orientation for new deep learning practitioners, as well as those seeking to innovate in the application of deep learning.

Chapter 15: The chapter discusses about the recent advancement of machine learning techniques in healthcare. The chapter explains the applications fields like Drug detection and Analysis, Assistive Technologies, Medical Image Diagnosis, Smart Health records and so on. The machine learning techniques plays a predominant role in healthcare and it will lead to a robotic healthcare all over the universe in future. The researchers and students in Engineering and Science can get a greater exposure on the applications of machine learning techniques in healthcare. It will create an impact for the researchers to do research in the machine learning techniques, implementing healthcare products, providing an exposure to the society, teaching to the public about the invents.

Chapter 16: Neural networks are very useful and are proving to be very beneficial in various fields. Biomedical applications such as breast cancer image classification, differentiating between the malignant and benign type of breast cancer, etc. are now seen to be making use of neural networks rapidly. Neural networks are showing remarkable results of their effectiveness in these biomedical applications and are proving to be immensely profitable. Another field such as agriculture, which is a very crucial field for survival of human life, can be benefitted from neural networks. Likewise various fields can gain enormous benefits from the usage of neural networks. In this chapter, titled "Contribution of Neural Networks in Different Applications", by the authors, shall explain neural networks in detail. Also, the authors shall provide a brief and detailed insight of the contribution of neural networks in different applications, along with its analysis.

Chapter 17: Deep learning refers to as part of machine learning. Learning here consists of various methods using neural network algorithm. Learning from the big vast data can be supervised or unsupervised. It enables the machine to learn gradually by itself from all the related situations or date provided. Nowadays, Deep Learning is playing vital role with greater success in various applications, such as Digital Image Processing, Human Computer interaction, Computer Vision and Natural Language Processing, Robotics, Biological Applications etc. Unlike traditional machine learning approaches, Deep Learning has effective ability of learning and makes better use of data set for feature extraction. Because of its repetitive learning ability, Deep Learning has become more popular in the present day research works

Chapter 18: Machine Learning (ML) is one of the exciting sub-fields of artificial intelligence (AI). The term Machine learning is generally stated as the ability to learn without being explicitly programmed. In recent years, Machine learning has become one of the thrust areas of research across various business verticals. The technical advancements in the field of big data have provided the ability to gain access over large volumes of diversified data at ease. This massive amount of data can be processed at high speeds in a reasonable amount of time with the help of emerging hardware capabilities. Hence the Machine learning algorithms have been the most effective at leveraging all of Big Data to provide almost near real-time solutions even for the complex business problems. This chapter aims in giving a solid introduction to various widely adopted machine learning techniques and its applications categorized into Supervised, Unsupervised and Reinforcement and will serve a simplified guide for the aspiring data and machine learning enthusiasts.

Chapter 19: Introduction to artificial intelligence is a book chapter about the science of artificial intelligence (AI). AI is the study of the design of intelligent computational agents. The book is structured to be accessible to a wide audience. We composed this book chapter since we are amped up for the development of AI as an incorporated science. Similarly as with any science being created, AI has an intelligent, formal hypothesis and a test wing. Here we balance hypothesis and examination and tell the best way to interface them together personally. We build up the investigation of AI together with its designing applications. We trust the aphorism, "There is nothing as down to earth as a decent hypothesis." The soul of our methodology is caught by the announcement, "Everything ought to be made as basic as would be prudent, however not less complex." We should manufacture the science on strong establishments; we present the establishments, yet just sketch, and give a few instances of, the unpredictability required to assemble valuable canny frameworks. The book chapter can be used as an introductory text on artificial intelligence for advanced undergraduate or graduate students in computer science or related disciplines such as computer engineering, philosophy, cognitive science, or psychology. It will appeal more to the technically minded; parts are technically challenging, focusing on learning by doing: designing, building, and implementing systems. Any curious scientifically oriented reader will benefit from studying the book.

Chapter 20: Machine Learning is the part of artificial intelligence that makes machines to learn without being expressly programmed and predict the future. Machine learning application built up the upcoming modern world. Machine learning techniques mainly classified into three techniques supervised, unsupervised and semi-supervised. Machine learning is an interdisciplinary field, which can be joined in different areas including science, business, and research. Supervised techniques applied in agriculture, email spam, malware filtering, online fraud detection, optical character recognition, natural language processing, and face detection. Unsupervised techniques applied in market segmentation, and sentiment analysis and anomaly detection. Deep learning is being utilized in a broad scope of filed such as sound, image, video, Time series, and Text. This chapter covers applications of various machine learning techniques, social media, agriculture and task scheduling in a distributed system.

Chapter 21: Machine learning provides the system to automatically learn without human intervention and improve their performance with the help of previous experience. It can access the data and use it for learning by itself. Even though many algorithms are developed to solve machine learning issues, it is difficult to handle all kinds of inputs data in-order to arrive at accurate decisions. The domain knowledge of statistical science, probability, logic, mathematical optimization, reinforcement learning and control theory plays a major role in developing machine learning based algorithms. The key consideration in selecting a suitable programming language for implementing machine learning algorithm includes performance, concurrency, application development, learning curve. This chapter deals with few of the top programming languages used for developing machine learning applications. They are python, R, and Java. Top three programming languages preferred by data scientist are: (1) Python more than 57%, (2) R more than 31% and (3) java used by 17% of the data scientist.

This edited book has specific salient features. They are:

- It deals with important and timely topic of emerging areas like Healthcare, Information Security, Medical Image Processing, agriculture and other unattended areas.
- It presents research findings and materials authored by global experts in the field.
- It serves as a comprehensive source of information and reference material on the topic machine learning.
- It presents latest development of the topic related to machine learning and its related areas.
- It presents the research findings in well organized and structured manner.
- Even though it is not a text book, it can serve as a complete reference material for data analysts.

- It can certainly be used as one for graduate courses and research oriented courses dealing with machine learning or data science.
- It can serve as light house of knowledge in machine learning research lab including data science lab.

This comprehensive and timely publication aims to be an essential reference source, building on the available literature in the field of machine learning to boost further research in this dynamic and challenging field. It is expected that this text book will provide the resources necessary for technology developers, scientists and manufacturer to adopt and implement new inventions across the globe.

In short, I am very happy with both experience and end product of our sincere efforts. It is certain that this book will continue as an essential and indispensable resource for all concerned for coming years.

With Regards

V. Sathiyamoorthi
Sona College of Technology, India

Acknowledgment

I am very much happy and thankful to IGI Global Inc., USA for giving me the opportunity to produce my first book on *Handbook of Research on Applications and Implementations of Machine Learning Techniques*, which is very much necessary in the present data driven internet world.

I express a deep sense of gratitude to the Jan Travers, Lindsay Wertman, Jordan Tepper, Halle N. Frisco, and other members of IGI Global Inc., USA who supported either directly or indirectly during book project development.

I am thankful to all authors who have contributed their valuable efforts and ideas in the form of chapters in the book. I would like to express my sincere thanks to all my reviewers for their continuous supports, guidance and encouragements in bringing this book project into successful one.

I am thankful to Chairman, Vice-Chairman, Principal and other faculty members of Sona College of Technology, Salem, Tamilnadu, India for their great support and kindness in completing this book.

I am very much thankful to my parents and family members for their support and encouragement in achieving this target goal in my academic career.

Finally, I am dedicating this work to my wife, K. Surya, and to my lovely son, S. Vikash.

Chapter 1
Analysis of Machine Learning Algorithms for Breast Cancer Detection

Aswathy M. A.
VIT University, India

Jagannath Mohan
ⓘ https://orcid.org/0000-0001-8953-118X
VIT Chennai, India

ABSTRACT

As per the latest health ministry registries of 2017-2018, breast cancer among women has ranked number one in India and number two in United States. Despite the fact that breast cancer affects men also, per-vasiveness is lower in men than women. This is the reason breast cancer is such a vital concern among ladies. Roughly 80% of cancer malignancies emerge from epithelial cells inside breast tissues. In breast cancer spectrum, ductal carcinoma in situ (DCIS) and invasive ductal carcinoma (IDC) are considered malignant cancers that need treatment and care. This chapter mainly deals with breast cancer and machine learning (ML) applications. All through this chapter, different issues related to breast cancer prognosis and early detection and diagnostic techniques using various ML algorithms are addressed.

INTRODUCTION

During the period of 2017-2018, health ministry is predicted that the breast cancer may reach 1797900 affected patients by 2020. An article in the journal consultant 360 says that every year approximately 200,000 or above new cases of breast cancer are reporting and 40,000 or above patients are dying with breast cancer in the United States (Estape, 2018). The incidence rate of breast cancer increases with the age of patients. Mostly 50% of new breast cancer diagnoses happening at an age of 65 years and older and the incidence of breast cancer rate increases till the 80s (Sharma, 2001). Usually pathologists detect breast cancer by manually adjusting region of interest and segmenting lesions from that selected area.

DOI: 10.4018/978-1-5225-9902-9.ch001

But chances of intra and inter observability variations will be there. In that context, it is very challenging to find a method that associates automatically selecting region of interests (ROIs) and differentiating ductal carcinoma in situ (DCIS) and invasive ductal carcinoma (IDC) from other normal cancers.

Traditionally cancer detection and the treatment were identified purely on pathologist's experience. These specialists were having above 15 years of practice in the medical field and have seen many patients in similar conditions. Still the accuracy was not 100%. With the evolution of machine learning and artificial intelligence, computer aided diagnosis of different types of cancer became easy. Machine intelligence (MI) or Artificial intelligence (AI) is defined as intelligence displayed by machines and adapt to the surroundings to perform actively to achieve its goals. Here the device imitates the "cognitive" functions correlated to human minds such as learning and perception. AI has exceptional impact in the field of image processing. Machine learning is a sub discipline of artificial intelligence and both are coming under computer science branch. The subject 'Machine learning' gained immense priority among pathologists and radiologists for its benefits in global health care industry and the curiosity boosted towards how the machine learning will strengthen medical specialists in their area of work. The study in machine learning makes healthcare engineering applications straightforward in acquiring and storing patient details in a database and possible to access these databases from anywhere in the world. Smart intelligent systems are there to help doctors and pathologists to interrogate and analyses these complex datasets. An article in Technology trends point out the world market of artificial intelligence including machine learning in various fields like medical imaging, health care, recognition and identification is estimated to reach 2 billion dollars in 2023 (Massat, 2018). Thus, the branch of artificial intelligence and machine learning became a valuable sphere in the healthcare industry.

Image processing became one of the fundamental elements in biomedical and medicinal research, laboratory areas etc. Image processing succeeds in processing a three-dimensional image and converts it into a two dimensional one using numerical data analysis. According to the last 7 years' market hype, artificial intelligence techniques like machine learning and other computer vision methods will change health care medical imaging industry in the stipulations like huge productivity, improved accuracy in diagnosis and good clinical outcomes (Massat, 2018). Hence machine learning would act as a mediator in between ever-growing figure of diagnostic image screening programs despite of harsh scarcity of radiologists and pathologists in many countries. Figure 1 shows the trend of using machine learning algorithms in the world market for various applications like computer vision and deep learning.

Among the vast variety of machine learning applications, cancer detection and prognosis diagnosis at its early stage is gaining high prominence in health care industry. Many researchers and specialists like IBM Watson had invested money and time in this field to make headway but lasted with little success in the history. Now Google came up with a machine learning system that incorporates microscope which helps doctors and pathologists in cancer detection. Similarly, there are many more algorithms that help in detecting any type of cancer with the help of machine learning and deep learning. Different AI techniques like fuzzy logic (FL), genetic algorithm, and neural network can be employed to solve many problems in the biomedical field. However, each method has its own constraints and can be used in certain circumstances only. In such situations, combination of these techniques might help in solving these problems. For example, neural network is just like a "black box" to the users. Users cannot access neural network interiors for understanding parameter revision. At the same time, fuzzy logic has issues in deciding membership functions (MFs). Artificial neural networks cannot parallelize and architecture selection is difficult. Genetic algorithm has an advantage of dealing complicated parameter optimization problems. Sometimes the combination of these techniques (hybrid systems) like neurofuzzy, neural

Figure 1. Statistics of usage of machine learning algorithms in various applications

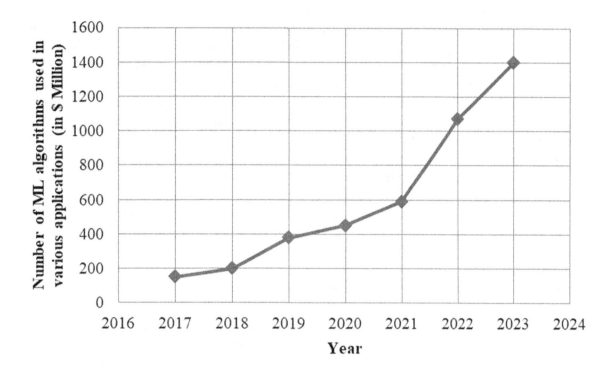

network combined with genetic algorithm etc., will guide to the optimal solution. Hence the major intension of this study is to realize different machine learning concepts, various architectures for image processing queries like segmentation, classification and pre-processing.

Repeated abscission rates for breast cancer partial mastectomy systems are as of now almost 25% because of specialists depending on unreliable techniques for assessing image specimens (Fancellu, 2019). This study is intended to find out how accurate automatic breast cancer detection from histopathology images through a set of machine learning algorithms. A patient's cancer can be characterized according to cancer stage, clinical result, and the decision of treatment by assuring oestrogen and progesterone hormone receptors and hormone epidermal growth factor 2 (HER2) (Malvia, 2017). Review and planned examinations propose that there is significant dissonance in receptor status among initial and final cancer stages. In spite of this proof and current proposals, the dissection of tissue from metastatic breast sites isn't standard practice. So, it leads to high rate of mastectomy in early breast cancer.

BACKGROUND AND MOTIVATION

There are many motivational reasons for researchers who are conducting studies in breast cancer field. Lynch (2017) used to observe and conduct experiments to know how exercise affects the life of a breast cancer patient, and how the lifestyle of patients impact on the further development of breast cancer. Everyone is very much interested to know about the risk factors and the surroundings that cause breast cancer like pollution, food adulteration etc. But the exciting matter is that the contributors of breast cancer are the things everyone has the ability to change. For example, overweight, lack of physical exercises and liquor consumption. Breast cancer is curable but early diagnosis makes it possible.

For many years, interpretation of microscopic images was one of the biggest challenge's humans faced. This is because microscopic images or histopathology images usually contains stain. Sometimes these stains may accumulate in one part and may be faint in color in other parts. Through the establishment of computer aided diagnosis (CAD), all these problems have been solved. Many experts in this area have tried to use professionally various techniques like machine learning, fuzzy logic, artificial neural network and genetic algorithms in order to expand the efficacy in diagnosing breast cancer. Now a days, doctors are taking much advices from pathologists and microscopic images i.e. histopathology images shows a significant role in CAD. Actually, to reduce inter and intra observer variability, pathologists need a second opinion. Here comes the significance of the CAD.

Sheshadri and Kandaswamy (2006) suggested a method for the detection of plague by using OTSU thresholding. Authors conducted the study on mini-MAIS (Mammogram Image Analysis Society) dataset. The entire study consists of segmenting the region of interest and detecting the micro calcification. Matlab software was used. Alhadidi, et al. (2007) presented a case study on mammogram images of breast cancer. The manuscript contains segmentation of cancer using watershed segmentation procedure. Elter and Held (2008) used feature extraction step with Wavelet transforms. Cell detection from histopathology images is quite difficult because of its confused structure. Existing methods uses textural features, color, contextual and edge features which are commonly known as hand-crafted low-level features. Bengio et al. (2013) suggested a new method of taking pixel level features which gives more information about shape and edge features. The deep learning (DL) technique offers the advantage of learning high level features from pixel intensities so that it will be easy for a classifier to learn and classify objects. Cruz-Roa et al. (2013) employed an autoencoder using convolutional neural network for learning image representation of histopathology images. One of the limitations of this paper was that the autoencoder has only one layer so that the high-level representation might not be accurate. Nedzved et al. (2000) recommended a segmentation method based on morphological approach for histopathology image cell detection. Al-Kofahi et al. (2010) put forwarded a hybrid model consisting graph cut binarization for nuclei count and detection.

Regarding segmentation and detection of breast cancer, histopathology images show different characteristics for various types of cancers. It includes variations in morphologies, dimensions, consistencies, and color. So, it is very hard to determine an overall pattern for histopathology image segmentation. Previously image segmentation algorithms are mainly based on texture features and their extraction, and Tashk et al. (2014) studied only about extracting these texture features. Belsare et al. (2016) suggested a segmentation method based on hyper-pixel generation. This technique was based on similarity, to develop the space-texture-color map combined with the text illustration of breast histopathology images. Xu et al. (2015) recommended a procedure based on sparse non-negative matrix factorization (SNMF) for reducing color variations in the breast images. But all these segmentation techniques lack the generality. That means all these designs are focused for peculiar types of cancer. They can't be generalizing.

With the progression of interdisciplinary fields like image processing and computer vision, a framework for cancer detection can be built by using various algorithms in machine learning. The metastatic and other harmful areas are consequently pinpoint by these systems. The oncologists are then empowered by this quantitative portrayal of the breast cancer to evaluate the prognosis, thereby analyzing customized medication, improved survival rate and enhanced personal satisfaction. Breast cancer detection system starts with segmentation and its segregation from other biological tissues. Cancer detection in metastasis stage from a segmented tissue can be done in both 2D and 3D geometries. The computer vision system has to face the challenge to extract the mathematical properties of the tumor and classify those structures into different stages. This classification task can be easily performing with the help of different classifiers like support vector machine (SVM), deep neural network, k-nn classifier etc. First there will be a concise review on the breast cancer and its various causative components. Next there will be a detailed explanation of different machine learning techniques in the breast cancer detection and last, the paper will be concluded with a detailed proposal of breast cancer detection using artificial intelligence.

STRUCTURE AND DEVELOPMENT OF THE BREAST

Breast of women has very complex structure and it is very difficult to understand the changes occurring inside the breast at each stages of body development. Breast starts to form at prenatal stage itself. Later it begins to change its shape and structure to show a feminine character from adolescence stage (Korde et al., 2010). Figure 2 shows the structure of a normal breast contains lobules, ducts, stroma, rib and other muscles (McGuire, 2016). Breast cancer is called the unwanted cellular growth inside the breast and its structures.

Breast cancer among men is very rare so that it is very difficult to study and realize in men. Less than 1% men affected with breast cancer. Usually women breasts go through many cellular and lobular transitions during adolescence, lactation and postmenopausal periods. But men don't have these changes unless changes due to the hormones viz: oestrogen and androgen (Taber et al., 2010). BRCA1 and BRCA2 are two human tumor destructive genes which are capable of repairing damaged DNA. The mutations in these hormones might cause high risk for breast cancer.

Breast cancer can be caused due to many reasons. The very important one is gene mutations as above said. The changes in BRCA1 and BRCA2 can be genetically inherited like germ line mutations that cause DNA damage. The other reasons are biological variations in the genes (somatic mutations that happen when gene changes because of some by-products reacted together due to some normal biological processes) during the life course of a person. The other reason for breast cancer is due to the external exposures like radiation, some food habits or after effects of some medical treatments.

TYPES OF BREAST CANCER

This section focused on different types of breast cancer such as invasive and non-invasive and even metastatic breast cancer (Figure 3). Cancer can happen anywhere inside breast like lobules, ducts or still in stroma or other tissues. Other than these cancers, Paget's disease which is affecting the nipple is a type of cancer. Then phyllodes lesions, metastatic cancer and molecular subtypes of breast cancer can all become life threatening.

Long Term Effects and Contentious Form of Breast Cancer

It is relentlessly increasing the rate of survival after the diagnosis of breast cancer. Of course, it is great information, however clinicians should likewise perceive this which takes out new objections to the medicinal world (Go, 2013). Breast cancer is a long-lasting disease or a disorder more than a life-

Figure 2. Anatomy of breast

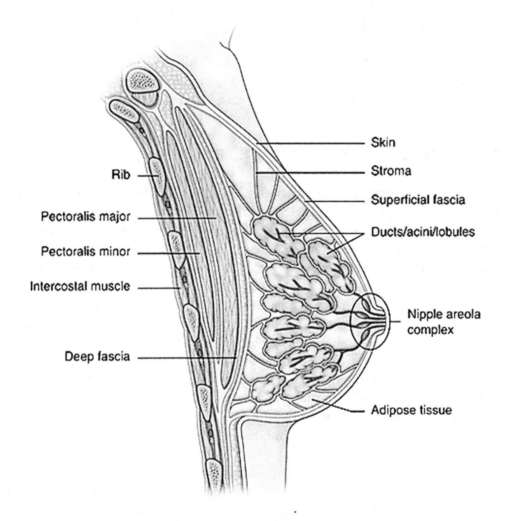

threatening condition because of early diagnosis methods and therapeutic treatments. But the doctors should manage and realize the long-term abnormalities of this disease due to the various medical treatments (Bodai & Tuso, 2015). Another important concern that demands immediate attention is in the number of teenagers (aged 25 to 38) who are affected with breast cancer is increasing. With the help of modern mammographic screening technologies and self-awareness among patients, it is easy to detect breast cancer at its early stage. But due to the most modern medical treatments, the survival rate became increased but the number of cardio vascular disease among breast cancer survivors also increased. The achievement of survival rate among breast cancer patients may leads to an unexpected increase in the death rate of patients affected with cardio vascular diseases (CVDs).

Last year many women who are breast cancer survivors cease into CVDs without prior to the stage or severity of cancer due to the various chemical treatments and diagnostic methods (Eifel et al., 2001). Recently studies have shown that CVD is a long-term effect of breast cancer (Canto, 2014). CVDs are now days became one of the foremost reasons of mortality amongst women in India. So, international

Figure 3. A hierarchical diagram of various types of breast cancer

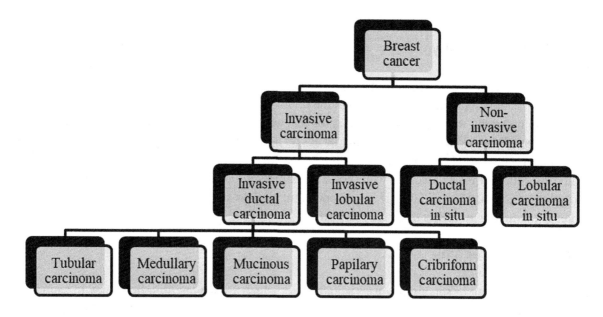

specialists in oncology department undertook a special task involving cardio-oncology specialty treatments for those who are affected with breast cancer and CVDs (Albini et al., 2010). Mostly half of the breast cancer survivors do not know that they are at high risk of CVD.

SCREENING METHODS

There are various screening methods for diagnosing breast cancer at its early stage. Screening means looking out a patient for hints of breast cancer before the symptoms start. These screening methods sometimes detect cancers which are very small in size and slowly expanding. These cancers are may be non-dangerous to the person. So, medical experts in this field are working seriously to find out people who are more prone to breast cancer. For that doctors will go through the patient's family history, exposure to radiations or other hormonal treatments during their course of life. According to their history, experts will suggest how often should the patient undergo screening tests and which screening methods are best suitable for the particular patient.

Self-Screening

Self-screening is nothing but a kind of early detection that a woman herself checking breasts for some kind of lumps or tumors or any discomfort. Studies are conducting whether self-examination is important or efficient enough to detect breast cancer early. In 2008, 400,000 women from Russia and China underwent a study on this statement. The study revealed that there is no any significant impact on early detection but women are undergoing unnecessary biopsies assuming they have breast cancer. So

American Cancer Society and some other organizations not recommending self-screening instead they are advising mammography.

Digital Mammography

Mammography is the primary screening method for women that help to detect breast cancer. This method uses an X-ray radiation that is passed through the breast and a digital image is captured on a recording plate. Mammography will use a low dose radiation that won't cause any health damages. Mammography can detect small lumps that a patient cannot detect by herself but it is not effective for all age groups. For younger women and pre-menopausal women, it is less effective that their breasts are very dense. Moreover, younger breast tissues are white color in mammogram and cancer lumps are also sees as white in mammogram. So, it is difficult to read their mammogram. As age increases, breast became fattier and darker in mammogram makes them easy to read.

Ultrasound Screening

Ultrasound screening or sonography uses sound waves which are having high frequency to capture an image. This method will capture sound waves produced by a transducer. This method is best suitable to differentiate solid lumps from liquid lumps (cysts that contain liquid which are non-cancerous). Ultrasound imaging can be used to find out the abnormalities detected in mammograms. It cannot be used as a screening method by itself but can be incorporated with mammography.

Magnetic Resonance Imaging (MRI)

MRI is not a regular screening method that everyone can undergo without proper suggestion. MRI uses strong magnetic field and radio frequency waves in which a computer will capture and processes to create the image of breast tissues. MRI has a disadvantage of increased rate of false positives. Invasive breast cancers are very malignant cancers and MRI is recommending for those who are at high risk of invasive breast cancer.

Positron Emission Tomography (PET)

Positron Emission Tomography is normally used to know the normal functioning of various organs and tissues. PET scans are using a nuclear material that injects into the patient's body or a part of body. PET scans are used to detect the prognosis and metastases of breast cancer rather than detecting a mass or lump. Doctors can understand the uptake of the nuclear material as it travels through the breast tissue. These scans show the malignant lumps as "hot spots" with high density.

Thermographic Screening

Thermography is not widely acceptable for screening breast cancer due to its inefficiency in clarity of images. This screening does not contain any type involvement of radiation. So, it is purely a non-invasive type screening. Thermal imaging involves the use of a temperature sensor to determine the temperature on breast skin. Due to the abnormal multiplication of cancer cells inside breast, the blood flow and en-

Figure 4. Hematoxylin and eosin (H & E) stained histopathology image specimen showing malignant characteristics

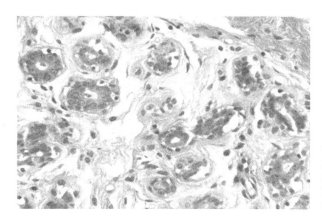 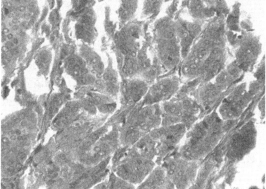

ergy increases. This will cause the temperature at that particular place to increase. This temperature is detecting by the sensor. Over decades, thermography is existing. But there is no enough proof to make thermography as a better screening tool to detect breast cancer early.

OVERVIEW OF BIOPSY

The origin of the word 'Biopsy' is from Greek words: "Bios" which means "life" and "opsis" means "a view". So, Biopsy is simply "to sight a living subject". Biopsy is the last word for cancer. After all these screening methods, if something found abnormal then the doctors will suggest a biopsy. Biopsy is a clinical process that requires very keen observation and strong experience in which a tissue is taken outside from the breast and examines under a microscope for further investigation. This procedure generally carried out by pathologists. The microscopic images are called as histopathology images and the procedure is called histopathology analysis. Authors in this study mainly focused on microscopic images (histopathology images).

To visualize different tissue structures and organelles in the microscopic slides, a process called staining has to be done. Most widely acceptable staining method is Hematoxylin and eosin (H&E). Hematoxylin stain is responsible for blue shade color for nuclear structures and eosin stain is responsible for purple or pink shade to other cytoplasmic structures. For example: two H&E stained images are given below which are taken from UCSB dataset (Aswathy & Jagannath, 2017).

Advantages

It is impossible to view the structures inside one living subject but biopsy makes it possible by offering a section of tissue for examining. Biopsy is frequently related to cancer but in some occasions, biopsy can be used to find out other diseases and their prognosis. Biopsy can be beneficial in the following cases:

- **Cancer:** If a patient found some abnormality or lumps or lesions during screening programs, biopsy can help to figure out whether that lump is malignant or benign.
- **Gastric Ulcer:** Non-steroidal anti-inflammatory drugs (NSAIDs) are one of the root causes for ulceration in stomach. Doctors very often use bowel biopsy to diagnose stomach ulcer. Main symptoms are celiac diseases, severe abdominal pain and gastric problems.
- **Liver Cirrhosis:** Biopsy is helpful in detecting liver cancer, liver cirrhosis and fibroid in the liver. Biopsy is usually conducting when the liver is fully damaged because of alcohol consumption. In the case of hepatitis, biopsy is useful to know the response of patients against various treatments.
- **Bacterial Infection:** Biopsy also helps to locate various infections in the body and the corresponding bacteria causing it.

Rarely biopsy is conducting on transplanted organs to confirm the body is going well with the organ and there is no tendency for rejection.

HISTOPATHOLOGY IMAGE ANALYSIS

The progress of compatible and precise machine-supported systematic approaches to medical imaging allows more computational power and enhanced image evaluation. As digital scanners became more prominent the histological slides can be transformed into digital image easily. Due to this, the machine learning and computerized techniques handles digital histopathology images widely. It is well known the role of CAD algorithms in assisting radiologists. Similar way for recent years CAD algorithms is also useful in assisting pathologists for detecting tumors, lesions etc. Figure 5 depicts the workflow of histopathology image analysis that consists of several steps such as pre-processing, segmentation, feature extraction and classification.

Pre-Processing Normalization

Spectral and illumination normalization is one of the biggest steps in histopathology image analysis. The normalization procedure helps in mitigating the variations in tissue specimen due to the stain and camera conditions. Illumination normalization is for correcting light variations caused due to camera fluctuations. This can be possible by calculating illumination patterns and try to match it with a reference image or by using calibration methods. Otherwise histogram matching is also a normalization method. Sometimes while staining a microscopic slide, some parts of the slide may get stained more so that the cells in that place may get clogged together makes it difficult to visualize. Most of the bright field companies now supplying a package that normalizes both light and stain variations with the help of software called one space software. Many algorithms are fully dependent on color space models. Hence, this will be helpful for such algorithms. Yang and Foran (2005) presented a LUV color space model for segmentation of histopathology images having color variations. Li et al. (2015) introduced a complete normalization technique that reduces the effect of both light and stain variations. They have used Non-Matrix factorization (NMF) and Statistical weighted histogram algorithms for the complete color normalization scheme. Some of the normalization techniques are given below:

Figure 5. Workflow of histopathology image analysis

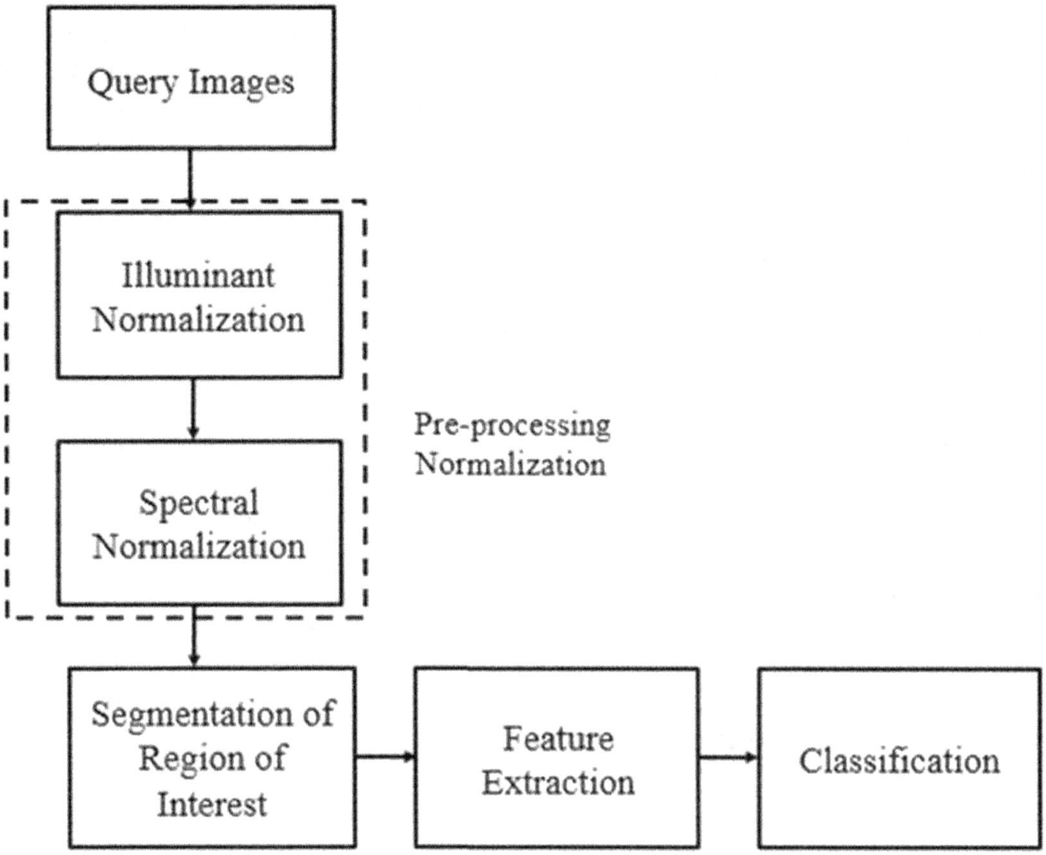

Based on Histogram Match

The basic set of color normalization algorithms are focused on Red Green Blue (RGB) color space histogram matching. But histogram matching has one problem in which it fully avoids the regional differences of image pixel variation and local color variations. Histogram matching is very poor in preserving histological data of the image so that it leads to redundant noises for further image analysis.

Color Cue Transfer

Instead of Red, Green and Blue channels, lαβ color space is there. The statistical properties like mean and variance of the query image are determined and match those with the properties of a reference image. Histopathological images are stained using more than one dye. So, after color cue transfer, the histological components of these images may get slightly changed. This difficulty can be addressed by dividing the whole image into different sections and each section having same histological details.

Spectral Matching

Initially the stain spectra of the image have been calculated by using adaptive methods or with the help of hardware. Then match those calculated spectra with that of a reference spectrum. Spectral matching has the benefit of preserving histological information. But this is possible only if color variation is due to stain variations only. If the color varied because of other reasons, the image's histological features may change after the normalization procedure.

Segmentation of the Region of Interest

Method Based on Markov Random Field (MRF)

In this method, the boundary abstraction on a saliency map conducted initially with the help of Loopy Back Propagation (LBP) algorithm on MRF. This detection method accomplished by using tensor voting. This framework can be used for both histopathology images and frames of images. LBP algorithm is usually used to find out an approximate solution for Markov random field. A saliency map is very essential to know the pixel's unique characteristics. Tensor voting is a kind of parallel marching which helps to find out features nicely. In a site, one input will communicate the message, a tensor, with its neighborhood node and assigns a vote. Hence, the site will collect all those tensor votes and evaluate and assign new tensor vote.

Watershed Segmentation With Connected Component Labeling (CCL)

Connected-component labeling is a subset of graph theory. CCL is also called as blob labeling. The sub disciplines of connected components are uniquely assigned based on a given empirical data. Connected-component labeling is usually performed with other segmentation algorithms. Watershed segmentation algorithm works well if background and foreground regions can separately mark.

Texture Segmentation

Guzmán et al. (2013) used a segmentation algorithm based on texture thresholding for the early detection of breast cancer. This algorithm was tested on several datasets of mammogram images for discriminating calcifications and small masses from background areas using morphological operations. This segmentation method is based on intensity features extracted from various machine learning algorithms.

Segmentation Algorithm Based on Feature Pyramid

Qin et al. (2018) suggested a segmentation procedure built on ResNet50-GICN-GPP feature pyramid for histopathological image segmentation. The framework consists of three points: (1) reduces the large training data size by sampling using patch wise technology (2) a multi stage GICN structure consisting different feature levels to resolve the paradox amongst classification and pixel position (3) a multi-scale feature pyramid by using average pooling along with several sizes that enables the combination of appropriate evidence on various sizes and locations. This method is purely an image semantic algorithm on ResNet50-GICN-GPP pyramid. Primarily, the image was resampled by using a patch sampling method thereby reduced the single image sample size. Then increase the training sample size. Next, a convolutional neural network (CNN) was designed on ResNet50 to acquire feature region data, then for assimilating multi-stage features, a GICN structure has been used along with a deconvolutional network. A GPP structure was finally introduced to solve the problem of neglecting minor things by GICN structures. It is also useful for acquiring the multi-scale semantic data. The anticipated feature pyramid accomplishes 63% of average segmentation accuracy on two datasets viz: Camelyon16 and Gastric WSIs Data.

Feature Extraction

Feature extraction is very essential before classification and widely used in machine learning, computer vision and image processing. The features are some informative attributes that are derived from some initial measured data and are helpful in training and testing phases. Feature extraction also helps to increase efficiency in human interpretations. On the other hand, feature extraction can be used for reducing dimensionality. An initial measured data is reduced to a new set of data for manipulation which is fully describing the original data. If the original data contains some redundant information, feature extraction reduces the redundancy and makes easy the processing of data. There is first order, second order and higher order statistic features. First order statistic features are those properties of distinct pixels neglecting the spatial relationship between neighbour pixels whereas second order and higher order statistic features are those properties collecting from two or pixels in a specific location. Some important statistical features that can be extracted are given below:

Mean

Arithmetic mean is simply referred as "mean". It is the average of all values or attributes given in a study. In image processing, mean is the average value of all neighboring pixels in a window of an image. It is calculated by summing up all the values in a sample space and then dividing the total samples by the number of samples in the space. Mathematically mean can be represented as in Equation (1).

$$\overline{X} = \frac{\sum X}{N}$$

(1)

where $\overline{X}$ is the mean of the population, $\sum X$ is the summation of all the samples in the population and N is the total number of samples.

Variance

Variance is a property fulfilled by a normal distribution. It is the average of squared deviation of all points in a population. It is a measure showing how far each pixel in an image from its mean. Variance gives knowledge on the pixels spread in an image. The variance represented as (σ^2) is calculated by summing up the squared distances of each sample (X) in the sample space from the mean (μ). Then this value is divided by the total number of samples in the space (N). Mathematically variance can be represented as in Equation (2).

Figure 6. Positive and negative distribution of skewness

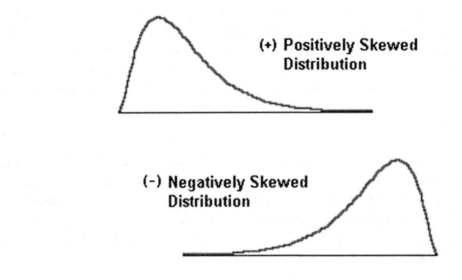

$$\sigma^2 = \frac{\sum X^2}{N} - \mu^2 \tag{2}$$

Skewness

Skewness is a property that tells about symmetry, or the absence of equilibrium. A population or sample space is said to be balanced if the left and right portions of its center pixel is same. The normal distribution has zero skewness, and all balanced data have skewness more or less equal to zero. That means skewness can take values either positive or negative. If it is positive, it shows that the population is skewed right and otherwise it says the population is skewed left. Negative values for the skewness indicate data that are skewed left and positive values for the skewness indicate data that are skewed right. Figure 6 shows the distribution of positive and negative skewed data.

Entropy

Entropy is a measure of randomness. As an example, the entropy of gas is higher than that of a solid because particles are not free to move in a solid whereas particles are freely moving in gas. It is a thermodynamic property that measures the originality of groups with regard to the given group labels. The entropy of a set of groups can be calculated from the class distribution of the images from each group.

Kurtosis

In a frequency distribution curve, kurtosis is a measure of sharpness of the peak. Kurtosis determines the data has a peak or flat pattern compared to a normal distribution. That is, sample points having high kurtosis has sharp peak around the mean.

Contrast

Contrast is defined as the variations in the color cue that creates an image (or its representation in an image display) unique. In the view of human perception, contrast is the difference in the color hue and brightness of the substance and other substances inside the same field.

There are other geometrical features like centroid, area and gradient features like orientation can also be used for feature extraction.

Classification

In our modern life, now computer applications make possible to collect and co-ordinate flood of information at very high speed. But to manipulate all this information smoothly, the need of machine learning and deep learning techniques increased. The field of machine learning focuses on building up various algorithms for determining patterns or yield results from experimental data. Many experts from different professions and industries are implementing adaptive structures using ML to optimize several processes. Moreover, one of the biggest challenges in this category that everyone facing is information classification. Here, authors were concentrated on breast cancer classification. Some classifiers, their advantages and disadvantages, application scenario were discussed below.

Artificial Neural Network (ANN)

An artificial neural network (ANN) is constructed similarly as a human neural system. Human nervous system is responsible for remembering patterns, replicating these patterns and identify correctly next time. Figure 7 shows the typical architecture of ANN. During first phase, an artificial neural network is trained to learn some patterns. This phase is called training phase. Next stage is the testing phase. During testing phase, neural network is tested with some unknown patterns. Hence, a neural network classifier should classify these unknown patterns correctly according to the previous patterns that the neural network is trained for. Different applications are voice detection, pattern recognition, abnormality detection etc.

Support Vector Machine (SVM)

SVMs are constructed on decision boundaries that are defined by decision planes. That means a decision boundary which separates two classes. Figure 8 shows an example of SVM classifier in which all red balls belongs to one class and other green balls belongs to another class. SVM normally comes under a supervised learning method. It can be used for analyzing both classification and regression problems. But SVMs are known for classification tasks. Like ANNs, SVMs are also trained with datasets which are clearly labelled one or categories. Then SVMs will build a model that categories the new data clearly. It is also called as a non-probabilistic linear binary classifier. Various applications of SVMs are handwriting categorization, image classification, permutation and combination models etc.

Decision Tree

Decision trees are flow charts modeled in a tree like structure that contain both decision and the corresponding consequences. Usually decision trees are employed for application like decision analysis

Figure 7. Architecture of artificial neural network

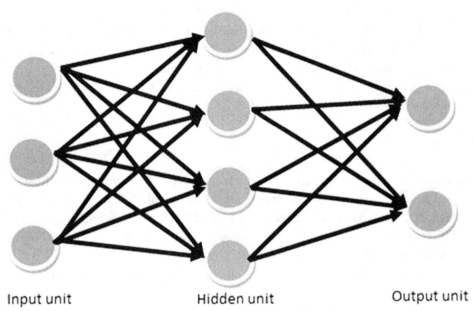

Input unit   Hidden unit   Output unit

especially operations research. But in rare cases, they can be used in machine learning applications. Three types of structures are there in a decision tree: Decision nodes that typically represent a test on an instance, a branch node that typically represents the result of a test and a leaf node that typically represents the category after calculating all attributes. The main disadvantage is that decision trees are not suitable for continuous variables.

K-Nearest Neighbour Classifier (K-NN)

K-NN algorithm is another supervised algorithm. The targets are known to us but no previous knowledge about the pattern. The K-NN model classifies the instances according to the Euclidean distance between

Figure 8. Example of SVM classifier

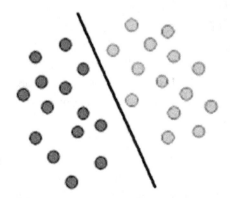

cluster nodes. That means if an instance wants to be labelled, calculate the k values to the all clusters. Then determine the cluster to which the instance is more belongs to. The main disadvantage is that the algorithm is very time consuming. That is why k-NN classifier is called as "lazy classifier". To solve a multiclassification task, a combination of features and binary classifiers will be useful.

FUTURE RESEARCH DIRECTIONS

Around the planet, 14 million new cancer patients are diagnosed by pathologists every year. That means the uncertainty of life is increasing in millions of people every year. Pathologists are diagnosing cancer with approximately 98% accuracy. They are very good in this concern. But the biggest challenge pathologists are facing in prognosis part. For predicting the progress of disease, pathologists have only about 68% accuracy (Sayed, 2018). So, pathologists have to take next level of pathology. That is machine learning. This nucleus branch of artificial intelligence feed data first, discover patterns, then trains using the input data and finally declares a decision. Then also, the scientists have a doubt that how machine can perform better than experienced pathologists. Initially, the machines can execute things much faster than human being. Even in matter of seconds, machines will finish hundreds to thousands of biopsies whereas one biopsy itself takes 5 to 10 days for pathologists to complete. Next is about accuracy. Now days, there are a lot of data out in this world. It is very difficult to manipulate all those data by a human. But a machine can do that with the help of Internet of Things (IoT) technology. Similarly, a machine can do large number of iterations without getting tired whereas humans see this a s a tiresome task. So, future of cancer prediction is machine learning.

CONCLUSION

This chapter is fully based on machine learning, breast cancer detection and prognosis. Authors started the chapter with breast cancer statistics and motivations followed by a literature review. For better understanding on breast cancer, authors discussed the structure of breast, different types of cancer and various screening methods. The chapter only deals with histopathology images. Therefore, an overview of biopsy was explained along with histopathology image analysis using various machine learning techniques. If things are going like this, ML will replace the pathologists tomorrow. Still machine learning has way more to go in the sense that models lack enough data and absence of good bias. But machine learning is the next altitude to reach by pathology and it would provide a new dimension to the field of investigating the breast cancer.

REFERENCES

Al-Kofahi, Y., Lassoued, W., Lee, W., & Roysam, B. (2010). Improved automatic detection and segmentation of cell nuclei in histopathology images. *IEEE Transactions on Biomedical Engineering, 57*(4), 841–852. doi:10.1109/TBME.2009.2035102 PMID:19884070

Albini, A., Pennesi, G., Donatelli, F., Cammarota, R., De Flora, S., & Noonan, D. M. (2010). Cardio-toxicity of anticancer drugs: The need for cardio-oncology and cardio-oncological prevention. *Journal of the National Cancer Institute, 102*(1), 14–25. doi:10.1093/jnci/djp440 PMID:20007921

Alhadidi, B., Zubi, M. H., & Suleiman, H. N. (2007). Mammogram breast cancer image detection using image processing functions. *Information Technology Journal, 6*(2), 217–221. doi:10.3923/itj.2007.217.221

Aswathy, M. A., & Jagannath, M. (2017). Detection of breast cancer on digital histopathology images: Present status and future possibilities. *Informatics in Medicine Unlocked, 8*, 74–79. doi:10.1016/j.imu.2016.11.001

Belsare, A. D., Mushrif, M. M., Pangarkar, M. A., & Meshram, N. (2016). Breast histopathology image segmentation using spatio-colour-texture based graph partition method. *Journal of Microscopy, 262*(3), 260–273. doi:10.1111/jmi.12361 PMID:26708167

Bengio, Y., Courville, A., & Vincent, P. (2013). Representation learning: A review and new perspectives. *IEEE Transactions on Pattern Analysis and Machine Intelligence, 35*(8), 1798–1828. doi:10.1109/TPAMI.2013.50 PMID:23787338

Bodai, B. I., & Tuso, P. (2015). Breast cancer survivorship: A comprehensive review of long-term medical issues and lifestyle recommendations. *The Permanente Journal, 19*(2), 48–79. doi:10.7812/TPP/14-241 PMID:25902343

Canto, J. G., & Kiefe, C. I. (2014). Age-specific analysis of breast cancer versus heart disease mortality in women. *The American Journal of Cardiology, 113*(2), 410–411. doi:10.1016/j.amjcard.2013.08.055 PMID:24210676

Cruz-Roa, A., Gilmore, H., Basavanhally, A., Feldman, M., Ganesan, S., Shih, N. N. C., ... Madabhushi, A. (2017). Accurate and reproducible invasive breast cancer detection in whole-slide images: A Deep Learning approach for quantifying tumor extent. *Scientific Reports, 7*(1), 46450. doi:10.1038rep46450 PMID:28418027

Eifel, P., Axelson, J. A., & Costa, J. (2001). National institutes of health consensus development conference statement: Adjuvant therapy for breast cancer. *Journal of the National Cancer Institute, 93*(13), 979–989. doi:10.1093/jnci/93.13.979 PMID:11438563

Elter, M., & Held, C. (2008). Semi-automatic segmentation for the computer aided diagnosis of clustered microcalcifications. Proceedings of. SPIE 2008, 6915, 691524-691524.

Estapé T. (2018). Cancer in the elderly: Challenges and barriers. *Asia-Pacific Journal of Oncology Nursing, 5*(1), 40-42.

Go, A. S., Mozaffarian, D., & Roger, V. L. (2013). Heart disease and stroke statistics -- 2013 update: A report from the American Heart Association. *Circulation, 127*, e6–e245. PMID:23239837

Guzmán-Cabrera, R., Guzmán-Sepúlveda, J. R., Torres-Cisneros, M. D., May-Arrioja, D. A., Ruiz-Pinales, J., Ibarra-Manzano, O. G., ... Parada, A. G. (2013). Digital image processing technique for breast cancer detection. *International Journal of Thermophysics, 34*(8-9), 1519–1531. doi:10.100710765-012-1328-4

Lynch, B. (2017). *what-motivates-our-researchers*. Retrieved from https://nbcf.org.au/news/research-blog/what-motivates-our-researchers/

Malvia, S., Bagadi, S. A., Dubey, U. S., & Saxena, S. (2017). Epidemiology of breast cancer in Indian women. *Asia Pacific Journal of Clinical Oncology*, *13*(4), 289–295. doi:10.1111/ajco.12661 PMID:28181405

Massat, M. B. (2018). A Promising future for AI in breast cancer screening. *Applied Radiology*, *47*(9), 22–25.

McGuire, K. P. (2016). Breast Anatomy and Physiology. In *Breast Disease*. Cham: Springer. doi:10.1007/978-3-319-22843-3_1

Nedzved, A., Ablameyko, S., & Pitas, I. (2006). Morphological segmentation of histology cell images. *Proceedings of IEEE International Special Topic Conference on Information Technology in Biomedicine*, *1*, 500–503.

Qin, P., Chen, J., & Zeng, J. (2018). Large-scale tissue histopathology image segmentation based on feature pyramid. *EURASIP Journal on Image and Video Processing*, *75*, 1–9.

Sayed, S. (2018). *Machine learning is the future of cancer prediction*. Retrieved from https://towards-datascience.com/machine-learning-is-the-future-of-cancer-prediction-e4d28e7e6dfa

Sharma, C. S. (2001). *India still has a low breast cancer survival rate of 66%: study*. Retrieved from https://www.livemint.com/Science/UaNco9nvoxQtxjneDS4LoO/India-still-has-a-low-breast-cancer-survival-rate-of-66-st.html

Sheshadri, H. S., & Kandaswany, A. (2006). Computer aided decision system for early detection of breast cancer. *The Indian Journal of Medical Research*, *124*(2), 149–154. PMID:17015928

Taber, J. K. A., Morisy, L. R., & Osbahr, A. J. III. (2010). Male breast cancer: Risk factors, diagnosis, and management. *Oncology Reports*, *24*(5), 1115–1120. PMID:20878100

Tashk, A., Helfroush, M. S., & Danyali, H. (2014). A novel CAD system for mitosis detection using histopathology slide images. *Journal of Medical Signals and Sensors*, *4*(2), 139–149. PMID:24761378

Xu, J., Xiang, L., Wang, G., Ganesan, S., Feldman, M., Shih, N. N. C., ... Madabhushi, A. (2015). Sparse non-negative matrix factorization (SNMF) based color unmixing for breast histopathological image analysis. *Computerized Medical Imaging and Graphics*, *46*, 20–29. doi:10.1016/j.compmed-imag.2015.04.002 PMID:25958195

Yang, L., Meer, P., & Foran, D. (2005). Unsupervised segmentation based on robust estimation and color active contour models. *IEEE Transactions on Information Technology in Biomedicine*, *9*(3), 475–486. doi:10.1109/TITB.2005.847515 PMID:16167702

KEY TERMS AND DEFINITIONS

Artificial Intelligence: The intelligence revealed by computers or machines like humans show intelligence.

Biopsy: The analytical procedure through which a tissue is taken from the breast using a needle for the microscopic examination.

Breast Cancer: The abnormal and uncontrolled growth of cells inside the breast tissue.

Computer-Assisted Diagnosis: The diagnosis of a disease with the help of various computer-aided algorithms.

Haemotoxylin and Eosin (H&E): Two stains that are used for staining the biopsy specimen for clarity of tissues and other structures.

Histopathology: The analysis of a biopsy specimen under the microscope for the study of internal tissue and structures.

Normalization: The procedure used to mitigate the problems caused by the light and stain variations in a breast tissue for clear visualization.

Chapter 2
Cognitive-Based Cover Image Selection in Image Steganography

Sangeetha K. N.
JSS Academy of Technical Education Bangalore, India

Usha B. Ajay
BMS Institute of Technology and Management, India

ABSTRACT

The chances of data getting lost while it is being transferred between the sender and receiver is very high these days. Since these data are very sensitive whose security cannot be compromised, there is a need for highly secure systems to transfer the data without compromising the content and the quality. Steganography techniques help us to achieve these objectives. In the present time, various organizations and industries are using cover image arbitrarily. In such cases, it does not provide personalized approach to the whole process of data hiding. Thus, as a result of this limitation, there is motivation to build such an application in which the system selects which image is most suitable for hiding data accordingly. The main algorithm being used here is the regression algorithm which consists of other algorithms like linear regression, decision tree regression. This application also extracts the hidden data from the generated stego image.

INTRODUCTION

Information hiding in digital images in the form of text, audio or video can be done using Image Steganography technique. In comparison with cryptography, steganography is not used to hide information from others but it is used to make others believe that the information does not even exist. Using steganography, the user can conceal/hide information in ways which will prevent the hidden message to be detected. In steganography, the information or encrypted information is hidden inside a digital host before being transferred through a network, thus existence of the hidden information is scarce. Image Steganography can be used for a wider number of applications such as copyright protection for digital media such as audio, video and images.

DOI: 10.4018/978-1-5225-9902-9.ch002

Steganography essentially cheats human perception, human senses have not been trained to keep an eye for files that may have hidden information inside them, there are a variety of available programs that can do Steganalysis (Detecting the use of Steganography.) Steganography is regularly used to hide one file into another file. When this hiding of files is performed, the hidden data is usually protected by a password.

A cognitive system performs the work of knowing, understanding, planning, deciding, problem solving, analyzing, synthesizing, assessing, and judging as it is fully integrated with perceiving and acting. In cognitive inspired image steganography, the algorithms employed are used to find the similarity ratio between the image before and after steganography is used. This is measured based on the SSIM ratios for each of the various images.

The main objective of using image steganography is to choose a suitable image for hiding the information so that any person trying to find encrypted information is unable to do so. The image that has been selected to hide the data should have a small SNR after steganography is performed on the image. Thus, the user gets an image which hides the encrypted data.

LITERATURE SURVEY

Khandare et al. (1996) discuss about data hiding technique called Steganography. Their paper presents a survey on various data hiding techniques in steganography along with the comparative analysis of these techniques. Their paper presents both traditional and novel techniques for addressing the data-hiding process and evaluates these techniques in light of three applications: copyright protection, tamper proofing, and augmentation data embedding. The authors have discussed about steganography and presented some notable differences between steganography and cryptography. They also surveyed various data hiding techniques in steganography and provided a comparative analysis of these techniques.

Goel et al. (2013) attempted to work on most of the prominent algorithms. Their work was mostly related to finding out the parameters that steganography can be based on and their comparison. Their paper deals with hiding information using LSB, DCT and DWT techniques. These algorithms are measured based on their MSE and PSNR values. Along with these, two other parameters are used to measure the effectiveness of these algorithms. They are Robustness and Capacity payload. The authors have successfully implemented the algorithms proposed in this paper and the results have been documented. From their results, they came to the conclusion that DCT having higher PSNR provides best quality of images.

Chen Ming et al. (2006) made a comparative study on different steganalysis techniques. They have implemented Markov Chains to try and test various techniques and made their conclusions.

Zöllner et al. (1998) studied SVM and its variation RBF to achieve the best possible results. According to his findings, the best result obtained was the usage of RBF as it was automatic and very versatile.

Joachims et al. (2000) has studied the effect steganography has on certain image features after the data has been embedded. They found out that certain statistical measures are different for cover images and stego images.

Fridrich et al. (2001) proposed a steganalysis method using the Histogram Characteristic Function (HCF) as a feature to distinguish the cover and stego images. This method is efficient in detecting the LSB replacement for RGB color bitmaps, but ineffective in detecting the LSB matching for grayscale images.

Harmsen et al. (2001) present different techniques for steganalysis of images that have been potentially embedded with data, using both active warden and passive warden framework. They used different image quality measures in order to detect the presence of stego images.

Dumitrescu et al. (2003) present another novel method for detection of steganographic data in image for LSB algorithm. It works on the principle that for a stego image, the histogram of the image will have local extrema in the grey level histogram.

Ali Al-Ataby et al. (2010) had worked on modifying the steganography algorithm so that the embedding is more secure. It does this by making sure that the statistical features of the stego image are kept as close to the features of the cover image as possible. It makes use of error correcting codes, which allows the algorithm to choose which pixel to change so that there will be minimum changes throughout the images.

Cachin et al. (1998) presented a new object method to quantify the visibility of errors between the modified image and the original image. SSIM take in account not only the per pixel differences between the images but also the structural similarity between them. This includes the textures of the image. Hence this is an ideal medic to gauge which image is least effected by embedding the data.

MOTIVATION

Software can easily be stolen these days by any third party.

The chances of data to get lost are very common these days while it is being transferred between the sender and receiver. Since these data are very sensitive whose security cannot be compromised therefore there is a much need for highly secure system for the data to be transferred without compromising on the content and the quality of data. Steganography techniques helps us to achieve these objectives.

In the present time, various organizations and industries are using cover image arbitrarily. In such cases, it does not provide personalized approach to the whole process of data hiding. Thus, as a result of this limitation the motivation to build such an application, in which the system selects which image is most suitable for hiding data accordingly. The main algorithm being used here is the regression algorithm which consists of other algorithms like linear regression, decision tree regression. This application also extracts the data hidden from the generated stego image. In cryptography, cognitive science has been used, so as similar to cognitive cryptography there is an expansion in the project from cryptography to steganography and cognitive science is used to predict the suitable image to be used for steganography.

Problem Statement

The present steganography applications does not provide suitable cover image selection, this project aims to build an application which incorporates selecting of cover images, cover images are selected behind which information is to be hidden, the different features of these cover images is extracted and using the best suitable algorithm for steganography to embed the data i.e., hide the data over an image using different steganography algorithms considering different parameters, the SSIM is calculated to be sure that the image before and after steganography has not be altered.

Objectives

- Creating a data set of cover images and embedded images from which the suitable image will be selected for hiding data or any secret information to prevent it from the third party interference.
- Training a ML regression model which can help predict expected secrecy, SSIM.
- Using ML model to help decide between multiple cover images, the optimum one to use. The more optimum the image, the less is the chance of data loss during transmission between a sender and a receiver.

Scope

The project deals with the selection of suitable cover image for information hiding, the information is hidden behind these images that can then be transferred through a network where someone monitoring the network will not know whether the image contains hidden information or not, the project has numerous applications in different varying field.

Apart from choosing suitable cover image, calculation of the SSIM of the image is also done. Higher the SSIM, more is the image similar to the original one used before steganography was performed on the image and the image will not look altered, hence, detecting hidden information will be difficult.

Methodology

- Collect image dataset with images of different size, textures, etc. More will be the number of images, the model will get a broad view of the features and can train of different features of the image making it more and more optimum for data hiding.
- Embed data using LSB spatial image steganography algorithm. The Least Significant Bit is one of the main techniques in spatial domain image steganography. It works on the fact that the precision level in several image formats is greater than that perceivable by average human being. So, a variant image with little changes in its colors will be non-differential from the original by a human, just by seeing at it. In LSB technique, just four bytes of pixels are sufficient to hold one message byte. Rest of the bits in the pixels is the same.
- Calculate the features for each cover image (Entropy, Histogram, No. of colors etc.). Machine learning can't be applied directly on an image so their features need to be extracted for applying machine learning on it and find a suitable image for particular data.
- For each stego-image, calculate the mean difference, PSNR, expected secrecy. To find out the difference in the final image and the original image.
- Train a regression model (linear/ logistic) using the previous data. The previous data is taken from the already made dataset with different size images.
- Use model to select optimum cover image from a group. The data can be securely hidden in that image without any threat of hacking and completely secure.

OVERVIEW OF COGNITIVE BASED COVER IMAGE SELECTION IN IMAGE STEGANOGRAPHY

Computer vision is a range of software engineering that includes strategies for programming a computer to see high dimensional information from this present reality with the point of delivering helpful data. It is an interdisciplinary field identified with manmade brainpower, machine learning, mechanical technology, flag preparing and geometry. Archive arrangement is an indispensable piece of machine vision.

Text File

Content records includes printed information or data which may be spared in plain content or rich content organizations. While a large number of the content records are reports produced and spared by clients, they can likewise be used by programming software engineers to store program as information. Word preparing archives, email messages, and log records are some of basic cases of such information. A computer document that is molded as an accumulation of lines of electronic content is only a content record. The sort of plain content that is being considered here is unstructured information.

There are various different document formats including: .TXT, .RTF, .LOG, .DOCX, .PDF, and so forth. A content record is put away either in ASCII or paired arrangement for every single working framework, for example, UNIX, Macintosh, Microsoft Windows, DOS, and different frameworks. Records with .txt augmentation are the simplest to be understood by the machine which makes them a stage free all-inclusive arrangement.

Unstructured Data

Unstructured information is a sort of printed information which is not composed in a pre-characterized set way or doesn't go under pre-outlined information display. Unstructured information is significantly message particular, yet may contain other data, for example, dates, measurements, diagrams, figures and truths moreover.

Image Features

Image features refers to the various image parameters that are calculated using different image processing algorithms. They are used to detect and separate various desired portions or image characteristics of a digital image or video stream, so that different operations can be applied to it.

Entropy

The entropy (E) of any given image represents the entropy of any given grayscale image. The given entropy is a statistical measure of randomness that can be used to characterize the texture of the given input image. As shown in Figure 1, it is observed that in places where the entropy of the grayscale image is low, are homogeneous regions and are represented by the black color in the resultant image and at other places where the entropy is high, white color is in the resultant image. Entropy is defined as:

Figure 1. Entropy feature of an image

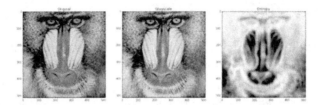

-sum(p.*log2(p))

where p contains the histogram counts.

Edge Detection

The Roberts cross administrator is utilized in image processing and computer vision for detecting the different edges in an image. It was one of the primary edge detectors used to identify edges in an image.

The consequences of this operation will highlight several changes in intensity in a diagonal direction. Most significant aspect of this operation is its simplicity; the kernel contains integers and is small. Roberts Cross operator performs a quick to compute, simple and a 2-D spatial gradient measurement on an image. It underlines regions of high spatial frequency which often correspond to different edges. In its most simple and common usage, the input to the operator is a grayscale image, as is the output. Pixel values at each point in the output represent the estimated absolute magnitude of the spatial gradient of the input image at that point.

To perform the detection of edge the algorithm needs to convolve the image, with the two kernels:

$$\begin{bmatrix} +1 & 0 \\ 0 & -1 \end{bmatrix} \text{and} \begin{bmatrix} 0 & +1 \\ -1 & 0 \end{bmatrix}$$

Let,

{\displaystyle I(x,y)}I(x,y) = a point in the original image and {\displaystyle G_{x}(x,y)}

Gx (x, y) = a point in an image formed by convolving with the first kernel and

Gy(x,y) {\displaystyle G_{y}(x,y)} = = = = = a point in an image formed by convolving with the second kernel.

The gradient can then be well defined as:

$$\nabla I\left(x,y\right) = G\left(x,y\right) = \sqrt{G_x^2 + G_y^2} \tag{1}$$

Total Number of Colors in the Image

The image that has been provided, the algorithm checks the number of colors that are present in the given image in which the secret information is to be embedded. More the number of colors, more the information that can be embedded in the image. The lesser the number of colors in the image the more is the insecurity in embedding the secret information.

Regression

Regression is a data mining function that predicts an unknown value based on some known values. Benefit, deals, contract rates, house estimations, square film, temperature, or separation all be predicted using regression techniques. For example, a model on regression can be used to predict the value of a house on the basis of its location, number of rooms and many other factors.

A regression task starts with a set of data in which the target values are known beforehand. For example, a regression model that predicts house values could be easily developed based on some observed data for several houses over a certain period of time. In addition to the value, the data might track the age of the house, square film, number of rooms, assessments, school locale, nearness to strip malls, and so on. House value would be the target, the other attributes would be the predictors, and the data for each house would constitute a case.

In the model build (training) process, the regression algorithm takes an estimate of the value of the target as a function of the predictors for each case within the build data. This relationship between the predictors and target are then consolidated in a model, this model can then be applied to different data sets in which the target values are unknown.

The testing of regression models is done by computing various statistics which measure the difference between the predicted values and the expected values. The data is divided into two data sets for a regression project: one for building the model and the other for testing.

Regression modeling has numerous applications in trend analysis, business planning, marketing, financial forecasting, time series prediction, biomedical, drug response modeling and environmental modeling.

Regression analysis aims at determining the values of the parameters for a function that causes the function to find the best fit for a set of data observations that have been provided. The following equation expresses these relationships in symbols. It shows that regression is the process of estimating the value of a continuous target (y) as a function (F) of one or more predictors ($\mathbf{x}_1, \mathbf{x}_2, ..., \mathbf{x}_n$), a set of parameters ($\theta_1, \theta_2, ..., \theta_n$), and a measure of error (e)

$$y = F\left(\mathrm{x}, \theta\right) + e \tag{2}$$

The predictors are understood as independent variables and the target as a dependent variable. The error, also called the residual, is the difference between the expected and predicted value of the dependent variable. The regression parameters are also known as regression coefficients.

The process of training a regression model involves finding the parameter values that minimize a measure of the error.

Figure 2. Simple linear regression with a single predictor

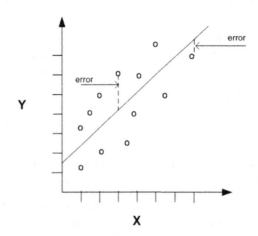

Linear Regression

This linear regression technique is brought into use if the relationship between predictors and the target can be approximated with the help of a straight line. Regression with a single predictor is the easiest to visualize. Simple linear regression with a single predictor is shown in Figure 2.

Support Vector Machines (SVM)

Support Vector Machines (SVM) is a capable, cutting edge calculation with solid theoretical establishments which depend on the Vapnik-Chervonenkis theory. SVM has solid regularization properties. Regularization implies the speculation of the model to new information. SVM utilizes an epsilon-insensitive loss function to take care of regression problems. SVM regression tries to locate a constant capacity to such an extent that the greatest number of information focuses exist within the epsilon-wide insensitivity tube. Predictions falling inside epsilon distance of the genuine target system are not translated as errors. The epsilon component is a regularization setting for SVM regression. It balances the margin of error with model robustness to achieve the best generalization to new data. SVM models have similar working as the neural networks and radial basis functions, both are very popular data mining techniques. However, neither of these algorithms has the well-founded theoretical approach to regularization that forms the basis of SVM. The quality of generalization and ease of training of SVM is far beyond the capacities of these more traditional methods.

SVM can model complex, real-world problems such as text and image classification, hand-writing recognition, and bioinformatics and bio sequence analysis.

SVM performs well on data sets which have a lot many attributes, even if there are very few cases on which to train the model. There is no upper limit on the number of attributes; but the hardware poses a constraint.

Decision Tree Algorithm

The Decision Tree algorithm, like Naive Bayes, is based on conditional probabilities but unlike Naive Bayes, decision trees generate rules. A rule is a conditional statement which is easy to be understood by humans and is easy to apply within a database to identify a set of records.

In some applications of data mining, the only thing that really matters is the accuracy of a prediction. It may not be important to know as to how the model works. In others, the ability to explain the reason for a particular decision can be very important. For example, a Marketing professional would require complete descriptions of all customer segments in order to launch a successful marketing campaign. The Decision Tree algorithm is ideal for such type of applications.

The Decision Tree algorithm produces an accurate and interpretable model with relatively little user intervention. The algorithm can be used for both binary and multiclass classification problems.

Decision tree scoring is especially fast. The tree structure, which is created in the model build, is used for a series of simple tests. Each test is based on a single predictor. It is a membership test: either IN or NOT IN a list of values (categorical predictor); or LESS THAN or EQUAL TO some value (numeric predictor). A decision tree predicts a target value by asking a sequence of questions. At a given stage in the sequence, the question that is asked depends upon the answers to the previous questions. The goal is to ask questions which, taken together, uniquely identify specific target values. Graphically, this process forms a tree structure which is shown in Figure 3.

Cryptography

Cryptography evolves from the Greek words 'Krypto's' meaning hidden and 'graphein' meaning writing. It is the study of techniques for safe communication between two parties and presence of a third party. Various issues like data confidentiality, data integrity and authentication are crucial to modern cryptography which exists in the disciplines of mathematics, computer science and electrical engineering.

It is analogous to encryption, the art of converting information from a readable state to apparent nonsense. The creator of an encrypted message shares the decoding technique only with legitimate recipients, thereby debarring the illegitimate persons from recovering the original message.

Figure 3. Decision tree formation

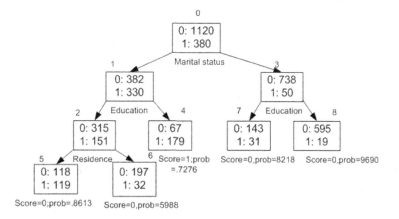

Cryptography algorithms are supposed to be extremely robust and imperceptible so that they are hard to be broken by any eavesdropper. Cryptanalysis is exactly opposite of cryptography involving methods for cracking the encrypted message or their implementations. Symmetric key cryptography is a type in which both the sender and the receiver share the same key. Even if the keys are different, they are related in a manner that is easily computable. Symmetric key ciphers are implemented as either block cipher or stream cipher. A block cipher encrypts input in blocks of plain text. A stream cipher on the other hand uses individual characters. In public key cryptosystems, every participating individual is distributed freely with the public key while its corresponding private key remains a secret. Here the public key is used for encryption whereas the private key is used for decryption.

Cognitive Cryptography

As a new scientific area, it focuses on building intelligent cryptographic protocols using cognitive information processing approaches. Such systems use the semantic analysis of encrypted data to select the suitable encryption method. Traditional cryptography is the art of hiding information using symmetric or asymmetric methods. Here, the best keys for data encryption are random keys which includes no extra information measured quantitatively.

Such algorithms are very secure but they do not allow the whole encryption process to be personalized and made dependent on the requirements of the client. In order to overcome this problem, the need for cognitive cryptography arises. That is when the user wants to create encryption keys that are not random sequences of bits but in which some personal information about the user is also encoded. This not only hides the data but also identifies the owner who has performed the task. Such features are very useful during authenticating parties and sharing secret information. Such a system semantically analyses selected patterns and extracts various unique features which can then be used to perform the most suitable cryptography algorithm.

Steganography

It is a practice of hiding a file, message, image, or video within another file, message, image or video. It is a combination of two Greek words 'Steganos' which means "covered or protected", and "graphein" means writing. The advantage of steganography over cryptography is that the secret message does not catch attention as an object of investigation. While cryptography is the practice of protecting the contents of a message, steganography hides the fact that a secret message is being transferred as well as hiding the contents of the message. Embedding data in any medium requires two files: the first one being the cover file and the other being the secret message. Secret message can be either plain text, cipher text or an image. The file obtained after embedding is called the stego file.

Wax covered tablets, hidden tattoos, invisible inks, microfilms, microdots were used traditionally for steganography. Various types of steganography are image steganography, audio steganography, video steganography or text steganography. In Image steganography the cover medium is an image file i.e. data to be hidden is done in the pixels of an image file. There are two most widely used image steganography techniques: Spatial Domain and Transform Domain.

In spatial Domain method secret bits are embedded straight away in the cover file. Most widely used spatial domain method is Least Significant Bit (LSB). In this, the data to be hidden is embedded in the least significant bit of the cover image file. There are two types under it: LSB Matching & LSB

Replacement. In LSB Matching if the message is same as the least significant bit of the cover image's pixel then it is remaining unchanged otherwise it is incremented or decremented by one in a random fashion. In case of LSB replacement simply the least significant bit of cover pixel is replaced with the message to be protected.

In the case of transform domain technique, hiding of secret bits is done in the significant portions of the cover image file. The various methods under this technique are Discrete Cosine Transform (DCT) and Discrete Wavelet Transform (DWT). In DCT, every color component in the JPEG image format makes use of discrete cosine transform to make transformation from successive 8x8 pixel blocks of image into every 64 DCT coefficients. Under DWT, secret data is stored the least important coefficients of each 4x4 transformed blocks of pixels.

The following criteria has been proposed for the imperceptibility of an algorithm.

- **Invisibility:** The strength of an algorithm lies in its ability to be unnoticed by the human eye. The moment anyone can make out even a minute difference in an image, the algorithm is compromised.
- **Payload Capacity:** Any steganography algorithm should satisfy sufficient embedding capacity.
- **Robustness against Statistical attacks:** Steganography algorithms leave behind a signature while embedding information that can be easily detected through statistical analysis. A robust algorithm is the one that outwits steganalysis.
- **Mean Square Error (MSE):** is a risk function corresponding to expected value of squared error. If {\displaystyle {\hat {Y}}}$\hat{Y}$ is a vector of *{\displaystyle n}n* predictions, and {\displaystyle Y} **Y** is the vector of observed values corresponding to the inputs to the function which generated the predictions, then the MSE of the predictor can be estimated by

$$\text{MSE} = \frac{1}{n}\sum_{i=1}^{n}(Y_i - Y_i)^2 \tag{3}$$

- **Peak Signal to Noise Ratio**: PSNR is the ratio between maximum possible power and corrupting noise that affects the representation of the image. It is a measure of quality reconstruction of an image.

$$= 20 \bullet \log_{10}\left(MAX_I\right) - 10 \bullet \left(MSE\right) \tag{4}$$

Here, *MAX$_I$* is the maximum possible pixel value of the image and **MSE** is the Mean Square Error.

- **Time Complexity**: Any fast steganography algorithm takes less time to embed and encode any information.

Least Significant Bit

LSB is one of the main techniques in the field of spatial domain image steganography. LSB is nothing but the lowest significant bit in the byte value of the image pixel. The secret information is embedded in the least significant bits of pixel values of the cover image in LSB based steganography. The concept is very simple. It reiterates the fact the level of precision in many image formats is far greater than that which can be perceived by an average human brain. Therefore, any modified image with slight variations in its colors will be indistinguishable from the original image by a human being if he is just looking at it. Any conventional LSB technique requires 8 bytes of pixels to store one byte of secret data.

HIGH LEVEL DESIGN OF COGNITIVE BASED COVER IMAGE SELECTION IN IMAGE STEGANOGRAPHY

High level Design refers to the design overview of the entire system architecture, where all the subcomponents involved in the working of the project are identified along with the constraints and the restrictions pertaining to them. The various designs which are mentioned in the following chapters are used in the development of the system. The design constraints and restrictions on the various parts of the system are taken under consideration and multiple modules are drawn out. Furthermore, the data flow for the modules are specified.

Design Considerations

The design process of the system is highly pipelined, with some considerations and assumptions which have to be taken into account between the various parts of the pipelines, as each stage of the pipeline is shaped according to the ones prior to them in the stages of development. This defines a method/approach which the programmer decides to take for the system which helps us shape the various stages of the pipeline so that all the various constraints can be addressed before arriving at a universal solution.

General Constraints

There are various constraints, limitations and exceptions which have to be addressed properly before the design process begins.

- Input document should not be of pdf format as only textual documents are considered valid inputs
- Training dataset must be selected so that it has a broader spectrum

There is always the possibility of the user aborting the session, so the system cannot be left in an inconsistent state.

Development Methods

Software development methods refers to the division of the development into various stages/phases with considerations before and after at each stage of the iterative process. For the implementation of our approach, the application makes use of the Scikit-learn, which is a predefined library which used for the various Machine Learning aspects, Scikit-image for the various operations to be done on the images for feature extractions, and numpy, which will allow for swifter mathematical operations respectively.

Architectural Strategies

The design decisions or strategies that affect the overall organization of the system and its higher-level structures are explained. These strategies provide insight into the key generalizations and mechanisms which have been used for the system architecture.

Programming Language

The programming language selection is essential to the implementation of the all the requirements of the various subcomponents in analysis and pipeline design. Keeping all these factors in consideration, Python was selected as the platform for programming of this project as it contains a large amount of already existing libraries.

User Interface Paradigm

The user interface is the subcomponent of the application which is used to make available the various functionalities of the project. An attractive, easy-to-use and efficient tends to get better results from the user of the program.

This project broadly comprises of two sections of user interface; when the data image is accepted, and at the end stage when the encrypted message is decrypted at the receiver end and the original message is received.

System Architecture

- . The project had started with the collection of an image dataset of 400 images covering a broad spectrum of features in terms of size, edge difference, entropy, histogram variance, texture, colors etc.
- From this database, a dataset module was created which contained all the various image feature vectors for all the images in the original dataset.
- Using the data obtained from this module a regression module was trained which took the image feature vector and returned the SSIM (Structural Similarity Index Matrix) based on the dataset module.
- Now the data file to be embedded and the image was passed to this regression model which used multiple regression techniques such as linear, SVM, Decision tree regression and the structural similarity with the stego image was determined.

As per the similarity the suitable cover images are determined and the data which is to be secretly transferred is hidden in the stego-image using methods such as random spatial LSB embedding. The complete system architecture is shown in Figure 4.

Figure 4. System architecture

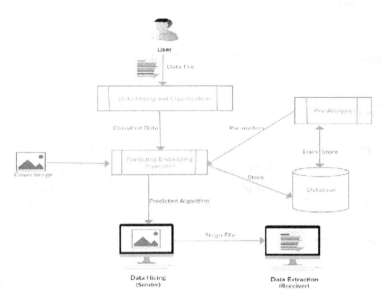

DETAILED DESIGN OF COGNITIVE BASED COVER IMAGE SELECTION IN IMAGE STEGANOGRAPHY

Detailed design is the part where further details and algorithmic designs of each of the modules is specified. The internal logic of each of the modules specified in high level design is also specified. All low-level components and other sub-components are described in detail as well. Each algorithm is described below in a step-wise manner. This chapter also discusses the control flow between different modules. The functionality, input and output of each module is also given in detail.

Functional Description of the Modules

This section lists and explains the functioning of each system module. Since the functioning of the software system as a whole is purely sequential, the entire working depends on each module equally.

The following are the modules in the project: Stego module, dataset module, Image features, Regression module.

1. **Stego Module:**
    a. **Purpose**: The purpose of this module is to take an input images and the text and apply random spatial LSB, and then return the stego image to the user
    b. **Functionality**: The system takes the input, and accepts the text to be hidden in the document, then generates random pixel positions whose RGB values are extracted and the system uses random spatial LSB embedding technique to embed the data in those selected pixels. The flowchart for this stego module is shown in Figure 5.
    c. **Input**: Image and text to be embedded
    d. **Output**: Stego-image returned to the user with the secret data hidden in the stego image.

2. **Image Features:**
    a. **Purpose**: Is used to process a given image and retrieve the various feature vectors associated with it.
    b. **Functionality**: Takes the image and processes the various properties such as entropy, edge difference, no of colors, histogram variance and stores these properties so that can be later used. The flowchart of the image feature module is shown in Figure 6.
    c. **Input**: Image
    d. **Output**: Values of the various feature vectors.
3. **Dataset Module:**
    a. **Purpose**: The purpose of this module is to take the image dataset which is going to be used for the training of the regression model and to store the feature vectors for all of the images in the database.
    b. **Functionality**: Contains all the images and the feature vectors of all the images contained in the dataset. Is also where the 1600 images generated from the 400 initial dataset images are contained.
    c. **Input**: Image dataset to be used for training.
    d. **Output**: Image feature vector dataset.
4. **Regression Module:**
    a. **Purpose**: The purpose of this module is to take the selection of input images and text to be embedded from the user and to determine the SSIM (Structural Similarity) of the stego image to the real image.
    b. **Functionality**: The system takes the selection of images and the text to be secretly camouflaged and enters it into the module which further enters it into the regression model. The module then extracts the various feature vectors and uses it to determine the structural similarity of the stego image to the real image. The flowchart of the regression module is shown in Figure 7.
    c. **Input**: Images and p value
    d. **Output**: Expected SSIM of the image.

IMPLEMENTATION OF COGNITIVE BASED COVER IMAGE SELECTION IN IMAGE STEGANOGRAPHY

The most crucial part of a project is its implementation which is based on several important decisions such as selection of platform, the language used, etc. To run the project smoothly, several factors such as the real environment in which the system works, the speed that is required, other implementation specific details, etc. have to be taken care of.

Programming Language Selection

The programming language chosen plays a major role in the development of the project. The key to picking a good programming language is to look at how efficiently the implementation can be done with that particular language, and compare it with the effort taken to code or prototype the project.

Figure 5. Flowchart of the stego module   *Figure 6. Flowchart of the image features model*

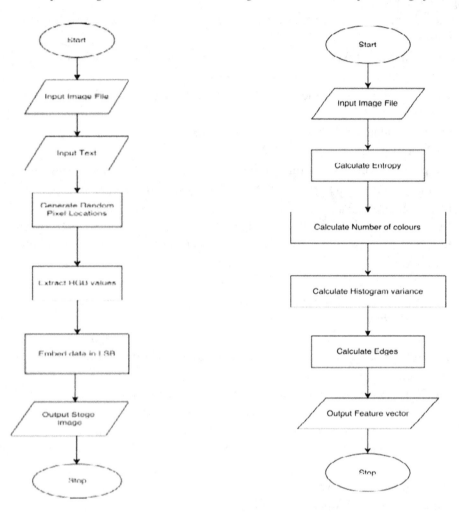

Python is a widely used high-level, general-purpose, interpreted, dynamic programming language. Its design philosophy emphasizes code readability, and its syntax allows programmers to express concepts in fewer lines of code than possible in languages such as C++ or Java. The language provides constructs intended to enable writing clear programs on both a small and large scale. Python supports multiple programming paradigms, including object oriented, imperative and procedural styles. It features a dynamic type system and automatic memory management and has a large and comprehensive standard library. Python interpreters are available for many operating systems, allowing Python code to run on a wide variety of systems.

One of the main reasons for selecting Python as the primary language for this project is because the comprehensive support and libraries ecosystem that Python has, especially in the domain of machine learning and data mining.

Figure 7. Flowchart of the regression model

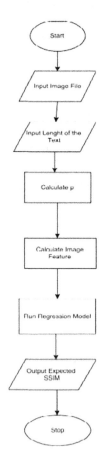

Platform Selection

Anaconda, a Python distribution is used for coding the software. The development environment was Windows 10, with all the coding being done on Sublime Text editor. It contains many image processing libraries which is useful for this project. The Python platform is optimized for solving engineering and scientific problems. The desktop environment invites experimentation, exploration, and discovery. These Python tools and libraries are all rigorously tested and designed to work together.

Code Conventions

Coding conventions refer to a set of practices and guidelines that are followed while writing code, in order to ensure uniformity and readability in the code. It also ensures that certain standards of style are upheld in the code.

The conventions that are followed in the project include organization of files, indentation of code, comments in the code, statements and declarations, whitespaces used, conventions for naming classes and variables, best practices for programming, principles of programming, rules of thumb of programming, and best architectural practices. The coding conventions are done in a systematic and organized manner so as to adopt a more object-oriented approach, thus resulting in improved software structural quality. These conventions may be formalized in a documented set of rules that an entire team or company follows, or may be as informal as the habitual coding practices of an individual.

Naming Conventions

All the class names, functions and variable names have been chosen bearing in mind that they must reflect the purpose of that class/function/variable. The naming is as short as possible and underscore is used to separate the words in a name. The variable names of a packet fields are in capitals to distinguish them from regular variables.

Establishing a naming convention for a group of developers can become ridiculously contentious. This section describes a commonly used convention. It is especially helpful for an individual programmer to follow a naming convention. Variables The names of variables should document their meaning or use. Variable names should be in mixed case starting with lower case.

The naming conventions used in Python are:

1. **General**
   a. Avoid using names that are too general or too wordy. Strike a good balance between the two.
   b. Good: user_profile, menu_options, word_definitions
   c. When using Camel Case names, capitalize all letters of an abbreviation (e.g. HTTPServer)
2. **Modules**
   a. Module names should be all lower case.
   b. When multiple words are needed, an underscore should separate them.
   c. It is usually preferable to stick to 1 word names.
3. **Classes**
   a. Class names should follow the UpperCaseCamelCase convention.
   b. Python's built-in classes, however are typically lowercase words.
   c. Exception classes should end in "Error".
4. **Global (Module-Level) Variables**
   a. Global variables should be all lowercase.
   b. Words in a global variable name should be separated by an underscore.
5. **Instance Variables**
   a. Instance variable names should be all lower case.
   b. Words in an instance variable name should be separated by an underscore.
   c. Non-public instance variables should begin with a single underscore.
   d. If an instance name needs to be mangled, two underscores may begin its name.
6. **Methods**
   a. Method names should be all lower case.
   b. Words in a method name should be separated by an underscore.
   c. Non-public method should begin with a single underscore.
   d. If a method name needs to be mangled, two underscores may begin its name.
7. **Method Arguments**
   a. Instance methods should have their first argument named 'self'.
   b. Class methods should have their first argument named 'cls'.

8. **Functions**
   a. Function names should be all lower case.
   b. Words in a function name should be separated by an underscore.
9. **Constants**
   a. Constant names must be fully capitalized.
   b. Words in a constant name should be separated by an underscore.

File Organizations

Structuring code, both among and within files is essential in making it understandable. Thoughtful partition in and ordering increase the value of the code.

- **Modularize**: The best way to write a big program is to assemble it from well-designed small pieces (usually functions). This approach enhances readability, understanding and testing by reducing the amount of text which must be read to see what the code is doing. Code longer than two editor screens is a candidate for partitioning. Small well designed functions are more likely to be usable in other applications.
- **Make Interaction Clear:** A function interacts with other code through input and output arguments and global variables. The use of arguments is almost always clearer than the use of global. Structures can be used to avoid long lists of input or output arguments.
- **Partitioning:** All sub functions and many functions should do one thing very well. Every function should hide something.
- **Use Existing Functions:** Developing a function that is correct, readable and reasonably flexible can be a significant task. It may be quicker or surer to find an existing function that provides some or all of the required functionality. as a function. It is much easier to manage changes if code appears in only one file.
- **Sub Function:** A function used by only one other function should be packaged as its sub function in the same file. This makes the code easier to understand and maintain.
- **Test Scripts:** Write a test script for every function. This practice will improve the quality of the initial version and the reliability of changed versions. Consider that any function too difficult to test is probably too difficult to write. More than the act of testing, the act of designing tests is one of the best bug preventers known.

Difficulties Encountered and Strategies Used to Tackle Them

There were a lot of challenges that were faced while implementing the project. Some of these major problems are stated in brief in following section along with their solutions.

- For steganography very few datasets are available which contain both the cover image and the embedded stego – image.
  Solution: We created our own dataset by utilizing the ImageNet Classification dataset. From the dataset, a random set of images were selected and their corresponding stego – image for different p values were generated.

- Inconsistent values when we were deciding the list of images features to be used for regression. **Solution:** A graph of each image feature along with actual SSIM of the image was plotted to see which image features had high correlation and only those features were used.
- Initially the accuracy we were getting from Linear and SVM regression were not satisfactory. **Solution:** After trying the Decision Tree regression, we got the accuracy that was required.

EXPERIMENTAL RESULT AND ANALYSIS OF COGNITIVE BASED COVER IMAGE SELECTION IN IMAGE STEGANOGRAPHY

This chapter lists the results of the project and the inferences made from the testing results. The evaluation enlisted and the results accordingly quantified.

Evaluation Metric

The main metric used in the project is the coefficient of determination calculated based on the comparison the structural similarity of the stego image to that of the actual image entered by the user. The stego images are trained by a regression algorithm which considers the various feature vectors such as entropy, edge difference, histogram variance, no of colors and the embedding factor for the training of the regression model.

Embedding was done for the values 0.3 and 0.5 and the various feature comparisons are shown below in Figure 8, Figure 9 and Figure 10. It is clearly observed that entropy versus SSIM graph has the narrowest curve which means they are highly correlated. Hence, entropy was chosen to be the primary feature for the training of the regression model.

Figure 8. Graph of entropy vs SSIM

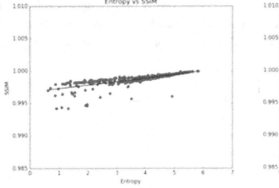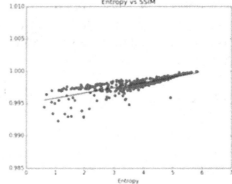

Figure 9. Graph of histogram variance vs SSIM

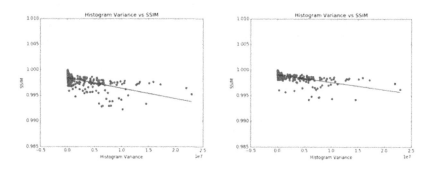

Figure 10. Graph of edges vs SSIM

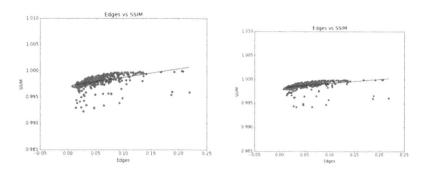

Experimental Dataset

The project uses an image dataset of about 400 images which was obtained online. All these images are unique and of different sizes and textures. These 400 images are used and with embedding values ranging from 0.2-0.5, namely 0.2,0.3,0.4,0.5, another image dataset of 1600 images is created which is used to train the regression model used in the project.

The user enters the selection of images through which he wants to secretly transfer the data and the approximate length of the secret message. The model then uses the regression algorithm trained so as to determine which images are suitable for embedding the data. The selection in order of best SSIM is returned to the user. The user then enters the secret data he wishes to transfer and the stego-images with the secret data embedded are shown to the user.

Performance Analysis

To determine the accuracy of the program and to analyze the result given for a given input, the SSIM (Structural Similarity Index Matrix) of the cover image and stego - image is taken into consideration. The actual SSIM obtained is compared to the SSIM which was predicted by the regression model, which uses linear, support vector and decision tree regression algorithms. In Figure 11, 12 and 13 it is clearly inferred from the graphs that decision tree algorithm is the most accurate among the various regression algorithms that were used.

Figure 11. Graph of predicted vs actual data for linear

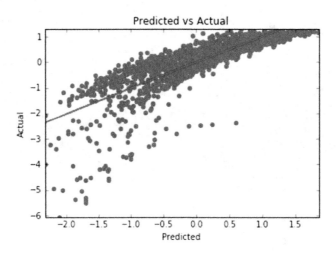

Figure 12. Graph of predicted vs actual data for support vector

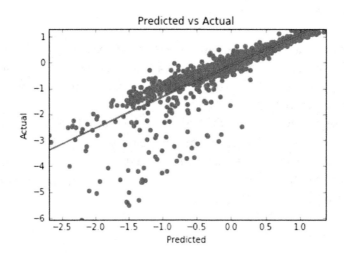

Figure 13. Graph of predicted vs actual data for random trees

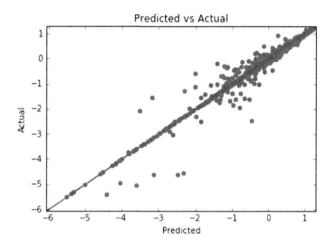

Inference From the Result

From the experimental analysis done and the results obtained, it is clearly obvious that decision tree algorithm is the best method to train the regression model and the stego images obtained had no visual difference from the original image, the Figure 14 is showing that our method is effective and the algorithm trained is suitable for camouflaging the data.

As shown in Figure 15 the graph of average difference between the actual SSIM and the predicted SSIM is plotted by varying the amount of data embedded in 50 random test images. Again it is observed that the Decision Tree regression algorithm has the lowest difference between the actual and predicted values, thus being more accurate.

Figure 14. Graph of accuracy of the regression algorithms

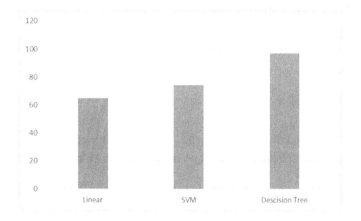

Figure 15. Graph of comparison of the regression algorithms

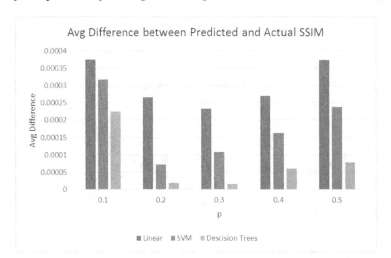

CONCLUSION

In a world where data thefts and attacks are increasing the need for data security is highly required. This project aims at suggesting the best suitable image for a given data based on vectors like payload, invisibility and robustness. Selecting a suitable cover image can help protect against statistical steganalysis. Till date, ML is used to decide between the different algorithms for steganography to hide the data but the user still has to manually select image in which user wishes to embed the secret data. Using machine learning to train model which will help determine which cover image will be best for embedding the secret file depending upon the required secrecy and size of data.

- Though LSB and its variations are vulnerable to image manipulations, they have a fast execution time.
- The image selection and steganography methods produced expected results.

Limitations

The main limitation of the project is that the dimension of the cover image should not exceed 4096x4096. If the dimensions of the cover image goes beyond 4096x4096, noise will creep into the stego image. User cannot enter PDF file format.

FUTURE ENHANCEMENT

- The project can be extended to include all types of cover images and large number of datasets can be created. Since execution time for the large images is very long parallelism needs to be introduced in the project.
- Different more types of image features can be included for regression.
- Other than text files, improvements can be made to also embed other files like audio, video, etc.

REFERENCES

Al-Ataby, A., & Al-Naima, F. (2010). A Modified High Capacity Image Steganography Technique Based on Wavelet Transform. *The International Arab Journal of Information Technology, 7*(4).

Cachin, I. (1998). An information-theoretic model for steganography. *Proceedings of the 2nd International Workshop on Information Hiding, 15,* 68-88.

Dumitrescu, S., Wu, X., & Wang, Z. (2003). *Detection of LSB Steganography via sample pair analysis. IEEE Trans, 51,* 128–136.

Fridrich, J., Goljan, M., & Du, R. (2001). Reliable Detection of LSB Steganography in Color and Grayscale Images. *Proc. of ACM Workshop on Multimedia and Security, 32,* 198-231. 10.1145/1232454.1232466

Goel, S., Rana, A., & Kaur, M. (2013a). A review of comparison techniques of image steganography. *Global Journal of Computer Science and Technology Graphics & Vision, 13*(4), 9–14.

Goel, S., Rana, A., & Kaur, M. (2013b). ADCT-based robust methodology for image steganography. *International Journal of Image, Graphics and Signal Processing, 5*(11).

Harmsen, J. J., & Pearlman, W. A. (2001). Steganalysis of LSB embedding using Image Metrics. *Proceedings of SPIE Security and Watermarking of Multimedia Contents V, 48,* 118–131.

Joachims, T., & Kaufman, M. (2000). Estimating the Generalization Performance of a SVM Efficiently. *Proceedings of the International Conference on Machine Learning (ICML), 15,* 28-54.

Khandare, P., Kambale, P., Narnavar, P., Galande, G., & Narnavar, J. (2014). Data hiding technique using steganography. *International Journal of Computer Science and Information Technologies, 5*(2), 1785–1787.

Ming, C., Ru, Z., Xinxin, N., & Yixian, Y. (2006). Analysis of Current Steganography Tools: Classifications & Features. *International Conference on Intelligent Information Hiding and Multimedia Signal Processing.*

Zöllner, J., & Federrath, H. (1998). Modeling the security of steganographic systems. *Proceedings of the 2nd Workshop on Information Hiding, 17,* 228-256.

Chapter 3
Disease Identification in Plant Leaf Using Deep Convolutional Neural Networks

Venu K.
Kongu Engineering College, India

Krishnakumar B.
Kongu Engineering College, India

Natesan Palanisamy
Kongu Engineering College, India

Sasipriyaa N.
Kongu Engineering College, India

ABSTRACT

Early detection of disease in the plant leads to an early treatment and reduction in the economic loss considerably. Recent development has introduced deep learning based convolutional neural network for detecting the diseases in the images accurately using image classification techniques. In the chapter, CNN is supplied with the input image. In each convolutional layer of CNN, features are extracted and are transferred to the next pooling layer. Finally, all the features which are extracted from convolution layers are concatenated and formed as input to the fully-connected layer of state-of-the-art architecture and then output class will be predicted by the model. The model is evaluated for three different datasets such as grape, pepper, and peach leaves. It is observed from the experimental results that the accuracy of the model obtained for grape, pepper, peach datasets are 74%, 69%, 84%, respectively.

INTRODUCTION

Motivation

Agriculture plays an important role in the global economy. Latest technologies have provided human society the facility to harvest adequate food to meet the requirement of more than 7 billion people. On the other hand, food safe keeping remains in danger by a number of factors such as change in climate, the decline in pollinators, plant diseases and others. Among these factors plant diseases are not only a threat to food security at the international level but can also have dreadful effect on small scale cultivators whose subsistence depends on safe and sound crops. Smallholder agriculturist bring about more than

DOI: 10.4018/978-1-5225-9902-9.ch003

80 percent of the agricultural production in the evolving world. Farmers are facing more than 50% of yield loss because of pests and disease. Hence identification of plant disease and do the needful in time is one of the most primitive and vital activity in agricultural field. Fungi and micro-organisms are the major origin for plant disease. The metabolism of micro – organisms are unfit to predict at early stage because a few diseases do not show any symptoms during early stage and are expressed only at the final stage. These types of diseases are causing major reduction in the yield.

Traditional Methodologies

In order to reduce crop loss due to disease several attempts have been developed from the olden days. Ancient way of widespread application of pesticides have in the past decade increasingly been supplemented by integrated pest management (IPM) approaches. Usage of chemicals such as bactericides, fungicides, and nematicides to control plant diseases can cause the development of long-term resistance of the pathogens, severely reducing the ability of the soil to fight back and produce adverse effects in the agro-ecosystem. Hence diagnosing a disease properly at its first appearance and provided appropriate remedial action is an important process for efficient disease management. In most of the cases diagnoses is performed visually by observing the symptoms through naked eye by the farmers or person from by agricultural extension organizations or other institutions, such as local plant clinics. Due to the enormous cultivated Crops and their existing phytopathological problems, even experienced agricultural experts and plant pathologists may often decline to victoriously diagnose specific diseases and are therefore led to misguided conclusions and concern solutions.

Interrelating Technologies With Agriculture

An automated systems are invented nowadays to support farmers for determining plant diseases by the plant's appearance and visual symptoms. This could provides an immense service to the beginners in the gardening process and also trained professionals can be used as a confirmation system in disease diagnostics. The process of precise plant protection has been enhanced and expanded by the opportunities provided via advancement in the computer vision. In recent years computer vision applications are widely used in the field of agriculture which provides better accuracy compared to other historical methods.

Trustworthiness of the disease diagnosis can be enriched by employing data analysis through innovative technologies such as Artificial Intelligence (AI). Machine learning the subarea of AI. Machine leaning is a field of research that formally focuses on the theory, performance, and properties of learning systems and algorithms. It is a highly interdisciplinary field building upon ideas from many different kinds of fields such as artificial intelligence, optimization theory, information theory, statistics, cognitive science, optimal control, and many other disciplines of science, engineering, and mathematics. Because of its implementation in a wide range of applications, machine learning has covered almost every scientific domain, which has brought great impact on the science and society. It has been used on a variety of problems, including recommendation engines, recognition systems, informatics and data mining, agriculture and autonomous control systems. There are several machine learning algorithms such as Support Vector Machine (SVM), Artificial Neural Network (ANN) and Deep Neural Network are used to extract hidden patterns from large volume of data and also the meta heuristics algorithms are employed to optimize the performance of these machine learning algorithms.

In machine learning, Neural Network (NN) is a computational technique used in computer science and other research disciplines. It is designed by the way in which biological nervous systems of the brain to process the information and to recognize patterns. This approach outshines in the field where the feature detection is troublesome to express in a conventional computer program. Rather than explicitly programmed this technique is based self- learning and training from the observational data which provides better accuracy in data analysis.

Prior versions of neural network are composed of swallower architecture with few hidden layers. Nowadays deep neural network with large number of processing layers has emerged and it is used in Deep learning techniques. Deep learning is a subset of machine learning which refers to Deep Artificial Neural Networks (DNN). Deep artificial neural networks are a set of algorithms that is applied for many important problems, such as image recognition, sound recognition, recommender systems and it is evident from many research works that it provides high accuracy. The technical term deep refers to the number of layers in a neural network. Deep neural networks learn features of the data with the help of multiple hidden layers. It is called as feature hierarchy since simple features from one layer is recombined to form complex features of the next layer. Neural network with large number of layers pass input data (features) through more mathematical operations when compared to neural networks with few layers. Hence training process is more computational intensive in deep learning and it is one reason why GPUs are in demand to train deep-learning models. It Provides higher accuracy, require more hardware or training time, and perform exceptionally well on machine perception tasks that involved unstructured data such as blobs of pixels or text. Deep learning is used in the applications where large amount of data analysis is required.

In recent years agriculture has been benefited from deep learning technologies. It is employed in agricultural production systems such as crop management, yield prediction, disease detection, weed detection crop quality, and species recognition livestock management, water management and soil management. Nowadays many real time artificial intelligence involved programs contributes to rich recommendations and insights for farmer decision support and action by employing learning to sensor data, farm management systems. Recently these deep learning techniques are stepped particular in the field of plant disease diagnosis to produce better results

Convolution Neural Network (CNN) is one the deep learning tools which excels in performing image processing task so it is used in agricultural applications. The current generation of convolutional neural networks (CNNs) has achieved remarkable results in the field of image classification. CNNs incorporates one of the most powerful system for modeling complex processes and performing pattern recognition in applications which consist of large amount of data, like the one of pattern recognition in images. A CNN is composed of three main parts which are convolution, pooling and fully connected layers. The convolution and pooling layers performs feature extractors operation from the input images while the fully connected layer acts as a classifier. These networks have grown in the number of layers leading to architectures such as RestNet and AlexNet that have been trained on images such as Cifar-10 and then fined tune to other problems, such as plant classification.

In the agricultural field CNN is trained with healthy and diseased leaves so that it is used in the disease detection diagnosis system to classify simple leaves images as healthy and diseased leaves in various plants with sufficient accuracy. Faster and accurate prediction of leaf disease in crops could help to develop an early treatment technique in the agricultural field.

The main target in the proposed system is to model a deep convolutional neural network to observe whether a plant leaf is healthy or not healthy by analyzing leaves of the those plant. If the plant is not healthy then the proposed model will identify the disease which affects the plant. The next section provides the literature survey on various methodologies used in detecting the disease in different plants.

RELATED WORKS

In Mohanty et al. (2016) deep learning model is trained for diagnosing 14 crop species and 26 crop diseases. Feature extraction and classification of images both can be achieved with the help of the same convolutional neural network architecture. Mohanty et al. (2016) compared the performance of two popular and established architectures of CNNs namely AlexNet and GoogLeNet, for plant disease dataset. The model is trained for classifying crop species and also to identify disease on the leaf by using two training mechanisms such as transfer learning and training from the scratch. The results were obtained at the success rate upto 99.35%. This methodology can be used in smartphone – based crop disease diagnosis systems by using large amount of data. The main drawback is the model is trained for single leaves, facing upwards on a similar background but in real world application it should able classify the image of the disease as it present on the plant itself.

In Sladojevic et al. (2016), the model is trained with the two classes of images such as healthy leaves and background images to provide accurate results. Here 30880 image were taken for training purpose and 2589 images for validation. It Uses CaffeNet Model, deep CNN which is available from an open source deep learning framework Caffe computes features from input image. The model uses the set of weights taken from the ImageNet and Graphics Processing Unit (GPU) mode for the training of the CNN. The overall accuracy is bring about to be 96.3%. It is found from the paper that fine tuning the hyper parameters has not exposed any significant changes in the overall accuracy but augmentation mechanism had shown greater impact to achieve good results.

In Furnetes et al. (2017) disease and pest identification is done with the help of deep meta architectures such as Faster Region-Based Convolutional Neural Network (Faster R-CNN), Single Shot Multibox Detector (SSD), and Region-based Fully Convolutional Networks (R-FCN), and feature extractor. Region of Interest (ROI) in the image which correlate with the affected areas of the plant is determined with the help of meta architecture. It can readily learn disease and pests found in the different part of the plant using deep feature extractor. This system is capable of detecting status of the infection whether it is earlier or last, finding the affected part of the plants from the given input image with different background conditions. It is identified from this paper that the number of samples is an important fact that controls the results. At most all the current image-based crop disease recognition algorithms depend on extracting different kinds of features from the affected plants leaf images. The main drawback of all these techniques is that all the features extracted from the leaf images are usually handled as equally important in the process of classification.

In Zhang et al. (2017) a different way of cucumber disease recognition is proposed. It consist of following three pipelined strategy for image classification: K- means clustering for segmenting leaf images which are diseased by classifying input image pixels into K classes based on the set of features, eliciting shape and color features from lesion data, Sparse Representation is used to classify the leaf image with disease. SR based classification method consist of training data from a single class lie on a subspace and test data are expressed as a sparse linear consolidation of the training samples. Decreasing the computation cost and increasing the recognition performance are the primary advantage in this method of classification using SR space. Cucumber leaf with disease image dataset is take for evaluation. The proposed methodology is compared with four other feature extraction techniques such as Texture feature (TF) based classification, Support Vector Machine, Plant leaf image (PLI) based classification, K-Means based segmentation followed by neural network based classification(KMSNN).The proposed method in this paper outperformed well when compared with other techniques in identifying seven major cucumber disease. The recognition rate is found to be 85.7%. The main drawback of this approach is that the complete dictionary of SR cannot be constructed efficiently.

An automated recognition of disease in cucumber leaf is proposed in Guo, Liu, and Li (2014) 2- Dimensional maximum entropy principle is used to generate threshold value for image segmentation and the value is optimized using different evolution algorithms. The cucumber diseased leaf images are segmented by using the generated threshold value. The lesion with large area from the segmentation results is picked up and given as representative lesion. The color features and texture features are extracted by analyzing the representative lesions of the affected images. With the extracted features from the lesion Bayes Classifier model is built for the recognition cucumber disease. This methodology is applied for recognition of anthracnose leaf image, cucumber powdery mildew leaf image, botrytis leaf images which were taken under natural conditions. Experimental outcome represents that this automated recognition method for cucumber disease leaf images are able to recognize affected images without involving human interaction and also it provides good performance.

In agriculture automated determination of the indication of foliage disease in the vast field of crops can be done effectively with the help of decision support systems. In this paper a decision support system has been devised and executed for small tomatoes manufacturers. In the proposed work (Vianna, Oliveira & Cunha, 2017), a model with a couple of multilayer perceptron neural network is developed. It is used for the study of digital photographs of tomatoes to pinpoint the late blight disease in the plant. The output generated by the neural network can be used to develop repainted tomato photographs in which the damage on the plant has been highlighted. The output can also be used to measure the illness level of each and every plant. A situation map of the field is created by making use of the measured damaged level of the plants in the farm. Then a cellularautomata triggers the outbreak progression over the fields. The various pesticides actions can be tested with the help of simulator within turn helps to make decision on when to start spraying the pesticides. It also helps to investigates losses and gains of every preferred action. The proposed pattern recognition method based on neural network for identifying late blight disease in tomato plant provides 97.99% prediction accuracy in pixel classification.

The technique of classifying disease in banana eaves automatically is proposed in this paper by using deep learning- based approaches. Amara, Bouaziz, and Algergawy (2017) use LeNet architecture as a convolutional neural network for the process of classifying large amount of image data sets. This method uses stochastic gradient descent as optimization algorithm to learn the values for weights used in the model with the learning rate of 0.001. The activation function used in the proposed work is Sigmoid function which is used in the classification process and RELU function is used in convolution layers. In order to increase the speed of the deep learning algorithms GPUs were used. It is evident from the test results that the proposed approach can produce better accuracy under challenging conditions such as illumination, complex background, different resolution, size, pose, and orientation of real scene images. The drawback of this method is that it can classify only two popular banana disease such as banana sigatoka and banana speckle. It cannot maintain the same accuracy level for more than two disease classification. Then the automated measurement of the level of damage in the detected disease type is also not addressed in this work.

BACKGROUND

Working of Convolution Neural Network

The ordinary neural Networks is not efficient enough in handling images. Images are made up of pixels, so when images are given as input to neural network then each pixel value should be given as input to each neurons which results in thousands of neurons in the input layer leads to very complex and expensive computations. Recently Convolutional Neural Networks, a kind of neural networks architecture specially designed to deal with images in a distinct fashion is introduced. It plays an efficient role in the areas such as image recognition and classification. CNN proceeds from the general concept of neural networks made up of neurons with learnable weights and biases. Input to the neural networks is a vector whereas in CNN input is multi-channeled images (3 channeled in the case of coloured image).

In order to reduce the size of the image without losing the original representation and to extract the important features from the images many new layers such as convolutional, pooling (downsampling), and fully connected layers, are used in CNN. In all these layers images are organised in 3 dimensions: width, height and depth. Further, only a small region of neurons in one layer connects to a neuron in the subsequent layer.

Convolutional Layer

Image is given as input to the convolution network. It observers the images as volumes (three dimensional objects as width * height * depth). For example let the dimension of input image be 124 *124* 3, since the given input image is colored the depth is 3. These depth layers are indicated as channels. Each pixel of an images represents the intensity by a number. These numbers are the raw features given as input to the convolution network. Features which significantly helps in classifying the images are extracted from the given image by the first layer called convolution layer.

Features such as horizontal edges, vertical edges, etc., are detected from the image by using filters in the convolution layer. Filters are just a square matrix of values also called as kernals or weight which are trained by the model to detect pattern in the image. Number of channels in the filter should be same as the number of channels in the input to the convolution layer. For example, if the input is of size 124*124*3 then the filter can be of size 5*5*3 (width and height are 5 pixel each, depth is 3 pixel) since the input images is with 3 layer depth the filter should also contain 3 layer depth. Any number of filters can be used at each convolution layers. Number of filters denotes the numbers of features to be extracted from the image. At the time of forward pass, the filter is stride over each part of the image in order to check whether the feature which is meant to detect is present or not. While striding, the dot product (element – wise product and the sum between two matrices) of the entries from the selected region of the input(first 5*5 region in the input) and the filter is computed in order to produce single entry in the output as shown in the Figure 1. The output represents how confident that the feature is present. If the output value is high then the feature is present in that input region, when it is low then the feature is not present. As we move the filter over the image fully then the output will be 2 – D activation map that provides the responses for that filter at every location. This is called as convolution operation.

In one convolution layer there will be n filters in order to detect n features from the input. As each filter produces one 2 – D activation map or feature map, n filters will produce n activation maps. This n represents the depth of the output volume. The width and height of the output volume is calculated by

Figure 1. Computation of the convolved image in the convolution layer

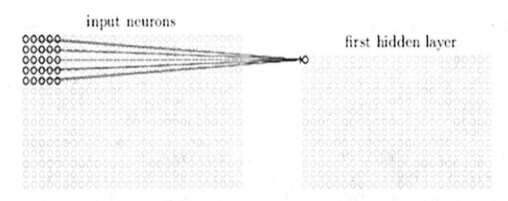

using stride value and padding values. The stride value represents the number of pixel be to moved by the filter while striding over the image at each step. When the stride value is one then the filter is moved by 1 pixel at a time. Padding is used to increase the input volume of the image by adding zeros at the border. Padding value 2 represents that 2 borders of zeros were added. Width and Height are calculated by using the following formula:

$$width\,or\,height = \frac{W - F + 2P}{S + 1}.$$

Where,

W = Input size (Eg: 124)
F = Filter size / receptive field size (Eg: 5)
P = Padding value(Eg: 1)
S = Stride value (Eg: 1)

Therefore width/ height = 121.For the above mentioned example after completing one convolution layer the given input image 124*124*3 is converted as 121*121*40 if 40 filters are used. By using a greater number of filters, we are able to preserve the spatial dimensions better. First convolution layer detects only the low-level features such as edges and curves. The output feature map from the convolution layer is summed up with a bias term and then passed through a non- linear activation function.

Activation Function

Complex data such as images and video could be modelled and learned by the CNN only with the help of activation function. It is responsible for deciding whether the value present in a neuron is needed for further processing or not. The most commonly used activation function in the hidden layers of CNN is RELU activation function. Its is just R(x) = max(0,x) i.e if x < 0, R(x) = 0 and if x >= 0, R(x) = x. If the value present in the neuron is less than zero it is changed as zero. If the value is positive then the value is taken as it is. RELU is most simple and effective technique and also it avoids vanishing gradient problem. In CNN positive values gets processed further compared to negative values so the RELU activation function is chosen to inactivate the neurons having negative value which leads to faster learning by the cnn. The next step is pooling layer it is a building block of CNN. The work of this layer is to regularly dimish the spatial size of the representation. This is done in order to decrease the amount of parameters, memory consumed and computation in the network and to speed up the training process. Each and every feature map are independently operated by the pooling layer. Max pooling is the most common approach used in CNN

For the first convolution layer the input is the original image whereas for the second convolution layer the input is the activation map or feature map that results as output from the first convolution layer. So each layer in the input for the second convolution layer is just the one which describes the location of low level features in the original image. Now on applying filters to the feature map will results in activation map that produce somewhat higher-level features. Example: detection of semicircles ie., circle and horizontal or vertical edge. Applying more number of convolution layers will result in the detection of complex features from the image. These features are given as input to the Multi-Layer Perceptron, which is nothing but a neural network. It is referred to as Fully – Connected Layer.

Fully – Connected Layer

In Fully – Connected Layer the input is flattened ie., all the rows of the multiple layers in the input is concatenated into a single feature vector and it is passed through the multiple dense layers to find the output probabilities of N different classes. Fully Connected layer looks for high level features that strongly corresponds to a particular class and has specific weights so that it will result in correct probabilities for various classes.

Output Layer

Output layer consist of N different neurons for N classes. The output class will be the class corresponding to the neuron with highest probability value.

Training Phase

Initially the filters in the convolution layer and weight in the fully connected layers are randomly chosen. Training image is given as an input to the model. It is processed by the model and produce with some probabilities for each class. This is called as forward pass. As the given data is training data the class label for that particular data is given. With the class label the loss function value is calculated by comparing the predicted output and the class label. The next step is backward pass which is used to find the weight which contribute most to the loss and then those weights and filter values are updated through back propagation techniques to reduce the error.

The process of forward pass, loss function calculation, backward pass and the parameters updation is represented as one training iteration. This process is repeated for fixed number of iteration for each set of training images. So that the network will be well trained and the parameters will be tuned correctly. Now the testing image will be given as input and the output class for the data will be predicted by the trained model.

There are several build in models are available such as VGG16, VGG19,GoogleNet, AlexNet,DenseNet etc..

VGG16 And VGG19

VGG16 is a persistent convolutional neural network which uses 3 X 3 convolution filters with stride value as 1 and pad value also as 1. The size of the input image does not diminish due to the first convolution layer. Max pooling with size 2 X 2 and a stride value of 2 is used in the model. Combination of two 3 X 3 conv layer will have an efficient receptive field same as 5 X 5. In the same way combination of three 3 X 3 conv layer will have an efficient receptive field same as 7 X 7. Thus the model gets the benefits of larger filter which keeping the smaller filter. Using smaller size filter will reduce the number of parameters. Totally in this model there are 181 parameters are involved to train and test the model. Nonlinearity becomes more because of using two RELU layers instead of one. VGG16 contains 16 weight layers where as VGG19 contains 19 weight layers and it is deeper version of VGG16.

DenseNet

DenseNet is expressed by sequence of dense blocks. In DenseNet ongoing layer has to perform the batch normalization, Relu activation function operation, convolution operation. After completing these three operation the output value is to be concatenated with the input vector and thus output of one layer is generated and it is given as input to the next layer.In Dense Net each layer is connected with other layers in a feed-forward fashion.

AlexNet Architecture

AlexNet architecture consist of five convolution layers. Normalization and pooling layers are present after the first two convolution layers. Then a single pooling layer is present after last convolutional layer, followed by the convolutional layer fully connected layer and a softmax layer are used in order to classify the given data. In each and every convolutional layer RELU activation function is used. The dropout value in this methodology is fixed as 0.4.

GoogleNet Architecture

The GoogleNet Architecture is deeper and wider architecture than any other architectures. It consists of 22 layers but considerably lesser number of parameters compared to AlexNet architecture. One of the key features of GoogleNet architecture is the application of network in network architecture in the form of inception module. This modules consist of parallel $1 \times 1, 3 \times 3$, and 5×5 convolution associated with a Max – Pooling layers in order to provide dimensionality reduction. Because of this parallel inception modules large amount of features can be extracted by the model. At last output from all the layers are concatenated into a single layer and given as input to fully connected layers.

PROPOSED METHODOLOGY

Dataset Description

Dataset Collection

Plants are affected by various breads of disease. Temperature, rainfall, season, type of the plant plays a major role for the disease occurrence. Disease may affect the different parts of the plant. So the Image used for training and testing the CNN model has been collected from plant village dataset. In the proposed work three different plant leaves such as peach leaves, grape leaves and pepper leaves images were taken for analysis to check whether the leaf is healthy or not healthy. If the leaf is unhealthy the model will tell the type of the disease that has affected that plant. For the three plant leaves the types of disease classes and their respective count taken for this work is shown in the Table 1.

Totally 2048 pepper leaf images, 2390 Grape leaf images, 2126 Peach leaf images were used in the proposed system. Lot of variations has been considered in the dataset since variations can generalize the model so that it can perform well on any type of data. Because of which the system becomes more robust.

Dataset Preprocessing

For training convolutional neural network large number of training images for each class is needed in order to build an efficient image classifier. Image augmentation is the technique which is used to generate images artificially from the existing images. Thus image augmentation helps in increasing the size of the dataset. Image augmentation is done by random rotation, shifting the images, shear, flips etc... Random combination of these augmentation methods are used to construct more images related to each image in the dataset. In the proposed method this augmentation technique is just used to preprocess the image by rotation, rescaling, zooming, horizontal flipping techniques. The variety of training data helps the model to learn all the features from the data efficiently moreover it avoids the problem of overfitting which may leads to poor accuracy.

Table 1. List of disease classes and its sample count for each plant leaf

Type of the Plant Leaf	Class Name	No. of Collected Images
Pepper Leaf	Bellhealthy	1139
	Earlyblight	800
	Healthy	109
Grape Leaf	Black_Rot	944
	Esca	1107
	Healthy	339
Peach Leaf	Bacterial_Spot	1838
	Healthy	288

Figure 2. Overview of the proposed methodology

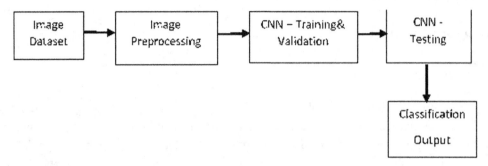

Proposed Method

The proposed method will classify healthy and unhealthy plant along with class type. The overview of the system is shown in the above Figure 2. Image dataset will be captured from the field. Then the images will be preprocessed. Each and every image to be processed should be resized to a constant size for example. 128*128 pixel. Randomly 80% of the data from various classes is chosen for training and 20% for generating validation dataset. Table 2 shows the distribution of images under different sets. The Convolution Neural Network model is trained will the given dataset so that it will learn features from the data. Then the model will be tested for a set of new image. The output generated will be healthy or if it is unhealthy plant it will tell the category of the disease.

Model Construction

The architecture of the Convolution Neural Network used in the proposed methodology is shown in the Figure 3. The model consists of four convolution layers. The convolution layers are used to extract features from the input image. Features are extracted with the help of 3 * 3 filters used in the convolution layers. The number of filters used in the first, second, third, fourth convolution layers are 16,32,64,64 respectively. So after the first convolution layer 16 features map are extracted. These feature maps are passed into the RELU activation function inorder to obtain nonlinearity.

Then Batch normalization is done to reduce the covariate shift. Next the output is passed into the pooling layer here in this model Maxpooling with pooling size 2* 2 is used. 25% of the neurons are dropout before passing the output of the first convolution layer to the next layer. Each and every convolution layers are followed by the batch normalization, pooling layer. Then dropout is also carried out after the

Table 2. Distribution of image for training, validation and testing for different dataset

Dataset Name	No. of Collected Images		
	Training Set	Validation Set	Test Set
Pepper Leaf	1528	383	137
Grape Leaf	1844	462	84
Peach Leaf	1654	414	58

Figure 3. Architecture of the CNN Model

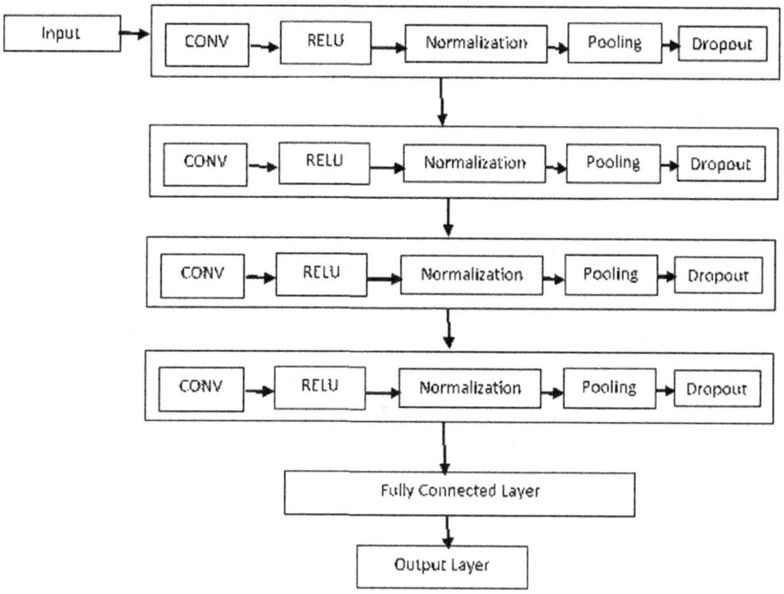

pooling layer. At last the output values from the convolution layers are flattened and passed to a fully connected layer with 50 neurons. Then again batch normalization and dropout has been done and the output is passed to the next layer which contains the number of neurons corresponding to the number output classes. The last layer is called as output layer.

Experimental Setup

Hyperparameter Tuning

Hyperparameters are the one in which the values are not trainable whereas the values for those parameters is to be fixed. The fixed value should be same throughout training, validating and testing phase. Dropout Rate is one of the hyperparameter considered mainly in this work.

DropoutRate

Overfitting problem is decreased by using Dropout technique.Only when the overfitting is reduced the model can learn the training samples correctly instead of memorizing the data. This will result in high accuracy while handling test data from real life scenario. Dropout layers are inserted after each and every dense layers. During the training phase some neurons will be randomly chosen and it is not considered during forward and backward pass of the training phase this process is called as Dropout. A dropout of 0.4 means that 40% of the neurons are ignored from the previous layers. In this method various dropout value has been fixed and checked for accuracy and it is found that Dropout rate of 0.25 produce better accuracy and so it is fixed for all the CNN architectures used in the proposed method.

Loss Function

Categorical crossentropy function is used for the classification of pepper and grape dataset since it has three output classes. Whereas Binary crossentropy function is used for the Peach leaf dataset classification because it contains only two classes.

Learning Rate

How fast the model weights are adjusted to get the local or global minima of the loss function is fixed by the learning rate. The convergence become faster at higher learning rate but it may results in the divergence from the minima due to larger steps over the loss function. With the smaller learning rate the probability of convergence is high but it will lead to larger number of training epochs. The model has been tested for different values of learning rate and it is finalized that 0.001 produces better result. This learning rate is fixed for all the CNN architectures.

Optimizer

Adaptive Moment Estimation (Adam) is used for training the model. Adam optimization techniques is an expansion of traditional stochastic gradient descent optimization algorithm. Optimization algorithms are used to update the parameters of the model such as weights or filter values iteratively in order to train the model using the training data. In stochastic gradient method learning rate is fixed and it is not changed during the training process. Whereas in Adam optimization technique different adaptive learning rate has been computed using the first and second moments. Adam method combines the advantage of both Adaptive Gradient Algorithm (AdaGrad) and Root Mean Square Propagation(RMSProp) for maintain per-parameter learning rate. There are several Adam configuration parameters used such as alpha, beta1, beta2, epsilon. Alpha indicates the learning rate or stepsize. In the proposed system it is maintained as 0.001. Beta1 denotes the first moment estimate's exponential decay rate. Whereas beta2 refers to the exponential decay rate for the second – moment estimates. Epsilon is a small number which is used to restrict any division by zero error during the implementation process. In the proposed system these parameters are fixed with their default values such as beta1=0.9, beta2=0.999, epsilon=1e-08. Adam optimization techniques has several benefits such as computationally efficient, requires little memory, best suited for problems with sparse gradients etc.,

PERFORMANCE METRIC

Accuracy is used as a performance metric. Model weights of each architecture are saved at an epoch at which best validation accuracy is reached. In the proposed method 10 epoch are used to train the model.

Model Accuracy and loss during training and validation phase is shown in the Table 3, 4 and 5 below for various dataset used in proposed system.

Precision, recall, f1-score, support, confusion matrix, accuracy are the various metrics which are used to measure the performance of the model for the given three datasets.

Table 3. Accuracy and loss for pepper leaf dataset

Epoch Number	Training Accuracy	Validation Accuracy	Training Loss
1	78%	89%	60%
2	90%	84%	29%
3	93%	70%	22%
4	93%	54%	18%
5	94%	49%	15%
6	94%	45%	16%
7	94%	48%	15%
8	94%	47%	16%
9	94%	46%	15%
10	94%	45%	13%

Table 4. Accuracy and loss for peach leaf dataset

Epoch Number	Training Accuracy	Validation Accuracy	Training Loss
1	67%	93%	80%
2	81%	96%	48%
3	91%	96%	33%
4	94%	98%	21%
5	95%	94%	18%
6	95%	92%	16%
7	95%	90%	14%
8	96%	92%	14%
9	97%	98%	12%
10	97%	94%	10%

Table 5. Accuracy and loss percentage for grape leaf dataset

Epoch Number	Training Accuracy	Validation Accuracy	Training Loss
1	68%	23%	94%
2	8%	23%	56%
3	84%	22%	43%
4	85%	26%	40%
5	85%	32%	40%
6	86%	25%	36%
7	87%	33%	34%
8	88%	25%	31%
9	89%	30%	30%
10	90%	34%	26%

Precision

Precision is the ratio of correctly predicted observations to the total predicted observations

$$Precision = \sum_{i=1}^{n} \frac{TPi}{TPi + FPi} .$$

Where,

i refers to each class in the dataset

TP is the number of true positive (No. of samples which are classified correctly)

FP is the number of false positive. (No. of samples which are wrongly classified)

Recall

Recall is the ratio of correctly predicted observations to the total correct observation of one particular class.

$$Recall = \sum_{i=1}^{n} \frac{TPi}{TPi + FNi}.$$

Where,

i refers to each class in the dataset
TP is the number of true positive (No. of samples which are classified correctly)
FN is the number of false negative (No. of samples which are wrongly classified)

F1 Score

F1 Score is the weighted average of Recall and Precision. The formula to calculate F1 Score is given below,

$$F1Score = 2 * \left(Recall * Precision \right) \left(Recall + Precision \right).$$

Support

The support is defined as the total number of occurrences of each class in the groud truth dataset.
    The Precision, Recall, F1-Score, Support for each dataset is shown in following Table 6.

Confusion Matrix

Confusion Matrix refers to a table which is used to represent the performance of the classification model on a set of testing data for which the ground truth value is already known. Confusion Matrix is very simple and easy to understand.

Table 6. The precision, recall, f1-score, support for each dataset

Dataset	Disease Class	Precision	Recall	F1-Score	Support
Pepper	Bellhealthy	1.00	0.07	0.13	44
	Earlyblight	0.90	1.00	0.95	81
	Healthy	0.25	0.92	0.39	12
Grape	Black_Rot	0.67	0.91	0.77	33
	Esca	1.00	0.53	0.69	40
Peach	Healthy	0.61	1.00	0.76	11
	Bacterial_Spot	0.83	1.00	0.90	40
	Healthy	1.00	0.50	0.67	18

Table 7. Confusion matrix for grape dataset

Actual Class Type	Predicted Class Type		
	Bellhealthy	Earlyblight	Healthy
Bellhealthy	3	8	33
Earlyblight	0	81	0
Healthy	0	1	11

Table 8. Confusion matrix for grape dataset

Actual Cass Type	Predicted Class Type		
	Black_Rot	Esca	Healthy
Black_Rot	30	0	3
Esca	15	21	4
Healthy	0	0	11

Table 9. Confusion matrix for peach dataset

Actual Class Type	Predicted Class Type	
	Bacterial_Spot	Healthy
Bacterial_Spot	40	0
Healthy	9	9

Confusion matrix for the model for Pepper dataset is shown in Table 7.
Confusion matrix for the model for Grape dataset is shown in Table 8.
Confusion matrix for the model for Peach dataset is shown in Table 9.

Accuracy

Accuracy is the most important performance measure. It is defined as the ratio of corrected predicted observations to the total number of observations. The formula for calculating the accuracy is shown below,

$$Accuracy = \sum_{i=1}^{n}(TPi + TNi) / \left(TPi + FPi + FNi + TNi\right)$$

Where,

i refers to each class in the dataset,
TP = Number of True Positive samples,
TN = Number of True Negative samples,
FP = Number of False Positive samples,
FN = No. of False Negative samples

The accuracy value of the model for grape dataset with three classes is 74%, Pepper dataset which consist of three classes is 69% and for Peach dataset with two classes is 84%.

CONCLUSION AND FUTURE WORK

In this work, deep Convolutional Neural Network based classifier has been proposed for disease recognition in various plant leaves. Analysis on different classes of disease has been done for three different datasets. The proposed model is trained for each dataset seperately and provides an accuracy of 74% on grape leaf dataset, 69% on pepper leaf dataset, 84% on peach leaf dataset for the disease classification task. The CNN model can effectively categorize the class of disease when the input is a unhealthy plant. Further the proposed method can be extended for providing the measurement level and the pesticide preferred for the diseases identified. The model can also expanded for classifying more number of diseases by maintaining the accuracy level.

REFERENCES

Amara, J., Bouaziz, B., & Algergawy, A. (2017). *A deep learning-based approach for banana leaf diseases classification*. Lecture Notes in Informatics.

Fuentes, A., Yoon, S., Kim, S. C., & Park, D. S. (2017). A robust deep-learning-based detector for real-time tomato plant diseases and pest recognition. *Sensors (Basel)*, *17*, 2022. doi:10.339017092022

Guo, P., Liu, T., & Li, N. (2014). Design of automatic recognition of cucumber disease image. *Inf. Technol. J.*, *13*(13), 2129–2136.

Mohanty, S. P., Hughes, D. P., & Salathé, M. (2016). Using deep learning for image - based plant disease detection. *Frontiers in Plant Science*, *01419*, 1419. doi:10.3389/fpls.2016.01419 PMID:27713752

Sladojevic, S., Arsenovic, M., Anderla, A., Culibrk, D., & Stefanovic, D. (2016). *Deep neural networks based recognition of plant diseases by leaf image classification*. Computat. Intelligence Neurosci; doi:10.1155/2016/3289801

Vianna, G.K., Oliveira, G.S., & Cunha, G.V. (2017). A neuro-automata decision support system for the control of late blight in tomato crops. *World Acad. Sci., Eng. Technol., Int. J. Comput., Electr., Autom., Control Inform. Eng.*, *11*(4), 455–462.

Zhang, S., Wu, X., You, Z., & Zhang, L. (2017). Leaf image based cucumber disease recognition using sparse representation classification. *Computers and Electronics in Agriculture*, *134*, 135–141. doi:10.1016/j.compag.2017.01.014

Chapter 4
Genetically–Modified K–Medoid Clustering Algorithm for Heterogeneous Data Set

Dhayanithi Jaganathan
Sona College of Technology, India

Akilandeswari Jeyapal
Sona College of Technology, India

ABSTRACT

In recent days, researchers are doing research studies for clustering of data which are heterogeneous in nature. The data generated in many real-world applications like data form IoT environments and big data domains are heterogeneous in nature. Most of the available clustering algorithms deal with data in homogeneous nature, and there are few algorithms discussed in the literature to deal the data with numeric and categorical nature. Applying the clustering algorithm used by homogenous data to the heterogeneous data leads to information loss. This chapter proposes a new genetically-modified k-medoid clustering algorithm (GMODKMD) which takes fused distance matrix as input that adopts from applying individual distance measures for each attribute based on its characteristics. The GMODKMD is a modified algorithm where Davies Boudlin index is applied in the iteration phase. The proposed algorithm is compared with existing techniques based on accuracy. The experimental result shows that the modified algorithm with fused distance matrix outperforms the existing clustering technique.

INTRODUCTION

The nature of data with high fluctuation and different characteristics are called heterogeneous data. In general, integrating the heterogeneous data is very difficult to meet the business information requirements. In recent days the data generated from IoT are often heterogeneous nature. The heterogeneous data are further classified into four different characteristics namely, numeric, binary, nominal and ordinal. The data are in measurable form or numeric forms are called numerical data. The data that falls on two states 0 or 1 are called binary data. The data which simply names or label something without any

DOI: 10.4018/978-1-5225-9902-9.ch004

ordered is called Nominal data. Ordinal data are extension of nominal data is follows an order. Apart from the characteristics of the data, it also important to know much about those data is in the form of metadata management. For the better interpretation of heterogeneous data detailed metadata information are required. In many cases it is difficult to collect those metadata.

Grouping objects into similar clusters is the prime motive of any clustering techniques. Similarity or Dissimilarity is measured by how far the objects are close enough together. Majority of similarity measure have been studied and tested in the literature. The similarity measure are falls in two categorized first the data with numerical value and second the data with conceptually categorical. The similarity measures available for one type of data are not suitable for other type of data. The challenges of clustering heterogeneous data concentrate on designing in tackling the difficulties raised by complex and dynamic characteristics, volume of data, and defining the good similarity measure to know the similarity between the objects in order to group them together. More focused research on similarity or dissimilarity measure for heterogeneous dataset was already carried out by many researchers. Study is needed for defining perfect similarity or dissimilarity measures of heterogeneous types.

Machine learning is the design of algorithms that permit machines to develop behaviors based on empirical data. Most of research work carried out in machine learning is that make the computer to automatically learn by themselves. Machine Learning is defined as any algorithm can learn by themselves based on the Experience (E) obtained from certain Task (T) and the Performance measure (P) of that Task T is keep on improving by their Experience (E). Based on the outcome of the algorithm machine learning can be classified in to two types namely, supervised and unsupervised. In supervised learning, function generates to map the input to desired outputs and in unsupervised learning, a set of inputs were modeled like clustering. Machine Learning is performed by various strategies and techniques namely, Inductive Logic Programming, Simulated Annealing, Neural Nets and Evolutionary Strategies. The first three techniques are beyond the scope of this chapter and an only evolutionary strategy is currently focused.

Genetic Algorithm is a heuristic search which is widely used in search optimization and finding the optimal solution based on natural evolution. Genetic Algorithm is a subset of evolutionary algorithm in which the offspring of the next generation is incurred by fittest individuals of current generation. Genetic Algorithm comprises of five phases namely, Population Initialization, fitness function, selection, cross over and mutation. It is necessary to incorporate Genetic Algorithm with clustering techniques because clustering is the key task in the process of acquiring knowledge. The cluster analysis is usually observed by measuring the natural association of members in the clusters i.e., the natural association of members within the group is high compared to the members in different group. Even for a small set of elements (25) to be clustered in small set of groups (5) arise a very large number of possibilities (2,436,684,974,110,751). The clustering task is incorporated with Genetic Algorithm leads to minimize the within cluster variance.

This paper focuses on two aspects, 1) Formulate the fused distance matrix for the heterogeneous data types and 2) Genetically modified K-Mediod clustering algorithm with modified Davies Bouldin Index as the fitness function.

BACKGROUND

There is no common definition used for data heterogeneity in the literature, meanwhile based on the data produced in different domains researchers define the heterogeneity accordingly. For example, (Skillicorn & David, 2007) describes datasets are collected from sensors, engineering, medical, scientific and social applications is heterogeneous in nature. In order to cluster the heterogeneous dataset, generalized cost function is required (Harikumar & Surya, 2015). In any data sets the objects are grouped together based on the similarity or dissimilarity between the objects. There is no universal similarity measure available for all the characteristics of data. (Huang, 1998) proposed different similarity measure for the attributes in categorical form and the main drawback of this approach is only one attribute object will acts as a cluster center. In the Haung's approach for the binary attributes hamming similarity measure is used but the similarity value is depends on the relative frequency of data points within a class (Ahmad & Dey, 2007). In this approach if the data representation is not proper it leads to incorrect results. The Huangs Similarity Function is further extended (Ahmad & Dey, 2007) by proposing a generalized similarity function for the categorical attributes. This work fortifies the drawbacks of (Huang, 1998). A new similarity measure based on entropy is used in (Ordonez & Carlos, 2003) in which the traditional Manhattan similarity measure is replaced. In the Unsupervised Classification of heterogeneous data (Rohit Rastogi, Agarwal, Gupta, & Jain, 2015) Euclidean similarity measure is used to find the similarity between any two objects irrespective to various characteristics of attributes.

Fusing of data has been classified into three types (Maragos, Gros, Katsamanis, Athanassios, & Papandreou, 2008) namely, early integration, late integration and intermediate integration. The fusing can take place in all the stages. In the intermediate integration the Fusing of data is applied through similarity or dissimilarity calculations. Fusing of data is one of the most popular approaches in the field of heterogeneous dataset. Fusing of data is referred as the process of integrating different data and knowledge from the same real world object into an accurate, consistent and useful representation (Mojahed, Bettencourt-Silva, H, Wenjia, & la, 2015). Fusing of data has been evolved for long time in the field of multi sensor research (Hall, L, Llinas, & James, 1997; Khaleghi, Khamis, Karray, & Razavi, 2013), robotics and machine learning (Meurant & Gerard, 1992; Faouzi, et al., 2011). Meanwhile, applying data mining technique for the fused heterogeneous dataset is shown little interest by the researchers until recently. (Mojahed, Bettencourt-Silva, H, Wenjia, & la, 2015) extended their work by evaluating similarity fusion matrix using the K-means algorithm to cluster heterogeneous data. The main drawback of those methods is the identification of optimal number of clusters for applications when no external knowledge of the clustering is available and also the development of appropriate weighting schemes.

There are variety of clustering techniques are available and the most commonly used technique is K-Means algorithm (Forrest, 1993) it will optimize the distance criterion either by minimize within cluster variance or by maximize the intra cluster separation. There are other clustering technique are also available like Hierarchical, Graph Theoretical etc. There is no general strategy to be followed for clustering for all problem domians. (Harikumar & Surya, 2015) proposed K-medoid clustering for heterogeneous dataset in which L1 norm, L2 norm and Hamming distance measures are used for numeric, categorical and binary attributes respectively. In this work the ordinal attributes are treated as categorical and K value for the K-medoid is predicted earlier (Huang & Zhexue, 1997). In the typical centroid based clustering of heterogeneous data, a K-prototypes technique is used. In this approach Hamming and Euclidean similarity measure is used for non-numeric and numeric attributes respectively. The hamming similarity measure is needs to set and modified manually. If the hamming and Euclidean measure combined linearly it leads to unnecessary problem. In order to resolve this problem, Kullback–Leibler information fuzzy c-means combined with Gauss-multinomial distribution (KLFCM-GM) has been proposed (Chatzis & Sotirios, 2011). This method is also needs some manual control to maintain the fuzziness. An improved K-Prototypes (Ji, Bai, Zhou, Ma, & Wang, 2013) was proposed by extending the fuzzy K-Prototypes (Ji, Pang, Zhou, Han, & Wang, 2012). This approach is optimizing the weight for each numeric and non-numeric attribute sequentially. To measure the similarity this method still need to combine the Euclidean and Hamming similarity measures.

Applying clustering technique in the fused heterogeneous data was initially investigated by (Yu, Moor, & Moreau, 2009). It is difficult to define an ideal similarity measure for the clustering process (Santos, RL, Zrate, & Luis, 2015). In most of the algorithms mentioned above either Euclidean based similarity metrics or identical similarity metrics are used to find the similarity between two different objects and this yields incompatible results for the large heterogeneous dataset. Most of the algorithms available in the literature are to cluster the datasets with only numeric attributes or only non-numeric attributes or a combination of numeric and non-numeric attributes. Incorporating Genetic Algorithm with clustering technique will form appropriate clustering. If the number of inputs is very large, then the traditional non GA based clustering algorithm is not efficiently and automatically form the clusters. In those approaches, choosing of initial centroid is another major problem. (Rahman & Islam, 2014) proposed a novel clustering techniques by combining K-Means with Genetic Algorithm called GenClust technique. This approach yields better cluster quality without receiving any input from the user like cluster number (K). (Chang, Zhang, & Zheng, 2009) suggest a new clustering algorithm called Genetic Algorithm with Gene Rearrangement (GAGR). In order to reduce the degeneracy causes by various chromosomes gene rearrangement were used. Further, they introduced path based crossover to generate new offspring. To resolve the problem of stuck in local optima, GAGR clustering algorithm used adaptive possibilities of crossover and mutation. (Pizzuti & Procopio, 2016) integrate the Genetic Algorithm and K-Means algorithm to partition the data sets in certain range of groups. In this approach, group based crossover is used to generate new offspring's and the experimental results are compared with traditional K-Means algorithm.

MAIN FOCUS OF THE CHAPTER

In the field of Data Analysis, clustering is very important and it will determine the core grouping among the data available. There is no any common criterion for a good clustering. Different users choose different criterions based on their requirements. Many clustering techniques are discussed in the literature is majorly focuses on clustering homogenous data and very less work done on clustering heterogeneous data. This chapter was focuses on clustering heterogeneous data. First, a unified distance measure is chosen based on the characteristics of attributes. Once the distance matrix is derived for all the attributes, Fused Distance Matrix (FDM) technique is applied. In FDM the fusing is performed based on different distance threshold. Next, the K-Medoid algorithm is modified by incorporating Genetic Algorithm. It takes FDM and number of clusters to be formed as input. The convergence of the proposed clustering algorithm is done through modified Davies-Bouldin index. The entire algorithm is tested over four different heterogeneous data sets. The performance of the algorithm is compared with other clustering algorithm discussed in the literature.

Problem Definition

Let H be the heterogeneous data-set which consists of M attributes such that $H=A_1,A_2,A_3,\ldots A_M$ where A_1 is the first attribute and M is the total number of attributes in the heterogeneous data-set. The attributes are classified as Numeric (Nu), Binary (Bi), Nominal (No) and Ordinal (Or). The attributes in Heterogeneous dataset are falls in any of those categories. Each attribute has N elements and it is defined as $A_M^c.\xi^N = A_M^c.\xi^1, A_M^c.\xi^2,\ldots.A_M^c.\xi^N$, where $c\epsilon\{Nu,Bi,No,Or\}$ and $M\epsilon\{1,2,\ldots M\}$. Therefore, $A_2^{Nu}.\xi^3$ is denoted as third element of second attribute which is numeric in nature.

Distance Measure and Fusing Technique

Once the heterogeneous dataset is properly represented, fused distance matrix is obtained by adopting suitable distance measures DM for each attributes individually based on its characteristics. If the attributes are characterized as numeric then Manhattan distance measure as specified in Equation 1 is applied for all pair of objects ($\forall i,j\epsilon\{1,2,\ldots N\}$) and the resultant value is normalised using min-max normalization technique.

$$DM\left(A_M^{Nu}.\xi^i, A_M^{Nu}.\xi^j\right) \leftarrow \left|A_M^{Nu}.\xi^i - A_M^{Nu}.\xi^j\right| \tag{1}$$

$$NuDM\left(NXN\right) \leftarrow \frac{DM\left(A_M^{Nu}.\xi^i, A_M^{Nu}.\xi^j\right) - \min\left(DM\left(A_M^{Nu}.\xi^i, A_M^{Nu}.\xi^j\right)\right)}{\max\left(DM\left(A_M^{Nu}.\xi^i, A_M^{Nu}.\xi^j\right)\right) - \min\left(DM\left(A_M^{Nu}.\xi^i, A_M^{Nu}.\xi^j\right)\right)} \tag{2}$$

Simple matching coefficient is considered for measuring the distance between binary attributes and it is given in Equation 3. Cosine distance measure is chosen for measuring the distance between Nominal attributes which is specified as Equation 4, because it is efficient and only non-zero dimensions are need to be considered.

$$BiDM\left(NXN\right) \leftarrow DM\left(A_M^{Bi}.\xi^i, A_M^{Bi}.\xi^j\right) \leftarrow \frac{p+s}{p+q+r+s} \tag{3}$$

where p=number of non zero variables for both elements, q=number of non zero variable for i^{th} elements and zero variable for j^{th} elements, r=number of zero variable for i^{th} elements and non zero variable for j^{th} elements, s=number of non zero variables for both elements.

$$NoDM\left(NXN\right) \leftarrow 1 - SM\left(A_M^{No}.\xi^i, A_M^{No}.\xi^j\right) \leftarrow \frac{A_M^{No}.\xi^i * A_M^{No}.\xi^j}{\parallel A_M^{No}.\xi^i \parallel \parallel A_M^{No}.\xi^j \parallel} \tag{4}$$

Ordinal attributes are also called as rank order in which the original element is converted to rank (r). Further the value is normalised using min-max normalisation technique and it is derived using Equation 5. After determining the normalised value for the ordinal attribute, Manhattan distance measure is applied to identify the distance between ordinal values as specified in Equation 6.

$$RA_M^{Or}.\xi^N = \frac{r-1}{R+1}, where R = \max\left(r\right) \tag{5}$$

$$OrDM\left(NXN\right) \leftarrow DM\left(A_M^{Or}.\xi^i, A_M^{Or}.\xi^j\right) \leftarrow \left|R\xi_{O_i}^{\delta_d} - R\xi_{O_j}^{\delta_d}\right| \tag{6}$$

Once the Distance Matrix are derived for all the attributes, Fused Distance Matrix FDM(N X N) is derived by aggregating distance matrix value of each pair of object in all the attributes with respect to different distance threshold (τ) ranges from 0.1 to 0.9 and it defined in Equation 7.

$$FDM\left(NXN\right) \leftarrow \frac{1}{M}\sum_{\tau} NuDM\left(NXN\right), BiDM\left(NXN\right), NoDM\left(NXN\right), OrDM\left(NXN\right) \tag{7}$$

The Fused Distance Matrix of N rows and N columns as shown below are taken as input for the clustering algorithm which is explain in the next section.

$$\mathbf{FDM\left(NXN\right)} = \begin{bmatrix} \mathbf{FDM}\left(1,1\right) & & & \\ \mathbf{FDM}\left(2,1\right) & \mathbf{FSM}\left(2,2\right) & & \\ \vdots & & & \\ \mathbf{FDM}\left(N,1\right) & \mathbf{FDM}\left(N,2\right) & \dots & \mathbf{FDM}\left(N,N\right) \end{bmatrix}$$

GENETICALLY MODIFIED K MEDOID CLUSTERING ALGORITHM

In any clustering technique it is important to determine the similarity between the objects. After determine the Fusing Distance Matrix as defined in previous section clustering algorithm was applied to group the similar data objects together. In this section, Genetically Modified K-Medoid Clustering Algorithm (GMODKMD) is described that can efficiently evolve suitable grouping of heterogeneous objects. The algorithm is described below in detail.

Data Representation and Initialize Population

In most cased the data objects are represented as numeric or binary and clustering of those objects are done explicitly based on the value of numeric or binary codes. It leads to the problem of context sensitivity. Therefore Genetic operators have to be deliberate to improve those problems. In this work, each individual objects are considered as allele gene taking the value from 1,2,..M. Each allele gene corresponds to a medoid of the chosen objects and total length of the individual relates to cluster number. For example, the individual (3,45,56,128,228) encodes 5 clusters where 3rd, 45th, 56th,128th, and 228th objects are selected as medoids. This kind of genetic representation leads to context sensitive with the available genetic operators. Initial number of clusters is randomly determined based on number of classes available for those data objects. No duplicate objects are considered to be included in the initial population.

Fitness Function

The fitness function process comprised of two different phases. In the first phase, clusters are formed based on the Fused Similarity Matrix. Each individual data objects are assigned to one of the medoid based on its similarity values. In the second phase, fitness of the clusters is evaluated. To formulate the effective fitness function modified Davies-Bouldin index is determined. The DB index is the ratio of sum of within cluster scatter to between cluster separations. This function is popularly used for cluster validation. It requires mean of the clusters is to be defined but it is difficult to define mean of the cluster in K-Medoid model. Therefore, DB index is modified to validate the clusters generated by the K-Medoid model. To determine the scatter within the ith cluster, S_i is defined as,

$$S_i \leftarrow \frac{1}{C_i} \sum_{x \int C_i} FDM\left(x, M_i\right) \tag{8}$$

where C_i is the total number of objects in the cluster I and M_i denotes the ith cluster medoid. The similarity between two different clusters Ci and Cj is written as $D_{ij} = DM(M_i, M_j)$. Now, R_i is computed as follows,

$$R_i \leftarrow \max\left\{ \frac{D_i + D_j}{D_{ij}} \right\} \tag{9}$$

Finally the modified davies bouldin index is defined as,

$$MDBI \leftarrow \frac{1}{K} \sum_{i=1}^{K} R_i \tag{10}$$

A good cluster is always being dense and well parted, with minimum value of the Modified Davies Bouldin index. The objective is to minimize the MDB index to achieve suitable clustering.

Genetic Operators

- **Selection**: The selection operator is used to select the parent pairs from the available population pool. w-fold tournament is commonly used selection operator which selects parent pairs by randomly selecting set of individual with size w from the available population. Goldberg and Richardson (1987) showed that allocating exponential number of mating chances to those individuals from the population that display better than expected survival qualities is certifiably not a good procedure for a careful investigation of complex hunt space. Therefore, in this paper the selection procedure is implemented with reduced pressure as follows. First parent is selected by 2-fold tournament selection, and its mate is selected by randomly from the population. This selection procedure aims for better performance and reduces the selection pressure of traditional tournament selection.

- **Crossover**: The new offspring for the next generation is crossover by exchanging information between a pair of parent. The crossover operator is applied with probability (pc) to ensure the newly generated offspring are between two to Kmax medoids. It should also ensure to avoid newly generated offspring is not identical to the parents and no duplicate offspring is produced. The crossover operator is defined as follows for given a pair of parent individuals I_1 and I_2 with K_1 and K_2 medoids, respectively. Imix is obtained by mixing one parent individual (I_1) to other individual (I_2) and the resulting medoids Pmix is scrambled randomly. Generate two new medoids K_3 and K_4 based on two offspring I_3 and I_4 respectively as follows, $K_3 = \text{RandInt}(\max(2, K_1 + K_2 - K_{max})$, $\min(K_1 + K_2 - 2, K_{max}))$, $K_4 = K_1 + K_2 - K_3$. Build the offspring I_3 with K_3 medoids by coping features from Imix starting at the leftmost feature and going feature-wise to the right, subject to the condition that features already in I_3 are skipped. Build the offspring I_4 in the same way as I_3, however starting at the rightmost feature of I_{mix} and going feature-wise to the left.

- **Mutation**: After crossover, a probability p_m of flip mutation will be applied to the offspring. Flip mutation replaces the chosen feature by another randomly generated feature, subject to the restriction that the new feature is not presented in the current individual. The mutation operator is useful to add new features to the offspring individuals and allow them to search other areas that have not been explored by the algorithm.

GMODKMD Algorithm

Genetically Modified K-Medoid Clustering Algorithm (GMODKMD) which is summarised in Algorithm 1. The algorithm takes the input as number of clusters (K) to be formed and Fused Distance Matrix FDM(N×N) . The Best Fitness value is initially considered as null. The GMODKMD is repeated until the Best Fitness value is evaluated. For the K-Medoid clustering approach the fused similarity values and K value are taken as input. M and M_{new} denotes the randomly initialized array of K-Medoid indices and its copy respectively. In each iteration, the data points are is assigned to the closest medoid based on the simialarity measure considered from Fused Similarity Matrix.

Once the medoid is selected, a new medoid for each cluster is identified by object minimization. The current medoid in each cluster is replaced with the new medoid. The fitness of clusters is evaluated using Modified Davies Bouldin Index as explained in previos section. The fitness function of newly formed clusters is compared with the best fitness value. If the newly formed clusters fitness is grreater than best fitness then apply crossover and mutation to produce the new Medoids. The algorithm is iterated until the clusters with best fitness were determined.

The significant contributions of the proposed algorithm are to choosing individual distance measure for the heterogeneous objects and apply fusing technique to form Fused Similarity Matrix. The GMOD-KMD is never stops until the best fitness clusters are evaluated. This significance leads the algorithm to form better clusters.

Genetically Modified K-Modified Clustering Algorithm

```
function GMODKMD(K, K, FDM(N×N))
    Input - K: Total Cluster Number, DM(N×N) : Fused Similarity Matrix
    Output - C₁,C₂,…C_K (Clusters)
    { Data Representatin and Initialize Population}
    Best Fitness = ∞
    Intialize Population and Selection
    M← Randomly choose K objects as initial medoids
    repeat
        M_new←M
        Each Individual Objects are assigned to a Medoid (M_new) based on FDM
        J←np.argmin(FDM[:,M])
        for P ← 1 to K do
            C[P] ← np.where(J==i)[0]
        end for
        {Update the cluster medoid}
        for P ← 1 to K do
            J ←np.medoid(FDM[n-.ix(C[P],C[P])])
            j ←np.argmin(J)
           M_new[P]←C[P][j]
        end for
        np.sort(M_new)
        {Update the cluster membership}
        for P ← 1 to K do
            J = np.argmin(FDM[:,M], axis=1)
            {C= C₁,C₂,…C_K  Clusters}
            C[P] ← np.where(J==i)[0]
        end for
        Fitness Function = Fitness(C₁,C₂,…C_K )
        if Fitness Function ≤ Best Fitness then
            Best Fitness = Fitness Function
            Exit
        else
            Apply Single Point Crossover in M_new and M
            Each Chromosome under Mutation with a fixed propbalbity (p_m)
            M is updated with new generation  Best Fitness Function is determined
        end if
        until Best Fitness Function is determined
end function
```

RESULTS AND DISCUSSION

Four different real world heterogeneous dataset were used to evaluate the performance of proposed Genetically Modified K-Medoid Clustering Algorithm and compared with existing technique. The description of the dataset is shown in Table 1. Once the individual distance Measure is obtained on each attribute of the heterogeneous dataset, Fused Distance Matrix (FDM) is derived as explained in section 3. The resultant FDM is taken as input for GMODKMD along with number of clusters to be formed. The proposed approach provides an intuition of giving better accuracy when clustering the heterogeneous objects.

The proposed algorithm were coded with Java and Python2.7 and implemented in a computer with Intel(R) Core(TM)2 DuoCPU, 2.09Ghz and 2.99GB of RAM.

In the Heart statlog dataset (HD1), constits of 270 instances with 13 attributes and it classified as 6 Numeric, 3 Binary, 3 Nominal and 1 Ordinal. The Australian credit data set (HD2) comprises of 690 data objects with 14 attributes in which each objects is classified as 6 numeric, 4 binary, 2 nominal and 2 ordinal. In the Heart Cleveland dataset (HD3), 303 samples are considered for clustering without any missing values. The 13 attributes of HD3 are classified as 6 Numeric, 3 Nominal, 1 Ordinal and 3 Binary. Zoo data set (HD4) is the complete binary data set having 101 data objects with 16 binary attributes were considered for clustering. The characterstics of the data set are explained in Table 1.

The effectiveness of any clustering algorithm is determined by evaluating the quality of clusters. In this paper, the quality of cluster is determined by summing the amount of truly classified class per cluster over the sample size and it is determined in Equation 11.

$$c\left[n\right] = \frac{1}{N} \sum_{i=1}^{K} \left(\max\left[w_k \cap c_k\right] \right)$$

(11)

where w_k be cluster k, and c_j be class j. The result of GMODKMD is compared with simple K-Medoid and extended K-Means algorithmbecause they have similar framework and procedure so that the accuracy of the proposed work can be easily evaluated. Table 2 shows the Clustering accuracy of the heterogenous data-sets varied among different clustering algorithms.

The main reason to choose GMODKMD is to determine the efficient cluster with the Fused Distance Matrix technique. In each heterogeneous data-set the accuracy of the cluster is mainly depends on the Fused Distance Matrix determined by applying suitable distance measure for the heterogeneous dataset. In the proposed approach the clustering algorithm is iterated until the best fitness is evaluated. In general the fitness function is determined based on Davies Bouldin Index in which Euclidean measure is used to determine the similarity of inter and intra cluster. In GMODKMD, the similarity of the fitness func-

Table 1. Characteristics of heterogeneous data set

SI No	Dataset	Nu	Bi	No	Or
1	Heart statlog(HD1)	6	3	3	1
2	Australian credit(HD2)	6	4	2	2
3	Heart Cleveland dataset (HD3)	6	3	1	3
4	Zoo (HD3)	0	16	0	0

Table 2. Cluster accuracy comparison with cluster numbers for different data set

Dataset	Algorithm	Clusters		Accuracy (%)
Heart Statlog	GMODKMD ($\tau \rightarrow 0.8$)	124 (Present)	19 (Present)	83.4
		26 (Absent)	101 (Absent)	
	K-Medoid	114 (Present)	28 (Present)	76.35
		36 (Absent)	92 (Absent)	
	Extended K-Means	107 (Present)	32 (Present)	72.3
		43 (Absent)	88 (Absent)	
Australian Credit	GMODKMD ($\tau \rightarrow 0.5$)	306 (Credit +ve)	3 (Credit +ve)	93.74
		34 (Credit -ve)	337 (Credit -ve)	
	K-Medoid	296 (Credit +ve)	13 (Credit +ve)	90.28
		54 (Credit -ve)	327 (Credit -ve)	
	Extended K-Means	288 (Credit +ve)	19 (Credit +ve)	88.2
		62 (Credit -ve)	321 (Credit -ve)	
Heart Cleveland	GMODKMD ($\tau \rightarrow 0.8$)	125 (Present)	39 (Present)	77.25
		30 (Absent)	109 (Absent)	
	K-Medoid	No data available		
	Extended K-Means	No data available		
Zoo	GMODKMD ($\tau \rightarrow 0.8$)	35 (True)	6 (True)	87.69
		6 (False)	54 (False)	
	K-Medoid	41 (True)	0 (True)	100
		0 (False)	60 (False)	
	Extended K-Means	33 (True)	8 (True)	84.1
		8 (False)	52 (False)	

tion is derived from the SMF approach. The better accuracy of 83.4% is achieved for the Heart statlog data set which have the Fused Distance Matrix derived at distance threshold 0.8. In Australian credit data set have the best cluster accuracy of 93.74% at the Fused Distance Matrix is derived at the distance threshold 0.5. The optimal value of MDBI is 0.31 for the Australian creidt data set and this shows that our proposed approach have increased cluster compactness. The heart clevland data set have the better accuracy of 77.25% with distance threshold is set as 0.8. In Zoo data set FDM is derived at distance threshold 0.8 having the maximum cluster accuracy of 87.69 %. The K-Medoid approach proposed by (Harikumar & Surya, 2015) has the accuracy of 100 %. Based on the result, it is observed that the Fusing technique is not suits for data set with binary attribute alone. Further, the cluster accuracy is compared with other clustering algorithm discussed in the literature and it is shown in Figure 1. The consolodated results of accuracy and Modified DBI measures of various heterogenous data set using GMODKMD is shown in Figure 2.

Figure 1. Cluster Accuracy comparison with existing approach

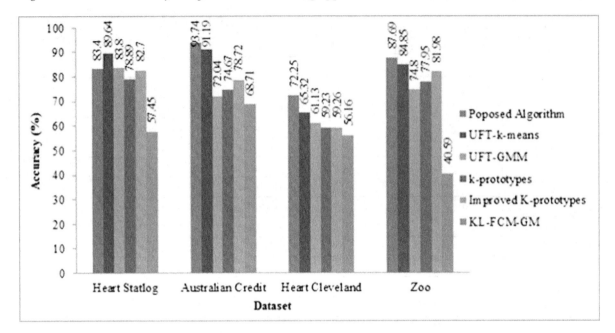

Figure 2. MDBI and Accuracy evaluation for the proposed algorithm

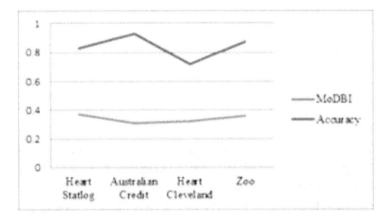

CONCLUSION AND FUTURE WORK

In this chapter, Genetically Modified K-Medoid clustering algorithm is proposed for object s with heterogeneous nature. A Fused Similarity Matrix is computed based on the distance between any heterogeneous objects are formulated and this matrix has been employed to conceive a GMODKMD. The algorithm performance is improved and best clusters have been formed due to the Fused Distance Matrix and Modified DBI evaluation. The proposed algorithm never changes the characteristics of heterogeneous data and also it ensures that there is 0% information loss. The MDBI index and accuracy are computed on different heterogeneous dataset shows that the proposed algorithm outperforms the existing techniques.

REFERENCES

Ahmad, A., & Dey, L. (2007). A k-mean clustering algorithm for mixed numeric and categorical data. *Data & Knowledge Engineering, 63*(2), 503–527. doi:10.1016/j.datak.2007.03.016

Chang, D.-X., Zhang, X., & Zheng, C. (2009). A genetic algorithm with gene rearrangement for K-means clustering. *Pattern Recognition, 42*(7), 1210–1222. doi:10.1016/j.patcog.2008.11.006

Chatzis, & Sotirios, P. (2011). A fuzzy c-means-type algorithm for clustering of data with mixed numeric and categorical attributes employing a probabilistic dissimilarity functional. *Expert Systems With Applications, 38*(7), 8684-8689.

Faouzi, E., Leung, H., & Kurian, A. (2011). Data fusion in intelligent transportation systems: Progress and challenges--A survey. *Information Fusion, 12*(1), 4–10. doi:10.1016/j.inffus.2010.06.001

Hall, L. D., & Llinas, J. (1997). An introduction to multisensor data fusion. *IEEE, 85*, 6-23.

Harikumar, S., & Surya, P. (2015). K-Medoid Clustering for Heterogeneous DataSets. *Elsevier Procedia Computer Science, 70*, 226–237. doi:10.1016/j.procs.2015.10.077

Huang, Z. (1998). Extensions to the k-means algorithm for clustering large datasets with categorical values. *Data Mining and Knowledge Discovery, 2*(3), 283–304. doi:10.1023/A:1009769707641

Huang & Zhexue. (1997). Clustering large data sets with mixed numeric and categorical values. In *Proceedings of the 1st Pacific-Asia conference on knowledge discovery and data mining (PAKDD)* (pp. 21-34). Academic Press.

Ji, J., Bai, T., Zhou, C., Ma, C., & Wang, Z. (2013). An improved k-prototypes clustering algorithm for mixed numeric and categorical data. *Neurocomputing, 120*, 590–596. doi:10.1016/j.neucom.2013.04.011

Ji, J., Pang, W., Zhou, C., Han, X., & Wang, Z. (2012). A fuzzy k-prototype clustering algorithm for mixed numeric and categorical data. *Knowledge-Based Systems, 30*, 129–135. doi:10.1016/j.knosys.2012.01.006

Khaleghi, B., Khamis, A., Karray, F. O., & Razavi, S. N. (2013). Multisensor data fusion: A review of the state-of-the-art. *Information Fusion, 14*(1), 28–44. doi:10.1016/j.inffus.2011.08.001

Maragos, P., Gros, P., Katsamanis, A., & Papandreou, G. (2008). Cross-modal integration for performance improving in multimedia: A review. *Multimodal Processing and Interaction*, 1-46.

Meurant & Gerard. (1992). *Data Fusion in Robotics and Machine Intelligence*. Academic Press.

Mojahed, A., Bettencourt-Silva, H. J., & Wenjia, W. (2015). Applying clustering analysis to heterogeneous data using similarity matrix fusion (smf). In *International Workshop on Machine Learning and Data Mining in Pattern Recognition* (pp. 251-265). Springer. 10.1007/978-3-319-21024-7_17

Ordonez, C. (2003). Clustering binary data streams with K-means. In *Proceedings of the 8th ACM SIGMOD workshop on Research issues in data mining and knowledge discovery* (pp. 12-19). ACM.

Pizzuti, C., & Procopio, N. (2016). *A K-means Based Genetic Algorithm for Data Clustering*. SOCO-CISIS-ICEUTE.

Rahman, M. A., & Islam, M. (2014). A Hybrid Clustering Technique Combining a Novel Genetic Algorithm with K-Means. *Knowledge-Based Systems*, *71*, 345–365. doi:10.1016/j.knosys.2014.08.011

Rohit Rastogi, P., Agarwal, K., Gupta, R., & Jain, S. (2015). GA Based Clustering of Mixed Data Type of Attributes - Numeric, Categorical, Ordinal, Binary and Ratio Scaled. *BVICAM's International Journal of Information Technology*, *7*(2), 861–865.

Santos, D. (2015). Categorical data clustering: What similarity measure to recommend? *Elsevier Expert Systems with Applications*, *42*(3), 1247–1260. doi:10.1016/j.eswa.2014.09.012

Skillicorn, D. (2007). *Understanding complex datasets: data mining with matrix decompositions*. Chapman and Hall/CRC.

Yu, S., Moor, B., & Moreau, Y. (2009). Clustering by heterogeneous data fusion: framework and applications. *NIPS Workshop*.

Chapter 5
Implementation of Deep Learning Neural Network for Retinal Images

R. Murugan

(iD) https://orcid.org/0000-0002-9341-3810

National Institute of Technology Silchar, India

ABSTRACT

The retinal parts segmentation has been recognized as a key component in both ophthalmological and cardiovascular sickness analysis. The parts of retinal pictures, vessels, optic disc, and macula segmentations, will add to the indicative outcome. In any case, the manual segmentation of retinal parts is tedious and dreary work, and it additionally requires proficient aptitudes. This chapter proposes a supervised method to segment blood vessel utilizing deep learning methods. All the more explicitly, the proposed part has connected the completely convolutional network, which is normally used to perform semantic segmentation undertaking with exchange learning. The convolutional neural system has turned out to be an amazing asset for a few computer vision assignments. As of late, restorative picture investigation bunches over the world are rapidly entering this field and applying convolutional neural systems and other deep learning philosophies to a wide assortment of uses, and uncommon outcomes are rising constantly.

INTRODUCTION

The eye is an important organ that allows human to observe, react and adapt to surrounding environments. It also enables to interpret shapes, colours and dimensions of objects visualized. Eye contains three major layers, an outer layer sclera in continuation with cornea, a vascular layer choroid and the neurosensory component retina. The visible parts of the eye also include the colour (blue, green, brown or a mixture of these) iris, and an opening in the iris, the normally black pupil. A ray of light, after passing through the cornea, which partially focuses the image, passes through the anterior chamber, the pupil, lens, vitreous and is then focused on the retina. The retina is supported by pigment epithelium, which is normally opaque (Livingstone & Hubel, 1988). The Anatomy of human eye is shown in Figure 1.

DOI: 10.4018/978-1-5225-9902-9.ch005

Figure 1. Anatomy of human eye (Source: Livingstone & Hubel 1988)

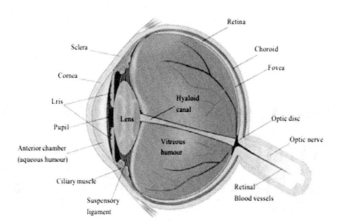

The neurosensory retina, usually called retina, is the largest part of the fundus which is the interior surface of the eye. The retina is a multi-layered sensory tissue that lines the back of the eye. The fundus includes the retina, the optic disc, and the macula. The retina is located in the eyeball as shown in Figure 2. The retina contains millions of photo-receptors that capture light rays and converts them into electrical impulses. These impulses travel along the optic nerve to the brain. The brain then "interprets" the electrical message sent to it, resulting in vision (Foracchia et al. 2004)

There are two types of photo-receptors in the retina: rods and cones, named after their shape. The retina contains approximately 6 to 7 million cones and about 125 million rods. Rods are the photo-receptors that are more responsive to light than the cones. Whether the cones or rods are used, depends on the amount of incoming light. In daylight the cones are the most active, under dark circumstances the rods are the most active and at dusk a combination of the two are used. In the human eye there are three distinct types of cones, and each type of cone responds to a different part of the colour spectrum. When the three different types of cones are located in a small area of the retina, the responses are combined. This enables us to see colors from the color spectrum. The rods, on the other hand, are not sensitive to color (Youssif et al. 2008).

When light enters the pupil, it is focused by the cornea and lens, and is projected onto the retina. The retina converts light into electrical impulses by use of the rods and cones, but the cells that transmit the neural signal to the brain are the ganglion cells. The axons of these ganglion cells make up the optic

Figure 2. Location and appearance of the retina (Source: Foracchia et al. 2004)

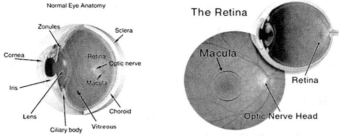

nerve, the single route by which information leaves the eye. When examining the back of the eye a portion of the optic nerve called the optic disc can be seen. At the optic disc the retina contains no photo-receptors. The result of having no photo-receptors at the optic disc is that light cannot be converted to neural signals and this creates a hole in our vision. That is why the optic disc is often called the blind spot (Hoover at al.2003).

Normally each eye covers for the blind spot of the other, and the brain fills in missing information with whatever pattern surrounds the hole. That is also the reason why we are not consciously aware of the existence of the blind spot. The retinal vessels branch out from the optic disc toward the retinal periphery. Normally, the vessels end about one or two mm before the retinal periphery. Two of the large vessels branching out of the optic disc are located around the center of the retina, called the vascular arch. The center of the retina is called the macula and can be recognized as the region within these two vascular branches. The macula has approximately the same size as the optic disc and has a darker colour than the rest of the retina. The macula is also the thickest portion of the retina with a thickness of 0.22 mm, except for the fovea, which is only 0.10 mm thick. The thickness and the dark colour of the macula are due to pigment granules, other parts of the retina have less of these pigment granules. The fovea is a small circular area (diameter $\approx$ 1500μm) within the macula. The retina is at its thinnest at the fovea, only small blood vessels lie in the fovea and the central area of the fovea is even devoid of blood vessels. At the fovea the retina consists exclusively of cones, and the density of the cones and ganglion cells is very high in contrast to other parts of the retina. These properties of the fovea all contribute to the same purpose, and that is to make sure that as much light as possible reaches the cones and to optimize the conversion from light to electrical impulse. The result of these properties is a region of high visual acuity (Walter & Klein 2001).

The fovea will always be directed to the object one studies, because of its possibility to determine small details. But in a dark environment, the light directed onto to fovea results in a very low response, because of the lack of rods in the fovea. In this case it is therefore better to look next to an object, because then the reflection of the object is directed onto a part of the retina with rods with the result that the object can be seen more clearly (Li & Chutatape 2001)

The retina is a unique site where the microcirculation can be imaged non-invasively providing an opportunity to study the structure and pathology of human blood circulation. Embryologically, retina is part of the central nervous system, readily accessible to examination and can be investigated with relative ease by both scientists and clinicians. Moreover, an estimated 80% of all sensory information in human is thought to be of retinal origin, indicating the importance of retinal function for the ability to interact with the outside world. Light sensitive, multi-layered retina comprises of various significant anatomical structures such as optic disc, macula and blood vessels. Variations in these structures are found to be correlated with pathological changes and provide information on severity or state of various diseases. The retina is the only location where blood vessels can be directly captured noninvasively in vivo. OD is a structure in retina, which is seen as a pale, round or slightly vertical oval disc. A distinguishing feature of the OD is that, it is the region of convergence for the blood vessel network. The change in the shape, colour or depth of OD is an indicator of various ophthalmic pathologies (Niemeijer at al 2009).

The Blood Vessel (BV) Segmentation is a fundamental advance in the medicinal finding of retinal fundus pictures (shown in Figure 3) as it helps in the determination of visual infections like Diabetic Retinopathy (DR) (Gupta & Chhikara 2018)). DR is an intricacy of diabetes and is a noteworthy reason for visual deficiency in created nations. The patients probably won't see lost vision until the point that it turned out to be excessively extreme, henceforth early determination and opportune treatment

Figure 3. Retinal images landmarks with blood vessels

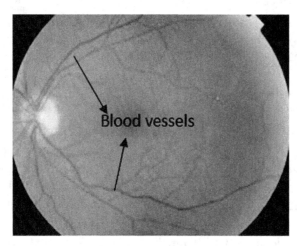

is fundamental to defer or anticipate visual impede and even visual impairment (Kawasaki et al 2018). The BV Segmentation can improve screening for retinopathy by lessening the quantity of false positive. It chiefly influences about 80% of patients experiencing diabetics for a long time or more (Amissah & Mensah 2018).

DR mainly occurs due to changes in blood vessels of retina, as the blood glucose level increases (Wang et al 2019). The walls of the blood vessels will then become weak and starts to break and leaks the blood around them. Afterward, the cells in the retina will bite the dust from an absence of sustenance and the vessels may quit conveying blood for all time (Akbar et al 2019). Accordingly, old vessels do not work appropriately and new but rather unusual ones will develop to take their place. They can't support the retina legitimately and may develop into the straightforward internal piece of the eye, and further influence vision (Shown in Figure 4). However, manual BV Segmentation isn't reasonable on the grounds that the vessels in a retinal picture are mind boggling and have low contrast (Ker et al. 2018).

Figure 4. DR and its stages with the effect of blood vessels (Source: http://rachellelefevre.us/diabetic-retinopathy-stages.html/diabetic-retinopathy-stages-about)

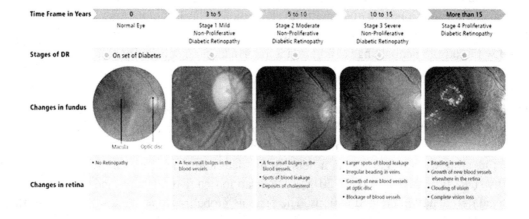

This paper presents a computerized BV segmentation in the human retina. The remaining part of the paper is organized as follows, the fundamental concepts of deep learning is presented in section 2. The related works are presented in section 3. In section 4. presents the methodology. The results and discussion are discussed in section 5 and 6 respectively. The conclusions and future work is found in section 7.

DEEP LEARNING

Generally, machine learning models are prepared to perform helpful assignments dependent on physically structured highlights removed from the crude information, or highlights learned by other basic machine learning models. In deep learning, the PCs learn valuable portrayals and highlights naturally, straightforwardly from the crude information, bypassing this manual and troublesome step. By a wide margin the most well-known models in profound learning are different variations of fake neural systems, however there are others (Ker et al. 2018).

The fundamental normal for profound learning strategies is their attention on highlight adapting: consequently learning portrayals of information. This is the essential contrast between profound learning methodologies and that's only the tip of the iceberg "traditional" machine learning. Finding highlights and playing out an assignment is converged into one issue, and in this way both improved amid the equivalent preparing process. The general outlines of the field in retinal imaging the enthusiasm for deep learning is for the most part activated by convolutional neural systems (CNNs). It an incredible approach to learn helpful portrayals of pictures and other organized information. Before it wound up conceivable to utilize CNNs proficiently, these highlights ordinarily must be built by hand, or made by less incredible machine learning models. When it wound up conceivable to utilize highlights gained straightforwardly from the information, a significant number of the carefully assembled picture highlights were ordinarily left by the wayside as they ended up being nearly useless contrasted with highlight indicators found by CNNs. There are some solid inclinations installed in CNNs based on how they are built, which encourages us comprehend why they are so ground-breaking. Let us hence investigate the building squares of CNNs (Mechelli 2018)

Convolutional Neural Network

While applying neural systems to pictures one can on a basic level utilize the straightforward feed forward neural systems talked about above. In any case, having associations from all hubs of one layer to all hubs in the following is incredibly wasteful. A watchful pruning of the associations dependent on area information, for example the structure of pictures, prompts much better execution (Razak et al. 2018)

A CNN is a specific sort of counterfeit neural system went for safeguarding spatial connections in the information, with not many associations between the layers. The contribution to a CNN is orchestrated in a matrix structure and afterward encouraged through layers that protect these connections, each layer activity working on a little district of the past layer (Fig. 5). CNNs can frame very productive portrayal of the information data, appropriate for picture arranged assignments. A CNN has different layers of convolutions and enactments, regularly scattered with pooling layers, what's more, and is prepared utilizing back propagation and angle plummet as for standard fake neural systems. In expansion, CNNs ordinarily have completely associated layers at the end, which process the last yields (Ker et al. 2018)

Convolutional Layers

In the convolutional layers(conv) the enactments from the past layers are convolved with a set of little parameterized channels, oftentimes of size 3×3, gathered in a tensor $W(j,i)$, where j is the channel number furthermore, i is the layer number. By having each channel share the identical loads over the entire info area, for example translational equivariance at each layer, one accomplishes an intense decrease in the quantity of loads that should be learned. The inspiration for this weight-sharing is that highlights showing up in one piece of the picture likely additionally show up in different parts. On the off chance that you have a channel equipped for recognizing even lines, state, at that point it very well may be utilized to recognize them wherever they show up. Applying all the convolutional channels at all areas of the contribution to a convolutional layer produces a tensor of highlight maps.

Activation Layer

The element maps from a convolutional layer are nourished through nonlinear enactment capacities. This makes it feasible for the whole neural system to estimate practically any nonlinear capacity. The actuation capacities are commonly the extremely straightforward amended direct units, or ReLUs, characterized as $ReLU(z) = max(0, z)$, or variations like defective ReLUs or parametric ReLUs, for more data about these and other initiation capacities. Sustaining the element maps through an enactment work delivers new tensors, commonly too called highlight maps.

Pooling

Each component map created by encouraging the information through at least one convolutional layer is then ordinarily pooled in a pooling layer. Pooling activities take little matrix areas as info and produce single numbers for each locale. The number is generally processed by utilizing the maximum work (max-pooling) or the normal capacity (normal pooling). Since a little move of the information picture results in little changes in the enactment maps, the pooling layers gives the CNN some translational invariance. An alternate method for getting the down sampling impact of pooling is to utilize convolutions with expanded walk lengths. Evacuating the pooling layers rearranges the arrange design without essentially yielding execution

Figure 5. Building blocks of a typical CNN (Source: https://towardsdatascience.com/applied-deep-learning-part-4-convolutional-neural-networks-584bc134c1e2)

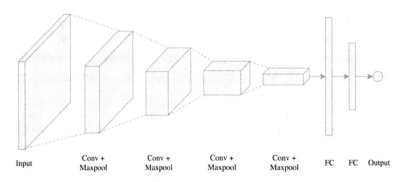

Dropout Regularization

A basic thought that gave an immense support in the execution of CNNs. By averaging a few models in a troupe one will in general show signs of improvement execution than when utilizing single models. Dropout is an averaging system dependent on stochastic examining of neural networks. By arbitrarily evacuating neurons amid preparing one winds up utilizing somewhat unique systems for each bunch of preparing information, and the loads of the prepared organize are tuned dependent on improvement of numerous varieties of the system.

Batch Normalization

A basic thought that gave a tremendous support in the execution of CNNs. By averaging a few models in an outfit one will in general show signs of improvement execution than when utilizing single models. Dropout is an averaging procedure dependent on stochastic examining of neural networks. By haphazardly evacuating neurons amid preparing one winds up utilizing somewhat extraordinary systems for each cluster of preparing information, and the loads of the prepared arrange are tuned dependent on streamlining of different varieties of the system. In the design of new and improved CNN architectures, these components are combined in increasingly complicated and interconnected ways, or even replaced by other more convenient operations. When architecting a CNN for a particular task there are multiple factors to consider, including understanding the task to be solved and the requirements to be met, figuring out how to best feed the data to the network, and optimally utilizing one's budget for computation and memory consumption.

RELATED WORKS

This literature analysis provides the most generally proposed vessel segmentation algorithms to segment blood vessels in the retinal fundus images. The first of vessel segmentation algorithm is pre-processing, which generally presents noise removal, contrast improvement, image normalization and color image to gray scale conversion. The necessary of pre-processing steps is to characterize the image features from various image modalities such as contrast, resolution and noise etc. (Moccia et al. 2018). This literature survey presents an overall work flow of existing vessel segmentation algorithms. Furthermore the existing segmentations are categorized in to four different sections such as vessel enhancement, machine learning, deformable models and tracking of vessels (shown in Figure 6). The vessel upgrade approaches, the nature of vessel discernment is enhanced, e.g. by expanding the vessel diverge from regard to the foundation and other non-enlightening structures. A solid and set up writing on vessel upgrade approaches as of now exists. Examples include matched filtering (Singh & Srivastava 2018), vessels-based approaches (Sazak et al 2019), Wavelet (Garcia et al. 2018) and diffusion filtering (Shalaby et al 2018). These methods provide the optimal resolution and contrast in both time and frequency domains. There are two principal classes of machine learning approaches: unsupervised (Xiao et al. 2018) and supervised (Nekovei et al.1995). Provide broad definitions and discussions of the topic and incorporate views of others (literature review) into the discussion to support, refute, or demonstrate your position on the topic.

The previous finds a model ready to depict shrouded plan of information picture inferred highlights, with no earlier learning or supervision, while the last takes in a piece of information demonstrate from a lot of effectively marked highlights. The deformable models think about bends or surfaces, characterized inside the picture space, that can move and disfigure affected by interior and outside forces. The previous are intended to keep smooth amid the disfigurement while the last draw in toward the vessel limit. Deformable model methodologies can be isolated in edge-based (Xu et al. 2000) and region based (Chan & Vese 2001). Tracking of vessels calculations, for the most part, comprise in the meaning of seed focuses pursued by a development procedure guided by picture inferred imperatives. Seed focuses can be either physically characterized or gotten through vessel upgrade approaches. Following methodologies are especially valuable to fragment associated vascular trees, for which the division can be accomplished utilizing a predetermined number of seed focuses. The tracking methods can be isolated in template matching (Carrillo et al 207), model based (Friman et al 2010), finding minimum cost path (Cohen et al 1997) and cost function estimation (Deschamps & Cohen 2001). The blood vessel segmentation algorithms are tabulated in Table 1. In view of the survey distinctive BV segmentation methods are right now utilized in DR screening and a proper decision of the segmentation algorithm is compulsory to manage BV segmentation attributes such as resolution, noise and vessel contrast. Hence this paper has introduced to adopt the BV segmentation attributes.

Methodology

The deep CNN has to utilize to segment BV in retinal fundus images. In more explicitly CNN which rather than sub-sampling or down-inspecting layers have a max-pooling layer. The CNN comprise of a succession of convolutional max-pooling and fully connected layers. The max-pooling layer can delineate input tests into yield class probabilities utilizing a few various leveled layers to remove highlights, and fully connected layers to group removed highlights. Amid the preparation of the system, parameters of highlight extraction and arrangement are mutually upgraded. The architecture of deep CNN is shown in Figure 7.

Figure 6. General blood vessel segmentation methods

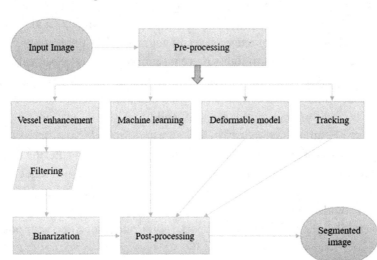

Table 1. Blood vessel segmentation algorithms

Main category	Algorithms	Interpretation
Vessel enhancement	• Matched filtering • Vesselness approach. • Wavelet approach. • Diffusion filtering	Provides the optimal resolution and contrast in both time and frequency domains.
Machine learning	• Un-supervised • Supervised	A model able to describe hidden arrangement of input image derived features without any prior knowledge
Deformable model	• Edge based • Region based	It considers vessel is either curve or surface with in the image domain that can move and deform under the influence of internal and external forces
Tracking	• Template matching • Model based • Minimum cost path • Cost function	It consist of fixing seed points followed by a growth process guided by image derived constraints

Figure 7. Architecture of CNN

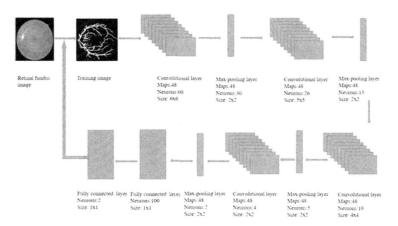

The novelty of this proposed methodology is the pre-processing is not required to segment BV. It is made of predefined non-variable filters. The filtering is connected between info pictures and a bank of channels in each convolutional layer. It results in a new set of pictures (signified as maps). As in fully connected input-output portrayal maps are additionally directly joined. From that point forward, it is connected a nonlinear enactment work (linear unit). In forwarding proliferation, if in the front convolutional layer will be the layer of size n × n, the m × m channel ω has used in this method. At that point size of the convolutional layer yield is (n − m + 1) × (n− m + 1). The pre-non linearity contribution to some unit x_{ij}^{l} considers:

$$x_{ij}^{l} = \sum_{a=0}^{m-1} \sum_{a=0}^{m-1} w_{ab} y_{(i+a)(j+b)}^{l-1} \tag{1}$$

$$y_{ij}^{l} = \sigma(x_{ij}^{l}) \tag{2}$$

Intently the forward and back propagation ventures of the max-pooling layer which are in subtleties depicted. The max-pooling layers are fixed and they are not prepared. They take square squares of convolution layers and lessen their yield into a solitary element. The chose to highlight is the most encouraging as max-pooling is done over the convolution layers. The fully connected layers are the standard neural arrange layers where the yield neurons are associated with all the information neurons, with each connection having a load as a parameter. So as to do segmentation, picture squares are taken (with an odd number of pixels – the focal the pixel in addition to the neighborhood) to decide the class (vessel or non-vessel) of the focal pixel. System training is performed on patches separated from a set of pictures for which a manual division exists. After such training, the system can be utilized to group every pixel in the new instances of pictures.

Subsequent to substituting four stages of the convolutional layer and max-pooling layer layers two fully connected layers further join the yields into a 1D include vector. The last layer is dependably a fully connected layer with one neuron for every class (two for our situation due to twofold characterization). In the yielding layer by utilizing Soft-max initiation work every neuron's yield actuation can be taken as the likelihood of a specific pixel. In fig.1 shows, the 10-layer design for the system with quantities of maps and neurons, the channel estimate for each layer, loads and associations for the convolutional layer and fully connected layers

Additionally, to the strategy portrayed to prepare the classifier, we utilized all BV pixels as positive models, and the equivalent a measure of pixels arbitrarily examined among all non-BV pixels. This guarantees a decent preparing set. The positive and negative examples are interleaved while producing the preparation tests. We utilize the green channel of the information pictures as it is well known from the writing that the green channel contains the most complexity in fundus photos.

Meterials

An ophthalmologist is a medicinal specialist that works in the structure, capacity, and ailments of the human eye. Amid a clinical examination, an ophthalmologist notes discoveries that are unmistakable according to the subject. The ophthalmologist at that point utilizes these discoveries to reason about the wellbeing of the subject. For example, a patient may display staining of the optic nerve, or a narrowing of the veins in the retina. An ophthalmologist utilizes this data to analyze the patient, as having for example Coats sickness or a focal retinal supply route impediment.

An optical camera is utilized to see through the understudy of the eye to the back inward surface of the eyeball. An image is taken appearing optic nerve, fovea, encompassing vessels, and the retinal layer. The ophthalmologist would then be able to reference this picture while thinking about any watched discoveries. This exploration concerns a framework to consequently analyze illnesses of the human eye. The framework takes as info data recognizable in a retinal picture. This data is detailed to copy the discoveries that an ophthalmologist would note amid a clinical examination. The principle yield of the framework is a determination planned to imitate the end that an ophthalmologist would reach about the wellbeing of the subject. In this segment, we give a concise outline on the databases, for example, DRIVE, STARE, MESSIDOR, DIARETDB0 and University of Lincoln utilized for veins location.

Digital Retinal Images for Vessel Extraction (DRIVE)

The photos for the DRIVE database were acquired from a diabetic retinopathy screening program in The Netherlands. The pictures were gained utilizing a Canon CR5 non-mydriatic 3CCD camera with a 45 degree field of view (FOV). Each picture was caught utilizing 8 bits for every shading plane at 768 by 584 pixels and compacted in JPEG position. Forty photos have been arbitrarily chosen, 33 don't hint at any diabetic retinopathy and 7 hint at gentle early diabetic retinopathy. The arrangement of 40 pictures has been separated into preparing and test set, both containing 20 pictures. For the preparation pictures, a solitary manual division of the vasculature is accessible. For the experiments, two manual divisions are accessible. Every single human eyewitness that physically fragmented the vasculature were told and prepared by an accomplished ophthalmologist (ISI, n.d.).

Methods to Evaluate Segmentation and Indexing Techniques in the Field of Retinal Ophthalmology (MESSIDOR)

The MESSIDOR database has been built up to rearrange examines on PC helped determinations of diabetic retinopathy. The 1200 eye fundus shading numerical pictures of the back post for the MESSIDOR database were created by 3 ophthalmologic divisions utilizing a shading video 3CCD camera on a Topcon TRC NW6 non-mydriatic retinograph with a 45-degree field of view. The pictures were caught utilizing 8 bits for every shading plane at 1440*960, 2240*1488 or 2304*1536 pixels. Around 800 pictures were procured with student enlargement and 400 without expansion (ADCIS, n.d.).

Structured Analysis of the Retina (STARE)

The STARE (STructured Analysis of the Retina) Project was considered and started in 1975 by Michael Goldbaum, M.D., at the University of California, San Diego. It was supported by the U.S. National Institutes of Health. Our methodology breaks the issue into two parts. The main part concerns naturally handling a retinal picture to indicate the vital discoveries. The second segment concerns consequently thinking about the discoveries to decide a determination. Extra yields incorporate point by point estimations of the anatomical structures and injuries obvious in the retinal picture. These estimations are helpful for following infection seriousness and the assessment of treatment advance after some time. By gathering a database of estimations for an expansive number of individuals, the STARE venture could bolster clinical populace studies and understudy preparing. The pictures in STARE database are assigned in XXXX where XXXX is a four digit number. The accessible pictures are numbered from 0001 to 0402 (Clemson, n.d.).

Standard Diabetic Retinopathy Database: Calibration level 0 (DIARETDB0)

The DIARETDB0 database comprises of 130 shading fundus pictures of which 20 are typical and 110 contain indications of the diabetic retinopathy. The pictures were taken in the Kuo-pio college medical clinic. Pictures were caught with few 50 degree field-of-see advanced fundus cameras with obscure camera settings (streak power, shade speed, gap and increase). The arrangement of 130 pictures were partitioned into 5 picture classifications, and a fixed number of haphazardly chosen pictures were taken from every classification to shape the preparation set. Whatever is left of the pictures create the test set. The picture classes were shaped to affirm that every diabetic retinopathy discovering type is incorporated into the both preparing and test sets (Imageret, n.d.).

University of Lincoln Dataset

This dataset contains 99 fundal pictures taken from 50 patients haphazardly examined from a diabetic retinopathy screening program; 96 pictures have discernable Optic Nerve Head (ONH). The subjects are from different ethnic foundations (Asian 20%, Afro-Caribbean 16%, Caucasian half and Unknown 14%); 19 have sort 2 diabetes mellitus, while the diabetes status was inaccessible for the remaining 31. The pictures were obtained utilizing a Canon CR6 45MNf fundus camera, with a field edge focal point of 45 degrees, goals 640 x 480. Pictures were changed over to dark scale by removing the Intensity part from the HSI portrayal. There is impressive quality variety in the pictures, with numerous attributes that can influence division calculations. The ONH focus has been increased a clinician. At that point, four clinicians denoted the ONH edge where it crosses with outspread spokes (at 15 degree edges) transmitting from the designated focus. These various selections of the edge can be utilized to describe the level of abstract vulnerability in the edge position (University of Lincoln, n.d.).

RESULT AND DISCUSSION

The Database used for blood vessel segmentation is as shown in Table 2. Thus, a set of 1550 retinal pictures is tried in which 679 pictures are ordinary and 871 pictures are strange for a mechanized segmentation of vessels in the retina.

A MATLAB (2018b) prototype was used to run the algorithm developed for training of blood vessels in retinal images for each image on a Dell Alienware, i7 6th gen, GTX 1080 GPU, 64 GB DDR4 RAM. In the BV segmentation, the result is a pixel-based arrangement result. Notice that we don't depend on any base up division since we treat semantic division as pixel characterization, where every pixel is depicted by its neighborhood. Along these lines, the technique isn't influenced by the blunders of base up the division. In Figure 8 we can perceive how a run of the mill yield picture resembles. We can see that regions having a place with veins have a higher likelihood of being a piece of veins.

Table 2. Dataset and images applied for blood vessel segmentation

S.No	Dataset	Total images	Normal images	Abnormal images
1	STARE	81	31	50
2	DRIVE	40	33	7
3	MESSIDOR	1200	546	654
4	DIARETDB0	130	20	110
5	UNIVERSITY OF LINCOLN	99	49	50
Total		**1550**	**679**	**871**

Figure 8. BV segmented images (a)-(c) STARE dataset,(d)-(f) DRIVE dataset,(g)-(i) MESSIDOR dataset,(J)-(L) DIARETDB0 dataset,(m)-(O) UNIVERSITY OF LINCOLN dataset.

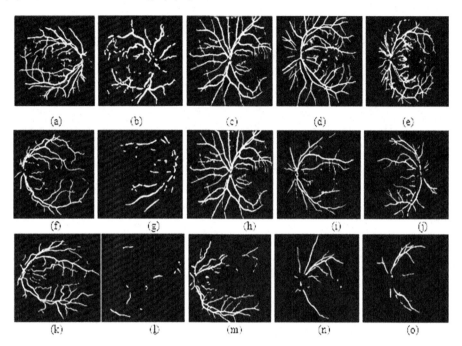

Performance Analysis

The performance of the proposed blood vessel segmentation method was evaluated by means of the Receiver Operating Characteristic (ROC) curve stated by University of Nebraska, Medical Center, and Department of Internal Medicine. The ordinate of the ROC curve is the sensitivity, which is the capacity of the technique to characterize the irregular pictures and the abscissa is identified with the explicitness, which is the capacity to arrange the typical pictures. The values of the sensitivity and the specificity have been obtained by Equation 3 and 4 respectively, the value of the area under the ROC curve (AUC) is described using dice similarity co-efficient by Equation 5. The AUC curve was generated for tested datasets such as STARE, DRIVE, MESSIDOR, DIARETDB0 and University of Lincoln that can be found in fig.9.

$$\text{Sensitivity} = \frac{TruePositive}{Truepositive + FalseNegative} \tag{3}$$

$$\text{Specificity} = \frac{TrueNegative}{TrueNegative + FalsePositive} \tag{4}$$

$$\text{AUC} = \frac{2Truepositive}{FalsePositive + FalseNegative + 2TruePositive} \tag{5}$$

Figure 9. ROC curve of (a) STARE (b) DRIVE(c) MESSIDEO (d) DIARETDB0 (e) University of Lincoln datasets

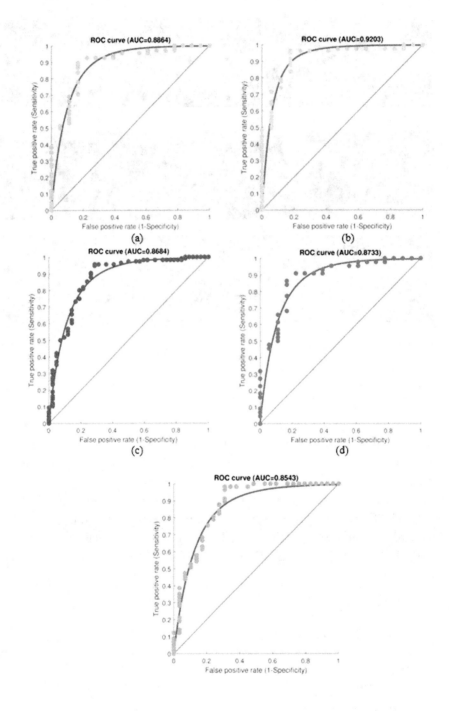

Table 3. AUC performance comparison on DRIVE database with state of the art works

Author	Algorithm	AUC
Abdurrazaq et al. 2008	Morphology approach	0.9059
Mendonca et al. 2006	Morphological reconstruction	0.7315
Zhang et al. 2016	locally adaptive derivative frame	0.7743
Azzopardi et al. 2015	Trainable cosfire filters	0.7655
Zhao et al. 2015	Active contour model	0.8620
Jiang et al. 2017	Morphology-based global thresholding	0.8375
Fraz et al. 2012	Bit planes and centerline detection	0.7242
Wang et al. 2015	Ensemble learning	0.8431
Li et al. 2016	Cross-modality learning	0.7273
Martin et al. 2011	Gray-level and moment invariants-based features	0.7067
Soomro et al. 2017	Convolutional neural network	0.8310
Proposed	**Convolutional neural network**	**0.9203**

Comparative Analysis

This section will give the execution examination the related cutting edge takes a shot at the DRIVE database. Table 3 introduces the execution correlation in the DRIVE database. In the execution comparison Wang et al. (2015) displayed the CNN however the AUC esteem is lower than proposed technique.

CONCLUSION AND FUTURE WORK

This paper proposes a novel BV segmentation algorithm for retinal fundus images. The segmentation of the BV in the retina has been an intensely inquired about territory in later a long time. Albeit numerous strategies and calculations have been created, there is still space for further enhancements. We introduced a methodology utilizing deep max-pooling convolutional neural systems with GPU execution to section veins and results demonstrate that it is a promising strategy. Our strategy yields the most elevated announced AUC for the STARE, DRIVE, MESSIDOR, DIARETDB0 and UNIVERSITY OF LINCOLN databases.

Future work is improving the calculation by different techniques like recreating more information for preparing: utilizing all channels (not just green), to pivot, scale and perfect representations and so forth. Maybe a few pre-processing and post-processing would upgrade results and doubtlessly averaging more systems would improve results. Conceivably foveation or non-uniform inspecting is likewise an approach to improve results. Preparing on a set with more pictures with pathological changes might improve results.

REFERENCES

Abdurrazaq, I., Hati, S., & Eswaran, C. (2008, May). Morphology approach for features extraction in retinal images for diabetic retionopathy diagnosis. In *2008 International Conference on Computer and Communication Engineering* (pp. 1373-1377). IEEE. 10.1109/ICCCE.2008.4580830

ADCIS. (n.d.). Retrieved from: http://www.adcis.net/en/third-party/messidor/

Akbar, S., Sharif, M., Akram, M. U., Saba, T., Mahmood, T., & Kolivand, M. (2019). Automated techniques for blood vessels segmentation through fundus retinal images: A review. *Microscopy Research and Technique*, *82*(2), 153–170. doi:10.1002/jemt.23172 PMID:30614150

Amissah-Arthur, K. N., & Mensah, E. (2018). The past, present and future management of sickle cell retinopathy within an African context. *Eye (London, England)*, 1. PMID:29991740

Azzopardi, G., Strisciuglio, N., Vento, M., & Petkov, N. (2015). Trainable COSFIRE filters for vessel delineation with application to retinal images. *Medical Image Analysis*, *19*(1), 46–57. doi:10.1016/j.media.2014.08.002 PMID:25240643

Carrillo, J. F., Hoyos, M. H., Dávila, E. E., & Orkisz, M. (2007). Recursive tracking of vascular tree axes in 3D medical images. *International Journal of Computer Assisted Radiology and Surgery*, *1*(6), 331–339. doi:10.100711548-007-0068-6

Chan, T. F., & Vese, L. A. (2001). Active contours without edges. *IEEE Transactions on Image Processing*, *10*(2), 266–277. doi:10.1109/83.902291 PMID:18249617

Clemson. (n.d.). Structured analysis of the retina. *Clemson University*. Retrieved from: http://cecas.clemson.edu/~ahoover/stare/

Cohen, L. D., & Kimmel, R. (1997). Global minimum for active contour models: A minimal path approach. *International Journal of Computer Vision*, *24*(1), 57–78. doi:10.1023/A:1007922224810

Deschamps, T., & Cohen, L. D. (2001). Fast extraction of minimal paths in 3D images and applications to virtual endoscopy. *Medical Image Analysis*, *5*(4), 281–299. doi:10.1016/S1361-8415(01)00046-9 PMID:11731307

Foracchia, M., Grisan, E., & Ruggeri, A. (2004). Detection of optic disc in retinal images by means of a geometrical model of vessel structure. *IEEE Transactions on Medical Imaging*, *23*(10), 1189–1195. doi:10.1109/TMI.2004.829331 PMID:15493687

Fraz, M. M., Barman, S. A., Remagnino, P., Hoppe, A., Basit, A., Uyyanonvara, B., ... Owen, C. G. (2012). An approach to localize the retinal blood vessels using bit planes and centerline detection. *Computer Methods and Programs in Biomedicine*, *108*(2), 600–616. doi:10.1016/j.cmpb.2011.08.009 PMID:21963241

Friman, O., Hindennach, M., Kühnel, C., & Peitgen, H. O. (2010). Multiple hypothesis template tracking of small 3D vessel structures. *Medical Image Analysis*, *14*(2), 160–171. doi:10.1016/j.media.2009.12.003 PMID:20060770

Garcıa-Tarifa, M. J., Martınez-Murcia, F. J., & Górriz, J. M. (2018, June). Retinal Blood Vessel Segmentation by Multi-channel Deep Convolutional Autoencoder. In *International Joint Conference SOCO'18-CISIS'18-ICEUTE'18: San Sebastián, Spain, June 6-8, 2018 Proceedings* (Vol. 771, p. 37). Springer.

Gupta, A., & Chhikara, R. (2018). Diabetic Retinopathy: Present and Past. *Procedia Computer Science*, *132*, 1432–1440. doi:10.1016/j.procs.2018.05.074

Hoover, A., & Goldbaum, M. (2003). Locating the optic nerve in a retinal image using the fuzzy convergence of the blood vessels. *IEEE Transactions on Medical Imaging*, *22*(8), 951–958. doi:10.1109/TMI.2003.815900 PMID:12906249

Imageret. (n.d.) DIARETDB0-Standard diabetic retinopathy database calibration 1.0. *Imageret*. Retrieved from: http://www.it.lut.fi/project/imageret/diaretdb0/

ISI. (n.d.). DRIVE: Digital retinal images for vessel extraction. *ISI*. Retrieved from: https://www.isi.uu.nl/Research/Databases/DRIVE/

Jiang, Z., Yepez, J., An, S., & Ko, S. (2017). Fast, accurate and robust retinal vessel segmentation system. *Biocybernetics and Biomedical Engineering*, *37*(3), 412–421. doi:10.1016/j.bbe.2017.04.001

Kawasaki, R., Kitano, S., Sato, Y., Yamashita, H., Nishimura, R., Tajima, N., & Japan Diabetes Complication and its Prevention prospective (JDCP) study Diabetic Retinopathy working group. (2018). Factors associated with non-proliferative diabetic retinopathy in patients with type 1 and type 2 diabetes: the Japan Diabetes Complication and its Prevention prospective study (JDCP study 4). *Diabetology International*, 1-9.

Ker, J., Wang, L., Rao, J., & Lim, T. (2018). Deep learning applications in medical image analysis. *IEEE Access: Practical Innovations, Open Solutions*, *6*, 9375–9389. doi:10.1109/ACCESS.2017.2788044

Li, H., & Chutatape, O. (2001, October). Automatic location of optic disk in retinal images. In *Proceedings 2001 International Conference on Image Processing (Cat. No. 01CH37205)* (Vol. 2, pp. 837-840). IEEE. 10.1109/ICIP.2001.958624

Li, Q., Feng, B., Xie, L., Liang, P., Zhang, H., & Wang, T. (2016). A cross-modality learning approach for vessel segmentation in retinal images. *IEEE Transactions on Medical Imaging*, *35*(1), 109–118. doi:10.1109/TMI.2015.2457891 PMID:26208306

Livingstone, M., & Hubel, D. (1988). Segregation of form, color, movement, and depth: Anatomy, physiology, and perception. *Science*, *240*(4853), 740–749. doi:10.1126cience.3283936 PMID:3283936

Marín, D., Aquino, A., Gegúndez-Arias, M. E., & Bravo, J. M. (2011). A new supervised method for blood vessel segmentation in retinal images by using gray-level and moment invariants-based features. *IEEE Transactions on Medical Imaging*, *30*(1), 146–158. doi:10.1109/TMI.2010.2064333 PMID:20699207

Mechelli, A. (2018). 202. Deep Learning Technology: Concepts and Applications in Biological Psychiatry. *Biological Psychiatry*, *83*(9), S81–S82. doi:10.1016/j.biopsych.2018.02.221

Mendonca, A. M., & Campilho, A. (2006). Segmentation of retinal blood vessels by combining the detection of centerlines and morphological reconstruction. *IEEE Transactions on Medical Imaging*, *25*(9), 1200–1213. doi:10.1109/TMI.2006.879955 PMID:16967805

Moccia, S., De Momi, E., El Hadji, S., & Mattos, L. S. (2018). Blood vessel segmentation algorithms—Review of methods, datasets and evaluation metrics. *Computer Methods and Programs in Biomedicine*, *158*, 71–91. doi:10.1016/j.cmpb.2018.02.001 PMID:29544791

Nekovei, R., & Sun, Y. (1995). Back-propagation network and its configuration for blood vessel detection in angiograms. *IEEE Transactions on Neural Networks*, *6*(1), 64–72. doi:10.1109/72.363449 PMID:18263286

Niemeijer, M., Abràmoff, M. D., & Van Ginneken, B. (2009). Fast detection of the optic disc and fovea in color fundus photographs. *Medical Image Analysis*, *13*(6), 859–870. doi:10.1016/j.media.2009.08.003 PMID:19782633

Razzak, M. I., Naz, S., & Zaib, A. (2018). Deep learning for medical image processing: Overview, challenges and the future. In *Classification in BioApps* (pp. 323–350). Cham: Springer. doi:10.1007/978-3-319-65981-7_12

Sazak, Ç., Nelson, C. J., & Obara, B. (2019). The multiscale bowler-hat transform for blood vessel enhancement in retinal images. *Pattern Recognition*, *88*, 739–750. doi:10.1016/j.patcog.2018.10.011

Shalaby, A., Mahmoud, A., Mesbah, S., El-Baz, M., Suri, J. S., & El-Baz, A. (2018). Accurate Unsupervised 3D Segmentation of Blood Vessels Using Magnetic Resonance Angiography. In Cardiovascular Imaging and Image Analysis (pp. 71-94). CRC Press.

Singh, N. P., & Srivastava, R. (2018). Extraction of retinal blood vessels by using an extended matched filter based on second derivative of gaussian. *Proceedings of the National Academy of Sciences, India Section A: Physical Sciences*, 1-9.

Soomro, T. A., Afifi, A. J., Gao, J., Hellwich, O., Khan, M. A., Paul, M., & Zheng, L. (2017, November). Boosting sensitivity of a retinal vessel segmentation algorithm with convolutional neural network. In *2017 International Conference on Digital Image Computing: Techniques and Applications (DICTA)* (pp. 1-8). IEEE. 10.1109/DICTA.2017.8227413

University of Lincoln. (n.d.). Review: Retinal Vessel Image set for estimation widths. *University of Lincoln*. Retrieved from: http://www.aldiri.info/REVIEWDB/REVIEWDB.aspx

Walter, T., & Klein, J. C. (2001, October). Segmentation of color fundus images of the human retina: Detection of the optic disc and the vascular tree using morphological techniques. In *International Symposium on Medical Data Analysis* (pp. 282-287). Springer. 10.1007/3-540-45497-7_43

Wang, S., Yin, Y., Cao, G., Wei, B., Zheng, Y., & Yang, G. (2015). Hierarchical retinal blood vessel segmentation based on feature and ensemble learning. *Neurocomputing*, *149*, 708–717. doi:10.1016/j.neucom.2014.07.059

Wang, X., Jiang, X., & Ren, J. (2019). Blood vessel segmentation from fundus image by a cascade classification framework. *Pattern Recognition*, *88*, 331–341. doi:10.1016/j.patcog.2018.11.030

Xiao, R., Ding, H., Zhai, F., Zhou, W., & Wang, G. (2018). Cerebrovascular segmentation of TOF-MRA based on seed point detection and multiple-feature fusion. *Computerized Medical Imaging and Graphics*, *69*, 1–8. doi:10.1016/j.compmedimag.2018.07.002 PMID:30142578

Xu, C., Pham, D. L., & Prince, J. L. (2000). Image segmentation using deformable models. Handbook of Medical Imaging, 2, 129-174.

Youssif, A. A. H. A. R., Ghalwash, A. Z., & Ghoneim, A. A. S. A. R. (2008). Optic disc detection from normalized digital fundus images by means of a vessels' direction matched filter. *IEEE Transactions on Medical Imaging, 27*(1), 11–18. doi:10.1109/TMI.2007.900326 PMID:18270057

Zhang, J., Dashtbozorg, B., Bekkers, E., Pluim, J. P., Duits, R., & ter Haar Romeny, B. M. (2016). Robust retinal vessel segmentation via locally adaptive derivative frames in orientation scores. *IEEE Transactions on Medical Imaging, 35*(12), 2631–2644. doi:10.1109/TMI.2016.2587062 PMID:27514039

Zhao, Y., Rada, L., Chen, K., Harding, S. P., & Zheng, Y. (2015). Automated vessel segmentation using infinite perimeter active contour model with hybrid region information with application to retinal images. *IEEE Transactions on Medical Imaging, 34*(9), 1797–1807. doi:10.1109/TMI.2015.2409024 PMID:25769147

KEY TERMS AND DEFINITIONS

Blood Vessels: A retinal vessel occlusion is a blockage in the blood vessel of your eye that can result in sight loss. There are two types of retinal blood vessels, arteries and veins.

Convolutional Neural Network: In deep learning, a convolutional neural network is a class of deep neural networks, most commonly applied to analyzing visual imagery. CNNs use a variation of multilayer perceptrons designed to require minimal preprocessing.

Deep Learning: Deep learning (also known as deep structured learning or hierarchical learning) is part of a broader family of machine learning methods based on learning data representations, as opposed to task-specific algorithms. Learning can be supervised, semi-supervised or unsupervised.

Diabetic Retinopathy: Diabetic retinopathy is the most common cause of vision loss among people with diabetes and a leading cause of blindness among working-age adults. DME is a consequence of diabetic retinopathy that causes swelling in the area of the retina called the macula.

Glaucoma: Glaucoma is a group of related eye disorders that cause damage to the optic nerve that carries information from the eye to the brain. The increased pressure, called intraocular pressure, can damage the optic nerve, which transmits images to your brain. If the damage continues, glaucoma can lead to permanent vision loss. Without treatment, glaucoma can cause total permanent blindness within a few years.

Machine Learning: Machine learning is an application of artificial intelligence (AI) that provides systems the ability to automatically learn and improve from experience without being explicitly programmed. Machine learning focuses on the development of computer programs that can access data and use it learn for themselves.

Retina: The retina is a thin layer of tissue that lines the back of the eye on the inside. It is located near the optic nerve. The purpose of the retina is to receive light that the lens has focused, convert the light into neural signals, and send these signals on to the brain for visual recognition.

Chapter 6
Intensity Inhomogeneity Correction in Brain MR Images Based on Filtering Method

C. Helen Sulochana
St. Xavier's Catholic College of Engineering, India

S. A. Praylin Selva Blessy
Bethlahem Institute of Engineering, India

ABSTRACT

Brain tumor is a mass of abnormal growth of cells in the brain which disturbs the normal functioning of the brain. MRI is a powerful diagnostic tool providing excellent soft tissue contrast and high spatial resolution. However, imperfections arising in the radio frequency field and scanner-related intensity artifacts in MRI produce intensity inhomogeneity. These intensity variations pose major challenges for subsequent image processing and analysis techniques. To mitigate this effect in the intensity correction process, an enhanced homomorphic unsharp masking (EHUM) method is proposed in this chapter. The main idea of the proposed EHUM method is determination of region of interest, intensity correction based on homomorphic filtering, and linear gray scale mapping followed by cutoff frequency selection of low pass filter used in the filtering process. This method first determines the ROI to overcome the halo effect between foreground and background regions. Then the intensity correction is carried out using homomorphic filtering and linear gray scale mapping.

INTRODUCTION

Brain tumor is a life-threatening disease that arises due to abnormal growth of cells in the brain. The diagnosis and treatment of brain tumor is based on the clinical symptoms and its radiological appearance. Brain tumor segmentation is a potential investigation tool used for partitioning abnormal tissues from the normal regions. Magnetic Resonance Imaging (MRI) is a non-invasive medical imaging modality used for revealing the anatomical structure of brain tumor. The prime intention of magnetic resonance brain tumor imaging investigation is to draw out the vital clinical knowledge that would improve clini-

DOI: 10.4018/978-1-5225-9902-9.ch006

cal diagnosis and treatment of disease. Due to its excellent soft tissue contrast and novel innovative acquisition sequences, Magnetic Resonance Imaging has become one of the most popular imaging modalities in health care. However, associated acquisition artifacts can significantly reduce image quality. Consequently, these imperfections can disturb the assessment of the acquired images. In the worst case, they may even lead to false decisions by the physician. Moreover, they can negatively influence an automatic processing of the data such as image segmentation or registration. If possible, the sources of artifacts have to be removed during the acquisition process. In many cases, however, this cannot be achieved due to physical or financial issues. Then, they have to be dealt with using appropriate correction methods. Some of the artifacts can even simulate pathologies that are invisible in the artifact free case. Even though many artifacts do not create false pathologies in the images, they make the diagnosis process much more complicated for the radiologist. Most mentionable artifacts in MRI are intensity non-uniformities, also denoted as signal intensity variations. Generally, these variations are very smooth, and in many cases a human observer is not able to recognize them. Figure 1 shows the sample MR images affected by intensity inhomogeneity.

Intensity inhomogeneity is a smooth intensity change referred to as intensity non-uniformity, intensity variations, bias field or gain field. Intensity variations in MR data are due to the combined effect of the imaged object, the MR pulse sequence and the imaging coils. These intensity variations pose major challenges for subsequent image processing and analysis techniques. The signal intensity variations make it impossible to predefine standard transfer functions to visualize certain tissue classes. The radiologist has to perform the adjustment manually in every single case and even for different regions within the images. This process can be very time consuming. These artifacts change the appearance of structures within the images and have a significant influence on the quality of the results of image processing techniques. Many segmentation techniques assume that objects to be segmented have homogeneous intensity characteristics. If these are altered due to imaging artifacts, many techniques will perform significantly worse or even fail. The intensity inhomogeneties in MR images make the segmentation of brain tumor a challenging task.

In the last decades, many researchers in the field of medical imaging have developed significant approaches for the correction of intensity inhomogeneities in MRI. Generally, the corrections are done focusing on two main directions, namely prospective and retrospective. Prospective methods regard inhomogeneity as an error acquired during the imaging process, and the intensity correction is based on adjustments of hardware and acquisition methods such as phantom-based calibration and multichannel transmit scanning (Clare, Alecci & Jezzard, 2001). These methods provide a good solution to intensity correction by gaining information from the scanner system. However, in many cases, they require additional scans which increase the cost and the time complexity. Moreover, these methods are often

Figure 1. Examples of intensity inhomogeneity in MR images

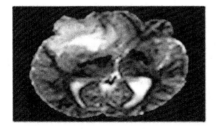 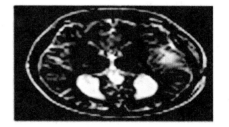

limited to a small area of application (Likar, Viergever & Pernus, 2001). For these reasons, retrospective methods are concentrated. In retrospective methods, the intensity correction process takes place after the acquisition and reconstruction of images. The retrospective methods are classified into surface fitting method, segmentation-based method, histogram-based method and filtering method (Likar, Viergever & Pernus, 2001). Surface fitting methods provides good approximation to intensity inhomogeneities in MR images. These methods provide good intensity correction for large homogeneous brain region but fail to provide correction for tumor regions (Li, John & Davatzikos, 2014). N3 algorithm is a popular histogram-based method for intensity correction by assigning default parameter. However, in certain applications, it cannot fully eliminate the inhomogeneity, which requires semi-automatic post-processing (Florian, 2010). Segmentation based methods increase the computational complexity (Tustison et al., 2010). Filtering-based methods are simple and commonly used intensity correction methods. Methods based on the filtering of the acquired images rely on the assumption that the inhomogeneities do not contain any high frequency information at all. The image content, on the other hand, is assumed to be composed of high frequency signals. Thus, the image content and the inhomogeneities can be separated using low pass filtering. This implies that there is no frequency overlap between both classes. In general, this assumption is not valid. Consequently, new artifacts are introduced due to the filtering operation. Brinkmann et al. developed a median based filtering method and proved kernel size of typically 65x65 or larger provided better results (Aitalissdia et al., 2016). Even though this method is commonly used, problem arises in the selection of kernel dimension. George, Kalaivani, and Sudhakar (2017) proposed a non-iterative multi-scale approach that does not involves prior knowledge and segmentation. This algorithm extracts bias field at different scales using a Log-Gabor filter bank followed by smoothing operation. They are then combined to fit a third-degree polynomial to estimate the bias field. Munendra et al (2017) proposed an intensity inhomogeneity correction of Diffusion-Weighted MR Images of Neonatal and Infantile Brain Using Dynamic Stochastic Resonance to achieve a homogeneous field over a small region of interest. Dynamic stochastic resonance uses the coefficient of discrete cosine transform of an image for brightness normalization and image enhancement simultaneously. Particle swarm optimization is used to tune bistability parameters associated with dynamic equation for the entropy minimization of different group of tissues individually. Both these methods provide better results but the use of polynomial and parameters complicates the process. Axel et al. introduced the most prominently used and simple Homomorphic Unsharp Masking (HUM) filtering method for intensity variation correction (Axel, Constantini & Listerud, 1987). HUM method assumes a multiplicative model of bias field and uses LPF to remove bias field. To maintain the image mean or median, the resulting image is multiplied by a constant relating the image mean or median. The advantage of HUM method is that it can be easily implemented very efficiently. Apart from the choice of using the mean or the median as multiplicative constant, the only parameter that has to be chosen is the size of the masking kernel. Unfortunately, this filter-based method produces halo effects in the MR image which degrades the performance of the intensity correction process. A medical image often consists of a dark background and a light foreground. Generally, halo effect occurs between the borders of these two different regions. To overcome this effect, Guillemaud has extracted only the region of interest (foreground) where the information exists and then follows the HUM procedure for intensity correction (Brinkmann, Manduca & Robb, 1998). Guillemaud scheme efficiently overcomes the halo effect between the background and foreground region of the medical image. But the halo effect between the ventricular system and white matter corrupts the white matter intensities. Ardizzone et al. (2008) developed an intensity inhomogeneity correction comprising an automatic cutoff frequency selection process (Guillemaud, 1998). Even though this method eliminates the manual intervention for cut off frequency selection, the above-mentioned halo effect problem remains unsolved. Halo Compensated Homomorphic Unsharp Masking scheme mitigates this effect by using an appropriate non-linear mapping of the filtered image to sustain the white matter intensity (Ardizzone, Pirrone & Gambino, 2008). This method reduces its performance in the case of images with tumor. To overcome this effect, Enhanced Homomorphic Unsharp Masking (EHUM) method is proposed in this chapter. The proposed method first determines the ROI to overcome the halo effect between foreground and background regions. Then the intensity correction is carried out using homomorphic filtering and linear gray scale mapping.

In the remaining part of this chapter, the proposed EHUM approach for intensity inhomogeneity correction is described which is followed by the experimental results. Finally, a brief conclusion of the proposed method is given.

THE PROPOSED EHUM METHOD

The normal brain tissue intensities are altered significantly over a certain region for images affected with disease. Under this circumstance, the existing methods are not fully effective in attaining good intensity correction. In an attempt to overcome this problem, an EHUM method is proposed for intensity inhomogeneity correction in MR images. The main idea of the proposed EHUM method is determination of region of interest, intensity correction based on homomorphic filtering and linear gray scale mapping followed by cutoff frequency selection of low pass filter used in the filtering process. The block diagram for the correction method is shown in Figure 2.

Determination of Region of Interest (ROI)

The proposed algorithm makes use of binary image characterizing the ROI to mitigate the halo effect between foreground and background regions that occurs while applying the conventional homomorphic filtering principle to any image with dark background. ROI represents a binary image R in which all foreground pixels are set to 1, and all background pixels are set to 0. ROI is determined using a simple thresholding operation. A threshold level T is identified, and based on Equ. (1) binary image R is determined.

$$R = R\left(x,y\right) = \begin{cases} 1 & if\, P\left(x,y\right) \geq T \\ 0 & if\, P\left(x,y\right) < T \end{cases} \tag{1}$$

Threshold T is determined using Otsu's method (Otsu, 1979). Threshold T is identified based on the fact that almost high intensity pixels belong to the brain and others to the background. The largest connected component of each thresholder result is extracted and produced as a binary image which represents the ROI. ROI prevents the halo effect and also suppresses the effect of noisy background pixels from being enhanced while applying filtering.

Figure 2. Block Diagram of the proposed EHUM method

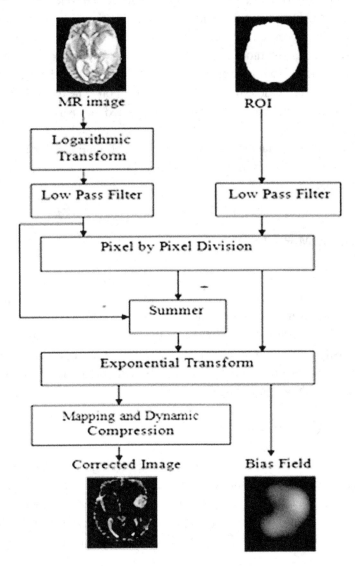

MRI Intensity Correction

In the proposed approach, intensity inhomogeneity is modelled as a multiplicative relationship. A logarithmic transform is applied to the original image *P* to transform the multiplicative model into an additive model for further processing. Equation 2 shows the result of applying log transform to original image *P*.

$$P_{log} = log(P) \tag{2}$$

Another effect of logarithmic transform on the image is that it makes transitions between tissue compartments smoother.

To perform filtering, Low Pass Filter (LPF) is applied to the ROI and the log transformed original image. In this work a Butterworth low pass filter is used for filtering. The proposed filtering scheme makes use of a Butterworth filter that is defined by the frequency response function as shown in Equation 3.

$$B_{lp} = \frac{1}{1 + \left(\left(\sqrt{2}\right) - 1\right)\left[\frac{D(u,v)}{D_0}\right]^{2n}} \tag{3}$$

where $D(u,v)$ represents the Euclidean distance from the origin of frequency domain, n and D_0 represent the filter order and filter cutoff frequency respectively. The Butterworth filter is a recognized filter applied in many areas including image processing which performs better than other widely used filters (Ardizzone, Pirrone & Gambino, 2014). The cutoff frequency selection is easy in Butterworth filter and it has a profile similar to a Gaussian filter.

The log transformed original image, the following equations are obtained,

$$R_L = LPF\left(ROI\right) \tag{4}$$

$$P_{Llog} = LPF\left(P_{log}\right) \tag{5}$$

To separate actual reflectance component from illumination component, pixel by pixel division I_D is performed between the filtered images in Equation (4) and Equation (5),

$$I_D = \frac{P_{Llog}}{R_L} \tag{6}$$

Using Equ.(6), bias field in the original image is estimated as

$$I_b = exp\left(log\left(I_D\right)\right) \tag{7}$$

As a result of homomorphic unsharp filtering, the original image is restored as shown in Equation 8,

$$I_s = exp\left(P_{log} - I_D\right) \tag{8}$$

In the restored image I_s due to the effect of ROI and HUM, the halo between foreground and background and the halo between CSF (Cerebrospinal Fluid) and WM (White Matter) are reduced. But the halo artifacts still cause certain significant impact on MR images with abnormalities such as tumor. Generally in MRI modalities, the tumor regions are represented contrast to other normal regions. In such cases, while applying homomorphic filtering, halo occurs between the boundary of tumor and normal tissues, which results in the corruption of tumor pixel intensities. Although the tumor region can be identified the differentiation between normal and tumor regions are not clearly visible. If the resulting image is used for further image analysis such as segmentation, it produces deviations in the results. Therefore to overcome this halo effect and to restore the intensities of tumor, a linear mapping is employed. The linear mapping function enhances the appearance of image and thus removes the halo effect. The linear mapping of the restored image intensity Rx from the interval $[P_1,P_2]$ (P_1 and P_2 representing the range of intensities of interest) to standard scale $[S_1,S_2]$ (S_1 and S_2 are the minimum and maximum intensities) is expressed in Equation 9.

$$Y = S_1 + \frac{Rx - P_1}{P_2 - P_1}\left(S_1 - S_2\right) \tag{9}$$

Here, Y indicates the image obtained from the intensity mapping. The standard scale $[S_1,S_2]$ is formulated based on the generalized scale (g-scale) (Ganzetti, Wenderoth & Mantini, 2016). The g-scale at any pixel in a slice is defined as the largest set of pixels connected to that pixel that satisfy some homogeneity criteria. The linear mapping function maps each pixel gray level into another gray level at the same position and enhances the difference between tumor and normal region.

The intensity mapped image is normalized to the original gray level dynamics using dynamic compression. The corrected image I_C is restored from the mapped image using the dynamic compression expression in Equation 10.

$$I_C = \frac{Y - \min\left(Y\right)}{\max\left(Y\right) - \min\left(Y\right)}\max\left(Y\right) \tag{10}$$

Cut-Off Frequency Selection

The cut-off frequency of the Butterworth low pass filter used in the homomorphic filtering process imposes certain impact on corrected image. Higher value of cut-off frequency results in loss of tissue contrast while no effect is visible on the corrected image if it is too low.

The original MR image is composed of uncorrupted image information and redundant bias field, therefore according to information theory point of view filtering process employed in the proposed EHUM algorithm can be considered as a sort of redundant information transfer. Therefore in the proposed algorithm, the cut-off frequency of the filter is determined based on Shannon entropy measure. Shannon's entropy measure for any image histogram 'x' with probability p(x) is given in Equation 11.

$$H = -\sum p\left(x\right)\log_2 p\left(x\right) \tag{11}$$

Based on this Shannon's entropy measure the cut off frequency is automatically tuned (Ardizzone, Pirrone & Gambino, 2014). The overall approach for intensity inhomogeneity correction is summarized below:

1. Determine region of interest 'R' of original Image 'P'
2. Compute log transform of original Image 'P'
3. Apply low pass filter to both original Image and region of interest. Let it be $\mathbf{P}_{Llog}$ and $\mathbf{R}_L$
4. Compute pixel by pixel division of $\mathbf{P}_{Llog}$ and $\mathbf{R}_L$
5. Compute the difference between the images obtained in Step 2 and Step 4 and write in exponential form
6. Compute Bias field
7. Map the intensities x of image $\mathbf{I}_s$ from the interval $[\mathbf{P}_1,\mathbf{P}_2]$ ($\mathbf{P}_1$ and $\mathbf{P}_2$ representing the range of intensities of interest) to $[\mathbf{S}_1,\mathbf{S}_2]$ ($\mathbf{S}_1$ and $\mathbf{S}_2$ are the minimum and maximum intensities)
8. Perform dynamic compression to obtain the bias corrected image

EXPERIMENTAL RESULTS AND DISCUSSION

In this section, experiments for quantitative and qualitative evaluation of EHUM algorithm are presented and compared with some reported filtering-based methods such as HUM, Guillemeud scheme, HC-HUM and other state-of-the-art intensity correction methods. To demonstrate the efficacy of the EHUM algorithm, experiments are carried out on BRATS database and clinical MRI brain images discussed in the following section. All the experiments are computed using MATLAB 2010Rb software with 2.6 GHz Pentium processor. The order of Butterworth low pass filter is chosen as one.

Database

Brain tumor image dataset used in this work is obtained from the "Challenge on Multimodal Brain Tumor Segmentation BRATS2012" (BRATS Challenge, n.d.). The dataset is composed of multi-contrast MR scans of 50 glioma patients (with both low-grade and high-grade). For each patient in the dataset, different MRI modalities such as T1, T2, FLAIR, and T1C MR images are present. In addition to patient image, it consists of simulated images for 25 high-grade and 25 low-grade glioma subjects. The simulated images in the dataset pursue the conventions employed for the real data, except that their file names begin with "SimBRATS" and are all available in Brain Web space. The normal MR brain images used for the evaluation of the proposed intensity correction method is obtained from Brain web space (BrainWeb, n.d.).

Qualitative Evaluation

Evaluation plays a vital role in validation process. Qualitative evaluation provides visual comparison of original and corrected images. In this section, the results demonstrating qualitatively the performance of EHUM method for different MRI brain images are discussed. The proposed intensity correction method is applied to normal MR images and MR images with tumor.

The example illustrated in Figure 3 shows the application of the proposed EHUM method to four sample T1 MRI slices. In Figure 3(a), the first two row shows the MR images with brain tumor and the last two rows shows the normal MR. Corresponding ROI, estimated bias field, and intensity corrected images are shown in Figure 3(b) to Figure 3(d). The intensities of the original image within each tissue become quite homogeneous in the intensity corrected images. After correction, pixels having the same

Figure 3. Examples of Intensity inhomogeneity correction results (a) MR images(T1) (First two rows shows images with tumor and last two rows shows normal images) (b)ROI (c)Bias field (d)Bias corrected images

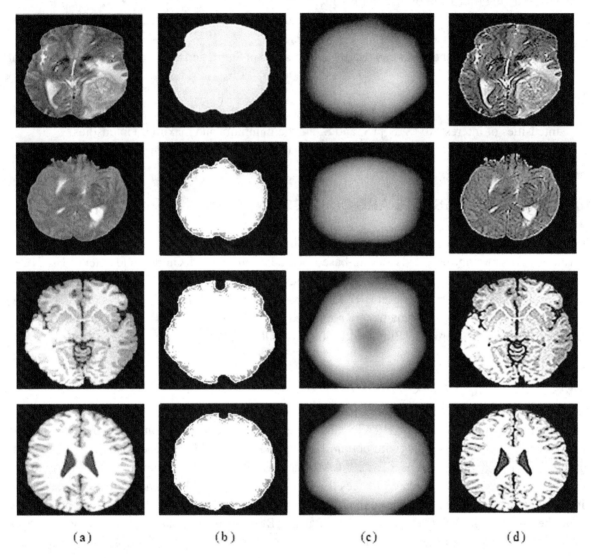

intensity value are more likely to contain the same kind of tissue. Since EHUM has no parameters whose values are to be adjusted for different situations by using priors, the automatic mode becomes feasible on MRI images.

The performance of the proposed method is compared with other filtering-based methods such as HUM, Guillemaud scheme and HC-HUM methods for three normal T1 MRI slices as shown in figure 4. Figure 4(a) represents the original image, and corrected scene of the original image produced by HUM, Guillemaud, HC-HUM and the proposed EHUM methods are shown in Figure 4(b), Figure 4(c), Figure 4(d) and Figure 4(e) respectively. From the figure, it can be seen that in HUM method halo effect is seen between the background and the foreground. It can also be noticed that Guillemaud scheme overcomes the halo effect but it corrupts the white matter intensities. Further, the HC-HUM method and the proposed method provide good results for intensity inhomogeneity correction.

Figure 4. Intensity correction results for normal MR brain images (a) Original MR images(T1) (b)HUM (c)Guillemaud (d)HC-HUM and (e)Proposed EHUM method

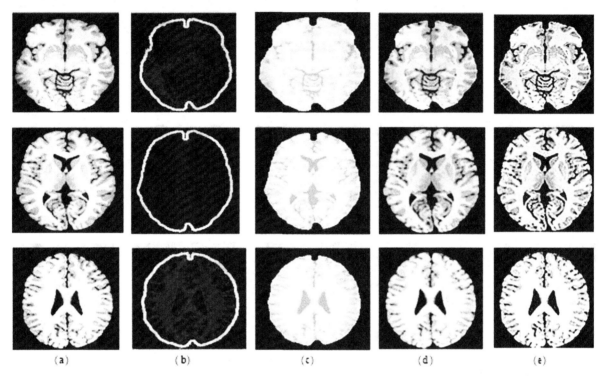

In Figure 5, evaluation of the proposed intensity correction method with other homomorphic filtering methods such as HUM, Guillemaud scheme and HC-HUM methods for three T1 MR images with tumor is shown.

Figure 5(a) represents the original scene, and the same slice of the corrected scene produced by HUM, Guillemaud, HC-HUM and Proposed EHUM methods are shown in Figure 5(b), Figure 5(c), Figure 5(d) and Figure 5(e) respectively. This figure implies that the HUM and the Guillemaud scheme produce similar results as that of normal images. But the performance of HC-HUM method degrades in case of images with tumor as shown in Figure 5(d). Figure 5(e) gives a qualitative indication of the effectiveness of EHUM in suppressing background intensity variation. The linear mapping of the intensities overcomes the halo effect and corrects the intensity variations efficiently. The qualitative evaluation implies the variation in the degree of correction quality of different methods. However, it is difficult to determine the effectiveness of a method using visual examination alone. Hence the quantitative evaluation of the proposed method is presented in the next section.

Quantitative Evaluation

Quantitative evaluation is performed based on the assessment of different validation measures. The performance of the EHUM correction method is quantitatively examined by two sets of measures, namely Coefficient of Variation (CV) and Coefficient of Joint Variation (CJV) (Ardizzone, Pirrone & Gambino, 2014; Ganzetti, Wenderoth & Mantini, 2016).

Figure 5. Intensity correction results for MR brain images with tumor (a)Original MR images(T1) (b) HUM (c)Guillemaud (d)HC-HUM and (e)Proposed EHUM method

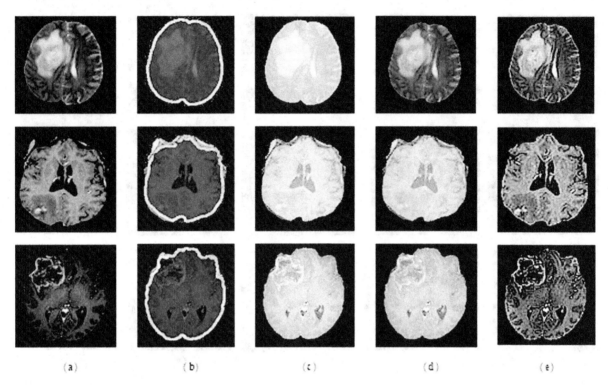

(a) (b) (c) (d) (e)

Coefficient of Variation of a tissue class C denotes the normalized standard deviation within a single class. The normalization σ is performed using its mean μ and is given in Equation 12.

$$CV = \frac{\sigma}{\mu} \tag{12}$$

The quantity CV represents the normalized standard deviation in a given tissue class and is invariant to uniform multiplicative intensity transformation.

Coefficient of Joint Variation (CJV) given in Equation 13 is used to represent the tissue overlap and describes the separability of tissue classes c_1 and c_2.

$$CJV = \frac{\sigma(c_1) + \sigma(c_2)}{\left| \mu(c_1) - \mu(c_2) \right|} \tag{13}$$

CJV estimates the overlap between GM and WM. It is invariant to linear uniform intensity transformation. Lower values of CV and CJV denote the region of interest has lower variation of intensity and thus the better performance of the correction method.

Table 1. Evaluation of the proposed method using CV and CJV in T1 MR images for GM

Methods	MR Images					
	1 (70%)		2 (40%)		4 (20%)	
	CV	CJV	CV	CJV	CV	CJV
Original Image	9.7	64.2	10.3	77.2	11.3	121.2
HUM [1]	9.7	64.1	10.1	76.8	11.2	121
Guillemaud [16]	9.4	62.2	9.9	76.6	10.8	119.3
HC HUM [5]	9.3	59.4	9.8	76.1	10.1	120.1
Proposed EHUM	9.2	58.3	9.7	75.3	10.1	119.9

Table 2. Evaluation of the proposed method using CV and CJV in T1 MR images for WM

Methods	MR Images					
	1 (70%)		2 (40%)		4 (20%)	
	CV	CJV	CV	CJV	CV	CJV
Original Image	9.9	67.2	10.7	85.2	11.9	120.8
HUM [1]	9.9	67.1	10.7	84.7	11.8	120.1
Guillemaud [16]	9.8	64.2	10.5	83.6	11.5	119.3
HC HUM [5]	9.5	58.4	10.4	80.1	10.8	112.1
Proposed EHUM	9.4	57.2	10.1	78.3	10.3	111.4

Table 3. Evaluation of the proposed method using CV and CJV in T1 MR images for tumor tissues

Methods	MR Images					
	1 (70%)		2 (40%)		4 (20%)	
	CV	CJV	CV	CJV	CV	CJV
Original Image	9.5	61.12	103	77.2	11.5	90.2
HUM [1]	9.5	61.11	10.2	75.7	11.3	90.2
Guillemaud [16]	9.5	60.9	10.1	72.6	10.9	90.1
HC HUM [5]	9.4	60.1	10.1	72.1	10.5	90.1
Proposed EHUM	9.1	56.2	9.8	68.3	10.1	84.4

Table 1, Table 2 and Table 3 imply the performance of the proposed EHUM method and other filtering methods on different tissues such as GM, WM and tumor using *CV* and *CJV* measures at different intensity inhomogeneity levels such as 20%, 40% and 70%. *CV* and *CJV* relate a scalar value level of intensity variation in a tissue. In a region affected by bias field, there is increased intensity variation. From the tables, one can view that the *CV* and *CJV* for the conventional HUM method in all the three tissues is almost nearer to that of the original image. Thus the conventional HUM method fails to produce reasonable results on these three types of tissues. The *CV* and *CJV* in Table 1 and Table 2 show that the Guillemaud scheme and HC-HUM methods provide good results for WM and GM. At the same time both the methods limit their performance in case of tumor which is clearly shown in the Table 3. The proposed method achieves better results in all tissues when compared to the other methods. The results in tables indicate a consistent and significant reduction of *CV* and *CJV* before and after correction using the proposed method. Also, the reduction in *CV* and *CJV* is more pronounced for tumor tissues than for other tissues.

The performance of the proposed EHUM method is compared with some of the state-of-the-art methods using T2 image using the *CV* and *CJV* measures available as shown in Table 4.

The DAC method (Vovk, Pernus & Likar, 2007), N3 method (Likar, Viergever & Pernus, 2001) and MICO method (Madabhushi & Udupa, n.d.) are the renowned methods employed for intensity correction and proved to perform well in any normal brain MR images. The performance evaluation of the proposed method with these state-of-the-art methods is shown in Table 4. As this study is focused on brain tumor segmentation in MR images, the performance is assessed with special concentration on brain tumor tissues. Even though the state-of-the-art methods mentioned above performs well for normal tissues regions, the *CV* and *CJV* values in Table 4 show that the proposed method outperforms these methods in case of tumor tissues.

CONCLUSION

Intensity inhomogeneity in MR images can negatively influence any automatic process such as segmentation. In this chapter, a filtering-based intensity correction method is developed to minimize the impact of intensity inhomogeneties in the MR images. The conventional homomorphic filter produces halo effects in the MR image which degrade the performance of the intensity correction process. Generally, the halo effect between the tumor and other tissue regions corrupts the tumor intensity. The EHUM filtering scheme presented in this chapter allows for compensating halos in bias correction tasks. It is easy to implement and can be used as an image pre-processing method to help physicians' findings. The method has been applied successfully on different images in MRI datasets. EHUM requires very few parameters to be set and does not require any prior information about processed images, tissues, and organs under investigation. The performance of EHUM intensity correction algorithm is validated using Coefficient of Variation and Coefficient of Joint Variation measures and compared with other filtering-based methods and state-of-the-art methods such as DAC, N3 and MICO methods. The results show that EHUM method outperforms the other state-of-the-art methods.

Table 4. CV and CJV measures of tumor tissues in different T1 images

Methods	MR Images					
	1 (70%)		2 (40%)		4 (20%)	
	CV	CJV	CV	CJV	CV	CJV
Original Image	9.7	63.2	10.4	79.2	10.9	121.2
DAC Method [19]	9.6	69.2	10.4	89.7	10.8	130.2
N3 Algorithm [4]	9.5	61.2	10.2	92.6	10.7	139.3
MICO Method [2]	9.8	58.4	10.1	80.1	10.4	132.1
Proposed EHUM	9.4	56.2	10.1	79.3	9.9	124.4

REFERENCES

Aitalissdia, N., Hassan, M., Cherradi, M. B., Abbassi, A. E., & Bouattane, O. (2016). Parallel Implementation of Bias Field Correction Fuzzy C-Means Algorithm for Image Segmentation. *International Journal of Advanced Computer Science and Applications, 1*(3), 375–383.

Ardizzone, E., Pirrone, R., & Gambino, O. (2008). Bias Artifact Suppression on MR Volumes. *Computer Methods and Programs in Biomedicine, 92*(1), 35–53. doi:10.1016/j.cmpb.2008.06.005 PMID:18644657

Ardizzone, E., Pirrone, R., & Gambino, O. (2014). Illumination correction in Biomedical Images. *Computer Information, 33*, 175–196.

Axel, L., Costantini, J., & Listerud, J. (1987). Intensity Correction in Surface Coil MR Imaging. *AJR. American Journal of Roentgenology, 148*(2), 418–420. doi:10.2214/ajr.148.2.418 PMID:3492123

BrainWeb. (n.d.). *Brain web: Simulated Brain Database.* Retrieved from http://www. brainweb.bic.mni.mcgill.ca/brainweb

BRATS Challenge. (n.d.). Retrieved from https://www.smir.ch/BRATS

Brinkmann, B. H., Manduca, A., & Robb, R. A. (1998). Optimized Homomorphic Un-sharp Masking for MR Greyscale Inhomogeneity Correction. *IEEE Transactions on Medical Imaging, 17*(2), 161–171. doi:10.1109/42.700729 PMID:9688149

Clare, S., Alecci, M., & Jezzard, P. (2001). Compensating for B1 inhomoge-neity using active transmit power modulation. *Magnetic Resonance Imaging, 19*(10), 1349–1352. doi:10.1016/S0730-725X(01)00467-2 PMID:11804763

Florian, J. (2010). *Normalization of Magnetic Resonance Images and its Application to the Diagnosis of the Scoliotic Spine* (Ph.D. thesis). University of Erlangen.

Ganzetti, M., Wenderoth, N., & Mantini, D. (2016). Intensity Inhomogeneity Correction of Structural MR Images: A Data-Driven Approach to Define Input Algorithm Parameters. *Frontiers in Neuroinformatics, 10*(10). PMID:27014050

George, M. M., Kalaivani, S., & Sudhakar, M. S. (2017). A non-iterative multi-scale approach for intensity inhomogeneity correction in MRI. *Magnetic Resonance Imaging, 45*, 43–59. doi:10.1016/j.mri.2017.05.005 PMID:28549883

Guillemaud, R. (1998). Uniformity Correction with Homomorphic Filtering on Region of Interest. *IEEE International Conference on Image Processing, 2*, 872-875. 10.1109/ICIP.1998.723695

Li, C., John, C. G., & Davatzikos, C. (2014). Multiplicative intrinsic component optimization (MICO) for MRI bias field estimation and tissue segmentation. *Magnetic Resonance Imaging, 32*(32), 913–923. doi:10.1016/j.mri.2014.03.010 PMID:24928302

Likar, B., Viergever, M. A., & Pernus, F. (2001). Retrospective correction of MR intensity inhomogeneity by information minimization. *IEEE Transactions on Medical Imaging, 20*(12), 1398–1410. doi:10.1109/42.974934 PMID:11811839

Madabhushi, A., & Udupa, J. K. (n.d.). New methods of MR Image Intensity Standardization Via Generalized Scale. *Proceedings of SPIE Medical Imaging*, *5747*, 1143-1154.

Otsu, N. (1979). A Threshold Selection Method from Gray-level Histograms. *IEEE Transactions on Systems, Man, and Cybernetics*, *9*(1), 62–66. doi:10.1109/TSMC.1979.4310076

Singh, M., Sharma, S., Verma, A., & Sharma, N. (2017). Enhancement and Intensity Inhomogeneity Correction of Diffusion-Weighted MR Images of Neonatal and Infantile Brain Using Dynamic Stochastic Resonance. *Journal of Medical and Biological Engineering*, *37*(4), 508–518. doi:10.100740846-017-0270-0

Tustison, N. J., Avants, B. B., Cook, P. A., Zheng, Y., Egan, A., Yushkevich, P. A., & James, C. (2010). N4ITK: Improved N3 Bias Correction. *IEEE Transactions on Medical Imaging*, *29*(6), 1310–1320. doi:10.1109/TMI.2010.2046908 PMID:20378467

Vovk, U., Pernus, F., & Likar, B. (2007). A Review of Methods for Correction of Intensity Inhomogeneity in MRI. *IEEE Transactions on Medical Imaging*, *26*(3), 405–421. doi:10.1109/TMI.2006.891486 PMID:17354645

Chapter 7
Machine Learning and Its Use in E-Commerce and E-Business

Mamata Rath

ⓘ https://orcid.org/0000-0002-2277-1012

Birla Global University, India

ABSTRACT

Electronic commerce associated with highly powerful web technology and mobile communication is currently dominating the business world. Current advancements in machine learning (ML) have also further coordinated to creative business applications and e-commerce administrations to reason about complex system and better solutions. In the course of recent years, the business security and machine-learning networks have created novel strategies for secured business frameworks based on computationally learned models. With the improvement of the internet and digital marketing, every financial platform has been more secured and user friendly for monetary transactions.

INTRODUCTION

Electronic commerce associated with highly powerful web technology and mobile communication is currently dominating the Business world. While electronic commerce keeps on profoundly affecting the worldwide business condition, advancements and applications have started to concentrate more on versatile processing and the wireless We b. With this prototype comes another arrangement of issues and issues particularly identified with wireless web based business. At last, specialists and engineers must figure out what undertakings clients truly need to perform whenever from anyplace and choose how to guarantee that data and usefulness to help those errands are promptly accessible and effectively open. This paper gives a diagram of a portion of the significant advances, applications, and issues in the generally new field of wireless webbased business. Wireless online business (additionally called portable commerce or m-commerce) is the advancement, purchasing, and offering of products and ventures through electronic information correspondence arranges that interface with wireless (or versatile) gadgets. Wireless web based business is a subset of wireless figuring, which is the getting to of data

DOI: 10.4018/978-1-5225-9902-9.ch007

frameworks by wireless means. A significant number of the issues that influence wireless registering all in all likewise influence wireless online business. Technologists have been anticipating for a considerable length of time that organizations are on the cusp of a flood in profitability however, up until now, this has not occurred. Most organizations still use individuals to perform monotonous undertakings in records payable, charging, finance, claims the executives, client support, offices the board and the sky is the limit from there.

To put in a leave ask for, we need to navigate twelve stages, every one expecting to enter data the framework should definitely know or settle on a choice that the framework ought to most likely make sense of from your goal. To decide why the financial plan endured a shot for the current month, we need to troll through a hundred columns in a spreadsheet you've physically separated from your account framework. Your frameworks ought to almost certainly figure out which columns are strange and present them. When we present a buy request for another seat, we realize that Bob in obtainment needs to physically settle on a cluster of little choices to process the structure -, for example, regardless of whether your request should be sent to HR for ergonomics endorsement or would it be able to be sent directly to the money related approver.

These little choices make defers that make we and your partners less responsive than we need to be and less powerful than your organization needs we to be. We trust we will before long have much better frameworks at work. Machine learning applications will robotize the majority of the little choices that hold up procedures. It is an imperative subject on the grounds that, over the coming decade, organizations that can turn out to be progressively robotized and increasingly beneficial will surpass those that can't. Also, machine learning will be one of the key empowering influences of this change. Before we get into how machine learning can make your organization increasingly beneficial, we should look why actualizing frameworks in your organization is more troublesome than receiving frameworks in your own life. Accept your own funds for instance. We may utilize a cash the board application to follow your spending. The application reveals to we the amount we spends and what we spend it on and it makes proposals on how we could expand your investment funds. It even naturally gathers together buys to the closest dollar and puts the extra change into your investment account. Cost the executives is an altogether different involvement with work. At work, to perceive how your group is following against their financial plan, we put a demand into the money group and they hit we up the next we ek. In the event that we need to penetrate down into specific details in your financial plan, you're in a tight spot.

E-COMMERCE AND E-BUSINESS SYSTEM

Purchase and Supply Chain in E-Commerce

This primary activity Includes identifying vendors, evaluating vendors, selecting specific products, placing orders. Supply chain is part of an industry value chain that precedes a particular strategic business unit. Procurement includes all purchasing activities, plus monitoring of all elements of purchase transaction. Supply management is a term used to describe procurement activities. Portable web based business additionally incorporates the utilization of gadgets such handheld and PCs interface with figuring resources through wired synchronization. We don't consider this wired type of versatile online business in this paper mainly in light of the fact that it is probably going to be supplanted by wireless gadgets later on. Our emphasis here is on the wireless types of portable commerce.

Production Process and E-Commerce

There are three general approaches to production

1. **Make-to-Stock Items:** Made for inventory (the "stock") in anticipation of sales orders
2. **Make-to-Order Items:** Produced to fill specific customer orders
3. **Assemble-to-Order Items:** Produced using a combination of make-to-stock and make-to-order processes

Problems associated with Production are as follows.

1. Inventory problems
    a. Production manager lacks systematic method for:
        i.   Meeting anticipated sales demand
        ii. Adjusting production to reflect actual sales
2. Accounting and purchasing related problems
    b. **Standard Costs**: Normal costs of manufacturing a product. Production and Accounting must periodically compare standard costs with actual costs and then adjust the accounts for the inevitable differences.

Planning in Production

Three important principles for production planning are as follows. Figure 1 represents the detail flow of information in production planning.

1. Work from sales forecast and current inventory levels to create an "aggregate" ("combined") production plan for all products
2. Break down aggregate plan into more specific production plans for individual products and smaller time intervals
3. Use production plan to determine raw material requirements.

Sales Forecasting - Whenever a sale is recorded in Sales and Distribution (SD) module, quantity sold is recorded as a consumption value for that material. Simple forecasting technique includes use of a prior period's sales and then adjust those figures for current conditions. Sales and operations planning (SOP) takes input as sales forecast provided by Marketing and gives the output of production plan designed to balance market demand with production capacity.

Marketing Strategy in E-Commerce

When creating a marketing strategy Managers must consider both the nature of their products and the nature of their potential customers. Most office furnish their product stores on the We b and believe customers organize their needs into product categories. There are Four Ps of marketing as follows and also depicted in fig.2.

Figure 1. Production planning process   *Figure 2. Four P of marketing*

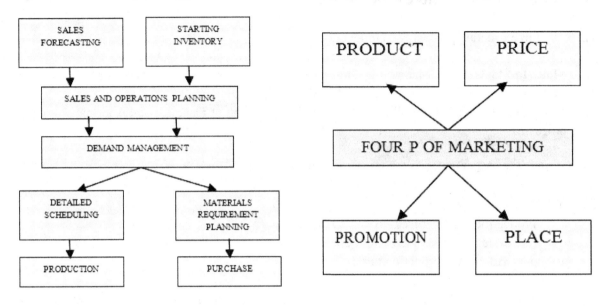

- **Product**: Physical item or service that company is selling
- **Price**: Amount customer pays for product
- **Promotion**: Any means of spreading the word about product
- **Place**: Need to have products or services available in different locations

Different types of marketing strategies in e-commerce are as follows.

1. **Good First Step in Building a Customer-Based Marketing Strategy**: Identify groups of customers who share common characteristics
2. **Customer-Based Marketing Approaches:** More common on B2B sites than on B2C sites
3. **B2B Sellers**: More aware of the need to customize product and service offerings to match their customers' needs.
4. **Identifying Groups of Potential Customers:** The first step in selling to those customers
5. **Media Selection**: Can be critical for an online firm
6. **Challenge for Online Businesses:** Convince customers to trust them

Segmentation of Marketing Task refers to targeting specific portions of the market with advertising messages such as Segments which usually defined in terms of demographic characteristics and Micromarketing that performs marketing by targeting very small market segments. Further there can be Geographic segmentation which is done by creating different combinations of marketing efforts for each geographical group of customers or Demographic segmentation that uses age, gender, family size, income, education, religion, or ethnicity to group customers. Behavioral segmentation means creation of separate experiences for customers based on their behavior, Occasion segmentation can be done when behavioral segmentation is based on things that happen at a specific time and Usage-based market segmentation refers to customizing visitor experiences to match the site usage behavior patterns of each visitor.

Retention and Attracting Customers

In marketing some costs are involved in retention and attracting customers such as acquisition cost that refers to Money a company spends to draw one visitor to site. Conversion cost refers to Converting first-time visitor into a customer, Conversion cost means Cost of inducing one visitor to make a purchase, sign up for a subscription, or register and Retained customers are they who return to the site one or more times after making their first purchases. Marketing managers are required to have a good sense of how their companies acquire and retain customers. Further a Funnel model is used as a conceptual tool to understand the overall nature of a marketing strategy, very similar to the customer life-cycle model.

Advertisement and E-Commerce

In E-Commerce different methods are used for advertisement such as Banner ad small rectangular object on a We b page, Interactive marketing unit (IMU) ad formats which are standard banner sizes that most We b sites have voluntarily agreed to use, banner exchange network means software used for coordinates ad sharing. Sometimes banner advertising network are also used which acts as a broker betwe en advertisers and We b sites that carry ads. Following metrics are used for advertisement in the web. Cost per thousand (CPM) - Pricing metric used when a company purchases mass media advertising. Trial visit - First time a visitor loads a We b site page. Page view - Each page loaded by a visitor counts. Impression - Each time the banner ad loads.

Email-marketing are also a new methods of marketing in e-commerce. It refers to sending one e-mail message to a customer which costs less than one cent if the company already has the customer's e-mail address. Conversion rate refers to the percentage of recipients who respond to an ad or promotion. Opt-in e-mail refers to practice of sending e-mail messages to people who request information on a particular topic. Table 1. Shows Ecommerce based research and security details.

The intension of e-business is to improve business exercises over the we b by accomplishing worldwide deals and achieving a bigger market gathering. In the UK, 37% of retail organizations have e-business applications on the we b and 22% of the UK populace utilize these frameworks to buy retail things (Rath et.al, 2018). It is conceivable to enhance e-business slant by extending it over to m-commerce. The development of mobile gadgets makes it conceivable to upgrade business exercises through web based business exchanges. Internet business is portrayed as a subset of e-business where online business works at the back end of the e-business condition managing electronic exchanges of the purchasing and offering procedure of e-business. Mobile gadgets can help in web based business on the grounds that the larger part of 79% of youthful grown-ups of the UK populace possesses a mobile telephone (Rath et.al, 2017). Most basic buy through mobile telephones are mobile Ringtones and benefits of up to $600 million have been created by acquiring mobile telephone Ringtones (Rath et.al, 2019). This business idea can be connected to mobile telephones, since the new third generation of mobile telephones have enhanced show screen with better hues and backings HTML content which empowers buys of CD or books on the mobile gadget straightforwardly. An ongoing study showed that 18% of respondents propose that the utilization of mobile innovation can enhance CRM action (Rath et.al, 2018). Nissan automobiles are additionally utilizing wireless PDAs to enhance their nature of administration where staff individuals furnished with their PDAs can manage client enquiries concerning save parts. The businessperson can check costs and hardware accessibility on the spot and give guide input to the client (A. Agah et.al, 2006). The utilization of mobile application programming has helped insurance agency Drive Assists in

Table 1. Ecommerce based research and security details

Sl. No	Literature	Year	Ecommerce based techniques in business
1	A. Herzberg et.al	2013	TCP Ack storm DoS attack
2	A.Agah	2006	Security in wireless sensor network
3	I. Almomani et.al	2013	Logic based security architecture in multi-hop communication
4	Z. Bankovic et.al	2011	Improvinf security in WMN with reputation
5	A. Boukerche et.al	2008	Trust based security system for ubiquitous and pervasive computing
6	Abdellaui J. et.al	2018	Multi-point relay selection through estimated spatial relation in smart city
7	A. Sharma et.al	2014	Assessment of QoS based multi-cast routing protocols
8	L.Cuizhi et. al	2011	Key technologies in the development of e-commerce
9	T.Wongkhamdi et.al	2017	Mobile learning readiness in rural area
10	Tao Li et.al	2016	Privacy preserving express delivery with fine grained attribute based access control
11	W. Zhu et.al	2015	Anomaly detection on ecommerce based on variable length behaviour sequence
12	P. Parvinen et.al	2015	Ecommerce engagement and social influence
13	V. Shankara Raman et.al	2014	Enterprise systems enbling smart commerce
14	E. Seth et.al	2014	Mobile commerce with broad perspective
15	B. Fuchs et.al	2011	E-commerce and e-shopping with interactivity and individualization

sparing street voyaging every year with the utilization of their mobile gadgets (I. Almomani et.al, 2013). The John Hopkins Hospital spared $1,000 multi day by utilizing PDAs to transfer pharmaceutical data to the drug specialists progressively and Addenbrooke's Hospital in Cambridge, UK, could finish 176 effective kidney and liver transplants on account of the forward data of organ givers by means of their Blackberry PDAs (A. Boukerche et.al, 2008). The utilization of mobile gadgets can profit e-business applications by enhancing their efficiency rate. Mobile Commerce or m-Commerce is portrayed as the "blast" or the broad utilization of mobile applications (J. Abdellaoui et.al, 2018), or then again might be depicted as making an exchange or buy using a mobile gadget. In the business world the significance of speed and dependability of data is urgent key of accomplishment and mobile telephones can give that upper hand. A study of 400 IT chiefs recommends that 36% of representatives depend on the utilization of mobile gadgets to browse their messages, 24% utilize mobile applications to change reports while in travel and half of the organizations proposes it is fundamental to enhance mobile data transmission so as to advance mobile business applications .

TECHNOLOGICAL USAGE OF E-COMMERCE

The World Wide We b Consortium (W3C), a not-for-profit group that maintains standards for the Web. It presented its first draft form of XML in 1996; the W3C issued its first formal version recommendation in 1998. Thus, it is a much newer markup language than HTML. In 2000, the W3C released the first version of a recommendation for a new markup language called Extensible Hypertext Markup Language (XHTML).

Companies are using the Internet to connect specific software applications at one organization directly to software applications at other organizations. The W3C defines We b services as software systems that support interoperable machine-to-machine interaction over a network.

The violation of an organization's rights that occurs when a company capable of supervising the infringing activity fails to do so and obtains a financial benefit from the infringing activity.A copyright is a right granted by a government to the author or creator of a literary or artistic work. The right is for the specific length of time provided in the copyright law and gives the author or creator the sole and exclusive right to print, publish, or sell the work.

A patent is an exclusive right granted by the government to an individual to make, use, and sell an invention. In the United States, patents on inventions protect the inventor's rights for 20 years. To be patentable, an invention must be genuine, novel, useful, and not obvious given the current state of technology. In the United States, Congress enacted the Children's Online Protection Act (COPA) in 1998 to protect children from "material harmful to minors." This law was held to be unconstitutional because it unnecessarily restricted access to a substantial amount of material that is lawful, thus violating the First Amendment. Congress was more successful with the Children's Online Privacy Protection Act of 1998 (COPPA), which provides restrictions on data collection that must be followe d by electronic commerce sites aimed at children. This law does not regulate content, as COPA attempted to do, so it has not been successfully challenged on First Amendment grounds.

In 2001, Congress enacted the Children's Internet Protection Act (CIPA). CIPA requires schools that receive federal funds to install filtering software on computers in their classrooms and libraries. Filtering software is used to block access to adult content We b sites. In 2003, the Supreme Court held that CIPA was constitutional. The Internet Engineering Task Force (IETF) worked on several new protocols that could solve the limited addressing capacity of IPv4, and in 1997, approved Internet Protocol version 6 (IPv6) as the protocol that will replace IPv4.

English auctions that offer multiple units of an item for sale and allow bidders to specify the quantity they want to buy are called Yankee auctions. When the bidding concludes in a Yankee auction, the highest bidder is allotted the quantity he or she bid. If items remain after satisfying the highest bidder, those remaining items are allocated to successive lower (next highest) bidders until all items are distributed. Although all successful bidders (except possibly the lowest successful bidder) receive the quantity of items on which they bid, they only pay the price bid by the lowest successful bidder.

Web Portals are very common means of business platforms. Some companies have been successful using the general interest strategy by operating a We b portal. A portal or We b portal is a site that people use as a launching point to enter the We b (the word "portal" means"doorway"). A portal almost always includes a We b directory or search engine, but it also includes other features that help visitors find what they are looking for on the We b and thus make the We b more useful.

Most portals include features such as shopping directories, white pages and yellow pages searchable databases, free e-mail, chat rooms, file storage services, games, and personal and group calendar tools. Ex - AOL, Google. Bing

Electronic Data Interchange (EDI)

Electronic data interchange (EDI) is a computer-to-computer transfer of business information between two businesses that uses a standard format of some kind. The two businesses that are exchanging information are trading partners. Firms that exchange data in specific standard formats are said to be EDI compatible.

EDI was first developed In 1987 and United Nations published first standards under the title EDI for Administration, Commerce, and Transport (EDIFACT, or UN/EDIFACT). Then in late 2000 ASC X12 organization and UN/EDIFACT group agreed to develop one common set of international standards.

Figure 3 depicts basic function of EDI syatem. EDI Implementation can be complicated, but it can be easily understood from the following example. Consider a company that needs a replacement for one of its metal-cutting machines Paper-based purchasing process, Buyer and vendor are not using any integrated software, Information transfer between buyer and vendor is paper based. EDI replaces postal mail, fax and email. While email is also an electronic approach, the documents exchanged via email must still be handled by people rather than computers. Having people involved slows down the processing of the documents and also introduces errors. Instead, EDI documents can flow straight through to the appropriate application on the receiver's computer (e.g., the Order Management System) and processing can begin immediately. A typical manual process looks like this, with lots of paper and people involvement.

- Direct connection EDI

  - Requires each business in the network to operate its own on-site EDI translator computer
  - EDI translator computers are connected directly to each other using Modems and dial-up telephone lines or dedicated leased lines. Figures 4 and 5 depicts direct and indirect EDI.

Indirect EDI are used for business document transfer from one entity to another business entity. These are any of the documents that are typically exchanged betwe en businesses. The most common documents exchanged via EDI are purchase orders, invoices and advance ship notices. But there are many, many others such as bill of lading, customs documents, inventory documents, shipping status documents and payment documents. Because EDI documents must be processed by computers rather than humans, a standard format must be used so that the computer will be able to read and understand the documents. A standard format describes what each piece of information is and in what format (e.g., integer, decimal, mmddyy). Without a standard format, each company would send documents using its company-specific format and, much as an English-speaking person probably doesn't understand Japanese, the receiver's computer system doesn't understand the company-specific format of the sender's format.

Figure 3. Basic function in EDI System

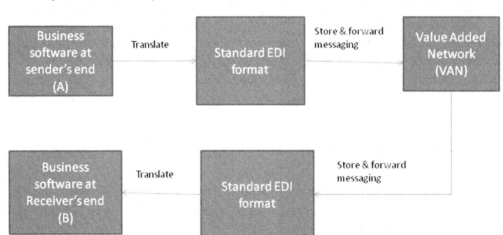

Figure 4. Direct connection EDI

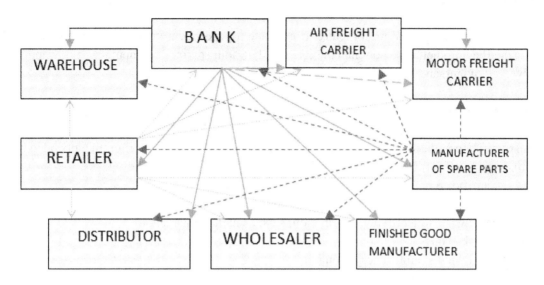

Figure 5. Indirect connection EDI

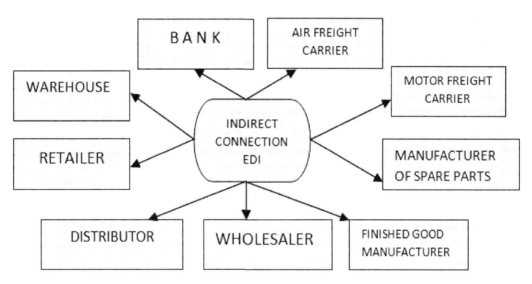

There are several EDI standards in use today, including ANSI, EDIFACT, TRADACOMS and ebXML. And, for each standard there are many different versions, e.g., ANSI 5010 or EDIFACT version D12, Release A. When two businesses decide to exchange EDI documents, they must agree on the specific EDI standard and version.Businesses typically use an EDI translator – either as in-house software or via an EDI service provider – to translate the EDI format so the data can be used by their internal applications and thus enable straight through processing of documents.The exchange of EDI documents is typically betwe en two different companies, referred to as business partners or trading partners. For example, Company A may buy goods from Company B. Company A sends orders to Company B. Company A and Company B are business partners.

E Mail in Business Communication

The process of using a person or computer to generate a paper form, mailing that filled form to the party, and then having another person enter the data into the trading partner's computer was slow, inefficient, expensive, redundant, and unreliable.

Digital Certificate

A digital certificate or digital ID is an attachment to an e-mail message or a program embedded in a We b page that verifies that the sender or We b site is who or what it claims to be.

A digital certificate includes six main elements, including:

- Certificate owner's identifying information, such as name, organization,
- address, and so on
- Certificate owner's public encryption key
- Dates betwe en which the certificate is valid
- Serial number of the certificate
- Name of the certificate issuer
- Digital signature of the certificate issuer

E Cash and E Wallets

Electronic cash (also called e-cash or digital cash) is a general term that describes any value storage and exchange system created by a private (nongovernmental) entity that does not use paper documents or coins and that can serve as a substitute for government-issued physical currency. A software utility that holds credit card information, owner identification and address information, and provides this data automatically at electronic commerce sites; electronic wallets can also store electronic cash. An electronic wallet (sometimes called an e-wallet), serving a function similar to a physical wallet, holds credit card numbers, electronic cash, owner identification, and owner contact information and provides that information at an electronic commerce site's checkout counter. Electronic wallets give consumers the benefit of entering their information just once, instead of having to enter their information at every site with which they want to do business.

Search Engine in the WEB

A search engine is a We b site that helps people find things on the We b. Search engines contain three major parts. The first part, called a spider, a crawler, or a robot (or simply bot), is a program that automatically searches the We b to find We b pages that might be interesting to people. When the spider finds We b pages that might interest search engine site visitors, it collects the URL of the page and information contained on the page. This information might include the page's title, key words included in the page's text, and information about other pages on that We b site. In addition to words that appear on the We b page, We b site designers can specify additional key words in the page that are hidden from the view of We b site visitors, but that are visible to spiders. These key words are enclosed in an HTML tag set called meta tags. The spider returns this information to the second part of the search engine to be stored. The storage element of a search engine is called its index or database.

Different Card Types Used in E-Commerce

Payment Cards

Businesspeople often use the term payment card as a general term to describe all types of plastic cards that consumers (and some businesses) use to make purchases. The main categories of payment cards are credit cards, debit cards, and charge cards.A credit card, such as a Visa or a MasterCard, has a spending limit based on the user's credit history; a user can pay off the entire credit card balance or pay a minimum amount each billing period. Credit card issuers charge interest on any unpaid balance.

Debit Card

A debit card looks like a credit card, but it works quite differently. Instead of charging purchases against a credit line, a debit card removes the amount of the sale from the cardholder's bank account and transfers it to the seller's bank account. Debit cards are issued by the cardholder's bank and usually carry the name of a major credit card issuer, such as Visa or MasterCard, by agreement betwe en the issuing bank and the credit card issuer. By branding their debit cards (with the Visa or MasterCard name), banks ensure that their debit cards will be accepted by merchants who recognize the credit card brand names.

Charge Card

A charge card, offered by companies such as American Express, carries no spending limit, and the entire amount charged to the card is due at the end of the billing period. Charge cards do not involve lines of credit and do not accumulate interest charges. (Note: In addition to its charge card products, American Express also offers credit cards, which do have credit limits and which do accumulate interest on unpaid balances.) In the United States, many retailers, such as department stores and oil companies that own gas stations, issue their own charge cards.

Smart Card

A smart card is a stored-value card that is a plastic card with an embedded microchip that can store information. Credit, debit, and charge cards currently store limited information on a magnetic strip. A smart card can store about 100 times the amount of information that a magnetic strip plastic card can store. A smart card can hold private user data, such as financial facts, encryption keys, account information, credit card numbers, health insurance information, medical records, and so on.

Electronic Cash in E Commerce System

Although credit cards dominate online payments today, electronic cash shows promise for the future. Electronic cash (also called e-cash or digital cash) is a general term that describes any value storage and exchange system created by a private (nongovernmental) entity that does not use paper documents or coins and that can serve as a substitute for government-issued physical currency. A significant difference betwe en electronic cash and scrip is that electronic cash can be readily exchanged for physical cash on demand. Because electronic cash is issued by private entities, there is a need for common standards among all electronic cash issuers so that one issuer's electronic cash can be accepted by another issuer. This need has not yet been met. Each issuer has its own standards and electronic cash is not universally accepted, as is government-issued physical currency.

Electronic cash has another factor in its favor: Most of the world's population does not have credit cards. Many adults cannot obtain credit cards due to minimum income requirements or past debt problems. Children and teens—eager purchasers representing a significant percentage of online buyers—are ineligible, simply because they are too young. People living in most countries other than the United States hold few credit cards because they have traditionally made their purchases in cash. For all of these people, electronic cash provides the solution to paying for online purchases. Even though there have been many failures in electronic cash, the idea of electronic cash refuses to die. Electronic cash shows particular promise in two applications: the sale of goods and services priced less than $10—the lowe r threshold for credit card payments—and the sale of all goods and services to those persons without credit cards.

Perhaps the most important characteristic of cash is convenience. If electronic cash requires special hardware or software, it is not convenient for people to use. Chances are good that people will not adopt an electronic cash system that is difficult to use. A company currently in the electronic cash business is Internet Cash.

MACHINE LEARNING APPROACHES IN E-COMMERCE AND E-BUSINESS

Machine learning permits ecommerce businesses to make a progressively customized client experience. Today, clients not just like to speak with their most loved brands by and by, howe ver they have generally expected personalization. Truth be told, an investigation by Janrain uncovered that 73% of clients are tired of being given insignificant substance. Man-made reasoning and machine learning offer retailers the capacity to customize every communication with their clients, along these lines furnishing them with a superior ordeal. Through machine learning, retailers can diminish client administration issues before they even happen. Thus, truck deserting rates ought to be lowe r and deals ought to be higher. What's more, not normal for people, client administration bots can give unprejudiced arrangements nonstop.

Machine Learning and Search

Results Improving list items offers tremendous adjustments for retailers. Machine learning can improve ecommerce indexed lists each time a client shops on the site, considering individual inclinations and buy history. Rather than utilizing customary inquiry strategies like watchword coordinating, machine learning can produce a look positioning dependent on pertinence for that specific client. This is particularly imperative for monsters, for example, eBay. With more than 800 million things recorded, the retailer is exploiting man-made reasoning and information to foresee and show the most significant list items.

Computerized Reasoning and Product Recommendation

Omnichannel is the new typical for retail, so we can anticipate that computerized reasoning should utilize not exclusively clients' advanced information, yet in addition break down their in-store conduct. Quite a long time ago, surveillance cameras were just expected to fend off shoplifters, however soon, with the assistance of face acknowledgment calculations, we may begin seeing promotions online for that new ice chest we looked at available. Machine learning can be utilized to prescribe ecommerce items as per different examples in shopping conduct, which will enable we to expand your change rates. By breaking down client information from various channels, the calculation can recognize conduct and acquiring designs which can be utilized to foresee what your clients really need. Individual customers have dependably been related with top of the line shoppers, however on account of computerized reasoning, everybody can exploit virtual ones. Open air item organization The North Face has assembled its own virtual individual customer utilizing the IBM Watson stage. The administration utilizes clients' vocal questions, shopping needs and touring plans as info and prescribes things that meet clients' criteria, but at the same time are reasonable for the area the client intends to utilize them—notwithstanding considering the we ather forecasting.

Artificial Neural Networks as Guidance for Marketing

Neural systems can gain as a matter of fact, perceive designs and anticipate patterns, so they can be utilized to discover what individuals react to, what ought to be changed and what ought to be wiped out from an advertising effort. Microsoft had the capacity to increment direct mailing open rate from 4.9% to 8.2% by utilizing BrainMaker, a neural system programming to augment returns on an advertising effort. Machine Learning Can also Eliminate Fraud.The more information we have, the less demanding it is to spot oddities. Along these lines, we can utilize machine learning to distinguish designs in information, realize what is 'ordinary' and what isn't and get advised when something isn't right. The most widely recognized application for this would be misrepresentation discovery. Retailers are frequently looked with clients who purchase vast sums utilizing stolen cards or withdraw their installments after the things have just been conveyed.

Ecommerce Targeting and Optimization of Price

Dissimilar to in a physical store where we can converse with your clients to discover what they need or need, online shops are hit with enormous measures of client information. Accordingly, client division turns out to be critical for online business, as it enables organizations to adjust their correspondence methodologies for each client. Machine learning can be utilized to comprehend your client's needs and make a customized shopping knowledge. Machine Learning can also play role in Price Optimization .Machine learning calculations can help we not just gather data in regards to valuing patterns, your rivals' costs and interest for different things, howe ver it can consolidate this data with client conduct to decide the best cost for every one of your items. Streamlining your costs will enable we to fulfill your customers just as increment your ROAS.

Product Recommendation

With the development of information, it is a standout amongst the most critical difficulties of current businesses to create information driven frameworks. Logical leaps forward in computerized reasoning (AI) have opened the entryway for a wide scope of utilizations, which can use immense measures of information into genuine business esteem. Driving AI specialist Andrew Ng says that AI is the new power as it will on a very basic level change every modern area, Forrester predicts that AI speculations will develop by 300% in 2017, and Barack Obama noticed that his successor will oversee a nation being changed by AI. Initially, the promotion around huge information and AI was very overpowering and organizations were not by any means beyond any doubt how to respond. Item suggestion is ordinarily the main thing individuals have as a top priority when they consider machine learning for online business. Highlights like "on the off chance that we like item x, we will presumably additionally like item y" have been appeared to work astoundingly we ll, and they can fill in as a significant instrument to control clients through the consistently expanding masses of choices accessible to them. Generally, suggestions have been included by hand based hard-coded item classifications, yet this is very tedious, mistake inclined, and rapidly out-dated.

Search Ranking IN Web Portals

Machine learning can help with highlights like hunt positioning, which permits arranging indexed lists by their evaluated significance. This estimation can consider frequencies of explicit hunt terms just as the specific client profile (for example age go, past item sees, expressing propensities, or past hunt terms). To put it plainly, seek calculations turn out to be less about posting all items that coordinate a given arrangement of letters, and increasingly about anticipating what clients may really need to see, notwithstanding when they probably won't know it yet. Another essential component is question extension, in which the no doubt seek term fruitions are proposed while the client is as yet composing. Aside from commonplace content based pursuit, picture based hunt is turning into an inexorably reasonable alternative. Logical advances in picture acknowledgment through profound neural systems currently give the innovation to utilize pictures of items to discover comparable things on the we b. Notwithstanding that, these techniques can be utilized to characterize outward appearances and perceive feelings. However, despite the fact that the possibility of progressively adjusting commerce administrations to the current passionate condition of a client absolutely appears to be important, organizations still have not exactly made sense of how to incorporate this.

Endeavouring to get help for clients can frequently be a significant baffling background. Clients regularly whine about exceedingly long holding up times, clarifying and re-clarify their concern on numerous occasions, inadequate guidance, or worried workers. Given the high measure of assets that are required to give solid client administration, it isn't amazing that these issues can happen. Machine learning can automatize this procedure through robots that can answer telephone calls. While past frameworks were just ready to manage a thin scope of issues and had visit false impressions, late advances in discourse acknowledgment and common language preparing by means of profound learning have made it conceivable to have a progressively adaptable and characteristic collaboration with robots. Essentially, these techniques have appeared in considering relevant data. Rather than dissecting a discourse sound or a solitary word in seclusion, present day approaches consider data from the entire information and look at it against much of the time happening designs, which has helped the exactness of machine learning models. Aside from telephone calls, machine learning can likewise add to other help stations, for example, naturally noting messages, sorting messages (for example grumbling versus question versus ask for) or offering help by means of chatbots. Chatbots specifically have motivated an assortment of AI new companies that need to change correspondence channels for promoting, counselling, or enlisting.

CONCLUSION

It is a very technical question that comes to the mind of general people that how can machine learning techniques help in electronic commerce. Many things have changed in ecommerce over the last few years and machine learning is getting more involved in such e-commerce activities more and more. Both AI (Artificial Intelligence) and ML (Machine Learning) are the future of ecommerce. AI includes the machine that can complete tasks using human cognition pattern and similar approaches, while machine learning is a section of AI that uses methods to improve the performance of the required system through learning and experiencing over a period of time. Currently, artificial intelligence and machine learning have been used entirely by global companies due to their not so available price. However, it is predicted through survey that by 2020 over 80% of all customer interactions will be handled by AI. Virtual technologies are likely to raise conversion rates and remove online shopping returns. We are already seeing those technologies being used by cosmetics, fashion and furniture companies and by the end of 2020 Augmented Reality will be generating $120 billion in revenue. The above chapter focuses on Ecommerce activities in conventional systems and how they have been improved and automated using machine learning system with special focus on areas in which the e-business has improved using ML techniques.

REFERENCES

Abdellaoui, J. E., & Berradi, H. (2018). Multipoint relay selection through estimated spatial relation in smart city environments. *2018 International Conference on Advanced Communication Technologies and Networking (CommNet)*, 1-10. 10.1109/COMMNET.2018.8360273

Abramov, R., & Herzberg, A. (2013). TCP Ack storm DoS attacks. *Computers & Security*, *33*, 12–27. doi:10.1016/j.cose.2012.09.005

Adnane, A., Bidan, C., & de Sousa Júnior, R. T. (2013). Trust-based security for the OLSR routing proto-col. *Computer Communications*, *36*(10), 1159–1171. doi:10.1016/j.comcom.2013.04.003

Agah, A., Basu, K., & Das, S. K. (2006). Security enforcement in wireless sensor networks: A framework based on non-cooperative games. *Pervasive and Mobile Computing*, *2*(2), 137–158. doi:10.1016/j.pmcj.2005.12.001

Almomani, I., Al-Banna, E., & Al-Akhras, M. (2013). Logic-Based Security Architecture for Systems Providing Multihop Communication. *International Journal of Distributed Sensor Networks*, *2013*, 1–17.

Bankovic, Z., Fraga, D., Manuel Moya, J., Carlos Vallejo, J., Malagón, P., Araujo, Á., ... Nieto-Taladriz, O. (2011). Improving security in WMNs with reputation systems and self-organizing maps. *Journal of Network and Computer Applications*, *34*(2), 455–463. doi:10.1016/j.jnca.2010.03.023

Bansal & Rishiwal. (2014). Assessment of QoS based multicast routing protocols in MANET. *2014 5th International Conference - Confluence The Next Generation Information Technology Summit (Confluence)*, 421-426.

Boukerche, A., & Ren, Y. (2008). A trust-based security system for ubiquitous and pervasive computing environments. *Computer Communications, 31*(18), 4343–4351. doi:10.1016/j.comcom.2008.05.007

Chaturvedi, S., Mishra, V., & Mishra, N. (2017). Sentiment analysis using machine learning for business intelligence. *IEEE International Conference on Power, Control, Signals and Instrumentation Engineering (ICPCSI)*, 2162-2166. 10.1109/ICPCSI.2017.8392100

Cuizhi, L., & Yunkang, Y. (2011). A study on key technologies in the development of mobile e-commerce. *2011 International Conference on E-Business and E-Government (ICEE)*, 1-4. 10.1109/ICEBEG.2011.5886779

Feng, C., Wu, S., & Liu, N. (2017). A user-centric machine learning framework for cyber security operations center. *IEEE International Conference on Intelligence and Security Informatics (ISI)*, 173-175. 10.1109/ISI.2017.8004902

Fuchs, B., Ritz, T., Halbach, B., & Hartl, F. (2011). Blended shopping: Interactivity and individualization. *Proceedings of the International Conference on e-Business*, 1-6.

Li, Rui, & Yanchao. (2016). PriExpress: Privacy-preserving express delivery with fine-grained attribute-based access control. *2016 IEEE Conference on Communications and Network Security (CNS)*, 333-341.

Parvinen, P., Kaptein, M., Oinas-Kukkonen, H., & Cheung, C. (2015). Introduction to E-Commerce, Engagement, and Social Influence Minitrack. *2015 48th Hawaii International Conference on System Sciences*, 3257-3257. 10.1109/HICSS.2015.393

Seth, E. (2014). Mobile Commerce: A Broader Perspective. *IT Professional, 16*(3), 61–65. doi:10.1109/MITP.2014.37

Shankararaman, V., & Kit, L. E. (2014). Enterprise Systems Enabling Smart Commerce. *2014 IEEE 16th Conference on Business Informatics*, 50-53. 10.1109/CBI.2014.17

Wan, Y., & Wu, C. (2009). Fitting and Prediction for Crack Propagation Rate Based on Machine Learning Optimal Algorithm. *International Conference on E-Learning, E-Business, Enterprise Information Systems, and E-Government*, 93-96. 10.1109/EEEE.2009.31

Wongkhamdi, T., Cooharojananone, N., & Khlaisang, J. (2017). The study of mobile learning readiness in rural area: Case of North-Eastern of Thailand. *2017 International Symposium on Computers in Education (SIIE)*, 1-6. 10.1109/SIIE.2017.8259665

Zhang, S.-H., Gu, N., Lian, J.-X., & Li, S.-H. (2003). Workflow process mining based on machine learning. *Proceedings of the 2003 International Conference on Machine Learning and Cybernetics (IEEE Cat. No.03EX693)*, 2319-2323. 10.1109/ICMLC.2003.1259895

Zhao, L., & Li, F. (2008). Statistical Machine Learning in Natural Language Understanding: Object Constraint Language Translator for Business Process. *IEEE International Symposium on Knowledge Acquisition and Modeling Workshop*, 1056-1059. 10.1109/KAMW.2008.4810674

Zhu, Fu, & Han. (2015). Online anomaly detection on e-commerce based on variable-length behavior sequence. *11th International Conference on Wireless Communications, Networking and Mobile Computing (WiCOM 2015)*, 1-8.

Chapter 8
Machine Learning in Python:
Diabetes Prediction Using Machine Learning

Astha Baranwal
VIT University, India

Bhagyashree R. Bagwe
VIT University, India

Vanitha M
VIT University, India

ABSTRACT

Diabetes is a disease of the modern world. The modern lifestyle has led to unhealthy eating habits causing type 2 diabetes. Machine learning has gained a lot of popularity in the recent days. It has applications in various fields and has proven to be increasingly effective in the medical field. The purpose of this chapter is to predict the diabetes outcome of a person based on other factors or attributes. Various machine learning algorithms like logistic regression (LR), tuned and not tuned random forest (RF), and multilayer perceptron (MLP) have been used as classifiers for diabetes prediction. This chapter also presents a comparative study of these algorithms based on various performance metrics like accuracy, sensitivity, specificity, and F1 score.

INTRODUCTION

Diabetes is a disease which happens when the glucose level of the blood becomes high, which eventually leads to other health problems such as heart diseases, kidney disease etc. Several data mining projects have used algorithms to predict diabetes in a patient. Though, in most of these projects, nothing is mentioned about the dangers of diabetes in women post-pregnancies. While data mining has been successfully applied to various fields in human society, such as weather prognosis, market analysis, engineering diagnosis, and customer relationship management, the application in disease prediction and medical data analysis still has room for improvement in accuracy.

DOI: 10.4018/978-1-5225-9902-9.ch008

Machine learning relates closely to Artificial Intelligence (AI) and makes software applications predict outcomes through statistical analysis. The algorithms used allow for reaching an optimal accuracy rate in predicting the output from the input data. Machine learning follows similar processes used in data mining and predictive modeling. They recognize patterns through the data entered and then adjust the actions of the program accordingly.

Machine learning algorithms are categorized as supervised learning and unsupervised learning. Supervised learning requires input data and the desired output data to build a training model. The training model is built by a data analyst or a data scientist. A feedback is then furnished concerning the accuracy of the model and other performance metrics during algorithm training. Revising is done as needed. Once the training phase is completed, the model can predict outcomes for new data. Classification is one of the many data mining tasks. Classification comes under supervised learning which implies that the machine learns through examples in Classification. In classification, every instance from the dataset is classified into a target value. Classification can either be binary or multi-label. Sometimes, one particular instance can also have multiple classes known as multi-class classification. Classification algorithms are majorly used for prediction and come under the category of predictive learning.

Unsupervised learning is used to draw inferences from the input data which do not have any labeled responses. This data is not categorized, labeled or classified into classes. Clustering analysis, one of the most common unsupervised learning method, is used to find hidden patterns in data or to form groups based on the input data.

While machine learning models have been around for decades, they have gained a new momentum with the rise of AI. Deep learning models are now used in most of the advanced AI applications. If these models are implemented for medical uses, they could be revolutionary for the society. Diagnosis of diseases like diabetes would be easier than ever. Machine learning in medical diagnosis applications fall under three classes: Pathology, Oncology and Chatbots. Pathology deals with the diagnosis of diseases with the help of machine learning models created with the data of diagnostic measurements of the patients. Oncology uses deep learning models to determine cancerous tissues in patients. Chatbots designed using AI and machine learning techniques can identify patterns in the symptoms of the patients and suggest a potential diagnosis or it can recommend further courses of action. This chapter falls under the pathological uses of machine learning as the model created will give diagnosis of whether a patient is diabetic or not.

This chapter focuses on implementing machine learning algorithms on the diabetes dataset in python. Python is a great language to support machine learning. It was created by Guido van Rossom. It is powerful, multipurpose, and simple and has an easy to use syntax. The length of a python code is generally relatively short. It is not overly strict. It is a fun language to work with because it lets us focus on the problem rather than the syntax. Python is a general purpose language with applications in a wide range of fields like web development, mathematical computing, graphical user interfaces, etc. These wide range of applications python most suitable for implementing machine learning algorithms. It is possible to implement some machine learning algorithms in python and later deploy the web service for it. Or it is also possible to create a graphical user interface for the deployed web service. This all becomes possible due to the diverse nature of the language. Various python libraries like, NumPy, SciPy, Matplotlib, Keras, Pandas, TensorFlow, and etc support machine learning in python. Scikit-learn library supports almost all the major machine learning classification, clustering and regression models. The Flask python web framework is used to create web apps from APIs created using the machine learning models. This web app can perform real-time predictions for individual and batch data inputs.

Background

About one in every seven U.S. adult citizen has diabetes currently, as per the Centers for Disease Control and Prevention. According to statistics, this rate could skyrocket to as many as one in three by the year 2050. Hence, it is of utmost importance that a proper diabetes prediction system should be built with high prediction accuracy. Several prior studies have proposed various models for the prediction of diabetes on the PIMA Indian Dataset. Accuracy up to 95.42% (proposed by Han Wu et al. 2018) has been obtained by first clustering the data using K-Means algorithm and removing the outliers and then creating the classification models. Patil et al. (2010) proposed a similar model with C4.5 algorithm as the final classifier model. They obtained an accuracy of 92.38%. Kandhasamy et al. (2015) applied machine learning classification techniques like Decision Tree J48, KNN Classifier, Random Forest and Support Vector Machine and obtained 86.46% accuracy. The paper proposed by the Sisodias (2018) applied three classification algorithms: Decision Tree, SVM and Naive Bayes and reported highest accuracy (76.30%) with the Naïve Bayes model.

Linear Discriminant Analysis (LDA) and Adaptive Network Based Fuzzy Inference System (ANFIS): LDA-ANFIS was proposed by Dogantekin et al. (2010) with an accuracy of 84.61%. R. Aishwarya et al. (2013) used Support Vector Machine to build the classification model. Temurtas et al. (2009) used a multilayer neural network structure which was trained by Levenberg–Marquardt (LM) algorithm. The accuracy stated was 82.37%.

Fatima and Pasha (2017) provided a comparative analysis of various machine learning algorithms and techniques for the diagnosis of serious diseases such as diabetes, heart diseases, liver diseases, dengue and hepatitis diseases. K Saravananathan and Velmurugan (2016) in the paper Analyzing Diabetic Data using Classification Algorithms in Data Mining use J48, support vector machine (SVM), classification and regression tree (CART) and K-Nearest Neighbor (KNN) to categorize the dataset that included 10 attributes from 545 patients in Weka. Kavakiotis et al. (2017) discovered that 85% of papers used supervised learning approaches and 15% by unsupervised ones, association rules, more specifically. Support vector machines (SVM) was stated as the most successful and popularly used algorithm. M. P. Gopinath and Murali (2017) provided a comparative study between various classification algorithms, namely Naive Bayes (NB), Support Vector Machine (SVM), Decision Tree (DT), Bayes net, etc, in their paper. Yasodha and Kannan (2011) used WEKA tool to classify the dataset and the 10-fold cross validation is used for evaluation and the results are compared. D. Nanthini and Thangaraju (2015) in their paper propose a method for building a hybrid on the diabetes dataset using three variations of the classification algorithm Decision Tree namely, C4.5, J48 and the FB tree.

Many other papers have reported a classification accuracy ranging from 50% to 80% on the PIMA Indians Diabetes dataset using various machine learning techniques. Research is underway for better accuracy rates using different advanced machine learning and deep learning algorithms and techniques.

MAIN FOCUS OF THE CHAPTER

Issues, Controversies, Problems

Medical diagnosis of Diabetes is possible only after the patient has acquired the disease and not before. This completely cuts down the possibility of prevention of the disease. This is an issue of the medical field. This problem can be sorted by aiding the medical field with the Information Technology sector.

Machine Learning algorithms are used in this chapter to predict if a person will have diabetes or not. This prediction is done based on some other lifestyle attributes of the person. The machine learning task used here is classification. Classification comes under supervised learning. Supervised learning is when the machine learns based on examples, like a human being, using the training dataset. In supervised leaning it is required that the data has a class label or a target value as an independent variable into which the instances will be classified. With respect to the PIMA diabetes dataset, the target variable is the outcome value which predicts whether the person will have diabetes or not. It is for this variable that the classification is carried out. If it is somehow possible to predict in advance if the person is going to contract diabetes or not, some preventive measures can be taken in order to avoid contraction of diabetes.

Thus, in this way, the use of machine learning in the medical field can help solve some critical issues and aid medical science in more ways than expected.

Section-Wise Description

1. **Platform Details:** This section provides a description about the platform used.
    a. Anaconda.
    b. Jupyter
    c. Python
    d. NumPy
    e. Pandas
    f. SciPy
    g. Matplotlib
    h. TensorFlow and Keras
2. **System Architecture:** This section briefly explains how the system works and how it is built using a flowchart and a textual description.
3. **Dataset Description:** This section gives a description about the selected PIMA diabetes dataset. It gives information about the datatype of the attributes along with their explanation.
4. **Data Cleaning:** This section shows how the data was preprocessed and cleaned using Weka. This included various processes like finding missing values and replacing them with suitable values.
5. **Data Visualization:** In this section the data was visualized using the Python Jupyter platform. Data visualization helps us in getting a better understanding of the data.
6. **Random Forest Model (Not Tuned):** This section explains how the basic random forest model is built on the PIMA diabetes dataset using machine learning in python. It also shows the results produced by this classifier.
7. **Random Forest Model (Tuned):** This section explains how the tuned random forest model is built on the PIMA diabetes dataset using machine learning in python. It also shows the results produced by this classifier.

8. **Checking with different Hyper parameter tuning:** This sections tests for random values of the three selected parameters namely, n_tree, max_features and max_depth for hyper parameter tuning.
9. **Logistic Regression (LR):** This section explains Logistic Regression classifier model is built on the PIMA diabetes datasetusing machine learning in python. It also shows the results produced by this classifier.
10. **Multilayer Perceptron:** This section explains how the multilayer perceptron (MLP), a type of Artificial Neural Network (ANN) is built on the PIMA diabetes dataset using machine learning in python. It also shows the results produced by this classifier.
11. **Performance Metrics**: This section gives a detailed information about the various performance metrics used for evaluating and comparing the various classifier models built on the PIMA diabetes dataset.
12. **Comparison between the models using various performance metrics**: This section provides a tabular comparison between the various classifier models built for predicting the outcome on the PIMA diabetes dataset.

SOLUTIONS AND RECOMMENDATIONS

Platform Details

Anaconda

Anaconda is a professional data science platform which we can use as a GUI as well as a console. Anaconda is a Python distribution which brings a lot of useful libraries with it, which are not included in Python standard library like Jupyter, NumPy, Pandas, SciPy, Matplotlib, etc. It can create different Python version environments.

Jupyter

The Jupyter Notebook is an open-source web app that allows the creation and sharing of documents that contain equations, live code, visualizations and narrative text in form of markdowns. It is included in the Anaconda distribution.

WEKA (Waikato Environment for Knowledge Analysis)

Weka is a software that is built in Java and can run on almost every platform. Weka gives provisions for various machine learning algorithms and can be used for data cleaning and data visualization.

Python

Python is a widely used high-level programming language which is interpreted, general-purpose, and dynamic.

The Python libraries used for data analysis, visualization and machine learning are:

NumPy

NumPy is a Python library that adds support for large and multi-dimensional arrays. It supports matrices.

Pandas

Pandas is a Python package designed to make the work with labeled and relational data be very simple and intuitive. It is designed for fast and easy data manipulation, visualization and aggregation.

SciPy

SciPy contains modules for statistics, linear algebra, optimization and integration. The principal functionality of SciPy library is based upon NumPy, and hence its arrays make considerable use of NumPy.

Matplotlib

Matplotlib is a Python library for 2D plotting which produces quality figures in a variety of hardcopy formats and interactive environments across platforms.

Tensorflow and Keras

Tensorflow is a Python Deep Learning library.

Keras is a simple neural networks library designed for high-level neural networks. It is written in Python and works as a wrapper to Tensorflow.

System Architecture

This chapter uses the PIMA Indians Diabetes Dataset for diabetes prediction by various machine learning models. The dataset is first explored. Data visualization helps to understand the data significance by identifying any useful patterns or abnormalities that are revealed in the data points of the dataset. Data visualization is done and correlation between each and every attribute is examined. The values of attributes are represented by binning for all the instances. The target variable 'Outcome' contains positive (1) and negative (0) values. The count of positive and negative instances can be identified.

The data cleaning involves removal of zero and missing (null) values from the dataset. This is done using the Weka Explorer software. Next, feature engineering is done. Feature engineering involves determination of useful attributes. The attributes which do not contribute much in predicting the outcome accurately are discarded. No attribute is discarded in making the models in this chapter. SkinThickness contributes the least in prediction of diabetes for the dataset but it is considered nonetheless. Logistic Regression (LR), Random Forest (RF) and Multilayer Perceptron (MLP) are selected for model building because they all are powerful machine learning algorithms which can be further hyper parameter tuned to obtain optimal accuracy. Multilayer perceptron classifier is a type of Artificial Neural Network (ANN). Confusion matrix and classification report for each model is generated. The results of the models are then compared based on various performance metrics.

Figure 1. The system architecture

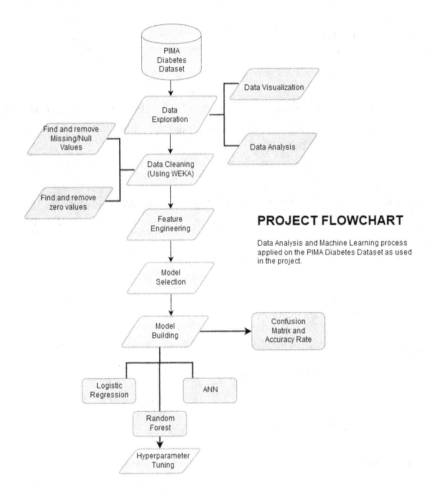

PROJECT FLOWCHART

Data Analysis and Machine Learning process applied on the PIMA Diabetes Dataset as used in the project.

Dataset Description

The dataset used is originally contributed by the National Institute of Diabetes and Digestive and Kidney Diseases. It has 768 instances and 9 attributes. The goal is to predict whether a patient has diabetes based on diagnostic measurements. The datasets consist of several medical predictor (independent) variables and one target (dependent) variable, Outcome.

Several constraints were placed on the selection of these instances from a larger database. In particular, all patients here are females at least 21 years old of Pima Indian heritage.

Data Cleaning

The missing values and the null values are cleaned:

- There are instances with BloodPressure as 0. Blood pressure of a living person can never be 0.
- Plasma glucose levels, even after fasting, can never be 0.

Table 1. Attribute description for the diabetes dataset

Sr. No.	Attribute	Description	Datatype
1	Pregnancies	Number of times pregnant	int64
2	Glucose	Plasma glucose concentration	int64
3	BloodPressure	Diastolic blood pressure (mm Hg)	int64
4	SkinThickness	Triceps skin fold thickness (mm)	int64
5	Insulin	2-Hour serum insulin (mu U/ml)	int64
6	BMI	Body mass index (weight in kg/(height in m)^2)	float64
7	DiabetesPedigreeFunction	Diabetes pedigree function	float64
8	Age	Age of patient (in years)	int64
9	Outcome	Class variable. 1 for diabetic and 0 for non-diabetic.	int64

- Skin Fold Thickness cannot be 0.
- BMI of a person can never be 0 as it is weight/height^2
- Insulin is never 0 in normal cases and there are about 374 instances with 0 insulin.

They are replaced by means of the values of the concerned attributes. The cleaned dataset has 768 instances and 9 attributes.

Data Cleaning of the "Pima Indian Diabetes Dataset" by WEKA Explorer

Mark Missing Values

Attributes such as BloodPressure and BMI (Body Mass Index) have values of zero, which is impossible. These examples of corrupt or missing data must be marked manually. Since zero values are not considered as missing values by Weka, this needs to be fixed first.

Weka marks zero values as missing values by the NumericalCleaner filter. The steps below show how to use this filter to mark the missing values on the Pregnancies,BloodPressure, Glucose, SkinThickness, BMI and Insulin attributes:

The Pima Indians diabetes dataset is loaded in the Weka Explorer.

NumericalCleaner filter is selected. It is under unsupervized.attribute.NumericalCleaner. This filter is further configured.

TheattributeIndicies is set to 1-6. This is the indices of the attributes with 0 values. The minThreshold is set to 0.1E-8 (close to zero), which is the minimum value allowed for the attribute. The minDefault is set to NaN, which is unknown and will replace values below the threshold.

The filter configuration is applied on the dataset. The transformation for the BloodPressure attribute is shown for each step.

Notice that the attribute values that were formally set to zero are now marked as Missing.

Figure 2. The initial dataset

No	1: Pregnancies	2: Glucose	3: BloodPressure	4: SkinThickness	5: Insulin	6: BMI	7: DiabetesPedigreeFunction	8: Age	9: Outcome
	Numeric	Numeric	Numeric	Numeric	Numeric	Numeric	Numeric	Numeric	Numeric
1	6.0	148.0	72.0	35.0	0.0	33.6	0.627	50.0	1.0
2	1.0	85.0	66.0	29.0	0.0	26.6	0.351	31.0	0.0
3	8.0	183.0	64.0	0.0	0.0	23.3	0.672	32.0	1.0
4	1.0	89.0	66.0	23.0	94.0	28.1	0.167	21.0	0.0
5	0.0	137.0	40.0	35.0	168.0	43.1	2.288	33.0	1.0
6	5.0	116.0	74.0	0.0	0.0	25.6	0.201	30.0	0.0
7	3.0	78.0	50.0	32.0	88.0	31.0	0.248	26.0	1.0
8	10.0	115.0	0.0	0.0	0.0	35.3	0.134	29.0	0.0
9	2.0	197.0	70.0	45.0	543.0	30.5	0.158	53.0	1.0
10	8.0	125.0	96.0	0.0	0.0	0.0	0.232	54.0	1.0
11	4.0	110.0	92.0	0.0	0.0	37.6	0.191	30.0	0.0
12	10.0	168.0	74.0	0.0	0.0	38.0	0.537	34.0	1.0
13	10.0	139.0	80.0	0.0	0.0	27.1	1.441	57.0	0.0
14	1.0	189.0	60.0	23.0	846.0	30.1	0.398	59.0	1.0
15	5.0	166.0	72.0	19.0	175.0	25.8	0.587	51.0	1.0
16	7.0	100.0	0.0	0.0	0.0	30.0	0.484	32.0	1.0
17	0.0	118.0	84.0	47.0	230.0	45.8	0.551	31.0	1.0
18	7.0	107.0	74.0	0.0	0.0	29.6	0.254	31.0	1.0
19	1.0	103.0	30.0	38.0	83.0	43.3	0.183	33.0	0.0
20	1.0	115.0	70.0	30.0	96.0	34.6	0.529	32.0	1.0
21	3.0	126.0	88.0	41.0	235.0	39.3	0.704	27.0	0.0
22	8.0	99.0	84.0	0.0	0.0	35.4	0.388	50.0	0.0
23	7.0	196.0	90.0	0.0	0.0	39.8	0.451	41.0	1.0
24	9.0	119.0	80.0	35.0	0.0	29.0	0.263	29.0	1.0
25	11.0	143.0	94.0	33.0	146.0	36.6	0.254	51.0	1.0
26	10.0	125.0	70.0	26.0	115.0	31.1	0.205	41.0	1.0
27	7.0	147.0	76.0	0.0	0.0	39.4	0.257	43.0	1.0
28	1.0	97.0	66.0	15.0	140.0	23.2	0.487	22.0	0.0
29	13.0	145.0	82.0	19.0	110.0	22.2	0.245	57.0	0.0
30	5.0	117.0	92.0	0.0	0.0	34.1	0.337	38.0	0.0
31	5.0	109.0	75.0	26.0	0.0	36.0	0.546	60.0	0.0
32	3.0	158.0	76.0	36.0	245.0	31.6	0.851	28.0	1.0
33	3.0	88.0	58.0	11.0	54.0	24.8	0.267	22.0	0.0
34	6.0	92.0	92.0	0.0	0.0	19.9	0.188	28.0	0.0
35	10.0	122.0	78.0	31.0	0.0	27.6	0.512	45.0	0.0
36	4.0	103.0	60.0	33.0	192.0	24.0	0.966	33.0	0.0
37	11.0	138.0	76.0	0.0	0.0	33.2	0.42	35.0	0.0
38	9.0	102.0	76.0	37.0	0.0	32.9	0.665	46.0	1.0

Relation: pima_diabetes

Figure 3. The BloodPresuure attribute before data cleaning

Name: BloodPressure		Type: Numeric	
Missing: 0 (0%)	Distinct: 47	Unique: 8 (1%)	

Statistic	Value
Minimum	0
Maximum	122
Mean	69.105
StdDev	19.356

Remove Missing Data

Now that missing values are marked in the data, they need to be handled. An easy way to deal with missing data in the dataset is to remove those data points that have one or more missing values.

This can be done in Weka using the RemoveWithValues filter.

However, this leads to loss in some data instances. It is advisable to impute the missing values instead of removing these instances altogether from the dataset.

Figure 4. Configuring the NumericalCleaner filter

Figure 5. The BloodPressure attribute after applying NumericalCleaner

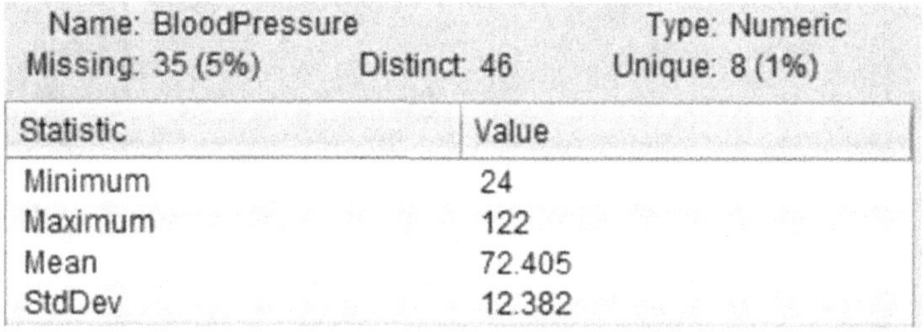

Name: BloodPressure		Type: Numeric
Missing: 35 (5%)	Distinct: 46	Unique: 8 (1%)

Statistic	Value
Minimum	24
Maximum	122
Mean	72.405
StdDev	12.382

Impute Missing Values

It is not necessary to remove the instances with missing values; the missing values can be replaced instead with some other value.

This is called imputing missing values.

It is not uncommon to impute missing values with the mean of the numerical distribution of an attribute. This can be done easily in Weka using the ReplaceMissingValues filter.

Figure 6. The BloodPressure attribute after ReplaceMissingValues filter

Name: BloodPressure		Type: Numeric	
Missing: 0 (0%)	Distinct: 47	Unique: 8 (1%)	

Statistic	Value
Minimum	24
Maximum	122
Mean	72.405
StdDev	12.096

Missing values can be imputed by theReplaceMissingValues filter. It is under the unsupervized.attribute.ReplaceMissingValues path.

The filter is applied on appropriate attributes.

The missing values are gone. They are replaced by means of the values of concerned attributes.

Figure 7. The final dataset after data cleaning

Relation: pima_diabetes-weka.filters.unsupervised.attribute.NumericCleaner-min1.0E-8-min-defaultNaN-max1.7976931348623157E308-r

No.	1: Pregnancies	2: Glucose	3: BloodPressure	4: SkinThickness	5: Insulin	6: BMI	7: DiabetesPedigreeFunction	8: Age	9: Outcome
	Numeric	Numeric	Numeric	Numeric	Numeric	Numeric	Numeric	Numeric	Numeric
1	6.0	148.0	72.0	35.0	155.5...	33.6	0.627	50.0	1.0
2	1.0	85.0	66.0	29.0	155.5...	26.6	0.351	31.0	0.0
3	8.0	183.0	64.0	29.153419593...	155.5...	23.3	0.672	32.0	1.0
4	1.0	89.0	66.0	23.0	94.0	28.1	0.167	21.0	0.0
5	4.49467275...	137.0	40.0	35.0	168.0	43.1	2.288	33.0	1.0
6	5.0	116.0	74.0	29.153419593...	155.5...	25.6	0.201	30.0	0.0
7	3.0	78.0	50.0	32.0	88.0	31.0	0.248	26.0	1.0
8	10.0	115.0	72.405184174...	29.153419593...	155.5...	35.3	0.134	29.0	0.0
9	2.0	197.0	70.0	45.0	543.0	30.5	0.158	53.0	1.0
10	8.0	125.0	96.0	29.153419593...	155.5...	32.4...	0.232	54.0	1.0
11	4.0	110.0	92.0	29.153419593...	155.5...	37.6	0.191	30.0	0.0
12	10.0	168.0	74.0	29.153419593...	155.5...	38.0	0.537	34.0	1.0
13	10.0	139.0	80.0	29.153419593...	155.5...	27.1	1.441	57.0	0.0
14	1.0	189.0	60.0	23.0	846.0	30.1	0.398	59.0	1.0
15	5.0	166.0	72.0	19.0	175.0	25.8	0.587	51.0	1.0
16	7.0	100.0	72.405184174...	29.153419593...	155.5...	30.0	0.484	32.0	1.0
17	4.49467275...	118.0	84.0	47.0	230.0	45.8	0.551	31.0	1.0
18	7.0	107.0	74.0	29.153419593...	155.5...	29.6	0.254	31.0	1.0
19	1.0	103.0	30.0	38.0	83.0	43.3	0.183	33.0	0.0
20	1.0	115.0	70.0	30.0	96.0	34.6	0.529	32.0	1.0
21	3.0	126.0	88.0	41.0	235.0	39.3	0.704	27.0	0.0
22	8.0	99.0	84.0	29.153419593...	155.5...	35.4	0.388	50.0	0.0
23	7.0	196.0	90.0	29.153419593...	155.5...	39.8	0.451	41.0	1.0
24	9.0	119.0	80.0	35.0	155.5...	29.0	0.263	29.0	1.0
25	11.0	143.0	94.0	33.0	146.0	36.6	0.254	51.0	1.0
26	10.0	125.0	70.0	26.0	115.0	31.1	0.205	41.0	1.0
27	7.0	147.0	76.0	29.153419593...	155.5...	39.4	0.257	43.0	1.0
28	1.0	97.0	66.0	15.0	140.0	23.2	0.487	22.0	0.0
29	13.0	145.0	82.0	19.0	110.0	22.2	0.245	57.0	0.0
30	5.0	117.0	92.0	29.153419593...	155.5...	34.1	0.337	38.0	0.0
31	5.0	109.0	75.0	26.0	155.5...	36.0	0.546	60.0	0.0
32	3.0	158.0	76.0	36.0	245.0	31.6	0.851	28.0	1.0
33	3.0	88.0	58.0	11.0	54.0	24.8	0.267	22.0	0.0
34	6.0	92.0	92.0	29.153419593...	155.5...	19.9	0.188	28.0	0.0
35	10.0	122.0	78.0	31.0	155.5...	27.6	0.512	45.0	0.0
36	4.0	103.0	60.0	33.0	192.0	24.0	0.966	33.0	0.0
37	11.0	138.0	76.0	29.153419593...	155.5...	33.2	0.42	35.0	0.0
38	9.0	102.0	76.0	37.0	155.5	32.9	0.665	46.0	1.0

Data Visualization

Importing the libraries and the dataset:

```
import numpy as np
import pandas as pd
import matplotlib.pyplot as plt
%matplotlib inline
import seaborn as sns
diabetes = pd.read_csv('pima_diabetes.csv')
```

Visualize the distribution of positive and negative instances for the Outcome attribute in the diabetes dataset:

```
diabetes.groupby('Outcome').size()
sns.countplot(diabetes['Outcome'],label="Count")
```

It can be identified that out of the 768 persons, 500 are labeled as 0 (Non-Diabetic) and 268 as 1 (Diabetic)

```
def plot_corr(df, size=11):
corr = df.corr()
    fig, ax = plt.subplots(figsize=(size, size))
ax.matshow(corr)
plt.xticks(range(len(corr.columns)), corr.columns)
plt.yticks(range(len(corr.columns)), corr.columns)
plot_corr(diabetes)
```

Figure 8. Positive and negative instances for the Outcome attribute in the diabetes dataset

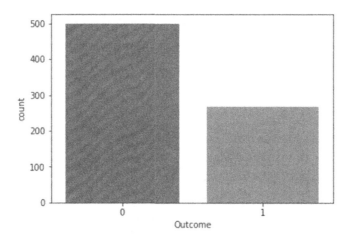

Figure 9. The correlation between various attributes of the diabetes dataset

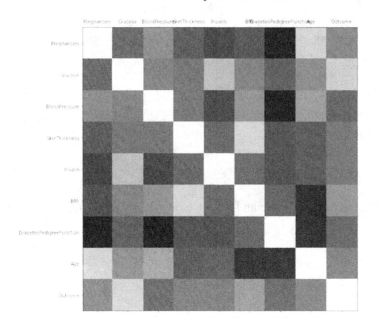

In the above visualization plot, lighter color represents maximum correlation and darker color represents minimum correlation. We can see none of the variable have proper correlation with any of the other variables.

Binning of the instances in dataset as per attributes:

```
diabetes.hist(figsize=(12,8),bins=20)
```

Model Selection: Comparison of Calibration of Classifiers

Model selection is the phase where the model with the best calibration and reliability estimate for the data set at hand is selected.

The "Classification Accuracy (Testing Accuracy)" of a given set of classification models is calculated with their default parameters to predict which model can perform better with the PIMA diabetes data set.

Seven classifiers namely K-Nearest Neighbors, Support Vector Classifier, Logistic Regression, Decision Tree, Gaussian Naive Bayes and Random Forest and Multilayer Perceptron are to be the contenders for the best classifier.

```
models = []

models.append(('KNN', KNeighborsClassifier()))
models.append(('SVC', SVC()))
models.append(('LR', LogisticRegression()))
models.append(('DT', DecisionTreeClassifier()))
models.append(('GNB', GaussianNB()))
```

Figure 10. The values of attributes in the diabetes dataset represented by binning

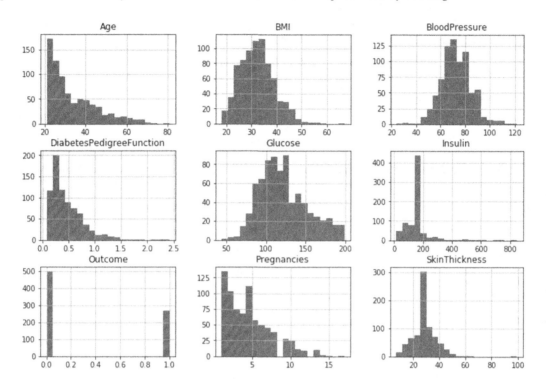

```
models.append(('RF', RandomForestClassifier()))
models.append(('ANN', MLPClassifier()))

from sklearn.model_selection import train_test_split
from sklearn.metrics import accuracy_score
X_train, X_test, y_train, y_test = train_test_split(X, y, stratify = diabetes.
Outcome, random_state=0)

names = []
scores = []

for name, model in models:
model.fit(X_train, y_train)
y_pred = model.predict(X_test) #prediction of models
scores.append(accuracy_score(y_test, y_pred))
names.append(name)

tr_split = pd.DataFrame({'Name': names, 'Score': scores})
print(tr_split)

axis = sns.barplot(x = 'Name', y = 'Score', data = tr_split)
```

```
axis.set(xlabel='Classifier', ylabel='Predicted Accuracy')

for p in axis.patches:
    height = p.get_height()
axis.text(p.get_x() + p.get_width()/2, height + 0.005, '{:1.4f}'.
format(height), ha="center")

plt.show()
```

Logistic Regression is the best contender based on the plot obtained. Random forest gives a decent performance. ANN or the Multilayer Perceptron (MLP) classifier can use standard scalar to increase the accuracy.

Random Forest Model (Not Tuned)

```
from sklearn import model_selection

# random forest model creation
rfc = RandomForestClassifier()
rfc.fit(X_train,y_train)

# predictions
rfc_predict = rfc.predict(X_test)

from sklearn.model_selection import cross_val_score
from sklearn.metrics import classification_report, confusion_matrix
rfc_cv_score = cross_val_score(rfc, X, y, cv=10, scoring='roc_auc')
```

Figure 11. Predicted Accuracy vs contender Classifiers

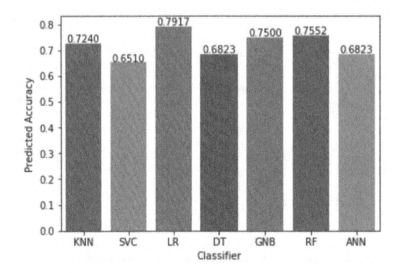

```
print("Model Accuracy: {0:.4f}".format(metrics.accuracy_score(y_test, rfc_pre-
dict)))

print("Confusion Matrix")
print(confusion_matrix(y_test, rfc_predict))
print('\n')

print("Classification Report")
print(classification_report(y_test, rfc_predict))
print('\n')
```

Random Forest Model (Tuned): Hyper Parameter Tuning the Random Forest Model

```
from sklearn.model_selection import RandomizedSearchCV

# number of trees in random forest
n_estimators = [int(x) for x in np.linspace(start = 200, stop = 2000, num =
10)]

# number of features at every split
max_features = ['auto', 'sqrt']

# max depth
max_depth = [int(x) for x in np.linspace(100, 500, num = 11)]
max_depth.append(None)

# create random grid
random_grid = {
 'n_estimators': n_estimators,
 'max_features': max_features,
```

Figure 12. Classification report for the Random Forest (not tuned) model

```
Model Accuracy: 0.7559
Confusion Matrix
[[146  30]
 [ 32  46]]


Classification Report
              precision   recall  f1-score   support

           0       0.82     0.83      0.82       176
           1       0.61     0.59      0.60        78

 avg / total       0.75     0.76      0.76       254
```

```
'max_depth': max_depth
 }


# Random search of parameters
rfc_random = RandomizedSearchCV(estimator = rfc, param_distributions = random_
grid, n_iter = 100, cv = 3, verbose=2, random_state=42, n_jobs = -1)


# Fit the model
rfc_random.fit(X_train, y_train.ravel())


# print results
print(rfc_random.best_params_)
```

The results are: 'n_estimators' = 1200; 'max_features' = 'auto'; 'max_depth': 180. Now these parameters can be plugged back into the model to see whether it improved the performance.

Checking With Different Hyper Parameter Tuning

```
import numpy
from matplotlib import pyplot
x = numpy.array([400,600,800,1000,1200,1400])
y = numpy.array([0.8299330484330485, 0.829940170940171, 0.8296937321937321,
0.8276780626780628, 0.8307606837606837, 0.8289601139601139])


fig = pyplot.figure()
ax = fig.add_subplot(111)
ax.set_ylim(0.80,0.85)
pyplot.plot(x,y)
pyplot.show()
```

Figure 13. Classification report for the random forest (tuned) model

```
Confusion Matrix
[[147  29]
 [ 30  48]]


Classification Report
              precision    recall  f1-score   support

           0       0.83      0.84      0.83       176
           1       0.62      0.62      0.62        78

avg / total       0.77      0.77      0.77       254
```

Figure 14. Area Under the Curve (AUC) score versus the number of trees (n_tree) in the Random Forest

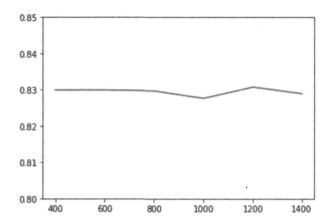

Clearly, at n_tree = 1200; max_features = 'auto'; max_depth: 180, the AUC score is highest and this, hence, will give the highest accuracy rate

Logistic Regression

```
from sklearn.linear_model import LogisticRegression

diab_lr_model = LogisticRegression(C=0.7, random_state=52)
diab_lr_model.fit(X_train, y_train.ravel())
lr_test_predict = diab_lr_model.predict(X_test)

print("Model Accuracy: {0:.2f}".format(metrics.accuracy_score(y_test, lr_test_
predict)))
print("")
print("Confusion Matrix")
print(metrics.confusion_matrix(y_test, lr_test_predict, labels=[1, 0]))
print("")
print("Classification Report")
print(metrics.classification_report(y_test, lr_test_predict, labels=[1, 0]))
```

Multilayer Perceptron

```
from sklearn.neural_network import MLPClassifier
from sklearn.model_selection import train_test_split

X_train, X_test, y_train, y_test = train_test_split(diabetes.loc[:, diabetes.
columns != 'Outcome'], diabetes['Outcome'], stratify=diabetes['Outcome'], ran-
dom_state=66)
from sklearn.preprocessing import StandardScaler
```

Figure 15. Classification report for the Logistic Regression (LR) model

```
Model Accuracy: 0.77

Confusion Matrix
[[ 37  30]
 [ 14 111]]

Classification Report
             precision    recall   f1-score   support

         1       0.73      0.55       0.63        67
         0       0.79      0.89       0.83       125

avg / total      0.77      0.77       0.76       192
```

```
scaler = StandardScaler()
X_train_scaled = scaler.fit_transform(X_train)
X_test_scaled = scaler.fit_transform(X_test)

mlp = MLPClassifier(random_state=0)
mlp.fit(X_train_scaled, y_train)

print("Accuracy on test set: {:.4f}".format(mlp.score(X_test_scaled, y_test)))
```

Performance Metrics

Performance metrics play an important role in the evaluation of the various machine learning models built. Choice of performance metrics determine how the machine learning models are compared and measured. This chapter compares the models based on the four performance metrics namely – Accuracy, Specificity, Sensitivity and the F1 score.

Figure 16. Classification report for the Multilayer Perceptron (MLP) classifier

```
Model Accuracy: 79.87012987012987%
Confusion Matrix
[[88 19]
 [11 36]]
Classification Report
             precision    recall   f1-score   support

         1       0.65      0.77       0.71        47
         0       0.89      0.82       0.85       107

avg / total      0.82      0.81       0.81       154
```

A confusion matrix is a performance metric table that is used to analyze the performance of a classification model (or "classifier") on a set of test data for which the true target attribute values are already known. It is also called as the error matrix.Python has confusion matrix and classification report functions under the sklearn.metrics library. Confusion matrix contains:

True Positive: The instances which are classified as positive and are actually positive.
True Negative: The instances which are classified as negative and are actually negative.
False Positive: The instances which are classified as positive but are actually negative.
False Negative: The instances which are classified as negative but are actually positive.

Sensitivity (True Positive Rate)

If a person has diabetes, how often will the classifier be able to predict it?

It is the ratio of true positives to the sum of the true positive and false negative. A highly sensitive test helps rule out diabetes. If the test is highly sensitive and the test result is test result is negative, it becomes nearly certain that the particular person doesn't have diabetes.

Sensitivity = True Positive / (True Positive + False Negative)

Specificity (True Negative Rate)

If a person doesn't have diabetes, how often will the classifier be able to predict it?

It is the ratio of true negatives to the sum of the true negatives and false positives. A highly sensitive test helps rule in diabetes. If the test is highly specific and the test result is test result is positive, it becomes nearly certain that the particular person has diabetes.

Specificity = True Negative / (True Negative + False Positive)

Accuracy

It is a metric used to predict the correctness of a machine learning model. The model is trained using the train data and a classifier is built. The test data is used to cross validate the classifier model. The percentage of correctly classified instances is termed as Accuracy.

F1 Score

F1 score is a combination function of precision and recall. It is used when we need to seek a balance between precision and recall.

Precision = True Positives / (True Positives + False Positives)

Here, the denominator (True Positives + False Positives) is the total predicted positives.

Table 2. Comparison between various classifiers based on performance metrics

Algorithm	Accuracy	Specificity	Sensitivity	F1-Score
Random Forest (before hyper parameter tuning)	0.7559	0.8295	0.5897	0.5974
Random Forest (after hyper parameter tuning)	0.7677	0.8352	0.6153	0.6193
Logistic Regression	0.7789	0.7872	0.7255	0.6271
Artificial Neural Networks (ANN)	0.7987	0.8224	0.7659	0.7058

Recall = True Positives / (True Positives + False Negatives)

Here, the denominator (True Positives + False Negatives) is the total actual positives.

F1 Score = 2 * (Precision * Recall) / (Precision + Recall)

Accuracy vs F1 Score

In cases where there is an uneven class distribution i.e. there are large number of actual negatives, F1 Score might prove to be better than accuracy. Accuracy only checks the correctness of a model while F1 score strikes a balance between precision and recall.

The model architecture is defined by several parameters. These parameters are referred to as hyper parameters. The process of searching for an ideal model architecture for optimal accuracy score is referred to as hyper parameter tuning. In this chapter, hyper parameter tuning of Random Forest model is done to give a better accuracy. At n_tree = 1200; max_features = 'auto'; max_depth: 180, the AUC (Area Under the Curve) score is highest and this, hence, gives the highest accuracy rate.

After building the models, Multilayer Perceptron (MLP) model gives the highest accuracy at 79.87%. Random Forest model was focused on to increase accuracy by Hyper-parameter Tuning. However, the highest accuracy obtained from it, i.e. 76.38%, could not exceed even the Logistic Regression model's accuracy (77.89%).

The neural network model built gives a better accuracy than LR and Random Forest classifier models. Diabetes is a huge threat to the modern world and devising an algorithm that tackles or even reduces its adversity can be a great help to diabetic patients.

Comparison Between the Models Using Various Performance Metrics

```
models = []
models.append(('LR', 0.7789))
models.append(('ANN (not tuned)', 0.7857))
models.append(('ANN (tuned)', 0.8052))
models.append(('Ensemble', 0.7512))
models.append(('Hybrid', 0.8377))
names = []
scores = []
```

```
for name, accuracy in models:
scores.append(accuracy)
names.append(name)
tb_split = pd.DataFrame({'Name': names, 'Score': scores})
print(tb_split)

axis = sns.barplot(x = 'Name', y = 'Score', data = tb_split, palette="GnBu_d")
axis.set(xlabel='CLASSIFIER', ylabel='ACCURACY SCORE')
sns.set(rc={'figure.figsize':(15,8)}, font_scale=1.5)
sns.set(font_scale=1.5)
for p in axis.patches:
    height = p.get_height()
axis.text(p.get_x() + p.get_width()/2, height + 0.005, '{:1.4f}'.
format(height), ha="center")
plt.show()
```

Clearly, accuracy of the Multilayer Perceptron (MLP) classifier is the highest at 79.87%, followed by the Logistic Regression model at 77.08%. Surprisingly, the Random forest did not perform better than the other two even after hyperparameter tuning the parameters. The accuracy of the Random Forest model increased only by 1.18% approximately after hyper parameter tuning.

The Logistic Regression model gives the lowest specificity rate at 78.72%. The best specificity rate is given by the Random Forest (hyperparameter tuned) model at 83.52%. The specificity determines how often a given classifier will be able to correctly predict if a person does not actually have diabetes.

The Random Forest (not tuned) model gives the lowest sensitivity rate at 58.97%. The best sensitivity rate is given by the Multilayer Perceptron (MLP) classifier model at 76.59%. The sensitivity determines how often a given classifier will be able to correctly predict if a person actually has diabetes.

The Logistic Regression model gives the lowest F1 score rate at 59.74%. The best F1 score is given by the Multilayer Perceptron (MLP) classifier model at 70.58%. The F1 score establishes a balance between the precision and recall values of a model.

Figure 17. Comparison between the accuracy score for each classifier

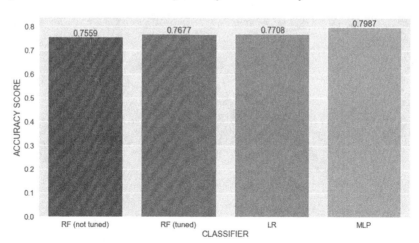

Figure 18. Comparison between the specificity for each classifier

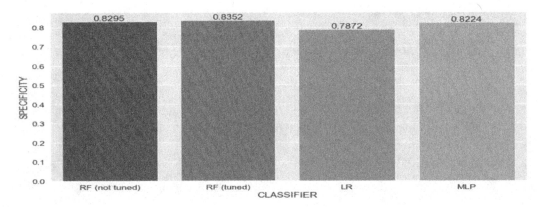

Figure 19. Comparison between the sensitivity for each classifier

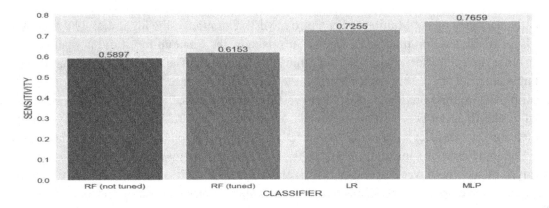

Figure 20. Comparison between the F1 score for each classifier

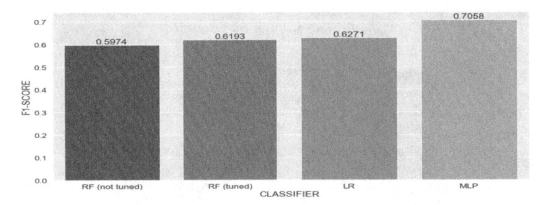

FUTURE RESEARCH DIRECTIONS

As a field of machine learning is progressing and improving day-by-day, researchers are diving into hybrid and ensemble modeling techniques. These complex hybrid and ensemble models are built by combining the traditional algorithms in a way that yields better performance metrics. Hybrid models are built in sequential blocks. The first block usually involves feature selection and is followed by blocks that contain various traditional classifiers. These classifiers can be further hyper parameter tuned. The ensemble model basically works on the concept of bagging. The prediction is made using multiple traditional algorithms and the class with the maximum number of votes is selected as the final prediction. Machine learning algorithms are giving rise to complex deep learning algorithms. Deep learning is a broader field of the machine learning family. It deals with learning data representations and pattern detection. The future neural network APIs in python libraries like PyTorch or Keras will just require a range of layers or parameters that are wanted in a customized neural network. Hyperparameter tuning by methods like Grid Search, Trial &Error, Random Search, Bayesian Optimization or Genetic Algorithm Optimization will increase the accuracy rate of these models. Batch size, epoch, activation function, number of hidden layers, units in each hidden layers, etc can result in distinct complex artificial neural networks.

Python is growing as the go-to language for data science, machine learning and is used even in big data. As the machine learning algorithms evolve, python is becoming the language of choice for most machine learning and data science professionals.

There are some limitations of the dataset taken in the chapter too which can be overcome to create an even more efficient and accurate diabetes prediction system/model. Considering the diabetes dataset taken is for women only, the complete scope of diabetes cannot be covered. Data for children, men, young and old people are not present in the PIMA diabetes dataset. There might be other risk factors that the dataset did not consider. Important factors like family history (i.e. if diabetes runs in the family), gestational diabetes, smoking; metabolic syndrome, inactive lifestyles, dietary patterns etc are not considered as attributes in the dataset. A proper model for prediction would need more data gathered from various sources to make the machine learning models more accurate. This can be attained by the collection of diabetes data from multiple sources, integrating these data and then generating a model from each dataset. The prediction model can be used as an API (Application Program Interface) for a Flask (python web framework) based web app which will give real-time prediction results of the entered data of a patient.

CONCLUSION

This chapter provides insights into various machine learning techniques used for classification. The code snippets demonstrate the use of python to build classifiers, hyper parameter tune them and visualize the data. It predicts the diabetes outcome based on other attributes. The classifiers like Logistic Regression (LR), Random Forest (RF) and Multilayer Perceptron (MLP) are used. It uses performance metrics like sensitivity, specificity, accuracy and F1 score to compare various classifiers and decide which gives the best results.

Python is one of the most suited languages to implement machine learning. It is easy and has a simple syntax to support diverse actions. Various python libraries make implementing machine learning a very easy process. The scikit-learn python library provides for almost all the major machine learning techniques and algorithms. Jupyter renders elegant graphical representations and code structures with results. Mark ups and headings provide further efficiency in presenting the work and code in a structured way. This chapter uses various python functions and libraries to implement the machine learning algorithms in order to build prediction models for the PIMA Indians Diabetes dataset.

The process of building a classifier starts with procuring data to train the model. The dataset selected for building classifiers in this chapter is the PIMA diabetes dataset. This dataset has attributes like number of pregnancies, glucose, blood pressure, skin thickness, insulin levels, the body mass index (BMI), the diabetes pedigree function and age. This dataset also has an independent or target variable namely outcome which predicts whether a person will have diabetes or not. Once the data is procured, the next step is data preprocessing. Data preprocessing includes, data cleaning, data reduction, data integration, data transformation, feature selection, dimensionality reduction, discretization and generating concept hierarchies. Data in the real world is dirty meaning it is incomplete, noisy and inconsistent. This makes data preprocessing inevitable. Low quality data is bound to produce low quality results. Thus, before building the classifier in this chapter, the data is preprocessed. It is made sure that all the attributes have the correct data types. Next, the missing values are found and replaced with some suitable values. Once the data is preprocessed, it is ready for the process of classification. Here, three classification algorithms are used, namely, Random Forest (RF), Logistic Regression (LR) and Multilayer Perceptron (MLP). Before the application of every algorithm, the dataset is divided into train and test dataset using percentage split technique for cross validation. Next, the algorithms are applied on the dataset and certain performance metrics like accuracy, F1 score, sensitivity and specificity are used to evaluate the performance of the algorithms.

The results show that the Multilayer Perceptron (MLP) performs the best with an accuracy of 79.87%, exceeding the second best performer – Logistic Regression (LR) by almost two percent. The Multilayer Perceptron (MLP) model gave the highest F1 score as well.

ACKNOWLEDGMENT

This work was supported by Vanitha M, Associate Professor, School of Information Technology and Engineering, Vellore Institute of Technology, Vellore. This research received no specific grant from any funding agency in the public, commercial, or not-for-profit sectors.

REFERENCES

Aishwarya, R., Gayathri, P., & Jaisankar, N. (2013). A Method for Classification Using Machine Learning Technique for Diabetes. *IACSIT International Journal of Engineering and Technology*, *5*(3), 2903–2908.

Dogantekin, E., Dogantekin, A., Avci, D., & Avci, L. (2010, July). An intelligent diagnosis system for diabetes on Linear Discriminant Analysis and Adaptive Network Based Fuzzy Inference System: LDA-ANFIS. *Digital Signal Processing*, *20*(4), 1248–1255. doi:10.1016/j.dsp.2009.10.021

Fatima, M., & Pasha, M. (2017). Survey of Machine Learning Algorithms for Disease Diagnostic. *Journal of Intelligent Learning Systems and Applications*, *9*(1), 1–16. doi:10.4236/jilsa.2017.91001

Gopinath, M. P., & Murali, S. (2017). Comparative study on Classification Algorithm for Diabetes Data set. *International Journal of Pure and Applied Mathematics, 117*(7), 47–52.

Hayashi, Y., & Yukita, S. (2016). Rule extraction using Recursive-Rule extraction algorithm with J48graft combined with sampling selection techniques for the diagnosis of type 2 diabetes mellitus in the Pima Indian dataset. *Informatics in Medicine Unlocked, 2*, 92–104. doi:10.1016/j.imu.2016.02.001

Kavakiotis, I., Tsave, O., Salifoglou, A., Maglaveras, N., Vlahavas, I., & Chouvarda, I. (2017). Machine Learning and Data Mining Methods in Diabetes Research. *Computational and Structural Biotechnology Journal, 15*, 104–116. doi:10.1016/j.csbj.2016.12.005 PMID:28138367

Nanthini, D., & Thangaraju, P. (2015, August). A Hybrid Classification Model For Diabetes Dataset Using Decision Tree. *International Journal of Emerging Technologies and Innovative Research, 2*(8), 3302–3308.

Patil, B. M., Joshi, R. C., & Toshniwal, D. (2010, December). Hybrid prediction model for Type-2 diabetic patients. *Expert Systems with Applications, 37*(12), 8102–8108. doi:10.1016/j.eswa.2010.05.078

Pradeep Kandhasamy, J., & Balamurali, S. (2015). Performance Analysis of Classifier Models to Predict Diabetes Mellitus. *Procedia Computer Science, 47*, 45–51. doi:10.1016/j.procs.2015.03.182

Ramezani, Maadi, & Khatami. (2018). Analysis of a Population of Diabetic Patients Databases in Weka Tool. *International Journal of Scientific and Engineering Research, 2*(5).

Saravananathan & Velmurugan. (2016). Analyzing Diabetic Data using Classification Algorithms in Data Mining. *Indian Journal of Science and Technology, 9*(43).

Sisodia, D., & Sisodia, D. S. (2018). Prediction of Diabetes using Classification Algorithms. *Procedia Computer Science, 132*, 1578–1585. doi:10.1016/j.procs.2018.05.122

Temurtas, H., Yumusak, N., & Temurtas, F. (2009, May). A comparative study on diabetes disease diagnosis using neural networks. *Systems with Applications, 36*(4), 8610–8615. doi:10.1016/j.eswa.2008.10.032

Wu, H., Yang, S., Huang, Z., He, J., & Wang, X. (2018). Type 2 diabetes mellitus prediction model based on data mining. *Informatics in Medicine Unlocked, 10*, 100–107. doi:10.1016/j.imu.2017.12.006

Yasodha & Kannan. (2011). A novel hybrid intelligent system with missing value imputation for diabetes diagnosis. *Alexandria Engineering Journal, 57*(3).

ADDITIONAL READING

Dey, A. (2016). Machine Learning Algorithms: A Review. *International Journal of Computer Science and Information Technologies, 7*(3), 1174–1179.

Pedregosa, F., Varoquaux, G., Gramfort, A., & Michel, V. (2011). Scikit-learn: Machine Learning in Python. *Journal of Machine Learning Research*.

Simon, A., Deo, M. S., Selvam, V., & Babu, R. (2015). An Overview of Machine Learning and its Applications. *International Journal of Electrical Sciences and Engineering*, *1*(1), 22–24.

Van der Walt, S., Colbert, S. C., & Varoquaux, G. (2011). The NumPy array:a structure for efficient numerical computation. *Computing in Science & Engineering*, *11*, 2011.

Zito, T., Wilbert, N., Wiskott, L., & Berkes, P. (2008). Modular toolkit for Data Processing (MDP*): A Python data processing framework. Frontiers in Neuroinformatics*, *2*, 2008. doi:10.3389/neuro.11.008.2008 PMID:19169361

KEY TERMS AND DEFINITIONS

Accuracy: It is a metric used to predict the correctness of a machine learning model. The model is trained using the train data and a classifier is built. The test data is used to cross validate the classifier model. The percentage of correctly classified instances is termed as accuracy.

Area Under the Curve (AUC) Score: Area under the curve (AUC) is a binary classification metric. It considers all the possible thresholds. Different threshold values result in distinct true positive/false positive rates. As the threshold is decreased, more true positives (but also more false positives) instances are discovered.

F1 Score: F1 score is a combination function of precision and recall. It is used when we need to seek a balance between precision and recall.

Hyper-Parameter Tuning: The model architecture is defined by several parameters. These parameters are referred to as hyper parameters. The process of searching for an ideal model architecture for optimal accuracy score is referred to as hyper parameter tuning.

Logistic Regression: Logistic regression is a classification algorithm that comes under supervised learning and is used for predictive learning. Logistic regression is used to describe data. It works best for dichotomous (binary) classification.

Multilayer Perceptron: Multilayer perceptron falls under artificial neural networks (ANN). It is a feed forward network that consists of a minimum of three layers of nodes- an input layer, one or more hidden layers and an output layer. It uses a supervised learning technique, namely, back propagation for training. Its main advantage is that it has the ability to distinguish data that is not linearly separable.

Random Forest: Random forest is a supervised learning algorithm and is used for classification and regression. It is an ensemble learning method that operates by constructing multiple decision trees and merges them together to obtain an accurate and stable prediction. Generally, it produces great results even without hyper parameter tuning.

Recall: Recall is the ratio of true positives to the sum of true positives and false negatives.

Sensitivity/Precision: It is the ratio of true positives to the sum of the true positive and false negative.

Specificity: It is the ratio of true negatives to the sum of the true negatives and false positives.

Supervised Learning: Machine learning is broadly classified into two: supervised learning and unsupervised learning. In supervised learning, the machine learns from examples. Historical or train data is needed which is given as an input to the machine and a classifier model is formed. A supervised algorithm also needs a target value. On the contrary, unsupervised learning algorithms need neither the train data nor the target value.

Chapter 9
Medical Reports Analysis Using Natural Language Processing for Disease Classification

Sumathi S.
St. Joseph's College of Engineering, India

Indumathi S.
Jerusalem College of Engineering, India

Rajkumar S.
HCL Technologies Ltd., India

ABSTRACT

Text classification in medical domain could result in an easier way of handling large volumes of medical data. They can be segregated depending on the type of diseases, which can be determined by extracting the decisive key texts from the original document. Due to various nuances present in understanding language in general, a requirement of large volumes of text-based data is required for algorithms to learn patterns properly. The problem with existing systems such as MedScape, MedLinePlus, Wrappin, and MedHunt is that they involve human interaction and high time consumption in handling a large volume of data. By employing automation in this proposed field, the large involvement of manpower could be removed which in turn speeds up the process of classification of the medical documents by which the shortage of medical technicians in third world countries are addressed.

INTRODUCTION

Text classification refers to the activity of classifying Natural Language texts from the predefined set of available categories. In a basic way of defining Text classification, it can be defined as the process of finding out generic tags from a document which is a collection of huge number of words. Classification of the document into generic tags enables the users of the application or product to easily access the desired information within the application without facing any kind of problems or troubles. Without the

DOI: 10.4018/978-1-5225-9902-9.ch009

usage of these classified tags, it is a tedious activity for the users to navigate through loads of information to locate the required document. Text classification in medical domain could result in an easier way of handling large volumes of medical data. They can be segregated depending on the type of diseases, which can be determined by extracting the decisive key texts from the original document. This classification has the potential to assist both the end-users and the experts involved in the medical domain and hence could improve the efficiency of document classification significantly.

Text classification has been proposed for a long time now and its introduction could ease out things for both users and professionals involved in the application. However due to various nuances present in understanding language in general, a requirement of large volumes of text-based data is required for algorithms to learn patterns properly. So, text classification can be employed whenever there are several classification tags to enable the mapping of large volume of textual data.

The introduction of Text classification in Healthcare could turn out to be productive if they are implemented carefully. One of the major sources for data related to healthcare is the Internet. The number of pages available in the Internet is significantly growing every year which in turn increases the amount of data related to health. Medical information has attracted a wide range of audience since its introduction in the electronic form. Health related information is now widely available for use to the public. They are being provided by several health organizations, medical universities and government institutions in a validated form which can be readily used by the public users.

The users of the medical domain can either be end-users or the professionals involved in medicine. The end-users navigate through the medical documents when they have to search for the desired information related to a particular disease. On the other hand, professional experts require Text classification to ease their hectic processes of locating the documents which may be required during case studies of similar diseases.

One of the popularly used medical database is Medline (Medical Literature Analysis and Retrieval System Online), which constitutes the primary medical repository of the U.S. National Library of Medicine (NLM), including approximately 20 million computer readable records. The above-mentioned data is drastically increasing and is forecasted to gain several more millions in upcoming years. It consists of a rich source of medical and biological information which requires an efficient method of mining to produce useful insights.

Since databases like Medline is used by both layman users and professional experts, classification has to be carried out to satisfy both types of users. The professional experts are well versed with the medical terminologies and tend to use those texts for searching information in the web. But the end-users are generally not aware of the complex medical terms and most often surf the internet using Natural Language terms. The existing systems such as MedScape, MedLinePlus, Wrappin and MedHunt (maintained by HON, the Health on Net Foundation, and a non-profit organization) provide the service of answering queries raised by both classifications of users. But, the problem with the above-mentioned systems is that they involve human interaction.

Initially we require professionals and domain experts to sort the documents manually without which the services cannot run properly. These systems are highly dependent on those experts to carry out the manual classification which has a potential threat of high time consumption. Hence these systems fail when there are large volumes of documents as it becomes impossible to manually classify every single document in a short span of time.

PubMed of NLM can be used for the proposed purpose as it helps to access the Medline document abstracts and also to articles in selected life sciences journals not included in MedLine, for free. Once a free access to these documents is made, they can be used to carry out automation in classification of those documents. By employing automation in this proposed field, the large involvement of manpower could be removed which in turn speeds up the process of classification of the medical documents.

Hence, the implementation of the proposed system could prove to be decisive in the field of Medicine and could enhance the existing efficiency of classification by removing the human interaction. The final resultant of the system helps both the layman users and professional experts to locate their desired documents with ease and hence the scope of the proposed system is much wider in practice.

Despite many innovations in classification algorithms, there is one defining issue with textual data. Textual data cannot be used as such in many text classification algorithms as all of them require text to be encoded in some form so that every word or document is represented as a vector of numbers. Word embedding models such as bag-of-words, Word2Vec, GloVe, etc. have been useful in capturing various meanings from words into simple vectors, yet active research is being done to better represent textual data. Recent strides in Deep Learning have led us to represent words and documents based on their contexts and when done with large corpora of text, these models will be able to provide word representations that can generalize well with other datasets as well. Prior to performing word embedding, it is a good idea use pre-processing steps such as stemming, lemmatizing, tagging, etc . to improve the output of our word embedding models.

After embedding this text, we can conveniently start building knowledge graphs or use classification algorithms. Few years ago, we were using Machine Learning Algorithms such as Support Vector Machines, Naïve Bayes, etc. to classify text, especially for sentiment analysis. Yet, the NLP landscape did remain stagnant for a long time due to the nuances involved with textual data. After the ImageNet challenge in 2012, when Deep Learning took its pace and algorithms such as RNNs, LSTMs, etc started analyzing patterns from large corpora of texts. Advances in Machine Comprehension (A subset in Natural Language Processing) largely remained stagnant until the re-introduction of Deep Learning and Bidirectional Transformers are now considered state of the art for Machine Comprehension.

Despite huge strides with new algorithms and techniques, practical applications of these methods in the field of medicine are quite stranded due to the lack of structured information for generalized models. By collection of large amounts of medical documents with relevant information about multiple diseases and using recently developed techniques, we can build intelligent systems that can match diseases with various kinds of medical documents which can address the shortage of medical technicians in third world countries.

MAIN FOCUS OF THIS CHAPTER

In recent years, a considerable amount of text processing approaches are proposed and implemented by the researchers to examine the medical document datasets. The recent works on medical document classification is done by using neural networks. The procedures involved in classification along with many classifiers are explained in this chapter.

Text Preprocessing

Text pre-processing is changing of text from text from human language to machine-readable format for further processing (Meystre & Haug, 206).

After a text is obtained, normalization of text is started. It covers

- Converting all letters to lower or upper case
- Converting numbers into words or removing numbers
- Removing punctuations, accent marks and other diacritics
- Removing white spaces
- Expanding abbreviations
- Removing stop words, sparse terms, and particular words
- Text canonicalization

It also includes steps such as normalization, tokenization, stemming, lemmatization, chunking, part of speech tagging, named-entity recognition, Coreference resolution, collocation extraction, and relationship extraction.

1. **Convert text to lowercase:** The text document is converted from uppercase to lowercase
2. **Remove numbers:** Regular Expression is used to remove numbers if they are not relevant to the analyses.
3. **Remove punctuation:** Set of symbols such as [!"#$%&'()*+,-./:;<=>?@[\]^_`{|}~] are removed
4. **Remove whitespaces:** Using Strip function leading and ending spaces are removed
5. **Tokenization:** Tokenization is the method of ripping the given text into smaller items known as tokens. Words, numbers, punctuation marks, et al. may be thought-about as tokens. NLTK may be a tokenization tool used.
6. Remove stop words

The words which don't carry necessary meaning and are sometimes faraway from texts are called Stop words that are removed using natural language Toolkit (NLTK). "Stop words" are the foremost common words in an exceedingly language like "the", "a", "on", "is", "all". NLTK is a collection of libraries and programs for symbolic and statistical natural language process.

7. Remove sparse terms and particular words

Sparse terms or explicit words from texts should be removed. This task may be done using stop words removal techniques considering that any cluster of words may be chosen as the stop words.

8. Stemming

Stemming could be a method of reducing words to their word stem, base or root type (for example, books — book, looked — look). The two algorithms are Porter stemmer (removes common morphological and inflexional endings from words and Lancaster stemmer (a lot of aggressive stemming algorithm)

9. Lemmatization

The aim of lemmatization, like stemming, is to scale back inflectional types to a typical base form. As hostile stemming, lemmatization doesn't merely chop off inflections. Instead it uses lexical data bases to urge the proper base types of words.

Some Lemmatization tools are NLTK (WordNet Lemmatizer), spaCy, TextBlob, Pattern, gensim, Stanford CoreNLP, Memory-Based Shallow Parser (MBSP), Apache OpenNLP, Apache Lucene, General Architecture for Text Engineering (GATE), Illinois Lemmatizer, and DKPro Core.

10. Part of speech tagging (POS)

Part-of-speech tagging assign elements of speech to every word of a given text (such as nouns, verbs, adjectives, and others) supported its definition and its context. There are several tools containing POS taggers as well as NLTK, spaCy, TextBlob, Pattern, Stanford CoreNLP, Memory-Based Shallow programme (MBSP), Apache OpenNLP, Apache Lucene, General architecture for Text Engineering

11. Chunking (shallow parsing)

Chunking could be a tongue method that identifies constituent elements of sentences (nouns, verbs, adjectives, etc.) and links them to higher order units that have distinct grammatical meanings (noun teams or phrases, verb teams, etc.) chunking tools are NLTK, TreeTagger chunker, Apache OpenNLP, General architecture for Text Engineering (GATE), FreeLing.

12. Named entity recognition

Named-entity recognition (NER) aims to classify the named entities into pre-defined classes (names of persons, locations, organizations, times, etc.). Named-entity recognition tools are NLTK, spaCy, General architecture for Text Engineering (GATE) — ANNIE, Apache OpenNLP, Stanford CoreNLP, DKPro Core, MITIE, Watson natural language Understanding, TextRazor

13. Coreference resolution (anaphora resolution)

Pronouns and different referring expressions ought to be connected to the proper people. Coreference resolution finds the mentions during a text that see the same real-world entity. For instance, within the sentence, "Andrew aforementioned he would get a car" the pronoun "he" refers to the same person, specifically to "Andrew". Coreference resolution tools ar Stanford CoreNLP, spaCy, Open port, Apache OpenNLP.

14. Collocation extraction

Collocations are word combos occurring along a lot of typically than would be expected inadvertently. Collocation examples are "break the foundations," "free time," "draw a conclusion," "keeps in mind," "get prepared," and then on.

15. Relationship extraction

Relationship extraction permits getting structured info from unstructured sources like raw text. Strictly expressed, it's distinctive relations (e.g., acquisition, spouse, employment) among named entities (e.g., people, organizations, locations). As an example, from the sentence "Mark and Emily married yesterday," we are able to extract the data that Mark is Emily's husband.

After the text pre-processing is done, the result may be used for more complicated NLP tasks, for example, machine translation or natural language generation.

AUTOMATIC DOCUMENT CLASSIFICATION

For automatic document classification Machine learning (ML), is divided into Supervised machine learning and Unsupervised machine learning.

Supervised machine learning is one where classifications are carried out based on pre-determined categorical classes or labels. Examples of supervised ML methods include:

Decision Tree Classifiers

Random Forest

Multiple decision trees are built and are merged together to obtain accurate and stable predictions (Parlak & Uysal, 2015). One amazing feature about Random Forests is that despite being able to fit complex models, it is quick and performs really good even in CPUs. From indiscriminately selected set of training set Random forest classifier creates a collection of decision trees. It then aggregates the votes from completely different decision trees to choose the ultimate class of the test object.

In Laymen's term, Suppose training set is given as: [X1, X2, X3, X4] with corresponding labels as [L1, L2, L3, L4], random forest may create three decision trees taking input of subset for example,

[X1, X2, X3]
[X1, X2, X4]
[X2, X3, X4]

So finally, it predicts based on the majority of votes from each of the decision trees made.

Figure 1 shows the visual representation of the random forest and how they are classified

Gradient Boosted Trees (XGBoost)

This technique employs the logic in which the subsequent predictors learn from the mistakes of the previous predictors (Chen & Guestrin, 2016). Therefore, the observations have an unequal likelihood of showing in subsequent models and ones with the very best error seem most. (So the observations don't seem to be chosen supported the bootstrap method, however supported the error).

Figure 1. Visual representation of random forests

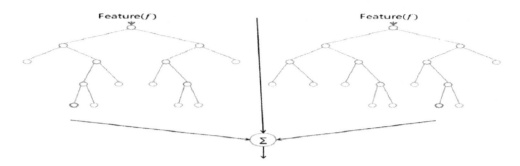

Rather than stochastic gradient descent, Gradient boosting solves a distinct problem. When optimizing a model using SGD, the architecture of the model is fastened. In Gradient Boost the parameters P of the model (in logistic regression, this might be the weights) are optimized. Mathematically, this would look like this as in Equation 1:

$$F(x|P) = \frac{\min}{P} Loss\Big(y, F(x|P)\Big) \tag{1}$$

Gradient boosting doesn't assume this fixed architecture. In fact, the complete purpose of gradient boosting is to search out the function that best approximates the information. It would be expressed like this as in Equation 2:

$$F(x|P) = \frac{\min}{F,P} Loss\Big(y, F(x|P)\Big) \tag{2}$$

The simple changes done are in addition to finding the best parameters P, to find the best function F. SGD trains a single complex model, gradient boosting trains an ensemble of simple models.

Gradient boosting is a method for optimizing the function F, but however it doesn't extremely care concerning h (since nothing concerning the improvement of h is defined). This implies that any base models h are often accustomed construct F.

Linear Classifiers

Logistic Regression

Logistic Regression is a powerful machine learning model based on the McCulloh Pitts Perceptron model (Hosner, Lemeshow & Sturdivant, 2013). Instead of using a threshold function as its activation, logistic regression uses the sigmoid activation function as in Figure 2 to obtain a smooth curve. This smoothness is what makes learning possible using simple gradient based mechanisms. Logistic Regression develops a probability space that we can use to map the test data.

Figure 2. Sigmoid Function

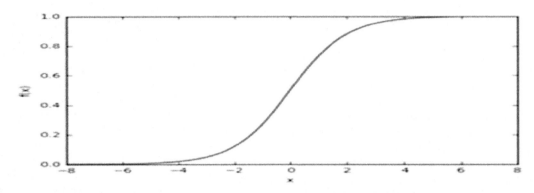

There are many types of Logistic Regression such as

1. **Binary Logistic Regression:** The categorical response has only two 2 possible outcomes. Example: Spam or Not
2. **Multinomial Logistic Regression:** Three or more categories without ordering. Example: Predicting which food is preferred more (Veg, Non-Veg, Vegan)
3. **Ordinal Logistic Regression:** Three or more categories with ordering. Example: Movie rating from 1 to 5

The Cost Function for Logistic Regression is as in equation 3.

$$\text{Cost}(h\Theta(x), Y(\text{actual})) = \begin{aligned} &-\log\big(h\Theta(x)\big) \ \text{if} \quad y = 1 \\ &-\log\big(1 - h\Theta(x)\big) \ \text{if} \quad y = 0 \end{aligned} \tag{3}$$

Linear regression uses mean squared error as its cost function. If this is used for logistic regression, then it will be a non-convex function of parameters (theta). Gradient descent will converge into global minimum only if the function is convex as shown in Figure 3.

Support Vector Machines (SVM)

Support vector machine is quite similar to Logistic Regression but differs with a varying cost function that requires a margin of at least one (Joachims, 1998). It was quite popular and when combined with Kernel functions, they can easily map data with large dimensions. It was quite popular in the 90s and the 2000s among statisticians. One huge advantage about SVMs is that it can be tuned to be robust enough even in the presence of outliers.

The learning of the hyper plane in linear SVM is done by transforming the problem using some linear algebra. This is where the kernel plays role.

Figure 3. Representation of convex and non-convex function

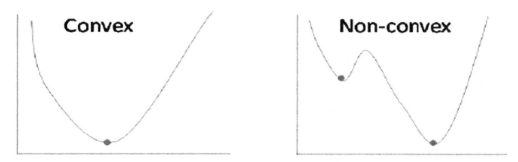

For linear kernel the equation for prediction for a new input using the dot product between the input (x) and each support vector (xi) is calculated as in equation 4:

$$f(x) = B(0) + sum(ai * (x,xi)) \tag{4}$$

This is an equation that involves calculating the inner products of a new input vector (x) with all support vectors in training data. The coefficients B0 and ai (for each input) must be estimated from the training data by the learning algorithm.

The polynomial kernel can be written as $K(x,xi) = 1 + sum(x * xi)^d$ and exponential as $K(x,xi) = exp(-gamma * sum((x—xi^2))$.

Figure 4 represents how does a hyper plane separated the data with maximum margin. Here it shows how the two groups are separated by means of hyper plane.

Neural Networks

Neural Networks are one of the most advanced robust available in the industry. They can fit almost curve for any kind of data. Neural Networks are however computationally heavy and require the usage of distributed systems and GPUs when being deployed in real time systems. They are basically a stack of multiple perceptron nodes having different activation functions. Deep neural networks have made huge strides in the industry, providing excellent results in cognitive tasks such as computer vision and Natural Language Processing.

Figure 4. Representation of hyper plane in SVM

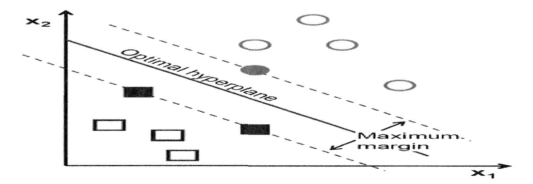

Figure 5. Schematic representation of neurons

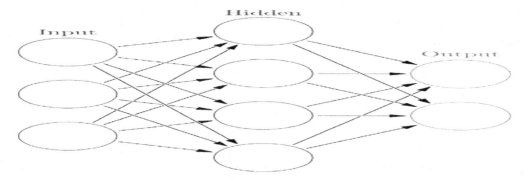

Figure 5 shows the schematic representation of neurons and their connections between them

Probabilistic Classifiers

Naïve Bayes

Naive Bayes is a simple, yet effective and commonly-used, machine learning classifier (Chen et al., 2009). It is a probabilistic classifier that makes classifications using the Maximum Posteriori decision rule in a Bayesian setting. It can also be represented using a very simple Bayesian network. Naive Bayes classifiers have been especially popular for text classification, and are a traditional solution for problems such as spam detection.

It is a classification technique supported Bayes' Theorem with a conjecture of independence among predictors. In clear-cut terms, a Naive Bayes classifier assumes that the presence of a specific feature in a very class is not related to the presence of the other feature. As an example, a fruit is also thought of to be an apple if it's red, round, and concerning three inches in diameter. Even if these options rely upon one another or upon the existence of the other options, all of those properties independently supply to the probability that this fruit is an apple which is why it's referred to as 'Naive'.

Naive Bayes model is simple to build and particularly helpful for very large data sets. Along with simplicity, Naive Bayes is known to top even greatly sophisticated classification methods.

Bayes theorem provides a way of calculating posterior probability P(c|x) from P(c), P(x) and P(x|c) as:

Likelihood   Class Prior Probability

$$P(c \mid x) = \frac{P(x \mid c)P(c)}{P(x)}$$

Posterior Probability   Predictor Prior Probability

$$P(c \mid X) = P(x_1 \mid c) \times P(x_2 \mid c) \times \cdots \times P(x_n \mid c) \times P(c)$$

Above,

- P(c|x) is the posterior probability of class (c, target) given predictor (x, attributes).
- P(c) is the prior probability of class.
- P(x|c) is the likelihood which is the probability of predictor given class.
- P(x) is the prior probability of predictor.

Bayesian Network

Bayesian Networks is kind of a Probabilistic Graphical Model that uses Conditional Probabilities and Bayesian Statistics to identify the probability of an event (Ikonomakis, Kotsiantis & Tampakas, 2005). Bayesian Networks can be quite powerful when we have enough prior and posterior probabilities along with enough number of states. Bayesian networks aim to model conditional dependence, and therefore causation, by representing conditional dependence by edges in a directed graph as in Figure 6.

Non-Parametric Classifiers

K-Nearest Neighbour Classifiers (k-NN): 2-NN...5-NN

K-Nearest Neighbour Classifier is a very simple algorithm that uses the Euclidean Distance to classify our data points (Cunningham & Delaney, 2007). It a non-parametric algorithm that compares our new data points with all of our existing points and use the nearest points to perform classification. It suffers from the curse of dimensionality and hence it isn't efficient when dealing with data of large dimensions.

Figure 7 shows the Representation of K-Nearest Neighbour Classifier with different values of K such as 5 and 9. The model shown in the figure is with 2 selected features.

Unsupervised machine learning (ML), where classifications are carried without pre-determined classes / category (labels) (Lloyd, Mohdeni & Rebentrist, 2013). Examples of unsupervised methods include:

Figure 6. Representation of graphs in Bayesian networks

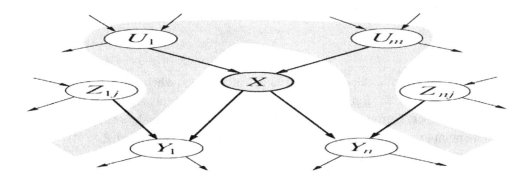

Figure 7. Representation of K-nearest neighbour classifier

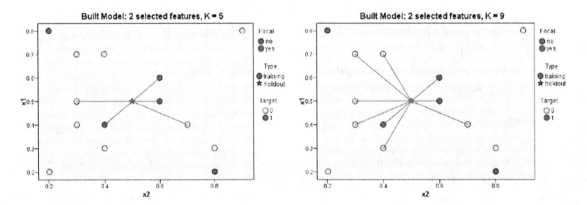

Dimensionality Reduction Techniques

Principal Component Analysis (PCA)

PCA is a simple technique that uses SVD (Singular Value Decomposition) as a means to reduce the dimensions of our given data. Using the output from SVD, we can identify the features that are highly correlated, which can be removed as they don't contribute much to the output. PCA is mostly used nowadays for data visualization purposes. PCA can also be used to prevent over fitting.

Principal component analysis (PCA) may be a method that uses an orthogonal transformation to convert a group of observations of presumably related to variables (entities every of that takes on varied numerical values) into a group of values of linearly unrelated variables referred to as principal elements (Abdi & Williams, 2010). If there are n observations with p variables, then the amount of distinct principal components is min (n-1, p) This transformation is outlined in such the simplest way that the primary principal components has the most important attainable variance (that is, accounts for the maximum amount of the variability within the information as possible), and every succeeding element successively has the best variance attainable underneath the constraint that it's orthogonal to the preceding elements. The ensuing vectors (each being a linear combination of the variables and containing n observations) are an unrelated orthogonal basis set. PCA is sensitive to the relative scaling of the first variables.

K-Means

K-Means clustering is a type of unsupervised learning, which is used when you have unlabeled data (i.e., data without defined categories or groups) (Jain, 2010). The goal of this algorithm is to find groups in the data, with the number of groups represented by the variable *K*. The algorithm works iteratively to assign each data point to one of *K* groups based on the features that are provided.

First group of randomly selected centroids are used as the beginning points for every cluster in K-Means. It then performs iterative (repetitive) calculations to optimize the positions of the centroids. It halts creating and optimizing clusters when both the centroids have stabilizedand there is no change in their values and thus the clustering has been successful and the defined numbers of iterations have been achieved. The Figure 8 shows the original unclustered data and clustered data which have been formed by K-Means Clustering

Figure 8. Representation of clusters in K-means clustering

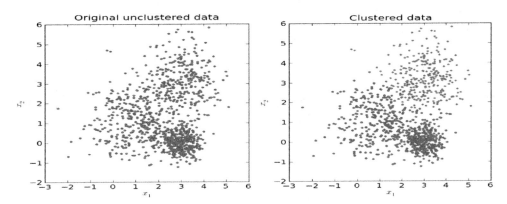

Convolutional Neural Network (CNN)

A Convolutional Neural Network (ConvNet/CNN) may be a Deep Learning algorithmic rule which might soak up an input image, assign importance (learnable weights and biases) to varied aspects/objects within the image and be able to differentiate one from the opposite (Kim, 2014). The pre-processing needed in a ConvNet is much lower as compared to alternative classification algorithms whereas in primitive strategies filters are hand-engineered, with enough training, ConvNets have the power to find out these filters/characteristics.

The Figure 9 shows the steps involved in Convolutional Neural Network. The inputs are feed through the convolution and relu activation is used and in next stage pooling is done and like this process goes on and afterwards it is flattened and given to softmax activation to classify the documents.

Recurrent Long Short-Term Memory (LSTM) Network

LSTMs are a type of Recurrent Neural Network which is modelled based on the Long Short Term Memory of the brain (Tang, Qin & Liu, 2015). As opposed to feed forward networks, the outputs of certain layers are fed to previous and same layers. LSTMs are used frequently for time series datasets. A

Figure 9. Steps involved in CNN

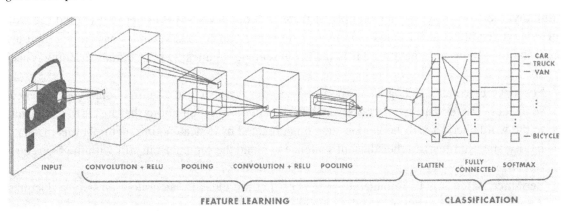

Figure 10. Schematic representation of RNN

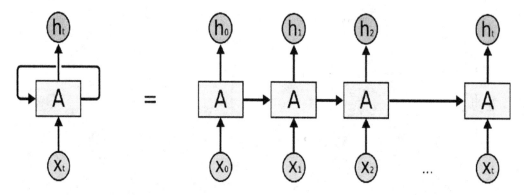

special kind of back propagation called back prop through time, which can capture the error that occur due to time series issue. RNN is a sequence of neural network blocks that are linked to each other's like a chain. Each one is passing a message to a successor.

The Figure 10 shows the Schematic representation of RNN. It gives the better understanding of RNN.

The hierarchical ATTENTION Network(HAN)

The hierarchical Attention Network(HAN) consists of several parts such as

1.   A word sequence encoder
2.   A word-level attention layer
3.   A sentence encoder
4.   A sentence-level attention layer

The above Figure 11 is used to understand the notations used in the following content.

1.   **Word Encoder**: A bifacial GRU is employed to urge annotations of words by summarising data from each directions for words and thereby incorporating the contextual data.
2.   **Word Attention**: Since all words doesn't contribute equally to a sentence's. An attention mechanism is employed to extract such words that are vital to the meaning of the sentence and combination.

Initially, the word is fed for annotation hit through a one-layer MLP to get unit (called the word-level context vector) as a concealed representation for hit. The context vector is basically a high-level representation of how edifying a word is in the given sentence and learned through the training process.

3.   **Sentence Encoder**: Analogous to the word encoder, here we use a bidirectional GRU to encode sentences. The forward and the backward hidden states are computations that are carried out similar to the word encoder and the hidden state h is obtained by concatenating them. At this instant the hidden state summarises the adjacent sentences around the sentence but still with the focus on the sentence.
4.   **Sentence Attention:**To remunerate sentences that are clues to accurately classify a document, Attention mechanism are paid at the sentence level.

Figure 11. Steps of HAN

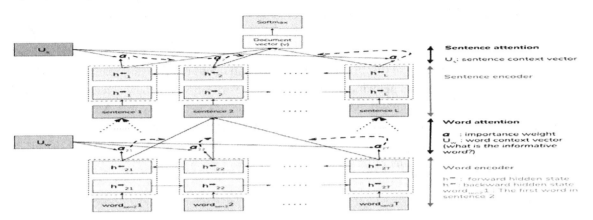

COMPARISON OF DIFFERENT CLASSIFIERS USING ML

Figures 12 below, shows some visualization from using ML classifiers with IRIS dataset in Python.

Classification of Medical Documents

For classification of medical documents along with Word2Vec a model of CNN with Word2Vec is proposed.

Word2Vec Word Embedding

Word2vec might be a two-layer neural net that processes text to line of feature vectors (words in corpus). While Word2vec isn't a deep neural network, it turns text into a numerical kind that deep nets will perceive. The aim and quality of Word2vec is to group the vectors of comparable words along in vector house. That is, it identifies similarities mathematically. Word2vec creates vectors that are dispersed numerical representations of word options like the context of individual words. It will perform without human intervention.

Figure 12. Visualization from using ML classifiers

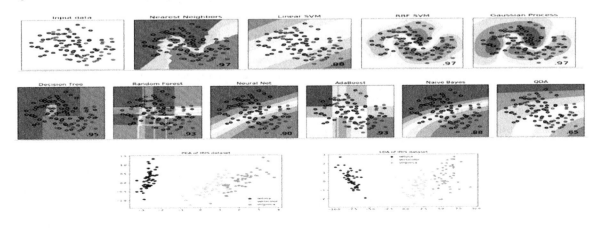

Exceedingly correct guess about a word's meaning based on past appearances will be done with enough information and its usage and contexts are given to Word2vec. With the support of the guesses word's association with dissimilar words, cluster of documents and classification can also be done (e.g. "man" is to "boy" what "woman" is to "girl"). Once cluster formation of documents it will be utilized in diverse fields like research, legal discovery, E-commerce and client relationship management. After the output of the Word2vec neural net which is a vector to the words in vocabulary is fed to deep neural network, a straightforward question will be used to ascertain the link between words. Measuring cosine similarity, the system is claimed to be completely overlap once the angle is zero and no similarity once ninety degree angle; i.e. Sweden equals Sweden, whereas Norway has a cosine distance of 0.760124 from Sweden, the uppermost of any other country.

CNN With Word2Vec

Sentence level classifier is trained with huge corpus of text and a smaller corpus of pre-categorized text. Two datasets are utilised from medical domain. Domain specific Word2vec algorithm's done by training domain specific Word2vec models to advance the performance. Thus, dataset from PubMed (online medical publication repository and contains published medical research across a very wide spectrum of clinical subjects. https://www.ncbi.nlm.nih.gov/pubmed) is used for training our Word2vec models. To coach our Word2vec models, 15k clinical research papers representing a extensive range of medical subjects are used.

For sentence level classification, it was essential to gather training data that had been pre-classified by medical professionals. Merck Manual dataset (Merck Manual is an online and offline resource containing encyclopaedic style articles describing a wide range of medical subjects (http://www.merckmanuals.com/)) contains articles from a range of topics like Brain, Cancer, etc. Each of these articles is classified under apparent header indicating a specific category of medical issues and conditions. In sum the dataset consisted of 26 medical categories and 4000 sentences that were selected at random for each category extracted from the Merck articles to use as the training data and to guarantee balance across all categories. The validation dataset consisted of 1000 sentences from each of the categories.

CNN-based approaches are applied to mechanically learn and classify sentences in toone of the 26 categories in the evaluation dataset. Using Convolutional Neural Networks each sentence is changed to a word level matrix where each row in the matrix is a sentence vector extracted from the Word2vec model. CNNs necessitate input to have astatic size and sentence lengths can vary greatly. Therefore, max word length is selected. During the training phase, a Word2vec hidden layer size of 100 is applied, hence giving the input feature a resolution of 100×50.

If a sentence enclosed less than 50 tokens, a special stop word was repeatedly appended to the end of the sentence to meet the 50-word requirement. If a sentence enclosed over50 words, only the first 50 were considered to be representative of that sentence therefore giving better output.

The accuracy is more in CNN with Word2Vec when compared to CNN models without Word2Vec.

Comparison of the model for two types of dataset is given in table 1 and from this it is very clear that CNN with word2Vec is better when compared to CNN for text classification.

Table 1. Comparison of the model

Dataset	Algorithm	Time/Epoch	Training Accuracy	Validation Accuracy
PubMed Dataset	CNN	170 Sec	95.76	95.23
	CNN with Word2Vec	48 sec	96.12	94.13
Merck Manual dataset	CNN	1800 sec	82.63	81.11
	CNN with Word2Vec	360 sec	87.88	83.76

CONCLUSION

In this chapter an entirely unique approach is proposed for sentence-level classification of medical documents. At this juncture it's shown the usage of CNNs in illustration of semantics of clinical text enabled semantic classification at sentence level. A lot of best options are produced during training phase in multi-layer convolutional deep networks when compared with superficial learning strategies. Every time semantic representations at sentence level are learned they'll be used for different tasks like text comparison and retrieval tasks as in computer vision. These approaches will be scaled to a paragraph or even document level with slight changes. In future, this system will be imposed at a bigger datasets with a lot of fine-grained set of clinical classifications with superior results like CNN for computer vision. Amid the medical domain, this hypothesis will be tested with a much bigger assortment of information collated from PubMed, relevant topics in Wikipedia, as well as medical books and journals. Furthermore, we intend to come up with a high level illustration of semantics of each patient with the illustration of feature generated from a patient's clinical notes. With the support of this for a patient, dense and enormously discriminative feature vector regarding medical conditions and coverings will be generated from their unstructured clinical notes pooled with structured knowledge.

REFERENCES

Abdi, H., & Williams, L. J. (2010). Principal component analysis. *Wiley Interdisciplinary Reviews: Computational Statistics, 2*(4), 433–459. doi:10.1002/wics.101

Chen, J., Huang, H., Tian, S., & Qu, Y. (2009). Feature selection for text classification with Naïve Bayes. *Expert Systems with Applications, 36*(3), 5432–5435. doi:10.1016/j.eswa.2008.06.054

Chen, T., & Guestrin, C. (2016, August). Xgboost: A scalable tree boosting system. In Proceedings of the 22nd *ACM SIGKDD* international conference on knowledge discovery and data mining (pp. 785-794). ACM.

Cunningham, P., & Delany, S. J. (2007). K-Nearest neighbour classifiers. *Multiple Classifier Systems, 34*(8), 1–17.

Hosmer, D. W., Jr., Lemeshow, S., & Sturdivant, R. X. (2013). *Applied logistic regression* (Vol. 398). John Wiley & Sons. doi:10.1109/SIU.2015.7130164

Ikonomakis, M. (2005). Sotiris Kotsiantis, and V. Tampakas. "Text classification using machine learning techniques. *WSEAS Transactions on Computers*, *4*(8), 966–974.

Jain, A. K. (2010). Data clustering: 50 years beyond K-means. *Pattern Recognition Letters*, *31*(8), 651–666. doi:10.1016/j.patrec.2009.09.011

Joachims, T. (1998, April). Text categorization with support vector machines: Learning with many relevant features. In *European conference on machine learning* (pp. 137-142). Springer. 10.1007/BFb0026683

Kim, Y. (2014). *Convolutional neural networks for sentence classification.* arXiv preprint arXiv:1408.5882

Lloyd, S., Mohseni, M., & Rebentrost, P. (2013). *Quantum algorithms for supervised and unsupervised machine learning.* arXiv preprint arXiv:1307.0411

Meystre, S., & Haug, P. J. (2006). Natural language processing to extract medical problems from electronic clinical documents: Performance evaluation. *Journal of Biomedical Informatics*, *39*(6), 589–599. doi:10.1016/j.jbi.2005.11.004 PMID:16359928

Parlak, B., & Uysal, A. K. (2015, May). Classification of medical documents according to diseases. In *2015 23nd Signal Processing and Communications Applications Conference (SIU)* (pp. 1635-1638). IEEE.

Tang, D., Qin, B., & Liu, T. (2015). Document modelling with gated recurrent neural network for sentiment classification. In *Proceedings of the 2015 conference on empirical methods in natural language processing* (pp. 1422-1432). Academic Press. 10.18653/v1/D15-1167

Chapter 10
Optimization of Evolutionary Algorithm Using Machine Learning Techniques for Pattern Mining in Transactional Database

Logeswaran K.
Kongu Engineering College, India

Suresh P.
Kongu Engineering College, India

Savitha S.
K. S. R. College of Engineering, India

Prasanna Kumar K. R.
Kongu Engineering College, India

ABSTRACT

In recent years, the data analysts are facing many challenges in high utility itemset (HUI) mining from given transactional database using existing traditional techniques. The challenges in utility mining algorithms are exponentially growing search space and the minimum utility threshold appropriate to the given database. To overcome these challenges, evolutionary algorithm-based techniques can be used to mine the HUI from transactional database. However, testing each of the supporting functions in the optimization problem is very inefficient and it increases the time complexity of the algorithm. To overcome this drawback, reinforcement learning-based approach is proposed for improving the efficiency of the algorithm, and the most appropriate fitness function for evaluation can be selected automatically during execution of an algorithm. Furthermore, during the optimization process when distinct functions are skillful, dynamic selection of current optimal function is done.

DOI: 10.4018/978-1-5225-9902-9.ch010

INTRODUCTION

There has been an explosive growth in the volume of data because of ease of storage, data collection and more computerization in various industries such as business, science and e-commerce. These huge volumes of data will not give enough knowledge. This entices to the method of automated analysis of such massive data to gather meaningful knowledge and the process is called data mining or knowledge discovery in database. Data mining can be construed as a non-trivial process of extracting interesting previously unknown and potentially useful patterns or knowledge from the huge amount of data. Data mining is a confluence of multiple disciplines such as database technologies, machine learning, pattern recognition, statistics, visualization, and other disciplines. Different types of knowledge can be obtained as an output from the data mining process which includes multidimensional concept description, pattern mining, classification, and prediction.

Sequential Pattern mining is a type of pattern mining used to determine the relationships between occurrences of frequently occurring ordered events or subsequences of patterns. Association rule mining is one of the methodologies used to mine such patterns, and correlated relations between them form a given database. There are many applications where pattern mining can be used. Typical examples include market basket analysis, customer shopping sequences analysis, analysis of biological sequences, healthcare and intrusion detection system.

BACKGROUND

Association Rule

In data mining, association rule mining is a popular and well-researched method for discovering interesting relationships between variables in a large database. Association rules are used to analyze and predict customer behavior but not restricted to healthcare, bioinformatics and etc. Association rule is if/then statement that helps to uncover relationships between unrelated data in the relational database or another information repository. It can be specified in linear implication expression like $X \Longrightarrow Y$. where X and Y are itemsets.

Association Rule Example: Consider a customer who buys bread is likely to buy butter also and this statement can be expressed as.

Bread$\Longrightarrow$Butter.

Such a statement can be used to express how items or objects are related to each other and how they tend to group together. Consider another example, if a customer buys a laptop and laptop sleeve then he likely to buy a wireless mouse. Such information can be used as a basis for marketing activities such as product promotion and product pricing.

Buys{Laptop, Laptop sleeve}$\Longrightarrow$buys{Wireless mouse}.

A different section of association rule includes Antecedent (if), Consequent (then), Support and Confidence. From earlier example

Bread$\Longrightarrow$Butter[10%,45%].

If a customer buys bread, then he likes to buy butter measured by percentage. In the above example, bread is antecedent, butter is consequent, 20% in support and 45% is confidence. Support and Confidence are two popular measurements used in association rule mining. Consider an association rule.

$A\Longrightarrow B$.

Support denotes the probability that contains both A and B. Confidence denotes the probability that a transaction containing A also contains B. For a better understanding of Confidence and Support consider another example. In the supermarket, the retailer wants to find the percentage of people who are buying bread by considering 100 total transactions. If 20 customer buys bread, then

$$Support = \left(\left(\frac{20}{100}\right) * 100\right) = 20\%.$$

Out of these 20 transactions, people who are buying bread also buy butter in 9 transactions, so confidence can be calculated as

$$Confidence = \left(\left(\frac{9}{20}\right) * 100\right) = 45\%.$$

Classification of Association Rule

- **Single Dimensional Association Rule:**

In single dimensional association rule, only one predicate or dimension is used. It means that an item in the rule refers to only dimension or predicate.

Buys(Bread) $\Longrightarrow$Buys(Butter).

Above rule specifies that customer who buys bread will also likely to buy butter, so only one predicate "Buys" is used.

- **Multidimensional Association Rule:**

As the name indicates, it has two or more predicate. Consider the example

Occupation(*IT*), Age(>22) $\Longrightarrow$Buys(Laptop).

In the above example, three predicate or dimensions such as Occupation, Age, and Buys are used. In a multidimensional association rule, predicates should not be repeated in the same rule.

- **Hybrid Dimensional Association Rule:**

It is an extended version of the multidimensional rule. Here single predicate or dimensions can be repeated for 'n' number of times in the same rule. Consider an example.

Time(5'Oclock), Buys(Tea) $\Longrightarrow$ Buys(Biscuits).

If a person buys tea in the morning at 05.00 am, then he is likely to buy biscuits. Here the predicate "Buys" is repeated for two times. So in hybrid dimension association rule repetition of the predicate is allowed.

Frequent Item Set Mining

Frequent patterns are itemsets, subsequences, or substructures that appear in a data set with a frequency no less than a user-specified threshold. The first step in discovering association rule is to detect frequent itemset in a given transactional database. An itemset is defined as a collection of items in a given transactional database. Frequent itemset mining determines the itemset which is popular and being purchased frequently by a customer.

Let $I=\{i_1,i_2,...,i_m\}$.be a finite set with m.distinct items. A quantitative database is a set of transactions $D = \{T_1.T_2...T_n\}$. in which each transaction $T_q \in D(1 \leq q \leq n)$ .is a subset of I and has a unique identifier q, called its Transaction ID(TID). Besides, each item i_j.in a transaction T_q.has a purchase quantity (a positive integer), denoted as $q(i_j,T_q)$.

Definition 1 (Itemset)

Itemset is a collection of one or more items.

Example: {a,b,c} is a itemset. Particularly it can be k itemset where k denotes the number of the item present in itemset.

Table 1. A quantitative transactional database

TID	Items with their quantities
T_1	a:1, b:2, c:4, d:3, e:8, f:2
T_2	a:3, b:3, c:8
T_3	a:2, b:5, d:5, e:7
T_4	a:4, c:4, f:2, g:12
T_5	a:5, b:2, c:3, d:5, f:8
T_6	e:1, f:1, a:3

Definition 2 (Support Count (σ))

The support count of an itemset X, denoted by X.σ in a transactional database T is the number of transactions in T that contains X. Assume that T has n transactions, then from Table 1, the support count for the occurrence of itemset {a,b} can be calculated as

$$\sigma\left(a \cup b\right) = \sigma\left(\{a,b\}\right) = 4.$$

Definition 3 (Support S)

The Support of an itemset X is denoted by S and it is defined as a fraction of transaction that contains the itemset X. It will normalize the support count by the total number of transactions. From Table 1, the support for itemset {a, b} can be calculated as

$$S\left(\{a,b\}\right) = \frac{\sigma\left(a \cup b\right)}{n} = \frac{4}{6} = 0.6 = 60\ \%.$$

Definition 4 (Frequent Itemset)

A frequent itemset is an itemset whose support (S) is greater than or equal to the minsup threshold value. Here, minsup threshold value should be manually assigned based on database size and transaction size.

Frequent Itemset(FI) = {if, $S(\{X\})$>minsup.

For example if minsup= 40%, then itmeset {a,b} is a frequent itemset in Table 1.

Definition 5 (Confidence)

Confidence is the proportion of the transactions containing item 'a' which also contains item 'b', and is calculated as

$$Confidence\left(A \Rightarrow B\right) = \frac{\sigma\left(a \cup b\right)}{\sigma\left(b\right)}.$$

For example from Table 1,

$$Confidence\left(a \Rightarrow b\right) = \frac{\sigma\left(\{a,b\}\right)}{\sigma\left(\{a\}\right)} = \frac{4}{5} = 0.8.$$

Given a set of transactions 'n', the goal of association rule mining is to find all rules having

```
support ≥ minsup threshold
confidence ≥ minconf threshold
```

Frequent itemset mining has major complications when applied to analyze the customers' transactions. . In Frequent Itemset Mining, only the frequency count is considered for mining the itemset which enables major drawback. This drawback can be evade by considering the quantity of an itemset.

In some cases, even if an itemset appears in very few transactions, it may be purchased for a larger number of quantity for every transaction in which it present. Thus, if a customer has bought 5kg of apple, 10kg of apple or 20kg of apple, it is viewed as the same. Another important hindrance is that all items in a transactional database are viewed as having the equal influence, utility of weight. For example, if a customer buys very expensive electronic gadgets or a cheap piece of slippers, it is viewed as being equally important.

Thus, frequent pattern mining may discover copious frequent patterns that are not even interesting. For example, one may identify that {slipper, milk} is a frequent pattern. However, from an e-commerce business perspective, it does not generate much profit as this pattern may be disinteresting. And also there may be a chance that frequent pattern mining may omit scarce pattern that will generate a high revenue such as perhaps {laptop, speaker}.

High Utility Mining

To eradicate these drawbacks, the problem of frequent itemset mining has been restructured as the problem of high-utility itemset mining. In this problem, interesting factors about each item in a transaction database is also considered along with the frequency of an item. Interesting factors of an item may include purchase quantity, price, negative profit, positive profit, on shelf time, recency, seasonal impact and other factors.

There are few senses that make the problem of high utility mining to be more interesting. First, from the perspective of growing business needs, high utility mining will ensure the high profit for e-commerce retailers. Second, from a research perspective, the problem of high utility mining is more confronting. Unlike frequent itemset mining, high utility mining does not have an anti-monotonicity property to prune the search space.

Table 2. A profit table

Item	a	b	c	d	e	f	g
Profit	2	6	5	2	7	4	2

Definition 6 (Item Utility)

The utility of an item i_j in a transaction T_q is denoted as $u(i_j, T_q)$. and defined as:

$$u\left(i_j T_q\right) = q\left(i_j, T_q\right) \times p\left(i_j\right).$$

where $q(i_j, T_q)$ is the purchased quantity of (i_j) .in the transaction T_q .and $p(i_j)$ .represent the profit value of (i_j) . For example in Table 1, the utility of (a) .in transaction T_1 .s calculated as $u(a)(=1\times2)=(2)$.

Definition 7 (Itemset Utility in a Transaction)

The utility of an itemset X.in a transaction T_q .is denoted as $u(X, T_q)$ .and defined as:

$$u\left(X, T_q\right) = \sum_{i_j \epsilon X \wedge X \subseteq T_q} u\left(i_j T_q\right).$$

For example in Table 1, the utility of the itemset (abcd) in T_1 .is calculated as $u(abcd, T_1)$ $(=1\times2+2\times6+4\times5+3\times2)$ $(=40)$.

Definition 8 (Itemset Utility in D)

The utility of an itemset X in a database D is denoted as u(X), and defined as:

$$u\left(X\right) = \sum_{X \subseteq T_q \wedge T_q \in D} u\left(X, T_q\right).$$

For example in Table 1, the utility of the itemset (ab) is calculated as u(ab)=u(ab,T1)+u(ab,T2)+u(ab,T3)+u(ab,T5)(=14+24+34+22) (=94).

Definition 9 (Transaction Utility)

The transaction utility of a transaction Tq is denoted as tu(Tq), and defined as:

$$tu\left(T_q\right) = \sum_{i_j \in X} u\left(i_j, T_q\right).$$

For example in Table 1, the utility of T1 is calculated astu(T$_1$) (=2+12+20+6+56+8)(=104).

Definition 10 (Total Utility in D)

The total utility of all transactions in a database D is denoted as TU, and defined as:

$$TU = \sum_{T_q \in D} tu\left(T_q\right).$$

For example in Table1, the total utility of the database is calculated as TU=tu(T_1)+tu(T_2)+tu(T_3)+tu(T_4)+tu(T_5)+tu(T_6) (=104+64+93+58+79+17) (= 415).

The above definitions are used in traditional HUIM. An itemset X is said to be a high-utility itemset (HUI) iffits utility in a database D is no less than a user-specified minimum high-utility count (minimum high-utility threshold multiplied by the total utility of the database), that is:

$$HUI \leftarrow \{X \mid u\left(X\right) \geq TU \times \delta\}.$$

where δ is the minimum high utility threshold.

In this example, assume that the minimum high-utilitythreshold is set to 14.7%. Hence, the minimum high-utility count is calculated as (415 × 14:7%)(=61). TheHUIs in the running example are thus: *{(ab:94), (abc:135), (abcd:87), (abcde:96), (abcdef:104), (ac:121), (ace:78), (acf:121), (bc:117), (bcd:75), (bcde:94), (bcdef:102), (c:95) and (ce:76) (e:112)}.*

In the above example, it is obvious that the utility of itemsets tends to be larger for itemsets containing more items. The problem of high average-utility itemset mining (HAUIM) was thus proposed using a novel measure called average-utility, to provide a more fair measurement of the utilities of itemsets that takes their lengths into account.HAUIM is defined by the following definitions.

Definition 11 (Average-Utility of an Item in a Transaction)

The average-utility of an item (i_j) in a transactionTq is denoted as au(i_j), and defined as:

$$au\left(i_j, T_q\right) = \frac{q\left(i_j, T_q\right) \times p(i_j)}{l} = \frac{u\left(i_j, T_q\right)}{l}.$$

For example in Table 1, the average-utility of the item (a) in transaction T1 is calculated as au(a,T1)= $\frac{2}{1}$. = (=2), which is equal to its utility in traditional HUIM.

Definition 12 (Average-Utility of an Itemset in a Transaction)

The average-utility of a k-itemset X in a transaction Tqis denoted as au(X, Tq), and defined as:

$$au\left(X, T_q\right) = \frac{\sum u\left(i_j, T_q\right)}{|X| = k}.$$

For example in Table 1, the average utility of the itemset (ab) in transaction T_1 is calculated as au(ab,

$T_1) = \dfrac{2+12}{2} \left(= 7\right).$

Definition 13 (Average Utility of an Itemset in D)

The average utility of an itemset X in a database D is denoted as au(X), and defined as:

$$au\left(X\right) = \sum_{X \subseteq T_q \wedge T_q \in D} au\left(X, T_q\right).$$

For example in Table 1, the average-utility of the itemset(ac) is calculated as:

Definition 14 (Traditional Problem Statement in HUI mining)

An itemset X is considered to be aHAUI iff its average-utility is no less than the minimum high average-utility count, that is:

$$HAUI \leftarrow \left\{X | au\left(X\right) \geq TU \times \delta\right\}.$$

Limitations of Traditional Approaches for Mining High Utility Mining

In recent years the data analysts are facing major challenges in mining High Utility Itemset(HUI) from a given transactional database using existing traditional techniques such as level-wise candidate generation and test method, approaches based on pattern growth and Frequent Pattern(FP) tree based utility mining algorithm. The challenges include exponentially growing search space for utility mining algorithms and existing utility mining algorithms assume that the minimum utility threshold appropriate to the given database should be fixed by the user which is not an easier task. To overcome these challenges, evolutionary algorithm based techniques are proposed to mine the high utility itemset from the transactional database. Evolutionary algorithms also called Bio Nature Inspired algorithms such as Genetic Algorithm (GA), Particle Swarm Optimization (PSO) and BAT algorithms are used to overcome the performance bottleneck of previous approaches. The existing bio-admired HUIM algorithms follow the traditional routine for selecting the optimal value in the current population and use that optimal value as a target value for the next population. Nonetheless, HUIM is entirely different from other optimization problems where itemset whose utility is not less than the minimum utility threshold should be discovered. Due to the uneven distribution of HUIs, examining for the best value in the current population and using it as the target value of the next population may lead to omitting of some results after a certain number of iterations.

Elemental Study of Evolutionary Algorithms

An evolutionary algorithm is a universal population-based trial and error method for solving the optimization problem. It is part of evolutionary computation. Evolutionary computation is a nature-inspired approach to optimization. It is the process of getting the most out of something and making it better.

During this process, a search for the best or optimal solution to a real-world problem is done. It is inspired by the idea of survival of the fittest from Darwinian evolution and modern genetics. The general idea behind the whole thing is that, if biological evolution is amazing as humans over many generations, then the same process can be used artificially to evolve optimal solutions for vehicles, aircraft, spaceships and much more. Evolutionary computation offers an approximation of optimal solutions to the difficult problems where artificial intelligence is required.

Any algorithm which includes reproduction and selection of candidate solutions which loosely mimics how an animal population evolves in nature will come under the category of an evolutionary algorithm. Based on the type of data structure and appropriate operations used, evolutionary algorithms are broadly classified as

- **Genetic Algorithm(GA):** A fixed-length binary string is used to represent the candidate solution. GA uses mutation operation as a driving force. GA also uses a recombination operator, which is the primary operator for the GA. The next selection operation is used. Selection operation applies evolutionary pressure either instinctive or preservative. In the GA, this operator selects individuals for breeding.
- **Evolutionary Strategies (ES):** A real value vector of fixed length is used to represent the candidate solution. ES uses mutation operation as a driving force. ES also uses a recombination operator. The next selection operation is used. Selection operation applies evolutionary pressure either instinctive or preservative. This operator determines which individuals will be excluded from the new population
- **Genetic Programming (GP):** Similar to ES, GP also uses a real value vector of fixed length. The next selection operation is used. Selection operation applies evolutionary pressure either instinctive or preservative. This operator determines which individuals will be excluded from the new population.

Genetic Algorithm Lifecycle

Genetic algorithms are biologically inspired stochastic meta-heuristic for combinatorial search and optimization. For any given problem, the genetic algorithm cycles through a series of steps as shown in Figure 1.

1. Creates a population of random chromosomes(solutions)
2. Score each chromosome in the population for fitness
3. Create a new generation through mutation and crossover
4. Repeat the process until if and only if the solution is good enough
5. Emit the fittest chromosome as the solution

There are huge benefits obtained from applying evolutionary algorithms for a given problem. One of the benefits is the resilience gain which means any complex problems can be solved using most of the evolutionary algorithm concepts. The objective target of the problem can also be met by the evolutionary algorithm. Evolutionary algorithms will never get locked with a particular solution due to the population of solution which makes the evolutionary algorithm to be applied for any optimization problem.

Figure 1. Genetic algorithm lifecycle

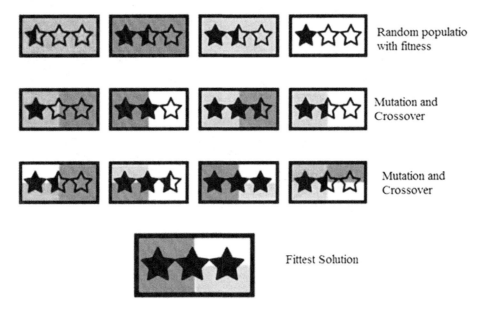

Reinforcement Learning (RL)

Machine learning is one among the applications of Artificial Intelligence (AI). Machine learning enables the systems to learn automatically and getting improved by experience without being explicitly programmed. Machine learning spots the development of computer programs that can access data and make use of the data to learn for themselves. Figure 2 shows the different classification of machine learning techniques.

Reinforcement learning is a machine learning method in which the system interacts with its environment by producing actions and discovers errors or rewards. The system or software agent would navigate through an uncertain situation to yield rewards. It maximizes the rewards along a particular dimension over many steps. For example, the player can win more points and won a game over many moves.

Reinforcement learning thriving towards rewards based on trial and error search method. To achieve maximum rewards the system and software agents automatically determine the principle behavior of the environment within specific circumstances. Reward feedback is used to analyze which action is best among the actions done by the agent. This feedback signal is referred to as a reinforcement signal. The reinforcement signal helps the agent to know the best possible path to reach maximum rewards.

Reinforcement learning is different from supervised learning. In supervised learning, the model is trained with the correct answer since the training data has the answer key with it. In reinforcement learning, there is no trained data and answer key. The reinforcement agent makes a decision that what has to be done to perform the given task. The reinforcement agent is bound to learn from its experience in the absence of a training dataset as shown in Figure 3.

Figure 2. Machine learning - classification

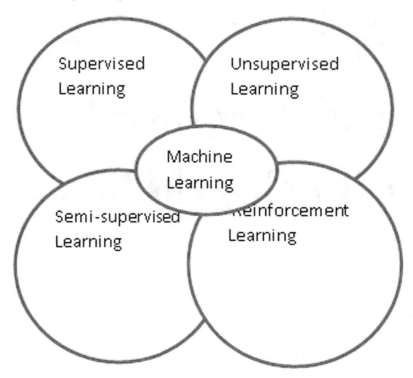

Figure 3. Participants of reinforcement learning

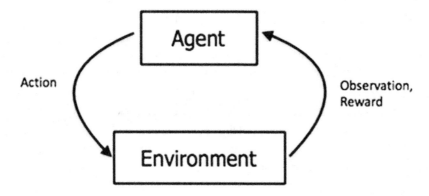

Key terms that describe the basic elements of an RL are:

1. **Environment:** It is the physical world in which the agent operates. The current state and action of the agent are taken as an input.
2. **Agent:** An agent takes actions
3. **Action:** Action is almost self-explanatory, but it should be noted that agents choose among a list of possible actions.
4. **Reward:** Positive or negative feedback from the environment

5. **Observation:** If the agent receives negative feedback, it will be recorded as knowledge for future use.

6. **Policy:** Method to map the agent's state to actions

7. **Value:** The future reward that an agent would receive by taking an action in a particular state

Example:

1. **Positive Reward**: Eat Vitamin A fruits because they taste good and will keep the better immune system in the body. Rewards are either short-term or long-term. The action of eating Vitamin A fruit tastes good results in a short term reward. The long-term reward is getting long and strong alive.

2. **NegativeReward**: Eating many oily foods will lead to body obesity and cardiac issues. (Actions based on short- and long-term rewards, such as the amount of fatty food causes body overweight, or the length of time you survive will be low.)

LITERATURE SURVEY

Tree Data Structure Based HUIM Algorithms

Frequent pattern mining is an elemental research topic in the area of discovering hidden patterns from various given application domains (Tseng et al, 2013) such as Web click-stream analysis (Chen, Park & Yum, 1998; Yun & Chen, 2000), bioinformatics (Creighton & Hanash, 2003; Georgii, Richter & Ru, 2005; Martinez, Pasquier & Pasquier, 2008) and mobile environments (Lee et al., 2007; Yun & Chen, 2007) and database of different kind such as streaming databases (Lin et al., 2005; Tanbeer et al., 2008),transactional databases (Agrawal & Sikrant, 1994; Han, Pei & Yin, 2000; Pei et al., 2007),time series databases (Eltabakh et al., 2008; Han, Dong & Yin, 1999). Nevertheless, the quantities of items and other important factors of each item in a transactional database are not taken into account. This problem will make the retailer to unable to find the itemset with high sales profit. The sale profit of an itemset is composed of unit profit and buying abundance of each item. To address these problems, mining high utility itemset from a database emerges as an important topic in the data mining field. Two elements can be considered to classify the utility of an item: 1) significance of dissimilar items, which is named as an external utility, and 2) the importance of items in the transaction, which is named as an internal utility. If the utility of an itemset is greater than the utility brink value, then it can be designated as high utility itmeset. In frequent itemset mining, downward closure property is used to prune the search space which is not applicable for high utility mining. To address this problem, a naïve method called principle of debilitation is used where list of all itmeset form database is considered. When databases contain lots of long transactions or a low minimum utility threshold is set, this method will be suffered by the problems of generating large search space. In order to efficiently capture all high utility itemset and effectively prune the search space, past studies (Ahmed et al., 2009; Erwin, Gopalan & Achuthan, 2008; Li et al., 2008; Li, Yeh & Chang, 2008; Liu, Liao & Choudhary, 2005; Shie et al., 2011; Tsent, Chu & Liang, 2006; Tsent et al., 2010) employed exaggerated methods to promote the performance of utility mining. In these approaches, potential high utility itemset (PHUIs) are generated initially and supplementary database scan is for finding their utilities. Yet existing approaches produce an extremely large set of PHUIs and this situation is worst when the database contains many long transactions and minimal threshold. This challenging problem will increase the processing time of algorithms.

To address this issue, transaction weighted downward closure (TWDC) (Liu, Liao & Choudhary, 2005) is proposed. TWDC is defined as, for any itemset X, if X is not a High Transaction Weighted Utility Itemset (HTWUI), any superset of X is alow utility itemset (Tseng et al., 2013). A global data structure called Utility Pattern Tree (UP Tree) is constructed by performing a dual scan of the actual database. Two strategies such as Discarding Global Unpromising Items (DGUI) and Discarding Global Node Utilities (DGNU) are used to decrease the overestimated utility of each item during the construction of a global UP-Tree. After constructing a global UP-Tree, Utility Pattern (UP) – Growth algorithm is used to mine the PHI from UP-Tree. UP-Growth incorporates two strategies called Discarding Local Unpromising Items (DLUI) and Decreasing Local Node Utilities (DLNU) during the construction of Local UP-Tree on the traditional FP-Growth (Han, Pei & Yin, 2000). These strategies will reduce overestimated utilities of itemset which will further decrease the number of PHUIs generated from UP-Tree.

Further to improve the performance of mining, UP-Tree and UP-Growth+ methods were used (Tseng et al., 2013). It eliminates the estimated utilities that are closure to the actual utility of unpromising items and descendant nodes which make the overestimated utilities to be closure the actual utilities. Minimal node utilities are used in UP-Growth+ to makes the estimated pruning values closer to real utility values of the pruned items in the database.

The majority of the pattern-growth algorithm which is used to mine the utility pattern adopts the UP- tree data structure for their working (Dawar & Goyal, 2015). Due to the availability of cramped information in UP-tree, huge numbers of candidate items are generated. A data structure named UP-Hist tree is constructed from the original database. UP-Hist tree maintains the histogram of item quantity with each node of the tree. The search space is effectively pruned by using histogram-based computation of estimated utility. UP-Hist Growth algorithm is used to mine the high utility pattern from the UP-Hist tree. Histograms are also used to remove unpromising items during the construction of the local UP-Hist tree. UP-Hist Growth algorithm will further reduce the overestimated utilities when compared with UP-Growth and UP-Growth+ (Tseng et al., 2013).

An item which is given as a free gift to promote the sale of another item with high cost or an item sold for the loss will have a greater impact in profit of the supermarket (Subramanian & Kandhasamy, 2015). These items are considered as an item with negative utility value. An item with negative utility value in a database is not considered by the existing HUI mining algorithms. To resolve this problem, Chu et al. (2009) designed a methodology for mining high utility itemsets with negative item value (HUINIV)-Mine from a given database. Tow phase (Liu et al., 2005) is used by HUINIV-Mine to mine the high utility itemset from the given database. In HUINIV-Mine significant number of candidates are generated which incurs huge time to mine the high utility itemset. A novel approach (Subramanian & Kandhasamy, 2015) called Utility Pattern-Growth approach for Negative Item Values (UP-GNIV) is used to discover high utility itemsets with negative item values from large databases efficiently and effectively.

High-utility itemset mining (HUIM) reveal patterns with high-utility. Frequent pattern mining spots in discovering frequent patterns (Lin, Ren & Fournier-Viger, 2017). High average-utility itemset mining (HAUIM) is derived from HUIM (Yao, Hamilton & Butz, 2004), which calculates the average utility, to select patterns in the view of their utilities and lengths. To reduce the amounts of memory and execution times, HAUIM utilizes the average-utility upper-bound model which overvalues the average utilities of itemsets (Lin, Hong & lu, 2010). To improve the performance of HAUIM, tighter upper-bound models are examined for mining HAUIs. The looser upper-bound model deemed the remaining-maximum utility in transactions to reduce the upper bound on the utilities of itemsets. The tighter upper-bound model ignores irrelevant items in transactions to further tighten the upper bound. Pruning strategies are implemented to reduce the search space for mining HAUIs.

As downward closure property cannot be directly applied to high utility mining, it is a really critical problem to reduce the search space in an efficient manner (Indumathi & Vaithiyanathan, 2014). The approaches discussed in this article (Indumathi & Vaithiyanathan, 2014) generate a huge number of candidate itemset and follow the overestimated method in order to mine the high utility itemset which adds complexity to the computation. Maximum Utility Growth and tree structure called Maximum Item Quantity (MIQ) are used here to address these problems. It generates a very less number of candidate itemset and improves the efficiency of the mining process. Also, an appropriate estimated utility of an itemset is calculated. Two strategies called Pruning 1-Itemset Candidates with Real Item Utilities and Pruning Candidates with Estimated Maximum Itemset Utility are followed to prune the number of candidate itemset.

Evolutionary-Based HUIM Algorithms

As the size of the database grows dynamically, the search space for mining high utility itemset also grows exponentially (Kannimuthua & Vaithiyanathan, 2014). Additionally, the threshold value used to specify the minimum value of item utility to become high utility itemset should be determined manually by the Data Specialist. The value of the minimum utility threshold will depend on the factors such as the size of the database, length of each transaction, the number of distinct itemset present in a database and other factors. So, the task of setting the value to the minimum utility threshold parameter by manually is not easier. To evade this problem evolutionary computation is used in the proposed approach. $HUPE_{UMU}$-GARM and $HUPE_{WUMU}$-GARM approaches are used to mine the high utility itemset with ranked motion using minimum utility threshold and without using minimum utility threshold respectively.

Particle Swarm Optimization (PSO) is also a type of evolutionary computation methodologies used to solve the optimization problems (Lin, Yang & Fournier-Viger, 2016a). By integrating the sigmoid renovation strategy and transaction weighted utility model, a discrete PSO algorithm called $HUIM\text{-}BPSO_{sig}$ is used. The traditional high utility itemset mining algorithms suffer from performance bottleneck when the size of the database is large, the length of the transaction is high and huge distinct itemset presents. This problem has been evaded in the proposed method by using TWU model to find the potential high utility itemset which further reduces the combinational problem.

Even though a traditional PSO algorithm used to mine the high utility itemset performs better than the traditional tree data structure based approaches, it is used to solve the general continuous domain problem of optimization (Lin, Yang & Fournier-Viger, 2016b). A discrete PSO is adopted in the proposed methodology to encode the particles as the binary variable value. The proposed methodology HUIM-BPSO also follows the basic steps of $HUIM\text{-}BPSO_{sig}$ to reduce the combinational problem. To reduce the invalid combination of discovered high utility itemset, a OR/NOR-tree structure is incorporated in HUIM-BPSO.

A traditional routine of the actual GA, PSO and BPSO is followed in (Kannimuthia & Vaithiyanathan, 2014; Lin, Yang & Fournier-Viger, 2016a, 2016b). In these nature inspired computing algorithms, the best values of one population are maintained in the next population which is not most appropriate for high utility itemset mining. High utility itemset mining has an uneven distribution over population. This may cause missing of some results when searching with the best value from the past population as a target within a certain number of iterations.

To address this problem, roulette wheel selection is incorporated in novel nature inspired algorithm based high utility mining framework and it called as Bio-HUIF (Song & Huang, 2018). Roulette wheel selection is used to determine the initial population of the next population from all discovered high utility itemset. Three algorithms called Bio-HUIF-GA, Bio-HUIF-PSO and Bio-HUIF-BA were derived from proposed Bio-HUIF and those algorithms employ GA, PSO, and the bat algorithm (BA), respectively.

PROBLEM STATEMENT

Genetic algorithms (GA) are often used for solving difficult optimization problems (Kannimuthia & Vaithiyanathan, 2014). To deal with performance bottleneck of traditional tree based approaches, Kannimuthu and Premalatha (2014) had recently proposed a bio-inspired algorithm GA to mine the high utility itemsets (HUIs) and particle swarm optimization (PSO) (Shie, et al., 2011; Tsent, Chu & Liang, 2006) has recently been applied to the mining of HUIs.

One of the drawbacks of using GA is that the process of optimization may take a long time. Generally, if an optimization problem with supporting functions is considered then testing each of the supporting functions is very inefficient. It allows to choose the most efficient fitness function automatically during the runoff the genetic algorithm. Moreover, when different functions are efficient at different stages of the optimization process, the method chooses the currently optimal function dynamically. Consider a set of fitness functions (FFs). The ambition of the genetic algorithm is to cultivate an individual with the most desirable value of one of these FFs, which is named as target FF. The leftover of the functions will be named as supporting FFs. The FF that is used in the genetic algorithm at an instance will be called as current FF. A model problem, where the use of different supporting functions at different stages of optimization is more efficient, is used to demonstrate that reinforcement learning (Creighton & Hanash, 2003) allows to choose the optimal current FF during the run of the GA for mining HUIs form given transactional database.

PROPOSED METHODOLOGY

Modeling GA based HUI Discovery with adaptive fitness function using Reinforcement Learning is proposed. Discovery of high utility itemset using Genetic algorithm with adaptive fitness function controlled by Reinforcement Learning. This methodology is being named as Reinforcement Learning based Genetic Algorithm (RLGA) for the discovery of high utility itemset from given databased is discussed in this section.

Initial Population

Before a genetic algorithm can be applied to any problem, the technique is needed to encode potential solutions to that problem in a form so that a computer can process. Figure 1 shows the configuration of the genes (items) in the chromosome. Binary encoding is used in this approach. Binary value '0'

Figure 4. Chromosome

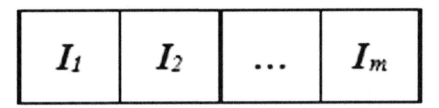

represents the absence of an item in an itemset and '1' represents the presence of an itemset. The length of the chromosome is fixed and it is equal to the number of dissimilar items (m) which is obtained from the transaction database. Figure 2 shows the example of chromosome representation for the itemset $\{i_1, i_2, i_4, i_8, i_9, i_{10}\}$.

Example: Bear an instance that, the length of the chromosome is 10 and the itemset length is 4. Arbitrary numbers generated by random number generator function is $\{1, 2, 4, 8, 9, 10\}$. The representation of a chromosome is shown in Figure 2.

Given an itemset length 'm', all the genes (item) in a chromosome are encoded as '0'. The initial population is produced using a random number generator function. The random generator function will generate a random number is 'r ', which represents the position of nth chromosome and it is encoded as '1'. This represents an item present in a chromosome (itemset). In this way, an itemset in a chromosome is generated randomly. Now the randomly generated item in a chromosome is compared against already existing items in the same chromosome and if the item is available, a fresh random number is generated until it is unique. This process is redone until generating 'k' unique random numbers. This process should hold the condition "k≤m".

Adaptive Fitness Function

A particular kind of objective function used to find an optimal solution in a GA is known as the fitness function. The main goal of this work is to generate high utility itemsets from the transaction database. Hence, the fitness function is essential for determining the chromosome (itemset) which prescribes the optimality. HUPEWUMU-GARM algorithm uses Yao et al's(2004) utility measure (u(X)) to calculate the fitness value. The fitness of the chromosome to be maximized is given in the equation (1).

Maximization of a certain target function is a critical problem in GA. Several supporting functions are computed for each calculation of the target function. Even though the target function decreases during the optimization process, it is more efficient to optimize a few supporting functions in certain phases of optimization. Part of supporting functions may relate mutually with the target function. Such problems often occur during the automation of performance test generation (Chen, Park & Yu, 1998).

Figure 5. Chromosome representation for the itemset

1	1	0	1	0	0	0	1	1	1

Assume an individual be a bit string of a permanent length n with xbits set to 1. The target fitness function of the chromosome to be maximized is given in equation (1).

$$f(i) \leftarrow \sum_{T_q \in D \wedge X \subseteq T_q} U(X, T_q).$$

(1)

$h_1(x) = \max(x, p)$ where p is switching point.

(2)

$h_2(x) = \max(x.p)$ where p is switching point.

(3)

Equation 2 and Equation 3 are the supporting fitness functions where p represents any positive integer. p is also called a switching point. Either $h_1(x)$.or $h_2(x)$.may be considered as the current fitness of the individuals based on the switching point value. If the number of bits in an individual is less than p then $h_1(x)$.ill be considered as the current fitness function. Otherwise, $h_2(x)$.will be considered as the current fitness function. The main objective of the proposed method is used to approximately exchange the current FF for GA in a dynamic manner. The dynamic switching is based on the kind of individuals in the current generation. Alternatively, the proposed methodology will fix the current FF to $h_1(x)$.initially and then switch it to $h_2(x)$.hen individuals in the current generation reach the switch point.

In the proposed model, a reinforcement learning task is used to represent the model problem. Fitness Function represents the actions done by agent $A = a, h_1, h_2$. Each action done by the agent is sketched as selecting the corresponding fitness function as the current fitness function. Now the GA will create a new generation of individuals. The state of environment relay upon the state of GA. Equation (4) describes the ordered value of fitness function. In equation (4), f is a measurement of the fitness function, x_p. represents the number of bit assigned as one in the prime individual from the former generation. x_c.represents the number of bits assigned to one in the best individual from the contemporary generation.

$$\left(f(x_c) - f(x_p) \right) / f(x_c).$$

(4)

Based on the change in the value of best individual determines the value of reward function. The best individual appears after creation of the next generation caused by the action of the agent. Equation (5) denotes the auxiliary function D_f.

$$D_f(x_1, x_2) = f(x) = \begin{cases} 0 & if\, f(x_2) - f(x_1) < 0 \\ 0.5 & if\, f(x_2) - f(x_1) = 0 \\ 1 & if\, f(x_2) - f(x_1) > 0 \end{cases}.$$

(5)

Equation (6) denotes the reward function $R(s,a)$.

$$R(s, a) = D_g(x_s, x_{s'}) + c\left(D_{h1}(x_s, x_{s'}) + D_{h2}(x_s, x_{s'}) \right).$$

(6)

where s, s' .are the previous and new state respectively. $c \in [0,1]$ .s a parameter of real-valued and used to shift the fitness function contribution to the reward s, s' . a.is a action that makes the transition from s to s' . The number of bits set to one in the best individual is represented by $x_s, x_{s'}$ .which corresponds to the states s, s' .respectively.

Inorder to have relatively low space and computational complexities, a Model-free incremental reinforcement algorithm such as ε-greedy Q-learning (Georgii et al., 2005) and Delayed Q-learning (Martinez, Pasquier & Pasquier, 2008) are used in the proposed model. These reinforcement algorithms will improves the performance of GA which solves the given model problem. Each stage of the model will have learning steps and GA steps. Learning steps allows the agent to choose the current fitness function and during GA step, current fitness function is used to generate next individuals. GA used to solve the model problem is controlled by as ε-greedy Q-learning and Delayed Q-learning.

Execution of the deployed algorithms is done with different either one of the combinations learning algorithm parameter values and model problem parameter values. In the proposed model Delayed Q-learning algorithm is used.

- **The parameters used in Delayed Q-learning algorithm are** (Martinez, Pasquier & Pasquier, 2008)
  - m - the update period of Q-value estimates
  - ε.- the bonus reward
  - γ.– the discount factor
- **ε-greedy Q-learning algorithm has following parameter**
  - ε.–the exploration probability
  - α.– the learning speed
  - γ.– the discount factor
- **Model problem parameters are**
  - *L - the length of an individual*
  - *P - the switch point;*
  - *k - the divisor in the target function g*

Classical Genetic Operation

1. **Selection:** Selection is the initial gait of genetic algorithm in which distinctive chromosome is selected from a population for subsequent breeding (crossover). By considering the value of fitness function, selection operation will filter the chromosome for next breeding. There are various approaches used for selection process of GA [R05]. Roulette wheel selection (Subramanian & Kandhasamy, 2015) is used in this work. n is the number of individuals in the population, X.s the fraction of the population to be replaced by crossover in each iteration and μ is the mutation rate.

   $(X \times n)$ .ndividuals need to be generated. It will form $\dfrac{\S \times n}{2}$ .pair of parents.

2. **Crossover:** Also called as recombination step of GA. It is genetic operator used generate new offspring of child by performing conjoin operation between two parents. First two parents to be mated are chosen and appropriate crossover point is opted from within those two genes. Based on the problem crossover point are chosen in different fashion as shown in Figure 6.

Figure 6. Crossover operation

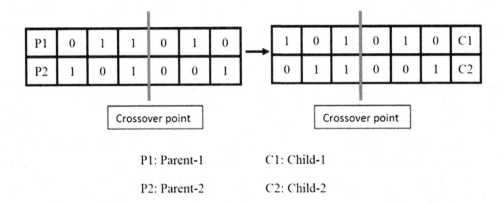

3. **Mutation:** A new generation of population is successfully created while stepping in to this process. $(1-X)\times$.) individuals have been cloned across, and $(X\times n)$ .individuals have been formed by a crossover operator. Now a assertive fraction μ.of the new generations are selected at random. This selection is done with consistent likelihood of occurrence. In each of the chosenindividuals a bit is chosen at random and this bit is inverted (flipped to the other value) when Mutation Probability $(P_m)\geq$ .randomly generated probability value.

Interpretation and Termination Precedent

Based on the value of adaptive fitness function chromosomes for next generation is selected. Interpretation step will select new population from chromosomes having highest fitness value. It is necessary to identify the termination criterion inorder to stop the process of GA. The possible conditions that are used to decide whether to continue search or stop the search of GA are listed below

- Number of generations created
- The highest ranking of a fitness at fixed number of generations.
- Physically examining the solution
- Any aggregation of the above criterions.

The Steps Involved in Discovering HUI Using GA With Adaptive Fitness Function

Figure 7 shows the different steps involved in the proposed model.

1. Number of distinct items (NDI) is determined by examining the given transaction database. The chromosome length (CL) is initiated with NDI.
2. Next generate a new chromosome of length CL
3. Individual chromosome is evaluated using calculated fitness value (fv)
4. Verify the population size, if it is equal to N then go to step 5, else go to step 2.

5. If the termination condition is satisfied, then it provides the mined utility itemset from the population which act as outcome of the GA and then terminate. Otherwise continue.

6. Choose m individuals by applying roulette wheel selection that will compute the future generate population of offspring with best parents.

7. Selected individuals of population is given to crossover operation

8. Based on the value of P_m. mutation operation is applied on the individuals of population. Fitness value (F_v) .is calculated again for the individuals

9. Check the size of new population. If the size is equal to N then go step 10, else go to step 6.

10. Evaluate the individuals

Figure 7. Flow of activities involved in discovering HUI using GA with adaptive fitness function_1

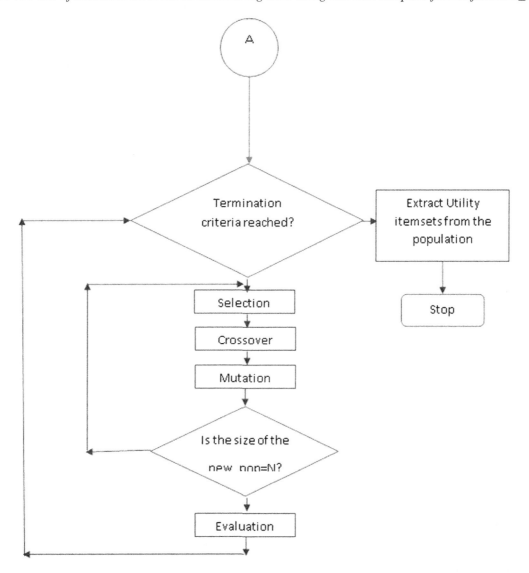

Figure 8. Flow of activities involved in discovering HUI using GA with adaptive fitness function_2

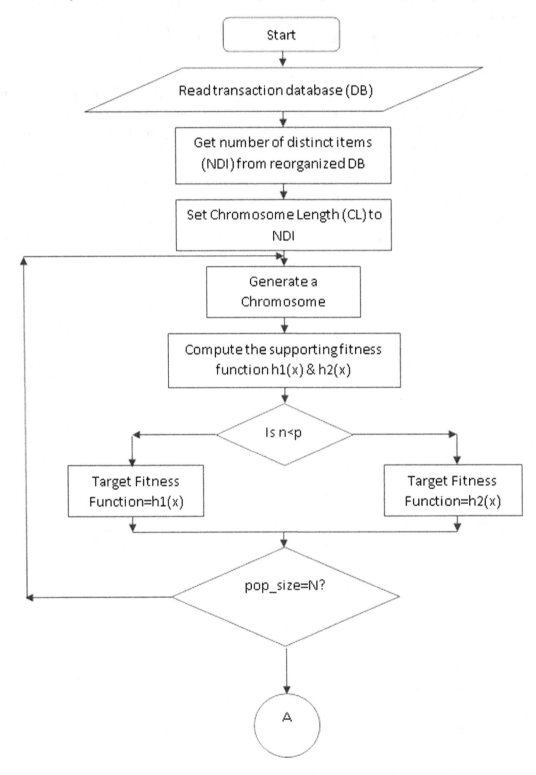

Algorithm for Discovering HUI Using GA With Adaptive Fitness Function

```
GA(n, χ, μ)
begin
Population initialize (n, k)
begin
i←0; .for i←0.to n do
begin
                pop[i]←0.end
while i≤k.do
begin
                rand_no←rand(k) .                    if pop[rand_no]≠1.then
                begin
                        pop[rand_no]←1.                      i←i+1
.               end
end
return pop;
end
```

P_k←population initialize(n,k) .// a population of n randomly-generated individuals;

//Evaluate P_k

Compute target fitness(i) for each i∈P_k. $f\left(i\right) \leftarrow \sum_{T_q \in D \wedge X \subseteq T_q} U\left(X, T_q\right)$ .Compute supporting

fitness functions

$h_1(x)$=max(x,p) where p is switching point . $h_2(x)$=max(x,p) where p is switching point .*if n<p.then*

```
begin
                target fitness(i)←h₁(x) .else then
                target fitness(i)←h₂(x) .end
do
begin
                //Create generation k+1:
//1. Copy:
                Select (1 - χ) × n members of Pₖ and insert into Pₖ₊₁;

                // 2. Crossover:
Select χ × n members of Pₖ;
pair them up;
produce offspring;
insert the offspring into Pₖ₊₁;

                // 3. Mutate:
```

```
Select μ × n members of P_{k+1};
invert a randomly-selected bit in each;

                // Evaluate P_{k+1}:
Compute fitness(i) for each i∈P_k.
                // Increment:
        k←k+1
end
while fitness of fittest individual in P_k is not high enough;
return fittest individual from P_k;
end
```

EMPIRICAL EVALUATION

Experimental Environment and Datasets

Significant experiment analysis has been done using GA which is controlled by Delayed Q-learning. Synthetic dataset T25.I10.D10K is used as input dataset for proposed methodology and the experiment is done on a machine with 2.40 GHz Intel® Core™ i5 CPU and 4GB RAMrunning on Windows 7.T25. I10.D10K dataset contains average transaction of size 25, an average size of the maximal significant frequent itemsets of 4 and 10000 synthetic transactions.

Figure 8 shows that the execution time of the proposed methodology gradually decreases as the minimum utility threshold percentage is increased.

Figure 9. Runtime vs minimum utility threshold

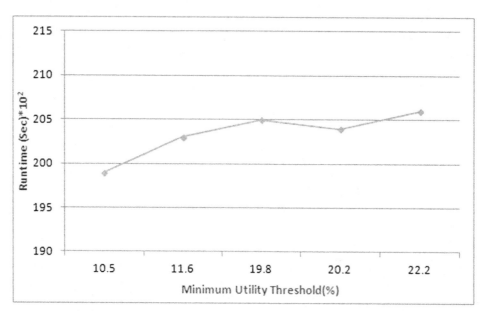

Figure 9 shows the plot between number of transactions and runtime. As the number of transactions increases, the runtime also increases.

Figure 10 shows the plot of number of patterns mined in different range of generations. It is identified from graph that as the number of generation increases the number of patterns mined also increases.

Figure 10. Runtime vs number of transactions

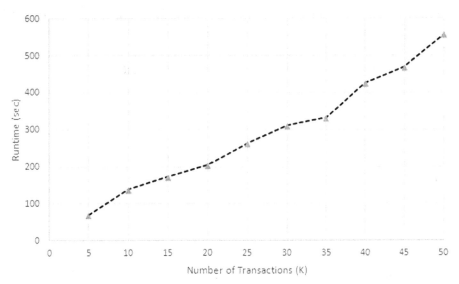

Figure 11. Number of patterns vs number of generations

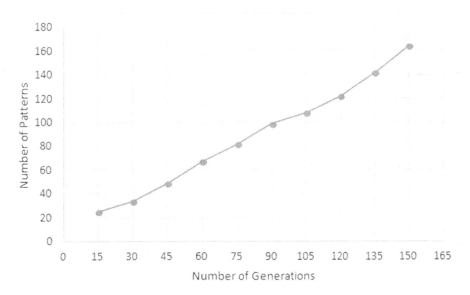

CONCLUSION

Mining high utility itmeset from given databased is one of the emerging research problem in recent years. It plays major roll in market basket analysis inorder to make profitable ecommerce business. Even though many traditional approaches using tree structure were proposed to mine high utility itmeset, the performance of those approaches are still questionable when database size and transaction size is huge. Only few approaches using evolutionary algorithms were used in recent years to improve the mining performance. In this article an methodology is described to dynamically choose the current fitness function in genetic algorithm by using reinforcement learning and is named as RLGA for high utility itmeset mining. This will improve the search speed of a best individual in genetic algorithm. In the proposed methodology the problem of HUI discovery was modeled from the perspective of the GA. The trivial task of selecting optimal minimum utility threshold value is automated by GA.

REFERENCES

Agrawal, R., & Srikant, R. (1994). Fast Algorithms for Mining Association Rules. *Proc. 20th Int'l Conf. Very Large Data Bases (VLDB)*, 487-499.

Ahmed, C. F., Tanbeer, S.-K., Jeong, B.-S., & Lee, Y.-K. (2009). Efficient Tree Structures for High Utility Pattern Mining in Incremental Databases. *IEEE Transactions on Knowledge and Data Engineering*, *21*(12), 1708–1721. doi:10.1109/TKDE.2009.46

Chen, M.-S., Park, J.-S., & Yu, P. S. (1998). Efficient Data Mining for Path Traversal Patterns. *IEEE Transactions on Knowledge and Data Engineering*, *10*(2), 209–221. doi:10.1109/69.683753

Creighton, C., & Hanash, S. (2003). Mining Gene Expression Databases for Association Rules. *Bioinformatics (Oxford, England)*, *19*(1), 79–86. doi:10.1093/bioinformatics/19.1.79 PMID:12499296

Dawar, S., & Goyal, V. (2015). UP-Hist Tree: An Efficient Data Structure for Mining High Utility Patterns from Transaction Databases. *Proc. of the 19th International Database Engineering & Applications Symposium (IDEAS '15)*, 56-61.

Eltabakh, M. Y., Ouzzani, M., Khalil, M. A., Aref, W. G., & Elmagarmid, A. K. (2008). *Incremental Mining for Frequent Patterns in Evolving Time Series Databases. Technical Report CSD TR#08-02.* Purdue Univ.

Erwin, A., Gopalan, R. P., & Achuthan, N. R. (2008). Efficient Mining of High Utility Itemsets from Large Data Sets. *Proc. 12th Pacific-Asia Conf. Advances in Knowledge Discovery and Data Mining (PAKDD)*, 554-561. 10.1007/978-3-540-68125-0_50

Georgii, E., Richter, L., Ruckert, U., & Kramer, S. (2005). Analyzing Microarray Data Using Quantitative Association Rules. *Bioinformatics (Oxford, England)*, *21*(Suppl 2), 123–129. doi:10.1093/bioinformatics/bti1121 PMID:16204090

Han, J., Dong, G., & Yin, Y. (1999). Efficient Mining of Partial Periodic Patterns in Time Series Database. *Proc. Int'l Conf. on Data Eng.*, 106-115.

Han, J., Pei, J., & Yin, Y. (2000). Mining Frequent Patterns without Candidate Generation. *Proc. ACM-SIGMOD Int'l Conf. Management of Data*, 1-12.

Indumathi, M., & Vaithiyanathan, V. (2016). Reduced Overestimated Utility and Pruning Candidates using Incremental Mining. *Indian Journal of Science and Technology*, 9(48). doi:10.17485/ijst/2016/v9i48/107990

Kannimuthua, S., & Vaithiyanathan, V. (2014). Discovery of High Utility Itemsets Using Genetic Algorithm with Ranked Mutation. Applied Artificial Intelligence: An International Journal, 337-359. doi:10.1080/08839514.2014.891839

Lee, S. C., Paik, J., Ok, J., Song, I., & Kim, U. M. (2007). Efficient Mining of User Behaviors by Temporal Mobile Access Patterns. Int'l J. *Computer Science Security*, 7(2), 285–291.

Li, H. F., Huang, H. Y., Chen, Y. C., Liu, Y. J., & Lee, S. Y. (2008). Fast and Memory Efficient Mining of High Utility Itemsets in Data Streams. *Proc. IEEE Eighth Int'l Conf. on Data Mining*, 881-886. 10.1109/ICDM.2008.107

Li, Y.-C., Yeh, J.-S., & Chang, C.-C. (2008). Isolated Items Discarding Strategy for Discovering High Utility Itemsets. *Data & Knowledge Engineering*, 64(1), 198–217. doi:10.1016/j.datak.2007.06.009

Lin, C.H., Chiu, D.Y., Wu, Y.H. & Chen, A.L.P. (2005). Mining Frequent Itemsets from Data Streams with a Time-Sensitive Sliding Window. *Proc. SIAM Int'l Conf. Data Mining (SDM '05)*.

Lin, C.-W., Hong, T.-P., & Lu, W.-H. (2010). Effciently mining high average utility itemsets with a tree structure. *Proc. Int. Conf. Intell. Inf.Database Syst.*, 131-139.

Lin, C.-W., Yang, L., Fournier-Viger, P., Hong, T.-P., & Voznak, M. (2016). *A binary PSO approach to mine high-utility itemsets*. Methodologies And Application Springer.

Lin, J. C.-W., Ren, S., Fournier-Viger, P., & Hong, T.-P. (2017). EHAUPM: Efficient High Average-Utility Pattern Mining With Tighter Upper Bounds. *IEEE Access: Practical Innovations, Open Solutions*, 5, 12927–12940. doi:10.1109/ACCESS.2017.2717438

Lin, J. C.-W., Yang, L., Fournier-Viger, P., Wu, J. M.-T., Hong, T.-P., Wang, L. S.-L., & Zhan, J. (2016). Mining high-utility itemsets based on particle swarm optimization. *Engineering Applications of Artificial Intelligence*, 55, 320–330. doi:10.1016/j.engappai.2016.07.006

Liu, Y., Liao, W., & Choudhary, A. (2005). A Fast High Utility Itemsets Mining Algorithm. *Proc. Utility-Based Data Mining Workshop*. 10.1145/1089827.1089839

Martinez, R., Pasquier, N., & Pasquier, C. (2008). GenMiner: Mining nonredundant Association Rules from Integrated Gene Expression Data and Annotations. *Bioinformatics (Oxford, England)*, 24(22), 2643–2644. doi:10.1093/bioinformatics/btn490 PMID:18799482

Pei, J., Han, J., Lu, H., Nishio, S., Tang, S., & Yang, D. (2007). H-Mine: Fast and Space-Preserving Frequent Pattern Mining in Large Databases. *IIE Trans. Inst. of Industrial Engineers*, 39(6), 593–605.

Shie, B.-E., Hsiao, H.-F., Tseng, V.-S., & Yu, P.-S. (2011). Mining High Utility Mobile Sequential Patterns in Mobile Commerce Environments. *Proc. 16th Int'l Conf. DAtabase Systems for Advanced Applications (DASFAA '11), 6587*, 224-238. 10.1007/978-3-642-20149-3_18

Song, W., & Huang, C. (2018). Mining High Utility Itemsets Using Bio-Inspired Algorithms: A Diverse Optimal Value Framework. *IEEE Access: Practical Innovations, Open Solutions, 6*, 19568–19582. doi:10.1109/ACCESS.2018.2819162

Subramanian, K., & Kandhasamy, P. (2015). UP-GNIV: An expeditious high utility pattern mining algorithm for itemsets with negative utility values. *International Journal of Information Technology and Management, 14*(1), 26–42. doi:10.1504/IJITM.2015.066056

Tanbeer, S. K., Ahmed, C. F., Jeong, B.-S., & Lee, Y.-K. (2008). Efficient Frequent Pattern Mining over Data Streams. *Proc. ACM 17th Conf. Information and Knowledge Management.* 10.1145/1458082.1458326

Tseng, V. S., Chu, C. J., & Liang, T. (2006). Efficient Mining of Temporal High Utility Itemsets from Data Streams. *Proc. ACM KDD Workshop Utility-Based Data Mining Workshop (UBDM '06).*

Tseng, V. S., Shie, B.-E., Wu, C. W., & Yu, P. S. (2013). Efficient Algorithms for Mining High Utility Itemsets from Transactional Databases. *IEEE Transactions on Knowledge and Data Engineering, 25*(8), 1772–1786. doi:10.1109/TKDE.2012.59

Tseng, V. S., Wu, C.-W., Shie, B.-E., & Yu, P. S. (2010). UP-Growth: An Efficient Algorithm for High Utility Itemsets Mining. *Proc. 16th ACM SIGKDD Conf. Knowledge Discovery and Data Mining (KDD '10)*, 253-262. 10.1145/1835804.1835839

Yao, H., Hamilton, H. J., & Butz, C. J. (2004). A foundational approach to mining itemset utilities from databases. *Proc. SIAM Int. Conf. Data Mining*, 482-486. 10.1137/1.9781611972740.51

Yun, C.-H., & Chen, M.-S. (2000). Using Pattern-Join and Purchase-Combination for Mining Web Transaction Patterns in an Electronic Commerce Environment. *Proc. IEEE 24th Ann. Int'l Computer Software and Application Conf.*, 99-104.

Yun, C.-H., & Chen, M. S. (2007). Mining Mobile Sequential Patterns in a Mobile Commerce Environment. IEEE Trans. Systems, Man, and Cybernetics-Part C. *Applications and Rev., 37*(2), 278–295.

Chapter 11
Prediction of High–Risk Factors in Surgical Operations Using Machine Learning Techniques

Anitha N.
Kongu Engineering College, India

Devi Priya R.
Kongu Engineering College, India

ABSTRACT

Prediction of risk during surgical operations is one of the most needed and challenging processes in the healthcare domain. Many researchers use clinical assessment tools to predict perioperative outcomes and postoperative factors in surgical operations. Even though traditional model yields better results, they are not able to achieve promising accuracy due to the enormous growth of data in medical domain. Since the data size grows seamlessly every day, some of the investigators over the past decade use machine learning techniques in their model to predict the risks before and after surgery. Most of the existing systems produced better accuracy by impute missing values in dataset through some common imputation method. However, in order to increase the accuracy level further, two new techniques proposed in this chapter to handle missing values using iterative deepening random forest classifier and identification of surgical risk by using iterative deepening support vector machine. Both of the methods worked well in experimental data set and obtained promising accuracy results.

INTRODUCTION

Surgical process is the most needful one to save human life from severe complications. Many standards of practice like AST standards are available to health care providers for proper surgical treatment. Everyone believes an effective surgeon is the only responsible person for successful surgery operations. However, making an informed decision in surgical process is the challenging one even by an expert surgeon. Even though, Chand et al (2007) determined that the decision making process in surgery has evolved over time, it still requires some qualitative support to treat the patients effectively and smoothly. Due to the

DOI: 10.4018/978-1-5225-9902-9.ch011

environment pollution and vast change in weather condition, rate of infection arises rapidly. To predict the infection risk for a patient during surgery is the complicated process. Pre-operative prediction and quantification of risks will support the patient as well as doctor for safe treatment. Stonelake et al (2015) recommended the huge number of clinical assessment tools are available to predict the risk. However, to provide an optimized solution for risk identification, many researchers use AI and machine learning techniques to make an instinctive decision-making.

Nowadays, there is a rapid growth of data in all sectors and especially in medical field, it grows enormously. Massive amount of data is generated every day and needs to be stored in Electronic health record (EHRs) data warehouse. In this digital era, huge number of genetic data and medical information is stored and manipulated using Machine learning and predictive modelling techniques. To handle those massive amount of data, many researchers preferred to use machine learning and data science technologies. Hence, Ehlers et al (2017) determined that the using machine learning technique in risk prediction during surgery will accurately detect risk and help to treat patients smoothly. When compared with traditional clinical methodologies, machine learning techniques can efficiently find features and nonlinear relationships that exist among them more accurately using predictor variables. Hence, machine learning techniques is widely used in many applications of health care like identification of diabetes, prediction of risks during surgical operations etc. Some health problems can be treated only with the help of surgeries which involve decisions made on collection of sensitive values. Most of the developed countries spend around billions of cost per year for surgical complications. Hence, health care organizations need an effective predictive modeling and accurate solution to detect high-risk individuals in surgery operations.

Classification is one of the supervised learning methods and helps to predict class labels or objects. It is used in many practical applications like image classification, document classification, and speech recognition and so on. Most commonly used algorithms in classification are Naive Bayes, Logistic regression, Decision-tree, Random Forest and SVM classifiers.

Brieman in the year 2001 has recommended Random Forest classifier (RF) which is one of the standard and ensemble classification algorithms. RF uses random subspace method in which each tree is constructed independently based on random samples. Based on training samples and features, a tree is constructed and the root node decision depends upon best split value of k randomly selected variables. Random forest is a well suitable method to handle large number of features in a dataset. As well as it is an efficient process to predict the attribute values even though dataset holds missing values. RF is widely used by many researchers in various fields and produce prominent classification results in health care domain. However, the result interpretation process is vague because of random tree construction process.

Nowadays, researchers uses ensemble classifiers in all domains especially in remote sensing applications. A complete review and future scope on RF classifiers in remote sensing field is prescribed by Belgiu & Dragut (2016). RF classifier is one of the best suitable classifiers for high dimensional data. In order to achieve effective text classification, Thiago et al (2018) have proposed an improved version of Random forest classifier. They eliminate the major issue of Random forest such as over fitting problem particularly in high dimensional data by using the nearest neighborhood training set projection. Thus, the modified RF classifier works better than the other classifiers in automatic text classification process. Random forest has also outperformed well in health care domains. Zhen et al (2019) have developed an integrated approach called LSTM-based ensemble malonylation predictor (LEMP) which is the combination of RF and deep learning network with one hot encoding mechanisms. They predict malonylation sites in substrates and proved that performance of this approach was promising compared to other standard classifiers.

Customer churn prediction is one of the famous applications in that both decision tree and logistic regression have shown strong and feasible performance. Instead of using a separate classifier in prediction, the author Arno et al (2018) have proposed a hybrid approach logit leaf model (LLM)by using the above popular algorithm in order to achieve better classification. LLM approach have shown that the comprehensibility performance was improved better rather than using decision tree and logistic regression separately. Hence, Random forest classifier is one of the popular and best techniques among different classifiers. Many researchers have widely used this technique for discriminating the features. RF is a powerful classifier since it constructs multiple trees based on the random input variables and summarize the estimated values of posterior probability from each tree. RF yields better results than other classification algorithms because of its statistical properties and well supported by mathematical concepts. Sometimes, it may fail when there is no efficient feature set.

SVM classifier is one of the best and famous algorithms to classify the data which contains 'n' number of features. It represents n features in n dimensional space by plotting each data as a coordinate point. SVM classifies the data points by finding hyper plane which helps to discriminate the classes effectively. This technique always produces better results and achieves promising accuracy. So, it can be widely used in many fields like text categorization, hand-written digit recognition, tone recognition, image classification and object detection, microarray gene expression data analysis and data classification. Rakhmetulayeva et al (2018) used SVM classifiers to detect the effectiveness of drug test treatment for tuberculosis. Diagnosis is one of the time consuming process in medical application. By using SVM classifier, the model reduces the burden of doctors to some extent in making their own assumptions and intuition about disease diagnosis methodology. Prediction process is not accurate in high dimensional data. Developing prediction model with noisy features present in high dimensional data is often a more challenging process. Ghaddar& Naoum-Sawaya (2017) have used SVM classifier to perform feature selection and tested with two real life problems like tumor classification and sentiment classification. The results have proved that the model used have reduced the issues in high dimensional dataset. Even though SVM yields better results, its performance is not satisfactory when there is a noisy dataset. To overcome this limitation, instead of directly assigning the dataset to SVM model, the dataset is first preprocessed and then cross-validation is performed.

Iterative- Deepening (ID) is one of the uninformed search methods and it inherits two characteristics from Breadth First Search (BFS) and Depth First Search (DFS). DFS shows space efficiency and BFS incorporates fast searching nature. The working principle of ID method is to visit the root nodes several times and leaf node once. Thus, the ID method eventually reduces the searching space complexity from exponential to linear and cost is not so expensive.

The data collected for surgery may contain large number of features and sometimes some of their values be missing which are very crucial for providing precise treatment. Many researchers have already used machine learning methods for identifying high risk factors. But, most of the methods have ignored the missing values and make decisions only from the data that is available which creates bias in surgical operations. Also, there is a cutting edge demand in a novel method for identifying high risk factors. In order to improve the classification accuracy in risk prediction of surgical data, we have proposed a method in which hybridization of RF with Iterative Deepening (ID) method is done to impute the missing values appropriately and SVM is combined with ID method for accurate classification. Hence, the proposed system addresses the above mentioned issues using machine learning techniques and makes two contributions: (i) Treatment of missing values using Iterative Deepening Random Forest method (IDRF) and (ii) Classification using Iterative Deepening Support Vector Method (IDSVM).

The proposed system is implemented in different kinds of large surgical datasets and the predictive accuracy was found to be improved. The chapter is organized as first describes the background information, then describes the proposed system, next discusses about the results and finally provides conclusion and further enhancement options.

BACKGROUND

Surgical risk prediction is one of the most needful and crucial applications in medical domain. Many researchers have worked on this area and produced promising results by using clinical assessment tools and modern technologies like AI and machine learning. When compared to other assessment tools, machine learning algorithms performs well in predicting the risk accurately during surgical operations.

Ehlers et al (2017) predicted Adverse Events (AE) or death risks more accurately by using Naïve Bayes algorithm. This method uses around 300 predictor variables and weight of each predictor is computed probabilistically rather than assignment of some manual values to variables. Over fitting problem is reduced by partitioning the dataset randomly into equal sized samples and finally aggregating them to assess model performance. Charlson comorbidity index statistical method is used to evaluate the prediction model and outperforms well.

Wong et al (2018) have used machine learning approaches to find delirium risk for newly hospitalized patients with high-dimensional EHR data at a large academic health institution. This method uses more than 796 variables which are highly related to delirium prediction. They have developed prediction model based on five different ML algorithms. When compared with the questionnaire-based scoring system, machine learning algorithms perform well even with large number of predictor variables.

A real time diagnostic and prognostic model was developed by Meyer et al (2018) using recurrent deep neural network to predict the risk in cardiac surgery involving many static and dynamic variables. Postoperative complication risk is a type of risk that was accurately predicted from EHR data repository by using machine learning methods. This method have shown accurate predictions when patients are shifted to ICU after surgery. The model performance were validated against MIMIC-III data set and standard clinical tools. Validation results have proved that this machine learning model surpasses the traditional assessment techniques.

An automatic clinical repository system was proposed by Corey et al (2018) to predict postoperative complication risk using machine learning methods. Lasso penalized regression model is used to assess the risk among 174 clinical features. To avoid generalization problem, cross validation is performed. Finally, a prediction model is built by using random forest and extreme gradient boosted decision trees. Compared to ACS NSQIP calculator a standard clinical tool, their method performs well and end ups with a strong prediction model.

Machine Learning methods are used to develop a model to predict mortality after elective cardiac surgery. Jérôme Allyn et al (2017) used five different ML algorithms and performed feature selection using Chi-Square filtering. When compared to the single ML algorithm, the ensemble results of five different ML algorithm have shown better accuracy. To validate the model, they have used ROC and Decision Curve Analysis (DCA) and it has been proven that ML algorithms predicts more accurately than the standard clinical assessment tool namely Euro SCORE II.

Composite kernel methods are used by Soguero-Ruiz, et.al (2016) to predict the common postoperative complication Anastomosis Leakage (AL). K Nearest Neighbor (KNN) algorithm is used for missing values imputation in datasets chosen from EHR repository. Feature selection algorithm is employed to choose best features from heterogeneous dataset. The powerful kernel classifiers are observed to predict AL risk at an early stage.

Todd C et al (2018) predicted postoperative factors in Pituitary adenomas proposed by is one of the challenging processes because of its heterogeneity nature. The developed model predict the postoperative outcomes with 87% accuracy than the clinical assessment tools. Thus with the help of machine learning algorithms highly improved the patient care who have the issues of pituitary adenoma. Dogan et al (2018) developed a DNA-based precision tool to predict the risk for incident coronary heart disease. The system eventually increased the accuracy level compared to traditional model.

Even though, the existing methods with the help of machine learning techniques produce promising results, still desired accuracy in prediction of risk is not achievable. Existing methods failed to address the missing values which is a major issue in all domains especially in health care applications. Since every value contains some valuable information, if any of the values is missed in dataset, then the prediction model is not accurate. Hence, proper way of handling missing values is very important which is considered and implemented by only few researchers.

The performance assessment for cardiac surgery Prediction Model was evaluated based on the effect of imputation of missing values. Karim et al (2017) used Bland-Altman method to assess the risks generated by two different approaches namely complete cases (CC) analysis and multiple imputation (MI) analysis. As a result shown that MI analysis yielded better prediction of mortality risk. But still many of the researchers either ignored the missing values or filled with null value, even though it was an important issue in healthcare domain .Only few work have done to handle missing value in an appropriate manner. As well as in development of prediction model many of them used Naïve Bayes, random forest, logistic regression and so on. Without preprocessing of data used algorithms directly for to predict the risk in surgical operations. This may lead to failure model.

RF has been widely used in surgical risk prediction application. Alexander et al (2016) have used the RF algorithm to categorize pre-operative predictors based on its importance to classify the postoperative complications. However, the system fails to impute missing value in a proper manner. Lee et al (2018) used many algorithms like decision tree, random forest, extreme gradient boosting, support vector machine and deep learning to predict the kidney infection after cardiac surgery. It has been proven that the ensemble random forest classifier have shown highest AUC curve and lower error-rate than the other algorithms.

SVM classifier is one of the excellent tools and widely used in medical research. Some of the investigators employs SVM classifier to predict the risk during surgery. The likelihood performance assessment in perioperative cardiac events is a difficult process. Kasamatsu et al (2008) used SVM classifiers and produced better accuracy results when compared to conventional model. This technique builds an effective hyper plane so that the patients are split into different groups based on prognostic values and higher predictive accuracy is obtained than other conventional linear model.

From the existing studies, it has been realized that identification of risks which are very critical during surgery is very much essential to reduce surgical complications. Traditional clinical tests and procedures cannot predict risks accurately because of large size, heterogeneous nature and high complexity of data involved. Machine learning tools support health care providers to accurately predict the patient's high risks of surgical complications than other conventional procedures. Even then, to improve the accuracy further and to address the missingness of data issue, a hybridization approach of RF with ID and SVM with ID have been proposed. The nature of ID will search for optimal results and hence combining RF with ID will handle missing values and ID with SVM will classify the risk appropriately.

PROPOSED METHODOLOGY

The aim of the proposed system is to achieve high accuracy in prediction of high risk factors in order to reduce complications during and after surgical operations. The system performs the task by implementing these two strategies. (i) Missing value treatment using Iterative Deepening Random Forest method (IDRF) and (ii) Prediction of High risk factors using Iterative Deepening Support Vector Machine (IDSVM).

In the proposed method used six different kind of datasets and implemented in Anaconda Environment using Python package. Since, there are different kinds of datasets with complex nature, the first Step is to preprocess the experimental datasets. Among six different types of surgical datasets, thoracic and post-operative dataset contains more number of categorical attributes. The thoracic dataset consists of 470 samples and 17 features in which 14 features are categorical attributes. Likewise post-operative dataset contains 90 samples and 9 categorical features. The most important crucial process in machine learning is handling of categorical attributes. In this proposed system, "one hot encoding" mechanism is used to handle categorical attributes. This method is used to map ordinal and nominal attribute values to numeric values in a proper way.

Figure 1. Proposed model IDRF_IDSVM

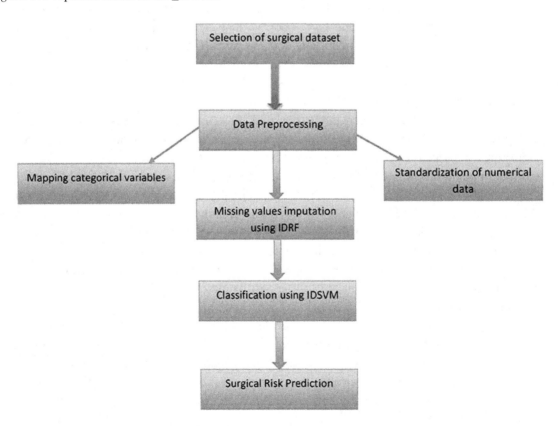

Next step is to impute the missing values using the proposed method IDRF. Before applying dataset to IDRF first temporarily delete 25% of original values in dataset. The input for this procedure is random features selected from those missing value datasets. The split node is calculated for to decide the root node in forest. In this proposed system, iterative deepening search mechanism is used to select the best split node. Suppose the split node contains missing value means then random value is used to fill that value which is taken from non missing values in data sets. The forest construction process is iteratively repeated until terminal nodes are reached. When there is a missing value occurs during construction process the values imputed based on the grown forest node values. The above process is repeated until all the missing values imputed through the random forest method.

Once the missing imputation process is over then the next step is to predict the risk in surgical operations. To develop a predict model, the proposed system uses IDSVM method .The most important process in classification is feature selection. Thus the IDRF method is used to select the important features from dataset during the process of missing imputation. In order to perform classification first cross validation method is used to split the samples into training and testing data. Next apply SVM algorithm to dataset for prediction of high risk factors. SVM classifier accuracy is depend upon the parameter selection. Therefore we used iterative deepening method for parameter selection. After selection process is over, model is fitted using training samples and predicted using test data. Finally fitness function is used to evaluate the predicted risk with selected features. Figure 1 depicts the proposed model of IDRF_IDSVM for surgical risk prediction.

Iterative Deepening Random Forest Method

Many researchers have found missingness issues in healthcare datasets like EHR, MIMIC-III datasets, etc., The standard Random forest classifier method has been commonly used for missing value treatment and it is chosen for this problem because it is one of the easiest and flexible techniques among machine learning methods and can be used for both classification (predicting discrete attributes) and regression (predicting continuous attributes). It always produces best result from randomness of data and choses the optimum result from random data instead of searching nodes in sequential manner. Even then, there is still scope for further enhancement and hence in order to improve the accuracy further, local search mechanism called iterative deepening search method is integrated with random forest classifier. In order to yield best results, the method fixes the threshold for each feature rather than searching for the best possible nodes in the tree. The exploitative capability of the random forest method is further enhanced by searching for the right value to be distributed in the missing hole. In IDRF, Iterative deepening method works in an iterative manner and the nodes are visited multiple times so that it produces best results.

Tang and Ishwaran (2017) proposed novel random forest approaches and revealed that the RF imputation is one of the best method to handle missingness of data and improved accuracy further. It works better even when there is a noisy dataset. In medical domain, especially prediction of risk during surgical operations faces many issues in noisy data. Hence, our objective is to handle missingness of data using RF imputation method with Iterative deepening local search mechanism.

IDRF method first preimpute missing values using random values taken from non-missing data samples. Next the split node is calculated using non-missing data and the best node is found using iterative deepening method. Then, the missing values are predicted in the existing forest and the predicted values are substituted. This process is repeatedly done until terminal nodes are reached.

Figure 2. Pseudocode for iterative deepening based random forest

```
Input: X ( m rows and n columns matrix), rmax and cmax

1: Check if there exists any column that has more than cmax missing values

2: If Yes

3:     Halt and report error

4: else

5:     log-transform the data

6: end if

7: for i = 1, ...,m do

8:   if row i has more than rmax missing values then

9:       Impute missing values by random value form the non-missing data

10: else

11:   if row i has at least one but no more than rmax missing values then

12:       pos ← record the positions where row i has missing values

13:       Find rows that have no missing values in column pos

14:       Calculate the split-statistic for splitting a tree node of row i with these rows

          using Iterative deepening

15:       Repeat steps 7 to 14 until terminal nodes are reached

16: end if

17: end if

18: end for
```

Iterative Deepening Support Vector Machine (IDSVM)

Now, the dataset contains complete records without any missing values and is ready for performing prediction. The dataset may contain many features some of which may be significant and some may be insignificant. SVM is a supervised learning technique that can be used to classify data by finding hyper planes in different classes. Classifiers can easily separate classes in linear hyper planes and not suitable for complex data. High risk factors are complex in nature. In order to handle those complex data, feature selection process is employed in IDRF missing imputation datasets. Feature Selection process is the most important process in preprocessing particularly which helps to obtain good accuracy results when there is a high dimensional dataset. SVM classifier is integrated with iterative deepening method to classify the risks in a very accurate manner and its fitness function is evaluated with the feature selected during IDRF process.

In order to identify the most significant features which carries high risks and influence surgical operations, a methodology called Iterative Deepening Support Vector Machine is proposed which is a hybrid combination of iterative deepening strategy with support vector machine. Both of the techniques work in parallel to predict the risk during surgical operations. Hence the objective of our proposed system in

Figure 3. Flow chart for iterative deepening based support vector machine

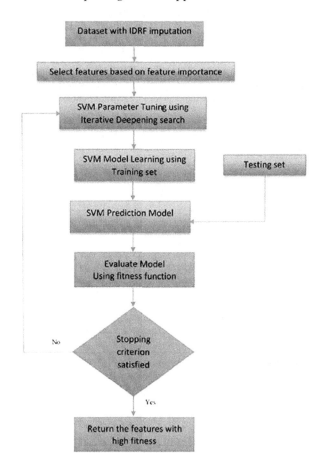

classification of risks is to use iterative deepening local search method with the SVM classifier to accurately predict high risk factors inducing surgical complications.

The process is performed iteratively and hence chances of the algorithm getting terminated without identifying the best solution is decreased to a great extent. The algorithm is run for multiple iterations and hence the solutions gets improved in each iteration. The algorithm is implemented in different kinds of surgical datasets and the risk is predicted in a very accurate manner.

EXPERIMENTAL RESULTS AND DISCUSSION

Data Set Description

Surgical datasets collected from UCI repository have been used in this proposed system to predict the risk during surgical operations. The proposed model uses six different types of surgical datasets for classification. Table 1 describes the characteristics of different data sets.

Table 1. Features overview in all six datasets

Name of the data set	Instances	Independent Attributes	Dependent Attributes
Thoracic Surgery	470	DgnCode, Fvc, Fev1, Performance Status, Pain Before Surgery, Haemoptysis Before Surgery, Dyspnoea Before Surgery, Cough Before Surgery, Weakness Before Surgery, Tnm(Size Of The Orginal Tumour), Diabetes Mellitus, Mi Upto 6 Months, Pad, Smoking, Asthma, Age At Surgery	Risk1y T stands for high risk and F stands for low risk
Breast Cancer	699	Clump Thickness, Uniformity of Cell Size, Uniformity of Cell Shape, Marginal Adhesion, Single Epithelial Cell Size, Bare Nuclei, Bland Chromatin, Normal Nucleoli and Mitoses	Identity 2 stands for benign and 4 stands for malignant
Crypo Therapy	90	Sex,Age,Time, Number_of_Warts, Area	Result_of_Treatment 0- 1-
Haberman's Surgery	306	Age of patient at time of operation, Number of positive axillary nodes detected, Patients year of operation	Survival status 1- 2-
Post-Operative Patient Data	90	L-Core(Patient's Internal Temperature In Celsius), L-Surf(Patient's Surface Temperature In Celsius), L-02 (Oxygen Saturation In Percentage), L-Bp (Last Measurement Of Blood Pressure), Surf-Stbl (Stability Of Patient's Surface Temperature), Core-Stbl (Stability Of Patient's Core Temperature), Bp-Stbl (Stability Of Patient's Blood Pressure), Comfort (Patient's Perceived Comfort At Discharge Measured As An Integer Between 0 And 20)	Decision Adm-Decs (Discharge Decision) S- A-
Lung Cancer	309	Gender,Age,Smoking, Yellow_Fingers, Anxiety, Peer_Pressure, Chronic Disease, Fatigue, Allergy, Wheezing, Alcohol Consuming, Coughing, Shortness Of Breath, Swallowing Difficulty, Chest Pain	Lung_Cancer Yes- No-

Table 2. Baseline characteristics of Habermans

BC	Age of patient at time of operation	Patients year of operation	Number of positive axillary nodes detected
count	306.000000	306.000000	306.000000
mean	52.457516	62.852941	4.026144
std	10.803452	3.249405	7.189654
min	30.000000	58.000000	0.000000
25%	44.000000	60.000000	0.000000
50%	52.000000	63.000000	1.000000
75%	60.750000	65.750000	4.000000
max	83.000000	69.000000	52.000000

The above tables represents the baseline characteristics of numeric features presented in datasets. From the above tables it was inferred that the thoracic and post-operative dataset contains many categorical attributes compared to other datasets.

Table 3. Baseline characteristics of cryotherapy

BC	sex	age	Time	Number of Warts	Type	Area	Result_of_ Treatment
count	90.000000	90.000000	90.000000	90.000000	90.000000	90.000000	90.000000
mean	1.477778	28.600000	7.666667	5.511111	1.700000	85.833333	0.533333
std	0.502304	13.360852	3.406661	3.567155	0.905042	131.733153	0.501683
min	1.000000	15.000000	0.250000	1.000000	1.000000	4.000000	0.000000
25%	1.000000	18.000000	4.562500	2.000000	1.000000	20.000000	0.000000
50%	1.000000	25.500000	8.500000	5.000000	1.000000	70.000000	1.000000
75%	2.000000	35.000000	10.687500	8.000000	3.000000	100.000000	1.000000
max	2.000000	67.000000	12.000000	12.000000	3.000000	750.000000	1.000000

Table 4. Baseline Characteristics of Breast Cancer

BC	Clump Thickness	Uniformity of Cell Size	Uniformity of Cell Shape	Marginal Adhesion	Single Epithelial Cell Size	Bland Chromatin	Normal Nucleoli	Mitoses	identity
count	699.00	699.00	699.00	699.00	699.00	699.00	699.00	699.00	699.00
mean	4.417740	3.134478	3.207439	2.806867	3.216023	3.437768	2.866953	1.589413	2.689557
std	2.815741	3.051459	2.971913	2.855379	2.214300	2.438364	3.053634	1.715078	0.951273
min	1.000000	1.000000	1.000000	1.000000	1.000000	1.000000	1.000000	1.000000	2.000000
25%	2.000000	1.000000	1.000000	1.000000	2.000000	2.000000	1.000000	1.000000	2.000000
50%	4.000000	1.000000	1.000000	1.000000	2.000000	3.000000	1.000000	1.000000	2.000000
75%	6.000000	5.000000	5.000000	4.000000	4.000000	5.000000	4.000000	1.000000	4.000000
max	10.000000	10.000000	10.000000	10.000000	10.000000	10.000000	10.000000	10.000000	4.000000

Table 5. Baseline characteristics of post-operative patient dataset

BC	l_core	l_surf	l_o2	l_bp	surf_stbl	core_stbl	bp_stbl	comfort	decision
count	90	90	90	90	90	90	90	90	90
unique	3	3	2	3	2	3	3	5	4
top	mid	mid	good	mid	stable	stable	stable	10	A
freq	58	48	47	57	45	83	46	65	63

Performance Measures

In this system the five different classification measures used to evaluate the model accuracy. Definitions:

True positive (TP) = the number of cases correctly identified as patient
False positive (FP) = the number of cases incorrectly identified as patient
True negative (TN) = the number of cases correctly identified as healthy

Table 6. Baseline characteristics of survey lung cancer dataset

BC	Age	Smoking	Yellow Fingers	Anxiety	Peer Pr.	Chronic Disease	Fatigue	Allergy	Wheezing	Alcohol Consuming	Coughing	Shortness of Breath	Swallowing Difficulty	Chest Pain
count	309.0	309.0	309.0	309.0	309.0	309.0	309.0	309.0	309.0	309.0	309.0	309.0	309.0	309.0
mean	62.67	1.563	1.569	1.498	1.501	1.504	1.673	1.556	1.556	1.556	1.579	1.640	1.469	1.556
std	8.210	0.496	0.495	0.500	0.500	0.500	0.469	0.497	0.497	0.497	0.494	0.480	0.499	0.497
min	21.00	1.0	1.0	1.0	1.0	1.0	1.0	1.0	1.0	1.0	1.0	1.0	1.0	1.0
25%	57.00	1.0	1.0	1.0	1.0	1.0	1.0	1.0	1.0	1.0	1.0	1.0	1.0	1.0
50%	62.00	2.0	2.0	2.0	2.0	2.0	2.0	2.0	2.0	2.0	2.0	2.0	2.0	2.0
75%	69.00	2.0	2.0	2.0	2.0	2.0	2.0	2.0	2.0	2.0	2.0	2.0	2.0	2.0
max	87.0	2.0	2.0	2.0	2.0	2.0	2.0	2.0	2.0	2.0	2.0	2.0	2.0	2.0

Table 7. Baseline characteristics of thoracic dataset

BC	FVC	FEV1	AGE
count	470.000000	470.000000	470.000000
mean	3.281638	4.568702	62.534043
std	0.871395	11.767857	8.706902
min	1.440000	0.960000	21.000000
25%	2.600000	1.960000	57.000000
50%	3.160000	2.400000	62.000000
75%	3.807500	3.080000	69.000000
max	6.300000	86.300000	87.000000

False negative (FN) = the number of cases incorrectly identified as healthy

1.   Precision also known as Positive Predictive Value (PPV) is calculated as

Precision = TP/(TP+FP)

Sometimes PPV will give biased results when there is an imbalanced classes.
2.   Sensitivity/Recall also known as the True Positive rate or Recall is calculated as,

Sensitivity = TP/(TP+FN)

Since the formula doesn't contain FP and TN, Sensitivity may give you a biased result, especially for imbalanced classes.
3.   Specificity, also known as True Negative Rate is calculated as,

Specificity = TN/(TN+FP)

Since the formula does not contain FN and TP, Specificity may give you a biased result, especially for imbalanced classes.

4. F1-Score is used to measure a test's accuracy and it lies between precision and recall. The range for F1 Score is [0, 1].

$$F1 = 2 * \frac{Precision \times Recall}{Precision + Recall}$$

5. Accuracy Score is used to test the performance of classifiers whether it correctly classified the instances.

$$Accuracy = \frac{TP + TN}{TP + TN + FP + FN}$$

RESULT AND DISCUSSION

Experimental data sets implemented in Anaconda Environment using Python package. The four different classifiers such as Random Forest, Support Vector Machine, K-Nearest Neighbor, and Logistic Regression classifiers are used to show how the classifiers accuracy improve over by using proposed IDRF missing imputation method. The following table represents the performance measures for all data sets for four classifiers by without imputation process of missing values and with IDRF imputation process.

Table 8. Performance measures of four different classifiers for without imputation of missing values and with using IDRF imputation for all datasets

Classifiers	Precision	Recall	F1-Score	Specificity	Accuracy
Performance Measures of Habermans dataset without missing values imputation					
RF	0.72	0.97	0.83	0.02	0.72
SVM	0.74	0.95	0.83	0.09	0.71
KNN	0.79	0.86	0.82	0.38	0.73
LR	0.86	0.40	0.54	0.83	0.51
Performance Measures of Habermans dataset with IDRF imputation					
RF	0.73	0.97	0.83	0.04	0.72
SVM	0.74	0.95	0.83	0.09	0.72
KNN	0.79	0.86	0.82	0.38	0.73
LR	0.86	0.45	0.56	0.80	0.53
Performance Measures of Cryotherapy dataset without missing values imputation					
RF	0.38	0.23	0.29	0.47	0.33
SVM	0.43	0.35	0.38	0.36	0.35
KNN	0.60	0.46	0.52	0.57	0.51

Table 8. Continued

Classifiers	Precision	Recall	F1-Score	Specificity	Accuracy
LR	0.40	0.31	0.35	0.36	0.33
Performance Measures of Cryotherapy dataset with IDRF imputation					
RF	0.40	0.24	0.30	0.40	0.35
SVM	0.44	0.35	0.40	0.33	0.38
KNN	0.62	0.48	0.53	0.50	0.53
LR	0.42	0.33	0.37	0.33	0.35
Performance Measures of Breast Cancer dataset without missing values imputation					
RF	1.00	0.96	0.98	0.98	0.96
SVM	0.78	0.97	0.86	0.10	0.76
KNN	0.76	0.72	0.74	0.25	0.61
LR	0.77	1.00	0.87	0.0	0.76
Performance Measures of Breast Cancer dataset with IDRF imputation					
RF	1.00	0.96	0.98	0.98	0.96
SVM	0.78	0.97	0.86	0.10	0.76
KNN	0.76	0.72	0.74	0.25	0.61
LR	0.77	1.00	0.87	0.0	0.76
Performance Measures of Survey Lung Cancer dataset without missing values imputation					
RF	0.88	1.00	0.93	1.0	0.87
SVM	0.96	0.95	0.96	0.73	0.92
KNN	0.89	0.99	0.94	0.15	0.88
LR	0.96	0.95	0.95	0.68	0.91
Performance Measures of Survey Lung Cancer with IDRF imputation					
RF	0.88	1.00	0.93	1.0	0.87
SVM	0.96	0.95	0.96	0.73	0.92
KNN	0.89	0.99	0.94	0.15	0.88
LR	0.96	0.95	0.95	0.68	0.91
Performance Measures of Thoracic dataset without missing values imputation					
RF	0.87	1.00	0.93	0.0	0.87
SVM	0.87	1.00	0.93	0.0	0.87
KNN	0.88	1.00	0.93	0.03	0.87
LR	0.88	0.98	0.93	0.06	0.86
Performance Measures of Thoracic dataset with IDRF imputation					
RF	0.87	1.00	0.93	0.0	0.87
SVM	0.87	1.00	0.93	0.0	0.87
KNN	0.88	1.00	0.93	0.03	0.87
LR	0.88	0.98	0.93	0.06	0.86

continued on following page

Table 8. Continued

Classifiers	Precision	Recall	F1-Score	Specificity	Accuracy
Performance Measures of Post-Operative Patient dataset without missing values imputation					
RF	0.75	0.88	0.81	0.09	0.68
SVM	0.76	0.94	0.84	0.09	0.73
KNN	0.75	0.79	0.77	0.18	0.64
LR	0.75	0.71	0.73	0.27	0.60
Performance Measures of Post-Operative Patient dataset with IDRF imputation					
RF	0.73	0.97	0.83	0.04	0.72
SVM	0.74	0.95	0.83	0.09	0.72
KNN	0.75	0.88	0.81	0.09	0.68
LR	0.76	0.72	0.74	0.25	0.61

Table 8 depicts the performance measures of four different classifiers such as Random Forest, Support Vector Machine, K-Nearest Neighbor and Logistic regression without imputation of missing values and with IDRF imputation for all six data sets. From the above table 8, it is observed that the missing values in dataset have predominant effect in classification accuracy. As well as table shows that the imputation of missing values using IDRF gradually improves the prediction model accuracy. Thus, the results have shown that the performance is slightly improved for all classifiers by using the proposed method IDRF.

In order to increase the accuracy level further, feature selection process is performed using Random Forest and then these important features are used for prediction of risks using proposed method IDSVM. The following figures represents the process of feature selection for all datasets.

Figure 4. Feature importances-Habermans

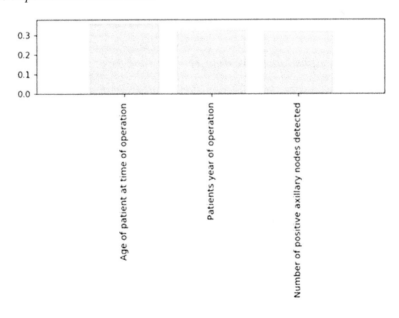

Figure 5. Feature importances-Cryotherapy

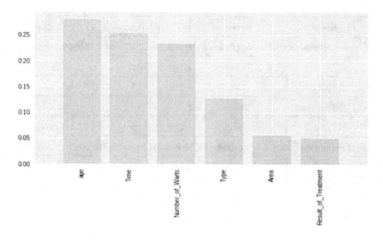

Figure 6. Feature importances-Breast Cancer

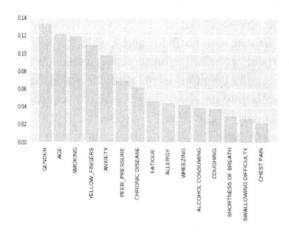

Figure 7. Feature importances-post-operative dataset

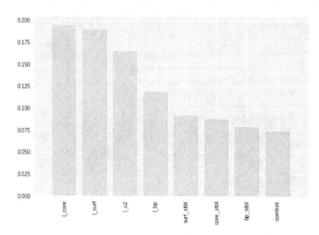

Figure 8. Feature importances-survey lung cancer

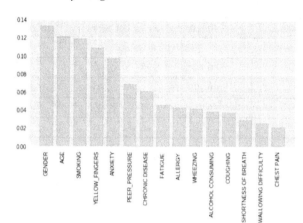

Figure 9. Feature importances-thoracic

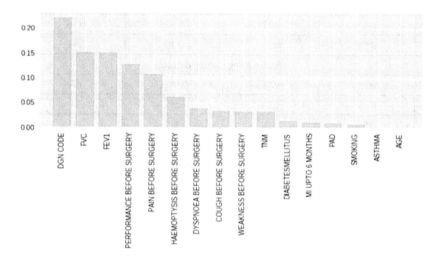

The following Table 9 demonstrates the classification measures for all datasets by comparing our proposed method IDRF based IDSVM (IDRF_IDSVM) with three different classifiers such as Recurrent Neural Network (RNN), least absolute shrinkage and selection operator (LASSO) penalized logistic regression and Extreme gradient boosted decision trees (EGBDT). The results depict that our proposed method performs better than the other compared classifiers by showing slight improvement in accuracy level.

From the above table 9, it is observed that the imputation of missing values using IDRF in the datasets have produced promising results in IDSVM classification accuracy as compared to other classifiers.

Table 9. Classification measures of different classifiers for all datasets

Classifiers	Precision	Recall	F1-Score	Specificity	Accuracy
Habermans dataset					
RNN	0.84	0.74	0.79	0.86	0.80
LASSO	0.75	0.79	0.77	0.18	0.64
EGBDT	0.75	0.71	0.73	0.27	0.60
IDRF_IDSVM	0.75	0.79	0.77	0.18	0.64
Cryotherapy dataset					
RNN	0.90	0.85	0.88	0.91	0.88
LASSO	0.75	0.88	0.81	0.09	0.68
EGBDT	0.75	0.88	0.81	0.09	0.68
IDRF_IDSVM	0.90	0.85	0.88	0.91	0.88
Breast Cancer dataset					
RNN	0.87	0.94	0.90	0.86	0.90
LASSO	0.44	0.35	0.40	0.33	0.38
EGBDT	0.62	0.48	0.53	0.50	0.53
IDRF_IDSVM	0.84	0.74	0.79	0.86	0.80
Survey Lung Cancer dataset					
RNN	0.75	0.88	0.81	0.09	0.68
LASSO	0.76	0.94	0.84	0.09	0.73
EGBDT	0.75	0.79	0.77	0.18	0.64
IDRF_IDSVM	0.75	0.71	0.73	0.27	0.60
Thoracic dataset					
RNN	0.84	0.74	0.79	0.86	0.80
LASSO	0.75	0.79	0.77	0.18	0.64
EGBDT	0.62	0.48	0.53	0.50	0.53
IDRF_IDSVM	0.84	0.74	0.79	0.86	0.80
Post-Operative Patient dataset					
RNN	0.84	0.74	0.79	0.86	0.80
LASSO	0.75	0.79	0.77	0.18	0.64
EGBDT	0.62	0.48	0.53	0.50	0.53
IDRF_IDSVM	0.87	0.94	0.90	0.86	0.90

DISCUSSION

Imputation of missing values using proposed Iterative deepening based Random forest (IDRF) method helps to increase the accuracy level of classifiers and table 8 shows that IDRF based classifier achieved a mean classification accuracy of 75% in all datasets. With the added support of cross validation folds in IDRF yields average Sensitivity 73% and Specificity 72% in all datasets. When compared to the existing imputation method, IDRF imputation slightly improved the classification accuracy as 5% in all data sets for all standard classifiers. Hence our proposed system IDRF based imputation of missing values have predominant effect in all standard classifiers for all datasets. IDRF method overcome the most important issues in medical domain particularly in prediction of risk during surgical operations. The results shown in the table 8 prove that the IDRF based classification with standard classifiers improves accuracy level than the other imputation based classification process. In order to further improve the accuracy level of prediction we used Iterative deepening based support vector machine. Our proposed system IDSVM produced a mean classification accuracy level of 78%.The results prove that the IDSVM works well in all types of data set and yields better results compared to standard classifiers. With the support of feature selection process IDSVM shows 5% improvement in classification accuracy compared to other classifiers. This method is new in the prediction of risk in surgical operations. Compared to standard classifiers IDRF based IDSVM classifiers yield better results.

CONCLUSION AND FURTHER ENHANCEMENT

Thus, two new contributions are proposed in this chapter in which the first method effectively imputes the missing values and the second one identifies high risk factors associated with surgical operations. Both these methods perform well in all the six datasets experimented and the performance measures like precision, recall, F1 score, specificity and classification accuracy of the proposed method is better than that of the state-of-the art methods. The features that are chosen for achieving better performance measures are identified as high risk factors for surgical operations. The proposed method using machine learning approaches will serve as a great boon for the doctors and clinical analysts in providing due importance to those high risk parameters. As a future work, novel deep learning architectures can be proposed to predict the factors which have close influence in the surgical operations.

REFERENCES

Allyn. (2017). *A Comparison of a Machine Learning Model with EuroSCORE II in Predicting Mortality after Elective Cardiac Surgery: A Decision Curve Analysis.* PLOS.

Belgiu, M., & Drăguţ, L (2016). Random forest in remote sensing: A review of applications and future directions. *ISPRS Journal of Photogrammetry and Remote Sensing, 114*, 24-31.

Chand, M., Armstrong, T., Britton, G., & Nash, G. F. (2007). How and why do we measure surgical risk. *Journal of the Royal Society of Medicine, 100*(11), 508–512. doi:10.1177/014107680710001113 PMID:18048708

Chen, Z., He, N., Huang, Y., Qin, W. T., Liu, X., & Li, L. (2019). Integration of A Deep Learning Classifier with A Random Forest Approach for Predicting Malonylation Sites. *Genomics, Proteomics & Bioinformatics*. PMID:30639696

Corey, K. M., Kashyap, S., Lorenzi, E., Lagoo-Deenadayalan, S. A., Heller, K., Whalen, K., ... Sendak, M. (2018). Development and validation of machine learning models to identify high-risk surgical patients using automatically curated electronic health record data (Pythia): A retrospective, single-site study'. *PLoS Medicine, 15*(11), e1002701–e1002701. doi:10.1371/journal.pmed.1002701 PMID:30481172

De Caigny, A., Coussement, K., & De Bock, K. (2018). *A New Hybrid Classification Algorithm for Customer Churn Prediction Based on Logistic Regression and Decision Trees*. Academic Press.

Dogan, M., Beach, S., Simons, R., Lendasse, A., Penaluna, B., & Philibert, R. (2018). Blood-Based Biomarkers for Predicting the Risk for Five-Year Incident Coronary Heart Disease in the Framingham Heart Study via. *Machine Learning*. PMID:30567402

Ehlers, A. P. (2017). Improved Risk Prediction Following Surgery Using Machine Learning Algorithms. *EGEMS, 5.*

Ghaddar, B., & Naoum-Sawaya, J. (2017). *High Dimensional Data Classification and Feature Selection using Support Vector Machines*. Academic Press.

Hollon. (2018). A machine learning approach to predict early outcomes after pituitary adenoma surgery. *Neurosurgical Focus, 45*(5).

Karim, M. N., Reid, C. M., Tran, L., Cochrane, A., & Billah, B. (2017). Missing Value Imputation Improves Mortality Risk Prediction Following Cardiac Surgery: An Investigation of an Australian Patient Cohort, Heart. *Lung and Circulation, 26*(3), 301–308. doi:10.1016/j.hlc.2016.06.1214 PMID:27546595

Kasamatsu, T., Hashimoto, J., Iyatomi, H., Nakahara, T., Bai, J., Kitamura, N., … Kubo, A. (2008). *Application of Support Vector Machine Classifiers to Preoperative Risk Stratification With Myocardial Perfusion Scintigraphy*. Academic Press.

Lee. (2018). Derivation and Validation of Machine Learning Approaches to Predict Acute Kidney Injury after Cardiac Surgery. *Journal of Clinical Medicine, 7.*

Meyer, A., Zverinski, D., Pfahringer, B., Kempfert, J., Kuehne, T., Sündermann, S. H., ... Eickhoff, C. (2018). Machine learning for real-time prediction of complications in critical care: A retrospective study. *The Lancet. Respiratory Medicine, 6*(12), 905–914. doi:10.1016/S2213-2600(18)30300-X PMID:30274956

Pantanowitz, A., & Marwala, T. (2009). Missing Data Imputation Through the Use of the Random Forest Algorithm. *Proceedings of the Advances in Computational Intelligence*, 53-62. 10.1007/978-3-642-03156-4_6

Pretorius, A., Bierman, S., & Steel, S. (2016). *A meta-analysis of research in random forests for classification*. Academic Press.

Rakhmetulayeva, S. B., Duisebekova, K. S., Mamyrbekov, A. M., Kozhamzharova, D. K., Astaubayeva, G. N., & Stamkulova, K. (2018). Application of Classification Algorithm Based on SVM for Determining the Effectiveness of Treatment of Tuberculosis. Procedia Computer Science, 130, 231-238.

Razzaghi, T., Safro, I., Ewing, J., Sadrfaridpour, E., & Scott, J. (2017). *Predictive models for bariatric surgery risks with imbalanced medical datasets*. Academic Press.

Salles, T., Gonçalves, M., Rodrigues, V., & Rocha, L. (2018). Improving random forests by neighborhood projection for effective text classification. Information Systems, 77, 1-21.

Soguero-Ruiz. (2016). Predicting colorectal surgical complications using heterogeneous clinical data and kernel methods. *Journal of Biomedical Informatics, 61*, 87-96.

Stonelake, S., Thomson, P., & Suggett, N. (2015). Identification of the high risk emergency surgical patient: Which risk prediction model should be used. *Annals of Medicine and Surgery (London)*, *4*(3), 240–247. doi:10.1016/j.amsu.2015.07.004 PMID:26468369

Tang, F., & Ishwaran, H. (2017). *Random forest missing data algorithms*. Academic Press.

Wong, A., Young, A. T., Liang, A. S., Gonzales, R., Douglas, V. C., & Hadley, D. (2018). Development and validation of an electronic health record–based machine learning model to estimate delirium risk in newly hospitalized patients without known cognitive impairment. *JAMA Network Open*, *1*(4), e181018. doi:10.1001/jamanetworkopen.2018.1018 PMID:30646095

Chapter 12
Privacy Preserving Machine Learning and Deep Learning Techniques:
Application – E-Healthcare

Divya Asok
Thiagarajar College of Engineering, India

Chitra P.
Thiagarajar College of Engineering, India

Bharathiraja Muthurajan
Indian Institute of Technology Madras, India

ABSTRACT

In the past years, the usage of internet and quantity of digital data generated by large organizations, firms, and governments have paved the way for the researchers to focus on security issues of private data. This collected data is usually related to a definite necessity. For example, in the medical field, health record systems are used for the exchange of medical data. In addition to services based on users' current location, many potential services rely on users' location history or their spatial-temporal provenance. However, most of the collected data contain data identifying individual which is sensitive. With the increase of machine learning applications around every corner of the society, it could significantly contribute to the preservation of privacy of both individuals and institutions. This chapter gives a wider perspective on the current literature on privacy ML and deep learning techniques, along with the non-cryptographic differential privacy approach for ensuring sensitive data privacy.

INTRODUCTION

In today's digital world, we are progressively relying on the internet for numerous applications. Especially online storage of our data for backup purposes or for real-time use which gives an anywhere, anytime

DOI: 10.4018/978-1-5225-9902-9.ch012

access. This has become a part of our routine day to day activity. Cloud Computing has recently achieved consistent growth in the field of computing. Consumers and businesses have started using the cloud as a platform or a service by virtue of its efficiency. Machine learning powers many of the products we use today, like social feeds, voice assistants, navigation maps, advertisements, and auto-complete.

Because machine learning is data famished, it can have a negative influence on data privacy. Accessing data for machine learning increases the outward area for attack. Data scientists are given access to data that may have been previously vaulted. Neural networks can memorize information from data sets that can be extracted through statistical inference attacks and GANs. Anonymized data is prone to re-identification attacks when they are de-anonymized.

The increasing utility of data from machine learning has a reverse effect on privacy too. Data that was seemingly safe through the eyes of a human suddenly produces perceptions and results that only a machine could deduce. The mosaic effect states "disparate pieces of information—although individually of limited utility—become significant when combined with other types of information". What happens when an E - company puts together your credit card transactions, location history, professional profile, and browser history?

These properties of machine learning seem adverse from the perception of privacy, but they are also mandatory fundamentals for deep learning that helps us to grow and transform our society. In healthcare, for example, this technology can save many lives, but this shouldn't have at our own risk of sensitive data.

The main concerns that come along with these practices are the security and privacy pitfalls as the user's data is stored out of his premises.

This chapter is divided into the following sections. Introduction, Privacy preservation approaches in Cloud environment, Privacy Preserving through Differential Privacy, Privacy Preserving Machine Learning, and Deep Learning Techniques. So, once we get a better picture of different privacy preservation methodologies, we explore how it is applicable in the e-healthcare system. In the next sections, we have briefed the introduction to the E-Healthcare architecture, Privacy preservation Approaches in the e-Healthcare environment, Privacy-Preserving Approach using Deep Learning: Differential Privacy for e-Health care data, and finally Concluded with the overall picture

BACKGROUND

Privacy Preservation Approaches in Cloud Environment

Privacy is when a person's information is fully secured and is free from all interference. Today, we have cloud playing a key role in providing services across various domains, e.g., - health care, online banking, social networking, etc., these utilize user's personal information. These privacy- sensitive data are residing out of user's premises, so privacy preservation of these data against leaks and attacks is of concern. According to the American Institute of Certified Public Accountants (AICPA) and Canadian Institute of Charted Accountants (CICA), the definition is "Privacy is the right and obligation of individuals and organizations concerning the collection, use, retention, and disclosure of personal information." Hence, privacy threats create insecurity among all cloud user. The research papers presents some of these issues in privacy which is as follows: lack of user control, training and expertise, unauthorized secondary usage, complexity of regulatory compliance, addressing trans-border data flow restrictions, litigation, legal uncertainty, oblique disclosure to the government, data security and disclosure of threats and leakage, data accessibility, location of data, transfer, and retention. Ample approaches have been proposed to preserve the privacy in the cloud especially in the e-Healthcare domain. As there is no proper classification of the privacy-preserving approaches, we categorize the privacy-preserving schemes used in the clouds into cryptographic and non-cryptographic approaches. The cryptographic methods help to ease the privacy risks by various encryption techniques. Conversely, non-cryptographic approaches mainly focus on policy-based authorization infrastructure that allows the data objects to have access control policies and using Machine Learning and Deep Learning techniques to achieve privacy through learning. Figure 1 describes the taxonomy of classification of cloud privacy preservation techniques. In the e-Healthcare cloud-based systems, the cryptographic approaches that are commonly used to protect data using encryption are techniques such as Public Key Encryption (PKE) and Symmetric Key Encryption (SKE). However, there are some advanced techniques like cryptographic primitives that help to preserve the privacy of the patient's data in the healthcare industry. These primitives comprise:

1. Searchable Encryption Technique,
2. Identity-Based Encryption,
3. Proxy Re-encryption,
4. Hierarchical Predicate Encryption, and
5. Fully homomorphic encryption technique.

The non-cryptographic approaches include Privacy-preserving machine learning schemes and deep learning techniques like differential privacy. These are elaborated and discussed in detail in the below sections. The following is a brief overview of the different methodology adopted to introduce privacy preservation in the cloud. It includes techniques such as anonymization, privacy-preserving database architecture, access control, authorization, policy-based authorization, data fragmentation, PccP approach, and metadata reconstruction.

Jiang Wang et al. (2008) method uses anonymization for preserving privacy; this method does not use the traditional key-based encryption. The algorithm proposed, anonymizes partially or completely before releasing in the cloud, the mining of this anonymous data is performed with the help of the background knowledge available on the data. This is a simple and flexible method of anonymization, but it serves only a limited number of services. Architecture based privacy preservation proposed by Greveler U et al. preserves user data privacy from both external and internal attacks. The architectural elements include cloud database, rule engine, user engine, and user interface. User requests and system responses are sent from secured identities, this along with machine-readable access rights preserves privacy.

Figure 1. Taxonomy of privacy preserving approaches

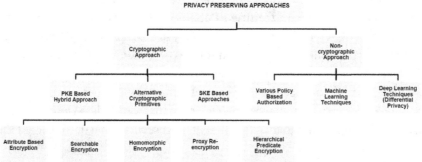

Miao Zhou et al. (2011) proposes user privacy preservation using a flexible access control method. The model consists of two-tier encryption; the first encryption is performed by data owner based on the local attributes and the cloud servers perform second encryption. Each cloud user is linked to specific attributes defining their access rights. And the Server re-encryption Mechanism(SRM) re-encrypts data in the cloud at the request of the data owner. This is helpful when there is an addition or removal of users. The user data is not compromised since the access policies of users remains hidden to the cloud server. Hence, privacy preservation is achieved by providing the data owner the complete access control and not providing the cloud provider any knowledge of the data. David W. Chadwick and Fatema (2012) have provided a policy-based authorization infrastructure for privacy preservation in the cloud. Data is labeled with user-defined access policies; these are enforced policy decision at policy enforcement points. A master Policy Decision Point(PDP) mediates the conflicts among different PDPs. This method trusts the cloud provider. The cloud provider notifies the access of data to the data owner who approves of the access of data.

PccP model implements user identity preservation and access to data content using three layers of the privacy-preserving mechanism. First, the consumer layer forms the base of the model, where the cloud users request access to cloud services. Second, the Network Interface or the Address Mapping layer modifies the IP address related to the access request; this implements anonymization to the user identity. Finally, the Privacy Preservation Layer has an associated Unique User Cloud Identity Generator which preserves the privacy of user's information by privacy check mechanism. Krishna R K N S et al. (2012) describes privacy constraints using a graph. The nodes represent the attributes, and the links represent the confidentiality to the connected nodes. The relation is fragmented vertically, and one part is held by the data owner and the other by an external server. Part of the two-dimensional graph can be reconstructed using universal ID. Thus, using fragmentation to attain privacy efficiently.

Privacy Preserving Through Differential Privacy

Differential Privacy Types

Classic anonymization techniques involve deleting user identifying information from datasets before public consumption. This method has been proven to be inefficient on anonymizing published data sets, with identifiers removed. Re-identification was possible using personal information of individuals and linking them using other public datasets. This information that can help to connect personal information to an identity is called background information. Linking movie datasets did similar de-anonymization by Narayanan using social networks for the background information. These show a need for an advancement in privacy preservation that can assure the safety of individuals information. Differential privacy addresses the privacy concern by releasing only an aggregated report of the data. The data collection and data analysis phase are divided by a trust boundary. Data collection is carried out by a trusted data curator and who handles all individual information. In the analysis phase, the data is disseminated to interested third party. Based on this differentiation there are different differential privacy methodologies

Differential Privacy for Location-Based Services

The abundance of location-based systems allows for untrusted servers to collect user location information. Here we will be looking at differential privacy in the context of such services. Differential privacy can provide privacy to participants by ensuring similar databases are not distinguishable. It could be achieved by protecting the user's location within a radius, by adding random noise to user location based on circular and non-circular noise function.

Privacy Preserving Machine Learning and Deep Learning Techniques

Recent advances in deep learning methods have led to the development of long-established Artificial Intelligent domains such as speech, image, and text recognition, language translation, etc. Meanwhile, the corporate sectors have taken immense advantage of the enormous amounts of training data collected from their customers(users) and the vast computational power of Graphical processing unit that are readily deployable.

The initial accuracy of the resulting models permits them to be used as the basis of many new services and applications, including reliable speech and image recognition that exceeds humans. While the utility of deep learning is definite, the same training data that has made it so successful also presents serious privacy concerns. Centralized accumulation of photos, audio, and video from millions of people are available with privacy risks. First, companies gathering this data keep it forever; users from whom the data was received can neither delete it, nor control its usage, nor influence what could be learned from it by machine learning or deep learning algorithms. Second, images and voice recordings often contain accidentally captured sensitive items—faces, license plates, computer screens, the sound of other people speaking and ambient noises, etc. Third, users' data kept by companies are subject to citations and permits, as well as warrantless spying by national-security and intelligence outfits.

Furthermore, the Internet giants' monopoly on "big data" collected from millions of users leads to their trust in the AI Models learned from this data. Users benefit from new services, such as powerful image search, voice-activated personal assistants, and machine translation of webpages in foreign languages, but the underlying models constructed from their collective data remain proprietary to the companies that created them.

Finally, in many domains, most notably those related to medicine, the sharing of data about individuals is not permitted by law or regulation. Consequently, biomedical and clinical researchers can only perform deep learning on the datasets belonging to their institutions. It is well-known that neural-network models become better as the training datasets grow more prominent and more diverse. Due to not being able to use the data from other institutions when training their models, researchers may end up with worse models. For example, data owned by a single organization (e.g., a particular medical clinic) may be very homogeneous, producing an overfitted model that will be inaccurate when used on other inputs. In this case, privacy and confidentiality restrictions significantly reduce utility.

Cryptographic Methodologies: Deep Learning via Additively Homomorphic Encryption

Le Trieu Phong et al. presented a privacy-preserving deep learning system over a combined dataset. They managed without revealing the local data to the central server. This system bridges deep learning and cryptography using asynchronous stochastic gradient descent along with homomorphic encryption. This paper contribution is the protection of gradients calculated using homomorphic encryption. The resulting system leaks no information of participants to the honest-but-curious cloud server. The accuracy showed no depreciation due to the use of homomorphic encryption.

A Comparative Study on Privacy Preserving Machine Learning approaches

Machine learning techniques are used in various domains like healthcare, finance, e-commerce, social networks, recommendation systems, malfunction detection, and authentication technologies. The data collected over a while is tremendous in size and also have produced solutions to many old problems. While the recent advancement improves in optimized storage, processing and computation on big data, combining data from different sources remains a significant challenge due to privacy and integrity threats. Secure Multiparty Computation (MPC) for privacy-preserving using machine learning techniques provides reassuring solutions by allowing multiple entities to train the model with all their data to achieve the result. For privacy preserving Machine learning algorithms, we use training linear regression, logistic regression, and neural networks models, and to adopt the two-server model regularly used by MPC. In the initial phase, the users, encrypt along with secret-share their data among two non-colluding servers. In the computation phase, the two servers prepare the training model by learning various models on the users' shared data. The state-of-the-art solutions for privacy-preserving linear regression are many orders of magnitude slower than plain text training.

Gilad-Bachrach et al. (2016) work on CryptoNets present neural networks that can be applied to encrypted data. Data owner can send data to the cloud in an encrypted format, where encrypted predictions are obtained by using neural networks and returned to the owner. The owner can decrypt the data to get the prediction from the cloud service without gaining any information about the raw data. Main ingredients in this method are homomorphic encryption and neural networks. Homomorphic encryption supports acting on data even when it is encrypted since homomorphism is a structure-preserving transformation. CryptoNets do not support training on encrypted data. Adding homomorphic encryption to the training process makes it at least an order of magnitude slower. An open research topic is finding efficient encoding schemes that allow for smaller parameters and hence faster homomorphic computation. For privacy sensitive data, the use of decentralized, federated learning was proposed. Here training data is left distributed on client computers (mobile devices). It involves learning shared models trained from rich data not centrally stored, but on multiple participating devices, i.e., clients. Here communication cost is the principal constraint. Holding even small anonymized dataset can cause user harm if they are joined with other data. Hence, federated learning only performs minimal update necessary to improve a model. Federated learning can be combined with differential privacy, and secure multi-party computation can be a potential future work. In Privacy-preserving deep learning method proposed by Shokri, R., And Shmatikov, V, (2015) multiple parties jointly learn an accurate neural network model for a given objective without sharing their input database. Parallelized optimization algorithm run asynchronously and sharing a small subset of their model's critical parameters during training. Here the data is not being shared, but all participants are benefited from the models and boosting the overall accuracy, which was unachievable on their data.

A detailed history of privacy-preserving machine learning techniques is discussed in the following section. Few have Proposed solutions based on secure multiparty computation (MPC) but appear to incur high-efficiency bottlenecks and lack implementation/evaluation strategies. Presents a privacy-preserving linear regression protocol on horizontally partitioned data combining LHE and garbled circuits and validates it across millions of dataset samples. Extend the results to vertically partitioned data and show improved performance. Still, both help to reduce the problem of solving a linear system which in turn introduces a significant overhead on the training time and does not work for non-linear models. Builds a framework for secure data exchange, and linear regression but that is not scalable for more massive datasets. They made an

Table 1. Comparison on different privacy preserving ML approaches

Technique	Advantage	Disadvantage
Privacy Preservation using decision trees	Secure multiparty computation for Privacy that is flexible to include complex problems and large inputs	Incurs high costs in terms of transactions in the database
Privacy Preservation using k-means clustering	Two-Party k-Means Clustering Protocol	Leakage of information arising from an insecure division algorithm
Privacy Preservation using SVM classification	Scalable solution for privacy-preserving SVM classification on vertically partitioned data with three or more participating parties, it securely computes the global SVM model, without disclosing the data or classification information of each party to the others	Does not achieve complete security as the global model cannot be split between parties
Privacy Preservation using linear regression	Helps the agencies wanting to conduct a linear regression analysis with complete records without disclosing values of their own attributes	Limitation of this work is due to the finite field assumption, which makes the computations different from original scientific computations
Privacy Preservation using logistic regression	To carry out "valid" statistical analysis for logistic regression with quantitative covariates on both horizontal and vertical partitioned databases that do not require actually integrating the data. This allows multiple parties to perform analyses on the global database while preventing exposure of details that are beyond those used in the joint computation.	No emphasize on data pre-processing.
Privacy preserving linear regression protocol on horizontally partitioned data using a combination of LHE and garbled circuits and vertically partitioned data	An extensive evaluation of MPC techniques includes conjugate gradient descent algorithm	High overhead on the training time and cannot be generalized to non-linear models. The problem of providing security guarantees against malicious adversaries for MPC functionalities.
Privacy preserving linear regression	A practical protocol for enabling SDE using Secure MultiParty Computation (MPC) in a novel adaptation of the server-aided setting hence efficient for a smaller dataset.	Does not scale for larger datasets
Privacy preserving logistic regression, which approximates the logistic function using polynomials, and train the model using LHE.	This approach achieves a good prediction accuracy compared with original logistic regression.	The accuracy of the model is degraded compared to using the logistic function and also the protocol is vulnerable to attacks.
instead of sharing the data, the two servers share the changes on a portion of the coefficients during the training	System is very efficient and accurate. (no cryptographic operation is needed at all)	The leakage of the coefficient changes is not well-explained and no formal security guarantees are obtained. In addition, this approach only works for horizontally partitioned data since each server needs to be able to perform the training individually on its portion in order to obtain the coefficient changes.
Privacy preserving predictions using neural networks Using fully homomorphic encryption, the neural network model can make predictions on encrypted data. In this case, it is assumed that the neural network is trained on plaintext data and the model is known to one party who evaluates it on private data of another	As the cloud service does not gain any information about the raw data nor about the prediction it made they allow high throughput, accurate, and private predictions	Bit slower homomorphic encryption with the throughput and latency to be improved by using GPUs and FPGAs to accelerate the computation
Introduces an additive noise to the data or the update function. The parameters of the noise are usually predetermined by the dimensions of the data, the parameters of the machine learning algorithm and the security requirement, and hence are data-independency is achieved	All the data still remains private during the training. Participants preserve the privacy of their respective data while still benefiting from other participants' models and thus boosting their learning accuracy beyond what is achievable solely on their own inputs. Built a connection between regularization and privacy: the larger the regularization constant, the less sensitive the logistic regression function is to any one individual example, and as a result, the less noise one needs to add to make it privacy-preserving. Therefore, regularization not only prevents overfitting, but also helps with privacy, by making the classifier less sensitive	To prevent a curious server from linking the updates of each participant, the design is under research To remove the restrictions from the class of optimization problems we consider.
Privacy preserving machine learning for linear regression, logistic regression and neural network training using the stochastic gradient descent method	Supports secure arithmetic operations on shared decimal numbers, and propose MPC-friendly alternatives to nonlinear functions such as sigmoid and SoftMax	For image processing tasks, the Neural Network algorithm is not an optimized one.

approximation for the logistic function using polynomials, and thus to train the model using LHE. But, the complexity rises to the exponential degree of the approximation polynomial, and the end accuracy is also affected when compared to the logistic function. Few more discusses privacy-preserving machine learning with neural networks that offer a solution where sharing of data is replaced by the implementation of two servers that shares the changes of the coefficients during the training module. As there is no cryptographic operation, the efficiency is tremendous, but the leakage is not explored still, and there are no solid security guarantees for them. Using fully homomorphic encryption, the neural network framework can make predictions on encrypted data but limited to plaintexts. Various researchers from 2005 discuss differential privacy, a non-cryptographic approach for achieving privacy. A general technique used in differentially privacy technique is to establish an additive noise to the data or the function. Parameters of the noise are usually encoded by the dimensions of the data, the parameters of the machine learning algorithm and the requirement needed for security, and hence they achieve data-independency. The model could also be built using the servers this can auto-generate the noise according to the public parameters and add it directly to the shared values in the training set. In this way, we can make the trained model be differentially private once reconstructed, while all the data being private during the training. Table 1 describes the precise view of the entire collection of work in privacy-preserving machine learning methodologies with the techniques, strengths, and weaknesses for all proposals made so far.

APPLICATION: E-HEALTHCARE

E-Healthcare Architecture

Based on the method of handling Electronic Health Record, e-Healthcare architecture design can vary. But it is essential to understand the e-Healthcare system to address the privacy issues involved. The major components of the e-healthcare environment include the following:

1.   Body sensors of patients and the extracted patient healthcare parameters.
2.   Users of the e-Healthcare system - Insurance provider, pharmacist, attending physician, etc.
3.   The core network is containing all the information and the servers.
4.   A communication link that connects all components to form a single system.

The interconnectedness of this system has been visualized in Figure 2. Another method adopted to define the e-Healthcare system is concerning the data. The different data sphere includes the user sphere comprising the patient and the body sensor network, the common field that consists of the cloud service provider and communication link and finally the recipient sphere that includes the attending physician, nurses, and pharmacists. Security requirement for all tier needs to be defined separately since different condition expects different handling. All the connected components require protection from threats when connecting to the e-Healthcare system, for example, health monitoring body sensors and mobile devices responsible for collecting healthcare data and each requires different security measure based on their threat environment. The protection need extends to the core network, once this PHI information reaches it. At this stage, the privacy-preserving, data confidentiality, access control come into play. e-Healthcare systems are widely deployed, and they need highly recognized, but with some exceptions, all of these systems have expressed vulnerabilities that should be addressed.

Figure 2. E-healthcare architecture overview

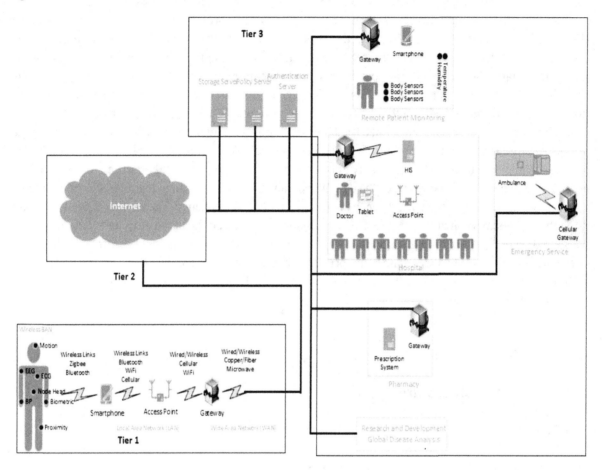

APPLICATION: E-HEALTH CARE

There has been active research in the field of information management in healthcare. Protocols proposed to address privacy preservation issues in healthcare include pseudo anonymization of user identity, data encryption, attribute-based encryption, dividing the cloud into public and private to handle sensitive data along with sanitized data, privacy-preserving data publishing, access control, data outsourcing, and data reconstruction. From past research, no single technique can handle the privacy and security requirements in the field of healthcare. So, there is a rise in the use of hybrid methods for addressing privacy concerns in healthcare.

Pseudonymization

Pseudonymization is the removal of all information identifying the patient associated with the data. Thus privacy preservation can be implemented. It improves the patient trust with the healthcare provider and also makes it convenient to share data for research. To meet the regulatory demand of the USA and EU, it is required to assign a pseudo-identity to the patient for use in all the task in the healthcare system. To trace back the pseudo-identity to the real only by answering a secret question, and with the knowledge of algorithm and key used in encryption. Pseudonymization was the only concern in the early stage of privacy preservation in healthcare, but since then it was discovered that it is possible to identify patient using their healthcare attributes. Privacy breaches identified include disclosure during transit or storage, weak authentication, poor access control scheme. Based on these breaches the requirements were determined to provide security and privacy were support of cross-system interaction, attribute-based encryption, different one or two-factor authentication.

Pseudonymization initially was concentrated on hiding the patient's identity. This approach was suitable when the information was shared with a trusted environment. Later as the need for this data in research became prevalent, it has become difficult using only pseudonymization to provide privacy. There is a need to strike a balance between maintaining the anonymity of the multiple patient information while still providing access to this data for research. Providing pseudonym for a patient every time makes it difficult to use the data for healthcare research. Providing multiple aliases for the same user at different stages of the healthcare system, and also deriving from the new pseudonym based on the parent pseudonym can offer a clear structure to pseudonymization with additional privacy strengthening. Finally, pseudonymization can also be provided by assigning group identities to each user, but this approach can still lead to the actual user by narrowing on the attributes. Data and user anonymization and pseudonymization necessary for sharing patient data outside the healthcare environment for research. Currently, the required amount of care needed to share medical data is not provided, this is visible from the literature we see.

Privacy-Preserving Access Control

Privacy-preserving access control is a technique usually used along with encryption-based privacy. Strict access control, in particular, hybrid access control is considered the best way to moderate access to information. By combining access control with data anonymization, it is expected to solve privacy preservation issues by obfuscating the user identity and also controlling the information flow. Access control schemes discussed by Narayanan and Günes (2011), it indicate that no single mechanism can provide a sufficient level of access control. They propose a role identity-based access, this does not have the excellent level of access control classifications that is required in real life scenarios. Sun et al.

A researcher proposed a patient-centric approach where the patients control access to their patient healthcare information (PHI). Based on the patient's preference multiple levels of access to the PHI is set up for the doctors, insurance companies and others in the healthcare system. Access to PHI is mediated by the patient and delegated to the doctor in charge of treatment. Zhou et al. (2015) have made the successful implementation of the access control requirements. It involves achieving authentication and privacy in a single procedure. To address privacy Zhou et al. (2015) have proposed an Authorized Accessible Privacy Model (AAPM). Here the patients encrypt their PHI with an access policy; this allows only the physicians who meet the criteria for access policy to decrypt the PHI. This method reduces the patients control over their choice of physician; also rouge actors can create profiles specific to PHI's interest to attract clients, thus compromising privacy.

Access control policies cannot be exhaustive; there will always be scenarios that cannot be handled by the control policy. So, there needs to be a fall-back mechanism that can handle irregularities and update the access control mechanism to reflect the newly observed scenario. There is potential for privacy violation or security issues when there is crucial improper handling by a third party. Chen et al. attempted to address the privacy and confidentiality concern arising when sharing among different healthcare service providers. This model uses homomorphic encryption for processing encrypted data, and this process ensures the confidentiality and privacy of the users. But the homomorphic encryption technique currently is not ready to be deployed in the healthcare system due to process power requirement from the system.

Privacy Preserving Approach Using Deep Learning: Differential Privacy For E-Health Care Data

Traditional cryptography anonymizes data with algorithms, these cannot provide personalized recommendations. A differentiated attack occurs when an attacker is able to gather background information on the dataset and use that to identify individual information. Differential privacy protects the data from such attacks. Differential privacy is especially suited for the protection of personal data also a suitable model for healthcare data. To disclose health data, many characteristics need to be considered to preserve privacy. These characteristics relate to e-Healthcare practices and the datasets involved. To release or analyze PHI, it is necessary that the privacy-preserving e-Healthcare system addresses all these issues. Healthcare data contains both categorical data (diagnosis codes, drugs prescribed, procedures codes, etc.) and numerical data (age, treatment duration, etc.). Therefore both types of variables need to be addressed. Health data is frequently released to end user, as analysts often require looking at the data. A non-interactive mechanism where statistics are computed without actual data publishing is a viable option for healthcare data. These are cases when a well-defined set of statistics needs to be calculated at regular intervals. In these cases, differentially private statistics can be easily calculated, but on other occasions, actual data would be required to be published. To implement a new mechanism to protect data, it is necessary to build trust in the privacy preservation system. These are the challenges that arise when we try to use differential privacy to address the healthcare problem.

CONCLUSION

The implementation of e-healthcare systems requires a fully developed privacy-preserving system for maintaining the patient's record which is considered as sensitive resources. The data handled by e-Healthcare systems are confidential, any leakage of this data is harmful to both the patient and the trust of the healthcare enterprise. This chapter reviews the current literature on privacy in the cloud, e-Healthcare architecture and privacy preservation techniques - both cryptographic and non-cryptographic techniques with particular focus on Machine Learning and Deep Learning approaches for preserving privacy for all kinds of e-Healthcare data. The chapter also explains, in brief, the various techniques' strengths and weaknesses available for privacy preservation in a tabular form and concludes with the adoption of differential privacy, a non-cryptographic approach for ensuring e-Healthcare data privacy.

REFERENCES

Abadi, M., Chu, A., Goodfellow, I., McMahan, H. B., Mironov, I., Talwar, K., & Zhang, L. (2016). Deep learning with differential privacy. *Proceedings of the ACM SIGSAC Conference on Computer and Communications Security ACM*, 308–318.

Bunn, P., & Ostrovsky, R. (2007). Secure two-party k-means clustering. In *Proceedings of the 14th ACM conference on Computer and communications security*. ACM.

Chadwick, D. W., & Fatema, K. (2012). A privacy preserving authorisation system for the cloud. *Journal of Computer and System Sciences, 78*(5), 1359–1373. doi:10.1016/j.jcss.2011.12.019

Chaudhuri, K., & Monteleoni, C. (2009). Privacy-preserving logistic regression. Advances in Neural Information Processing Systems, 289–296.

Chen, F. (2014). PRECISE: PRivacy-preserving cloud-assisted quality improvement service in healthcare. *Systems Biology (ISB), 2014 8th International Conference on.* 10.1109/ISB.2014.6990752

Du, W., & Atallah, M. J. (2001). Privacy-preserving cooperative scientific computations. CSFW, 1, 273.

Du, W., Han, Y. S., & Chen, S. (2004). Privacy-preserving multivariate statistical analysis: Linear regression and classification. SDM, 4, 222–233.

Dwork, C. (2006). Calibrating noise to sensitivity in private data analysis. In *Theory of cryptography*. Springer Berlin Heidelberg.

Fernández-Alemán, J. L., Señor, I. C., Lozoya, P. Á. O., & Toval, A. (2013). Security and privacy in electronic health records: A systematic literature review. *Journal of Biomedical Informatics, 46*(3), 541–562. doi:10.1016/j.jbi.2012.12.003 PMID:23305810

Gascon, A., Schoppmann, P., Balle, B., Raykova, M., Doerner, J., Zahur, S., & Evans, D. (n.d.). *Secure linear regression on vertically partitioned datasets*. Academic Press.

Gilad-Bachrach, R., Dowlin, N., Laine, K., Lauter, K., Naehrig, M., & Wernsing, J. (2016), Cryptonets: Applying neural networks to encrypted data with high throughput and accuracy. *Proceedings of The 33rd International Conference on Machine Learning*, 201–210.

Gilad-Bachrach, R., Laine, K., Lauter, K., Rindal, P., & Rosulek, M. (2016). *Secure data exchange: A marketplace in the cloud*. Cryptology ePrint Archive, Report 2016/620. Retrieved from http://eprint. iacr.org/ 2016/620

Gilad-Bachrach, R., Dowlin, N., & Laine, K. (2016). CryptoNets: applying neural networks to encrypted data with high throughput and accuracy. *International Conference on Machine Learning*, 201–10.

Jagannathan, G., & Wright, R. N. (2005). Privacy-preserving distributed k-means clus- tering over arbitrarily partitioned data. *Proceedings of the eleventh ACM SIGKDD international conference on Knowledge discovery in data mining ACM*, 593–599.

Lavanya & Valarmathie. (n.d.). *Big Data in Healthcare Using Cloud Database with Enhanced Privacy*. Academic Press.

Mohassel & Zhang. (2017). SecureML: A System for Scalable Privacy-Preserving Machine Learning. *IACR Cryptology ePrint Archive, 396.*

Narayanan, H. A. J., & Güneș, M. H. (2011). Ensuring access control in cloud provisioned healthcare systems. *Proc. IEEE Consum. Commun. Netw. Conf. (CCNC)*, 247–251. 10.1109/CCNC.2011.5766466

Nikolaenko, V., Weinsberg, U., Ioannidis, S., Joye, M., Boneh, D., & Taft, N. (2013). Privacy-preserving ridge regression on hundreds of millions of records. In *Security and Privacy (SP), 2013 IEEE Symposium on*. IEEE.

Privacy-Preserving Deep Learning via Additively Homomorphic Encryption. (2018). *IEEE Transactions on Information Forensics and Security, 13*(5), 1333-1345.

Rahaman, S. M., & Farhatullah, M. (2012). PccP: A Model for Preserving Cloud Computing Privacy. *International Conference on Data Science & Engineering (ICDSE)*, 166–170. 10.1109/ICDSE.2012.6281900

Rouse, W. B. (2008). *Health care as a complex adaptive system: implications for design and management*. Bridge-Washington-National Academy of Engineering.

Sahi, M., Abbas, H., Saleem, K., Yang, X., Derhab, A., Orgun, M., ... Yaseen, A. (2018). Privacy Preservation in e-Healthcare Environments: State of the Art and Future Directions. *IEEE Access: Practical Innovations, Open Solutions, 6*, 464–478. doi:10.1109/ACCESS.2017.2767561

Sanil, A. P., Karr, A. F., Lin, X., & Reiter, J. P. (2004). Privacy preserving regression modelling via distributed computation. In *Proceedings of the tenth ACM SIGKDD international conference on Knowledge discovery and data mining*. ACM.

Sayi, T. J. V. R. K. M. K., & Krishna, R. K. N. S. (2012). Data Outsourcing in Cloud Environments: A Privacy Preserving Approach. *9th International Conference on Information Technology- New Generations*, 361–366.

Shokri, R., & Shmatikov, V. (2015). Privacy-preserving deep learning. *Proceedings of the 22nd ACM SIGSAC Conference on Computer and Communications Security ACM*, 1310–1321.

Shokri, R., & Shmatikov, V. (2015). Privacy-preserving deep learning. In *Proceedings of the 22nd ACM SIGSAC Conference on Computer and Communications Security*. ACM.

Slavkovic, A. B., Nardi, Y., & Tibbits, M. M. (2007). Secure logistic regression of horizontally and vertically partitioned distributed databases. *Seventh IEEE International Conference on Data Mining Workshops (ICDMW)*, 723–728.

Song, S., Chaudhuri, K., & Sarwate, A. D. (2013). Stochastic gradient descent with dif- ferentially private updates. In *Global Conference on Signal and Information Processing (GlobalSIP)*. IEEE.

Sun, J., Fang, Y., & Zhu, X. (2010). Privacy and emergency response in e- healthcare leveraging wireless body sensor networks. *Wireless Communications, IEEE, 17*(1), 66–73. doi:10.1109/MWC.2010.5416352

The Conversation. (2018). *Explainer: what is differential privacy and how can it protect your data?* Available at: http://theconversation.com/explainer-what-is-differential-privacy-and-how-can-it-protect-your-data-90686

Vaidya, J., Yu, H., & Jiang, X. (2008). Privacy-preserving svm classification. *Knowledge and Information Systems, 14*(2), 161–178. doi:10.100710115-007-0073-7

Wu, S., Teruya, T., Kawamoto, J., Sakuma, J., & Kikuchi, H. (2013). Privacy- preservation for stochastic gradient descent application to secure logistic regression. *The 27th Annual Conference of the Japanese Society for Artificial Intelligence*, 1–4.

Yu, H., Vaidya, J., & Jiang, X. (2006). Privacy-preserving svm classification on vertically partitioned data. In *Pacific-Asia Conference on Knowledge Discovery and Data Mining*. Springer.

Zhou, J., Lin, X., Dong, X., & Cao, Z. (2015). PSMPA: Patient Self-Controllable and Multi-Level Privacy-Preserving Cooperative Authentication in Distributedm-Healthcare Cloud Computing System. *Parallel and Distributed Systems, IEEE Transactions on*, 26(6), 1693–1703. doi:10.1109/TPDS.2014.2314119

Zhou, M., & Mu, Y. (2011). Privacy-Preserved Access Control for Cloud Computing. *International Joint Conference of IEEE TrustCom-11/IEEE ICESS-11/FCST-11*, 83–90. 10.1109/TrustCom.2011.14

Chapter 13
Trend and Predictive Analytics of Dengue Prevalence in Administrative Region

Kannimuthu Subramanian
Karpagam College of Engineering, India

Swathypriyadharsini P.
Bannari Amman Institute of Technology, India

Gunavathi C.
VIT University, India

Premalatha K.
Bannari Amman Institute of Technology, India

ABSTRACT

Dengue is fast emerging pandemic-prone viral disease in many parts of the world. Dengue flourishes in urban areas, suburbs, and the countryside, but also affects more affluent neighborhoods in tropical and subtropical countries. Dengue is a mosquito-borne viral infection causing a severe flu-like illness and sometimes causing a potentially deadly complication called severe dengue. It is a major public health problem in India. Accurate and timely forecasts of dengue incidence in India are still lacking. In this chapter, the state-of-the-art machine learning algorithms are used to develop an accurate predictive model of dengue. Several machine learning algorithms are used as candidate models to predict dengue incidence. Performance and goodness of fit of the models were assessed, and it is found that the optimized SVR gives minimal RMSE 0.25. The classifiers are applied, and experiment results show that the extreme boost and random forest gives 93.65% accuracy.

INTRODUCTION

Dengue fever, also called as break bone fever is a disease rooted from dengue virus which is transmitted by Aedes mosquito. There are four kind of dengue infection such as DHF1, DHF2, DHF3 and DHF4.

DOI: 10.4018/978-1-5225-9902-9.ch013

The symptoms of dengue include low blood pressure, headache, joint pain, rashes, and low levels of blood platelets count which leads to critical dengue hemorrhagic fever. The major issue in dengue fever is that there is no particular antibiotic or medicine exists to care for it. Dengue fever takes place in form of cycles and which is exist inside the body of a patient for one or two weeks. This leads to bleeding, abdominal pain and dengue hemorrhagic fever

Mainly Aedes mosquito brings a virus in its saliva when it gnaws a healthy person. These viruses go into persons' body and mixed with body fluids of a healthy person. When dengue virus is blended with the white blood vessels, it begins reproducing inside the white blood cells (WBC) and thus starts the dengue virus cycle. If there is severe infection, the length of virus cycle is extended and thus has an effect on bone marrow and liver leading to less blood circulation in blood vessels and blood pressure turn out to be so low that is not able to supply adequate blood to all of the organs in a body. The main task of platelets is blood clotting which is affected because of dengue virus. Virus reduces platelets which causes increased risk of bleeding.

The primary aim of this chapter is dengue disease prediction in administrative region. The predictive analytics covers several statistical methods in data analytics and machine learning. It explores the present and past facts to make predictions about future or unknown events. In this chapter, a number of machine learning algorithms including the Support Vector Regression (SVR) algorithm, Step-down Linear Regression(SLR) model, Gradient Boosted Regression Tree (GBRT) algorithm, Negative Binomial Regression (NBM) model, Least Absolute Shrinkage and Selection Operator (LASSO) linear regression model and Generalized Additive Model (GAM)are utilized as candidate models to predict dengue incidence. Evaluation of performance and goodness of fit of the models were donewith the help of root-mean-square error (RMSE) and R-squared measures

The chief contributions of this chapter paper are:

1. To perform thorough review on data analysis on dengue diseases.
2. Comparative analysis of various machine learning algorithms on dengue dataset in an administrative region.
3. Make out the best performance algorithm for prediction of diseases through methodical investigation.

The remaining section of this chapter is organized as follows. Section 2 discusses about the literature review of dengue disease analysis. Section 3 briefs about methodology of dengue disease prediction. The experiment results are done and analyzed the performance of various predictive analytics approaches are done in section 4. Section 5 concluded the chapter.

LITERATURE REVIEW

In a study conducted by Long et al (2010) for dengue outbreaks, they identified the number of attributes to be used in determining outbreaks rather than using only case counts. They used multiple attribute value based on Apriori concept. The results were encouraging when they identified more than one attributes showing similar graph in vector-borne diseases outbreaks. Their proposed methods also outperform in term of detection rate, false positive rate and overall performance.

The mRNA expression levels of genes involved in dengue virus innate immune responses were measured using quantitative real time PCR (qPCR). A novel application of the support vector machines (SVM) algorithm was used to analyse the expression pattern of 12 genes in peripheral blood mononuclear cells (PBMCs) of 28 dengue patients (13 DHF and 15 DF) during acute viral infection. The SVM model was trained using gene expression data of these genes and achieved the highest accuracy of ~85% with leave-one-out cross-validation. This work was the first report of application of the SVM method to gene expression data from DF and DHF patients to better understand the role of the genes in DENV infection pathway. The results suggested the important role of seven genes in classifying DF and DHF patients: TLR3, MDA5, IRF3, IFN-α, CLEC5A, and the two most important MYD88 and TLR7 (Gomes et al, 2010).

Fathima et al (2011) summarized various machine learning techniques and data mining algorithms used for the diagnosis of chikungunya and dengue fever threat in Tropics.

Huy et al (2013) reported a development of a clinical rule for the prediction of dengue.They have used the data collected from Center for Preventive Medicine in Vinh Long province and the Children's Hospital No. 2 in Ho Chi Minh City, Vietnam. They used univariate and multivariate analyses and a pre-processing methodto estimate and choose 14 clinical and laboratory signs recorded at shock onset. The patient's data such as admission day, purpura/ecchymosis, ascites/pleural effusion, blood platelet count and pulse pressure were used as the variables.

A discussion about the social media system to prevent Dengue that integrates three concepts of public health prevention was given by Lwin et al (2014). It includes predictive surveillance component, the citizen engagement component and health communication component. The challenges, content validation and stakeholder collaborations were given in their paper. For the life threatening dengue fever categorization Naïve Bayes, REP Tree, Random forest, J48 and Self-organizing maps were used by Shaukat et al (2015). The have used WEKA tool for implementation.

Khan et al (2016) found the spectral differences between dengue positive and normal sera using machine learning techniques. The SVM models were built based on the three different kernel functions including Gaussian radial basis function (RBF), polynomial function and linear function. They employed the features obtained from Raman Spectra to classify the human blood sera. The classification model had been evaluated with the 10-fold cross validation method.

A predictive statistical model was built by Anna Kiefer (2017) using logistic regression, classification and cluster analysis to forecast dengue fever outbreaks in Latin America. NOAA's Global Historical Climatology Network temperature data, PERSIANN satellite precipitation measurements, NOAA's NCEP climate forecast system reanalysis precipitation measurements and satellite vegetation index for two cities prone to dengue, San Juan, PR and Iquitos, Peru are used for analysis in this work.

Khan et al (2017) presented the evaluation of Raman spectroscopy using random forest (RF) for the analysis of dengue fever in the diseased human sera. To understand the spectral differences between normal and infected samples, an effective machine learning system is developed that automatically learns the pattern of the shift in spectrum for the dengue compared to normal cases. It was able to predict the unknown class based on the known example. Dimensionality reduction was performed with the principal component analysis (PCA), while RF is used for automatic classification of dengue samples.

In Gambhir et al (2017), they have made an effort to devise a PSO-ANN based diagnostic model for earlier diagnosis of dengue fever. In their work, PSO technique is applied to optimize the weight and bias parameters of ANN method. Further, PSO optimized ANN approach is used to detect dengue patients. They have evaluated the measures such as accuracy, sensitivity, specificity, error rate and AUC parameters. Real time data on dengue fever and weather were collected from Ministry of Health, Malaysia were used by Rahim et al (2017). They have used Naïve bayes, D3, Support Vector Machine, CN2 and Random forest for the purpose of prediction.

Chatterjee et al (2018) proposed a modified bag-of-features method to identify the marker genes in the classification task. A modified cuckoo search optimization algorithm has been used to help the artificial neural (ANN-MCS) to separate the unknown subjects into three different classes namely, DF, DHF, and another class containing convalescent and normal cases. The results of the method have been compared with multilayer perceptron feed-forward network (MLP-FFN), artificial neural network (ANN) trained with cuckoo search (ANN-CS), and ANN trained with PSO (ANN-PSO).By varying the number of clusters different experiments were conducted for the initial bag-of-features-based feature selection phase. The hybrid ANN-MCS model has been used on the reduced dataset for the classification process.

Carvajal et al (2018) compared the predictive accuracy of the temporal pattern of Dengue incidence in Metropolitan Manila which was affected by the meteorological factors using general additive modelling, seasonal autoregressive integrated moving average with exogenous variables, random forest and gradient boosting. The meteorological factors used here are flood, precipitation, southern oscillation index, temperature, wind speed, relative humidity and direction.

Three important machine learning techniques namely Artificial Neural Network (ANN), Decision Tree (DT) and Naïve Bayes (NB) are evaluated for early detection and precise diagnosis of dengue disease (Gambhir et al, 2018). Different performance measures like accuracy, sensitivity, specificity and error rate were analyzed.A comparative study based on Classification and Regression Tree (CART), Multi-layer perceptron (MLP) and C4.5 algorithm was conducted by Sajana et al (2018) to classify the dengue samples.

Mutheneni et al (2018) collected the district-wise disease endemicity levels of Andhra Pradesh using geographical information system tools. The hot spots and cold spots were identified using spatial statistical analysis. Self-organizing map (SOM) of data mining was used to understand the endemicity patterns in study areas. The identified SOM clusters were projected in the geographical space according to the intensity of the disease and the intensity levels were classified into low, medium and high endemic areas.

The ensemble models made by the combination of two-dimensional method of analogues models including dengue and climate data, additive seasonal Holt-Winters models with and without wavelet smoothing and simple historical models were utilized by Buczak et al (2018) for dengue prediction.

Agarwal et al (2018) utilized multi-regression and Naïve Bayes approach to device a model that gives the relation between dengue cases and weather parameters like maximum temperature, rainfall and relative humidity. They have suggested a new spherical k-means clustering algorithm for finding the zones with similar transmission pattern.Dengue Hemorrhagic Fever (DHF) prediction based on Naïve Bayes method was used by Arafiyah&Hermin (2018) to reduce the misdiagnosis rate in Indonesia. The patient's medical data such as temperature, spotting and bleeding were used as inputs. They have suggested that optimization methods can be incorporated for improving the classification accuracy.

Artificial Neural Networks (ANN) was applied to predict dengue fever outbreak by Laureano-Rosario (2018). The sea surface temperature, precipitation, air temperature, humidity, previous dengue cases and population size were used as the input data for the process. They have used two models for predicting dengue based on the population at risk and the size of the vulnerable population.

METHODOLOGY

Supervised learning one of the most commonly used types of machine learning algorithms. In these types of ML algorithms, we have input and output variables and the algorithm generate a function that predicts the output based on given input variables. It is called 'supervised' because the algorithm learns in a supervised (given target variable) fashion. This learning process iterates over the training data until the model achieves an acceptable level. Supervised learning problems can be further divided into two parts:

- **Regression**: A supervised problem is said to be regression problem when the output variable is a continuous value such as "weight", "height" or "dollars."
- **Classification**: It is said to be a classification problem when the output variable is a discrete (or category) such as "male" and "female" or "disease" and "no disease."

A real-life application of supervised machine learning is the recommendation system used by Amazon, Google, Facebook, Netflix, Youtube, etc. Another example of supervised machine learning is fraud detection. Some examples for supervised algorithms include Linear Regression, Decision Trees, Random Forest, k nearest neighbours, SVM, Gradient Boosting Machines (GBM), Neural Network etc.

Since the nature of data is numeric, predictive model construction is performed by using regression-based algorithms. Regression models are realized as the one of the most fashionable and constructive tools in machine learning. Regression is a statistical method used for modeling and examination of numerical data which consist of dependent variable and of one or more independent variables. The following subsections discusses about various prominent regression approaches used for predictive analytics of dengue prevalence.

Machine learning algorithms are only a very small part of using machine learning in practice as a data analyst or data scientist. In practice, the process often looks like:

Start Loop
1. **Understand the Domain, Prior Knowledge, and Goals**: Talk to domain experts. Often the goals are very unclear. You often have more things to try then you can possibly implement.
2. **Data Integration, Selection, Cleaning, and Pre-Processing**: This is often the most time consuming part. It is important to have high quality data. The more data you have, the more it sucks because the data is dirty. Garbage in, garbage out.
3. **Learning Models**: The fun part. This part is very mature. The tools are general.
4. **Interpreting Results**: Sometimes it does not matter how the model works as long it delivers results. Other domains require that the model is understandable. You will be challenged by human experts.
5. **Consolidating and Deploying Discovered Knowledge**: The majority of projects that are successful in the lab are not used in practice. It is very hard to get something used.

End Loop

It is not a one-shot process, it is a cycle. It's a need to run the loop until getting a result that can be used in practice. Also, the data can change, requiring a new loop.

Support Vector Regression (SVR) Algorithm

Support Vector Machine (SVM) are the special kind of algorithms which are exemplified by the usage of kernels, number of support vectors, sparseness of the solution, etc. In SVM, each data item are plotted as a point in n-dimensional space with the value of every feature being the value of a specific coordinate.

Afterward, classification is done by finding the hyperplane that differentiate the classes very well. SVM can be used as a regression approach which maintains all the major features that distinguish the algorithm. SVR make use of same principles as used in SVM for data classification with a few minor differences. Since the nature of output is a real number it turn out to be very difficult to predict the future at hand, which possess many possibilities. A margin of tolerance is placed in approximation to the SVM which would have previously requested from the problem. The main theme of this kind of regression model is to minimize the error, maximizing the margin, characterize the hyperplane.

Step-Down Linear Regression (SLR) Model

Regression analysis is the task of estimating the relationship among features. It has several techniques for analyzing and modeling the variables. The main focal point of regression model is to find the relationship between the dependent variable and one or more independent variables. Step wise regression builds regression model from a set of candidate independent variables by including and removing predictors in a stepwise manner into the model in anticipation of there is no reasonable basis to enter or remove anymore. This will end up with a fruitful regression model.

Gradient Boosted Regression Tree (GBRT) Algorithm

Gradient Boosted Regression Tree (GBRT) is the one of the successful machine learning model for making predictions. It is a kind of additive model that makes forecasting by combining decisions from a set of base models. The formal representation of class of model is

$$g(x) = f_0(x) + f_1(x) + f_2(x) + ...$$

The ultimate classifier 'g' is the sum of simple base classifier f_i. GBRT uses a special kind of ensempling technique called Gradient boosting which is rooted from Gradient Descent in numerical optimization.

Negative Binomial Regression (NBM) Model

Negative Binomial Regression (NBM) approach is analogous to conventional regression model except that the dependent variable is an observed count that tag along the negative binomial distribution. Dependent variable can take up non-negative integers such as 0,1,2,3 and so on. NBM model is a generalization of Poisson regression which unties the restrictive assumption that the variance is equal to the mean ended by the Poisson model. NBM is rooted in the Poisson-gamma mixture distribution which is popular since it lets the modeling of Poisson heterogeneity using a gamma distribution.

Least Absolute Shrinkage and Selection Operator (LASSO) Linear Regression Model

Ridge and Lasso models in regression are more influential methods used for building thrifty models in existence of a large number of features. The meaning of 'large' here basically mean either of two things, large enough to augment the affinity of a model to overfit or Large enough to root computational challenges. The intrinsic properties and sensible use cases differentiate Ridge with Lasso models. Basically Ridge regression performs L2 regularization whereas Lasso performs L1 regularization. Hence, minimization objectives vary for two models.

Generalized Additive Model (GAM)

Generalized Additive Model (GAM) is a one kind of statistical models in which the customary linear relationship between the dependent and independent variables are replaced by several Non-linear smooth functions to model and confine the non linearity in the data. GAM helps us to fit the linear models which be either linearly or non-linearly dependent on many predictors

Decision Tree

Decision tree builds classification or regression models in the form of a tree structure. It breaks down a dataset into smaller and smaller subsets while at the same time an associated decision tree is incrementally developed. The final result is a tree with decision nodes and leaf nodes. A decision node has two or more branches Leaf node represents a classification or decision. The topmost decision node in a tree which corresponds to the best predictor called root node. Decision trees can handle both categorical and numerical data

The below are the some of the assumptions that made while using Decision tree:

- At the beginning, the whole training set is considered as the **root.**
- Feature values are preferred to be categorical. If the values are continuous then they are discretized prior to building the model.
- Records are distributed recursively on the basis of attribute values.
- Order to placing attributes as root or internal node of the tree is done by using some statistical approach.

Random Forest

Random Forest is a versatile machine learning method capable of performing both regression and classification tasks. It is a type of ensemble learning method, where a group of weak models combine to form a powerful model.

In Random Forest, multiple trees are grown as opposed to a single tree in CART / ID3 model. To classify a new object based on attributes, each tree gives a classification and it's called as the tree "votes" for that class. The forest chooses the classification having the most votes (over all the trees in the forest) and in case of regression, it takes the average of outputs by different trees.

It works in the following manner. Each tree is planted & grown as follows:

1. Assume number of cases in the training set is N. Then, sample of these N cases is taken at random but *with replacement*. This sample will be the training set for growing the tree.
2. If there are M input variables, a number m<M is specified such that at each node, m variables are selected at random out of the M. The best split on this m is used to split the node. The value of m is held constant while we grow the forest.
3. Each tree is grown to the largest extent possible and there is no pruning.
4. Predict new data by aggregating the predictions of the ntree trees (i.e., majority votes for classification, average for regression).

Boosting

Boosting is an ensemble technique that attempts to create a strong classifier from a number of weak classifiers. The algorithm for Boosting Trees evolved from the application of boosting methods to regression trees. The general idea is to compute a sequence of simple trees, where each successive tree is built for the prediction residuals of the preceding tree. At each step of the boosting (boosting trees algorithm), a simple (best) partitioning of the data is determined, and the deviations of the observed values from the respective means (residuals for each partition) are computed.

Boosting, the machine-learning method is based on the observation that finding many rough rules of thumb can be a lot easier than finding a single, highly accurate prediction rule. The boosting algorithm calls the "weak" or "base" learning algorithm repeatedly, each time feeding it a different subset of the training examples Each time it is called, the base learning algorithm generates a new weak prediction rule, and after many rounds, the boosting algorithm must combine these weak rules into a single prediction rule that, hopefully, will be much more accurate than any one of the weak rules

Support Vector Machine (SVM)

Support Vector Machines (SVM) rooted in statistical learning theory, developed by Vladimir Vapnik in the 1990s. This classifier requires only few examples for training, and it is very intensive to the number of dimensions. It is a novel method for the classification of both linear and non-linear data. SVM classification can be used to regression and classification problems. Like ANN, SVM is an example for "black-box" algorithm. SVM is most suitable algorithm for classification when compared to other algorithms. The primary task of an SVM is to separate classes with a surface that maximizes the margins between them. SVM is basically used to transform the training dataset into a higher dimension with the help of nonlinear mapping. SVM searches for the linear optimal separating hyperplane using the new dimension. If data is from two classes, then it is separated by a hyperplane. Hyperplane is identified by using support vectors (i.e., training tuples) and margins.

k-Nearest Neighbour Classification (k-NN)

k-Nearest Neighbour method is used to build a classification model with no supposition about the system of the function,

$$y=f(x_1,x_2, \ldots,x_p)$$

y-dependent variable
$x_1,x_2, \ldots,x_p$- Independent variable

Function is assumed to be a "smooth". It is different from linear regression that it does not involve assessment of parameters in an assumed function form. Machine Learning model is generated by using training data which has y value. y is the class to which training tuple belongs. y may be binary variable or discrete variable. K-NN method is used to identify k observations / tuples in the training tuples that are similar to a new observation called $(a_1,a_2, \ldots,a_p)$ that we want to classify and to use these tuples to classify the tuples into a particular class, C. This can be represented as

$C=f((a_1,a_2, \ldots,a_p)$

If we consider f is a smooth function, the task is to identify tuples in training data that are near it and find C from the values of y for these tuples. Identifying neighbours are like a measuring distance or dissimilarity that we can compute between observations. Distance based measures like Euclidean distance is used for this kind of classification.

Artificial Neural Networks (ANN)

The fundamental model of ANN is derived from the architecture of animal brains. ANN is based on the basic form of inputs and outputs. The core element of brain is neuron, a cell that can transmit and process electrical or chemical signals. One neuron is associated with other neuron to create a network. There is massive number of neurons interconnected with each other in human brain. Every neuron possesses an input, a cell body and an output. Output of one neuron is connected with other neurons and the network is developed. Complexity of neuron is very high when compared to the artificial neurons. Basically, neurons are stimulated when the electrochemical signal is directed through the axon. The cell body governs the weight of the signal, and, if a threshold is reached, the firing continues through the output, along the dendrite. Benefits of ANN are realized in many fields like Trading, Credit applications, Medical diagnosis, Robotics and etc.

Perceptrons

The basic element of a neural network is the *perceptron*. The main role of perceptron is to receive an input signal and then pass the value through some form of function. It outputs the result of the function. Perceptrons focus on numbers when a number or vector of numbers is sent to the input. It is then sent to a function that computes the outgoing value; this is called the *activation function*.

Experiment Results and Analysis

In this work, Data record, for each of 2000 administrative regions, whether or not dengue was recorded at any time between 1961 and 1990 is considered. This is derived from a data set in which the climate and tree cover information were given for each half degree of latitude by half degree of longitude pixel. It contains 13 attributes with 2000 records. The attributes description is given in Table 1.

The variable NoYes was given by administrative region. The climate data and tree cover data given here are 50th or 90th percentiles, where percentiles were calculates across pixels for an administrative region.

Preprocessing Dengue Dataset

A correlation between variables indicates that as one variable changes in value, the other variable tends to change in a specific direction. The extreme values of -1 and 1 indicate a perfectly linear relationship where a change in one variable is accompanied by a perfectly consistent change in the other. A coefficient of zero represents no linear relationship. As one variable increases, there is no tendency in the other variable to either increase or decrease. When the value is in-between 0 and +1/-1, there is a relationship,

Table 1. Dengue dataset

Attribute	Description
humid	Average vapour density: 1961-1990
humid90	90th percentile of humid
temp	Average temperature: 1961-1990
temp90	90th percentile of temp
h10pix	maximum of humid, within a 10 pixel radius
h10pix90	maximum of humid90, within a 10 pixel radius
trees	Percent tree cover, from satellite data
trees90	90th percentile of trees
Xmin	minimum longitude
Xmax	maximum longitude
Ymin	minimum latitude
Ymax	maximum latitude
NoYes	Was dengue observed? (1=yes)

but the points don't all fall on a line. As r approaches -1 or 1, the strength of the relationship increases and the data points tend to fall closer to a line.

The coefficient sign represents the direction of the relationship.

- Positive coefficients indicate that when the value of one variable increases, the value of the other variable also tends to increase.
- Negative coefficients represent cases when the value of one variable increases, the value of the other variable tends to decrease.

Figure 1 shows the density plots for the attributes humid, humid90, temp, temp90, h10pix and h10pix90. The impact of dengue is high in humid range from 25 to 30 and the temperature is 25-30 and it doesn't depend on number of trees. Similarly Figure 2 shows the distribution of attribute values for the class label NoYes for the attributes humid, humid90, temp, temp90, h10pix and h10pix90. From this the inference is the influence of dengue is highly dependent on humid and h10pix compared to trees.

Figure 3 shows the correlation analysis between the attributes of dataset. The correlation between h10pix, h10pix90, humid90 and humid are positively correlated with the class label NoYes. There is no correlation between the Dengue fever and minimum and maximum longitude. Minimum and maximum latitude are negatively correlated with Dengue fever.

Predictive Analysis

Prediction on Dengue Dataset

In this work, Linear Regression (LR) model, Support Vector Regression (SVR) algorithm, Optimimized SVR, Negative Binomial Regression (NBM)model, Quassi Poisson, Poisson Least Absolute Shrinkage

Figure 1. Density diagram for Dengue dataset attributes

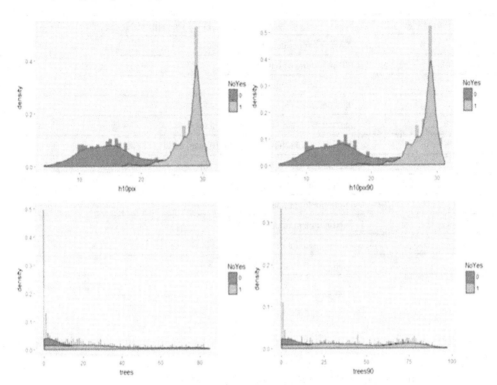

Figure 2. Scatter plot for Dengue dataset attributes

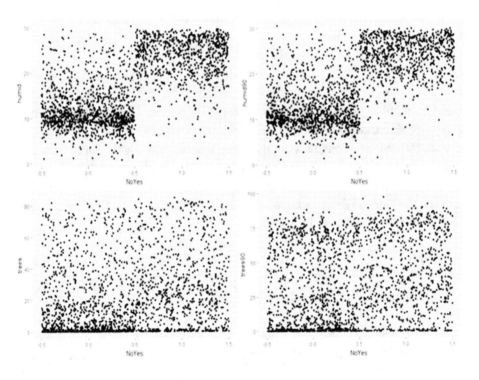

Figure 3. Correlation analysis on attributes

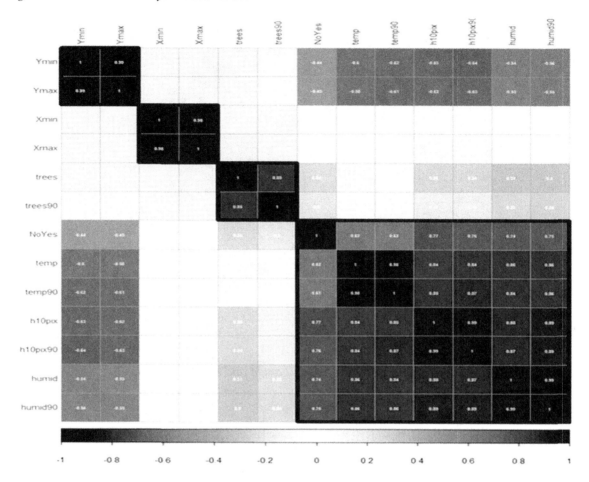

and Selection Operator (LASSO) linear regression model, Ridges and Elastic net are employed on the dengue dataset. and Generalized Additive Model (GAM) are as candidate models to predict dengue incidence. Performance and goodness of fit of the models were assessed using the root-mean-square error (RMSE).

Ridge and lasso regularization work by adding a penalty term to the log likelihood function. In the case of ridge regression, the penalty term is β_1^2 and in the case of lasso, it is β_1 Figure – shows the error as function of lambda. The plot shows that the *log* of the optimal value of lambda (i.e. the one that minimizes the root mean square error) is approximately -5. The plot displays the cross-validation error according to the log of lambda. The left dashed vertical line indicates that the log of the optimal value of lambda, which is the one that minimizes the prediction error. This lambda value will give the most accurate model In general though; the objective of regularization is to balance accuracy and simplicity. In the present context, this means a model with the smallest number of coefficients that also gives a good accuracy. Figure 4 shows the Lasso model for log(lamda) error values.

Figure 5 shows L1 norm and log(lambda) values of LASSO, Ridge and Elasticnet. In these plots, each colored line represents the value taken by a different coefficient in the model. Lambda is the weight given to the regularization term (the L1 norm), so as lambda approaches zero, the loss function of the model

Figure 4. Error as a function of lambda

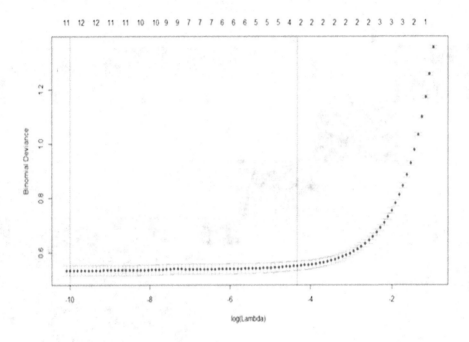

Figure 5. Ridge, Lasso and Elastic net model for log Lamda and L1-Norm values

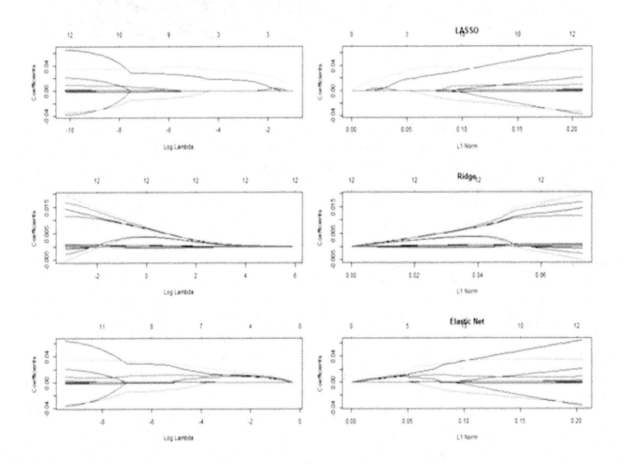

Figure 6. RMSE value for predictive models

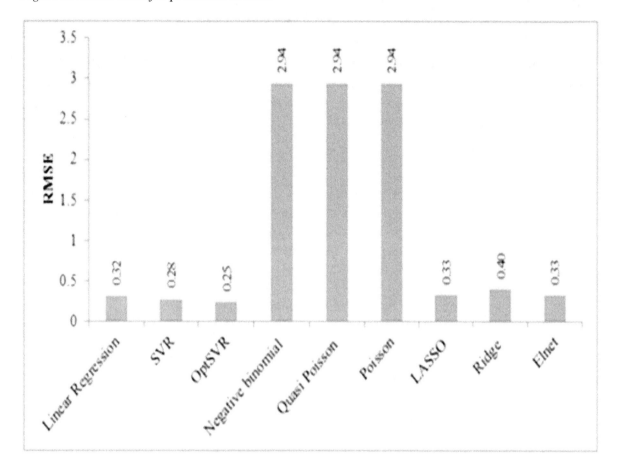

approaches the ordinary least squares (OLS)loss function. Therefore, when lambda is very small, the LASSO solution should be very close to the OLS solution, and all of the coefficients are in the model. As lambda grows, the regularization term has greater effect and a fewer variables in the model.

The left figure shows how the coefficients start to decrease and finally all drop to zero as the penalty becomes more important (larger log(lambda)). The right figure shows the same but plotted against the penalty.As the norm of the vector is small many of the coefficients are 0 or close to 0. As the norm increases the coefficients deviate from 0 and in the end all are different from 0.

Figure 6 shows the RMSE obtained from Linear regression, SVR, OptSVR, Negative binomial, Quasi Poisson, Poisson, LASSO, Ridge and Elastinet. It shows that, the RMSE value obtained byoptimalSVR is less compared to other methods considered in this work. Negative binomial, Quasi Poisson and Poisson gives the highest RMSE of 2.94.

Classification

Decision Tree

Figure 7 shows the decision tree model for dengue dataset. The root node of the tree is h10pix. In this, 59% of the records are less than 22 and 41% of the records are greater than 22. 98% of chance

```
1) root 1400 572 0 (0.59142857 0.40857143)
  2) h10pix< 22.19986 683  14 0 (0.97950220 0.02049780) *
  3) h10pix>=22.19986 717 159 1 (0.22175732 0.77824268)
    6) h10pix< 26.49222 196  93 1 (0.47448980 0.52551020)
     12) Ymax>=25.75 21   1 0 (0.95238095 0.04761905) *
     13) Ymax< 25.75 175  73 1 (0.41714286 0.58285714)
       26) Xmin< 65 148  70 1 (0.47297297 0.52702703)
         52) Ymax>=-3.75 88  32 0 (0.63636364 0.36363636)
           104) Xmin>=11.75 48   7 0 (0.85416667 0.14583333) *
           105) Xmin< 11.75 40  15 1 (0.37500000 0.62500000)
             210) Ymin>=14.75 15   3 0 (0.80000000 0.20000000) *
             211) Ymin< 14.75 25   3 1 (0.12000000 0.88000000) *
         53) Ymax< -3.75 60  14 1 (0.23333333 0.76666667) *
       27) Xmin>=65 27   3 1 (0.11111111 0.88888889) *
    7) h10pix>=26.49222 521  66 1 (0.12667946 0.87332054)
     14) Xmax< -92.5 12   2 0 (0.83333333 0.16666667) *
     15) Xmax>=-92.5 509  56 1 (0.11001965 0.88998035) *
```

Figure 7. Decision tree for Dengue dataset

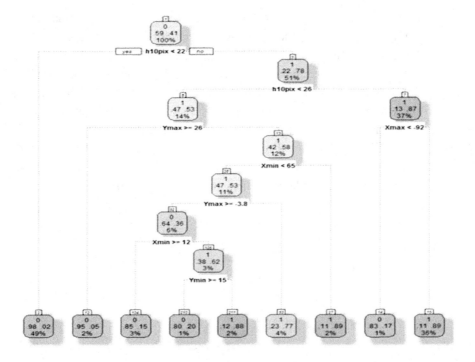

Random Forest

Random forest is used to fit many decision trees without overfitting. A random forest allows us to determine the most important predictors across the explanatory variables by generating many decision trees and then ranking the variables by importance. The complexity parameter (cp) is used to control the size of the decision tree and to select the optimal tree size. If the cost of adding another variable to the decision tree from the current node is above the value of cp, then tree building does not continue. That means the tree construction does not continue unless it would decrease the overall lack of fit by a factor of cp. Table 2 expresses cpvs relative error for random forest. Figure 8 shows cpvs relative error for random forest with number of trees.

Table 2. cpvs relative error for random forest

S. NO	CP	nsplitrel	error	xerror	xstd
1	0.7316486	0	1.00000	1.00000	0.026521
2	0.0216606	1	0.26835	0.28640	0.017425
3	0.0180505	2	0.24669	0.27798	0.017201
4	0.0150421	3	0.22864	0.26955	0.016972
5	0.0064180	7	0.16847	0.19976	0.014847
6	0.0048135	11	0.14200	0.18893	0.014474
7	0.0030084	12	0.13718	0.16606	0.013640
8	0.0026474	14	0.13117	0.16486	0.013594
9	0.0024067	19	0.11793	0.17088	0.013821
10	0.0010000	21	0.11312	0.170880	0.013821

Figure 8. Complexity parameter for Random Forest

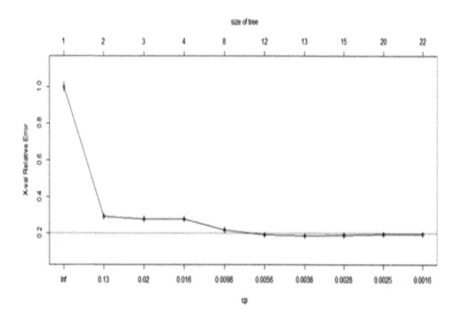

Figures 9-13 show the random forest with different number of splits and cp value.

Figure 9. Random forest for split 21 with cp=0.0010000

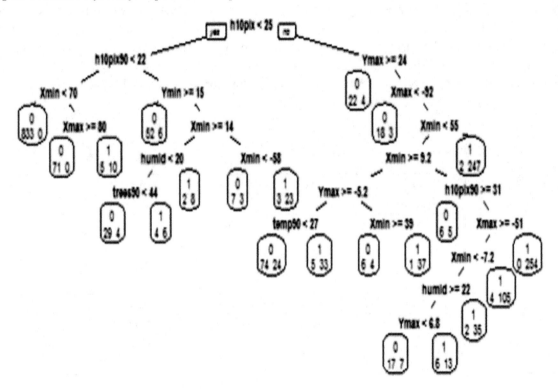

Figure 10. Random forest for split 21 with cp=0.0010000

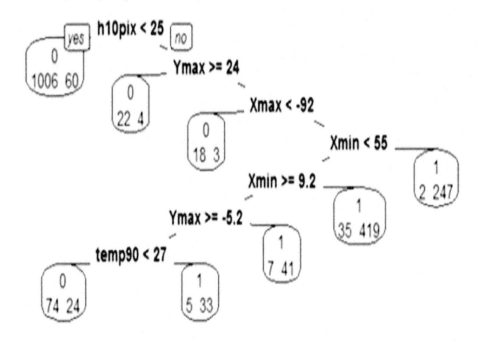

Figure 11. Random forest for split 2 with cp=0.0180505

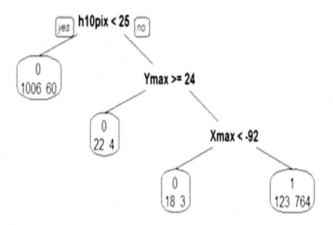

Figure 12. Random forest for split =1 with cp=0.0216606

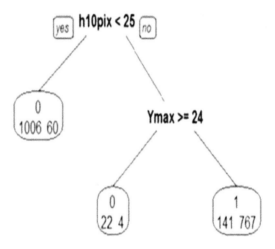

Figure 13. Random forest Tree for split =0 with cp=0.7316486

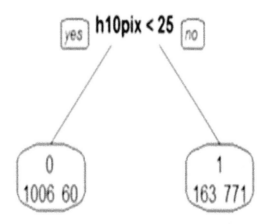

Neural Network

Neural network is an information-processing machine and can be viewed as analogous to human nervous system. Just like human nervous system, which is made up of interconnected neurons, a neural network is made up of interconnected information processing units. The information processing units do not work in a linear manner. In fact, neural network draws its strength from parallel processing of information, which allows it to deal with non-linearity. Neural network becomes handy to infer meaning and detect patterns from complex data sets.

Figure 14 and Figure 15 visualize the computed neural network. They have 1 neuron and 3 neurons in its hidden layer respectively. The black lines show the connections with weights. The weights are calculated using the back propagation algorithm. The blue line is the displays the bias term

A lift chart graphically represents the improvement that a mining model provides when compared against a random guess and measures the change in terms of a lift score. The best model is identified by comparing the lift scores for different models. It is also possible determine the point at which the model's predictions become less useful. Figure 16 shows the lift chart for decision tree, gradient boost, random forest SVM, linear model and neural network. The lift chart plots the relative increase in predictive performance against the rate of positive predictions.

Figure 14. Neural network with hidden node =1

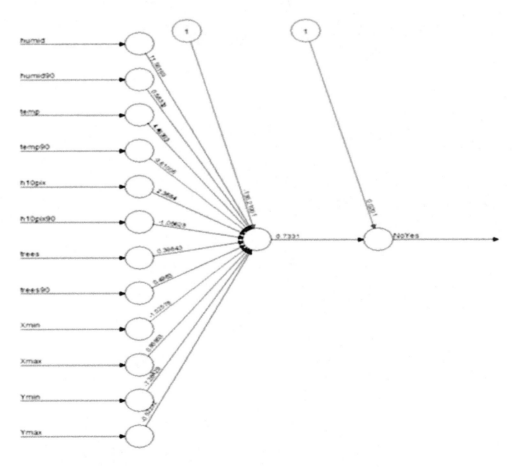

Figure 15. Neural Network with hidden node= 3

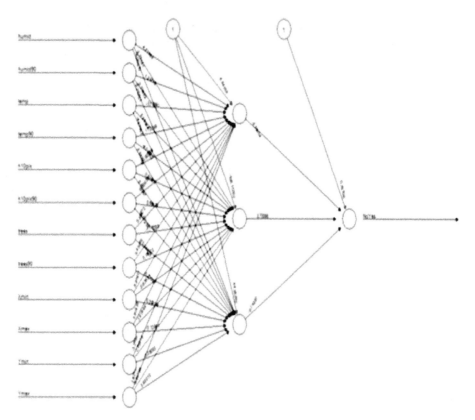

Figure 16. Lift chart for classifier models

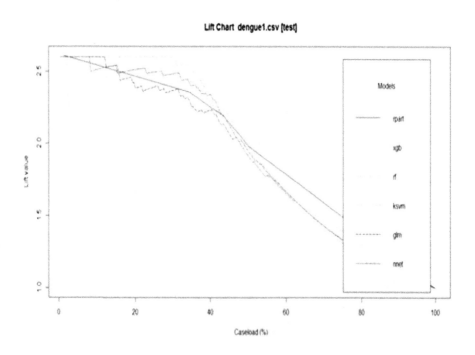

Figure 17. Precision / Recall chart for classifier models

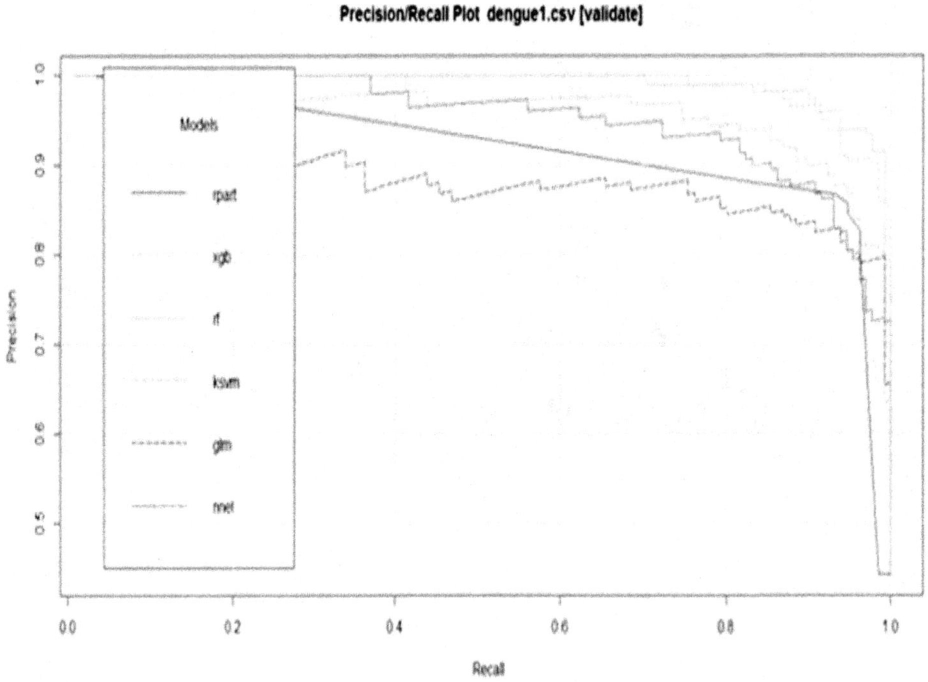

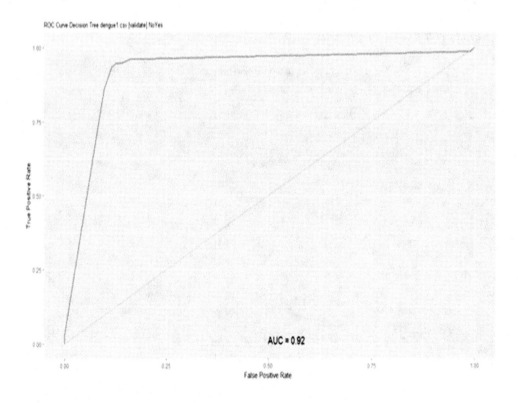

Figure 18. ROC for Decision Tree

Figure 19. ROC for Random Forest

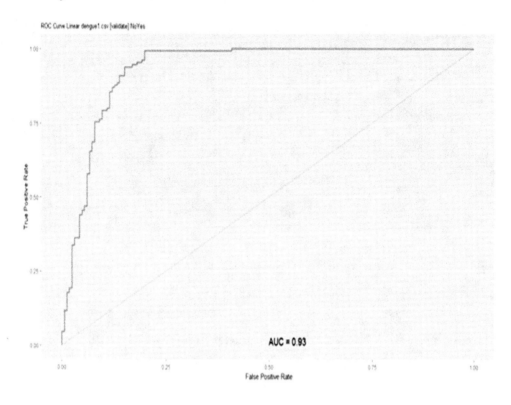

Figure 20. ROC for Linear Model

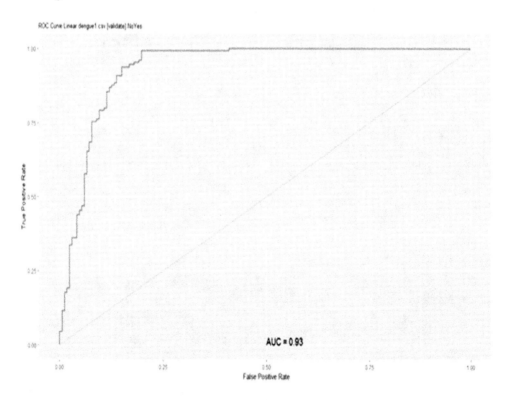

Figure 21. ROC for Extreme Boost Model

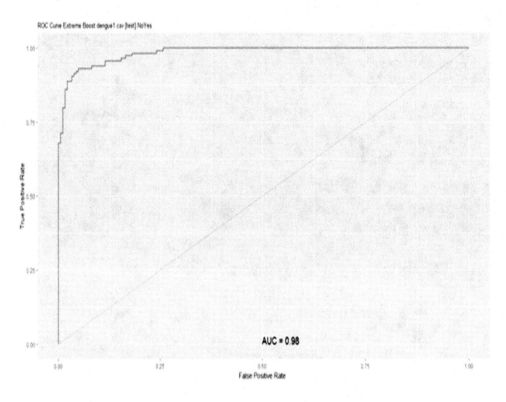

Figure 22. ROC for SVM

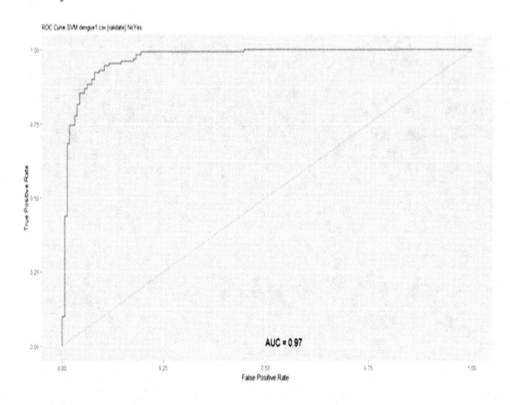

Figure 23. ROC for Neural Network

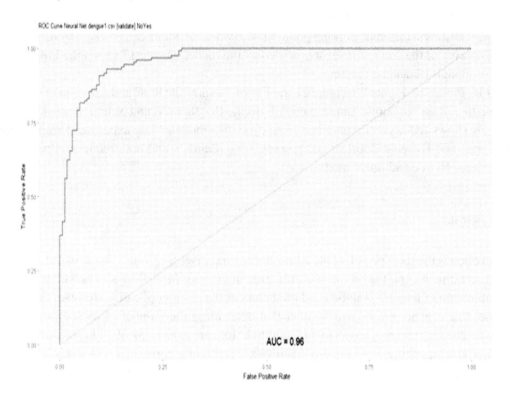

Figure 24. Performance analysis of classifier models

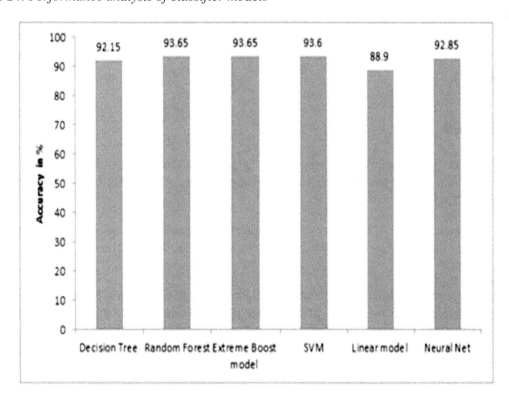

Precision/recall (PR) curves are visual representations of the performance of a classification model in terms of the precision and recall statistics. The curves are obtained by proper interpolation of the values of the statistics at different working points. These working points can be given by different cut-off limits on a ranking of the class of interest provided by the model. Figure 17 shows the Precision/Recall for classifier models of dengue dataset.

Figures 18, Figure 19, Figure 20, Figure 21 and Figure 22 show the ROC and Area Under Curve (AUC) for Decision tree, Random Forest, Linear model, Extreme Boost, SVM and Neural network respectively.

Figure 24 shows the accuracy obtained from classifier models. The experiment results show the Random Forest and Extreme Boost model gives 93.65% accuracy and both models outperform SVM, neural net, decision tree and linear model.

CONCLUSION

Dengue infection is the most prevalent mosquito-borne viral disease throughout the world—and there is no available treatment. And the problem is only growing worse. Modelling shows which features, and which combination of features, will be good predictors of the number of cases. However, it is important to remember that it is not the current weather that determines the number of mosquitos and thus the number of dengue fever cases. The weeks and months before provide the incubation period for mosquitos to flourish. The temperature and humidity features are positively correlated with dengue fever. In this work the predictive models and classifiers are applied to demonstrate the features mainly involved in dengue fever. Support Vector Regression (SVR) algorithm, Step-down Linear Regression (SLR) model, Gradient Boosted Regression Tree (GBRT) algorithm, Negative Binomial Regression (NBM)model, Least Absolute Shrinkage and Selection Operator (LASSO) linear regression model and Generalized Additive Model (GAM) are used to predict dengue incidence. The optimized SVR gives minimal RMSE 0.25. The classifiers Decision Tree, Random Forest, Linear Model, Extreme Boost, SVM and Neural networks are applied. The experiment results show that the Extreme Boost and Random Forest gives 93.65% accuracy.

REFERENCES

Agarwal, N., Koti, S. R., Saran, S., & Kumar, A. S. (2018). Data mining techniques for predicting dengue outbreak in geospatial domain using weather parameters for New Delhi, India. *Current Science*, *114*(11), 2281–2291.

Arafiyah, R., & Hermin, F. (2018, January). Data mining for dengue hemorrhagic fever (DHF) prediction with naive Bayes method. *Journal of Physics: Conference Series*, *948*(1), 012077. doi:10.1088/1742-6596/948/1/012077

Buczak, A. L., Baugher, B., Moniz, L. J., Bagley, T., Babin, S. M., & Guven, E. (2018). Ensemble method for dengue prediction. *PLoS One*, *13*(1), e0189988. doi:10.1371/journal.pone.0189988 PMID:29298320

Carvajal, T. M., Viacrusis, K. M., Hernandez, L. F. T., Ho, H. T., Amalin, D. M., & Watanabe, K. (2018). Machine learning methods reveal the temporal pattern of dengue incidence using meteorological factors in metropolitan Manila, Philippines. *BMC Infectious Diseases*, *18*(1), 183. doi:10.118612879-018-3066-0 PMID:29665781

Chatterjee, S., Dey, N., Shi, F., Ashour, A. S., Fong, S. J., & Sen, S. (2018). Clinical application of modified bag-of-features coupled with hybrid neural-based classifier in dengue fever classification using gene expression data. *Medical & Biological Engineering & Computing*, *56*(4), 709–720. doi:10.100711517-017-1722-y PMID:28891000

Fathima, A. S., Manimegalai, D., & Hundewale, N. (2011). A review of data mining classification techniques applied for diagnosis and prognosis of the arbovirus-dengue. *International Journal of Computer Science Issues*, *8*(6), 322.

Gambhir, S., Malik, S. K., & Kumar, Y. (2017). PSO-ANN based diagnostic model for the early detection of dengue disease. *New Horizons in Translational Medicine*, *4*(1-4), 1–8. doi:10.1016/j.nhtm.2017.10.001

Gambhir, S., Malik, S. K., & Kumar, Y. (2018). The Diagnosis of Dengue Disease: An Evaluation of Three Machine Learning Approaches. *International Journal of Healthcare Information Systems and Informatics*, *13*(3), 1–19. doi:10.4018/IJHISI.2018070101

Gomes, A. L. V., Wee, L. J., Khan, A. M., Gil, L. H., Marques, E. T. Jr, Calzavara-Silva, C. E., & Tan, T. W. (2010). Classification of dengue fever patients based on gene expression data using support vector machines. *PLoS One*, *5*(6), e11267. doi:10.1371/journal.pone.0011267 PMID:20585645

Huy, N. T., Thao, N. T. H., Ha, T. T. N., Lan, N. T. P., Nga, P. T. T., Thuy, T. T., ... Huong, V. T. Q. (2013). Development of clinical decision rules to predict recurrent shock in dengue. *Critical Care (London, England)*, *17*(6), R280. doi:10.1186/cc13135 PMID:24295509

Khan, S., Ullah, R., Khan, A., Sohail, A., Wahab, N., Bilal, M., & Ahmed, M. (2017). Random forest-based evaluation of raman spectroscopy for dengue fever analysis. *Applied Spectroscopy*, *71*(9), 2111–2117. doi:10.1177/0003702817695571 PMID:28862033

Khan, S., Ullah, R., Khan, A., Wahab, N., Bilal, M., & Ahmed, M. (2016). Analysis of dengue infection based on Raman spectroscopy and support vector machine (SVM). *Biomedical Optics Express*, *7*(6), 2249–2256. doi:10.1364/BOE.7.002249 PMID:27375941

Kiefer, A. (2017). Using machine learning to forecast local epidemics of dengue fever in Latin America. *6th International Conference on Biostatistics and Bioinformatics*, Atlanta, GA.

Laureano-Rosario, A., Duncan, A., Mendez-Lazaro, P., Garcia-Rejon, J., Gomez-Carro, S., Farfan-Ale, J., ... Muller-Karger, F. (2018). Application of artificial neural networks for dengue fever outbreak predictions in the northwest coast of Yucatan, Mexico and San Juan, Puerto Rico. *Tropical Medicine and Infectious Disease*, *3*(1), 5.

Long, Z. A., Bakar, A. A., Hamdan, A. R., & Sahani, M. (2010, November). Multiple attribute frequent mining-based for dengue outbreak. In *International Conference on Advanced Data Mining and Applications* (pp. 489-496). Springer. 10.1007/978-3-642-17316-5_46

Lwin, M. O., Vijaykumar, S., Fernando, O. N. N., Cheong, S. A., Rathnayake, V. S., Lim, G., ... Foo, S. (2014). A 21st century approach to tackling dengue: Crowdsourced surveillance, predictive mapping and tailored communication. *Acta Tropica*, *130*, 100–107. doi:10.1016/j.actatropica.2013.09.021 PMID:24161879

Mutheneni, S. R., Mopuri, R., Naish, S., Gunti, D., &Upadhyayula, S. M. (2018). Spatial distribution and cluster analysis of dengue using self organizing maps in Andhra Pradesh, India, 2011–2013. *Parasite Epidemiology and Control, 3*(1), 52-61.

Rahim, N. F., Taib, S. M., & Abidin, A. I. Z. (2017). Dengue fatality prediction using data mining. *Journal of Fundamental and Applied Sciences*, *9*(6S), 671–683. doi:10.4314/jfas.v9i6s.52

Sajana, Navya, Gayathri, & Reshma. (2018). Classification of Dengue using Machine Learning Techniques. *International Journal of Engineering & Technology, 7*(2), 212-218.

Shaukat, K., Masood, N., Mehreen, S., & Azmeen, U. (2015). Dengue fever prediction: A data mining problem. *Journal of Data Mining in Genomics & Proteomics*.

Chapter 14
Relative Analysis on Algorithms and Applications of Deep Learning

Senbagavalli M.
Alliance University Bangalore, India

Sathiyamoorthi V.
Sona College of Technology, India

D. Sudaroli Vijayakumar
ⓘD https://orcid.org/0000-0001-8270-6223
Alliance University Bangalore, India

ABSTRACT

Deep learning is an artificial intelligence function that reproduces the mechanisms of the human mind in processing records and evolving shapes to be used in selection construction. The main objective of this chapter is to provide a complete examination of deep learning algorithms and its applications in various fields. Deep learning has detonated in the public alertness, primarily as inspective and analytical products fill our world, in the form of numerous human-centered smart-world systems, with besieged advertisements, natural language supporters and interpreters, and prototype self-driving vehicle systems. Therefore, it provides a broad orientation for those seeking a primer on deep learning algorithms and its various applications, platforms, and uses in a variety of smart-world systems. Also, this survey delivers a precious orientation for new deep learning practitioners, as well as those seeking to innovate in the application of deep learning.

INTRODUCTION

In the past decade there has been a rapid paradigm shift in the field of computer science due to apex achievements in artificial intelligence (Pallis et al., 2008) .Machine learning which is a sub field of artificial intelligence has taken the capabilities of imparting the intelligence across various disciplines

DOI: 10.4018/978-1-5225-9902-9.ch014

beyond the horizon. In 1959, Arthur Samuel defined machine learning as a "Field of study that gives computers the ability to learn without being explicitly programmed" (Samuel 1959).The machine learning algorithms works on the fact that the learning happens persistently from the training data or with the past experience and can enhance their performance by synthesizing the underlying relationships among data and the given problem without any human intervention. In contrast with the optimization problems, the machine learning algorithms generally encompasses a well-defined function that can be optimized through learning. This optimization of the decision-making processes based on learning has led to rapid rise in employing automation in innumerable areas like Healthcare, Finance, Retail, E-governance etc. However, machine learning has been considered as the giant step forward in the AI revolution the development in neural networks has taken the AI to a completely new level. Deep learning which a subset of machine learning is incorporates neural networks as their building blocks have remarkable advances in natural language and image processing (Chen et al., 2003).

With big data landscape being able to store massive amount of data that is generated every day by various businesses and users the machine learning algorithms can harvest the exponentially growing data in deriving accurate predictions. The complexity raised in maintaining a large computational on primes infrastructure to ensure successful learning has been efficiently addressed through cloud computing by eliminating the need to maintain expensive computing hardware, software and dedicated space. The businesses have started adopting Machine Learning as a service (MLaaS) into their technology stacks since they offer machine learning as a part of their service, as the name suggests. The major attraction is that these services offer data modeling APIs, machine learning algorithms, data transformations and predictive analytics without having to install software or provision their own servers, just like any other cloud service. Moreover, MLaas can help manage big data better by collecting huge amounts of data to get insights by correlating the data, crunching numbers and understanding patterns of the data to helps business take quick decisions. As data sources proliferate along with the computing power to process them, going straight to the data is one of the most straightforward ways to quickly gain insights and make predictions (Ten et al., 2005). The combination of these two mainstream technologies yields beneficial outcome for the organizations. Machine learning is heavily recommended for the problems that involve complex learning. However, it is essential to remember that Machine learning is not always an optimal solution to every type of problem. There are certain problems where robust solutions can be developed without using Machine-learning techniques (Jyoti & Goel, 2009).

This chapter will explore the end-to-end process of investigating data through a machine-learning lens from how to extract and identify useful features from the data; some of the most commonly used machine-learning algorithms, to identifying and evaluating the performance of the machine learning algorithms. Section 2 introduces steps for developing suitable machine learning model and various paradigms of machine learning techniques such as supervised, unsupervised and reinforcement learning. Section 3 discusses about various applications of machine learning in various fields and then concludes whole chapter with research insights.

DEVELOPING A MACHINE LEARNING MODEL

As discussed, machine Learning is the field where an agent is said to learn from the experience with respect to some class of tasks and the performance measure P. The task could be answering exams in a particular subject or it could be of diagnosing patients of a specific illness. As shown in the Figure 1 given below, it is

Figure 1. Taxonomy of knowledge discovery

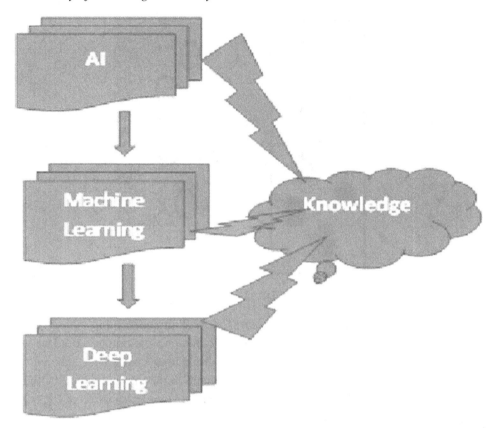

the subset of Artificial intelligence (AI) where it contains artificial neurons and reacts to the given stimuli whereas machine learning uses statistical techniques for knowledge discovery. Deep learning is the subset of machine learning where it uses artificial neural networks for learning process (Podlipnig & Boszormenyi, 2003).

Further, machine learning can be categorized into supervised, unsupervised and reinforcement learning. In any kind of tasks, the machine learning involves three components. The first component is, defining the set of tasks on which learning will take place and second is setting up a performance measure P. Whether learning is happening or not, defining some kind of performance criteria P is mandatory in machine learning tasks. Consider an example of answering questions in an exam then the performance criterion would be the number of marks that you get. Similarly, consider an example of diagnosing patient with specific illness then the performance measure would be the number of patients who did not have adverse reaction to the given drugs. So, there exists different ways for defining various performance metrics depending on what you are looking for within a given domain. The last important component machine learning is experience. For an example, experience in the case of writing exams could be writing more exams which means the better you write, the better you get or it could be the number of patient's in the case of diagnosing illnesses i.e. the more patients that you look at the better you become an expert in diagnosing illness. Hence, these are three components involved in learning; class of tasks, performance measure and well-defined experience (Silver, 2016). This kind of learning where you are learning to improve your performance based on experience is known as inductive learning. There are various machine-learning paradigms as shown in the Figure 2.

Figure 2. Categorization of various machine learning algorithms

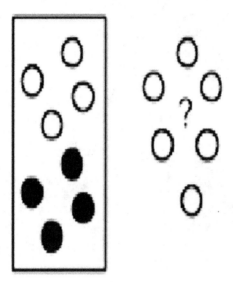

The first one is supervised learning where one learns from an input to output map. For an example, it could be a description of the patient who comes to the clinic and the output would be whether the patient has a certain disease or not in the case of diagnosing patients. Similarly, take an example of writing the exam where the input could be some kind of equation then output would be the answer to the question or it could be a true or false question i.e. it will give you a description of the question then you have to state whether it is true or false as the output. So, the essential part of supervised learning is mapping from the given input to the required output. If the output that you are looking for happens to be a categorical output such as whether he has a disease or does not have a disease or whether the answer is true or false then the learning is called supervised learning. If the output happens to be a continuous value like how long will this product last before it fails right or what is the expected rainfall tomorrow then those kinds of problems would be called as regression problems. Thus, classification and regression are called classes of supervised learning process (Woochul & Daeyeon, 2016).

The second paradigm is known as unsupervised learning problems where input to output is not required. The main goal is not to produce an output in response to the given input indeed it tries to discover some patterns out of it. Therefore, in unsupervised learning there is no real desired output that we are looking for instead it looks for finding closely related patterns in the data. Clustering is one such task where it tries to find cohesive groups among the given input pattern. For an example, one might be looking at customers who comes to the shop and want to figure out if they are into different categories of customers like college students or IT professionals so on so forth. The other popular unsupervised learning paradigm is known as association rule mining or frequent pattern mining where one is interested in finding a frequent co-occurrence of items in the data that is given to them i.e. whenever A comes to the shop B also comes to the shop. Therefore, one can learn these kinds of relationship via associations between data (Xin et al., 2016).

The third form of learning which is called as reinforcement learning. It is neither supervised nor unsupervised in nature. In reinforcement learning you have an agent who is acting in an environment, you want to figure out what actions the agent must take at every step, and the action that the agent takes is based on the rewards or penalties that the agent gets in different states.

Apart from these three types of learning, one more learning is also possible which is called as semi-supervised learning. It is the combination of supervised and unsupervised learning i.e. you have some labeled training data and you also have a larger amount of unlabeled training data and you can try to come up with some learning out of them that can work even when the training data is limited features(Yang et al., 2017).

Irrespective of domain and the type of leaning, every task needs to have some kind of a performance measure. In classification, the performance measure would be classification error i.e. how many instances are misclassified to the total number of instances. Similarly, the prediction error is supposed to be a performance measure in regression i.e. if I said, it's going to rain like 23 millimeters and then it would ends up raining like 49 centimeters then this huge difference in actual and predicted value is called prediction error. In case of clustering, it is little hard to define performance measures as we do not know what is a good clustering algorithm and do not know how to measure the quality of clusters. Therefore, there exists different kinds of clustering measures and so one of the measures is a scatter or spread of the cluster that essentially tells you how to spread out the points that belong to a single group. Thus, good clustering algorithms should minimize intra-cluster distance and maximize inter-cluster distance (Sathiyamoorthi,2017). Association rule mining use variety of measures called support and confidence whereas reinforcement learning tries to minimize the cost to accrue while controlling the system. There are several challenges exists when trying to build a machine learning solution to the given problem and few of these are given below.

First issue is about how good is a model and type of performance measures used. Most of the measures discussed above were finds to be insufficient and there are other practical considerations that come into play such as user skills, experience etc. while selecting a model and measures. The second issue is of course presence of noisy and missing data. Presence of these kinds of data leads to an error in the predicted value. Suppose medical data is recorded as 225. so what does that mean it could be 225 days in which case it is a reasonable number it could be twenty two point five years again is a reasonable number or twenty two point five months is reasonable but if it is 225 years it's not a reasonable number so there's something wrong in the data. Finally, the biggest challenge is size of the dataset since algorithms perform well when data is large but not all. The following are the basic steps to be followed while developing any kind of machine-learning applications. They are,

1. Formulating the Problem/ Define Your Machine Learning Problem
2. Collecting Labeled Data/ Gathering Data
3. Preparing that data/ Analyzing Your Data
4. Feature selection/ Feature Processing
5. Splitting the Data into Training and Evaluation Data
6. Choosing a model:
7. Training
8. Evaluation
9. Parameter Tuning
10. Prediction/ Generating and Interpreting Predictions

The following subsections will give a detailed scheme for developing a suitable machine-learning model for the given problem.

Describing the Problem

The first step in developing a model is to clearly define and describe the problem that need to be addressed with machine learning (Sathiyamoorthi, 2016). In other words formulating the core of the problem will help in deciding what the model has to predict. The formulation can be done in different ways such as understanding problem through sentence description, deriving problem from the solved similar problems from the past. Choosing how to define the problem varies depending upon the use case or business need. It is very important to avoid over-complicating the problem and to frame the simplest solution as per the requirement. The motivation for solving the problem is to be evaluated against how the solution would benefit the business. Some of the common ways of describing the problems are

Similar Problems

After detailed discussions with stakeholders, identifying the pain-points the common and most afford-able strategy is to derive the problem with previous similar experiences. Other problems can inform details about the current problem by highlighting limitations in the problem such as time dimensions and conceptual drift and can point to algorithms, data transformations that could be adapted to spot check performance (Sathiyamoorthi & Murali Bhaskaran, 2013).

Informal Description

The other simplest way is to describe the problems informally by highlighting the basic spaces of the problem in a sentence for initial understanding about the possible solution. However, this step must be considered only for initial level problem formation substituted with any other approach for detailed problem formation.

Using Assumptions

Creating a list of assumptions about the problem such as domain specific information that will lead to a viable solution that can be tested against real data .It can also be useful to highlight areas of the problem specification that may need to be challenged, relaxed or tightened.

Formalism

The most structured approach is Tom Mitchell's machine learning formalism. A computer program is said to learn from experience E with respect to some class of tasks T and performance measure P, if its performance at tasks in T, as measured by P, improves with experience E.

Use this formalism to define the T, P, and E for your problem.

- **Task** (T):
- **Experience** (E):

- **Performance** (*P*):

Data Collection

This step is the most expensive and most time-consuming aspect of any machine learning project because the quality and quantity of data that you gather will directly determine the success of the project .The paper published by Yuji Roh et al. (2018) discuss in detail about high level research landscape of data collection for machine learning such as data acquisition, data labeling and improve the labeling of any existing data. The Machine learning problems require many data for better prediction. With the rapid adoption of standard IOT solution enormous volume of sensor data can be collected from the industries for the Machine learning problems, other sources like social media and third party data providers can provide enough data for better solution predictions. The labeled data is a group of samples that have been tagged with one or more labels. Labeling typically takes a set of unlabeled data and augments each piece of that unlabeled data with meaningful tags that are informative. In supervised Machine learning, the algorithm teaches itself to learn from the labeled examples. Labeled data typically takes a set of unlabeled data and augments each piece of that unlabeled data with some sort of meaningful "tag," "label," or "class" that is somehow informative or desirable to know. Often, data is not readily available in a labeled form. Collecting and preparing the variables and the target are often the most important steps in solving a problem. The example data should be representative of the data that is used by the model to make a prediction. Unsupervised learning is the opposite of supervised learning, where unlabeled data is used because a training set does not exist. Semi-supervised learning is aimed at integrating unlabeled and labeled data to build better and more accurate models (Ramya & Sathiyamoorthi, 2014).

Data Preparation

Data preparation is the process of combining, structuring and organizing data so it can be analyzed through machine learning applications. Good enough visualizations of the data will help in finding any relevant relationships between the different variables and to find any data imbalances present. The Collected data is spilt into two parts. The first part that is used in training the model will be the majority of the dataset and the second will be used for the evaluation of the trained model's performance (Jati et al., 2016).

The data might need a lot of cleaning and preprocessing before it is feed into the machine learning system. The process of cleaning involves various processes such as getting rid of errors & noise and removal of redundancies to avoid ambiguities that arise out of the data. The preprocessing involves renaming categorical values to numbers, rescaling (normalization), abstraction, and aggregation (Sathiyamoorthi & Murali Bhaskaran, 2012a).

The appropriate usage of attributes can lead to unexpected improvements in model accuracy. Deriving new attributes from the training data in the modeling process can boost model performance. Similarly, removal of redundant or duplicate attributes can increase the performance. Transformations of training data can reduce the skewness of data as well as the prominence of outliers in the data. Outliers are extreme values that fall a long way outside of the other observations. The outliers in input data can skew and mislead the training process of machine learning algorithms resulting in longer training times, less accurate models and ultimately poorer results. Outliers can skew the summary distribution of attribute values in descriptive statistics like mean and standard deviation and in plots such as histograms and scatterplots, compressing the body of the data. Charu C. Aggarwal in his book "Outlier Analysis "suggests following methods such as,

- **Extreme Value Analysis**: Determine the statistical tails of the underlying distribution of the data. For example, statistical methods like the z-scores on univariate data.
- **Probabilistic and Statistical Models**: Determine unlikely instances from a probabilistic model of the data.
- **Linear Models**: Projection methods that model the data into lower dimensions using linear correlations.
- **Proximity-Based Models**: Data instances that are isolated from the mass of the data as determined by cluster, density or nearest neighbor analysis.
- **Information Theoretic Models**: Outliers are detected as data instances that increase the complexity (minimum code length) of the dataset.
- **High-Dimensional Outlier Detection**: Methods that search subspaces for outliers give the breakdown of distance-based measures in higher dimensions (curse of dimensionality).

Feature Engineering and Feature Selection

Feature engineering is about creating new input features from your existing ones. Feature engineering is the process of transforming raw data into features that had better represent the underlying problem to the predictive models, resulting in improved model accuracy on unseen data. An iterative process interplays with data selection and model evaluation, repeatedly, until better prediction is achieved. The process of involves the following steps

- **Brainstorm Features**: Examining the problem and data closely and by study feature engineering on other problems to extract similar patterns
- **Devise Features**: Decide on using use automatic feature extraction or manual feature construction and mixtures of the two.
- **Select Features**: Using different feature importance scorings and feature selection methods to prepare different view of the model.
- **Evaluate Models**: Estimate model accuracy on unseen data using the chosen features.

Feature selection is the process of selecting a subset of relevant features (variables, predictors) for use in machine learning model construction. Feature selection is also called variable selection or attributes selection. The data features are used to train the machine learning models have a huge influence on the performance. Hence choosing irrelevant or partially relevant features can negatively influence the model performance. A feature selection algorithm can be seen as the combination of a search technique for proposing new feature subsets, along with an evaluation measure, which scores the different feature subsets (Sathiyamoorthi & Murali Bhaskaran, 2012b). In real world, applications the models usually choke due to very high dimensionality of the data presented along with exponential increase in training time and risk of over fitting with increasing number of features. Identifying better features can provide the flexibility in even choosing a slightly wrong algorithm but ending up in getting good results. The three general classes of feature selection algorithms are filter methods, wrapper methods and embedded methods.

- **Filter Methods:** Filter feature selection methods apply a statistical measure to assign a scoring to each feature. The features are ranked by the score and either selected to be kept or removed from the dataset. Some examples of filter methods include Pearson's Correlation, Linear discriminant analysis, ANOVA, Chi-Square.
- **Wrapper Methods:** The Wrapper Methods generate considers the selection of a set of features as a search problem, where different combinations are prepared, evaluated and compared to other combinations. Some examples of wrapper methods include recursive feature elimination, forward feature selection, backward feature elimination.
- **Embedded Methods:** Embedded methods combine the qualities' of filter and wrapper methods. Algorithms that have their own built-in feature selection methods implement it. Some examples of embedded methods include regularization algorithms (LASSO, Elastic Net and Ridge Regression), Memetic algorithm, and Random multinomial logit.

Splitting Up the Data

The crux of any machine-learning model is to generalize beyond the instances used to train the model. In other words, a model should be judged on its ability to predict new, unseen data. Hence evaluating (testing) the model with the same data used for training will generally result in over fitting. It should be noted that the data should not either over fit or underfit. The common strategy is to take into consideration of all the available labeled data and split it into training and evaluation (testing) subsets. The Training set used to fit and tune the model while the test sets are put aside as unseen data to evaluate the model. The split is usually done with a ratio of 70-80 percent for training and 20-30 percent for evaluation based upon the nature of the problem and the model that is been adapted. One of the best practices that is adopted is to make this split before starting the training process in order to get reliable outcomes of the models performance. In addition, the test data should be kept aside until the model is trained good enough to handle unseen data. The performance comparison against the entire test dataset and training dataset will give a clear picture about the data over fits the model. Some of the common ways of splitting up the labeled data are

- **Sequentially Split:** Sequential split is the simplest way to guarantee distinct training and evaluation data split. This method is extremely convenient if the data holds date or time range since it retains the order of the data records.
- **Random Split:** Random split is the most commonly adopted approach since it is easy to implement. However, for models that are more complex the random selection will result high variance (Guyon et al., 2012).
- **Cross-Validation:** Cross-validation is a method for getting a reliable estimate of model performance using only the training data. There are several ways to cross-validate the commonly used method is k-fold cross-validation. In k-fold cross-validation the data is split into k-equally sized folds, k models are trained and each fold is used as the holdout set where the model is trained on all remaining folds.

Choosing an Appropriate Model

Choosing a suitable Machine-learning model can be very confusing because it depends on a number of following factors

- **Nature of Problem:** The nature of the problem can be a significant factor in deciding which Machine-learning model works best among the possible models.
- **Volume of the Training Set:** The training set volume can be helpful in selecting the Machine-learning models based on bias and variance factors
- **Accuracy:** Deciding on the level of accuracy can sometimes guide in determine the suitable model. If the project does not require most accurate results then approximate methods can be adopted. The approximation can provide better results due to reduces processing time and usually avoid overfitting.
- **Training Time:** The training time heavily depends on the accuracy and the volume of the dataset. If the training time is limited then it can be a considerable factor in picking a model particularly when the data set is large.
- **Number of Parameters:** The number of parameters can tamper the model behavior in various ways like error tolerance or number of iterations. Moreover, algorithms with large numbers parameters require the most trial and error to find a good combination.
- **Number of Features:** The amount of features incorporated in the datasets can be very large compared to the number of data points. The huge amount of features can pull down the efficiency some learning models, making training time very long.

The following two-step process can guide in choosing the model

Step 1: Categorize the Problem

The categorization of the problem can be by the input feed into the machine-learning model or the output expected out of the machine-learning model. If the input data is labeled then, supervised learning model can be a good choice in contrast if input data is unlabeled data then unsupervised learning model can be adopted. The reinforcement learning models can be used for optimizing the objective function interacting with the environment. Similarly, if the output of the model is a number then regression models suits best whereas the classification models can an ideal solution if the output of the model is a class. The clustering models will be most appropriate for models that output a set of input groups.

Step 2: Find the Available Algorithms

Once the categorization of the problem is completed, the apposite model can be pinpointed with ease. Some of the commonly used algorithms discussed below for better understanding. Classification of Machine Learning Algorithms as follow;

- Supervised learning
- Unsupervised learning
- Semi-supervised learning

- Reinforcement learning

Training the Model

The process of training works by finding a relationship between a label and its features. The training dataset is used to prepare a model, to train it. Each sample in the selected training data will define how each feature affects the label (Sathiyamoorthi & Murali Bhaskaran, 2012c). This data is used to incrementally improve the model's ability to predict. This process then repeated and updated to fit the data as best as possible. A single iteration of this process is called one training step. In general, a trained model is not exposed to the test dataset during training and any predictions made on that dataset are designed to be indicative of the performance of the model. Model training is the crux of machine learning that is done by fitting a model to the data. In other words, training a model with existing data to fit the model parameters. Parameters are the key to machine learning models since they are the part of the model that is learned from historical training data. There are two types of parameters that are used in machine learning models (Dongxia et al., 2018).

- **Model Parameters:** A model parameter is a configuration variable that is internal to the model and whose value can be estimated from data. These parameters are learnt during training by the classifier or other machine-learning model. The Model parameters provide the estimate of learning during the training. Example: The support vectors in a support vector machine.
- **Hyper Parameters:** A model hyper parameter is a configuration that is external to the model and whose value cannot be estimated from data. Hyperactive parameters are usually fixed before the actual training process begins. Example: number of clusters in a k-means clustering. In essence, a hyperactive parameter is a parameter whose value is set before the learning process begins. While the values of other parameters are derived via training. Model hyper parameters, on the other hand, are common for similar models and cannot be learnt during training but are set beforehand. The key distinction is that model parameters can be learned directly from the training data while hyperactive parameters cannot. Other training parameters are
- **Learning Rate:** The amount of change to the model during each step of this search process, or the step size, is called the *"learning rate"* and provides perhaps the most important hyperparameter to tune for your neural network in order to achieve good performance on your problem. The learning rate is an important parameter in Gradient descent.
- **Model Size:** Model size depends on the product being used and what is included in the model. This can vary from implementation to implementation, type of problem (classification, regression), algorithm (SVM, neural net etc.), data type (image, text etc.), feature size etc. Large models have practical implications, such as requiring more RAM to hold the model while training and when generating predictions. We can reduce the model size by using regularization or by specifically restricting the model size by specifying the maximum size.
- **Regularization:** Generalization refers to how well the concepts learned by a machine-learning model apply to specific examples not seen by the model when it was learning. Overfitting refers to a model that models the training data too well and performs poorly with unseen data. Regularization helps prevent models from overfitting training data examples by penalizing extreme weight values. Some of the common types of regularization techniques are L2 and L1 regularization, Dropout, Data augmentation and early stopping(Naseer & Burgard, 2017).

Figure 3. Popular machine learning algorithms

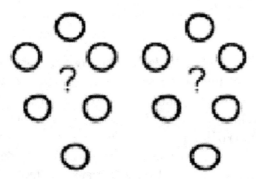

Figure 3 gives the most popular and widely used algorithms in machine learning based applications. The following subsections discusses in detail about these techniques.

Supervised Learning

As shown in the Figure 4, it is categorized into two types.

- Classification
- Regression

It is one of the machine learning techniques used for data analysis and used to construct the classification model. It is used to predict future trends analysis. It is also known as supervised learning(Mohamed, 2018).

Classification

The classification models used to predict categorical class labels whereas and prediction models predict continuous valued.

For example, classification model for bank is used to classify bank loan applications as either safe or risky one. A prediction model is used to predict the potential customers who will buy computer equipment given their income and occupation.

Some other examples of data analysis task of classification are given below.

- A bank loan officer wants to analyze the data in order to predict which loan applicant is risky or which are safe.
- A marketing manager at a company needs to analyze a customer with a given profile, who will buy a new computer as shown in Figure 3.

In both the cases, a model is constructed to predict the categorical labels. These labels are risky or safe for loan application and yes or no for marketing data.

Figure 4. Supervised learning algorithms

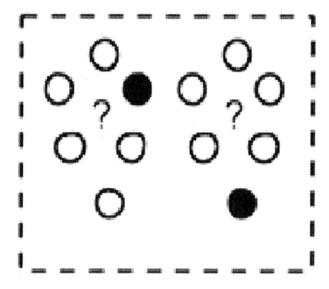

It is the task of building a model that describe and distinguish data class of an object. This is used to predict class label for an object where class label information is not available (Jiawei et al. 2006). It is an example of learning from samples. The first phase called model construction is also referred to as training phase, where a model is built based on the features present in the training data. This model is then used to predict class labels for the testing data, where class label information is not available. A test set is used to determine the accuracy of the model. Usually, the given data set is divided into training and test sets, with training set used to construct the model and test set used to validate it.

Decision trees are commonly used to represent classification models. A decision tree is similar to a flowchart like structure where every node represents a test on an attribute value and branches denote a test outcome and tree leaves represent actual classes. Other standard representation techniques include K-nearest neighbor, Bayesians classification algorithm, if-then rules and neural networks (Jiawei et al. 2006). It is also known as supervised learning process. Effectiveness of prediction depends on training dataset used to train the model.

The classification is two steps process. They are,

Phase I: Building the Classifier(Training Phase)
Phase II: Using Classifier (Testing Phase)

Phase I: Training Phase

This is the first step in classification and in this step a classification algorithm is used to construct the classifier model shown in Figure 6. The model is built from the training dataset which contain tuples called records with the associated class labels. Each tuple presents in the training dataset is called as category or class.

Consider that training dataset of a bank_loan schema contains value for the following attributes.

```
<Name, Age, Income, Loan_decision>
```

Figure 5. Decision tree

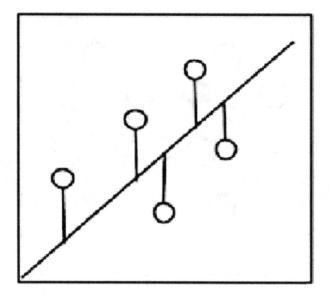

and class label here is Loan_decision and possible class label are risky, safe and low_risky. Say for an example, classification algorithm uses ID3 then classification model is the decision tree which is shown in Figure 5. A decision tree is a tree that includes a root node, branches and leaf nodes. Each internal node denotes a test on an attribute, each branch denotes the outcome of the test, and each leaf node holds a class label. The node without parent is the root node. Nodes without children is called leaf node and it represents the outcome.

Once the decision tree was built, then it uses the IF-THEN rules on nodes present in the node to find the class label of a tuple in the testing dataset.

May be following six rules are derived from the above tree.

1. If Age=young and Income=low then Loan_decision= risky
2. If Age=Senior and Income=low then Loan_decision= risky
3. If Age=Middle_Aged and Income=low then Loan_decision= risky
4. If Age=young and Income=High then Loan_decision= Safe
5. If Age=Middle_Aged and Income=High then Loan_decision=Safe
6. If Age=Senior and Income=High then Loan_decision= Low_risky

Once the model is built then next step is testing the classifier using some sample testing dataset which is shown in Figure 6. Here, the testing dataset is used to measure the accuracy of classification model shown in Figure 7. There are two different metrics such as precision and recall used for measuring accuracy of a classification model. Figure 8 gives the sample decision tree construction based on ID3 algorithm.

Figure 6. Training process of classification

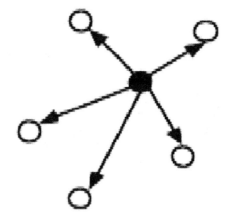

Figure 7. Testing process of classification

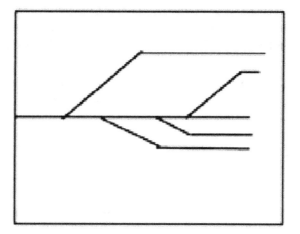

Figure 8. Sample decision tree using ID3 algorithm

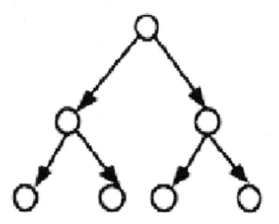

Phase II: Testing Phase

Regression

Prediction is an analytic process designed to explore data for consistent patterns or systematic relationships among variables and then to validate the findings by applying the detected patterns to new subsets of data. (Jiawei et al. 2006) uncover that the predictive data mining is the most common type of data mining and it has the most direct business applications.

The process of predictive data mining task consists of three stages:

- Data exploration
- Model building
- Deployment

Data Exploration usually starts with data preparation which may involve data cleaning, data transformations, selecting subsets of records and feature selection. Feature selection is one of the important operations in the exploration process. It is defined as reducing the numbers of variables to a manageable range if the datasets are with large number of variables performing some preliminary feature selection operations. Then, a simple choice of straightforward predictors for a regression model is used to elaborate exploratory analyses. The most widely used graphical and statistical method is exploratory data analysis. Model building and validation steps involve considering various models and choosing the best one based on their predictive performance. Deployment is the final step which involves selecting the best model in the previous step and applying it to a new data in order to generate predictions or estimates of the expected outcome (Honglak et al., 2017).

Both classification and prediction are used for data analysis but there exists some issues dealing with preparing the data for data analysis. It involves the following activities,

- **Data Cleaning**: Data cleaning involves removing the noisy, incomplete and inconsistent data and methods for handling missing values of an attribute. The noisy data is removed by applying smoothing techniques such as binning and then problem of missing values is handled by replacing a missing value with most commonly occurring value for that attribute or replacing missing value by mean value of that attribute or replacing the missing value by global constant and so on.
- **Relevance Analysis**: Datasets may also have some irrelevant attributes and hence correlation analysis is performed to know whether any two given attributes are related or not. All irrelevant attributes are removed.
- **Normalization**: Normalization involves scaling all values for given attribute in order to make them fall within a small-specified range. Ex. Min_Max normalization.
- **Generalization**: It is data generalization method where data at low levels are mapped to some higher level there by reducing the number of values of an attributes. For this purpose, we can use the concept hierarchies. Example is shown in figure 8.

Unsupervised Learning

Unsupervised learning is the process of grouping the objects based on the similarity present in it. It can be classified into three types as shown in the Figure 9.

- Clustering
- Association Rule
- Dimensionality Reduction

Clustering

Clustering is the process of grouping of objects into classes of similar objects based on some similarity measures between them (Sathiyamoorthi & Murali Baskaran 2011b). It is unsupervised leaning method.

Figure 9. Unsupervised learning categorization

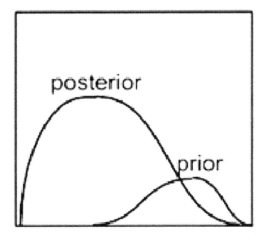

Figure 10. Popular algorithms in unsupervised learning

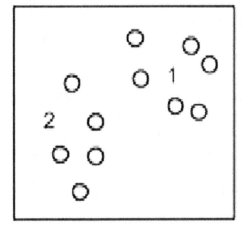

Figure 11. Types of clustering

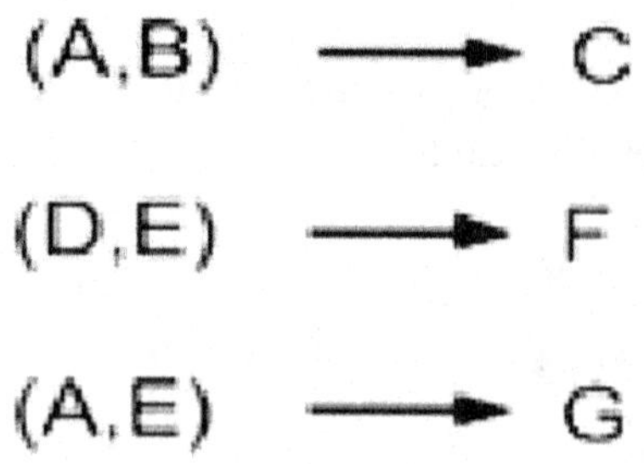

$$(A, B) \longrightarrow C$$

$$(D, E) \longrightarrow F$$

$$(A, E) \longrightarrow G$$

Each cluster can be represented as one group and while performing cluster analysis, first partition objects into groups based on the similarity between them and then assign the class labels to those groups (Fadlullah, 2017). The main difference between clustering and classification is that, clustering is adaptable to changes and helps select useful features that distinguish objects into different groups. Some of the popular algorithms are shown in the Figure 10.

All these algorithms will belong to any one of the following methods as shown in the Figure 11.

- Partitioning Method
- Hierarchical Method
- Density-based Method
- Grid-Based Method
- Model-Based Method
- Constraint-based Method

Partitioning Method

Given a database of 'n' objects and then the partitioning algorithm groups the objects into 'k' partition where k ≤ n. Each group should have at least one object. Also, objects in the same group should satisfy the following criteria.

- Each group contains at least one object.
- Each object must belong to exactly one group.
- Objects within clusters are highly similar and objects present in the different clusters are highly dissimilar.
- Kmeans algorithm is the most popular algorithm in this category. It works as follows.
- For a given number of partitions (say K), the Kmeans partitioning will create an initial partitioning representing K clusters using some distance measure.
- Then it uses the iterative technique to improve the partitioning by moving objects from one group to other. The problem with Kmeans algorithm is that K (number of partition) value is fixed before executing cluster and it does not change.
- Another algorithm is Kmedoid which is an improvement of Kmeans algorithm and provides better performance.

Hierarchical Clustering

In this method, it tries to create a hierarchical decomposition of given objects into various groups. There are two approaches used here for decomposition.

- Agglomerative Approach
- Divisive Approach

In agglomerative approach, clustering starts with each object forming a different group. Then, it keeps on merging the objects that are close to one another into groups. It repeats it until all of the groups are merged into one or until the termination condition holds. It is also known as bottom-up approach.

In divisive approach, clustering starts with all the objects representing a single cluster as a root. In each iteration, it tries to split the cluster into smaller clusters having similar i.e. objects that are close to one another. It proceeds towards down and split the cluster until each object in one cluster or the termination condition holds. This method is inflexible means that once a merging or splitting is done then it cannot be undone. It is also known as top-down approach.

- **Density-Based Clustering:** It is based on the concept of density i.e. each clusters should have minimum number of data objects within the cluster radius. Here a cluster is continuing growing as long as the density in the neighborhood exceeds some threshold.
- **Grid-Based Clustering:** In this clustering, the objects together form a grid. The object space is quantized into finite number of cells that form a grid structure. The main advantage of this approach is that it produces the cluster faster and takes less processing time.
- **Model-Based Clustering:** In this approach, a model is used to build each cluster and find the best fit of data object for a given clusters. This method locates the clusters by using the density function. It reflects spatial distribution of the data objects among the clusters. It determines the number of clusters based on statistics, taking outlier or noise into account. Also, it yields robust clustering algorithm.
- **Constraint-Based Clustering:** In this approach, the clustering is performed by incorporating the user and application constraints or requirements. Here, a constraint is the user expectation or the properties of desired clustering results. It is so interactive since constraints provide an interactive way of communication with the clustering process. Constraints can be specified by the user or by the application.

Association Rule Mining

As defined by (Jiawei et al. 2006), an association rule identifies the collection of data attributes that are statistically related to one another. The association rule mining problem can be defined as follows: Given a database of related transactions, a minimal support and confidence value, find all association rules whose confidence and support are above the given threshold. In general, it produces a dependency rule that predicts an object based on the occurrences of other objects.

An association rule is of the form X->Y where X is called antecedent and Y is called consequent. There are two measures that assist in identification of frequent items and generate rules from it. One such measure is confidence which is the conditional probability of Y given X, Pr(Y|X), and the other is

Figure 12. Evaluating association rules

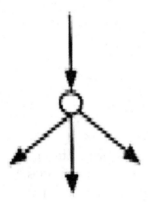

support which is the prior probability of X and Y, Pr(X and Y) (Jiawei et al 2006). It can be classified into either single dimensional association rule or multidimensional association rule based on number of predicates it contains (Jiawei et al. 2006). It can be extended to better fit in the application domains like genetic analysis and electronic commerce and so on. Aprior algorithm, FP growth algorithm and vertical data format are some of the standard algorithm used to identify the frequent items present in the large data set (Jiawei et al. 2006). Association rule mining metrics is shown in the Figure 12.

Algorithms used for association rule mining are given below.

- Aprior algorithm
- FP-Growth
- Vertical Data format algorithm

Issues Related to Clustering

- **Scalability**: Clustering algorithms should be scalable and can handle large databases.
- **Ability to Deal With Different Kinds of Attributes:** Clustering algorithms should be in such a way that it should be capable of handling different kinds of data such as numerical data, categorical, and binary data and so on.
- **Discovery of Clusters With Attribute Shape**: Clustering algorithms should be capable of producing clusters of arbitrary shape using different measures.
- **High Dimensionality:** Clustering algorithm should be designed in such way that it should be capable of handling both low as well as high dimensional data.
- **Ability to Deal With Noisy Data**: Data sources may contain noisy, missing or erroneous data. So presence of these data may leads too poor quality clusters. Hence clustering algorithm should be designed in such way that it should handle noisy, missing and error data and produce high quality clusters.
- **Interpretability**: The results of clustering should be readable, interpretable, comprehensible into different form and useful to the end users

Dimensionality Reduction

In statistics, machine learning, and information theory, dimensionality reduction or dimension reduction is the process of reducing the number of random variables under consideration by obtaining a set of principal variables. It can be divided into feature selection and feature extraction.

Principal Component Analysis(PCA) is one of the most popular linear dimension reduction. Sometimes, it is used alone and sometimes as a starting solution for other dimension reduction methods. PCA is a projection based method which transforms the data by projecting it onto a set of orthogonal axes.

Evaluating the Model

Choosing the right evaluation metrics for the machine learning models will help the model to learn patterns that generalize well for unseen data instead of just memorizing the data. This will help in evaluating the model performs and to select better parameters. However using all the different metrics available will create chaos due to different outputs generated from these metrics. The different machine learning tasks have different performance metrics so the choice of metric completely depends on the type of model and the implementation plan of the model. There are different metrics for the tasks of classification, regression, ranking, clustering, topic modeling, etc.

Underfitting vs. Overfitting

Underfitting

A statistical model or a machine-learning algorithm is said to have underfitting when it cannot capture the underlying trend of the data in other words model does not fit the data well enough. Overfitting occurs if the model or algorithm shows low bias but high variance.

Figure 13. Model evaluation based on overfitting and underfitting

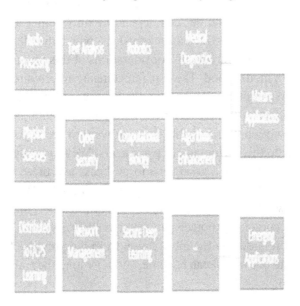

Overfitting

A statistical model is said to have overfitted, when trained with large data but the model cannot capture the underlying trend of the data. Underfitting occurs if the model or algorithm shows low variance but high bias. Both overfitting and underfitting lead to poor predictions on new data sets. Some of the commonly used metrics are Hold-Out Validation, Bootstrapping, Hyperparameter, Tuning, Classification Accuracy, Logarithmic Loss, Confusion Matrix, Area under Curve, F1 Score, Mean Absolute Error, and Mean Squared Error.

Tuning the Parameter

The machine models applied to vary according to the Machine learning models are parameterized so that their behavior can be tuned for a given problem. These models can have many parameters and finding the best combination of parameters can be treated as a search problem. However, this very term called parameter may appear unfamiliar to you if you are new to applied machine learning. Some of the parameters to tune when optimizing neural nets (NNs) include:

- Learning rate
- Momentum
- Regularization
- Dropout probability
- Batch normalization

Once the evaluation is over, any further improvement in your training can be possible by tuning the parameters. A few parameters were implicitly assumed when the training was done. Another parameter included is the learning rate that defines how far the line is shifted during each step, based on the information from the previous training step. These values all play a role in the accuracy of the training model, and how long the training will take.

For models that are more complex, initial conditions play a significant role in the determination of the outcome of training. Differences can be seen depending on whether a model starts training with values initialized to zeroes versus some distribution of values, which then leads to the question of which distribution is to be used. Since there are many considerations at this phase of training, it is important that you define what makes a model good. These parameters are referred to as Hyper parameters. The adjustment or tuning of these parameters depends on the dataset, model, and the training process. Once you are done with these parameters and are satisfied, you can move on to the last step.

Once you have done evaluation, it is possible that you want to see if you can further improve your training in any way. We can do this by tuning our parameters. We implicitly assumed a few parameters when we did our training, and now is a good time to go back, test those assumptions, and try other values. One example is how many times we run through the training dataset during training. What I mean by that is we can "show" the model our full dataset multiple times, rather than just once. This can sometimes lead to higher accuracies. Another parameter is "*learning rate*". This defines how far we shift the line during each step, based on the information from the previous training step. These values all play a role in how accurate our model can become, and how long the training takes (Sathiyamoorthi & Murali Bhaskaran, 2011b),

For more complex mode, initial condition plays a significant role in determining the outcome of training. Differences can be seen depending on whether a model starts off training with values initialized to zeroes versus some distribution of values, which leads to the question of which distribution to use. As you can see there are many considerations at this phase of training, and it is important that you define what makes a model "good enough", otherwise you might find yourself tweaking parameters for a very long time. These parameters are typically referred as "*hyper parameters*". The adjustment, or tuning, of these hyperactive parameters, remains a bit of an art, and is more of an experimental process that heavily depends on the specifics of your dataset, model, and training process. Once you're happy with your training and hyper parameters, guided by the evaluation step, it's time to finally use your model to do something useful!

Generating Predictions

Machine learning is using data to answer questions. The final step is where the model can predict the outcome and establish a learning path. The predictions can be generated in two ways real-time predictions and batch predictions.

- **Real-Time Predictions:** *The real-time predictions*, when you want to obtain predictions at low latency. The real-time prediction API accepts a single input observation serialized as a JSON string, and synchronously returns the prediction and associated metadata as part of the API response. You can simultaneously invoke the API more than once to obtain synchronous predictions in parallel.
- **Batch Predictions:** Use asynchronous predictions, or *batch predictions*, when you have a number of observations and would like to obtain predictions for the observations all at once. The process uses a data source as input, and outputs predictions into a .csv file stored in an S3 bucket of your choice. You need to wait until the batch prediction process completes before you can access the prediction results.

APPLICATIONS OF DATA MINING

Machine Learning applications include (Sathiyamoorthi & Murali Bhaskaran, 2011a),

- Market basket analysis and management
  - Helps in determining customer purchase pattern i.e. what kind of consumer going to buy what kind of products.
  - Helps in finding the best products for different consumers. Here prediction is a data mining technique used to find the users interests based on available data.
  - Performs correlations analysis between product and sales.
  - Helps in finding clusters of consumers who share the same purchase characteristics such as user interests, regular habits, and monthly income and so on.
  - Is used in analyzing and determining customer purchasing pattern.
  - Provides multidimensional analysis on user data and support various summary reports.
- Corporate analysis and risk management in industries
  - It performs cash flow analysis and prediction, contingent claim analysis to evaluate assets.

- ◦ Where it summarizes and compares the resource utilization i.e. how much resources are allocated and how much are currently available. it, helps in production planning and control system
  - ◦ Current trend analysis where it monitors competitors and predict future market directions.
- Fraud detection or Outlier detection
  - ◦ It is also known as outlier analysis which is used in the fields of credit card analysis and approval and telecommunication industry to detect fraudulent users.
  - ◦ In communication department, it helps in finding the destination of the fraud call, time duration of the fraud call, at what time the user made a call and the day or week of the calls and so on.
  - ◦ It helps in analyzing the patterns that are deviating from the normal behavior called outlier.
- Spatial and time series data analysis
  - ◦ For predicting stock market trends and bond analysis
  - ◦ Identifying areas that shares similar characteristics
- Image retrieval and analysis
  - ◦ Image segmentation and classification
  - ◦ Face recognition and detection
- Web mining
  - ◦ Web content mining
  - ◦ Web structure mining
  - ◦ Web log mining

CONCLUSION

In recent days, more and more researchers are focusing their research in field of machine and its related fields. From this literature study, it is evident that it is one of the emerging filed in computer science and its aligned branches. In addition, it presented various machine-learning algorithms and its implementation techniques in detail. It is used to retrieve pattern from the raw dataset either using statistical techniques or algorithms. The discovered pattern can be used in many fields.

REFERENCES

Chen, Y., Qiu, L., Chen, W., Nguyen, L., & Katz, R.H. (2003). Efficient and adaptive web replication using content clustering. *Selected Areas in Communications, IEEE Journal on, 21*(6), 979-994.

Dongxia, Z., Xiaoqing, H., & Chunyu, D. (2018). Review on the Research and Practice of Deep Learning and Reinforcement Learning in Smart Grids. *CSEE Journal of Power and Energy Systems, 4*(3).

Fadlullah, Z. M., Tang, F., Mao, B., Kato, N., Akashi, O., Inoue, T., & Mizutani, K. (2017). State-of-the-art deep learning: Evolving machine intelligence toward tomorrow's intelligent network traffic control systems. *IEEE Commun. Surveys Tuts., 19*(4), 2432–2455. doi:10.1109/COMST.2017.2707140

Guyon, I., Dror, G., Lemaire, V., Taylor, G., & Silver, D. (2012). Unsupervised and Transfer Learning Challenge: a Deep Learning Approach. *Workshop and Conference Proceedings*, 97–111.

Honglak, L., Richard, L., Xiaoshi, W., Satinder, S., & Xiaoshi, W. (2017). *Deep Learning for Real-Time Atari Game Play Using Offline Monte-Carlo Tree Search Planning*. Academic Press.

Jati, D., Mantau, A. J., & Wasito, I. (2016). Dimensionality reduction using deep belief network in big data case study: Hyperspectral image classification. *Proc. Int. Workshop Big Data Inf. Secur. (IWBIS)*, 71-76.

Joseph & Grunwald. (n.d.). Pre-fetching Using Markov Predictors. *Journal of IEEE Transactions on Computers, 48*(2).

Jyoti, S., & Goel, A. (2009). A novel approach for clustering web user sessions using RST. *Advances in Computing, Control, & Telecommunication Technologies, 2*(1), 656-661.

Mohamed, A.A. (2018). *Improving Deep Learning Performance Using Random Forest HTM Cortical Learning Algorithm*. Academic Press.

Naseer, T., & Burgard, W. (2017). Deep regression for monocular camera-based 6-DoF global localization in outdoor environments. *Proc. IEEE/RSJ Int. Conf. Intell. Robots Syst. (IROS)*, 1525-1530. 10.1109/IROS.2017.8205957

Pallis, G., & Vakali, A., & Pokorny, J. (2008). A clustering-based pre-fetching scheme on a web cache environment. *Science Direct, Computer & Electrical Engineering, 34*(4), 309–323.

Podlipnig, S., & Böszörmenyi, L. (2003). A survey of web cache replacement strategies. *ACM Computing Surveys, 35*(4), 374–398. doi:10.1145/954339.954341

Pons. (2006). Object Pre-fetching using Semantic Links. *Journal of ACM SIGMIS Database, 37*(1).

Sathiyamoorthi, V. (2016). A Novel Cache Replacement Policy for Web Proxy Caching System Using Web Usage Mining. *International Journal of Information Technology and Web Engineering, 11*(2), 1–12. doi:10.4018/IJITWE.2016040101

Sathiyamoorthi, V. (2017). *Improving the Performance of an Information Retrieval System through WEB Mining*. DOI: doi:10.1515/itc-2017-0004

Sathiyamoorthi, V., & Murali Bhaskaran, V. (2011a). Improving the Performance of Web Page Retrieval through Pre-Fetching and Caching. *European Journal of Scientific Research, 66*(2), 207–217.

Sathiyamoorthi, V., & Murali Bhaskaran, V. (2011b). Data Pre-Processing Techniques for Pre-Fetching and Caching of Web Data through Proxy Server. *International Journal of Computer Science and Network Security, 11*(11), 92-98.

Sathiyamoorthi, V., & Murali Bhaskaran, V. (2012). Optimizing the Web Cache performance by Clustering Based Pre-Fetching Technique Using Modified ART1. *International Journal of Computers and Applications, 44*(1), 51–60.

Sathiyamoorthi, V., & Murali Bhaskaran, V. (2013). Novel Approaches for Integrating MART1 Clustering Based Pre-Fetching Technique with Web Caching. *International Journal of Information Technology and Web Engineering, 8*(2), 18–32. doi:10.4018/jitwe.2013040102

Sathiyamoorthi, V., & Ramya, P. (2014). Enhancing Proxy based Web Caching system using Clustering based Pre-fetching with Machine Learning Technique. *International Journal of Research in Engineering and Technology.*

Silver, D., Huang, A., Maddison, C. J., Guez, A., Sifre, L., van den Driessche, G., ... Hassabis, D. (2016). Mastering the game of Go with deep neural networks and tree search. *Nature, 529*(7587), 484–489. doi:10.1038/nature16961 PMID:26819042

Ten, W., Chang, C.Y., & Chen, M.S. (2005). Integrating web caching and web pre-fetching in client-side proxies. *Parallel and Distributed Systems, IEEE Transactions on, 16*(5), 444-455.

Woochul K., & Daeyeon K. (2018). *DeepRT: A Predictable Deep Learning Inference Framework for IoT Devices.* Academic Press.

Xin, X., Haibo, H., Dongbin, Z., Shiliang, S., Lucian, B., & Simon, X. Y. (2016). *Machine Learning with Applications to Autonomous Systems.* Hindawi Publishing Corporation.

Xu, & Ibrahim. (n.d.). Towards Semantics-Based Pre-fetching to Reduce Web Access Latency. *Proceedings IEEE Computer Society Symposium, SAINT'03.*

Yang, X., Zhao, P., Zhang, X., Lin, J., & Yu, W. (2017). Toward a Gaussian mixture model-based detection scheme against data integrity attacks in the smart grid. *IEEE Internet Things J., 4*(1), 147–161.

Yi & Chen. (n.d.). Prediction of Web Page Accesses by Proxy Server Log. *ACM Journal of World Wide Web, 5*(1).

Chapter 15
Application of Machine Learning Techniques in Healthcare

Sathya D.
Kumaraguru College of Technology, India

Sudha V.
Kumaraguru College of Technology, India

Jagadeesan D.
Cherraan's Arts Science College, India

ABSTRACT

Machine learning is an approach of artificial intelligence (AI) where the machine can automatically learn and improve its performance on experience. It is not explicitly programmed; the data is fed into the generic algorithm and it builds logic based on the data provided. Traditional algorithms have to define new rules or massive rules when the pattern varies or the number of patterns increases, which reduces the accuracy or efficiency of the algorithms. But the machine learning algorithms learn new input patterns capable of handling complex situations while maintaining accuracy and efficiency. Due to its effectual benefits, machine learning algorithms are used in various domains like healthcare, industries, travel, game development, social media services, robotics, and surveillance and information security. In this chapter, the application of machine learning technique in healthcare is discussed in detail.

INTRODUCTION

In recent days, the people are using medical sensors and other health devices to monitor health status. Using the advanced medical devices the patients' health related parameters can be monitored continuously and in real time, and then processed and transferred to medical databases. This certainly improves patient's quality-of-care without disturbing their comfort and significantly reduces the hospital occupancy rates. At the same time, the enormous amount of health data collected using the sensors are difficult to analyse by the human beings. The advancement in technologies like machine learning when combined with health care helps the health care to move a step ahead. Machine learning infact helps us to improve the performance in health care from experience rather than programming.

DOI: 10.4018/978-1-5225-9902-9.ch015

Since the health data is more sensitive and any fault may affect person's life, it has to be processed and the health problem has to be predicted quickly. The human being's cannot process the data quickly using the conventional methods. So the machine learning techniques are used in these cases to find out the disease pattern and the cause. Similarly, the machine learning techniques are used in various applications like disease diagnosing systems, drug detection, and assistive technology. The benefits of machine learning algorithm includes accuracy, decision making, quick and powerful processing, handling complex data and cost effective. The objective of this study is to explore the current applications of AI techniques in health care systems in detail.

The applications of machine learning techniques in health systems are listed below:

1. Disease Diagnosing systems
2. Remote Health Monitoring Systems
3. Drug detection and analysis
4. Assistive Technologies
5. Medical Imaging Diagnosis
6. Smart Health Records
7. Clinical Trial and Research
8. Crowd sourced Data Collection
9. Better Radiotherapy
10. Outbreak Prediction

The chapter is organized as follows: Section 1 gives the brief Introduction on the uses and applications of AI, Section 2 explains the types of disease diagnosing systems, AI system in diagnosing stroke and cancer, Section 3 describes the Remote Health monitoring systems and AI in mobile Health, WMSN and Internet of Things (IoT), Section 4 discusses the AI in drug detection and analysis, Section 5 explains the Assistive technology devices and its use, Section 6 describes the Medical Imaging diagnosis, Section 7 presents the smart health records and its use, Section 8 briefs about the Clinical trial and research, Section 9 explains the crowd sourced data collection, Section 10 illustrates the radiotherapy and Section 11 briefs on outbreak prediction.

DISEASE DIAGNOSING SYSTEMS

In most of the disease diagnosing systems the AI techniques analyses the data from medical images, genetic test reports, electrophysiological data, and clinical notes etc. The clinical notes are the unstructured data which has to be processed before analysing. The AI techniques converts the unstructured data into machine readable Electronic Medical Record (EMR), which is analysed by the machine learning techniques easily (Fei et al. 2017).

The disease diagnosing systems are using the below given types (emrj.com):

- **AI-Chatbots:** The speech recognition techniques are used in AI- Chatbots to identify disease patterns and to advise a suitable course of action for the patients.
- **Oncology:** The researchers train the algorithm using deep learning to identify cancerous tissues specifically skin cancer.

- **Pathology:** Traditionally the pathologists use the microscope to diagnose disease, as well as it involves the diagnosing using body fluids like blood, urine etc. Deep learning techniques and machine vision algorithms are used to provide speed and accurate diagnosing results.
- **Unusual Diseases:** The genetic and other rare diseases are detected using facial recognition and deep learning techniques.

In Gillies et al. (2016), AI technologies are used for analysing medical images and to convert large set of images into minable data. By the subsequent analysis of these data, it provides better decision making for the diseases like tumour. In Shin et al. (2010), the Electrodiagnosis Support System is used for clinical decision making for neural injury in the upper limb. This system provides a Graphical User Interface (GUI), which picturize the neural structure. The user can input the electromyography test results in the GUI and can get the diagnosis results.

From the above discussion, we can conclude that the medical applications using AI falls into two categories (Fei et al. 2017):

1. The machine learning techniques analyse structured data like medical images, genetic data etc to diagnose the disease.
2. The machine learning techniques analyse unstructured data using Natural Language Processing (NLP) from medical notes, medical journals. The NLP algorithms produce a machine readable structured data which can be easily analysed.

AI System to Diagnose Stroke

AI techniques are used in three stages of stroke care: Early detection of stroke, treatment, result prediction and stroke prognosis evaluation (Fei et al. 2017).

Early Detection of Stroke

A movement detecting device was developed for early stroke prediction (Villar et al. 2015). The Principle Component Analysis (PCA) and genetic finite state machine are implemented in the device. If the movement of the patient is different from the normal value then the alert will be given for stroke treatment. In Mannini et al. (2016), the wearable device is used for detecting stroke. The wearable device collects the physiological status of the patients continuously. The collected data is processed by the SVM and hidden markov model algorithms and provides accuracy about 90.5%.

For stroke diagnosis, the machine learning techniques are applied on the neuro imaging data like Magnetic Resonance Imaging (MRI) and Computed Tomography (CT) scan image. In Rehme et al. (2015), the abnormal conditions are identified using Support Vector Machine (SVM) for the patients having stroke. The accuracy of SVM on MRI data is 87.6%.

Treatment

Intravenous thrombolysis (tPA) is the only approved treatment for ischemic stroke. tPA dissolves the clot and improves the blood flow to the brain. In (Bentley et al. 2014), the SVM is used to predict whether the tPA treatment would develop any intracranial haemorrhage. The intracranial haemorrhage is the type of bleeding occurs inside the skull. The CT scan is used as the input for SVM which performs better than conventional radiology based methods. In Ye at al. (2017), the interaction trees and subgroup analysis is used to predict the tPA dosage to be given to the patient based on the patient characteristics.

Result Prediction and Stroke Prognosis Evaluation

Compared with the conventional methods machine learning techniques provides better performance in evaluating stroke prognosis. In Zhang at al. (2013), used a logistic regression to predict the result of three months treatment by analysing the physical parameters of the patients for 48 hours after getting stroke. In Asadi at. Al (2014) and Sandeep (2018), the physiological information of 107 patients is stored in a database who undergone a intra-arterial therapy. The Neural network and SVM is implemented to predict the outcome of treatment which provides 97.5% accuracy.

AI System to Diagnose Cancer

The cancer biomarkers have been used for screening, diagnosis, risk assessment, prognosis of cancer, and detection of response to treatment. Currently many newer technologies are used for disease diagnosis. For detecting breast cancer, the gene expression patterns are used to detect the prognosis of the disease. Machine learning techniques like random forest classifier and SVM classifier are used for classifying normal and abnormal tissues. The SVM accuracy is better than random forest model in same-tissue testing. The random forest classifier performs better than SVM in across-tissue testing (Henry et al. 2012).

From the study, we can conclude that AI techniques concentrate more on diseases like cancer, cardiac disease and nervous system disease.

REMOTE HEALTH MONITORING SYSTEMS

Remote health monitoring collects the physiological data of the patients using digital technologies and transmits it to the hospital or to the doctors. (cloudtweaks.com) The patient can be monitored with the parameters like blood pressure, blood sugar levels, heart rate, weight, electrocardiogram (ECG) etc. It provides the continuous monitoring of patients with better accuracy at home place. It is used for the patients who suffer from chronic diseases, post-surgery patients, elderly people, and for the patients who are bedridden.

AI in Mobile Health

Nowadays, the wireless devices are used to support the healthcare in the form of mobile health or mHealth (Sandeep 2018; Barton 2012). Mobile health applications are widely used in the areas like diagnostic disease, remote patient monitoring, surveillance on the spread of disease, emergency support, patient information management system (Barton 2012; Mohammadzadeh at al. 2014). The AI techniques are widely used in the mHealth which is the reason for the successful development of mHealth. Recently the intelligent agents are used in mHealth for communication, dynamic resource management, predicting the solutions etc. The mHealth have been successfully used in remote patient monitoring systems for adults and sport's persons, clinical decision making, emergency care. The AI techniques is used in mHealth for predicting emergency care and suggesting the first aid medication for the patients.

AI in WMSN

The application of AI is also used in the Wireless Medical Sensor Networks (WMSN). The WMSN have the collection of biosensors connected to the patient body having chronic diseases or adults who needs continuous monitoring. The WMSN is also used to continuously monitor the sports person's activities. The health data collected using wireless medical sensors are transmitted to the hospital server (Sathya et al. 2017). The data aggregation is performed at the hospital server and it is communicated to the doctor's personal digital assistant for diagnosis. The AI techniques are used in filtration of data in sensors. Instead of sending all the monitored physiological data to the hospital server. The data can be filtered using the AI techniques in the sensors and the value above the threshold value or the abnormal values can alone be send to the hospital server.

AI in IoT

The application of AI is not only used in the mHealth and WMSN it has also been extended to the smart devices. The smart devices are connected to each other to form a pervasive network is called as IoT (Islam at al. 2015; Da Xu et al. 2014). IoT is used in smart health care for the persons who need remote monitoring of health and medicine intake. The AI techniques are used in this Ambient Assisted living. The diagnosing of patient conditions and medicine intake is possible by implementing AI techniques in the Ambient Assisted living (Sandeep 2018).

The advantage of Remote Health Monitoring is listed below:

1. **Reduced Healthcare Cost:** In WMSNs and in mhealth, the patients' health related parameters can be monitored continuously and in real time, and then processed and transferred to medical databases. This certainly improves patient's quality-of-care without disturbing their comfort and significantly reduces the hospital occupancy rates.
2. **Improved Quality:** The data taken by the sensors and medical devices are highly accurate.
3. **Emergency Care:** The patient sufferings from chronic diseases are remotely monitored and any emergency conditions will be intimated immediately to the medical professionals.
4. **Disease Diagnosis:** By continuous monitoring, the identification and assessment of medications can be improved.
5. **Future Reference:** The health data collected using digital devices can be stored and used for future clinical decision making and treatments.

DRUG DETECTION AND ANALYSIS

The machine learning and natural language processing helps the drug discovery scientists to discover new drugs. The machine learning is an AI technique which becomes skilled from trained data to determine patterns and make decisions based on these patterns. Whereas the natural language processing refers to computer system which program and analyze large amount of natural language data (technologyworks.com).

Before AI techniques come into existence virtual screening, molecular modelling and predicting how drug would be non-toxic to the patient body is a difficult process. This pre-clinical test is more expensive and time consuming. But using AI we can train the compounds with known properties and learn how to do associates with the matching molecules for the required application. AI techniques are used to reduce the running of experimental labs for drug discovery and running large scale experiments.

The AI and machine learning is applied in three major areas (technologyworks.com):

1.   Target Identification
2.   Lead Optimization
3.   Screening drug Candidates

The target identification provides validation and improves target areas for drug identification and compound screening. Lead optimization uses algorithms for simulating structure, simulating toxicity and binding. Screening drug candidate is used to assist the scientists in identifying pattern from the input image and also to identify the rare patterns from the large image datasets.

AI for Genetics and Genomics

The microarray genetic data or RNA-seq expression data can be analysed by using Supervised, semi-supervised and unsupervised machine learning algorithms (deepsense.ai). These algorithms are used to identify the genetic disease and the action of drugs. Many studies are on-going to analyse genomic data and to solve genomic sequencing problems. Finding the specific region in genomic sequencing and recognizing locations of transcriptomic sites is very difficult task in real time. Deep learning algorithms can be used for genome interpretation and analysis. The supervised heterogeneous algorithms can be used to address difficult biomedical prediction problems.

AI for Network Analysis of Biomedical Data

The analysis of genetic data would be helpful in identifying the drugs and its action (deepsense.ai). It will also be helpful for predicting the optimal combination of drugs and new drugs. The machine learning approaches for biological network analysis is used to identify the new class of genes for cancer disease. The combination of support vector machine (SVM) and machine learning assisted network interference is used to identify cancer gene pairs. This can be used to reorganise the new network for identifying key cancer genes in high dimensional data space.

ASSISTIVE TECHNOLOGIES

The Assistive technology is the life changing alternative developed for the disabled persons to make their life easier (newgenapps.com). Currently, the robots are used for disabled persons to make their life better. Robots are used by the people who are living alone. The people using the robots at home to satisfy their needs are called as home robots. The human can customize the robots to the individual needs. The home robots are used to make an emergency call to the hospital, reminding the appointments and medications.

AI in Assistive Technology

Smarter Glasses

The smarter glasses are invented by the neuroscientists and computer vision scientists in the Oxford University, UK. The smarter glass is the augmented reality glass focuses on specific part of sight. This will increase the image contrast which highlights the specific feature of an image (digitaltrends.com).

Google Glass

Google glass was introduced in the year 2013 and very useful for the visually impaired people. It assists the blind person's by describing their environment and helps to navigate. The intelligent agent has the dashboard of preferred data, maps, and the information of their surroundings. This information is helpful for the person's to know how long to travel to reach their target place (in.pcmag.com).

Cognitive Hearing Aids

The hearing aid with AI and sensors is released first time for hearing impaired patients by Livio AI (starkey.com). The head and the ear is the more appropriate place to measure our physical activity. So the Livio AI uses the 3D motion sensors like accelerometer and gyroscope to detect movements and gestures, track the activities. This hearing aid is used to help the people to treat hearing loss and also to understand and improve their overall health.

The features of Livio AI are discussed below (globenewswire.com):

1. Customizable adjustments to the sounds and programs
2. Remote controlling of the hearing aid
3. User interface with tap control
4. Hearing reality technology gives natural listening, speech clarity in the noisiest environment
5. Inertial sensors are used for fall detection.
6. Tracks the overall health and wellness.

Locked-In Syndrome

The patients with Locked-in syndrome have the full cognitive ability but they are not able to speak or move (healtheuropa.eu). The AI powered device for the locked-in syndrome patient's provides communication to the patients with eye movements.

The device tracks the eye movements by using head-mounted camera and translates into the audio communication viz a speaker (med-technews.com). The earpiece has the bone conduction element that provides the audio feedback to the user before sending to the output speaker. The device can be used without a screen, teach with personalised syntax, choose the range of output language, and can work with Bluetooth wireless technology.

Helen Paterson, speech therapist, Royal hospital, tested the device with her patient's. She said that the device is easy to wear, light weight, the patient need to move only the eyes up and down or side to side. The patient no need to have the device in front of them all the time.

Parkinson's Disease Balancing Application

Parkinson's Disease is the degenerative nerve disease that affects the motor system. The early symptoms of the disease are rigidity, shaking, difficulty in walking, slowness of movement. The advanced stages of the disease are sensory, sleepy, emotional problems, depression, anxiety. These abnormal motor symptoms are called as "parkinsonism".

The patient with Parkinson's disease suffers from loss of balance or they fall (digitaltrends.com). The University of Houston releasing the new project for the patient having loss of balance. The smarter balance system is wearable and connected with smart-phone. The smarter balance system has the special belt connected with vibrating actuators. These actuators have a customized program to map the patient movement. The patient movement is mapped like series of dots on the Smartphone. The smarter balance improves the postural stability by guiding patients through exercise. It decreases the number of falls and increases the user's confidence. The patients can have the virtual physical therapist at home which reduces the repeated visits to hospitals.

MEDICAL IMAGING DIAGNOSIS

Medical imaging is the procedure used for building a clear visual representation of the interior parts of the body that are hidden by skin and bones. This is also used for diagnosing the disease and treatment of the same. This can also be used for database construction. In a survey by IBM, it is found that about 90% of the medical database consists of images. Hence processing and analysis of medical images is a challenging task that exists in image processing.

The image diagnosing process is improved by applying Artificial Intelligence and Machine Learning algorithms. The application of machine learning to image diagnosis process dates back to 1990. In those days, the computation of the algorithm is done manually. Machine Learning algorithms are used for designing an automated image identification system and the same is presented in the market. Also, the cost of the diagnosing system and health care got reduced with the help of these technologies. One of the most significant challenges in constructing automated image diagnosing system is the data labelling and skills gap. The detailed discussion about this issue is done below.

When an image has to be processed by Machine Learning all the images must be pre processed by attaching labels to it. But including labels for all the images that are needed for constructing an innovative image recognition model is a labour-intensive process. Also, most of the medical data's are sparse. Available mining algorithms can be used for converting this sparse data set into reusable data sets. Though machine learning is applied to the medical data's by overcoming the above changes, another real life issue that exists is the knowledge level of the radiologists. Thus, to successfully apply machine learning in radiology along with automating the process, the knowledge about machine learning must be imparted to the radiologists. This skill gap can be filled by teaching the techniques to the radiologists by the data scientists.

It is predicted that in future by 2020, we may have a tool kit that automatically predict the image and serve the purpose for which it is designed. Along with improving the image diagnosing, machine learning techniques can be used to constructing a very good image acquisition system whose output can be used for further processing.

SMART HEALTH RECORDS

It is well known that prediction in medical field can be improved by applying machine learning techniques to it. But construction of medical database involves many issues. The primary issue is the collection of data. Though the above issue is addressed with the help of technologies, finding relationship among the data's is still a difficult task. Next issue is the database must include both image and genetic data. Some of the tools developed for this purpose are ePAD, and TCIA .

Personalized treatment to the patients are getting famous now-a-days. This is possible only if we have a system that stores the patient's record digitally and retrieve the needed information very quickly. Retrieval of information's can be personalized and optimized with the help of the machine learning algorithm: support vector machine.

The two constraints that are faced while applying machine learning over medical image is the heterogeneous raw data and small sample size. With the help of Electronic Health Record (EHR) and digital imaging the database size can be increased. These constraints can be solved by selecting proper data preprocessing and augmentation algorithms.

An important issue with the above proposed technique is not all the doctors are recording their prescriptions digitally and while few are not even aware of it. This drawback can be overcome by converting the characters in the hand written format to equivalent digital characters. Also, there is an ongoing research for converting the doctor's prescription and patient's health records into a digital record by applying Natural Language Processing (NLP) and ML.

Personalized treatment to the patients can be enhanced by applying predictive modelling to the EHR data. But, to apply the predictive algorithms the EHR data need to be pre-processed. This pre-processing is again a labour intensive task. A new representation is proposed in (Neil at al. 2018), for representing the EHR data created on the Fast Healthcare Interoperability Resources (FHIR) format. The application of predictive algorithms on these new formats enhances the treatment process. This proposed method is tested using the database obtained from the US academic medical centres.

From the test, it is predicted that the proposed model outperformed all the existing models. This model can be further used for creating different clinical scenarios. By applying neural network algorithms, this model is also used for retrieving relevant information about a patient.

CLINICAL TRIAL AND RESEARCH

A clinical trial is an experimental study on a person to invent new medicines. Also, it is used for deciding whether the newly invented medicine and treatment works for the purpose and does not cause any harm to the human beings when applied in future. Clinical trial plays a major role in health care as it is used for improving the research in terms of application and safety. They make researchers to learn what is working and what is not working while they are working for finding new drugs. It is also used for learning the side effects allied with the new drug, ways to manage and avoid it. Usually, clinical trials are divided into five stages. Though clinical trial procedures are speeded up, still few medicines takes even few years to reach the market. This time delay can be reduced by applying machine learning to clinical trials.

The clinical trial research can further be improvised by the application of Machine Learning. For instance, number of candidate's identification for applying clinical trial can be increased by using predictive analytics. Thus, by increasing number of participants better result can be obtained.

One of the important challenge of the clinical trial procedure lies in finding the corresponding patient for every clinical trial. Every stage in clinical trial can be improved with the help of Artificial Intelligence. The artificial intelligence algorithms can be applied to the patients record, compare it to find the matching ongoing trials. From the comparison, matching studies can be suggested. One of the main problem in following the above methodology is in maintaining the privacy and security of the patient's record. HIPAA is one of the law that is proposed for protecting the patient's record. It is difficult to apply sentiment analysis on clinical trial records. Intel proposed a solution for improving the clinical trial process using Artificial Intelligence and sensors.

Intel® Pharma Analytics Platform – the proposed solution makes use of wearable sensors to collect continuous data from the patient. On the collected data, analytics methods are applied to find important patterns and apply the suitable clinical trial on it. Few of the advantages of the above methods are: it reduces trial cost, improves data quality and improves patient experience.

Machine Learning can further be used for efficiently accessing the real-time data sets. The other applications of Machine Learning includes in identifying best trail data and aiding in maintaining electronic health records.

Machine learning algorithms can be applied on the data's collected from patients to predict the influence of the drug on the patient.

CROWDSOURCED DATA COLLECTION

Sometimes the data required for analysing and arriving for a conclusion may be insufficient. Now-a-days crowd sourcing helps the people to overcome the above constraints. Though many technologies come into the market, it is not possible for us to find relation between the big data and health care. Also, few of the health care data set lacks proper data set. But, to train a machine learning algorithm, proper data must be passed to it. This drawback is overcome with the help of crowdsourcing.

Crowdsourcing is a blooming technique that encompasses a large number of people cracking a problem or finishing a task for a single person or for an organisation. With the help of information technology, the crowd sourcing has advanced very vastly. A review of the application of crowd sourcing in health care is done in (Kerri 2018). Some of the fields in health care where crowd sourcing finds its application are surveillance; nutrition; public health and environment; education; genetics; psychology; and, general medicine/other.

The traditional way of data handling in the field like sociology and psychology are enhanced with the help of crowdsourcing and ML (Michael at al. 2011; Winter Mason at al. 2012). The following are the three advantages that are obtained by combining crowd sourcing and machine learning (allerin.com).

1. **Improves Sentiment Analysis:** The main objective of applying crowd sourcing and machine learning is to provide an impartial sentiment assessment.
2. **Improves Natural Language Processing (NLP):** In today's market, the customer review plays an important role. The existing machine learning algorithm concentrates much on the study of the reviews but not on analysing it. Thus by applying crowdsourcing in machine learning it is possible

to propose an efficient algorithm for analysing the customer reviews. Initially, pre-processing of the review data is done using some machine learning algorithms. The data's that are not processed by the ML algorithms are filtered and given to the humans for processing. Then, the final analysis result is obtained from the output of the machine learning and crowd sourcing algorithms.

3. **Improves Quality of Data:** Though varieties of data are available, machine learning algorithms yields better result when they are applied to labelled data. With the help of crowd sourcing and machine learning now most of the available data's are labelled data. Also crowd sourcing helps to improve the quality of data.

BETTER RADIOTHERAPY

One of the most important technique used in the cancer treatment is the Radiation therapy. There are three specialties in the cancer treatment. They are radiation oncology, surgical oncology and medical oncology. Among the above three, radiation oncology is used in the treatment of cancer by applying radiations over the cancer cells. Also, radiation oncology is well suited for applying machine learning concepts because of the huge amount of data that can be collected in a given time period. In addition to the above application, machine learning can also be used for studying the reaction of genes over radiations. The data set available for performing predictive analysis in radiation oncology is very limited. From the available data, prediction of the accurate place for applying radiation has to be identified. The success of the identification depends upon on how well the prediction is able to differentiate between the normal and the affected place (Reid et al.). Also, with the help of AI, it possible to integrate data's from various sources.

Radiation therapy includes the following stages in the cancer treatment.

1. Patient assessment,
2. Simulation, planning,
3. Quality assurance,
4. Treatment delivery,
5. Follow-up

All the above stages can be improved by applying machine learning techniques over it. From the images obtained from the patients, it is important to find the space over which radiations must be applied. In addition to it, the amount of radiations that need to be passed over the patients so that the purpose can be achieved with less toxic radiations. Radiation therapy when applied to the target place correctly, then it has a very powerful effect. Though radiation therapy found its application in the treatment of non-malignant disease, its most important application lies in the treatment of cancer. It makes use of waves in the treatment of cancer. Waves are nothing but the very powerful energy. Most of the cancer patients undergoing treatment will take radiation therapy treatment. Hence, there are huge amount of data available in radiation therapy. These data can be refined and information be extracted by applying ML algorithms.

In literature it is identified that there are a lot of opportunities exists in applying ML in the various phases of radiation oncology. For clinical practice, ML algorithms can be applied. A number of use cases can be supported with the help of applying ML to clinical practice. It is also inferred that an existing model can be fine-tuned to perform better on a small size dataset. In future, these technologies can save doctors time a lot.

Machine Learning has the capability to reduce the time of the radiation oncology team. Radiation oncology when combined with ML can give the world's best treatment. Machine Learning can even facilitate personalized radiation therapy treatment. One of the most important applications of radiology is the prediction of cancer. The cancer prediction process can be improved by combining imaging data with genetic data. Early prediction of cancer can be done by predicting for the existence of certain type of patterns of genes. This pattern prediction process can be improved by applying Natural Language Processing (NLP) to the genes when it is represented as characters.

OUTBREAK PREDICTION

An outbreak is an unexpected increase in number of incidents of a disease in a particular time and place. This outbreak will affect a little and localized group or some thousands of people across a continent. The outbreak may be epidemic i.e. fast spread of infectious diseases among a group of people in a very short period of time. Though the influence of outbreak is much among people, there are no formal methods proposed still now to predict the outbreak. Thus we are in need of a system that is capable of predicting the outbreaks. In this chapter, some of the existing technique used for predicting the outbreak that makes use of machine learning are discount breaks must be predicted. Outbreak prediction can be categorized in to three: probability of occurrence of particular disease; how fast it spreads and what kind of action need to be done to control the spread of the outbreak.

Epidemic diseases are the contagious diseases that spread out in a country in a particular time period when the quantity of the outbreak exceeds the minimum threshold level. Some of the well-known outbreaks are dengue, yellow fever, cholera, diphtheria, influenza, bird flu etc. By analysing the classical outbreaks, the technologist have come up with some advance methods in identifying the pattern and predicting the outbreaks. This prediction is further refined by the incoming dynamic data's.

Health predictive analysis is the new technology that is proposed for preventing contagious epidemic disease. Infectious disease spreads from affected animal or a person (Sangwon Chae at al. 2018). Here, infectious diseases are predicted using deep learning techniques. It is difficult to predict a pattern in infectious disease. Some of the disease outbreak prediction techniques are discussed in the following subsections.

Malaria Outbreak Prediction

Malaria is one of the epidemic diseases in India. It is important to predict the outbreak of this disease to prevent the life that is loosed because of it. In Vijeta (2015), a model using Machine learning is proposed. Here, two machine learning algorithms such as Support Vector Machine (SVM) and Artificial Neural Network (ANN) are used for predicting malaria disease. The data's collected from the Maharashtra state are used for training the model. The performance of these two models are compared here. As the result of the comparison, it is concluded that SVM outperforms ANN by providing more accurate results.

Another important issue that need to be addressed before applying machine learning algorithm is the incomplete data. When the collected data is incomplete, then we may not be able to derive an accurate solution. Thus, before applying the machine learning algorithm the data's need to be structured.

In (emerj.com), it proposed that initially by applying decision tree algorithm, prediction for the missing values can be obtained and later map-reduce algorithm can be applied to get the results for the queries in optimal time.

Surveillance or monitoring of the outbreak of a disease is very important for a public health department. Now-a-days public health departments are allowed to access the real time data's, but from the accessed data they could not conclude anything due to the number of instances of the data. Hence, some algorithms are developed that surveys the data and gives an alarm if there are any possibility for outbreak of any diseases.

Dengue Outbreak Prediction System

Dengue is an epidemic disease that is caused by the mosquito bite. Dengue is caused by the mosquito breed Aedes. Around 30% of the world population are under risk of getting affected by dengue. By earlier prediction of dengue. It is possible to save life many peoples.

Some of the machine learning algorithms used for the dengue prediction are discussed in Rajathi at al. (2018). Here, they have compared the various data mining algorithms using the data obtained from karuna medical hospital. Decision tree algorithm is used for dengue prediction in Buczak et al. (2012). A predictive model is constructed in Thitiprayoonwongse et al. (2012) using set annotated discharge summaries as input. This model predicts the presence or absence of the dengue fever from the summary. Multivariate Poisson regression - a statistics model is used (Nandhini et al. 2016) for dengue prediction by identifying the correlation between the existing dengue cases and mosquito data. Dengue prediction in tribal area is done in Ta-Chien Chan et al. (2015) using decision tree classification algorithm.

Risk prediction model is proposed in Padet Siriyasatien et al. (2016) for predicting dengue in some small area. The model proposed here can be applied for data's from any cities. In Yuhanis Yusof et al. (2011), Least Squares Support Vector Machines (LS-SVM) is proposed for predicting dengue outbreak. This proposed method is applied in five districts of Malaysian country for dengue prediction. SVM outperforms Neural Network in performance generalization. It is proved in Qisong et al. (2008), that the Least Squares Support Vector Machines (LS-SVM) prediction model outperforms Radial Basis Function (RBF) neural network predictor and Back Propagation (BP) neural network predictor in simulation and results.

Flu Outbreak Prediction

Flu - contagious disease affected by the influenza virus. It can easily spread from one person to another person by coughing, sneezing etc. In (Sangeeta Grover et al. 2014) (Ali et al. 2018), a predictive model is proposed for predicting swine flu based on the twitter data. Like the weather forecasting, it would be of greater help when flu can be identified from the existing weather data. In (veritone.com), Roni Rosenfeld proposed one such technique. In (Hongping Hu et al. 2018), artificial tree and neural network is used for flu prediction.

CONCLUSION

Machine learning is an emerging technology that has also become a predominant technology in today's world. Now-a-days all the fields have moved up a level with the application of Machine Learning. Among them, the application of Machine Learning in health care has revolutionized this area. As discussed in this chapter, the precision and performance of many areas in health care has improved by application of this technology. The discussion in this chapter shows that the machine learning techniques will have a greater advancement in health care applications in future. We can expect the Robotic healthcare system will be used by a common man in forthcoming era.

REFERENCES

Abhigna, B. S. (2018). Crowdsourcing– A Step Towards Advanced Machine Learning. *Procedia Computer Science*, *132*, 632–642.

Alessa, A., & Faezipour, M. (2018). *Preliminary Flu Outbreak Prediction Using Efficient Twitter Posts Classification and Linear Regression with Historical CDC Reports*. Preprint. doi:10.2196/12383

Asadi, H., Dowling, R., Yan, B., & Mitchell, P. (2014). Machine learning for outcome prediction of acute ischemic stroke post intra-arterial therapy. *PLoS One*, *9*(2), e88225. doi:10.1371/journal.pone.0088225 PMID:24520356

Asadi, H., Kok, H. K., Looby, S., Brennan, P., O'Hare, A., & Thornton, J. (2016). Outcomes and complications after endovascular treatment of Brain Arteriovenous Malformations: A Prognostication Attempt using artificial Intelligence. *World Neurosurgery*, *96*, 562–569. doi:10.1016/j.wneu.2016.09.086 PMID:27693769

Barton, A. J. (2012). The regulation of mobile health applications. *BMC Medicine*, *10*(1), 46. doi:10.1186/1741-7015-10-46 PMID:22569114

Bentley, P., Ganesalingam, J., Carlton Jones, A. L., Mahady, K., Epton, S., Rinne, P., ... Rueckert, D. (2014). Prediction of stroke thrombolysis outcome using CT brain machine learning. *NeuroImage. Clinical*, *4*, 635–640. doi:10.1016/j.nicl.2014.02.003 PMID:24936414

Buczak, A. L., Koshute, P. T., Babin, S. M., Feighner, B. H., & Lewis, S. H. (2012). A data-driven epidemiological prediction method for dengue outbreaks using local and remote sensing data. *BMC Medical Informatics and Decision Making*, *12*(1), 1. doi:10.1186/1472-6947-12-124 PMID:23126401

Chae, S., Kwon, S., & Lee, D. (2018). Predicting Infectious Disease Using Deep Learning and Big Data. *International Journal of Environmental Research and Public Health*, *15*(8), 1596. doi:10.3390/ijerph15081596 PMID:30060525

Chan, T.-C., Hu, T.-H., & Hwang, J.-S. (2015). Daily forecast of dengue fever incidents for urban villages in a city. *International Journal of Health Geographics*, *14*(1), 9. doi:10.1186/1476-072X-14-9 PMID:25636965

Créquit, P., Mansouri, G., Benchoufi, M., Vivot, A., & Ravaud, P. (2018). Mapping of Crowdsourcing in Health: Systematic Review. *Journal of Medical Internet Research*, *20*(5). PMID:29764795

Da Xu, L., He, W., & Li, S. (2014). Internet of things in industries: A survey. *IEEE Transactions on Industrial Informatics*, *10*(4), 2233–2243. doi:10.1109/TII.2014.2300753

Fei, J., Yong, J., Hui, Z., Yi, D., Hao, L., Sufeng, M., ... Yongjun, W. (2017). Artificial intelligence in healthcare: Past, present and future. *Journal of Neurology, Neurosurgery, and Psychiatry*, 2(4). Retrieved from https://emerj.com/ai-sector-overviews/machine-learning-medical-diagnostics-4-current-applications/

Gillies, R.J., Kinahan, P. E., Hricak, H. (2016). Radiomics: images are more than pictures, they are data. *Radiology*, 278(2), 563–77.

Grover, S., & Aujla, G. S. (2014). Prediction Model for Influenza Epidemic Based on Twitter Data. *International Journal of Advanced Research in Computer and Communication Engineering*, 3(7).

Henry, N. L., & Hayes, D. F. (2012). Cancer biomarkers. *Molecular Oncology*, 6(2), 140–146. doi:10.1016/j.molonc.2012.01.010 PMID:22356776

Hu, H., Wang, H., Wang, F., Langley, D., Avram, A., & Liu, M. (2018). Prediction of influenza-like illness based on the improved artificial tree algorithm and artificial neural network. *Scientific Reports*, 8(4895). PMID:29559649

Islam, S. M. R., Kwak, D., Kabir, H., Hossain, M., & Kwak, K. S. (2015). The Internet of things for health care: A comprehensive survey. *IEEE Access: Practical Innovations, Open Solutions*, 3, 678–708. doi:10.1109/ACCESS.2015.2437951

Kerri, W. (2018). Applications of crowdsourcing in health: An overview. *Journal of Global Health*, 8(1), 010502. doi:10.7189/jogh.08.010502 PMID:29564087

Mannini, A., Trojaniello, D., Cereatti, A., & Sabatini, A. M. (2016). A machine Learning Framework for Gait classification using inertial sensors: Application to Elderly, Post-Stroke and Huntington's Disease Patients. *Sensors (Basel)*, 16(1), 134. doi:10.339016010134 PMID:26805847

Mason, W., & Suri, S. (2012). Conducting behavioural research on Amazon's Mechanical Turk. *Behavior Research Methods*, 44(1), 1–23. doi:10.375813428-011-0124-6 PMID:21717266

Michael, B., Tracy, K., & Samuel, D. G. (2011). Amazon's Mechanical Turk: A new source of inexpensive, yet high-quality, data. *Perspectives on Psychological Science*, 6(1), 3–5. doi:10.1177/1745691610393980 PMID:26162106

Mitchell, T. (1997). *Machine Learning*. McGraw Hill.

Mohammadzadeh, N., & Safdari, R. (2014). Patient monitoring in mobile health: Opportunities and challenges. *Medieval Archaeology*, 68(1), 57. PMID:24783916

Nandini, V., Sriranjitha, R., & Yazhini, T. P. (2016). *Dengue detection and prediction system using data mining with frequency analysis. Computer Science & Information Technology.*

Neil, M., & Murthy, V. D. (2018). Machine learning, natural language programming, and electronic health records: The next step in the artificial intelligence journey? *The Journal of Allergy and Clinical Immunology*, 141(6), 2019–20121. doi:10.1016/j.jaci.2018.02.025 PMID:29518424

Qisong, C., Yun, W., & Xiaowei, C. (2008) Research on Customers Demand Forecasting for E-business Web Site Based on LS-SVM. *Proc. International Symposium in Electronic Commerce and Security*, 66-70.

Rajathi, N., Kanagaraj, S., Brahmanambika, R., & Manjubarkavi, K. (2018). Early Detection of Dengue Using Machine Learning Algorithms. *International Journal of Pure and Applied Mathematics*, *118*(18), 3881–3887.

Rehme, A. K., Volz, L. J., Feis, D. L., Bomilcar, F., Liebig, T., Eickhoff, S. B., ... Grefkes, C. (2015). Identifying neuroimaging markers of Motor Disability in acute stroke by machine Learning Techniques. *Cereb Cortex*, *25*(9), 3046–3056. doi:10.1093/cercor/bhu100 PMID:24836690

Reid, Thompson, Valdes, Fuller, Carpenter, Morin, ... Thomas, Jr. (n.d.). Artificial intelligence in radiation oncology: A specialty-wide disruptive transformation? In *Radiation and Oncology*. Elsevier.

Sandeep, R. (2018). Use of Artificial Intelligence in Healthcare Delivery. In eHealth - Making Health Care Smarter. Intechopen.

Sathya, D., & Ganesh Kumar, P. (2017). Secured Remote Health Monitoring System. *IET Healthcare Technology Letters*, *4*(6), 228–232. doi:10.1049/htl.2017.0033 PMID:29383257

Shin, H., Kim, K. H., Song, C., Lee, I., Lee, K., Kang, J., & Kang, Y. K. (2010). Electrodiagnosis support system for localizing neural injury in an upper limb. *Journal of the American Medical Informatics Association*, *17*(3), 345–347. doi:10.1136/jamia.2009.001594 PMID:20442155

Siriyasatien, P., Phumee, A., Ongruk, P., & Jampac, K. (2016). Analysis of significant factors for dengue fever incidence prediction. *International Journal of Pure and Applied Mathematics*, 3885. PMID:27083696

Thitiprayoonwongse, D. A., Suriyaphol, P. R., & Soonthornphisaj, N. U. (2012). Data mining of Dengue Infection using Decision Tree. *Entropy (Basel, Switzerland)*.

Vijeta, S. (2015). Malaria Outbreak Prediction Model Using Machine Learning. *International Journal of Advanced Research in Computer Engineering & Technology*, *4*(12), 4415–4419.

Villar, J. R., González, S., Sedano, J., Chira, C., & Trejo-Gabriel-Galan, J. M. (2015). Improving human activity recognition and its application in early stroke diagnosis. *International Journal of Neural Systems*, *25*(4), 1450036. doi:10.1142/S0129065714500361 PMID:25684369

Ye, H., Shen, H., & Dong, Y. (2017). *Using Evidence-Based medicine through Advanced Data Analytics to work toward a National Standard for Hospital-based acute ischemic Stroke treatment*. Mainland China.

Yusof, Y., & Mustaffa, Z. (2011). Dengue Outbreak Prediction: A Least Squares Support Vector Machines Approach. *International Journal of Computer Theory and Engineering*, *3*(4).

Zhang, Q., Xie, Y., & Ye, P. (2013). Acute ischaemic stroke prediction from physiological time series patterns. *The Australasian Medical Journal*, *6*(5), 280–286. doi:10.4066/AMJ.2013.1650 PMID:23745149

Chapter 16
Contribution of Neural Networks in Different Applications

Bhushan Patil
Mumbai University, India

Manisha Vohra
Mumbai University, India

ABSTRACT

Neural networks are very useful and are proving to be very beneficial in various fields. Biomedical applications such as breast cancer image classification, differentiating between the malignant and benign type of breast cancer, etc. are now seen to be making use of neural networks rapidly. Neural networks are showing remarkable results of their effectiveness in these biomedical applications and are proving to be immensely profitable. Another field such as agriculture, which is a very crucial field for survival of human life, can be benefitted from neural networks. Likewise, various fields can gain enormous benefits from the usage of neural networks. This chapter shall explain neural networks in detail. Also, the authors shall provide a brief and detailed insight of the contribution of neural networks in different applications, along with its analysis.

WHAT IS NEURAL NETWORK?

A system consisting of a combination of hardware and software platform which is developed and modelled on the basis of human brain neurons is called as neural network. It consists of artificial neurons. It is basically a type of deep learning technology. It has the human ability of learning things and it keeps on learning and acts accordingly.

DOI: 10.4018/978-1-5225-9902-9.ch016

OVERVIEW OF HISTORY OF NEURAL NETWORKS

Many people have contributed in the development of neural networks. Their contributions are as follows:

- **1943**: Warren McCulloch, a neurophysiologist and Walter Pitts, a mathematician came together and wrote regarding artificial neurons. They also developed and modeled neural network. This was the first time when neural networks were introduced to the world.
- **1949**: Donald O. Hebb wrote a book titled "The Organization of Behavior" which gave information regarding neural networks learning process and explained regarding neurons. It stated that connection of two neurons strengthens when both of them are activated at the same time.
- **1951**: Marvin Minsky developed a neurocomputer for neural networks that adjusted weights automatically but it was not implemented practically.
- **1956**: A memory network was developed and research regarding neural networks and neurons was continued.
- **1958**: Frank Rosenblatt developed and successfully implemented Mark I Perceptron which was a neurocomputer having the capability of recognizing different numerical using image sensor and it helped in cases where input classes were separable linearly.
- **1960**: Bernard Widrow and Marcian E. Hoff developed Adaptive Linear Neuron (ADALINE). It was the first commercially used neural network.
- **1961**: Karl Steinbuch implemented the concept of associative memory. These implementations are seen as the predecessors of present neural networks associative memory. He even explained various concepts for neural networks.
- **1965**: In this year, Nils Nilsson wrote a book titled Learning Machines which explained about neural networks and also stated regarding their progress.
- **1969**: Marvin Minsky and Seymour Papret published a discovery regarding Perceptron.
- **1972**: During this year, Teuvo Kohonen developed associative memory.
- **1973**: Christoph Malsburgh made use of a neuron model.
- **1974**: Paul Werbos introduced and developed a learning method called backpropagation of error.
- **1976**: Gail Carpenter and Stephen Grossberg introduced and developed adaptive resonance theory.
- **1982**: John Hopfield developed the energy network called the Hopfield energy network.
- **1985**: Hinton, Sejnowski and Ackley introduced and developed Boltzmann machine.
- **1986**: Hinton, Rumelhart and Williams introduced the generalized Delta rule.
- **1988**: In this year, Kosko introduced fuzzy logic concept in ANN and also introduced and developed Binary Associative Memory (BAM).

Time to time constant progress was made in development of neural networks and till today neural networks are constantly improving and are being included in various applications. The constant progress of neural networks are providing enormous opportunities to different sectors as neural networks can help and benefit different sectors to a great extent. Sectors like biomedical, agricultural, etc. can largely gain advantages from introduction of neural networks. These applications shall be viewed and explained in brief later on in this chapter.

REQUIREMENT OF NEURAL NETWORKS

Neural networks are capable of learning on their own and also have the capability of taking decisions according to the situation. Due to such beneficial capabilities of neural networks, they ease the human work and can be widely used in various applications. They give optimum desired results and they are highly efficient. This is why neural networks are required. They are largely used for classification of images, patterns, etc. They are also used in prediction of stock market and analysis of different sectors like finance sector. Along with it, neural networks are also used in controlling different things like controlling self-driving cars and different vehicles, etc. Besides, neural networks are also used in biomedical and agricultural sectors and are gaining popularity day by day.

NEURON

A neuron is a special nerve cell. It processes information in the brain. Each neuron comprises of a cell body which is also called as soma. Along with cell body, each neuron also comprises of dendrite and axon which are nerve fibres.

LEARNING PROCESS OF HUMAN BRAIN

Human brain learning process is complex to understand. The neurons present in human brain undertakes the work of gathering different signals. These signals are gathered through dendrites which are nerve fibres and an extension of nerve cell. The different impulses that are received from different cells at synapses i.e., a junction between two cells are sent to the cell body along with dendrites. Then via axon which is also a nerve fibre and a long structure of nerve cell through which impulses are conducted from cell body to different cells, neurons sends out signals. These signals through axon spilt into different branches. At the end of each branch, synapse transmits these signals to the next neuron present. This is how the information is processed and human brain learns through the information it is receiving via neurons.

ARTIFICIAL NEURON

An artificial neuron is a neuron which is modeled on the biological neuron and which functions the way the biological neuron functions in human brain. It has the human brain ability of processing information and learning new things. It is used in an artificial neural network.

WORKING OF NEURAL NETWORKS

Neural network comprises of artificial neurons. These artificial neurons are called as nodes. They are responsible for processing of information. They are also responsible for performing any kind of tasks. The neural network consists of three different part. They are as follows:

- Input layer
- Hidden layer
- Output layer

These all layers are having different roles. All these layers are explained as follows:

- **Input Layer**: The neural network is very flexible and capable of accepting different types of inputs. The input layer intakes or accepts data like audio files, written text, numerical data, images, etc.
- **Hidden Layer**: A neural network can comprise of one or more than one hidden layers. This part of neural network is having major responsibilities. This part is responsible for performing operations like analysis of different pattern, mathematical operation, extraction of features, etc.
- **Output Layer**: The output layer of neural network is responsible for generating output.

All the nodes are allotted certain values called as weights. The weighted sum of inputs are calculated using a transfer function. Also a bias is added to it. The output then received from transfer function is applied as input to activation functions. The functions which are having the role of deciding which nodes to fire are called as activation functions. There are various activation functions available for use. Examples of some of activation functions are hyperbolic tangent function denoted as Tanh, sigmoid or logistic, rectified linear units abbreviated as ReLu, etc. All these activation functions are used as per the requirement of the neural network. Depending on the nodes that are fired, the final output is generated by the output layer. Prior to generating the final output, there is always a predicted output. This predicted output is very useful as based on comparison with the predicted output, the generated final output can be judged for the amount of errors it is comprising. If there is a major difference in the predicted output and generated final output, it means that a huge amount of error is present in the generated final output. In order to keep the error at its least possible backpropagation is used. Backpropagation is a method which is used to reduce the error in the network. Backpropagation helps by providing feedback to reduce error. Cost function is used in back propagation. Cost function is a function that helps in calculation of error. The errors that are found are huge then backpropagation is used immediately in neural networks. The weights are then again adjusted on a random basis. The backpropagation method is repeated again and again till the time error between the predicted output and the generated output is very less, almost negligible.

LEARNING PROCESS OF NEURAL NETWORKS

Neural networks learn from the feedback they receive. Backpropagation method provides this feedback. The error is also reduced with the help of backpropagation method. Neural networks learn from their errors which even helps in reducing the errors. Besides this, neural networks also learn from the training they are provided with.

LEARNING TECHNIQUES OF NEURAL NETWORKS

There are different learning techniques of neural networks through which they are trained. These techniques are as follows:

- Supervised learning
- Unsupervised learning
- Reinforcement learning

Supervised learning: The name itself suggests that in this type of learning technique, a supervision is performed. A source which is an expert of some particular data or is having knowledge about certain particular data, feeds that data to the neural network. Then, if supposing the neural network is assigned with the work of recognizing pattern of this this fed data and classifying it, the neural network does this assigned work on the basis of assumptions and guess work. The person who is an expert, who has fed the data provides the correct answers to the neural network which then compares the assumption and guess work answers with the correct answers fed by the expert. As per the differences found in the answers, the neural network makes correction.

Unsupervised learning: In this type of learning, no supervision is performed. The neural network will be assigned with certain work. Unlike supervised learning technique there will not be any expert or any person having knowledge about the assigned work. The neural network will complete the assigned work based on the knowledge it is having through the existing datasets.

Reinforcement learning: This learning technique is quite different from supervised and unsupervised leaning technique. In this learning technique the neural network works by observing its surrounding area. It works as per its environment.

TYPES OF NEURAL NETWORKS

There are various types of neural networks present. All of them have some kind of differences in them with respect to their functioning. There are precisely six different types of neural networks present. They are as follows:

- **Feedforward Neural Network**: This type of neural network has a very simplified functionality. It is mostly used in classification kind of work where classification is difficult. This type of neural network being very simplified, utilizing it in complicated work proves to be very useful. It might or might not consist of hidden layers. The data traveling here, takes place in only one direction. It moves from input to output. It does not has backpropagation. There is a single layer feedforward network present in feedforward neural network. At this single layer feedforward network, the sum of products of inputs and weights are calculated and kept. The result obtained at this layer is fed to the output. If the output value is more than a certain fixed threshold value, where the threshold value is usually zero then neuron shall fire with an activated output i.e., mostly value one. In case when the neuron does not fire, the deactivated value i.e. negative (-1) is fired.
- **Radial Basis Function Neural Network**: This neural network considers the distance of any point with respect to the center. Radial basis functions have two layers. The features of neural network

are combined with radial basis function. They both are combined in the inner layer out of the two layers. The output received from these features is considered during computation of the same output in the next step i.e., a memory.

- **Convolutional Neural Network**: Convolutional neural networks are having similarity with feed forward neural networks. Alike the feedforward networks, the convolutional neural networks' neurons are having weights and biases which can learn. The convolutional neural network have application in image processing and signal processing.
- **Modular Neural Network**: These neural networks have a combination of various networks working independently and contributing towards the output. Every neural network consists of set of inputs that are unique in comparison with other networks which construct and perform sub-tasks. These networks have no interaction with each other and they do not help each other in completing their tasks. The most important merit of modular neural network is its ability to break a large process of computation into small parts. This helps in reducing the complexity involved in the whole process. Another advantage is the speed of computation increases as the computation is performed in small parts.
- **Recurrent Neural Network**: This neural network has a working principle of saving the output of a layer. This saved output is fed back to the input to help predict the result of the layer. The first layer is formed alike to the feed forward neural network along with the product of the sum of the weights and the features. The process of the neural network will start when the computation is done. So whenever the neuron will move from one step to another, it will have the memory of some information from its preceding step. In recurrent neural network, the work is done on the front propagation. If the prediction of this neural network is wrong then error correction or learning rate is used to make prediction. This helps by making correct prediction during back propagation.
- **Kohonen Self-Organizing Neural Network**: As the name suggests, this neural network is a self-organizing neural network. The aim of a Kohonen map is to input vectors of arbitrary dimension to discrete map comprised of neurons. Training is required by the map for the purpose of creating a self-organization of training data. There can be one or two dimensions. During training of map, the weights differ in accordance with the value but the location of neuron remains constant. This neural network is used to recognize patterns in data.

ADVANTAGES OF NEURAL NETWORKS

There are various advantages of neural networks. They are as follows:

- Neural networks can learn things like humans.
- Neural networks can act and make decisions as per the situation and as per their learning.
- Neural networks can be used in different sectors where analysis or prediction is required like stock market, finance sector, etc.
- Neural networks ensures the output is generated with the minimum possible error.

LIMITATIONS OF NEURAL NETWORKS

Along with great advantages of neural networks, there also exist some limitations of neural networks. They are as follows:

- Neural networks can sometimes prove to be quite complicated in terms of their computation, especially when handling a huge amount of data.
- Neural networks can sometimes make a prediction of a certain output which is way too far from the actual output.

The limitations of neural networks however do not overshadow the advantages of neural networks. In fact, owing to the advantages of the neural networks, they are widely used in various applications.

APPLICATIONS OF NEURAL NETWORKS

Neural networks can be widely used in various sectors like financial, biomedical, agricultural, etc. For gaining a better understanding of applications of neural networks, the following different case studies should be considered.

Case Study 1: Application of Neural Networks in Breast Cancer Image Classification

An image dataset consisting of cancerous and non-cancerous images was taken from the department of pathology of the Near East University of Nicosia, Cyprus, by a team of three authors Sertan Kaymak et al. (2018) for classification of breast cancer images using ANN. The authors took the image dataset and used Haar wavelets for training the neural network. Firstly, all the images of the dataset were taken and were converted to grey scale format and Gaussain filter was applied to the images. Then using the resulting images, Haar wavelets were calculated on them. After this, all the images were summed together and finally inverse wavelets were calculated for reconstructing new image. The neural network uses feedforward network and the architecture on which the ANN is trained is back propagation. Along with backpropagation ANN, another ANN is also used by the authors which is radial basis function ANN. The same number of images were taken from the dataset and were trained using these two ANN's. The results obtained using these both ANN's are illustrated below in table 1. Both the neural networks do

Table 1. Results of neural networks.

Neural Network	Back propagation	Radial basis
Training images	115	115
Test images	61	61
Classification result	59.02%	70.49%

Source: Sertan Kaymak et al. (2018), Procedia Computer Science.

really work well in breast cancer image classification. The only difference in both the ANN's is that the radial basis function ANN has better performance than the backpropagation ANN.

Case Study 2: Application of Neural Networks in Automating Irrigation

An irrigation system based on the ANN was developed and implemented by authors Raja Sekhar Reddy G. et al. (2013). Different parameters i.e. soil humidity, soil temperature, air humidity and radiation are sensed using different sensors. The values that are received from the sensors and the desired values of these different parameters taken from the agricultural research center database are given to the microcontroller and then the microcontroller compares both set of values of these parameters. Also, the actual required values of these parameters are calculated using ETo (evapotranspiration) equation and are given to ANN which minimizes the error present in these calculated values. These values received from ANN are also given to the microcontroller and a comparison is done between them and the actual required values of the different parameters. The results then obtained from this comparison are sent to the PC or laptop using zigbee module. The implemented system can be either operated in an automated manner, i.e. by automatically starting the pump for irrigation as soon as the soil moisture value reaches it threshold value or the system can be operated manually by giving commands from the PC or laptop to the microcontroller to switch on and off the pump.

Case Study 3: Application of Neural Networks in Breast Cancer Detection and Classification

A breast cancer dataset was taken by authors Chandra Prasetyo Utomo et al. (2014) from University of Wisconsin Hospital, Madison, United States from Dr. William H. Wolberg. The dataset consisted of benign and malignant cancer images and was tested by them using two different artificial ANN's. The first neural network used was based on backpropagation and was called as backpropagation artificial neural network (BP ANN) by the authors Chandra Prasetyo Utomo et al. (2014) and the second neural network used was based on extreme learning machine techniques, so they called it extreme learning machine artificial neural network (ELM ANN). The results obtained by testing the dataset using BP ANN and ELM ANN clearly made it evident that neural networks work very efficiently in breast cancer detection and classification. The only difference obtained in the performance of both the ANN's was one of them had better performance specifications. ELM ANN had better sensitivity and better accuracy rate than BP ANN while the specificity rate of BP ANN was slightly better than ELM ANN. It can be concluded from this case study that ANN's are very useful in breast cancer detection and classification.

Case Study 4: Application of Neural Networks in Predicting Groundwater Suitability for Irrigation

Authors Vasant Madhav Wagh et al. (2016) developed an ANN for predicting different values like sodium adsorption ratio (SAR), residual sodium carbonate (RSC), magnesium adsorption ratio (MAR), Kellys ratio (KR) and percent sodium (%Na) in the groundwater of Nanded tehsil. Exactly 50 groundwater samples were taken and analyzed for different physicochemical parameters such as pH, EC, TDS, Ca, Mg, Na, K, Cl, CO_3, HCO_3, SO_4 and NO_3, for the pre monsoon season 2012. All these parameters were taken as input variables in the ANN. The ANN, based on these parameters gives groundwater quality

Table 2. Descriptive statistics of measured and predicted values of irrigation water suitability indices

Parameter	Measured					Predicted				
	SAR	RSC	KR	MAR	%Na	SAR	RSC	KR	MAR	%Na
Min	0.67	-4.97	0.17	20.09	15.07	0.07	-4.97	-0.32	18.10	11.36
Max	9.46	-4.70	4.64	78.76	82.36	8.99	4.70	3.81	77.71	84.54
Average	3.30	-1.28	1.18	55.00	46.42	3.30	-1.28	1.18	55.00	46.42
SD	2.43	2.02	1.08	14.35	18.00	2.39	2.02	1.03	13.78	17.79

Source: Madhav Wagh et al. (2016), Modeling Earth Systems and Environment, Springer.

indices for irrigation suitability prediction. The ANN gave certain results which are seen in table 2 below. The measured values of SAR, RSC, KR, MAR and %Na are compared with the predicted values of the same parameters and are depicted in table 2. The minimum (min), maximum (max), average and standard deviation (SD) values for different parameters were obtained. From the obtained results, it can be concluded that ANN best suits the RSC value as the measured and predicted values are precisely the same. Parameters other than RSC do have some differences in the measured values as compared to the predicted values. The difference is however not drastically major. This proves that ANN's can efficiently contribute in predicting groundwater suitability.

Case Study 5: Application of Neural Networks in Rail Track Crack Detection

The authors R. Manikandan et al. (2017) developed a system that utilizes neural network classifier for crack detection in railway tracks. The rail track images are captured first and are preprocessed, after which gabor transform is used on the images. The rail track images are spatial domain images. These images need to be converted to mutli resolution images, which is done with the help of gabor transform. After performing gabor transform, gabor magnitude image is obtained. Grey Level Co-occurrence Matrix (GLCM) features are then extracted from gabor magnitude image in order to classify the crack containing images of the railway track. Feed Forward Back Propagation (FFBP) neural network (NN) classifier is used for detection of rail track images. The images detected are classified into two types. These two types are crack consisting images and non-crack consisting images. Morphological operations are performed on crack consisting images of the NN classifier to detect the cracks. This leads to erosion and dilation images which subtracts the eroded images from dilated images and ultimately gives crack segmented image. This system was evaluated and it was found that, it had an accuracy of 94.9%.

Case Study 6: Application of Neural Networks for Coal Mine Safety Production Forewarning Indicator System

Authors Wang Ying et al. (2015) established coal mine safety production forewarning indicator system from four aspects of personnel, equipment, environment and management. Improvement measures that included momentum method, particle swarm optimization algorithm, variable weight method, adaptive learning rate and asynchronous learning factor are utilized to optimize backpropagation neural network models. The gradient backpropagation (GBP), particle swarm optimization-backpropagation (PSO-BP), modified particle swarm optimization-backpropagation (MPSO-BP) neural network optimization models

Table 3. Error of the early warning indicators' simulation value in 2013

Method	GBP	PSO-BP	MPSO-BP
Standard error	4.7029	3.6364	2.3062
Average relative error (%)	-4.69	-5.44	-3.67

Source: Wang Ying et.al (2017), International Journal of Mining Science and Technology.

Table 4. Error analysis f MPSO-BP neural network

No.	Simulation output	Desired output	Error
1	(0.0000 0.9200 0.1100 0.1000 0.0481)	(01000)	0.0308
2	(0.0001 0.1092 0.9606 0.0062 0.1207)	(00100)	0.0281
3	(0.0000 0.0298 0.8524 0.0310 0.0786)	(00100)	0.0298
4	(0.0001 0.1224 0.8727 0.0139 0.1011)	(00100)	0.0416
5	(0.0001 0.0000 0.0000 0.9012 0.1402)	(00010)	0.0294
6	(0.0030 0.0200 0.0360 0.8798 0.1278)	(00010)	0.0325
7	(0.0084 0.0112 0.0300 0.9020 0.1900)	(00010)	0.0468
8	(0.0010 0.0614 0.0002 0.1600 0.9206)	(00001)	0.0357

Source: Wang Ying et.al (2017), International Journal of Mining Science and Technology.

were applied to coal mine safety production forewarning instances for the purpose of comparative study. Certain simulation results were obtained. These results can be seen in table 3 below. The comparison of simulation results of GBP, PSO-BP and MPSO-BP models show that the identification accuracy of MPSO-BP network model is higher than that of GBP model and PSO-BP model. Table 4 shows the error analysis of MPSO-BP neural network. The errors are very less. From table 3 and table 4, it can be stated that MPSO-BP has the best relative performance. MPSO-BP network model can effectively reduce the possibility that the neural network falls into a local minimum point. MPSO-BP network model's fast convergence and high accuracy provides basis for early warning and control of the safety accident in coal mine enterprises.

CONCLUSION FROM CASE STUDIES

The case studies above demonstrate the use of neural networks in different sectors like biomedical and agriculture. The use of neural network was found to be very useful in detection of breast cancer. Along with detection of breast cancer, classification of benign and malignant type of cancer was also very successfully performed with the help of neural network. Besides biomedical sector, agricultural sector, railway sector and coal mine also benefits from the use of neural networks. Automating irrigation process is possible with the help of ANN. Also, finding suitability of groundwater for irrigation purpose is also achievable with ANN. Hence, from the above case studies, it can be concluded that neural networks are great contributors in biomedical, agricultural, railways and coal mine sectors.

FUTURE POSSIBILITIES WITH NEURAL NETWORKS

As seen in the above case studies, the neural networks showcase a lot of potential. They can very well successfully be utilized in various different sectors. Their working capabilities and advantages shall prove to be of benefit in which ever sector they are used. Despite of their certain limitations, their capabilities and advantages do not get overshadowed. With the kind of potential shown by neural networks as seen through case studies in different sectors like medical, agricultural and rail, the neural networks sure have great future possibilities to be used in different sectors like industrial, mining, etc. and help create a difference for the enrichment and wellbeing of the society.

CONCLUSION

Neural networks are very useful in applications like biomedical and agricultural. Neural networks can be even introduced in other sectors as they provide enormous benefits. They have the human ability of learning things. They can very well learn things and act on the basis of their learning. Neural networks have constantly progressed and are still undergoing great progress and advancements which helps improve neural networks and thus allows the possibility of use of neural networks in various applications.

REFERENCES

Kaymak, S., Helwan, A., & Uzun, D. (2017). Breast cancer image classification using artificial neural networks. *Procedia Computer Science, 120,* 126–131. doi:10.1016/j.procs.2017.11.219

Raja Sekhar Reddy, G., Manujunatha, S., & Sundeep Kumar, K. (2013). Evapotranpiration model using AI controller for automatic irrigation system. *International Journal of Computer Trends and Technology, 4*(7), 2311–2315.

Utomo, C. P., Kardiana, A., & Yuliwulandri, R. (2014). Breast cancer diagnosis using artificial neural networks with extreme learning techniques. *International Journal of Advanced Research in Artificial Intelligence, 3*(7), 10–14.

Wagh, V. M., Panaskar, D. B., Muley, A. A., Mukate, S. V., Logale, Y. P., & Aamalawar, M. L. (2016). Prediction of groundwater suitability for irrigation using artificial neural network model: A case study of Nanded tehsil, Maharashtra, India. *Modeling Earth Systems and Environment, Springer, 2*(4), 1–10. doi:10.100740808-016-0250-3

Ying, W., Lu, C., & Zuo, C. (2015). Coal mine safety production forewarning based on improved BP neural network. *International Journal of Mining Science and Technology, 25*(2), 319–324. doi:10.1016/j.ijmst.2015.02.023

KEY TERMS AND DEFINITIONS

Artificial Neuron: It is an artificial replication of human brain neuron.

Neural Network: It is a system having functionality akin to the human brain. It incorporates and replicates some abilities of the human brain like the ability of learning.

Neuron: It is a nerve cell used for communication with other cells.

Chapter 17
Introducing the Deep Learning for Digital Age

Shaila S. G.
Dayananda Sagar University, India

Sunanda Rajkumari
Dayananda Sagar University, India

Vadivel Ayyasamy
SRM University AP Amaravati, India

ABSTRACT

Deep learning is playing vital role with greater success in various applications, such as digital image processing, human-computer interaction, computer vision and natural language processing, robotics, biological applications, etc. Unlike traditional machine learning approaches, deep learning has effective ability of learning and makes better use of data set for feature extraction. Because of its repetitive learning ability, deep learning has become more popular in the present-day research works.

INTRODUCTION

Deep Learning is a subset of Machine learning in Artificial Intelligence that simulates with the working nature of human brain in processing the unstructured or unlabeled data using unsupervised method and creating patterns which will be used further for decision making. Deep Learning also called Deep Neural Network uses neural networks. Deep Learning became popular in digital era because of an explosion of data from various parts of the world from various sources such as social media, internet search engines, e-commerce platforms, etc. And we simply call this data as Big Data which is unstructured in nature. Manual process of retrieving the relevant information from the Big Data takes decades. Hence it became necessary to develop automated models that adapt techniques of Machine Learning in Artificial Intelligence to retrieve wealthy information hidden in the Big Data. Thus, Deep Learning became popular nowadays as it learns the system in repetitive process deeply and supports in building automated models.

DOI: 10.4018/978-1-5225-9902-9.ch017

Artificial Neural Networks (ANN) is employed by Deep learning to assists the process of machine learning. The ANN in structure simulates the human brain with neuron nodes connected like a web. ANN is a multi layered network, input of the one layer is the output of the preceding layer in such way information is passed through each layer in the network. The initial layer of the network is the input layer and the layer at the end of the network is called an output layer. There are many layer called hidden layers between input and output layers consisting of neurons and they are connected to each other. Deep Learning operates on the data using nonlinear approach because of its hierarchical function the computers. The hierarchy of knowledge in deep learning for each layer represents a deeper level of knowledge. Hence, with increasing number of layers in neural network it will learn more complex features than a few layers of neural network. Learning occurs in two phases in Deep Learning. First phase consists creating a statistical model as output by applying a non linear transformation of the input. Second phase focus at improving the model with a mathematical method known as Derivative. These two phases are repeated hundreds to thousands of time until it has achieved decent level of accuracy. For example, Deep Learning nonlinear technique will adapt present or instance time, current position, IP address, and other attributes for detecting and identifying illegal activity. In Deep Learning, the first layer of the neural network processes takes raw data as input and passes through the second layer as output. The second layer will pass its output to the next layer along with the previous layer's output. The third layer takes the second layer's information and adds additional information and produces data patterns. The series of constructing data patterns continues through all levels of the neuron network.

Deep learning is making major advances in solving problems of the artificial intelligence community that have resisted the best, attempts for many years. It has turned out that in high-dimensional data deep learning is very good at finding complex structures and is therefore applicable to many domains of business, science and government. In addition it has done far more better in at predicting the activity of potential drug molecules, analyzing particle accelerator data, reconstructing brain circuits, and predicting the effects of mutations in non-coding DNA on gene expression and disease compared to other machine-learning techniques. It has produced extremely favorable results for various tasks in natural language understanding, classification of particularly topic, analysis of person sentiment, answering questions and language translation

Background

Deep learning was first emerged in 1940s with the development of Artificial Neural Network (ANN). McCulloch and Pitts (1943) by analyzing and summarizing the characteristics of neurons proposed the model of ANN named as McCulloch-Pitts (MP) model. Hebb (1949) in their work, proposed a cell assembly theory for describing cerebral neuron adaptation process during its learning, explaining the development of neural networks. To imitate the thought process of the cerebral neuron process they used a combination of algorithms and mathematics called "threshold logic". Deep Learning has been steadily evolving since then, with only two significant breaks in its development. Later, Rosenblatt (1958) developed an important concept of ANN called the perceptron algorithm. The author explains the perceptron algorithm as a binary classifier that adapts supervised learning. Widrow (1990), an author based on the MP model proposed a single layer artificial neural network which has the property of the adaptive linear element. Kunihiko Fukushima first used "convolutional neural networks". Neural networks with multiple pooling and convolutional layers was designed by Fukushima. In 1979, he developed an artificial neural network which used a hierarchical, multilayered design, called Neocognitro. It permitted the computer the "learn" to recognize pictures and visual patterns. The networks resembled modern versions, but were directed with reinforcement strategy of recurring activation in multiple layers, which became more advanced over time. Additionally, Fukushima's design, by increasing the "weight" of certain connections manually allowed important features to be adjusted.

Later in 1980's Hopfield (1982) proposed the Hopfield network which is ANN with advanced of both methods in theory and in application. An effective deep architectures training strategies had a breakthrough in 2006 with the development of training deep belief networks (DBN) algorithms (Hinton et al., 2006) and stacked auto-encoders (Ranzato et al., 2007; Bengio et al., 2007). These methods are all based on a similar approach, greedy layer-wise unsupervised pre-training followed by fine-tuning of the supervised. With an unsupervised learning algorithm each layer is pre-trained, the main variations in its input is captured by learning a nonlinear transformation of its input. A final training phase is set with this unsupervised pre-training where with respect to a supervised training criterion with gradient-based optimization the deep architecture is fine-tuned. While the pre-training strategy has improved the performance of trained deep models impressively, the mechanisms underlying this success is not known much.

DEEP LEARNING ALGORITHMS

Below are listed some of the popular Deep Learning algorithms:

Feed Forward Neural Network

A feed forward neural network is a grouping algorithm inspired biologically. It comprises of a number of simple neuron-like processing *units or also called as nodes*, organized in *layers*. Every unit in a layer is connected with all the units in the next layer. These connection may have a different strength or *weight* and are not all equal. The knowledge of a network are encoded on weight of the connections. Data enters at the inputs and passes through the multilayered network, layer by layer, until it arrives at the outputs. During normal operation, that is when it acts as a classifier, there is no feedback between layers so they are called *feedforward* neural networks.

This is the simplest type of ANN. In this neural network, information flows in single direction that is forward. The information flow initiates at input layer and passes on to hidden layer and ends at the output layer. This network does not have a loop. This is shown in Figure 1.

Figure 1. Feed forward neural networks

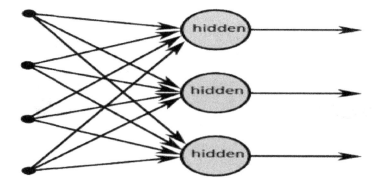

Single Layered Preceptron

Single-layer perceptron network consists of a single layer of output nodes and is the simplest kind of neural network . The inputs are fed directly to the outputs through a series of weights. Input is multi-dimensional i.e., it can be a vector. Let's take input $x = (I_1, I_2, .., I_n)$.Input units or nodes are connected to a node or multiple nodes in the next layer. The preceding layer node or unit takes a weighted sum of all its inputs:

$$\text{summed input } = \sum_i w_i I_i$$

In each node the sum of the products of the weights and the inputs is calculated. If the calculated value is observed to be above some threshold value, the neuron fires and takes the activated value typically 1 or else it takes -1 the deactivated value. This type of activation function of neurons are also called artificial neurons or linear threshold units. As long as the threshold value lies between the two a perceptron can be created using any values for both the activated and deactivated states. Delta rule, a simple learning algorithm can trained the perceptrons. It calculates the errors between sample output data and calculated output, and adjusts the weights accordingly, thus implementing a form of gradient descent. Marvin Minsky and Seymour Papert in 1969, showed that it was impossible for a single-layer perceptron network to learn an XOR function in a famous monograph entitled perceptrons. Single-layer perceptrons are only capable of learning linearly separable patterns.

The limitations of the single layer network led to the development of multi-layer feed-forward networks, it has one or more hidden layers, called multi-layer perceptron (MLP) networks. MLP networks overcome many of the limitations of single layer perceptrons, and can use the back-propagation algorithm for training. The back-propagation technique was invented independently several times.

There is one input layer of processing unit and one output layer of processing unit in Figure 2. No feedback connections e.g., single layered preceptron.

Figure 2. Single layered preceptron

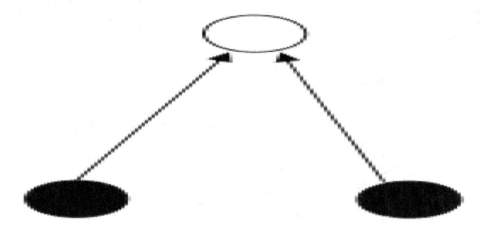

Multilayered Preception

In 1974 Werrbos developed a backpropagation training algorithm. However, Werbos' work remained almost unknown in the scientific community until 1985 when Parker rediscovered the technique. Rumelhart, Soon after Parker published his findings, Hinton and Williams also rediscovered the technique. Rumelhart and the other members of the Parallel Distributed Processing (PDP) group efforts that make the back-propagation technique a backbone of neuro-computing. Until now, back-propagation networks are the most popular neural network model among all the existing models and have attracted most research interest. Multi-layered network used various learning techniques, the most accepted being *back-propagation*. In this method, to compute the value of some predefined error-function the output values are compared with the correct answer. Using various techniques the error is then fed back through the network. In order to reduce the value of the error function by some small amount with the information obtained, the algorithm adjusts the weights of each connection. The process is carried on for particularly a huge number of training cycles, the network will eventually come to a state where the error of the calculations is minimal. In such case, the network has learned a certain target function. One applies gradient descent a general method for non-linear. For this method, the networks calculates the derivative of the error function with respect to the network weights, and it changes the weights to reduce error. For this reason, only back-propagation can be applied by networks with differentiable activation functions.

In Figure 3 shows the mutli-layered preceptron, there is one input layer, one output layer, and one or more hidden layers of processing units and no feedback connections.

Figure 3. Multilayered preceptron

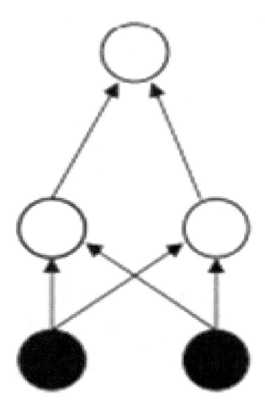

Recurrent Neural Network

Recurrent Neural Network(RNN) is a multilayered neural network which includes loops i.e, the output is sent back to itself. This is depicted in Figure 4, for processing sequence of inputs these neural networks are used. It is a class of artificial neural network commonly adapted for natural language processing (NLP) and speech recognition. RNNs are outline to identify a data's sequential characteristics and the patterns is utilized to guess the next possible scenario. Currently Recurrent Neural Networks (RNN) are the most approving algorithms, it is the only algorithm that has internal memory so they are kind of powerful and robust neural networks. RNN's are able to recollect significant things about the input they received because of their internal memory, which made them to be very accurate in predicting next coming outcome. Compared to other algorithms sequential data like text, speech, audio, video, time series, financial data, weather and much more prefer RNN algorithm. The reason is that they can form a much deeper understanding of a sequence and its context. Some of its applications are time series analysis, chatbots, detection of fraud credit card transaction.

RNNs are adapted for deep learning and in the development of models that reflects the performances of neurons in the human brain. They are especially powerful in use cases in which context is critical to predicting an outcome. They use feedback loops to perform a sequence of data that notify about the final output, which can also be a sequence of data which make them distinct from other types of artificial neural networks. These feedback loops allow information to be preserved.

Over last few years, in deep learning models recurrent neural networks have become one of main architectures. However, pure recurrent networks often result limited to address many real-world deep learning scenarios. Various issues in recurrent neural networks implementations due to the lack of recursive connections or backward feedback loops. Researchers have created variations of recurrent neural networks to address those issues that have been widely implemented in popular open source deep learning frameworks. Among them are bidirectional and deep RNNs which are often used in more sophisticated scenarios that deal with sequential data.

Figure 4. Recurrent neural networks

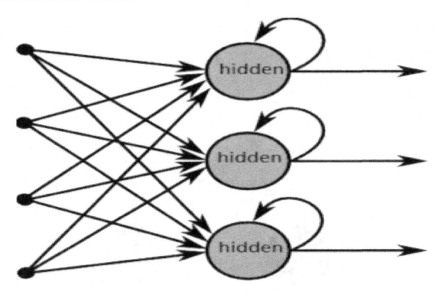

Bidirectional Recurrent Neural Networks (BRNN)

BRNN model design is shown in Figure 5, the same output is connected to two hidden layers of opposite directions. In this type of the model of deep learning, the information or data can be supplied to the output layer from backwards i.e., past and forward i.e., future states simultaneously. The inputs of the opposite direction states are not connected to these forward and backward states' output. Contrary to standard RNN, input information from the previous and latter of the current time frame can be utilised by using two time directions whereas in RNN, it needs to detain for including future information. The use case for bidirectional recurrent neural networks is focus on scenarios in which the execution of nodes state at a future time affects the state of a node. Whereas, in the traditional RNN architecture the state of the network at any given time is based on a very simple computation graph and is based solely on information about the past. Schuster and Paliwal invented it in 1997, it increases the volume of input information present in the network. For example, time delay neural network (TDNNs) and multilayer perceptron (MLPs) have limitations on the input data flexibility as they require their input data to be fixed. Standard recurrent neural network (RNNs) also have limitations as the future input information cannot be reached from the current state whereas, BRNNs do not require their input data to be fixed. Besides, from the current state the future input information is attainable.

BRNN are mostly applicable when the context of the input is required. For example, in handwriting recognition, the knowledge of the letters position is increased before and after the current letter can enhanced the performance.

Deep Recurrent Neural Network

Deep neural network has multiple number of hidden layers. In a recurrent neural network the hidden layer has recurrent (feedback) connection. In that hidden layer each hidden unit is connected to itself and also to all other nodes. Hence deep recurrent neural network consists of multiple recurrent hidden layers in the network hierarchy.

Issues that deep neural network has are also supported by recurrent neural network suffers because of the recurrent connections. Present RNNs are still not deep models compared to other models regarding representation learning. Pascanu et al. in 2013 formalizes the idea of constructing deep RNNs by expanding current RNNs. A deep recurrent neural network can be constructed in three different directions as shown in Figure 6, by increasing the layers of the input component Figure 6(a), recurrent component Figure 6 (b) and output component Figure 6(c) respectively.

Figure 5. Bidirectional recurrent neural network

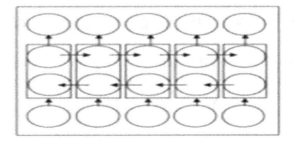

Figure 6. Three different formulation of deep RNN

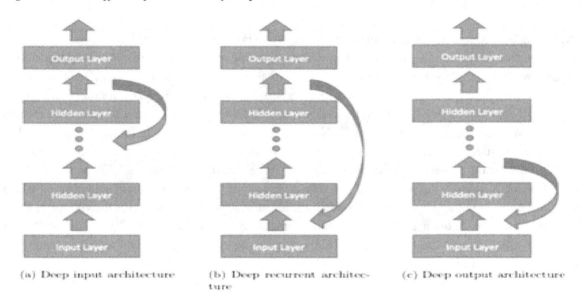

(a) Deep input architecture   (b) Deep recurrent architecture   (c) Deep output architecture

Convolutional Neural Network

Convolutional neural networks are deep artificial neural networks that are used primarily to classify images and visual patterns, cluster them by sameness and conduct object recognition within scenes. These algorithms can identify street signs, faces, person, platypuses, tumors, and many other features of visual data. Convolutional neural networks implement optical character recognition (OCR) on analog and hand-written documents to digitize text and make natural-language processing achievable. CNNs can also support audio when it is represented visually as a spectrogram. Convolutional networks have been applied straight to text analytics together with graph data with graph convolutional networks recently. The polpularity of convolutional nets (ConvNets) in image recognition is a reason of the rise for the success of deep learning. They are the major reasons for advances in computer vision (CV), which has various applications for surveillance, drones, roboitcs, self-driving cars, medical puposes and many more applications.

Convolutional Neural Network (CNN) is a multilayered neural network designed which uses unstructured datasets to extract increasingly complex features of data at each layer and to determine the output and extracted the information from it. CNN is a combination of feature learning and classification. This is depicted in Figure 7.

DEEP LEARNING VS TRADITIONAL MACHINE LEARNING

Deep learning requires advanced and costly machines comparatively to traditional machine learning algorithms. In present scenarios, for the performance of any Deep Learning algorithm Graphic Processing Unit (GPU) has become a main part. A huge advantages of deep learning algorithm is trying to learn

Figure 7. Convolution neural networks

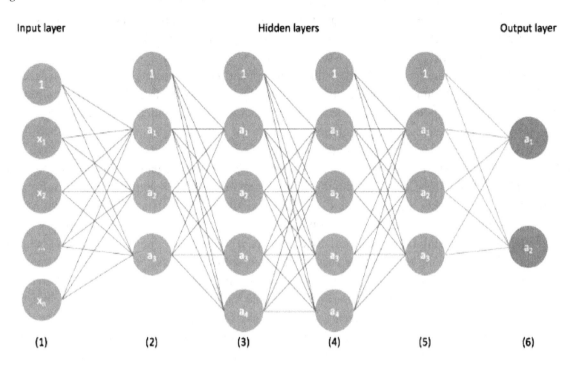

high-level features from data in an incremental manner. Hence removing the requirement of domain expertise extraction and hard core feature.

The methods used for problem solving of deep Learning and Machine Learning is another major dissimilarity between them. Machine learning techniques usually try to solve the problem statements by first breaking it down to various parts and finally merge their result whereas Deep Learning techniques solve the problem end to end. For example, for a multiple object detection problem, Machine Learning algorithms like Support Vector Machine (SVM), to specify all available objects to have the HOG as input to the learning algorithm, a bounding box object detection algorithm is first needed to recognize relevant objects. While techniques like Yolo of Deep Learning net it produces the present position and name of objects at output by acquring the image as input.

Deep Learning algorithm usually maximum time to learn than Machine learning algorithm due to huge number of parameters. Deep Learning algorithm Residual Network (ResNet) algorithm at least takes weeks to train completely from the start. Whereas, it only take less time comparatively maybe an hour or a second for traditional Machine Learning algorithms to train. In testing phase, the scenario is completely opposite.

It is true in all situation, lets us take k-nearest neighbors a type of machine learning algorithm, where the test time is directly proportional to the size of the data. The test time increases with the increase in the size of the data whereas Deep Learning algorithm at test time takes much less time to run. Some of the machine learning algorithm may have less testing times but it is not applicable on all machine learning algorithms.

Generally, the traditional Machine Learning algorithms requires complex feature engineering. Initially a through data analysis is performed on the dataset. Then for easier processing a dimensionality reduction might be performed. Finally, the best characteristic is chosen cautiously to address the machine learning algorithm. While in case of deep network a better performance can be attained by simply sending the data directly to the network. Thus it totally removes the whole process from large and challenging feature engineering stage.

Deep learning techniques can easily take a different application and domains than traditional Machine Learning algorithms. Within the same domain pre-trained deep networks for different applications are made functional to be applied by transfer learning. For example, in computer vision feature extraction front-end to object detection and segmentation networks are usually performed by pre-trained image classification networks. The application of the pre-trained networks as front-ends has made more comprehensible the full model training and assists in achieving higher performance in a shorter amount of time. In addition, using the same underlying techniques and ideas of deep learning in various domains are entirely interchangeable. For example, if one understands the fundamentals of deep learning idea and theory for the domain of speech recognition learning and apprehend how to apply deep networks to natural language processing is not that hard, since the underlying knowledge is identical. Whereas for traditional machine learning this isn't the case since for different domains and applications the underlying knowledge of traditional ML varies and often requires throughout specialized study within each individual area. Hence, to build high-performance Machine Language models both domain specific and application specific ML features engineering and techniques are needed.

An important factor of comparison between machine learning and deep learning is interpretability. It is the reason industry have doubts on using deep learning algorithm. For example, suppose deep learning is used to give automated scoring to essays. The performance it gives in scoring is near human performance and quite excellent. But an issue may arises. It is not known to why the scores are given. Mathematically activate nodes of a deep neural network can be find, but what these layers of neurons collectively can performed is not known and what there neurons were supposed to model. So the results interpretation has failed. As for machine learning algorithms like decision trees it provides a fresh rules as to what it chose why it chose, such that the interpretation of the reasoning behind the particular essay becomes easy. Because of this reason, in industry for interpretability algorithms like decision trees and linear/logistic regression are primarily used.

APPLICATIONS OF DEEP LEARNING

Artificial Intelligence

The main aim of deep leaning algorithms is to extraction of representations from the data automatically. Deep learning utilized the raw unsupervised data to automatically remove complex information. The traditional goal of the artificial intelligence is to master and examine and make decision like the human's brain and it is achieved by using these algorithm. The task related to these complex challenges has been the main focus of Deep Learning algorithms. Decision trees, support vector machines, and case-based reasoning are some of the algorithms used as different models on shallow learning architectures. But these models are not sufficient enough to extract useful information from complex structures and relationships in the input data. However, deep learning architectures has the capability to issue learning methods and relationships to the immediate neighbors and beyond in the data.

Deep learning is a breakthrough for artificial intelligence. It makes the machines work with no human intervention and supply with the complex data representation fit for AI tasks. It support the aim of AI that is to extract data representation directly from unsupervised data automatically without human intervention.

Data Mining

Deep learning algorithms as discuss it consist of multilayered, it provides a representation in its output by applying to each layer a nonlinear transformation on its input. The objective is to learn complex and abstract representation of the data in a hierarchical fashion by advancing the data through several transformation layers and for each layer the input of the next layer is provided with the output of the previous layer. The basic design of deep learning algorithms is building up the nonlinear transformation layers. The nonlinear transformations constructed gets more complex with the increases in the number of layers the data goes through in the deep architecture. The final representation received is a mostly non-linear function of the input data. For the transformation algorithms in the layers of the deep structure linear transformation like PCA cannot be apply because the arrangement of linear transformations produces another linear transformation.

Big Data Analytics

Deep Learning algorithms extract complex information from raw data through series of multilayered interconnected network, where in a higher-level more abstract and complicated representations are learnt based on the few abstract concepts and representations in the bottom level of the learning hierarchy. It is essentially appealing for learning from large quantity of unsupervised data, for Deep Learning and used for extracting significant patterns and representations from Big Data.

Deep Learning algorithms are perceived to execute better at isolating non-local and global correlations and patterns in the data, contrast to relatively shallow learning architectures. Important properties of the acquire abstract representations by Deep Learning include: (a) from the more complex and more abstract data representations acquired relatively simple linear models can perform effectively with the knowledge received, (b) various types of data such as image, textural, audio, etc., applications are enabled from increased automation of data representation extraction from unsupervised data and (c) relational and semantic knowledge can be obtained at the higher levels of abstraction and representation of the data.

Deep Learning algorithms and architectures are mostly appropriate to specify the issues regarding Volume and Variety of Big Data Analytics, taking each the features of Big Data into consideration i.e., Volume, Variety, Velocity, and Veracity. Algorithms with shallow learning hierarchies fail to explore and understand the higher complexities of data patterns but Deep Learning inherently exploits the availability of massive amounts of data, i.e. Volume in Big Data. It is probably suited for analyzing raw data represented in different formats or from different sources, i.e. Variety in Big Data, since Deep Learning associates with data abstraction and representations, and may minimize requirement for input from human experts to extract features from every fresh data type observed in Big Data. With various issues for most conventional data analysis techiques, Data Analytics provides important algorithms to resolved problems particularly for Big Data. For example, Deep Learning extracted representations can be considered as the knowledge source for information retrieval, decision-making, semantic indexing and other operations in Big Data Analytics. Simple linear modeling techniques can be observed when complex data is represented in higher forms of abstraction for Big Data Analytics.

Speech and Audio Recognition

The speech signals is highly feasible so for translating of spoken words into text i.e automatic speech recognition is still a difficult task. For example, people may have various different pronunciations of the same word, accents, dialects, and speak at different rates, in different styles. There exist various disturbances such as environmental noise, resonance, different microphones and recording devices results in additional variability. Gaussian mixture model (GMM) based hidden Markov models (HMMs) are used in conventional speech recognition systems. Typically, a combination of Gaussian are used by each HMM state to model a spectral representation of the sound wave. HMMs-based speech recognition systems are simple, feasible to utilized for computation and can be trained automatically. One of the limitation of Gaussian mixture models are statistically not sufficient enough for modeling data that lie on or near a non-linear manifold in the data space, whereas Neural networks make no particular speculation about feature statistical properties as it is done in HMMs. Neural networks due to its inability to model temporal dependencies are hardly successful for continuous recognition tasks regardless of their effectiveness in classifying short-time units such as isolated words and individual phones. For this reason neural networks is used as a pre-processing is an alternate approach e.g. dimensionality reduction, feature transformation for the HMM based recognition. Deep learning is a new area of Machine Learning often known as unsupervised feature learning or representation learning. Deep Learning is becoming a mainstream technology for speech recognition and has replaced Gaussian mixtures for speech recognition and feature coding.

Video and Image Processing

A video is a sequence of consecutive images or frames and if form a continuous and smooth impression to the human eye. Video analysis tries to understand the various image features and their behavior in time. The Harris-3D detector and the Cuboid detector are probably the most used space-time salient points detectors from a traditional classical computer vision point of view. They are highly problem dependent due to the fact that they rely on hand-crafted features. Therefore, recent research has made interest on learning low level and mid level features unsupervised or supervised learning. Following the huge success of deep learning and especially CNNs with images, the extension to the video domain is clear. However, there has been few work and innovating success on video analysis compared to the image counterparts. One of the clear is that due to the video's additional temporal dimension it increases the complexity.

The computer vision organization has been executing different video analysis for years and handled various problems such as event and video recovery, recognizing irregurarity, action detection, and activity understanding. Mainly human action identification has many applications in a variety of fields including customer attribute, intelligent video surveillance and analyzing shopping behavior. However, task cause of disarranged backgrounds, obstructions, and viewpoint differences perfect recognition of actions is a mostly challenging. The C3D project of Tran et al., is a very demonstrative example for action recognition which perform sports classification on the Sports-1M dataset.

The image domain has already seen great success and there has been work on semantic video analysis, in terms of activity understanding. It can be understood as features being combined as objects, whose appearances are kept track of in a period of time. This data is then processed e.g., into video descriptions with the use of RNNs. There are different favorable concepts emergences in different publications. Architectures that model local or global motion can generally be distinguish. Strictly speaking, a local motion only covers short periods of time and tries to draw an inference from them. The important information is probably encoded in the local details if the task is e.g., to differentiate between different arm gestures. However, an additional global approach is needed, if the task is to capture information about the plot of a movie, a longer time window. A fusion between both approaches can be found in other architectures. The method how the temporal dimension is included into the network is another major distinction. The usage of optical flow, RNNs, and connection via fully connected layers besides 3D convolution, have been proposed.

Biomedical Applications

Deep learning has started to impact biological research and biomedical applications as a result of its ability to integrate vast dataset and the medical domain has huge amount of data available. For instance, a large amount of genes across the whole human genome are available and in typical academic labs, a whole-genome gene expression profiling is still very expensive by considering a large number of conditions, such as genetic perturbations. Deep learning utilizing the big data in bioinformatics has been widely used in drug discovery, protein structure prediction, gene expression regulation, and so on. It is different from bioinformatics that applies informatics methods in biology and genetics, biomedical informatics is "the inter-disciplinary field that studies and pursues the effective uses of biomedical data, information, and knowledge for scientific inquiry, decision making and problem solving, driven by efforts to improve human health". Electronic Health Records (EHR) is a decision making typical kind of biomedical data that maintain information about an individual's health status and health care. Deep learning to biomedical informatics research applications mainly focus on how to leverage EHR data for clinical decision support. In EHR one of the important resources stored are medical images. Researchers following the traditional routine train deep learning models for feature representations and apply the pre-trained features to high-level tasks, such as classification, detection, and segmentation. Some of the few examples are for tumor architecture classification, learning the features of histopathology tumor images with a deep neural net could improve the classification accuracy use of convolutional neural networks (CNNs) identification of different types of pathologies in chest x-ray images could be improve even on non-medical image. For learning hierarchical representations of images for segmentation of tibial cartilage in low field knee MRI scans CNNs is used, a unified deep learning framework is developed for feature representation and automatic prostate MR segmentation. These studies show that researchers have attempted to apply deep learning models to clinical radiology research to assist physicians.

In genomic sequencing and gene expression analyses Deep learning has an important role. The National Institute of Health(NIH) Integrated Network-based Cellular Signatures (LINCS) program, Chen et al. presented D-GEX, a deep learning method with dropout as regularization, which significantly outperformed linear regression (LR) in terms of prediction accuracy on both microarray and RNA-seq data to infer the expression profiles of target genes based on approximately thousand landmark genes. To model structural binding preferences by using a multimodal DBN and applying the primary sequence as well as the secondary and tertiary structural profiles to speculated binding areas of RNA-binding proteins (RBPs).From the amino acid sequence composition found the 3D structure of proteins is determined. However, the computational prediction of 3D protein from the 1D sequence obtained is difficult. An inappropriate structures can lead to a wide range of diseases hence correct 3D structure of a protein is key to its function. Deep learning technologies have shown great capabilities in the area of protein structure prediction, which aims to predict the secondary structure of a protein.

CNNs are most commonly used in the biomedical image analysis domain due to their excellent capacity in analyzing spatial information. Whereas, RNN-based architectures are used for sequential data, and in dynamic biomedical signals and for sequencing data, but occasionally in static biomedical images. In present, since more attention are paid for the usage deep learning for biomedical information new applications of each schema may be uncovered in the future.

Self-Driving Car

The force that brings autonomous driving came to life is because of Deep learning. are fed to a system. To build a model a system is fed with a million sets of data, to train the machines for learning, and then testing the results in a safe environment. The Uber AI Labs at Pittsburg is not only working on making driverless cars but also integrating many other smart features such as food delivery options with the use of driverless cars. Handling unprecedented scenarios is the major concern for autonomous car developers. Safe driving with more and more exposure to millions of scenarios is ensure by regular cycle of testing and implementation typical to deep learning algorithms. To help create succinct and sophisticated models to navigate through traffic, signage, identify paths, pedestrian-only routes, and real-time elements like traffic volume and road blockages data from cameras, sensors, geo-mapping.

Natural Language Processing (NLP)

One of the hardest tasks for humans to learn is understanding the complexities associated with language whether it is expressions, semantics, syntax, tonal nuances, or even sarcasm. Humans develops appropriate responses and a personalized form of expression to every scenario with constant training since birth and exposure to various different social settings. By training machines to catch linguistic nuances and frame appropriate responses NLP is trying to achieve the same thing through Deep Learning. Using and testing of Document summarization widely in the Legal sphere making paraprofessionals outdated. All subsets of natural language processing are answering questions, classifying text, language modeling, twitter analysis, or sentiment analysis at a broader level these are the areas deep learning is gaining momentum. Previously, to build time-consuming complex models logistic regression or Support Vector Machine (SVM) were used but now distributed representations, recurrent and recursive neural networks, convolutional neural networks, reinforcement learning, and memory augmenting strategies are serving to achieve greater maturity in NLP.

Marketing

Deep Learning tool provides good support for customer service management. Improved speech recognition in call center management and call routine results a seamless experience for customers. Voice and speech analysis using Deep Learning allows a system to assess customer emotions and in automated email marketing and target identification. It is used to find new markets, target within markets, increase effectiveness of marketing, personalization by marketing person and also be used to enhance products or even create new products with AI and NN at its core. It is used by Business person to analyze how to make company money, save costs, increase margins, find new markets or opportunities. It also can be used to analyze massive quantities of data to find trends and predictors, and develop new models for any industry.

Deep learning and neural networks can be utilized to solved most of the problems. It can help find opportunities, solutions, and insights and can be applied to any kind of operation. Some of the other applications and fields that uses deep learning:

- In academics, refinement of existing models, creation of new models, algorithm development, and more intelligent neural networks are forthcoming and there's a wide open area of opportunities for academics to help progress in AI.
- In Computer Vision it is used for different applications like facial recognition and vehicle number plate identification and.
- It is used in ML and Al for various applications like search engines, both image and text search for Information retrieval.

CHALLENGES OF DEEP LEARNING

Deep Learning has various issues though it is an effective machine learning system. Deep Learning techniques needs a large training data sets to train the model and learn progressively using the data set. The large dataset ensures that the machine convey desired results. The artificial neural network requires a huge amount of data as the human brain needs a lot of experiences to learn and deduce information . A large parameters need to be tuned for the more robust abstraction required and more data are required for more parameters. For example, a speech recognition application would require huge amount of data from different demography, various different dialects and time scales. Researchers supply terabytes of data for the algorithm to learn a particular language. It is a time-consuming process and also requires a huge data processing capabilities. To some extent, the availability of huge amount of data to train on is the scope of solving a problem through Deep Learning.

The complexity of deep neural networks is very huge it can be in the range of millions whereas for a neural network through a number of parameters it is enough to expressed. For neural networks, the amount of data needed for training will be much higher compared to other ML algorithms. The reason behind it is that the task of a deep learning algorithm is two steps. It learns about the domain first and only then solve the problem. The algorithm starts from scratch when the training begins. Deep Learning also learns complex interdependencies between input and output features without representing relationship between a cause and an effect.

CONCLUSION

The chapter discuss about the Deep Learning, as it plays vital role in various applications. Nowadays, Deep Learning has become very effective machine learning approach as it has the ability of learning deep or repeatedly, and makes better use of datasets for feature extraction. The chapter gives the exposure to the concepts of Deep Learning and its algorithms, background of Deep Learning, tools and its applications in present days. The authors also discuss the limitations of Deep Learning. Practically deep learning helps in extracting complex data representation automatically from large volumes of unsupervised data. It is the base tool for data analytics which involves data analysis from a collection of very large raw data which are mostly un-categorized and unsupervised.

REFERENCES

Baldi, P., & Pollastri, G. (2004). The principled design of large-scale recursive neural network architectures-DAG-RNNs and the protein structure prediction problem. *Journal of Machine Learning Research, 4,* 575–602.

Bengio, X. (2010). *Glorot, Understanding the difficulty of training deep feedforward neuralnetworks.* AISTATS.

Chen, Li, Narayan, Subramanian, & Xie. (2016). Gene expression inference with deep learning. *Bioinfarmatics, 32,* 1832-1839.

Di Lena, P., Nagata, K., & Baldi, P. (2012). Deep architectures for protein contact map prediction. *Bioinformatics (Oxford, England), 28*(19), 2449–2457. doi:10.1093/bioinformatics/bts475 PMID:22847931

Eickholt, J., & Cheng, J. (2013). DNdisorder: Predicting protein disorder using boosting and deep networks. *BMC Bioinformatics, 14*(1), 88. doi:10.1186/1471-2105-14-88 PMID:23497251

Hebb, D. O. (1949). The organization of behavior. *Journal of Applied Behavior Analysis, 25,* 575-577.

Hopfield, J. J. (1982). Neural networks and physical systems with emergent collective computational abilities. *Proceedings of the National Academy of Sciences of the United States of America, 79*(8), 2554–2558. doi:10.1073/pnas.79.8.2554 PMID:6953413

Lena, P. D., Nagata, K., & Baldi, P. F. (2012). Deep spatio-temporal architectures and learning for protein structure prediction. *Advances in Neural Information Processing Systems,* 512–520.

Li, P., & Huang, H. (2016). *Clinical information extraction via convolutional neural network.* Academic Press.

Li, Y., & Shibuya, T. (2015). Malphite: a convolutional neural network and ensemble learning based protein secondary structure predictor *Proc IEEE Int Conf Bioinformatics Biomed,* 1260-1266.

Liao, S., Gao, Y., Oto, A., & Shen, D. (2013). Representation learning: A unified deep learning framework for automatic prostate MR segmentation. *Med Image Comput Comput Assist Interv, 16,* 254–261. PMID:24579148

Lin, Z., Lanchantin, J., & Qi, Y. (2016). MUST-CNN: A multilayer shift-and-stitch deep convolutional architecture for sequence-based protein structure prediction. *Proceedings of the AAAI Conference on Artificial Intelligence, 8.*

Lv, X., Guan, Y., Yang, J., & Wu, J. (2016). Clinical relation extraction with deep learning. *Int J Hybrid Inf Technol, 9,* 237–248.

Ma, X., & Hovy, E. (2016). *End-to-end sequence labeling via bi-directional lstm-cnns-crf.* arXiv preprint arXiv:1603.01354

McCulloch, W. S., & Pitts, W. (1943). A logical calculus of the ideas immanent in nervous activity. *The Bulletin of Mathematical Biophysics, 5*(4), 115–133. doi:10.1007/BF02478259

Pollastri, G., & Baldi, P. (2002). Prediction of contact maps by GIOHMMs and recurrent neural networks using lateral propagation from all four cardinal corners. *Bioinformatics (Oxford, England)*, 18. PMID:12169532

Pollastri, G., Przybylski, D., Rost, B., & Baldi, P. (2002). Improving the prediction of protein secondary structure in three and eight classes using recurrent neural networks and profiles. *Proteins*, *47*(2), 228–235. doi:10.1002/prot.10082 PMID:11933069

Rosenblatt, F. (1958). The perceptron: A probabilistic model for information storage and organization in the brain. *Psychological Review*, *65*(6), 386–408. doi:10.1037/h0042519 PMID:13602029

Santos, C., Guimaraes, V., Niterói, R. J., & de Janeiro, R. (2015) Boosting named entity recognition with neural character embeddings. *Proceedings of NEWS 2015 the Fifth Named Entities Workshop*. 10.18653/v1/W15-3904

Shin, Orton, Collins, Doran, & Leach. (n.d.). *Autoencoder in time-series analysis for unsupervised tissues characterisation in a large unlabelled medical image dataset*. Academic Press.

Sønderby, S.K., & Winther, O. (n.d.). *Protein secondary structure prediction with long short term memory networks*. arXiv1412.7828

Troyanskaya, O. G. (2014). Deep supervised and convolutional generative stochastic network for protein secondary structure prediction. *Proc 31st Int Conf Mach Learn*, *32*, 745–53.

Wang, S., Li, W., Liu, S., & Xu, J. (2016). RaptorX-Property: A web server for protein structure property prediction. *Nucleic Acids Research*, 44. PMID:27112573

Wang, S., Weng, S., Ma, J., & Tang, Q. (2015). DeepCNF-D: Predicting protein order/disorder regions by weighted deep convolutional neural fields. *International Journal of Molecular Sciences*, *16*(8), 17315–17330. doi:10.3390/ijms160817315 PMID:26230689

Widrow, B., & Michael, L. A. (1990). 30 years of adaptive neural networks: Perceptron, madaline, and backpropagation. *Proceedings of the IEEE*, *78*(9), 1415–1442. doi:10.1109/5.58323

Xu, Y., Mou, L., Li, G., Chen, Y., & Peng, H. (2015). Classifying relations via long short term memory networks along shortest dependency path. *Proceedings of Conference on Empirical Methods in Natural Language Processing*. 10.18653/v1/D15-1206

Chapter 18
Introduction to Machine Learning and Its Implementation Techniques

Arul Murugan R.
Sona College of Technology, India

Sathiyamoorthi V.
Sona College of Technology, India

ABSTRACT

Machine learning (ML) is one of the exciting sub-fields of artificial intelligence (AI). The term machine learning is generally stated as the ability to learn without being explicitly programmed. In recent years, machine learning has become one of the thrust areas of research across various business verticals. The technical advancements in the field of big data have provided the ability to gain access over large volumes of diversified data at ease. This massive amount of data can be processed at high speeds in a reasonable amount of time with the help of emerging hardware capabilities. Hence the machine learning algorithms have been the most effective at leveraging all of big data to provide near real-time solutions even for the complex business problems. This chapter aims in giving a solid introduction to various widely adopted machine learning techniques and its applications categorized into supervised, unsupervised, and reinforcement and will serve a simplified guide for the aspiring data and machine learning enthusiasts.

INTRODUCTION

In the past decade there has been a rapid paradigm shift in the field of computer science due to apex achievements in artificial intelligence .Machine learning which is a sub field of artificial intelligence has taken the capabilities of imparting the intelligence across various disciplines beyond the horizon. In 1959, Arthur Samuel defined machine learning as a "Field of study that gives computers the ability to learn without being explicitly programmed" (Samuel 1959).The machine learning algorithms works on the fact that the learning happens persistently from the training data or with the past experience and can enhance their performance by synthesizing the underlying relationships among data and the given

DOI: 10.4018/978-1-5225-9902-9.ch018

problem without any human intervention. In contrast with the optimization problems, the machine learning algorithms generally encompasses a well-defined function that can be optimized through learning. This optimization of the decision-making processes based on learning has led to rapid rise in employing automation in innumerable areas like Healthcare, Finance, Retail, E-governance etc. However, machine learning has been considered as the giant step forward in the AI revolution the development in neural networks has taken the AI to a completely new level. Deep learning which a subset of machine learning is incorporates neural networks as their building blocks have remarkable advances in natural language and image processing.

With big data landscape being able to store massive amount of data that is generated every day by various businesses and users the machine learning algorithms can harvest the exponentially growing data in deriving accurate predictions. The complexity raised in maintaining a large computational on primes infrastructure to ensure successful learning has been efficiently addressed through cloud computing by eliminating the need to maintain expensive computing hardware, software and dedicated space. The businesses have started adopting Machine Learning as a service (MLaaS) into their technology stacks since they offer machine learning as a part of their service, as the name suggests. The major attraction is that these services offer data modeling APIs, machine learning algorithms, data transformations and predictive analytics without having to install software or provision their own servers, just like any other cloud service. Moreover MLaas can help manage big data better by collecting huge amounts of data to get insights by correlating the data, crunching numbers and understanding patterns of the data to helps business take quick decisions. As data sources proliferate along with the computing power to process them, going straight to the data is one of the most straightforward ways to quickly gain insights and make predictions. The combination of these two mainstream technologies yields beneficial outcome for the organizations. Machine learning is heavily recommended for the problems that involve complex learning. However, it is essential to remember that Machine learning is not always an optimal solution to every type of problem. There are certain problems where robust solutions can be developed without using Machine-learning techniques.

This chapter will explore the end-to-end process of investigating data through a machine-learning lens from how to extract and identify useful features from the data; some of the most commonly used machine-learning algorithms, to identifying and evaluating the performance of the machine learning algorithms. Section 2 introduces steps for developing suitable machine learning model and various paradigms of machine learning techniques such as supervised, unsupervised and reinforcement learning. Section 3 discusses about various applications of machine learning in various fields and then concludes whole chapter with research insights.

DEVELOPING A MACHINE LEARNING MODEL

As discussed, machine Learning is the field where an agent is said to learn from the experience with respect to some class of tasks and the performance measure P. The task could be answering exams in a particular subject or it could be of diagnosing patients of a specific illness. As shown in the figure 1 given below, it is the subset of Artificial intelligence (AI) where it contains artificial neurons and reacts to the given stimuli whereas machine learning uses statistical techniques for knowledge discovery. Deep learning is the subset of machine learning where it uses artificial neural networks for learning process.

Figure 1. Taxonomy of Knowledge Discovery

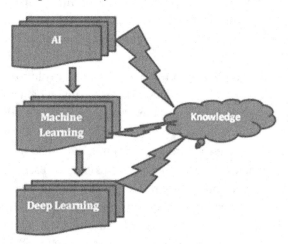

Further, machine learning can be categorized into supervised, unsupervised and reinforcement learning. In any kind of tasks, the machine learning involves three components. The first component is, defining the set of tasks on which learning will take place and second is setting up a performance measure P. Whether learning is happening or not, defining some kind of performance criteria P is mandatory in machine learning tasks. Consider an example of answering questions in an exam then the performance criterion would be the number of marks that you get. Similarly, consider an example of diagnosing patient with specific illness then the performance measure would be the number of patients who did not have adverse reaction to the given drugs. So, there exists different ways for defining various performance metrics depending on what you are looking for within a given domain. The last important component machine learning is experience. For an example, experience in the case of writing exams could be writing more

Figure 2. Categorization of Various Machine Learning Algorithms

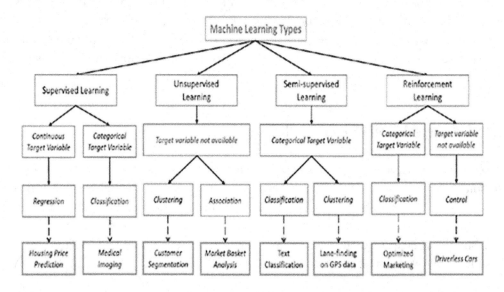

exams which means the better you write, the better you get or it could be the number of patient's in the case of diagnosing illnesses i.e. the more patients that you look at the better you become an expert in diagnosing illness. Hence, these are three components involved in learning; class of tasks, performance measure and well-defined experience. This kind of learning where you are learning to improve your performance based on experience is known as inductive learning. There are various machine-learning paradigms as shown in the figure 2.

The first one is supervised learning where one learns from an input to output map. For an example, it could be a description of the patient who comes to the clinic and the output would be whether the patient has a certain disease or not in the case of diagnosing patients. Similarly, take an example of writing the exam where the input could be some kind of equation then output would be the answer to the question or it could be a true or false question i.e. it will give you a description of the question then you have to state whether it is true or false as the output. So, the essential part of supervised learning is mapping from the given input to the required output. If the output that you are looking for happens to be a categorical output such as whether he has a disease or does not have a disease or whether the answer is true or false then the learning is called supervised learning. If the output happens to be a continuous value like how long will this product last before it fails right or what is the expected rainfall tomorrow then those kinds of problems would be called as regression problems. Thus, classification and regression are called classes of supervised learning process.

The second paradigm is known as unsupervised learning problems where input to output is not required. The main goal is not to produce an output in response to the given input indeed it tries to discover some patterns out of it. Therefore, in unsupervised learning there is no real desired output that we are looking for instead it looks for finding closely related patterns in the data. Clustering is one such task where it tries to find cohesive groups among the given input pattern. For an example, one might be looking at customers who comes to the shop and want to figure out if they are into different categories of customers like college students or IT professionals so on so forth. The other popular unsupervised learning paradigm is known as association rule mining or frequent pattern mining where one is interested in finding a frequent co-occurrence of items in the data that is given to them i.e. whenever A comes to the shop B also comes to the shop. Therefore, one can learn these kinds of relationship via associations between data.

The third form of learning which is called as reinforcement learning. It is neither supervised nor unsupervised in nature. In reinforcement learning you have an agent who is acting in an environment, you want to figure out what actions the agent must take at every step, and the action that the agent takes is based on the rewards or penalties that the agent gets in different states.

Apart from these three types of learning, one more learning is also possible which is called as semi-supervised learning. It is the combination of supervised and unsupervised learning i.e. you have some labeled training data and you also have a larger amount of unlabeled training data and you can try to come up with some learning out of them that can work even when the training data is limited features.

Irrespective of domain and the type of leaning, every task needs to have some kind of a performance measure. In classification, the performance measure would be classification error i.e. how many instances are misclassified to the total number of instances. Similarly, the prediction error is supposed to be a per-formance measure in regression i.e. if I said, it's going to rain like 23 millimeters and then it would ends up raining like 49 centimeters then this huge difference in actual and predicted value is called prediction error. In case of clustering, it is little hard to define performance measures as we do not know what is a good clustering algorithm and do not know how to measure the quality of clusters. Therefore, there exists different kinds of clustering measures and so one of the measures is a scatter or spread of the cluster that essentially tells you how to spread out the points that belong to a single group. Thus, good clustering algorithms should minimize intra-cluster distance and maximize inter-cluster distance. Association rule mining use variety of measures called support and confidence whereas reinforcement learning tries to minimize the cost to accrue while controlling the system. There are several challenges exists when trying to build a machine learning solution to the given problem and few of these are given below.

First issue is about how good is a model and type of performance measures used. Most of the measures discussed above were finds to be insufficient and there are other practical considerations that come into play such as user skills, experience etc. while selecting a model and measures. The second issue is of course presence of noisy and missing data. Presence of these kinds of data leads to an error in the predicted value. Suppose medical data is recorded as 225. so what does that mean it could be 225 days in which case it is a reasonable number it could be twenty two point five years again is a reasonable number or twenty two point five months is reasonable but if it is 225 years it's not a reasonable number so there's something wrong in the data. Finally, the biggest challenge is size of the dataset since algorithms perform well when data is large but not all. The following are the basic steps to be followed while developing any kind of machine-learning applications. They are,

A.   Formulating the Problem/ Define Your Machine Learning Problem
B.   Collecting Labeled Data/ Gathering Data
C.   Preparing that data/ Analyzing Your Data
D.   Feature selection/ Feature Processing
E.   Splitting the Data into Training and Evaluation Data
F.   Choosing a model:
G.   Training
H.   Evaluation
I.   Parameter Tuning
J.   Prediction/ Generating and Interpreting Predictions

The following subsections will give a detailed scheme for developing a suitable machine-learning model for the given problem.

Describing the Problem

The first step in developing a model is to clearly define and describe about the problem that need to be addressed with machine learning. In other words formulating the core of the problem will help in deciding what the model has to predict. The formulation can be done in different ways such as understanding problem through sentence description, deriving problem from the solved similar problems from the past. Choosing how to define the problem varies depending upon the use case or business need. It is very important to avoid over-complicating the problem and to frame the simplest solution as per the requirement. The motivation for solving the problem is to be evaluated against how the solution would benefit the business. Some of the common ways of describing the problems are

Similar Problems

After detailed discussions with stakeholders, identifying the pain-points the common and most afford-able strategy is to derive the problem with previous similar experiences. Other problems can inform details about the current problem by highlighting limitations in the problem such as time dimensions and conceptual drift and can point to algorithms, data transformations that could be adapted to spot check performance.

Informal Description

The other simplest way is to describe the problems informally by highlighting the basic spaces of the problem in a sentence for initial understanding about the possible solution. However, this step must be considered only for initial level problem formation substituted with any other approach for detailed problem formation.

Using Assumptions

Creating a list of assumptions about the problem such as domain specific information that will lead to a viable solution that can be tested against real data .It can also be useful to highlight areas of the problem specification that may need to be challenged, relaxed or tightened.

Formalism

The most structured approach is Tom Mitchell's machine learning formalism. A computer program is said to learn from experience *E* with respect to some class of tasks *T* and performance measure *P*, if its performance at tasks in *T*, as measured by *P*, improves with experience *E*.

Use this formalism to define the *T*, *P*, and *E* for your problem.

- **Task** (*T*):
- **Experience** (*E*):
- **Performance** (*P*):

Data Collection

This step is the most expensive and most time-consuming aspect of any machine learning project because the quality and quantity of data that you gather will directly determine the success of the project .The paper published by Yuji Roh et al. (2018) discuss in detail about high level research landscape of data collection for machine learning such as data acquisition, data labeling and improve the labeling of any existing data. The Machine learning problems require many data for better prediction. With the rapid adoption of standard IOT solution enormous volume of sensor data can be collected from the industries for the Machine learning problems, other sources like social media and third party data providers can provide enough data for better solution predictions. The labeled data is a group of samples that have been tagged with one or more labels. Labeling typically takes a set of unlabeled data and augments each piece of that unlabeled data with meaningful tags that are informative. In supervised Machine learning, the algorithm teaches itself to learn from the labeled examples. Labeled data typically takes a set of unlabeled data and augments each piece of that unlabeled data with some sort of meaningful "tag," "label," or "class" that is somehow informative or desirable to know. Often, data is not readily available in a labeled form. Collecting and preparing the variables and the target are often the most important steps in solving a problem. The example data should be representative of the data that is used by the model to make a prediction. Unsupervised learning is the opposite of supervised learning, where unlabeled data is used because a training set does not exist. Semi-supervised learning is aimed at integrating unlabeled and labeled data to build better and more accurate models.

Data Preparation

Data preparation is the process of combining, structuring and organizing data so it can be analyzed through machine learning applications. Good enough visualizations of the data will help in finding any relevant relationships between the different variables and to find any data imbalances present. The Collected data is spilt into two parts. The first part that is used in training the model will be the majority of the dataset and the second will be used for the evaluation of the trained model's performance.

The data might need a lot of cleaning and preprocessing before it is feed into the machine learning system. The process of cleaning involves various processes such as getting rid of errors & noise and removal of redundancies to avoid ambiguities that arise out of the data. The preprocessing involves renaming categorical values to numbers, rescaling (normalization), abstraction, and aggregation.

The appropriate usage of attributes can lead to unexpected improvements in model accuracy. Deriving new attributes from the training data in the modeling process can boost model performance. Similarly, removal of redundant or duplicate attributes can increase the performance. Transformations of training data can reduce the skewness of data as well as the prominence of outliers in the data. Outliers are extreme values that fall a long way outside of the other observations. The outliers in input data can skew and mislead the training process of machine learning algorithms resulting in longer training times, less accurate models and ultimately poorer results. Outliers can skew the summary distribution of attribute values in descriptive statistics like mean and standard deviation and in plots such as histograms and scatterplots, compressing the body of the data. Charu C. Aggarwal in his book "Outlier Analysis "suggests following methods such as,

- **Extreme Value Analysis**: Determine the statistical tails of the underlying distribution of the data. For example, statistical methods like the z-scores on univariate data.
- **Probabilistic and Statistical Models**: Determine unlikely instances from a probabilistic model of the data.
- **Linear Models**: Projection methods that model the data into lower dimensions using linear correlations.
- **Proximity-based Models**: Data instances that are isolated from the mass of the data as determined by cluster, density or nearest neighbor analysis.
- **Information Theoretic Models**: Outliers are detected as data instances that increase the complexity (minimum code length) of the dataset.
- **High-Dimensional Outlier Detection**: Methods that search subspaces for outliers give the breakdown of distance-based measures in higher dimensions (curse of dimensionality).

Feature Engineering and Feature Selection

Feature engineering is about creating new input features from your existing ones. Feature engineering is the process of transforming raw data into features that had better represent the underlying problem to the predictive models, resulting in improved model accuracy on unseen data. An iterative process interplays with data selection and model evaluation, repeatedly, until better prediction is achieved. The process of involves the following steps

- **Brainstorm features**: Examining the problem and data closely and by study feature engineering on other problems to extract similar patterns
- **Devise features**: Decide on using use automatic feature extraction or manual feature construction and mixtures of the two.
- **Select features**: Using different feature importance scorings and feature selection methods to prepare different view of the model.
- **Evaluate models**: Estimate model accuracy on unseen data using the chosen features.

Feature selection is the process of selecting a subset of relevant features (variables, predictors) for use in machine learning model construction. Feature selection is also called variable selection or attributes selection. The data features are used to train the machine learning models have a huge influence on the performance. Hence choosing irrelevant or partially relevant features can negatively influence the model performance. A feature selection algorithm can be seen as the combination of a search technique for proposing new feature subsets, along with an evaluation measure, which scores the different feature subsets. In real world, applications the models usually choke due to very high dimensionality of the data presented along with exponential increase in training time and risk of over fitting with increasing number of features. Identifying better features can provide the flexibility in even choosing a slightly wrong algorithm but ending up in getting good results. The three general classes of feature selection algorithms are filter methods, wrapper methods and embedded methods.

Filter Methods

Filter feature selection methods apply a statistical measure to assign a scoring to each feature. The features are ranked by the score and either selected to be kept or removed from the dataset. Some examples of filter methods include Pearson's Correlation, Linear discriminant analysis, ANOVA, Chi-Square.

Wrapper Methods

The Wrapper Methods generate considers the selection of a set of features as a search problem, where different combinations are prepared, evaluated and compared to other combinations. Some examples of wrapper methods include recursive feature elimination, forward feature selection, backward feature elimination.

Embedded Methods

Embedded methods combine the qualities' of filter and wrapper methods. Algorithms that have their own built-in feature selection methods implement it. Some examples of embedded methods include regularization algorithms (LASSO, Elastic Net and Ridge Regression), Memetic algorithm, and Random multinomial logit.

Splitting up the Data

The crux of any machine-learning model is to generalize beyond the instances used to train the model. In other words, a model should be judged on its ability to predict new, unseen data. Hence evaluating (testing) the model with the same data used for training will generally result in over fitting. It should be noted that the data should not either over fit or underfit. The common strategy is to take into consideration of all the available labeled data and split it into training and evaluation (testing) subsets. The Training set used to fit and tune the model while the test sets are put aside as unseen data to evaluate the model. The split is usually done with a ratio of 70-80 percent for training and 20-30 percent for evaluation based upon the nature of the problem and the model that is been adapted. One of the best practices that is adopted is to make this split before starting the training process in order to get reliable outcomes of the models performance. In addition, the test data should be kept aside until the model is trained good enough to handle unseen data. The performance comparison against the entire test dataset and training dataset will give a clear picture about the data over fits the model. Some of the common ways of splitting up the labeled data are

Sequentially Split

Sequential split is the simplest way to guarantee distinct training and evaluation data split. This method is extremely convenient if the data holds date or time range since it retains the order of the data records.

Random Split

Random split is the most commonly adopted approach since it is easy to implement. However, for models that are more complex the random selection will result high variance.

Cross-validation

Cross-validation is a method for getting a reliable estimate of model performance using only the training data. There are several ways to cross-validate the commonly used method is k-fold cross-validation. In k-fold cross-validation the data is split into k-equally sized folds, k models are trained and each fold is used as the holdout set where the model is trained on all remaining folds.

Choosing an Appropriate Model

Choosing a suitable Machine-learning model can be very confusing because it depends on a number of following factors

Nature of Problem

The nature of the problem can be a significant factor in deciding which Machine-learning model works best among the possible models.

Volume of the Training Set

The training set volume can be helpful in selecting the Machine-learning models based on bias and variance factors

Accuracy

Deciding on the level of accuracy can sometimes guide in determine the suitable model. If the project does not require most accurate results then approximate methods can be adopted. The approximation can provide better results due to reduces processing time and usually avoid overfitting.

Training Time

The training time heavily depends on the accuracy and the volume of the dataset. If the training time is limited then it can be a considerable factor in picking a model particularly when the data set is large.

Number of Parameters

The number of parameters can tamper the model behavior in various ways like error tolerance or number of iterations. Moreover, algorithms with large numbers parameters require the most trial and error to find a good combination.

Number of Features

The amount of features incorporated in the datasets can be very large compared to the number of data points. The huge amount of features can pull down the efficiency some learning models, making training time very long.

The following two-step process can guide in choosing the model

Step 1: Categorize the problem

The categorization of the problem can be by the input feed into the machine-learning model or the output expected out of the machine-learning model. If the input data is labeled then, supervised learning model can be a good choice in contrast if input data is unlabeled data then unsupervised learning model can be adopted. The reinforcement learning models can be used for optimizing the objective function interacting with the environment. Similarly, if the output of the model is a number then regression models suits best whereas the classification models can an ideal solution if the output of the model is a class. The clustering models will be most appropriate for models that output a set of input groups.

Step 2: Find the available algorithms

Once the categorization of the problem is completed, the apposite model can be pinpointed with ease. Some of the commonly used algorithms discussed below for better understanding. Classification of Machine Learning Algorithms as follow;

- Supervised learning
- Unsupervised learning
- Semi-supervised learning
- Reinforcement learning

Training the Model

The process of training works by finding a relationship between a label and its features. The training dataset is used to prepare a model, to train it. Each sample in the selected training data will define how each feature affects the label. This data is used to incrementally improve the model's ability to predict. This process then repeated and updated to fit the data as best as possible. A single iteration of this process is called one training step. In general, a trained model is not exposed to the test dataset during training and any predictions made on that dataset are designed to be indicative of the performance of the model. Model training is the crux of machine learning that is done by fitting a model to the data. In other words, training a model with existing data to fit the model parameters. Parameters are the key to machine learning models since they are the part of the model that is learned from historical training data. There are two types of parameters that are used in machine learning models.

Model Parameters

A model parameter is a configuration variable that is internal to the model and whose value can be estimated from data. These parameters are learnt during training by the classifier or other machine-learning model. The Model parameters provide the estimate of learning during the training. Example: The support vectors in a support vector machine.

Hyper Parameters

A model hyper parameter is a configuration that is external to the model and whose value cannot be estimated from data. Hyperactive parameters are usually fixed before the actual training process begins. Example: number of clusters in a k-means clustering. In essence, a hyperactive parameter is a parameter whose value is set before the learning process begins. While the values of other parameters are derived via training. Model hyper parameters, on the other hand, are common for similar models and cannot be learnt during training but are set beforehand. The key distinction is that model parameters can be learned directly from the training data while hyperactive parameters cannot. Other training parameters are

Learning Rate

The amount of change to the model during each step of this search process, or the step size, is called the "*learning rate*" and provides perhaps the most important hyperparameter to tune for your neural network in order to achieve good performance on your problem. The learning rate is an important parameter in Gradient descent.

Model Size

Model size depends on the product being used and what is included in the model. This can vary from implementation to implementation, type of problem (classification, regression), algorithm (SVM, neural net etc.), data type (image, text etc.), feature size etc. Large models have practical implications, such as requiring more RAM to hold the model while training and when generating predictions. We can reduce the model size by using regularization or by specifically restricting the model size by specifying the maximum size.

Regularization

Generalization refers to how well the concepts learned by a machine-learning model apply to specific examples not seen by the model when it was learning. Overfitting refers to a model that models the training data too well and performs poorly with unseen data. Regularization helps prevent models from overfitting training data examples by penalizing extreme weight values. Some of the common types of regularization techniques are L2 and L1 regularization, Dropout, Data augmentation and early stopping.

Figure 3 gives the most popular and widely used algorithms in machine learning based applications. The following subsections discusses in detail about these techniques.

Supervised Learning

As shown in the figure 4, it is categorized into two types.

- Classification
- Regression

Figure 3. Popular Machine Learning Algorithms

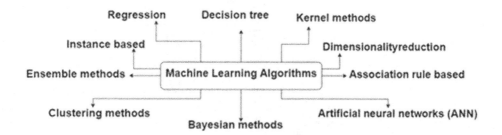

It is one of the machine learning techniques used for data analysis and used to construct the classification model. It is used to predict future trends analysis. It is also known as supervised learning.

Classification

The classification models used to predict categorical class labels whereas and prediction models predict continuous valued.

For example, classification model for bank is used to classify bank loan applications as either safe or risky one. A prediction model is used to predict the potential customers who will buy computer equipment given their income and occupation.

Some other examples of data analysis task of classification are given below.

- A bank loan officer wants to analyze the data in order to predict which loan applicant is risky or which are safe.
- A marketing manager at a company needs to analyze a customer with a given profile, who will buy a new computer as shown in figure 3.

In both the cases, a model is constructed to predict the categorical labels. These labels are risky or safe for loan application and yes or no for marketing data.

It is the task of building a model that describe and distinguish data class of an object. This is used to predict class label for an object where class label information is not available (Jiwei et al. 2006). It is an example of learning from samples. The first phase called model construction is also referred to as training phase, where a model is built based on the features present in the training data. This model is then used to predict class labels for the testing data, where class label information is not available. A test set is used to determine the accuracy of the model. Usually, the given data set is divided into training and test sets, with training set used to construct the model and test set used to validate it.

Figure 4. Supervised Learning Algorithms

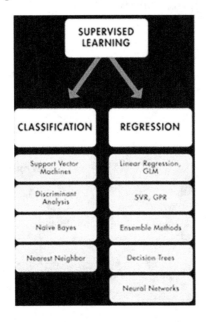

Decision trees are commonly used to represent classification models. A decision tree is similar to a flowchart like structure where every node represents a test on an attribute value and branches denote a test outcome and tree leaves represent actual classes. Other standard representation techniques include K-nearest neighbor, Bayesians classification algorithm, if-then rules and neural networks (Han et al. 2006). It is also known as supervised learning process. Effectiveness of prediction depends on training dataset used to train the model.

The classification is two steps process. They are,

Phase I: Building the Classifier(Training Phase)
Phase II: Using Classifier (Testing Phase)

Phase I: Training Phase

This is the first step in classification and in this step a classification algorithm is used to construct the classifier model shown in figure 6. The model is built from the training dataset which contain tuples called records with the associated class labels. Each tuple presents in the training dataset is called as category or class.

Consider that training dataset of a bank_loan schema contains value for the following attributes.

```
<Name, Age, Income, Loan_decision>
```

Once the decision tree was built, then it uses the IF-THEN rules on nodes present in the node to find the class label of a tuple in the testing dataset.

May be following six rules are derived from the above tree.

1.   If Age=young and Income=low then Loan_decision= risky
2.   If Age=Senior and Income=low then Loan_decision= risky
3.   If Age=Middle_Aged and Income=low then Loan_decision= risky
4.   If Age=young and Income=High then Loan_decision= Safe
5.   If Age=Middle_Aged and Income=High then Loan_decision=Safe
6.   If Age=Senior and Income=High then Loan_decision= Low_risky

Figure 5. Decision Tree

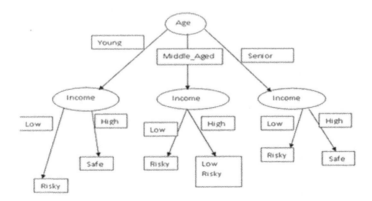

Figure 6. Training Process of Classification

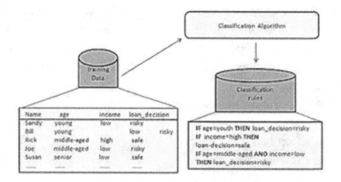

Figure 7. Testing Process of Classification

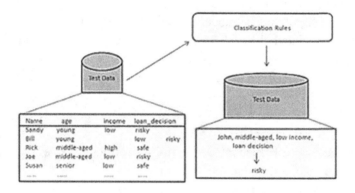

Figure 8. Sample Decision tree using ID3 Algorithm

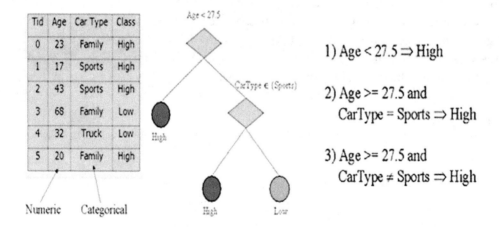

Once the model is built then next step is testing the classifier using some sample testing dataset which is shown above figure. Here, the testing dataset is used to measure the accuracy of classification model shown in figure 7. There are two different metrics such as precision and recall used for measuring accuracy of a classification model. Figure 8 gives the sample decision tree construction based on ID3 algorithm.

Phase II: Testing Phase

Regression

Prediction is an analytic process designed to explore data for consistent patterns or systematic relationships among variables and then to validate the findings by applying the detected patterns to new subsets of data. (Jiawei et al. 2006) uncover that the predictive data mining is the most common type of data mining and it has the most direct business applications.

The process of predictive data mining task consists of three stages:

- Data exploration
- Model building
- Deployment

Data Exploration usually starts with data preparation which may involve data cleaning, data transformations, selecting subsets of records and feature selection. Feature selection is one of the important operations in the exploration process. It is defined as reducing the numbers of variables to a manageable range if the datasets are with large number of variables performing some preliminary feature selection operations. Then, a simple choice of straightforward predictors for a regression model is used to elaborate exploratory analyses. The most widely used graphical and statistical method is exploratory data analysis. Model building and validation steps involve considering various models and choosing the best one based on their predictive performance. Deployment is the final step which involves selecting the best model in the previous step and applying it to a new data in order to generate predictions or estimates of the expected outcome.

Both classification and prediction are used for data analysis but there exists some issues dealing with preparing the data for data analysis. It involves the following activities,

- **Data Cleaning:** Data cleaning involves removing the noisy, incomplete and inconsistent data and methods for handling missing values of an attribute. The noisy data is removed by applying smoothing techniques such as binning and then problem of missing values is handled by replacing a missing value with most commonly occurring value for that attribute or replacing missing value by mean value of that attribute or replacing the missing value by global constant and so on.
- **Relevance Analysis:** Datasets may also have some irrelevant attributes and hence correlation analysis is performed to know whether any two given attributes are related or not. All irrelevant attributes are removed.
- **Normalization:** Normalization involves scaling all values for given attribute in order to make them fall within a small-specified range. Ex. Min_Max normalization.

Figure 9. Unsupervised Learning Categorization

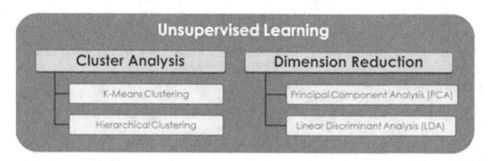

- **Generalization:** it is data generalization method where data at low levels are mapped to some higher level there by reducing the number of values of an attributes. For this purpose, we can use the concept hierarchies. Example is shown in figure 8.

Unsupervised Learning

Unsupervised learning is the process of grouping the objects based on the similarity present in it. It can be classified into three types as shown in the figure 9.

- Clustering
- Association Rule
- Dimensionality Reduction

Figure 10. Popular Algorithms in Unsupervised Learning

Clustering

Clustering is the process of grouping of objects into classes of similar objects based on some similarity measures between them (Sathiyamoorthi & Murali Baskaran 2011b). It is unsupervised leaning method. Each cluster can be represented as one group and while performing cluster analysis, first partition objects into groups based on the similarity between them and then assign the class labels to those groups. The main difference between clustering and classification is that, clustering is adaptable to changes and helps select useful features that distinguish objects into different groups. Some of the popular algorithms are shown in the figure 10.

All these algorithms will belong to any one of the following methods as shown in the figure 11.

- Partitioning Method
- Hierarchical Method
- Density-based Method
- Grid-Based Method
- Model-Based Method
- Constraint-based Method

Partitioning Method

Given a database of 'n' objects and then the partitioning algorithm groups the objects into 'k' partition where k ≤ n. Each group should have at least one object. Also, objects in the same group should satisfy the following criteria.

- Each group contains at least one object.
- Each object must belong to exactly one group.
- Objects within clusters are highly similar and objects present in the different clusters are highly dissimilar.
- Kmeans algorithm is the most popular algorithm in this category. It works as follows.

Figure 11. Types of Clustering

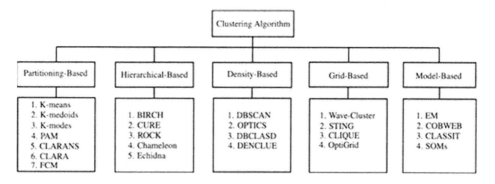

- For a given number of partitions (say K), the Kmeans partitioning will create an initial partitioning representing K clusters using some distance measure.
- Then it uses the iterative technique to improve the partitioning by moving objects from one group to other. The problem with Kmeans algorithm is that K (number of partition) value is fixed before executing cluster and it does not change.
- Another algorithm is Kmedoid which is an improvement of Kmeans algorithm and provides better performance.

Hierarchical Clustering

In this method, it tries to create a hierarchical decomposition of given objects into various groups. There are two approaches used here for decomposition.

- Agglomerative Approach
- Divisive Approach

In agglomerative approach, clustering starts with each object forming a different group. Then, it keeps on merging the objects that are close to one another into groups. It repeats it until all of the groups are merged into one or until the termination condition holds. It is also known as bottom-up approach.

In divisive approach, clustering starts with all the objects representing a single cluster as a root. In each iteration, it tries to split the cluster into smaller clusters having similar i.e. objects that are close to one another. It proceeds towards down and split the cluster until each object in one cluster or the termination condition holds. This method is inflexible means that once a merging or splitting is done then it cannot be undone. It is also known as top-down approach.

Density-Based Clustering

It is based on the concept of density i.e. each clusters should have minimum number of data objects within the cluster radius. Here a cluster is continuing growing as long as the density in the neighborhood exceeds some threshold.

Grid-Based Clustering

In this clustering, the objects together form a grid. The object space is quantized into finite number of cells that form a grid structure. The main advantage of this approach is that it produces the cluster faster and takes less processing time.

Model-Based Clustering

In this approach, a model is used to build each cluster and find the best fit of data object for a given clusters. This method locates the clusters by using the density function. It reflects spatial distribution of the data objects among the clusters. It determines the number of clusters based on statistics, taking outlier or noise into account. Also, it yields robust clustering algorithm.

Figure 12. Evaluating Association Rules

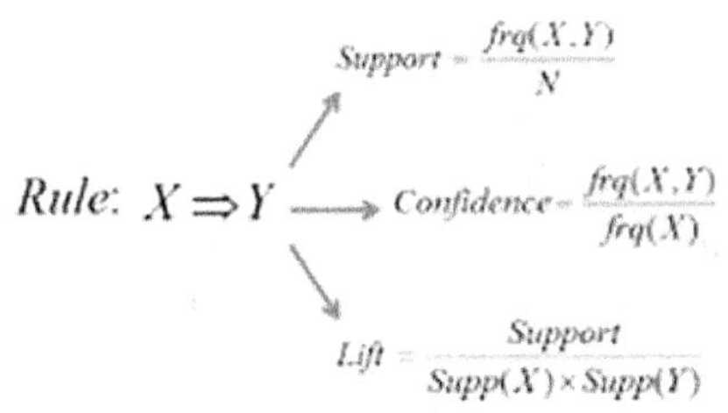

$$Rule: X \Rightarrow Y$$

$$Support = \frac{frq(X.Y)}{N}$$

$$Confidence = \frac{frq(X.Y)}{frq(X)}$$

$$Lift = \frac{Support}{Supp(X) \times Supp(Y)}$$

Constraint-Based Clustering

In this approach, the clustering is performed by incorporating the user and application constraints or requirements. Here, a constraint is the user expectation or the properties of desired clustering results. It is so interactive since constraints provide an interactive way of communication with the clustering process. Constraints can be specified by the user or by the application.

Association Rule Mining

As defined by (Han et al. 2006), an association rule identifies the collection of data attributes that are statistically related to one another. The association rule mining problem can be defined as follows: Given a database of related transactions, a minimal support and confidence value, find all association rules whose confidence and support are above the given threshold. In general, it produces a dependency rule that predicts an object based on the occurrences of other objects.

An association rule is of the form X->Y where X is called antecedent and Y is called consequent. There are two measures that assist in identification of frequent items and generate rules from it. One such measure is confidence which is the conditional probability of Y given X, Pr(Y|X), and the other is support which is the prior probability of X and Y, Pr(X and Y) (Jiawei et al 2006). It can be classified into either single dimensional association rule or multidimensional association rule based on number of predicates it contains (Jiawei et al. 2006). It can be extended to better fit in the application domains like genetic analysis and electronic commerce and so on. Aprior algorithm, FP growth algorithm and vertical data format are some of the standard algorithm used to identify the frequent items present in the large data set (Jiawei et al. 2006). Association rule mining metrics is shown in the figure 12.

Algorithms used for association rule mining are given below.

- Aprior algorithm
- FP-Growth
- Vertical Data format algorithm

Issues Related to Clustering

- **Scalability**: Clustering algorithms should be scalable and can handle large databases.

- **Ability to deal with different kinds of attributes: clustering a**lgorithms should be in such a way that it should be capable of handling different kinds of data such as numerical data, categorical, and binary data and so on.
- **Discovery of clusters with attribute shape**: Clustering algorithms should be capable of producing clusters of arbitrary shape using different measures.
- **High dimensionality:** Clustering algorithm should be designed in such way that it should be capable of handling both low as well as high dimensional data.
- **Ability to deal with noisy data**: Data sources may contain noisy, missing or erroneous data. So presence of these data may leads too poor quality clusters. Hence clustering algorithm should be designed in such way that it should handle noisy, missing and error data and produce high quality clusters.
- **Interpretability**: The results of clustering should be readable, interpretable, comprehensible into different form and useful to the end users

Dimensionality Reduction

In statistics, machine learning, and information theory, dimensionality reduction or dimension reduction is the process of reducing the number of random variables under consideration by obtaining a set of principal variables. It can be divided into feature selection and feature extraction.

Principal Component Analysis(PCA) is one of the most popular linear dimension reduction. Sometimes, it is used alone and sometimes as a starting solution for other dimension reduction methods. PCA is a projection based method which transforms the data by projecting it onto a set of orthogonal axes.

Evaluating the Model

Choosing the right evaluation metrics for the machine learning models will help the model to learn patterns that generalize well for unseen data instead of just memorizing the data. This will help in evaluating the model performs and to select better parameters. However using all the different metrics available will create chaos due to different outputs generated from these metrics. The different machine learning tasks have different performance metrics so the choice of metric completely depends on the type of model and the implementation plan of the model. There are different metrics for the tasks of classification, regression, ranking, clustering, topic modeling, etc.

Underfitting vs. Overfitting

Underfitting

A statistical model or a machine-learning algorithm is said to have underfitting when it cannot capture the underlying trend of the data in other words model does not fit the data well enough. Overfitting occurs if the model or algorithm shows low bias but high variance.

Figure 13. Model Evaluation based on Overfitting and Underfitting

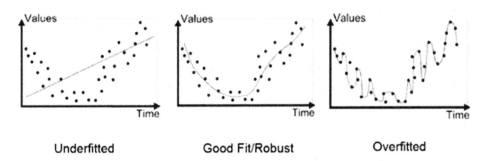

Underfitted   Good Fit/Robust   Overfitted

Overfitting

A statistical model is said to have overfitted, when trained with large data but the model cannot capture the underlying trend of the data. Underfitting occurs if the model or algorithm shows low variance but high bias. Both overfitting and underfitting lead to poor predictions on new data sets. Some of the commonly used metrics are Hold-Out Validation, Bootstrapping, Hyperparameter, Tuning, Classification Accuracy, Logarithmic Loss, Confusion Matrix, Area under Curve, F1 Score, Mean Absolute Error, and Mean Squared Error.

Tuning the Parameter

The machine models applied to vary according to the Machine learning models are parameterized so that their behavior can be tuned for a given problem. These models can have many parameters and finding the best combination of parameters can be treated as a search problem. However, this very term called parameter may appear unfamiliar to you if you are new to applied machine learning. Some of the parameters to tune when optimizing neural nets (NNs) include:

- learning rate
- momentum
- regularization
- dropout probability
- batch normalization

Once the evaluation is over, any further improvement in your training can be possible by tuning the parameters. A few parameters were implicitly assumed when the training was done. Another parameter included is the learning rate that defines how far the line is shifted during each step, based on the information from the previous training step. These values all play a role in the accuracy of the training model, and how long the training will take.

For models that are more complex, initial conditions play a significant role in the determination of the outcome of training. Differences can be seen depending on whether a model starts training with values initialized to zeroes versus some distribution of values, which then leads to the question of which distribution is to be used. Since there are many considerations at this phase of training, it is important that you define what makes a model good. These parameters are referred to as Hyper parameters. The adjustment or tuning of these parameters depends on the dataset, model, and the training process. Once you are done with these parameters and are satisfied, you can move on to the last step.

Once you have done evaluation, it is possible that you want to see if you can further improve your training in any way. We can do this by tuning our parameters. We implicitly assumed a few parameters when we did our training, and now is a good time to go back, test those assumptions, and try other values. One example is how many times we run through the training dataset during training. What I mean by that is we can "show" the model our full dataset multiple times, rather than just once. This can sometimes lead to higher accuracies. Another parameter is "*learning rate*". This defines how far we shift the line during each step, based on the information from the previous training step. These values all play a role in how accurate our model can become, and how long the training takes.

For more complex models, initial conditions can play a significant role in determining the outcome of training. Differences can be seen depending on whether a model starts off training with values initialized to zeroes versus some distribution of values, which leads to the question of which distribution to use. As you can see there are many considerations at this phase of training, and it's important that you define what makes a model "good enough", otherwise you might find yourself tweaking parameters for a very long time. These parameters are typically referred to as "*hyper parameters*". The adjustment, or tuning, of these hyperactive parameters, remains a bit of an art, and is more of an experimental process that heavily depends on the specifics of your dataset, model, and training process. Once you're happy with your training and hyper parameters, guided by the evaluation step, it's time to finally use your model to do something useful!

Generating Predictions

Machine learning is using data to answer questions. The final step is where the model can predict the outcome and establish a learning path. The predictions can be generated in two ways real-time predictions and batch predictions.

Real-time Predictions

The real-time predictions, when you want to obtain predictions at low latency. The real-time prediction API accepts a single input observation serialized as a JSON string, and synchronously returns the prediction and associated metadata as part of the API response. You can simultaneously invoke the API more than once to obtain synchronous predictions in parallel.

Batch Predictions

Use asynchronous predictions, or *batch predictions*, when you have a number of observations and would like to obtain predictions for the observations all at once. The process uses a data source as input, and outputs predictions into a .csv file stored in an S3 bucket of your choice. You need to wait until the batch prediction process completes before you can access the prediction results.

APPLICATIONS OF DATA MINING

Data mining applications include (Sathiyamoorthi, 2016),

- Market Basket Analysis and Management
  - Helps in determining customer purchase pattern i.e. what kind of consumer going to buy what kind of products.
  - Helps in finding the best products for different consumers. Here prediction is a data mining technique used to find the users interests based on available data.
  - Performs correlations analysis between product and sales.
  - Helps in finding clusters of consumers who share the same purchase characteristics such as user interests, regular habits, and monthly income and so on.
  - Is used in analyzing and determining customer purchasing pattern.
  - Provides multidimensional analysis on user data and support various summary reports.
- Corporate Analysis and Risk Management in Industries
  - It performs cash flow analysis and prediction, contingent claim analysis to evaluate assets.
  - Where it summarizes and compares the resource utilization i.e. how much resources are allocated and how much are currently available. it, helps in production planning and control system
  - Current trend analysis where it monitors competitors and predict future market directions.
- Fraud Detection or Outlier Detection
  - It is also known as outlier analysis which is used in the fields of credit card analysis and approval and telecommunication industry to detect fraudulent users.
  - In communication department, it helps in finding the destination of the fraud call, time duration of the fraud call, at what time the user made a call and the day or week of the calls and so on.
  - It helps in analyzing the patterns that are deviating from the normal behavior called outlier.
- Spatial and Time Series Data Analysis
  - For predicting stock market trends and bond analysis
  - Identifying areas that shares similar characteristics
- Image Retrieval and analysis
  - Image segmentation and classification
  - Face recognition and detection
- Web Mining
  - Web content mining
  - Web structure mining
  - Web log mining

REFERENCES

Aggarwal, C. C. (2016). *Outlier analysis*. New York: Springer.

Han, J., Kamber, M., & Pei, J. (2012). Data Preprocessing. *Data Mining,* 83-124. doi:10.1016/b978-0-12-381479-1.00003-4

Roh, Y., Heo, G., & Whang, S. E. (2018). *A survey on data collection for machine learning: a big data – AI integration perspective.* Retrieved from: https://arxiv.org/pdf/1811.03402.pdf

Samuel, A. L. (1959). Some Studies in Machine Learning Using the Game of Checkers. *IBM Journal of Research and Development, 44*(1), 210–229.

Sathiyamoorthi & Baskaran. (2011). Data pre-processing techniques for pre-fetching and caching of web data through proxy server. *International Journal of Computer Science and Network Security, 11*(1), 92–98.

Chapter 19
Introduction to the World of Artificial Intelligence

Shaila S. G.
Dayananda Sagar University, India

Vadivel A.
SRM University AP, India

Naksha V.
Dayananda Sagar University, India

ABSTRACT

Today, artificial intelligence is a technology which is completely advanced and very fast growingIt has a very strong and significant influence in our daily lives. Artificial intelligence have created tools and techniques linked to various disciplines such as computational logic, the theory of the probability, the theory of the decision, management science, linguistics and philosophy, etc. This technical area is a standout amongst the new fields in science and designing.

INTRODUCTION

Today, Artificial intelligence (AI) is a technology which is completely advanced and very fast growing, all this was possible only by the internet, which has a very strong and significant influence in our daily lives. Various trends on the search Artificial intelligence have created lot of tools and techniques linked to various disciplines such as formal logic, the theory of the probability, the theory of the decision, management science, linguistics and philosophy, etc. the most powerful method among the above is computation logic. The AI research was based on equipment and systems of a global range of orders that is, they include formal justification, hypothesis probability, and the idea of choice, the board science, phonetics and theory. However, the application of these disciplines in the Artificial intelligence has required the development of many improvements and extensions. Among the most powerful of these they are the methods of the computer logic. We call us Homo sapiens-wise humankind, in light of our insight and this knowledge is essential to us. For a huge number of years, we have attempted to

DOI: 10.4018/978-1-5225-9902-9.ch019

comprehend about our reasoning limit; for example as an insignificant bunch of issue would we be able to see, comprehend, predict and control a world exceptionally bigger and progressively confounded. The field of Artificial Intelligence or A I, never end: Artificial Intelligence looks for not exclusively to see, yet additionally assemble elements that are brilliant and wise.

The Artificial Intelligence is a standout amongst the most new fields in science and designing. The work started on the genuine piece 'after the second war world and a similar name was used in 1956. Together as science atomic, it is referred to that AI routinely as the "field in which I might want to be more" from researchers who had a place with others disciplines. A material science understudy could sensibly feel that all the smart thoughts as of now have taken by Galileo, Newton, Einstein and the rest. Computer based intelligence, then again, yet has its lead-ins for a few of Einstein and Edison work in full time. The Artificial insight at present covers an assortment of sub - fields, which are going from the general (learning and discernment) for the particular, such as playing chess, understanding scientific based theorem's, to compose verse, drive a vehicle in the busiest streets and analyze sicknesses. The Artificial intelligence is appropriate for any task which is intellectual; It certainly is a universal field. The chapter explains Artificial intelligence and intelligence computational in the form of agents. The chapter offers a clear view of different research strategies composed with algorithms. Also the chapter explains the role of the AI in different applications, trailed by certain limitations.

WHAT IS ARTIFICIAL INTELLIGENCE?

Today, Artificial intelligence (AI) is a multidisciplinary field whose target is to bring the automation environments without the intervention of intelligence human. The Intelligence functions of an artificial system are based on knowledge facts and rules that characterize the domain of the system. Applications in AI for several domains have built on the different tools and techniques disciplines such as formal logic, the theory of the probability, the theory of the decision, neuroscience, linguistics and philosophy.

The tool which is powerful amongst these is the technique similar to the computational logic. Therefore, AI concerns about forming informative systems, scientific data as It helps to analyze, to think, learn and to make decisions just as beings human who can accomplish all this at a greater speed. Artificial intelligence efforts to follow the process cognitive human such as to make decisions in order to reach a conclusion. Therefore, AI simulates the process of intelligence human in machines certain rules policies and perfect conclusions with correction.

Although it's easy for the human beings to apply the adjective intelligence in order to know the behavior from others human beings, with big abundant subjectivity .Several attempts to obtain accurate intelligent measures and the absence of a template process specific intellectual have been completed such as exercises in scale and correlation with others scores of the tests and based the performance "of the world in real". At this moment, we have to be content to learn about the goal and definition from targets obtained by searching artificial intelligence to level of judgment subjective human on which we operate normally in these problems. This is, in reality, the embodiment of the proposition of Turing to show the limit of the machine to test .From the initial step to the logical world in the logical field, the man-made reasoning is improved emphatically and had an effect in practically all fields of the cutting edge way of life. Consolidating hypothetical and connected qualities of the Computer science with the help of certain advances, for example, data innovation, hardware and correspondences, computerized reasoning has as of now an incredible capacity to discover the answers for all issues on this present reality, autonomous of multifaceted nature.

It is clear that artificial intelligence is a flexible open solution. It has a critical part in refining viability and the effectiveness of methodologies for answers for the issues dependent on the genuine world so as to make the existence progressively agreeable for the general population. Generally the numerical and intelligent philosophies in foundation have facilitated the adjustment of any critical thinking way to deal with the unsolved issues in various fields. Here, there is contrast between computerized reasoning and the other field of science in philosophical way, it's anything but an issue of improvement of astute frameworks. This component of multidisciplinary makes computerized reasoning as one of the hardest logical fields of things to come. In any case, uneasiness of news enhancements: i.e improvements have made individuals dependably to talk about on potential view that they are risky or dangerous for the presence of humankind or if nothing else their standard stable life on the Earth. Last however not the least, the field of man-made consciousness has found and model a tension is that has caused the presence of another field of hunt optional: Safety of Artificial Intelligence. The morals and arrangement producing Intelligence, Artificial Intelligence Safety centers around guarantee frameworks of wise protection, that I'm not unsafe for humankind and I'm viable in their extent of critical thinking.

The Birth of Artificial Intelligence

When we consider the literature associate, we can search problems related to safety. It responds with a bit concepts area of research such as Artificial / machine Ethics, future of Artificial Intelligence, Intelligence Artificial Compatible with human etc. all these six are the related concepts that are relative to the achievement of safe intelligent systems to ensure, to test, to discover approaches general rules, strategies and policies for to develop desired system oriented artificial intelligence. In detail, ethics of artificial intelligence works on the ethical confusions that occur in intelligent systems and some of the best ways to work on the dilemmas. It was basically anticipated for the literature.

Enthusiasm and Hope

Information Technology Progress Report 1963, 1960-1963 249 these data forms are superbly exploitable; that the route for this clarification is in the perception, experimentation, examination, demonstrating, approval of models, and so on.; and that advanced PCs, being general data handling gadgets, can be customized to play out any data forms are clarified. The researchers differ greatly in the time scale predicted for a program of this type. Two sub-targets in the investigation are distinguishable, although the thin line separating them is, in fact, confusing. A gathering of scientists are in charge of the recreation of the human data handling movement, with the look for explicit mental hypotheses of human subjective action. These analysts utilize the advanced PC as a methods for demonstrating. The PC is the device to practice the data preparing model, to create the remote and complex outcomes of the systems proposed in the model.

The intelligent behavior of the model is not evaluated alone; it has value only to the extent that it correctly predicts human behavior in the same tasks. A second gathering of analysts manages summoning the shrewd conduct of machines, paying little respect to whether the data forms utilized have anything to do with conceivable human psychological components. Here the conduct incited is, it could be said, an end in itself. These analysts are allowed to utilize the most dominant numerical, legitimate and informatics methods accessible in their ventures. It's a given that there has been a lot of cross-treatment of thoughts and loaning strategies between the two gatherings.

Figure 1. *The agents sense the environment through sensors and act on their environment through actuators. An AI agent can have mental properties such as knowledge, belief, intention, etc.*

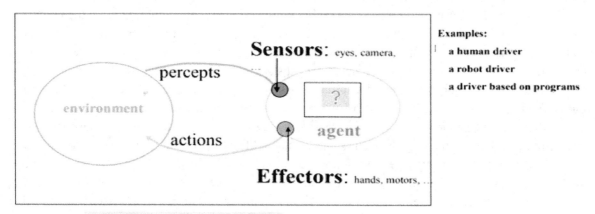

A generic agent diagram

ROLE OF AGENTS IN ARTIFICIAL INTELLIGENCE

An artificial intelligence system consists of rational agents in its environment. The role of AI depends on the study of rational agents. Rational agents can be anything like hardware or software components that perceives its condition through sensors and following up on that condition through effectors to make decisions. They perform an action with the best result after considering past and current perceptions.

To solve AI problems, Searching is the universal technique that is used. Some of the common Search Terminology includes:

1. **Problem Space**: This is the environment where search takes place. It may be set of states and set of operators that change these states.
2. **Problem Instance**: It includes: {Initial state + Goal state}.
3. **Problem Space Graph**: It is a graph that represents problem state. Here, states are represented by nodes and operators by edges.
4. **Depth of a Problem**: Length of a shortest path from Initial State to goal state.
5. **Space Complexity**: This relates to maximum number of nodes that are stored in memory.
6. **Time Complexity**: This relates to maximum number of nodes that are created.
7. **Admissibility**: This denotes the property of an algorithm to find the best optimal solution.
8. **Branching Factor**: Average number of child nodes in the problem space graph.

Examples of How Agents Work

Specialists end up after some time: they get tangible information after some time and perform activities over the long haul. The activity performed by an operator at a given minute is a component of his sources of info. First we think about the thought of time.

Let T be the set of time points. Suppose that T is totally ordered and has some metric that can be used to measure the temporal distance between two time points. Basically, we assume that T can be assigned to some subsets of the real line.

T is discreet if there is a finite number of a time point between two time points; For example, there is a point of time every hundredth of a second, or every day, or there may be time points whenever interesting events occur. T is dense if there is always another time point between two time points; this implies that there must be infinite points of time between any of the two points. Discreet time has the property that, for all times, except perhaps one last time, there is always a next time. Dense time does not have a "next time". Initially, suppose the weather is discrete and continues forever. So, for every moment there is a next time. We write t + 1 to be the next time after t; it does not mean that the time points are equidistant. Suppose that T has a starting point, which we arbitrarily call 0.

Suppose that P is the set of all possible precepts. A trace of perception, or a current of perception, is a function of T to P. Specifies what is observed at all times.

Suppose that C is the set of all commands. A command trace is a function from T to C. Specify the command for each time point.

Example 3.1

Consider a home dealer who controls the price of certain goods (for example, check online for special offers and price increases for toilet paper) and how much the family has in stock. You have to decide whether to buy more and how much to buy. The perceptions are the price and quantity in stock. The command is the number of units that the agent decides to buy (which is zero if the agent does not buy it). A specific perception tracks for each time point (for example, every day) the price at that time and the quantity existing at that time. Traces of perception are shown in Figure 1. A command track specifies how much the agent decides to purchase at any time. An example of a command track is shown in Figure 2.

The buying action actually depends on the command, but it can be different. For example, the agent could issue a command to purchase 12 rolls of toilet paper at a particular price. This does not mean that the agent actually purchases 12 rolls because there may be communication problems, the store may be running out of toilet paper or the price may change between the decision to buy and the actual purchase.

A trace of perception for an agent is, therefore, the sequence of all past, present and future precepts received from the controller. Hence the controller Is responsible for all the present past and the future commands. Commands can be a function of the chronology of precepts. This gives rise to the concept of transduction, a function that maps the traces of perception into traces of command.

Because all agents are in time, an agent cannot actually observe the complete traces of perception; at any time you've only experienced the part of the track so far. It is only possible to observe the trace value at the time t∈T when it reaches the time t. Your command can only depend on what you have experienced.

A transduction is causal if, for all times t, the command at time t depends only on the precepts up to and including t. The restriction of causality is necessary because the agents are in time; his command at time t cannot depend on the precepts after time t. A controller is an implementation of a causal transduction.

The agent history at time t is the agent's perception trace for all previous hours or time t and the agent's command trace before time t.

Thus, a causal transduction specifies a function of the agent history at time t to the command at time t. It can be seen as the most general specification of an agent.

Figure 2. The perceptions are the price and quantity in stock. A specific perception tracks for each time point. The price at that time and the quantity existing at that time

Figure 3. A command track specifies how much the agent decides to purchase at any time.

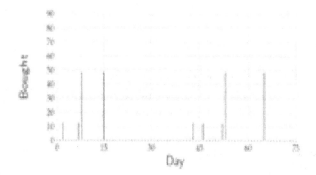

Example 2.2

Continuation of Example 2.1, a specific causal transduction, for each time, which quantity of the goods that the agent has to buy based on the price history, the chronology of which quantity of goods is in stock (including the current price and the price). (Quantity in stock) and the past history of purchase.

An example of causal transduction is as follows: buy four dozen rolls if there are fewer than five in stock and the price is less than 90% of the average price in the last 20 days; buy a dozen rolls if there are fewer than a dozen in stock; Otherwise, do not buy anyone.

Although a causal transduction is a function of an agent's history, it can not be implemented directly because an agent has no direct access to its entire history. He only has access to his current precepts and what he has remembered.

The state of belief of an agent at time t is all the information the agent has remembered from previous times. An agent has access only to his history which he codified in his state of faith. Therefore, the validation state encapsulates all the information on its history that the agent can use for current and future commands. At any time, an agent has access to his or her beliefs and perceptions.

The condition of conviction can contain any data, subject to the restrictions of memory and handling of the specialist. This is an extremely broad idea of conviction; now and again we utilize an increasingly explicit thought of conviction, for example, the operator's conviction about what is valid on the planet, the specialist's convictions about the elements of the earth, or the specialist's conviction about what he will do later on.

Different Cases of the Belief State

- The belief state for a specialist adhering to a fixed arrangement of directions might be a program counter that records its present position in the succession.
- The belief state may contain explicit certainties that are helpful, for instance, where the conveyance robot has left the bundle to recover the key or where it has effectively checked the key. It might be useful for the operator to recollect something that is sensibly steady and can't be watched right away.
- The condition of belief could code a model or a halfway model of the condition of the world. A specialist could keep up his best speculation about the present condition of the world or could have likelihood dispersion on the conceivable conditions of the world; to see.
- The condition of belief could be a portrayal of the elements of the world and the significance of its statutes, and the specialist could utilize his observation to figure out what is valid on the planet.
- The condition of belief could arrange what the operator needs, the objectives he still can't seem to accomplish, his convictions about the condition of the world and his expectations, or the means he plans to take to accomplish his objectives. These can be kept up when the specialist demonstrations and watches the world, for instance by taking out the objectives accomplished and supplanting aims when the most suitable advances are identified.

A controller must keep up the operator's conviction status and figure out which order to issue whenever. The data you have accessible when you ought to do this incorporates your present convictions and statutes.

A transition capacity of the conviction state for discrete time is a capacity remember: $S \times P \to S$

where S is the set of states of belief and P is the set of possible perceptions; $s(t + 1) = $ remember (st, pt) means that $st + 1$ is the state of belief that follows the state of belief st when observed pt.

A command function is a function

do: $S \times P \to C$

where S is the set of states of belief, P is the set of possible perceptions and C is the set of possible commands; $ct = $ do (st, pt) means that the controller issues the ct command when the belief state is st and when pt is observed.

The conviction state transition function and the command function specify a causal transduction for the agent. Note that a causal transduction is a function of the agent's history, to which the agent does not necessarily have access, but a command function is a function of the state of belief and perception of the agent to which he has access.

Example 3.3

To implement the causal transduction of Example 3.2, a controller must track the price history of the previous 20 days. By plotting the average (bird), you can update the media using

$$bird \leftarrow bird + (new-old) / \hspace{8cm} (20)$$

where new is the new price and the old is the oldest price mentioned. So you can discard the age. You must do something special during the first 20 days.

A simpler controller could, instead of remembering a mobile record to maintain the average, remember only the average and use the average as a substitute for the older element. The state of conviction can therefore contain a real number (bird). The state transition function to update the average could be

$$bird \leftarrow bird + (new-bird) / \hspace{8cm} (20)$$

This driver is much easier to implement and is not sensitive to what happened 20 units ago. This way of maintaining average estimates is the basis of time differences in learning through reinforcement.

In the event that there is a limited number of conceivable conviction expresses, the controller is known as a finite state or finite state machine. A considered portrayal is one in which conviction states, recognitions, or directions are characterized by attributes. On the off chance that there is a limited number of qualities and each element can have just a limited number of conceivable qualities, the controller is a limited state machine, figured. The more extravagant controllers can be made utilizing a boundless number of qualities or a boundless number of capacities. A controller that has numerous states can ascertain everything that can be determined from a Turing machine.

ARTIFICIAL INTELLIGENCE BACKGROUND

In 1950, Alan Turing, called the AI's father, proposed an approach related to machines and computer intelligence. The author developed the game of imitation between two subjects and the game is called the Turing test, which involved the written communication between the subjects without detecting the other subject. The test continued with the first topic in the identification of the second subject as human or machine with the help of written communication. When the first subject fails to distinguish perfectly or chooses the identification incorrectly, Turing states that the Turing test shows that even the machines can think. In 1980, John Searle proposed the China Room experiment, which uses the analogy of a native English speaker without knowledge of Chinese speaking, writing or reading and is assigned a set of rules in English. These rules correlate the Chinese voice and the release also in Chinese, although the translator was English. In this way, various research topics have been opened in machine learning and natural language processing.

History of Artificial Intelligence

Chess has for quite some time been viewed as a round of mind, and numerous PC pioneers thought about that a chess machine would be the sign of genuine computerized reasoning. While the Turing test is a noteworthy test to decide the insight of the machine, chess is likewise a decent objective, which luckily has been "illuminated" by AI specialists; delivering programs that can match, if worse, the best chess players on the planet. Be that as it may, even the best gaming machines don't comprehend the ideas of the diversion and are basically founded on beast drive ways to deal with play. The causes of automated chess and knowledge have dependably been associated; The capacity to play chess has even been utilized as a substantial thing to ask amid a turning test in the first Turing report. Numerous individuals envisioned that one day machines would almost certainly play chess, however it was Claude Shannon who initially composed an article about building up a chess program. Shannon's paper depicted two ways to deal with PC chess: Type A projects, which utilized unadulterated beast drive, inspected a great many developments and utilized a base most extreme pursuit calculation.

On the other hand, type B, programs that would utilize specific heuristics and vital computerized reasoning, analyzing just some key applicant developments. At first, type B (vital) programs were supported over sort An (animal power) since PCs were constrained amid the '50s and' 60s. Nonetheless, in 1973, engineers of the "Chess" program arrangement (which won the ACM PC chess title 1970-72) changed their program to Type-A. The new program, called "Chess 4.0", has won various future PC diversion titles from ACM. * WikiChess +. This change was a grievous hit to those wanting to locate a superior comprehension of chess through the advancement of sort B programs. There were a few essential elements to move far from the conceivably more astute structure of a sort B program for an idiotic person. The first was effortlessness. The speed of a machine has an immediate relationship with the limit of a sort A program, accordingly, since the propensity is that the machines turned out to be quicker consistently, it is less demanding to compose a program of sort A solid and "improve" a program to give more power parallelism or specific equipment. While a sort B program should show new guidelines and fundamental procedures, paying little respect to the measure of new vitality that is given. Moreover, there was the idea of consistency.

The creators of 'Chess' remarked on the pressure they encountered amid the competitions in which their sort B program would carry on unpredictably as per the diverse tenets of the hard code. Up to this point, type A (savage power) programs are the most vigorous applications accessible. There are savvy type B programs, yet it's simply too simple to even consider writing type A projects and get an outstanding diversion just with the speed of your PC. Type B ace dimension programs have not yet appeared, as further research is expected to comprehend and extract chess into (much more) tenets and heuristics. Execution Perhaps the best known sort A program is IBM Deep Blue. In 1997, Deep Blue tested and crushed world chess champion Gary Kasparov. The triumph of the 3.5/2.5 match was not a definitive triumph, however with the machines that expansion consistently.

Scientists Who Involved in Bringing Up AI

The scientist David G Stoke enlightened this concept of computational power predicted with: "Today, few of us feel profoundly threatened by a computer that surpasses a world chess champion, just as we do not do it on a motorcycle that defeats an Olympic Racer. ". Because Deep Blue is a type A program. Deep Blue has assessed around 200 million positions for every second and a normal hunt profundity of 8-12 levels. (Up to 40 under specific conditions). [CambleHsuHoane02] It is by and large considered 50 developments at different profundities. In the event that Deep Blue was a sort B program, maybe the triumph would have been all the more fascinating from the perspective of the machine's insight. Another fascinating ramification of Deep Blue's triumph was IBM's monetary benefit from the amusement. A few assessments property the estimation of Deep Blue's triumph to $ 500 million in free publicizing for IBM's Super PCs. Additionally, the fortuitous event caused an expansion in the cost of the IBM offers of $ 10 to a verifiable greatest then [ScaefferPlatt97]. Go as the following wilderness Computer chess keeps on creating to make all the more dominant machines with less particular equipment, in any case, there is little enthusiasm for sort B programs that endeavor to catch the crude information of human chess players.

With chess "understood" for some currently focusing on different amusements where PCs still need to test people, one diversion specifically emerges as the following wilderness of AI examine dependent on the amusement: the old Go to the Asian diversion. What sets go separated is the failure to relate the intensity of computation set up. While chess has a fanning variable of around 40, typically Go has a stretching component of 200. (The substantial moves a player can set aside a few minutes). [Muller00] what's more, there is no unmistakable condition for triumph. At the point when chess calculations look for a checkmate, the assurance of the last amusement in Go requires the assentation of the two players, just as a comprehensive inquiry to check whether the situation of the chessboard is terminal. Regardless of long stretches of research, there is still no reasonable calculation to decide whether a gathering of stones is alive or dead (a major idea of the diversion). Indeed, even with a $ 1,000,000 prize offered to any individual who can make a program equipped for vanquishing a solid Go player (the Ing prize), even the best projects are not ready to crush a powerless player at the dimension of club.

REPRESENTATION OF KNOWLEDGE IN ARTIFICIAL INTELLIGENCE

The representation of knowledge concerns how knowledge and facts of the world can be represented and what kind of reasoning can be done with that knowledge. Artificial intelligence is mainly concerned with the study of understanding, design and implementation of forms associated with the representation of knowledge in computers. Knowledge represents an individual's understanding of a subject. In every intelligent system, the representation of knowledge is a necessary technique for the codification of knowledge. The portrayal of information fuses the consequences of human brain science to take care of issues and speak to learning to structure formalisms that will make the frameworks planned and built increasingly mind boggling. The portrayal of information and thinking additionally fuses the aftereffects of rationale to robotize different kinds of thinking, for example, the use of standards and connections of sets and subsets. Although the vast majority of the ventures talked about so far have the portrayal of learning as a vital segment, the activities referenced in this segment are straightforwardly identified with it.

Representation of Visual Knowledge

We are examining strategies to speak to visual information in an arrangement of portrayal of learning coordinated with customary and propositional applied information. Visual learning is the information of how to envision objects, object characteristics and connections between items on a realistic terminal screen. At the most essential dimension, the visual type of an item is a Lisp work that draws the article on the screen when it is assessed. Be that as it may, visual learning can likewise be dispersed among the hubs in conventional pecking orders: the information of how to imagine a specific sledge can be remembered at the dimension of the mallet class; the learning of how to demonstrate an individual can be appropriated among the bunches for heads, arms, hands, and so on. The places of the gatherings are in respect to their totality. Item qualities can be viewed as practical that graphically change capacities. We utilize visual learning in the advancement of a flexible, master computerized circuit support framework (see Modeling gadgets for an adaptable upkeep framework depicted above) executed in the SNePS semantic system preparing framework (Shapiro, 1979). The cooperation with the client is brought out through realistic pictures, asking for and acquiring information, demonstrating dynamic hints of thinking and appearing last ends. This examination is an undertaking of the SNePS look into gathering and is supported by RADC and the Aeronautics Scientific Research Office through North-Eastern AIC and the South-Eastern Electrical Engineering Education Center.

Layout of learning association for mental analysis The intellectual displaying of the experience shown by a specialist amid an indicative session offers us the chance to address a portion of the focal issues of research in the field of AI. In this undertaking, we are building up an online automated associate that can enable a specialist to perform mental judgments. Specifically, we are contemplating,

1. The upsides of a PC partner on a total PC indicative framework,
2. The parameters of an area that demonstrate its reasonableness to acquire support from an IT associate.
3. An utilitarian determination for a PC right hand and
4. The limitations this determination forces on the most proficient method to compose the information base around handling offices.

As of now, the venture centers around the usage of the arrangement of conclusion, analysis and mental comprehension of common encounters (DUNE), had practical experience in emotional and on edge issue. Ridge depends on the possibility that a viable finding in a confused space includes the parallel pursuit of various speculations. Every theory is actualized as a gathering of processors and the framework gives expound self-assessment plans of the correspondence and the processor.

Concentrated semantics for propositional semantic systems A semantic system is a portrayal in which every idea (counting the relations between ideas) is spoken to by a particular hub, and the hubs are associated with one another by a little arrangement of curves. The SNePS semantic system preparing framework contains a derivation bundle that underpins forward, in reverse and bidirectional deduction utilizing the tenets spoke to in the SNePS arrange. It likewise gives intuitive illustrations to information and clarification, picture examination and common language interfaces. SNePS is one of only a handful couple of semantic frameworks of system handling that is totally serious as in hubs speak to just intentional elements. The past endeavors by certain specialists to give a semantic translation to the framework depended on the "semi-purposeful formalism of conceivable worldwide semantics." In this task, we give a semantic understanding utilizing a completely concentrated hypothesis dependent on the philosophical speculations of Alexius Meinong. This examination is a venture of the SNePS inquire about gathering and is bolstered by a give from the National Science Foundation.

AI ALGORITHMS

Reasoning of projects include reasoning of common sense, intuitive reasoning and belief revision.

Problem Solving

On the off chance that we need to naturally tackle an issue we need a portrayal of the issue calculations that utilization some methodology to determine the issue sketched out in that representation.

Problem Representation

1. General way to representation:
   a. **State Space**: A retardant is split into a collection of resolution steps from the initial state to the goal state
   b. **Reduction to Sub-Problems**: A retardant is organized into a hierarchy of sub-problems
2. Specific way of representation:
3. Game resolution
4. Constraints satisfaction

States

An issue is characterized by its components and their relations .In every moment of the goals of an issue, those components have explicit descriptors, so How to choose them? what's more, relations. A state may be a illustration of these components in a very given moment.

Two special states are defined:

- Initial state (starting point)
- Final state (goal state)

State Modification Successor Function

A successor perform is required to move between entirely unexpected states. A successor work is a portrayal of conceivable activities, a lot of administrators. It is transformations perform on a state representation, which converts it into another state. The successor work characterizes a connection of openness among states. Representation of the successor function:

- Conditions of applicability
- Transformation function

State Space

The state house is that the arrangement of all states receptive from the underlying state. It shapes a chart (or guide) inside which the hubs square measure states and in this way the circular segments between hubs square measure activities.

A way inside the state house might be a grouping of states associated by a succession of activities. The arrangement of the issue is a component of the guide molded by the state house

Problem Solution

An answer inside the state district could be a path from the hidden state to a target state or, all over, just a goal state. Way/game plan cost: work that doles out a numeric cost to each way, the cost of applying the directors to the states Solution quality is evaluated by the way cost limit, and a perfect course of action has the least path cost among all arrangements. Arrangements: any, a perfect one, all. Cost is vital retaliation on the issue and moreover the sort of answer required.

Problem Description

Components used for the description of a specific problem.

1. State space (explicitly or implicitly defined),
2. Initial state
3. Goal state (or the conditions it has to fulfill)
4. Available actions (operators to change state)
5. Restrictions (e.g., cost)
6. Elements of the domain which are relevant to the problem (e.g., incomplete knowledge of the starting point)

Type of Solution

1. Sequence of operators or goal state
2. Any, an optimal one (cost definition needed).

Example: 8- Puzzle

1. **State Space:** Configuration of the eight tiles on the board.
2. **Initial State:** Any configuration.
3. **Goal State:** Tiles in a specific order.
4. **Operators or Actions:** "Blank moves".
5. **Condition:** The move is within the board.
6. **Transformation:** Blank moves Left, Right, Up, or Down.
7. **Solution:** Optimal sequence of operators.

Example: NQUEENS(N = 4, N = 8)
Example: *n*queens(n = 4, n = 8)
State Space: configurations from 0 to n queens on the board with only one queen per row and column

1. **Initial State:** Configuration without queens on the board
2. **Goal State**: Configuration with n queens such that no queen attacks any other
3. **Operators or Actions**: Place a queen on the board
4. **Condition**: The new queen is not attacked by any other already placed
5. **Transformation**: Place a new queen in a particular square of the board

6. **Solution**: One solution (cost is not considered)

Structure of Space

The structure of the space is represented by using the Data structures:

- **Trees**: Only one path to a given node
- **Graphs**: Several paths to a given node

Operators: directed arcs between nodes. The search process explores the state space.In the worst case all possible paths between the initial state and the goal state are explored.

Search as Goal Satisfaction

In Satisfying a goal the Agent knows what the goal is and hence cannot evaluate intermediate solutions (uninformed).

The environment is:

1. Static
2. Observable
3. Deterministic

Example: Holiday in Romania

On vacation in Romania; presently in Arad Flight leaves tomorrow from Bucharest at 13:00
Let's configure this to be an AI problem

Tree Search Algorithms

Basic idea of Simulated exploration of state space is by generating successors of already explored states (Figure 4).

Algorithm General Search

```
Open_states.insert (Initial_state)
Current= Open_states.first()
  while not is_final?(Current) and not Open_states.empty?() do
    Open_states.delete_first()
    Closed_states.insert(Current)
    Successors= generate_successors(Current)
    Successors= process_repeated(Successors, Closed_states, Open_states)
    Open_states.insert(Successors)
    Current= Open_states.first()
```

Figure 4. Basic idea:-offline, stimulated exploration of state space by generating successors of already explored states.

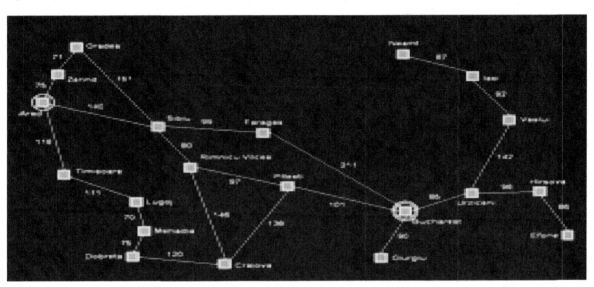

```
     eWhile
eAlgorithm
STATE
(Representation of) a physical configuration.
Node.
```

Data structure constituting part of a search tree. Includes parent, children, depth, path cost g(x). States do not have parents, children, depth, or path cost.

Search Strategies

A strategy is outlined by choosing the order of node growth. Strategies are evaluated along the following dimensions:

1. **Completeness**: Does it always find a solution if one exists?
2. **Time Complexity**: Number of nodes generated/expanded
3. **Space Complexity**: Maximum nodes in memory
4. **Optimality**: Does it always find a least-cost solution?
5. Time and area complexness square measure measured in terms of:
   a. **b**: Maximum branching factor of the search tree (may be infinite)
   b. **d**: Depth of the least-cost solution
   c. **m**: Maximum depth of the state space (may be infinite)

Figure 5. Breadth-first search treats the frontier as a queue. It always selects one of the earliest elements added to the frontier.

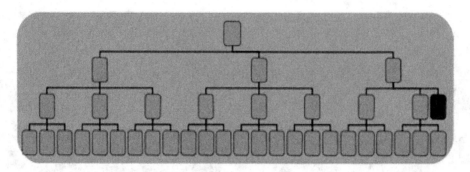

Uniformed Search Strategies

Uninformed strategies use only the information available in the problem definition such as

- Breadth-first search
- Uniform-cost search
- Depth-first search
- Depth-limited search
- Iterative deepening search.

Space Cost of BFS

Because you must be able to generate the path upon finding the goal state, all visited nodes must be stored in:

- $O(b^{d+1})$
- Complete?:-Yes (if b (max branch factor) is finite)
- Time?:-1 + b + b^2 + ... + b^d + b(b^d-1) = $O(b^{d+1})$, i.e., exponential in d
- Space?:-$O(b^{d+1})$ (keeps every node in memory)
- Optimal?:-Only if cost = 1 per step, otherwise not optimal in general
- Space is the big problem; it can easily generate nodes at 10 MB/s, so 24 hrs = 860GB!

Depth First Search

- Complete?:**-**No: fails in infinite-depth spaces, spaces with loops.
- Can be modified to avoid repeated states along path complete in finite spaces
- Time?:-$O(b^m)$: terrible if *m* is much larger than *d*, but if solutions are dense, may be much faster than breadth-first
- Space?:-$O(bm)$, *i.e., linear space!*
- Optimal:-No

Depth Limited Search

It is depth-first search with an imposed limit on the depth of exploration, to guarantee that the algorithm ends

Breadth-First

If the repeated state is in the structure of closed or open nodes, the actual path has equal or greater depth than the repeated state and can be forgotten.

Depth-First

If the repeated state is in the structure of closed nodes, the actual path is kept if its depth is less than the repeated state.

If the repeated state is in the structure of open nodes, the actual path has always greater depth than the repeated state and can be forgotten.

Iterative Deepening Search

The calculation comprises of iterative, profundity first pursuits, with a greatest profundity that increments at every emphasis. Most extreme profundity toward the start is 1. Behavior similar to BFS, but without the spatial complexity. Only the actual path is kept in memory; nodes are regenerated at each iteration.

DFS problems related to infinite branches are avoided. To guarantee that the algorithm ends if there is no solution, a general maximum depth of exploration can be defined.

Summary

All uninformed searching techniques are more alike than different.

- Breadth First Search initially has space issues, and potentially optimality issues.
- Depth First Search initially has time and optimality issues, and perhaps culmination issues.
- Depth limited search constrained hunt has optimality and fulfillment issues.
- Iterative developing is the best ignorant hunt we have investigated.

Uniformed Vs. Ununiformed

- Blind (or uninformed) search algorithms:
  ○ Solution cost is not taken into account.
  ○ Heuristic (or informed) search algorithms:
  ○ A solution cost estimation is used to guide the search.
  ○ The optimal solution, or even a solution, are not guaranteed.

Figure 6. BFS is a navigating algorithm where you should begin traversal from a chose hub (source or beginning hub) and navigate the chart layer savvy along these lines investigating the neighbor (hubs which are straightforwardly associated with source hub). Then move towards the following dimension neighbor hubs.

Figure 7. DFS is algorithm for looking through tree or chart information structures. The calculation begins at the root hub (choosing some discretionary hub as the root hub on account of a chart) and investigates beyond what many would consider possible along each branch before backtracking.

Figure 8. Iterative deepening search or all the more explicitly iterative deepening search .iterative deepening search is a state space/chart search technique in which a profundity constrained variant of profundity first pursuit is run over and over with expanding profundity limits until the objective is found.

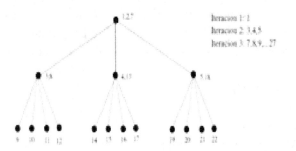

APPLICATIONS OF AI

The core fields such as finance sectors, medical care, education, transport, etc, needs AI, for the prediction about customers, disease, etc. The Air Operations Division (AOD) utilizes AI to construct master rule-based frameworks. Plane test systems use AI for recreating the flights by handling the information. Various AI tools are widely used in defense system, Speech and Voice Recognition, Text recognition, Gesture Recognition, Facial Expression Recognition Data Mining and Spam Filtering applications. Other applications are navigation with robots, obstacle avoidance and object recognition, etc. AI applications goes with Machine Translation and NLP techniques. From custom-constructed master frameworks to mass created programming and shopper hardware the AI applications run.

Competitive self-play is valuable in improving AI performance, from creating fake images to achieving superhuman performance at games. Offers straightforward interpretation of obtained results. AI is applied to related systems in computer networks, and is implemented in a programming format, which in turn enables related systems to have more targeted data analysis capabilities and computational capabilities and to improve computer data processing capabilities. With the use of intrusion detection technology, the operational status of the computer network can be monitored in real time, which can provide real-time protection for the computer network, improve the performance of the computer network, and enable the computer network to avoid external and internal attacks, so that the operation error can be avoided. Such as artificial neural network systems, expert systems, etc. have all started using intrusion detection technology and the effect is very good.

Use of counterfeit astute strategies in the plan of intensity supply stabilizers (PSS) Since the 1960s, PSSs have been utilized to add damping to electromechanical motions. The PSS is an extra control framework, which is regularly connected as a major aspect of an excitation control framework. The fundamental capacity of the PSS is to apply a flag to the excitation framework, delivering electric sets to the rotor in stage with contrasts in speed that hose the motions of the power. They work inside the generator excitation framework to make a piece of the electric torque, called damping torque, relative to the speed change. A CPSS can be displayed by a two-arrange (indistinguishable) organize, a forward postponement, spoken to by an increase K and two time constants T1 and T2. This system is associated with a washing circuit of a period steady Tw. The flag wash square goes about as a high-hang loose consistent Tw which permits the flag related with the motions of the rotor speed to pass unaltered. Moreover, it doesn't permit stable state changes to adjust terminal voltages. The stage remuneration hinders with time constants T1i-T4i give the fitting qualities of the stage conductor to make up for the stage contrast between the information and yield signals. The regularly utilized structure of PSS Structure of the PSS In the field of intensity framework task, PC programs are every now and again executed and altered by any variety. Computerized reasoning (AI) can deal with the high non-linearity of functional frameworks. The different advancements utilized in PSS improvement issues are ANN, FL, ES, and so forth.

ISSUES OF AI

AI is developing with an incredible speed. The analysts and engineers are anticipating that AI will develop so tremendously that it would wind up troublesome for people to control. People are building up the AI frameworks by filling however much knowledge as could be expected into them, by which now people themselves are getting undermined. Some of the threats are listed below:

1. **Unemployment**: Though AI drastically improves the world in various ways, there are certain concerns regarding the upcoming impacts of AI on employment and the workforce. The researchers and developers are predicting that millions of people loose jobs in the next decades in the areas of *markets, businesses, education, government.*

2. **Security**: Autonomous weapons are developed using AI techniques which are programmed to kill. If it falls in the hands of the wrong person, these weapons could be easily misused and cause mass casualties. Apart from this, AI arms race could lead to AI war which results in major loss.

3. **To Pump Information out of Complex Systems**, and then use that information to manipulate those same systems people are trying to use intelligent machines. Optimizing two or more machines of same complex system to different operator utility functions at the same time, virtues of the overall system that we did not understand well enough to deliberately, collectively protect are hollowed out by the machines in their arms race faster than we can react to the observation that it's happening and establish that collective protection.

4. AI systems can identify human faces and emotions and precisely track body movements, but it would not be able to tell a story explaining the motivations for a person's behavior.

FUTURE OF AI

Society will change massively with the utilization of AI innovation. There will be increment in security. The human way of life gets changed. Automatons will turn into a piece of human lives. Automatons will be utilized for Package conveyance, crisis reactions or pressing conveyance of restorative items, as they can move questions all around quickly through fly. Automatons are viewed as a main issue in the security field. Man-made intelligence will improve the human reasoning procedure by creating new thoughts that takes care of different complex issues. It is anticipated that in next couple of years, AI and apply autonomy will be totally coordinated in the business tasks. While empowering development approaches and procedures should address moral, security suggestions, and protection and should work to guarantee that the advantages of AI innovations will be spread extensively and decently. They will expand association's proficiency regarding new items and administrations dependent on AI, likewise new markets and clients will be made. In future, detecting calculations will accomplish super-human execution for capacities required for driving.

AI Assistant will become truly useful-ordering food and taxi booking, and choosing restaurants to visit are becoming increasingly streamlined and accessible. These are become high efficient at understanding their human users, as the natural language algorithms used to encode speech into computer-readable data, and vice versa is exposed to more and more information about how we communicate. However, the rapid acceleration of understanding in this field means that, we will be getting used to far more natural and flowing discourse with the machines we share our lives with. Execution outpaces wellbeing could be very risky if countries race to put into the field AI frameworks that are liable to mishaps. The results of AI for the world will probably surpass the ramifications for military power and the fate of war.

The effect of robotization on the fate of work could have huge financial and societal outcomes that will happen paying little respect to decisions that militaries make about whether to create, or not, AI applications for explicit military territories AI also solves the problems in education. High quality education in India is still concentrated in major cities so a lot of students from the rural and small town kids have to migrate to get good quality education and highly qualified teachers. Within its possible to scale the teaching methodologies of one good teacher to anybody and everybody.

CONCLUSION

The chapter discuss about the introduction to Artificial Intelligence and its agents. The chapter gives the exposure about the background of AI and also explains the importance of knowledge representation in AI. The chapter introduces various AI algorithms, its applications in present days. The authors also discuss the limitations of AI. Artificial intelligence system will keep on staying one of the most loved diagnostic instruments to extricate includes consequently in blame finding because of its exact, dependable and minimal effort arrangement nature. It very well may be utilized by individuals to improve their own human knowledge. It can likewise help them We infer that if the machine can effectively profess to know, it ought to be viewed as insightful. Computerized reasoning frameworks are presently normally utilized in different fields, for example, financial aspects, drug, designing and military, just as being coordinated into numerous basic programming applications, customary procedure diversions, and so on.

Artificial intelligence is an energizing and compensating discipline. Computerized reasoning is a part of software engineering that manages the mechanization of insightful conduct. The reexamined meaning of AI is - AI is the investigation of the components that underlie wise conduct through the development and assessment of relics that endeavor to apply such instruments. So it is presumed that it works like a counterfeit human cerebrum that has a mind boggling intensity of fake idea. Express their musings all the more plainly and soundly with settle on better decisions.

REFERENCES

Devi, K.K.A., Matthew, Y., & Sandra, L.A. (2012). Advanced Neural Network in Artificial Intelligence Systems. *IEEE Trans on Artificial Intelligence Systems, 4*(9), 100 – 120.

Lily, D., Chan, B., & Wang, T. G. (2013). A Simple Explanation of Neural Network in Artificial Intelligence. *IEEE Trans on Comtrol System, 247*, 1529–5651.

Shapiro, S. C. (1979). The SNePS Semantic Network Processing System. In N. V. Findler (Ed.), *Associative Networks* (pp. 179–203). New York: Academic Press. doi:10.1016/B978-0-12-256380-5.50011-6

Chapter 20
Machine Learning Techniques Application:
Social Media, Agriculture, and Scheduling in Distributed Systems

Karthikeyan P.
Presidency University Bangalore, India

Karunakaran Velswamy
Karunya Institute of Technology and Sciences, India

Pon Harshavardhanan
VIT Bhopal, India

Rajagopal R.
Vel Tech Multi Tech Dr. Rangarajan Dr. Sakunthala Engineering College, India

JeyaKrishnan V.
Saintgits College of Engineering, India

Velliangiri S.
CMR Institute of Technology, India

ABSTRACT

Machine learning is the part of artificial intelligence that makes machines learn without being expressly programmed. Machine learning application built the modern world. Machine learning techniques are mainly classified into three techniques: supervised, unsupervised, and semi-supervised. Machine learning is an interdisciplinary field, which can be joined in different areas including science, business, and research. Supervised techniques are applied in agriculture, email spam, malware filtering, online fraud detection, optical character recognition, natural language processing, and face detection. Unsupervised techniques are applied in market segmentation and sentiment analysis and anomaly detection. Deep learning is being utilized in sound, image, video, time series, and text. This chapter covers applications of various machine learning techniques, social media, agriculture, and task scheduling in a distributed system.

DOI: 10.4018/978-1-5225-9902-9.ch020

INTRODUCTION

Machine learning (ML) is a discipline of information technology that gives machines the ability to "learn" with data, without being expressly programmed, this means in other words that these programs change their behavior by learning from data. Machine learning is the future of computing. From home automation to landing a rover on a comet, everything is digitalized, and these are made possible only because of intelligent systems that use Machine learning and their associated applications (Wernick, Yang, Brankov, Yourganov, & Strother, 2010). With advances in ML, probabilistic standards and deep neural network machine can now promptly convert spoken conversion and written, identify and precisely caption photos, recognize faces and be a personal assistant for the consumers. The latest inventions in Artificial Intelligence (AI) are the result of core advances in AI, including improvements in ML, and perception, on a stage set by improvements in multiple fields of computer science. Processing power has raised and has compared to cloud computing. For the meantime, the extension of the web has produced chances to collect, store and share massive volumes of data (Hatcher & Yu, 2018). There also have been prominent strides in probabilistic modeling, in which processing system examine probabilities and make the best solution or suggestion, and ML in which a computer gets better at something based on the data that it collects. This process proves that the future of machine learning is heading in many ways making the lives of millions of people more comfortable, productive, and effective. Figure 1 depicts the Application of various Machine Learning Techniques.

Supervised Learning

Supervised learning algorithm train the model based on labeled training data. Supervised learning algorithms can be categorized as two primary classes: regression algorithms forecast the continuous value or classification algorithms forecast the discrete value. Regression: Regression learning algorithm try to obtain the best fit function for the training data. Classification: In contrast with regression machine learning algorithm that attempts to locate the best fit capacity for the training information Classification algorithms are dived into four types such as logistic regression, artificial neural networks(ANN), support vector machines(SVM), and decision trees. Logistic Regression: It is used as a binary classifier where the output belongs to true or false.

Decision Trees: This can categorize an input data, decision trees sort the input data down the tree from the root node to a particular leaf node. Support Vector Machines: Support Vector Machine (SVM) is principally a more tasteful strategy that performs arrangement assignments by building hyperplanes in a multidimensional space. Artificial Neural Networks: Artificial neural networks (ANN) used whenever we have rich labeled training data with numerous. ANN tries to impersonator the way our brain mechanism as it has been confirmed that the brain uses one ``learning algorithm'' for all its different purposes (Garcia-Ceja et al., 2018) . The real world application of supervised machine learning is listed below.

Spam Detection: Incoming Electronic mail (E-mail) in an inbox, recognize those E-mail messages that are spam and those that are most certainly not. Possessing a system of this issue will enable software to transmit non-spam messages in the inbox and leave spam messages to a spam envelope (Cohen, Nissim, & Elovici, 2018).

Face Detection: Given an excellent photo collection of a massive number of computerized photos, recognize those photographs that incorporate a given individual. A model of this choice procedure would

Figure 1. Application of various machine learning techniques

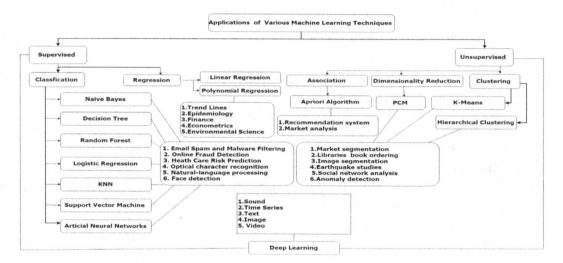

enable a program to sort out photographs by an individual. A few cameras and programming like iPhoto and Facebook has this ability.

MasterCard Fraud Detection: User uses their master card to exchanges money for their business operation or shopping. MasterCard Fraud Detection identifies those exchanges that were made by the client and those that were not. A performance with a model of this choice could discount those exchanges that were false.

Digit Recognition: it can be used in the postal divisions to identify the digit for each manually written character in the postcard or letter. A model of this issue would permit a PC program to peruse and comprehend manually written postal districts and sort wraps by geographic location.

Speech Understanding: Given a speech from a client, distinguish the specific demand made by the client. A model of this issue would enable a program to understand and make an attempt to satisfy that ask. Cortana and Google presently have this capacity.

Medicinal Diagnosis: Given the side effects displayed in a victim and a database of anonymized understanding records, anticipate whether the patient is probably going to have an ailment. A model of this choice issue could be utilized by a program to give choice help to therapeutic experts.

Stock Trading: Given the present and past value developments for a stock, decide if the stock ought to be purchased, held or sold. This model choice issue can give choice help to monetary experts.

Pattern Detection: Supplied a client hand drawing a pattern on a touch screen and a database of a known pattern, figure out which patterns the client was aiming to draw. A model of this choice would enable a program to demonstrate the non-romantic rendition of that pattern the client attracted to make new charts. The Instaviz iPhone application performs this (Wrzesień, Treder, Klamkowski, & Rudnicki, 2018).

Unsupervised Learning

The unsupervised learning techniques train model without labeled data. Unsupervised learning algorithms can be divided into three main categories: clustering, association and dimensionality reduction.

Clustering: One of the simplest ways to obtain knowledge of a set of data points is to cluster them, this performs the data more acceptable as it gives more formation to it by making a finite set of groups moderately than having a multitude of random data points. Unsupervised machine learning is extraordinarily significant in applications such as market segmentation and social network analysis.one of the widely used clustering is K-Means Algorithm.it is used for automatic data grouping into coherent clusters. Dimensionality Reduction: Dimensionality reduction is a distinctive crucial issue in the field of ML. The motive behind dimensionality reduction can be compiled as follows: i- Eliminate repeated data ii- Decrease the storage and processing need iii- Shorten the visualization of data by only taking a few features. Principal Component Analysis (PCM): PCM is the best example of dimensionality reduction. PCM main objective is discovery the subsection of features that top signifies the data. The real world application of unsupervised machine learning is listed below(Willcock et al., 2018).

Product Recommendation: Given a buying record for a client and a massive stock of items, recognize those items in which that client will be intrigued and prone to buy. A model of this choice procedure will enable a program to deliver proposals to a client and inspire item buys. Amazon has this ability to sell the product (Boselli, Cesarini, Mercorio, & Mezzanzanica, 2018).Customers Segmentation: Given the example of conduct by a client amid a time for testing and the past practices everything being equal, distinguish those clients that will change over to the paid rendition of the item and those that will not. A model of this choice issue would enable a program to trigger client mediations to induce the client to be undercover early or better participate in the preliminary. Deep Learning Use Cases: Deep learning excels at recognizing patterns in unstructured data, which most people know as media such as images, sound, video, and text.

The whole purposes of this chapter are itemized as follows:

a.   To highlight the machine learning application in social media services
b.   To analysis the existing approaches to social media service in sentiment analysis
c.   To classify the existing sentiment analysis techniques based on text, image, audio, and video.
d.   To summarize the machine learning application in agriculture
e.   To discuss the machine learning techniques that can be applied in the task scheduling in the distributed system.

The remaining of the chapter organized as follows: Section 2.1 discusses social media analysis framework, section 2.2 discuss the Sentimental analysis in social media, section 2.3 discuss the machine learning techniques in agricultural application and section 2.4 present the applying machine learning techniques for task scheduling in the distributed system. Finally we presented possible future direction for this research work and concluded.

MACHINE LEARNING TECHNIQUES IN SOCIAL MEDIA ANALYSIS APPLICATION

The social media analysis is playing a vital role in the business environment to improve their business process with its competitor. Social media analysis (SMA) is the art and science of mining valuable hidden information is from massive volumes of semi-structured and unstructured social media data to enable informed and perceptive decision making. Social media website like Twitter, YouTube, Facebook, and

Figure 2. The social media analysis framework

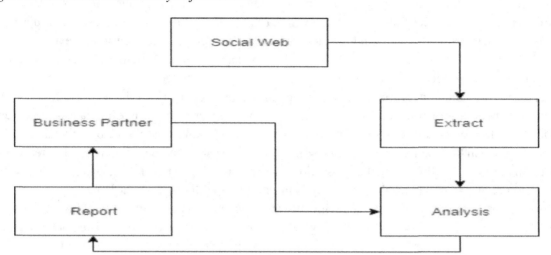

Google+ are used by billions of people to connect and share their knowledge, private opinions to other people in social media. The development of this website has provided organizations to find marketable strategies and concentrating on potential clients on social media to improve their business operations. Business is acknowledged by methods for the nearness of the organization on the web and by delivering content that will take the client's consideration. Consequently, clients share their assessments about specific items by leaving remarks on them and responding to the organization's posts. In this section, we discuss how ML techniques can be applied in social media analysis.

Social Media Analysis Framework

The initial phase in social media analytics framework is the extracting process .it is extracting appropriate business information form the web. Extensively, information extraction could have two distinct levels. For example, brand or crusade checking, the extension is all posts from whole online life universe that match to a defined set of catchphrases or hunt terms. Then again, for prerequisites, for example, execution estimation or aggressive knowledge, the extension is all posts from a characterized set of social media profiles. After extraction comes, the analyze step where we attempt to clean and comprehend the assembled information. This may include angles, for example, volume pattern investigation, positioning posts, positioning profiles, and so forth. Analyze steps performed all the time establishes a social networking listening program. Machine learning investigator or Data scientist generate the report that is communicated to the business partner. If a business partner is satisfied with the result, then they can use the report to improve their business activities, else they will give feedback to the Machine learning investigator or Data Scientist. Figure 2 depicts the social media analysis framework.

Sentimental Analysis

The sentimental analysis is instrumental in social media for monitoring purpose and as well as in the business field. It allows us to increase an overview of the broader public opinions behind specific top-

Figure 3. Classification of sentiment analysis

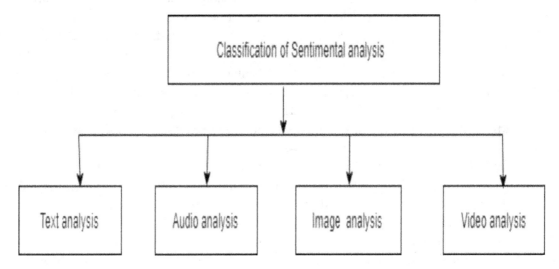

ics. The sentimental analysis is also named as the opinion mining. The sentimental analysis is generally expressed in terms of polarities, reviews. Generally, the sentimental analysis will ask the questions regarding customer satisfaction or dissatisfaction and get public opinions regarding the new products or brands which are going to launch.

The sentimental analysis is the most important research topic in real time applications like "Decision making. "One of the frequently visited social media sites around the world is "twitter" where they can share various opinions and thoughts regarding different domains like politics, brands, products, celebrities, etc. Early days the research had carried on the model and track public sentiments. Nowadays in the advancement of the research field, we can use it for interpreting the reasons for the change of public opinions on particular product and mining and summarizing the product reviews, and the latest one is to solve the polarity shift problems by performing the dual sentimental analysis. Figure 3 show is the classification of sentiment analysis.

Sentiment Analysis in Text

The extracting sentiment from the text is not a complicated process compared to video. Text examination comprises data retrieval, lexical analysis to frequency word recurrence circulations, design acknowledgment, labeling/comment, data removal, data mining systems investigation, perception, and prescient investigation. The broader goal is to modify content into information for examination, employing utilization of natural language handling natural language processing and diagnostic strategies.

Bo Pang et al (Bo Pang and Lillian Lee Shivakumar Vaithyanathan, 2002) was proposed sentimental classification analysis using machine learning technique for a movie review. The domain chooses by the author's is experimentally convenient because it is easy to collect a large number of reviews. The reviewers are often summaries their overall sentimental data with a machine-extractable rating indicator by the number of stars. They user expressed the review comments in the form either with a star or numerical values. The rating given by the user was automatically extracted and converted into the following three categories like positive, negative or neutral. They have used two of the classifiers to evaluating the performance of the proposed system, one is SVM classifier, and another one is Navie Bayes classifier. The author's claimed the SVM classifier provides better classification accuracy than Navie Bayes Classifier.

Wang et al. (Wang, Zhu, Jiang, & Li, 2013) discussed real-time event detection by social sensors. In this paper, the author takes an earthquake tweets, and they proposed an algorithm to monitor the tweets and detect the target event. To detect the target event, the authors develop a classifier of tweets based on the features such as keywords used in the particular sentence, the number of words used and their context. In this work, particle filtering and Kalman filtering are used for finding the event target location. The proposed particle filtering method will give better results than other compared methods in estimating the center of earthquakes and the trajectories of typhoons.

Deepayan Chakrabarti and Kunal Punera (Deepayan Chakrabarti & Kunal Punera, 2011) designed novel techniques on constructing real-time events from Twitter tweets. For this instance, the author's took the query about the online going game of American football. To understand the strong baseline on the play by play summary construction task they proposed an approach based on learning an underlying hidden state representing an event. The model has two steps: one is hidden Markov model that can segment the event timeline, depending on both business of the tweet stream and the word distribution used in the tweets and each segment represents one sub-event significantly. The overall study of summarizing events on Twitter gives a better improvement of sport in the future. Johan and Wang (John & Wang, 2015) have proposed a model called the ET-LDA, in this one the events and tweets are based on latent dirchlet Al-locaton as a baseline for the model to the aligning events in the tweeter feedback, for this author's used a large scale tweet dataset associated with two events from different domains. One is President Obama's Middle East speech and republican primary debate. They took the feedbacks of both the events on tweeter and evaluated with the model based on the quantitatively and qualitatively and proved that the proposed method provides significantly improved over the baseline method.

Bholane and Gore (Bholane & Gore, 2016) worked on the sentimental analysis of Twitter data using a support vector machine model. Early research was carried out to model and track the public sentiments. Nowadays in the advancement of the research, we can do mining and quickly summarize the product reviews. By using modeling and tracking of the public sentiment will not useful for decision making. In the proposed system, latent dirichlet approach is used for interpreting exact reasons present behind the sentiment tweets. In this work, SVM is compared with two baseline methods, one is senti strength+twitter sentiment, and another one is senti strength the proposed system provides better classification rate compared to the senti strength+twitter sentiment method and senti strength method.

Mountassir et al. (Mountassir, Benbrahim, & Berrada, 2012) have proposed a work, which deals with the problem of unbalanced data set in the sentimental analysis. Two types of data were considered in this work. First data is based on the Arab Muslim data (DSMR), it consists of 594 comments and second data is Arab support for Palestinian affair (DSPO). The author has proposed three different sampling methods for improving the performance of the overall system. The three different sampling methods can remove similar, farthest and cluster in the data. The experiment was carried out with different classifiers, and the result shows that SVM classifier is better than other classifiers for both DSMR and DSPO data.

Tan et al. (Tan et al., 2014) interpreted public sentimental variations on twitter. In this paper, the author has handled with two emerging topics one is a scientific article and another one is a product review data, and the author has investigated the problem of analyzing public sentiment variations and finding the possible reasons caused these variations. To solve this problem, the latent Dirichlet model called the RCB-LDA is proposed. In the experiment the proposed system is compared two other methods, one is TFIDF, and another method is LDA, and the result shows the proposed system is better in all aspect compared to LDA and TFIDF.

Trilla and Alias (Trilla & Alias, 2013) worked on sentence based sentimental analysis for descriptive text to speech. In the experiment, the semeval 2007 dataset is carried out, and it consists of a compilation of news headlines, and it contains nearly 250 headlines. From the 250 headlines, the proposed system found the positive and negative headlines and repeated words and the average length of the sentence, etc. Additionally, the proposed system will calculate the feature properties like unigram and bigrams from the overall sentence and found that unigrams perform the best result it will give 8% effective rate more than bigrams.

Xia et al. (Xia et al., 2015) worked on the dual sentimental analysis. It will consider the two sides of one review. The experiment is carried out on two tasks, one is the polarity classification, and another one is positive, negative sentimental classification and the experiment is evaluated by using across 9 sentimental datasets, three classification algorithms, two types of features and two kinds of antonym dictionaries. In this paper, the author is mainly focused on polarity shift problem in the sentimental analysis using the data expansion approach called DSA. DSA aims to reverse the review that is sentiment opposite to the original review. After many iterations, the experimental results concluded that DSA is very useful for polarity classification problems.

Patodkar and I.R (Patodkar & I.R, 2017) proposed a sentimental analysis on a television program by collecting the sample audience opinion from Twitter. The experiment was carried out by different algorithms and different methods on sentimental analysis for the polarity detection and sentimental summarization. Finally, the experiment results concluded that the random forest algorithm with 20 random trees gives better results than the naïve Bayes and support vector machine. With the help of better results obtained from the random forest will provide valuable feedback to producers and help them to find negative feedback from the viewers on that particular television show.

Parikh and Movassate (Parikh & Movassate, 2009) worked on the sentimental analysis of user-generated regarding tweets on the movie review. In the experiment for classification, they took equally 370 positive tweets and 370 negative tweets. The experiment is carried out by two classifiers. One is naïve, and another one is MaxEnt classifier. The classification result shows that naive Bayes algorithm is classified as follows 70% of negative tweets classified correctly and 48% of positive tweets classified correctly. The results concluded that the naive Bayes classifier provides better classification accuracy results compared to MaxEntclassifier.

Barbosa & Feng (Barbosa & Feng, 2010) created a robust sentimental detection approach on twitter from biased and noisy data. The data which they took consist of two-step sentimental analysis classification methods for Twitter, which will give as follows the first classification message as subjective and objective again the subjective tweets are divided in to positive and negative. The approach they have created has a more abstract representation as the raw words that were used in the previous approaches. The approach they used gives lower error rates than the previous methods. Bifet and Frank (Bifet & Frank, 2010) worked on sentimental knowledge discovery in Twitter streaming data. They focused on the challenges on twitter data poses and sentimental analysis of Twitter data for this they proposed a sliding window kappa statistic as an evaluating metric for data streaming. They used the data from two data streams one is from twittersentiment.appsport.com, and another one is Edinburgh Corpus with 1,600,000 instances. Moreover, they found that the Stochastic Gradient Descent model gives better accuracy results [20]. Agarwal et al. (Agarwal, 2014) worked on sentimental Analysis of Twitter data for this they used three types of models.1 Unigram model2. Feature-based model 3.tree kernel-based model. Unigram model is also known as the bag of words model. All these three models are compared.

Davidov et al. (Davidov, 2010) proposed enhanced sentimental learning using Twitter hashtags and smileys. In this work, the author has used 50 twitter tags and 15 smileys as the sentimental labels and its help to create a dozen of sentimental types. This study of sentimental labels used four different feature types called punctuations, words, n-grams, and patterns. With these data, they proposed a framework which allows the automatic identification and classification of various sentimental types in short text which is based on Twitter data and found best results without any labor- fast manually named training information.

Sentiment Analysis in Audio

The extracting sentiment from the audio is complex process compared to text. The following literature we discussed how machine learning techniques could be applied in the sentiment analysis in audio.

Perez-Rosas and Mihalcea (Pérez-Rosas & Mihalcea, 2013) investigated the task of sentiment analysis for spoken words, with an emphasis on the verbal part of the audits. Utilizing a novel dataset, comprising of video audits from two distinct filed, they performed assessments to: (1) decide the precision of a sentiment classifier that can be assembled utilizing just the verbal part of the audits (2) measure the pretended by the nature of the translation on the exactness of the classifier; and (3) think about the execution acquired with written versus spoken audits. This system discoveries demonstrate that while the utilization of programmed discourse acknowledgment can prompt sensibly exact supposition classifiers, with correctness's in the scope of 62-68%, the nature of the interpretation can in any case bigly affect the opinion investigation instrument, with misfortunes inexactness of up to 10% for programmed interpretations when contrasted with manual translations . Maghilnan and Kumar (Maghilnan S, 2017) proposed a model for sentiment analysis that utilizes features mined from the audio signal to discover the emotions of the speakers used in the dialogue. The scheme is precise in understanding the sentiment of the speakers in conversations. It ensures a few imperfections, at this moment the framework can deal with a discussion between two speakers and in the discussion just a single speaker should talk at a given time, it cannot comprehend if two individuals talk at the same time.

Luo et al. (Luo, Xu, & Chen, 2018) designed novel utterance-based deep neural network system named AFF-ACRNN, which has a parallel mix of Convolutional Neural Network (CNN) and Long Short-Term Memory (LSTM) based system, to get agent highlights named Audio Sentiment Vector (ASV), that can maximally reflect feeling data in an expression from a sound. This model can perceive sound is feeling decisively and rapidly, and show that our heterogeneous ASV is superior to customary acoustic highlights or vectors separated from other profound learning models. Wollmer et al. (Wöllmer et al., 2013) presented a framework for sentiment analysis of online videos containing motion picture surveys by non-professional speakers as controlled in a novel varying media database named Multi-Modal Movie Opinion (MMMO) corpus. The framework applies bidirectional Long Short-Term Memory neural systems for estimating the assumption (positive versus negative) conveyed in the audit recordings dependent on much sounds and video features and relevant data.

Sentiment Analysis in Image

Images are mostly posted in social media. Regardless of whether it is a picture, photograph, selfie, or connection to an article, our social feeds are progressively loaded up with more pictures and less content. Additional locks in image investigation can likewise recognize faces inside photographs to decide conclusion, sexual orientation, age, and that is only the tip of the iceberg. It can perceive different components inside a photograph in the meantime, including logos, faces, exercises, items, and scenes. The innovation can naturally subtitle pictures "man and lady remaining outside wearing Peter England shirts with bicycle and mountains out of sight." Moreover, that is only an essential subtleties. This section discusses the image analysis technology how it is used in social media analysis. Yuan et al. (Yuan, 2013) presented Sentribute, a novel picture sentiment forecast calculation dependent on mid-level traits. The unbalanced sacking approach is utilized to bargain with the lopsided dataset. To upgrade this forecast execution, used Eigen face-based feeling location calculation, which is essential yet incredible particularly in instances of recognizing outrageous outward appearances, to managing pictures containing faces and get an unmistakable increase in exactness over result dependent on mid-level characteristics as it were. This calculation investigates current visual substance based feeling examination approach by utilizing mid-level characteristics and without utilizing literary substance. Zhao, Yao, Gao, Ji, & Ding (Zhao, Yao, Gao, Ji, & Ding, 2017) proposed to predict personalized insights of image emotions by including numerous issues with visual content. Rolling multi-task hypergraph learning was offered to combine these issues jointly. A large-scale personalized emotion dataset of social images was constructed, and some baselines were provided. This model proves that they can attain significant performance gains on personalized emotion grouping, as compared to several advanced approaches.

Zhao, Yao, Gao, Ding, & Chua (Zhao, Yao, Gao, Ding, & Chua, 2018) developed a continuous probability distribution of image emotion via Multitask Shared Sparse Regression which can be seen as an underlying endeavor to quantify the general assessment of human feeling observations. This model exhibited shared inadequate relapse as the learning model and upgraded it by iteratively reweighted least squares. Moreover, above, different dimensions of feeling highlights were separated, and three benchmark calculations were given. Tests led on the Image-Emotion-Social-Net dataset supported the adequacy of the proposed strategy. The anticipated feeling dispersion can be investigated in numerous applications, for example, full of feeling picture recovery and feeling exchange.

Sentiment Analysis in Video

The considerable number of the video is uploaded in YouTube, and Facebook, in future performing Sentiment analysis in the video is a very cumbersome task due to some of the limitation in the current analysis process, which goes past the investigation of writings, and incorporates different modalities, for example, sound and visual information. Poria et al. (Poria, Cambria, Howard, Huang, & Hussain, 2016) demonstrated a multimodal sentiment analysis model, which incorporates sets of applicable highlights for content and visual information, just as a straightforward strategy for intertwining the highlights removed from various modalities. YouTube dataset demonstrate that the proposed multimodal framework accomplishes a precision of about 80%, beating all best in class frameworks by over 20%. Perez et al. (Perez Rosas, Mihalcea, & Morency, 2013) proposed Multimodal sentiment analysis, the exhibited technique incorporates etymological, sound, and visual highlights to recognize slant in online recordings. Specifically, tests center around another dataset comprising of Spanish recordings gathered

Table 1. Summary of the strength and challenge of sentiment analysis in social media

Type	Techniques	Strengths	Challenges
Text	Probabilistic spatiotemporal model	The system senses earthquakes on time and sends electronic mail to listed users. The announcement is distributed much quicker than the announcements that are broadcast by the Japan Meteorological Agency.	Location with less number of earthquakes
Text	SUMMHMM SUMMTIMEINT SUMMALLTEXT	Outperforms some intuitive and competitive baselines	Procedures that have long-running, and where users are expected to want a summary of all incidences so far, this method is frequently unsatisfactory
Text	Support Vector Machine	The accuracy of analysis of causes behind sentiment variations is improved by 23.24% using SVM than Twitter Sentiment tools.	Forming and following public sentiments is not beneficial for choice making.
Audio	Online Spoken Reviews	Automatic speech recognition can lead to reasonably precise sentiment classifiers, with accuracies in the range of 62-68%	The consequence of spoken reviews is not as much of perfect
Audio	Speaker Specific Speech Data	The scheme is precise in understanding the sentiment of the speakers in conversations	The model cannot recognize if two individuals talk at the same time.
Audio	Utterance-Based Audio Sentiment Analysis	This model demonstrates the cutting edge approach by 9.33% on Multimodal Opinion-level Sentiment Intensity dataset	This model cannot outperform in the multimodal sentiment analysis
Audio	Sentiment Analysis in an Audiovisual Context	Inspects speaker's sentiment in YouTube videos comprising movie reviews that language-independent audiovisual study can compete with linguistic analysis.	the more massive database was used in the system
Image	Sentribute	Better performance in terms of forecast accuracy	Attributes in the images need to be labeled
Image	Multitask Shared Sparse Regression	Sentiment distribution can be explored in much real-time application like emotional Image recovery and sentiment transfer.	large-scale Image-Emotion-Social-Net dataset was used
Image	Rolling multi-task hypergraph learning	Model prove that can attain important performance gains on personalized emotion grouping, as compared to several advanced approaches.	Modeling social connections of client vigorously and seeing attention prior by taking out connected private profile is complex.
Video	Multimodal system	YouTube dataset demonstrate that the proposed multimodal framework accomplishes a precision of about 80%, beating all best in class frameworks by over 20%.	Reducing the time complexities is complex.
Video	Multimodal Sentiment Analysis of Spanish Online Videos	Mixing of image, audio, and textual characteristics can increase significantly over the single use of individual modality at a moment	Number of features used by the algorithm

from YouTube that is explained for sentiment polarity. Table 1. Listed the Summary of the strength and challenge of Sentiment analysis in social media for the different type of data.

Machine Learning Techniques in Agricultural Application

Agricultural work generates much information, and this generated information need to be analyzed and generate the report to improve agriculture work. Handling and recovery of unique information in this plenitude of farming data is essential. Usage of data and interchanges innovation empowers mechaniza-

Figure 4. Classification different agriculture application in machine learning techniques

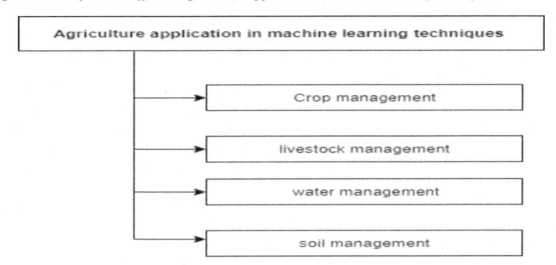

tion of removing tremendous information with an end goal to get learning and patterns, which empowers the end of manual undertakings and less demanding information extraction specifically from electronic sources, exchange to verify electronic arrangement of documentation which will empower generation cost decrease, higher yield, and higher market cost.

Agricultural analysis frameworks take large quantities of data including data about yields, consumers and soil. Utilization of ML techniques, important cases of data can be discovered in this data, which would be used for further investigation and report assessment. The critical inquiry is how to order a massive measure of information. Automatic characterization is done based on similarities present in the information. This kind of grouping is just valuable if the end procured is satisfactory for the agronomist or the end client. The issue of anticipating creation yield can be measured with machine learning strategies. It ought to be viewed as that the sensor information is accessible for some past tense, in which fitting creation yield was recorded. This data makes a lot of information which can be utilized for learning methods for characterizing future generation yields because new sensor information is accessible. Yield expectation is an outstanding issue of farming associations. Every agriculturist needs as quickly as time permits to realize how much respect anticipate. Throughout the years, yield expectation was directed dependent on rancher's understanding of certain farming societies and harvests. In any case, this data can be gained with the utilization of present-day innovations, similar to GPS.

The different application of machine learning strategies in agriculture has been summarized in this section. These processes will upgrade the efficiency of fields alongside a decrease in the info endeavors of the agriculturists. Classification different agriculture application is depicted in figure 4.

Crop Management

Crop management important function in agriculture are listed as follows. 1. The yield prediction 2.disease detection 3. Weed detection and 4. Species recognition. Crop Yield Prediction to amplify the yield, choice of the fitting yield that will be sown assumes a crucial job. It relies upon different components like the soil and its organization, atmosphere, geology of the district, crop yield, advertises costs and so on. Machine learning gives numerous viable calculations which can recognize the info and yield relationship in harvest choice and yield expectation. Systems like Artificial neural network (ANN), K-nearest neighbors (KNN) and Decision Trees have cut a specialty for themselves with regards to trim choice which depends on different elements. Harvest choice dependent on the impact of natural disasters like starvation-dependent on machine learning.

Ramos et al. (Ramos, Prieto, Montoya, & Oliveros, 2017) present a total calculating number of organic products on a branch in a non-ruinous manner by utilizing preparing calculations and pictures. The organic products are tallied, paying little mind to their development organize, differentiate between the branch and the foundation, or lighting conditions. The issues introduced in the gained pictures produce check mistakes more prominent than 6%, a rate which can be decreased by methods for a proper picture procurement.

Ali et al.(Ali, Cawkwell, Dwyer, & Green, 2017) combined multiple linear regression (MLR), artificial neural network (ANN) and adaptive neuro-fuzzy inference system (ANFIS) to calculate the grassland biomass estimation of farms in Ireland. The method that was proposed will better investigate the future inflow of remote detecting information from spaceborne sensors for the recovery of various biophysical parameters and with the dispatch of new individuals from satellite classes.

Disease Detection

A most critical worry in agriculture is disease prediction. The most broadly utilized practice in vermin and infection control is to splash pesticides over the editing zone consistently. This training, albeit successful, has a high monetary and huge ecological expense. Natural effects can be buildups in harvest items, reactions on groundwater pollution, impacts on nearby untamed life and eco-frameworks, etc. Pantazi et al. (Pantazi et al., 2017) discussed Vision-based pest detection method to detect the detect of thrips on the crop canopy images using the SVM technique. Mean square error (MSE), the root of mean square error (RMSE), mean absolute error (MAE) and mean percent error (MPE) were utilized for assessment of the method that was proposed. Results demonstrate that utilizing SVM strategy provide a mean percent mistake of under 2.25%. Pantazi et al. (2017) presented a Detection of nitrogen stressed, yellow rust infected and healthy winter wheat canopies. The strategy that was created was a hybrid classification. Three distinct models have considered: ANN supervised Kohonen networks (SKNs) and XY-combination.

Weed Detection

Weed detection is a special complex issue in agriculture. Numerous makers demonstrate weeds as the most immediate risk to crop generation. The exact location of weeds is of high significance to maintainable farming, since weeds are hard to distinguish and segregate from harvests. Binch & Fox (Binch & Fox, 2017) Automated robotic weeding would improve the profitability of dairy and sheep ranches while saving their surroundings. Past examinations have revealed consequences of machine vision strategies to isolate grass from field weeds; however, each utilization their very own datasets and report just execution of their calculation, making it difficult to look at them. An authoritative, vast scale autonomous examination is exhibited of all major realized field weed detection techniques assessed on another institutionalized informational index under a more extensive scope of condition conditions. This considers a reasonable, impartial, free and factually critical examination of these and future strategies out of the blue.

Species Recognition

The primary objective of Species Recognition is classified as the agriculture item from the utilization of human specialists, just as to decrease the order time. Grinblat et al. (Grinblat, Uzal, Larese, & Granitto, 2016) used a Deep Learning for plant classification using vein morphological exemplars. Deep learning method considerably increases the correctness of the denoted pipeline. The system shows that this correctness is extended by growing the depth of the model.

Livestock Management

The livestock production appreciates readings established for the correct forecast and assessment of farming constraints to optimize the financial efficiency of the manufacturing system. Grinblat et al. (Grinblat et al., 2016) reported that an SVM classifier method is surveyed by execution measurements, results plainly show that it is reachable to early caution issues in the bend of business laying hens. Spiral premise work bit with sigma esteem equivalent to 5, and a parameter C estimation of 0.15 is the one which accomplished the best execution, that is 0.9874 for exactness, 0.9876 for particularity, 0.9783 for affectability and 0.6518 for positive prescient esteem, as early cautioning at 0-day determining interim.

Water Management

Water management in horticultural and agricultural production requires important endeavors and plays a critical function in hydrological, climatological, and agronomical parity. Recently Patil& Deka (Patil & Deka, 2016) used machine learning methods like ANN are by and large broadly utilized for demonstrating the procedure of evapotranspiration. In any case, ANN faces issues like catching in neighborhood minima, moderate learning, and tuning of meta-parameters. In this examination, an improved extreme learning machine (ELM) calculation was used to assess week after week reference crop evapotranspiration (ETo). The investigation was completed for Jodhpur and Pali meteorological climate stations situated in the Thar Desert, India. The investigation assessed the execution of three diverse information mixes. The original information mix utilized locally accessible most extreme and least air temperature information while the second and third mix utilized ETo values from another station (outward contributions) alongside the locally accessible temperature information as data sources. The execution of ELM models was contrasted and the observational Hargreaves condition, ANN and least square support vector machine (LS-SVM) models.

Soil Management

The last classification of this concerns ML application on expectation distinguishing proof of agricultural soil properties, for example, the estimation of soil drying, condition, temperature, and dampness content. The soil is a different regular asset, with complicated procedures and systems that are hard to get it. Soil properties enable analysts to comprehend the elements of environments, what is more, the impingement in farming. Morellos et al. (Morellos et al., 2016) reported Machine learning methods, for example, Cubist and LS-SVM demonstrated a superior informative power than the tremendous multivariate relapse strategies, for example, PCR and PLSR. Consequently, they are suggested for soil spectroscopy investigations. Despite the fact that, for MC, the Cubist demonstrated the best model fitting, it had higher

Table 2 Applications of machine learning in agriculture

S.No	Machine learning applications in agriculture		
	Field of study	**Author & Year**	**Algorithms used**
1	Crop management	Ramos et al. 2017	SVM
2	Crop management	Ali et al. 2017	MLR, ANN,ANFIS
3	Crop management	Ebrahimi et al. 2017	SVM
4	Crop management	Pantazi et al. 2017	ANN/XY-Fusion
5	Crop management	Bench et al 2017	SVN
6	Crop management	Grinblat et al 2016	CNN
7	Livestock Management	Grinblat et al 2016	SVM
8	Water Management	Patil& Deka 2016	ANN/ELM
9	Soil Management	Morellos et al 2016	SVM/LS-SVM and Regression/ Cubist

RMSE and lower RPD than LS-SVM, and therefore LS-SVM was picked as the best performing model. The machine learning systems researched in this investigation can be utilized in field spectroscopy for the disconnected and on-line forecast of the dirt parameters examined in fields with corresponding soil type and fluctuation. Table 2 summarizes the application of machine learning technique in agriculture.

Applying Machine Learning Techniques for Scheduling In Distributed Systems

Application of machine learning techniques for scheduling in distributed systems is a contemporary field of research. In this chapter, such research contributions are brought to the light, and the proposed methods of using machine learning are explained.

Task vs. Virtual Machine Scheduling

In (George, Chandrasekaran, & Binu, 2016) cloud environment tasks are scheduled to processors by schedulers who will have to reduce the processing time and also to optimize the processing elements utilization. The objective of the designers of schedulers is to use the minimal number of processing components to complete the tasks in the expected time of completion.

Vengerov (Vengerov, 2009) has proposed a reinforcement learning method to optimize server utilization while scheduling jobs to servers. They formulated a value function, which calculates the future utility of resources. The reinforcement learning method is used to tune value function to present the state of servers to maximize server utilization with less number of servers to complete jobs.

In (Orhean, Pop, & Raicu, 2018) the authors have suggested a reinforcement learning algorithm for scheduling tasks in a distributed environment, typically in a cluster or a grid. The tasks are of various size and the dependencies also considered while mapping them onto different nodes of various type. The proposed method reduces total execution time while reducing utility usage by efficiently scheduling the tasks.

The directed acyclic graph (DAG) is used to model the tasks to be scheduled. The graph will represent the dependencies between tasks like tasks that are a parent, child, and sibling to other tasks. Dependent

Figure 5. DAG of tasks in a distributed system

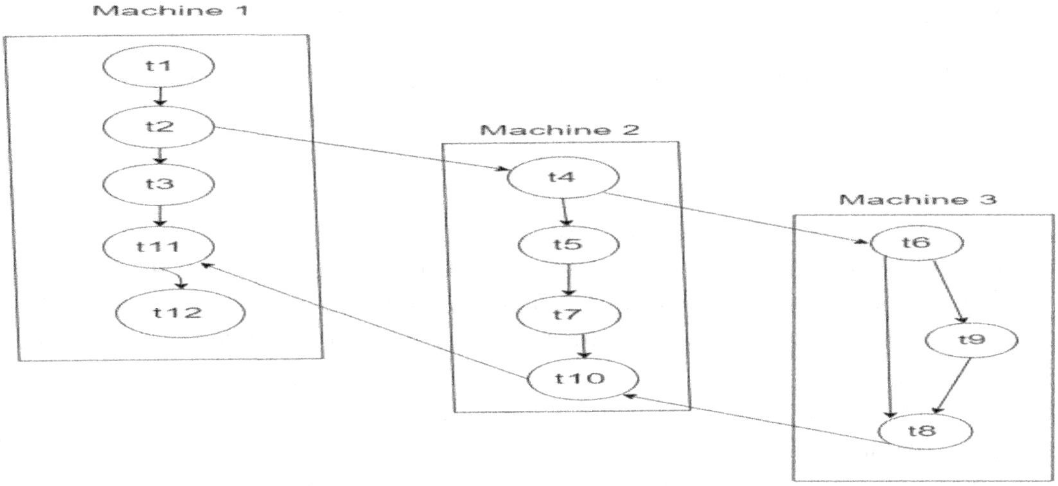

Tasks that cannot initiate until the tasks that they depend on had not completed. Child and sibling tasks can run in parallel, but tasks which are dependent can be paralleled with tasks that they depend on to finish the execution. Figure .5 depicts an example of the association between tasks in a distributed system represented in a DAG.

The DAG depicts not only the dependencies but also the mappings into different machines in the cluster or grid. The learning algorithms are divided into three namely, Q-learning, State-Action-Reward-State-Action (SARSA) and the Monte-Carlo technique. An agent chooses a particular scheduling policy based on his previous learning of scheduling similar tasks to nodes. Before understanding the algorithms, it is better to know the context of the scheduling environment.

Given a world of nodes, their resource state, actions taken on the nodes the following formula calculates utility value update when tasks are assigned to nodes during the scheduling. This utility update is the learning after allocating tasks to nodes and the corresponding updates in the state value. All of the three algorithms assume the following,

$S_{initial}$ and $S_{terminal}$ are the initial and final states of the nodes. They represent the state value before the initiation of tasks and after the completion of tasks during the scheduling of tasks to nodes. A set of actions A, maps the current set of states of nodes of the world (environment) to a new set represented as, T: S × A →S. Because of the set of actions A, the set of rewards is calculated as R: S ×A → R, set of utilities Q: S ×A → R and a policy is represented as π: S →A. The aim of an agent will be to increase the reward R by carrying out a set of actions A as part of the scheduling to learn a scheduling policy π.

For any given algorithm the objective is to calculate the utility value and learning the scheduling approach. The utility value can be calculated as,

$$Q [s, a] \leftarrow Q [s, a] + \alpha(r + d \cdot max_{a'} Q [s', a'] - Q [s, a]) \dots.. \qquad (1)$$

where α is learning rate, d is a discount factor.

The Q learning algorithm is to find the best scheduling policy, i.e., state action policy. It finds the best state action by finding the best state-action-rewards by calculating utilities to maximize reward.

The algorithm tries to improve the reward by finding optimum state-actions that results in efficient use of utilities.

$$Q [s, a] \leftarrow Q [s, a] + \alpha(r + d \cdot max_{a'} Q [s', a'] - Q [s, a]) \ldots \ldots \quad (2)$$

$$s \leftarrow s'$$

The algorithm tries to explore different paths from a current state to the next noticeable state by taking serious actions. For a known problem, when the algorithm uses the same path, it misses the opportunity to find a new optimum path for reaching a state. Also when algorithm explores a new path, it may stick indefinitely in it.

The next algorithm is SARSA, an on policy strategy when compared to Q-learning which is an off-policy strategy. Negative rewards are not considered in Q-learning hence called as off policy. SARSA takes the utility value update function from the path being explored than from the best path as it is in Q-learning.

$$Q [s, a] \leftarrow Q [s, a] + \alpha(r + d \cdot Q [s', a'] - Q [s, a]) \ldots \ldots \quad (3)$$

$$s \leftarrow s'$$

$$an \leftarrow a'$$

The Basic Q-learning Algorithm:

```
1:      function Q-learning (s_initial, s_terminal, α, d)
2:             initialize Q [S, A]
3:             s ← s_initial
4:             while s! = s_terminal do
5:                    select a
6:                    r = R(s, a)
7:                    s' = T (s, a)
8:                    Q [s, a] ← Q [s, a] + α(r + d · max_a' Q [s', a' ] -
                       Q [s, a])
9:             s ← s'
```

The next algorithm is SARSA, an on policy strategy when compared to Q-learning which is an off-policy strategy. Negative rewards are not considered in Q-learning hence called as off policy. SARSA takes the utility value update function from the path being explored than from the best path as it is in Q-learning.

Figure 6. Scheduling system with the third level of complexity

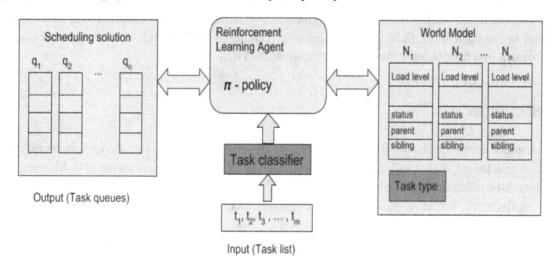

Levels of Complexities Considered

The proposed assumes three levels of complexity in implementing the policy. In the first level, all the tasks are assumed to be of the same size and complexity. To run a set of tasks represented in a DAG, the system in its first complexity level would require time to complete all the tasks will be equal to the time to complete each of the tasks sequentially.

Each node will be assigned with values of its load level, list of sibling tasks and parent tasks of that particular node's assigned tasks. The combination of all the nodes values form the world of states of the system given as, $S = \{\langle load\_level_i, parent_i, sibling_i \rangle | 1 \leq i \leq n\}$ ..... (4)

Figure 6 depicts the scheduling model with all three levels of complexities. In the first level task type and task classifier will not be available. It is a simple method to find optimum scheduling policy using only the node's load level, running task's parent and sibling tasks.

The second level of complexity includes a node's status information, and by consolidating the world of status, the tasks will be scheduled. This status will be updated whenever an agent schedules the tasks into the nodes.

Neither in the first level nor in the second level the complexity of the task is considered. The addition of a task type attribute in the world model will increase the proper scheduling of tasks onto nodes based on the complexity of tasks and load level of nodes. Introduction of a task classifier will also make the assignment of right tasks onto the right nodes efficient.

FUTURE RESEARCH DIRECTIONS

In this chapter, the merits, challenges of sentiment analysis in the text, image, audio, and video were discussed. However, there are some open problems presents that can be a foundation point for future research work. Sentiment analysis in the video is a real challenge still their open problem present. For example, if the customer visits any shopping complex, we can record the video and perform the sentiment analysis and predict the customer expectations to improve the business. Machine learning techniques can be applied in the weather forecasting, rain forecasting, automated water management, and soil management in the agriculture field. Machine learning techniques will be applied in automated resource management in a distributed system without using human help.

CONCLUSION

This chapters discussed the significance and effects of sentiment analysis challenges in social media based on text, image, audio, and video. The comparison of the techniques is summarized. Moreover, we discussed how machine learning techniques could be applied in the field of agriculture like crop management, livestock, soil management, and water management. Finally, we discussed task scheduling in the distributed system. Reinforcement learning based on the rewards given for better allocation of tasks while scheduling will improve the efficient utilization of nodes and completion of tasks in reduced time. Hence it has been a successful field of research.

REFERENCES

Agarwal, A. B. X. I. V. (2014). Sentiment analysis of twitter feeds. *Lecture Notes in Computer Science, 8883*, 33–52. doi:10.1007/978-3-319-13820-6

Ali, I., Cawkwell, F., Dwyer, E., & Green, S. (2017). Modeling Managed Grassland Biomass Estimation by Using Multitemporal Remote Sensing Data-A Machine Learning Approach. *IEEE Journal of Selected Topics in Applied Earth Observations and Remote Sensing, 10*(7), 3254–3264. doi:10.1109/JSTARS.2016.2561618

Barbosa, L., & Feng, J. (2010). Robust Sentiment Detection on Twitter from Biased and Noisy Data. Proceedings of the 23rd International Conference on Computational Linguistics: Posters. Association for Computational Linguistics, 36–44. 10.1016/j.sedgeo.2006.07.004

Bholane, S., & Gore, D. (2016). Sentiment Analysis on Twitter Data Using Support Vector Machine. *International Journal of Computer Science Trends and Technology, 4*(3), 365–370. Retrieved from https://sivaanalytics.wordpress.com/2013/10/10/sentiment-analysis-on-twitter-data-using-r-part-i/%5Cnhttps://sivaanalytics.wordpress.com/2013/10/18/step-by-step-sentiment-analysis-on-twitter-data-using-r-with-airtel-tweets-part-ii/%5Cnhttps://sivaanalytic

Bifet, A., & Frank, E. (2010). Twitter-crc.pdf. Discovery Science - 13th International Conference Proceedings.

Binch, A., & Fox, C. W. (2017). Controlled comparison of machine vision algorithms for Rumex and Urtica detection in grassland. *Computers and Electronics in Agriculture, 140*, 123–138. doi:10.1016/j.compag.2017.05.018

Boselli, R., Cesarini, M., Mercorio, F., & Mezzanzanica, M. (2018). Classifying online Job Advertisements through Machine Learning. *Future Generation Computer Systems, 86*, 319–328. doi:10.1016/j.future.2018.03.035

Chakrabarti & Punera. (2011). Event Summarization Using Tweets. ICWSM, 66–73. doi:10.1016/j.clgc.2012.04.004

Cohen, A., Nissim, N., & Elovici, Y. (2018). Novel set of general descriptive features for enhanced detection of malicious emails using machine learning methods. *Expert Systems with Applications, 110,* 143–169. doi:10.1016/j.eswa.2018.05.031

Davidov, D. (2010). Enhanced Sentiment Learning Using Twitter Hashtags and Smileys. Coling, 241–249.

Garcia-Ceja, E., Riegler, M., Nordgreen, T., Jakobsen, P., Oedegaard, K. J., & Tørresen, J. (2018). Mental health monitoring with multimodal sensing and machine learning: A survey. *Pervasive and Mobile Computing, 51,* 1–26. doi:10.1016/j.pmcj.2018.09.003

George, N., Chandrasekaran, K., & Binu, A. (2016). An objective study on improvement of task scheduling mechanism using computational intelligence in cloud computing. *2015 IEEE International Conference on Computational Intelligence and Computing Research, ICCIC 2015.* 10.1109/ICCIC.2015.7435660

Grinblat, G. L., Uzal, L. C., Larese, M. G., & Granitto, P. M. (2016). Deep learning for plant identification using vein morphological patterns. *Computers and Electronics in Agriculture, 127,* 418–424. doi:10.1016/j.compag.2016.07.003

Hatcher, W. G., & Yu, W. (2018). A Survey of Deep Learning: Platforms, Applications and Emerging Research Trends. *IEEE Access : Practical Innovations, Open Solutions, 6,* 24411–24432. doi:10.1109/ACCESS.2018.2830661

John, A., & Wang, F. (2015). *ET-LDA : Joint Topic Modeling for Aligning Events and their Twitter Feedback ET-LDA : Joint Topic Modeling for.* Academic Press.

Luo, Z., Xu, H., & Chen, F. (2018). Utterance-Based Audio Sentiment Analysis Learned by a Parallel Combination of CNN and LSTM. Retrieved from http://arxiv.org/abs/1811.08065

Maghilnan, S. (2017). *Sentiment Analysis on Speaker Specific Speech Data.* Academic Press.

Morellos, A., Pantazi, X. E., Moshou, D., Alexandridis, T., Whetton, R., Tziotzios, G., ... Mouazen, A. M. (2016). Machine learning based prediction of soil total nitrogen, organic carbon and moisture content by using VIS-NIR spectroscopy. *Biosystems Engineering, 152,* 104–116. doi:10.1016/j.biosystemseng.2016.04.018

Mountassir, A., Benbrahim, H., & Berrada, I. (2012). An empirical study to address the problem of unbalanced data sets in sentiment classification. Conference Proceedings - IEEE International Conference on Systems, Man and Cybernetics, 3298–3303. doi:10.1109/ICSMC.2012.6378300

Orhean, A. I., Pop, F., & Raicu, I. (2018). New scheduling approach using reinforcement learning for heterogeneous distributed systems. *Journal of Parallel and Distributed Computing, 117,* 292–302. doi:10.1016/j.jpdc.2017.05.001

Pang, B., & Lillian, L. S. V. (2002). Thumbs up? Sentiment Classification using Machine Learning Techniques. Proceedings of the Conference on Empirical Methods in Natural Language Processing (EMNLP), 57, 79–86. doi:10.3115/1118693.1118704

Pantazi, X. E., Moshou, D., Oberti, R., West, J., Mouazen, A. M., & Bochtis, D. (2017). Detection of biotic and abiotic stresses in crops by using hierarchical self organizing classifiers. *Precision Agriculture*, *18*(3), 383–393. doi:10.1007/s11119-017-9507-8

Parikh, R., & Movassate, M. (2009). Sentiment analysis of user-generated twitter updates using various classification techniques. *Business Marketing*, 1–18. Retrieved from http://nlp.stanford.edu/courses/cs224n/2009/fp/19.pdf

Patil, A. P., & Deka, P. C. (2016). An extreme learning machine approach for modeling evapotranspiration using extrinsic inputs. *Computers and Electronics in Agriculture*, *121*, 385–392. doi:10.1016/j.compag.2016.01.016

Patodkar, V. N., & I.R., S. (2017). Twitter as a Corpus for Sentiment Analysis and Opinion Mining. Ijarcce, 5(12), 320–322. doi:10.17148/IJARCCE.2016.51274

Pérez-Rosas, V., & Mihalcea, R. (2013). Sentiment analysis of online spoken reviews. Proceedings of the Annual Conference of the International Speech Communication Association, INTERSPEECH, 862–866.

Perez Rosas, V., Mihalcea, R., & Morency, L. P. (2013). Multimodal sentiment analysis of spanish online videos. *IEEE Intelligent Systems*, *28*(3), 38–45. doi:10.1109/MIS.2013.9

Poria, S., Cambria, E., Howard, N., Huang, G., & Hussain, A. (2016). Fusing audio, visual and textual clues for sentiment analysis from multimodal content. *Neurocomputing*, *174*, 50–59. doi:10.1016/j.neucom.2015.01.095

Ramos, P. J., Prieto, F. A., Montoya, E. C., & Oliveros, C. E. (2017). Automatic fruit count on coffee branches using computer vision. *Computers and Electronics in Agriculture*, *137*, 9–22. doi:10.1016/j.compag.2017.03.010

Tan, S., Li, Y., Sun, H., Guan, Z., Yan, X., Bu, J., ... He, X. (2014). Interpreting the public sentiment variations on Twitter. *IEEE Transactions on Knowledge and Data Engineering*, *26*(5), 1158–1170. doi:10.1109/TKDE.2013.116

Trilla, A., & Alias, F. (2013). Sentence-based sentiment analysis for expressive text-to-speech. *IEEE Transactions on Audio, Speech, and Language Processing*, *21*(2), 223–233. doi:10.1109/TASL.2012.2217129

Vengerov, D. (2009). A reinforcement learning framework for utility-based scheduling in resource-constrained systems. *Future Generation Computer Systems*, *25*(7), 728–736. doi:10.1016/j.future.2008.02.006

Wang, X., Zhu, F., Jiang, J., & Li, S. (2013). Earthquake Shakes Twitter Users: Real-time Event Detection by Social Sensors. *Lecture Notes in Computer Science*, *7923*, 502–513. doi:10.1007/978-3-642-38562-9-51

Wernick, M. N., Yang, Y., Brankov, J. G., Yourganov, G., & Strother, S. C. (2010). Medical imaging and machine learning. IEEE Signal Processing Magazine, 25–38. doi:10.1109/MSP.2010.936730 PubMed

Willcock, S., Martínez-López, J., Hooftman, D. A. P., Bagstad, K. J., Balbi, S., Marzo, A., ... Athanasiadis, I. N. (2018). Machine learning for ecosystem services. *Ecosystem Services*, *33*, 165–174. doi:10.1016/j.ecoser.2018.04.004

Wöllmer, M., Weninger, F., Knaup, T., Schuller, B., Sun, C., Sagae, K., & Morency, L.-P. (2013). You-Tube Movie Reviews: Sentiment Analysis in an Audio- Visual Context. *IEEE Intelligent Systems, 28*(3), 46–53. doi:10.1109/MIS.2013.34

Wrzesień, M., Treder, W., Klamkowski, K., & Rudnicki, W. R. (2018). Prediction of the apple scab using machine learning and simple weather stations. *Computers and Electronics in Agriculture*. doi:10.1016/j.compag.2018.09.026

Xia, R., Xu, F., Zong, C., Li, Q., Qi, Y., & Li, T. (2015). Dual Sentiment Analysis: Considering Two Sides of One Review. *IEEE Transactions on Knowledge and Data Engineering, 27*(8), 2120–2133. doi:10.1109/TKDE.2015.2407371

Yuan, J. (2013). *Sentribute: Image Sentiment Analysis from a Mid-level Perspective Categories and Subject Descriptors*. Academic Press.

Zhao, S., Yao, H., Gao, Y., Ding, G., & Chua, T. S. (2018). Predicting Personalized Image Emotion Perceptions in Social Networks. IEEE Transactions on Affective Computing, 9(4), 526–540. doi:10.1109/TAFFC.2016.2628787

Zhao, S., Yao, H., Gao, Y., Ji, R., & Ding, G. (2017). Continuous Probability Distribution Prediction of Image Emotions via Multitask Shared Sparse Regression. *IEEE Transactions on Multimedia, 19*(3), 632–645. doi:10.1109/TMM.2016.2617741

Chapter 21
Programming Language Support for Implementing Machine Learning Algorithms

Anitha Elavarasi S.
Sona College of Technology, India

Jayanthi J.
Sona College of Technology, India

ABSTRACT

Machine learning provides the system to automatically learn without human intervention and improve their performance with the help of previous experience. It can access the data and use it for learning by itself. Even though many algorithms are developed to solve machine learning issues, it is difficult to handle all kinds of inputs data in-order to arrive at accurate decisions. The domain knowledge of statistical science, probability, logic, mathematical optimization, reinforcement learning, and control theory plays a major role in developing machine learning based algorithms. The key consideration in selecting a suitable programming language for implementing machine learning algorithm includes performance, concurrence, application development, learning curve. This chapter deals with few of the top programming languages used for developing machine learning applications. They are Python, R, and Java. Top three programming languages preferred by data scientist are (1) Python more than 57%, (2) R more than 31%, and (3) Java used by 17% of the data scientists.

MACHINE LEARNING

Machine learning (ML) is one of the essential applications of artificial intelligence (AI) that makes the computer system to automatically learn and improve their performance from its own experience without being explicitly trained. ML refers to the set of techniques meant to deal with huge data in the most intelligent way in order to derive actionable insights. The purpose of ML is to automate the data analysis process by constructing algorithms and make appropriate prediction on the new input data that arrives their by enhancing the system performance. A computer program is said to learn from experience

DOI: 10.4018/978-1-5225-9902-9.ch021

E with respect to some class of tasks T and performance measure P, if its performance at tasks in T, as measured by P, improves with experience E (Singh, 2018). Machine learning algorithms are classified into four main types, such as:

- **Supervised Learning Algorithm**: Learning maps an input to an output based on the label value (i.e input-output pairs).
- **Unsupervised Learning Algorithm:** System learns from data which has not been labeled or categorized. Systems can infer a function to describe a hidden structure from unlabeled data.
- **Semi-supervised Learning Algorithm:** Combination of supervised and unsupervised learning. In this approach the system learns by make use of a small amount of labeled data for training from a large amount of unlabeled data in-order to maximize the learning capability.
- **Reinforcement Learning Algorithm**: System ought to take action in an *environment* so as to maximize the *reward*.

Steps Involved in Machine Learning

Machine learning is a method of data analysis that automates analytical model building. I t can learn from data identify patterns, and make decisions with minimal human interventions. The steps involved in solving the given problem are:

- Problem definition
- Data preparation
- Algorithm evaluation
- Performance analysis
- Visualizing results

LANGUAGES SUPPORT FOR MACHINE LEARNING

"Machine Learning – The Scorching Technology Fostering the Growth of several industries"

While you update technology news, you could probably see and hear machine learning everywhere from retail to space for any good reasons. Everyday a new app, product or service discloses that it is using machine learning to get smarter and useful results. It can be used at machine domains starting from on your way to work (Google Maps for suggesting Traffic Route, making an online purchase (on Amazon or Walmart), and for communicating with your friends online (Facebook). Figure 1 shows the popular machine learning languages and tools.

Case Study: Programming Languages and Healthcare Domain

The top healthcare applications that can influence Machine Learning in the world are

1. Medical Image Diagnosis

Figure 1. Popular Machine Learning tools

Computer vision has been one of the most ground-breaking inventions and has reformed the way medical diagnosis is being carried out. The medical image diagnosis has been one of the liveliest applications of machine learning in healthcare. Today, there are many companies that are functioning on using ML to diagnose diseases based on the images taken from various medical imaging instruments.

2.   Drug Discovery

Drug discovery is one of the most upfront and fast-growing applications of ML in healthcare. Several new drugs are regularly being discovered to treat various medical disorders. ML speed up this process of drug discovery and reduces the time necessary to develop new medicines. This application is advantageous to pharmaceutical companies which are under a constant pressure of outpacing their competitors, as ML helps them in rapidly developing effective drugs before somebody else in the market does.

3.   Robotic Surgery

Robotic surgery is one of the leading edge of ML applications in healthcare and is turning out to be one of the most trustworthy choices in this field. This technology empowers doctors to perform different types of complex surgeries with greater precision. Sometimes surgeries can get extremely complicated as there could be injuries in insignificant and tight areas, which are tough for the surgeons to work on it. Robotic surgery offers better visualization and greater access to such areas, making it easy for the surgeon involved. Although this technique is generally used for minimally invasive procedures, intermittently they are used in traditional open surgical procedures. ML is not directly used in such cases, however its applications, such as robotic and robot-assisted surgeries are proving to be highly beneficial for steadiness of the movement and motion of robotic arms, when being controlled by surgeons.

4.   Personalized Medicines

Personalized medicine, also known as precision medicine, is a procedure that differentiates patients into diverse groups, where the medications and treatment plans will be custom-made to an individual patient depending on their menace of disease or foreseen response. As every human being is different, even two people suffering from same illness may require different quantities of medicines. ML can be used to personalize each person's medicine dosage, based on various factors such as medical history, genetic lineage, age, weight, diet, patient history, stress levels, etc. This application also helps patients to decide whether they should undergo certain complicated treatments, such as chemotherapy, surgery, etc., based on factors such as medical history age, etc.

5.   Remote Healthcare Assistance

Machine learning is being progressively used in patient monitoring systems and in helping healthcare providers keep a track of the patient's condition in real time. The machine can identify patterns related to the patient's condition, follow-up with health status, detect improvements, and recommend treatments based on the patient's condition. Furthermore, these systems equipped with ML algorithms can call for help in case of any emergencies.

6.   Promoting Superior After Care and Healthy Lifestyle

Using ML, devices can be programmed to promote elderly person after care and healthy lifestyle among patients by providing suitable direction about the measures to be followed post treatment. The device can analyse the nature of the patients and the life style followed and appropriate measures to improve their health condition need to be suggested. ML technology can be used to improve quality of life.

Widespread Languages in Practice

Python

Python is a general-purpose, open source high level programming language developed by Python Software Foundation. It was first released in 1991 by Guido van Rossum. Code readability is emphasized by python. Using python, user can create anything from desktop software to web applications and frameworks. It supports dynamic type, automatic memory management, object-oriented programming paradigms, procedural, and standard library. Python programming language runs on any platform, ranging from Windows to Linux to Macintosh, Solaris etc. Machine learning Libraries and Packages included in python are:

- **Numpy** is used for its N-dimensional array objects.
- **Pandas** is a data analysis library that includes dataframes.
- **Matplotlib** is 2D plotting library for creating graphs and plots.
- **Scikit-learn** the algorithms used for data analysis and data mining tasks.
- **Seaborn** a data visualization library based on matplotlib.

Decision Tree Implementation Using Python

Decision tree (2019) uses a tree like model to classify the sample into two or more homogeneous sets based on a criterion. Each internal node represents a test on an attribute and each branch represents an outcome of the test. It is one of the supervised learning algorithms. This can be used for classification and prediction.

Steps Involved in Decision Tree (Analytics, 2016)

Step 1: Import necessary library like panda, numpy etc
Step 2: Create tree object using DecisionTreeClassifier
Step 3: Train the model
Step 4: Predict the output

Coding:

```
#Create Tree Object
1.        model = tree.DecisionTreeClassifier(criterion='gini')
#Train the model using predictor(X) and target(Y) - training data
2.        model.fit(X, y)
3.        model.score(X, y)
#Predict Output for the test data(x_test)
4.        predicted= model.predict(x_test)
```

R Programming Language

R is an open source programming language used for statistical analysis, graphics representation and reporting. R is freely available under the GNU General Public License. It run on a various platform such as Linux, Windows and Mac. R is an interpreted language. The data manipulation, calculation and graphical display facilities included in R [https://www.r-project.org/about.html] are:

- An effective data handling and storage facility.
- A suite of operators for calculations on arrays, in particular matrices.
- A large, coherent, integrated collection of intermediate tools for data analysis.
- Graphical facilities for data analysis and display either on /off -screen.
- A well-developed, simple and effective programming language which includes conditionals, loops, user-defined recursive functions and input and output facilities.

CRAN (Comprehensive R Archive Network), approximately 8,341 packages are available today. The users can install these ML packages simply by using the syntax: install.packages . Some of the machine learning packages included in R are:

- Package e1071 offer Functions for latent class analysis,fuzzy clustering, support vector machines, naive Bayes classifier etc,

- Package C50 offers decision trees and rule based models for pattern recognition application.
- Rpart for building regression trees.
- Deep learning and neural network can be practiced through packages such as nnet,rnn,deepnet etc.
- Package kernlab supports Kernel-based machine learning methods for classification, regression, clustering, dimensionality reduction. Among other methods it includes Support Vector Machines, Spectral Clustering, Kernel PCA etc.
- Optimization using Genetic Algorithms can be practiced through rgenoud, Rmalschains.
- Package arules provides implementations of Apriori, mining frequent itemsets, maximal frequent itemsets, closed frequent itemsets and association rules.
- Package frbs implements Fuzzy Rule-based Systems for regression and classification. Package RoughSets provides implementations of the rough set theory (RST) and the fuzzy rough set theory (FRST).

Linear Regression Implementation in R

Linear regression (Prabhakaran, n.d.) establishes a linear relationship between the predictor variable and the response variable. It is used to predict the value of an outcome variable based on one or more input predictor variables. The function used for building linear models is lm() which takes in two main arguments, namely: formula and data.

lm(sales ~ youtube, data = marketing)

Scatter plots can help visualize any linear relationships between the dependent and independent variables which can be drawn using

scatter.smooth(x=Attribute_x, y=Attribute_y, main="TitleX vs Y")

Correlation suggests the level of linear dependence between two variables. It can take values between -1 to +1. This can be calculated using cor().

Steps Involved in Linear Regression Process

Step 1: Load the data.
Step 2: Create the training and test data samples from original data.
Step 3: Develop the model on the training data and use it to predict it on the test data
Step 4: Evaluate the measures.
Step 5: Compute the prediction accuracy and error rates

Coding:

```
# Use the marketing data set which contains the impact of three
# advertising medias (youtube, facebook and newspaper) on sales.
# In-order to predict future sales based on advertising budget
# spent on youtube regression model is developed.
# load and inspect 4 rows of marketing data
```

```
1.          head(marketing, 4)

# linear model using lm()

2.          model <- lm(sales ~ youtube, data = marketing)

# Add regression line to the scatter plot

3.          ggplot(marketing, aes(x = youtube, y = sales)) +
 geom_point() +
   stat_smooth()
4.          correlation_acc <-cor(youtube, sales)
```

Java Machine Learning Library

Java-ML (Java machine learning library) consists of a collection of machine learning algorithms for classification, clustering, regression, filtering, etc (Abeel, de Peer, and Saeys, 2009). It provides a common interface for various machine learning algorithms. Well documented source code and plenty of code samples and tutorials for library 0.1.7 is available in the URL: http://java-ml.sourceforge.net/api/0.1.7/

A set of machine learning library and 170 data set from the well-known repositories (UCI Machine Learning Repository) is available in the URL: https://sourceforge.net/projects/java-ml/files/. Some of the machine learning library available in Java-ML are:

- **Net.sf.javaml.classification:** Provides several classification algorithms
- **Net.sf.javaml.classification.evaluation**: Provides algorithms and measures to evaluate classification algorithms.
- **Net.sf.javaml.clustering:** Provides algorithms to cluster data.
- **Net.sf.javaml.core.kdtree:** Provides a KD-tree implementation for fast range- and nearest-neighbors-queries.
- **Net.sf.javaml.featureselection:** Provides algorithms to evaluation the worth of attributes and attribute sets.
- **Net.sf.javaml.featureselection.ranking:** Provides feature ranking algorithms.

Clustering Implementation using Java ML

Clustering is the task of grouping a set of data objects such that objects in the same group are more similar to each other than to those in other groups. In other words data elements are cluster in such a manner that the distance between elements within a group should be minimum, and data element among different cluster should be maximum. It is one of the unsupervised learning algorithms.

Steps involved in k-means Clustering process:

Step 1: Loading the input file: Java-ML supports CSV, TSV and ARFF formatted files.

Dataset data = FileHandler.loadDataset(**new** File("iris.data"), 4, ",");

The first parameter of loadDataset is the file to load the data from. The second parameter is the index of the class label (zero-based) and the final parameter is the separator used to split the attributes in the file.

Dataset data = ARFFHandler.loadARFF(**new** File("iris.arff"), 4);

the ARFFHandler only has two arguments, the first one to indicate the file that should be loaded and the second one to indicate the index of the class label.

Step 2: Clustering process using k-Means Algorithm: C*reate four number of cluster using k-means algorithm*
Clusterer km=**new** KMeans(4);
Step 3: Cluster evaluation: *Create a measure for the cluster quality*
ClusterEvaluation sse= **new** SumOfSquaredErrors();

Java-ML provides a large number of cluster evaluation measures that are provided in the package net.sf.javaml.clustering.evaluation (Java.ml, n.d.).
Coding:

```
1.      Dataset data = FileHandler.loadDataset(new File("iris.data"), 4, ",");
2.      Clusterer km=new KMeans(4);
3.      Dataset[] clusters = km.cluster(data);
4.      ClusterEvaluation sse= new SumOfSquaredErrors();
5.      double score=sse.score(clusters);
```

Figure 2 shows the comparison of popular machine learning software between 2015 and 2017. More than 50% of the people use python and R language for their machine learning applications.

MACHINE LEARNING TOOL KIT

Weka

Weka is an open source **Java**-based workbench consist of a collection of machine learning algorithms for the purpose of data analysis, data mining and predictive modelling. It has tools for data preparation, classification, regression, clustering, association rules mining, and visualization. The algorithms can either be applied directly to a dataset or called from your own Java code. Weka can be downloaded from the URL http://www.cs.waikato.ac.nz/ml/weka/. Successful installation of weka (Aksenova, 2004) is shown in figure 2 with four different option for the user to select, such as:

- Simple CLI provides a simple command-line interface and allows direct execution of Weka commands.
- Explorer is an environment for exploring data.

Figure 2. Comparison of machine learning software

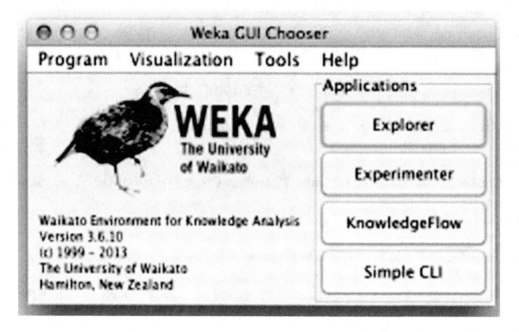

- Experimenter is an environment for performing experiments and conducting statistical tests between learning schemes.
- KnowledgeFlow is a Java-Beans-based interface for setting up and running machine learning experiments.

WEKA supports decision trees and lists, instance-based classifiers, support vector machines, multilayer perceptrons, logistic regression, and bayes' nets.

Implementation of Classification using Weka

Classification is the process of accurately predicting the data to a target class. For example to classify whether a person can be identified as low, medium, or high credit risks person. This approach uses class label in-order to categorise the person.

Steps Involved in Classification (Aksenova, 2004)

1. **Loading the Dataset:** It supports Attribute-Relation File Format (ARFF) file format.
2. **Choosing a Classifier:** Click on 'Choose' button in the 'Classifier' box just below the tabs and select the required algorithm (for example: C4.5 classifier WEKA -> Classifiers -> Trees ->J48.)
3. **Setting Test Options**: select the appropriate the test options given below
   a. Use training set. Evaluates the classifier on how well it predicts the class of the instances it was trained on.
   b. Supplied test set. Evaluates the classifier on how well it predicts the class of a set of instances loaded from a file. Clicking on the 'Set...' button brings up a dialog allowing you to choose the file to test on.

Figure 3. Weka Home screen

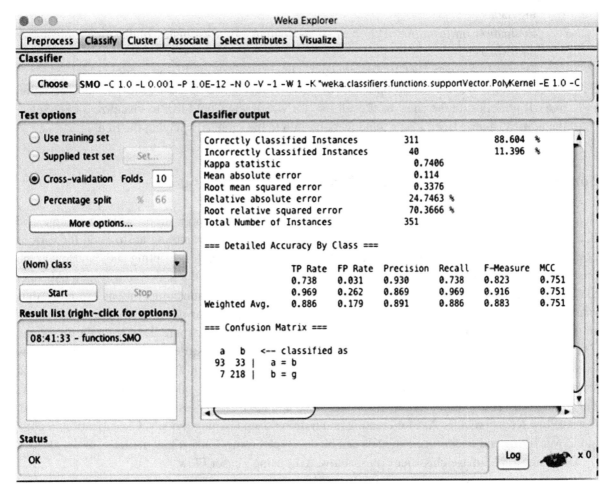

c. Cross-validation. Evaluates the classifier by cross-validation, using the number of folds that are entered in the 'Folds' text field.

d. Percentage split. Evaluates the classifier on how well it predicts a certain percentage of the data, which is held out for testing. The amount of data held out depends on the value entered in the '%' field.

Identify what is included into the output. In the 'Classifier evaluation options' make sure that the following options are checked (1) Output model (2) Output per-class stats, (3) Output confusion matrix, (4) Store predictions for visualization and (5) Set 'Random seed for Xval / % Split' to 1. Once the options have been selected, Click on 'Start' button to start the learning process. Figure 3 shows the classification output.

4. Analyzing
    ◦ Run Information indicate the algorithm used, no of instance and number of attribute used along with the split mode for training and test data used.

- ○ Classifier model is a pruned decision tree in textual form that was produced on the full training data.
- ○ Evaluation on test split. This part of the output gives estimates of the tree's predictive performance,
- ○ Detailed Accuracy By Class demonstrates the classifier's prediction accuracy.

5. **Visualization:** WEKA has an option of displaying the result in graphical format (classification tree). Right-click on the entry in 'Result list' for which you would like to visualize a tree. Select the item 'Visualize tree'; a new window comes up to the screen displaying the tree.

Tensorflow: A System For Large-Scale Machine Learning

TensorFlow is an open-source library used for machine learning applications which are large and heterogeneous in nature. It uses the notation of dataflow-based programming abstraction for various computation processes both within and across the machine. Wrapping of scripting and dataflow graph enables the user to make use of varied architecture without modifying the underlying system (Abadi et al., 2016). The dataflow graph expresses the communication between sub computations explicitly, thus making it easy to execute independent computations in parallel and to partition computations across multiple devices. Tensor Processing Units (TPUs) makes the architecture more flexible for the developer. The execution of Tensorflow application requires two phases, first phase defines the symbolic dataflow graph and the second phase executes an optimized version of the program. Performance can be improved with the help of multicore CPUs and GPUs running the deep learning algorithm and their by saving the power. TensorFlow offers various APIs to develop applications on desktop, mobile, web, and cloud. TensorFlow Keras provides API for creating and training deep learning models. Classification, regression, over fitting and under fitting models can be developed using TensorFlow model

Building simple image classifier (TensorFlow, n.d.) using Tensor Flow

Step 1: Import the TensorFlow library into your program
Step 2: Load and prepare the MNIST dataset. Convert the samples from integers to floating-point numbers
Step 3: Build the tf.keras model by stacking layers. Select an optimizer and loss function used for training
Step 4: Train and evaluate image classifier model:

Coding:

```
1.      import tensorflow as tf
2.
3.      mnist = tf.keras.datasets.mnist
4.      (x_train, y_train),(x_test, y_test) = mnist.load_data()
5.      x_train, x_test = x_train / 255.0, x_test / 255.0
6.
7.      model = tf.keras.models.Sequential([
8.        tf.keras.layers.Flatten(input_shape=(28, 28)),
9.        tf.keras.layers.Dense(512, activation=tf.nn.relu),
10.        tf.keras.layers.Dropout(0.2),
```

Figure 4. Classification output

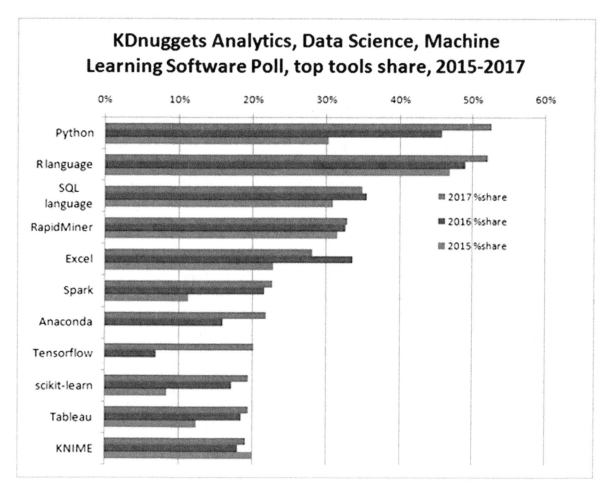

```
11.             tf.keras.layers.Dense(10, activation=tf.nn.softmax)
12.         ])
13.
14.         model.compile(optimizer='adam',
15.                     loss='sparse_categorical_crossentropy',
16.                     metrics=['accuracy'])
17.
18.         model.fit(x_train, y_train, epochs=5)
19.         model.evaluate(X_test,y_test)
```

Dlib-ml: A Machine Learning Toolkit

Dlib-ml is open source software developed by Davis E. King (2009). It contains a wide range of machine learning algorithms developed in C++ language. The Dlib-ml toolkit can be accessed from the URL -

http://dlib.net/ml.html. It can be used in both open source and commercial ways and is released as Boost Software License. This can be configured and installed on Windows, Linux and Mac operating system. It provides numerous library function for performing tasks related to image processing (management and manipulation of images ie feature extraction, object detection, filtering, scaling and rotation, visualization etc.), machine learning (algorithm for classification, regression, clustering, unsupervised and semi supervised algorithm, deep learning etc), networking (to provide network service- socket API), algorithms for sorting and finding cryptographic hashes, graph (provides tools for representing undirected and directed graphs) etc. Dlib-ml can be used in robotics, mobile phones high performance computing environment. Dlib-ml also provides certain python interface to perform the task of classification (binary classifier), image processing (face detection, jitter, face recognition), clustering, support vector machine (structural SVM, SVM rank) and video object tracking. Figure 5 shows the home page of Dlib library.

Scikit-learn: Machine Learning in Python

Scikit-learn an easy-to-use interface integrated with the Python language (Pedregosa et al., 2011) shown in figure 6 . It provides python based machine learning algorithm for both supervised and unsupervised problems. It has been given under simplified BSD (Berkeley Software Distribution) license to promote its usage both on academic and commercial sectors. BSD licenses are a family of permissive free software licenses, imposing minimal restrictions on the use and distribution of covered software (Scikt-learn, 2019). Scikit- learn can be accessed from the URL - http://scikit-learn.sourceforge.net. The features that differentiate Scikit- learn from other python based machine learning tool kit are (1) it depends only on numpy and scipy to facilitate easy distribution (2) it focuses on imperative programming (3) it incorporates compiled code. The technologies involved on scikit-learn are (1) Numpy the base data structure to handle data and model parameters, (2)Scipy provides algorithms for linear algebra, sparse matrix representation and basic statistical functions and (3) Cython combines C and Python to reach higher performance.

Orange: Data Mining Toolbox in Python

Orange is an open source data analysis tool kit released under General Public License (GPL) (Demsar et al., 2013). It runs on Windows, Mac OS and Linux operating system. Versions up to 3.0 include core components in C++ with wrappers in Python are available on GitHub. It provides a component-based design which is simple to use and ensure high interactivity through scripting. This can be used by any type of user such as experienced user, programmers, students etc. The features offered by orange are:

1. data management and preprocessing,
2. classification,
3. regression,
4. association,
5. ensembles,
6. clustering,
7. evaluation,
8. projections.

Figure 5. Home page of DLib library

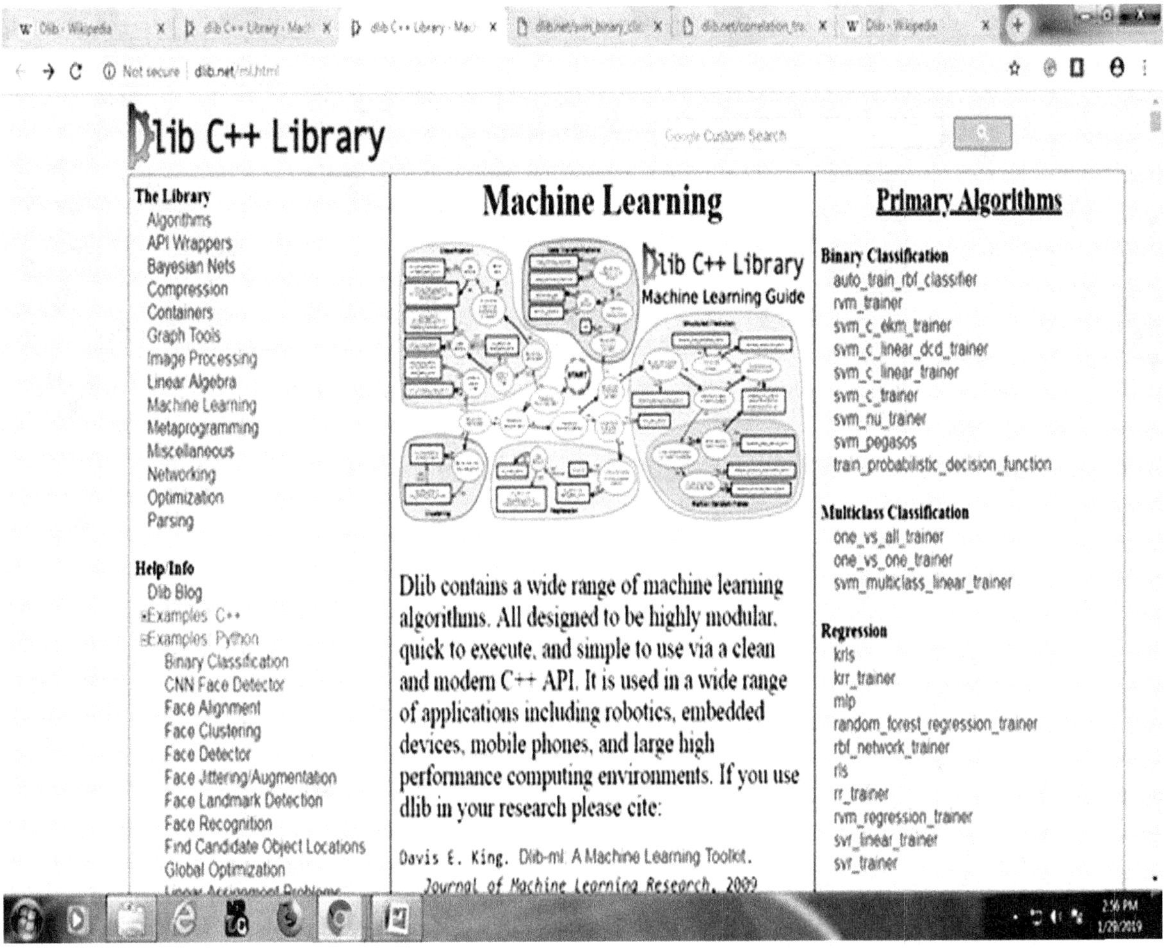

The popular Python libraries included in Orange are numpy for linear algebra operation, networkx for networks operation and matplotlib for visualization purpose. Figure 7 shows the home page of Orange.

Implementation of Naive Bayes using Orange

Naïve Bayes is a classification method based on the Bayes theorem. It is based on a probabilistic approach. Download and install Orange from github. On successful installation use the python environment or command line to import orange. Orange supports discrete attributes for naïve Bayes algorithm.

Steps to build naïve bayes

Step 1: Load the required library.
Step 2: Load the data set.
Step 3: Constructs naive Bayesian learner using the class NaiveBayesLearner.()

Coding

Figure 6. Home page of Scikit

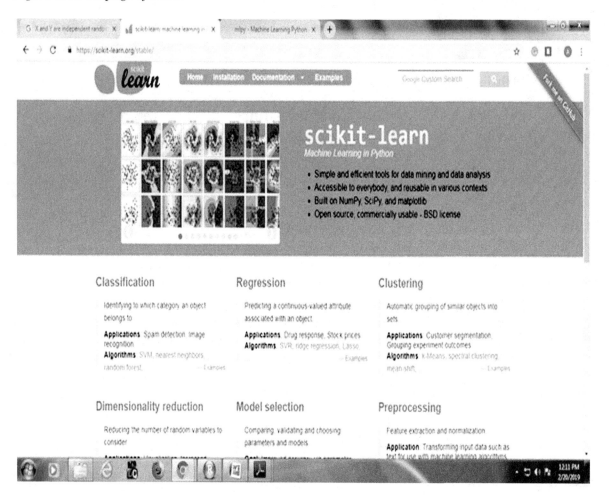

```
# Load the lenses dataset and constructs naive Bayesian learner
# Apply classifier to the first 100 data instances
import Orange
lenses = Orange.data.Table('lenses')
nb = Orange.classification.NaiveBayesLearner()
classifier = nb(lenses)
classifier(lenses[0:100], True)
```

MLPY: Machine Learning Python

Machine Learning Python (mlpy) (Albanese et al.., 2012) is an open source python machine learning library distributed under the GNU General Public License version 3. This can be accessed using the URL: http://mlpy.sourceforge.net and its home page is shown in figure8. mlpy is built on top of the NumPy/ SciPy packages. It supports methods for both supervised and unsupervised problems such as Support

Figure 7. Home page of Orange

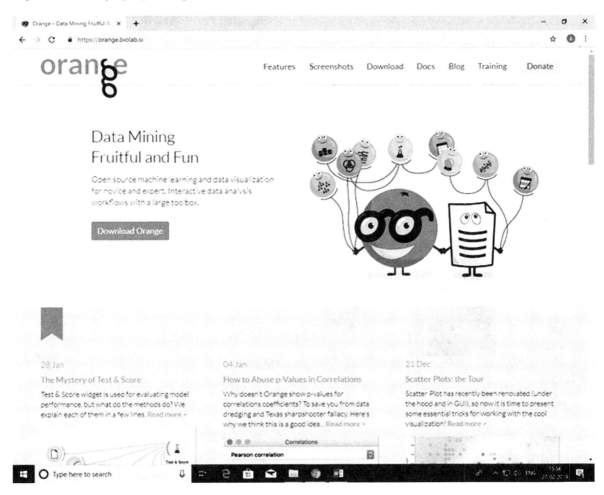

Vector Machines, Linear Discriminate analysis LDA, k-nearest neighbor, Hierarchical Clustering, k-means clustering, Principal Component Analysis (PCA), Wavelet Transform etc.

Table 1 shows the various popular machine learning algorithm supported by various toolkit.

Programming Language Selection for Healthcare Domain

JAVA

The language which is useful in providing solution to a healthcare problems (Krill, 2014) using machine learning is plenty. Most widely used languages would be java, Python, R etc. If the need is on maintaining (Electronic Health Record) EHR, and if no managerial restrictions and governance for what to use, then it is better to with Java. Since it consisting of wider range of API's that supports machine learning.

Java offers the widest collection of deliver options: desktop apps, server apps, web apps, cloud apps, etc. It's the language that creates the least number of conventions about what platform you're running, providing a reliable performance across multiple devices. Since medical data are highly secured, Java

Figure 8. Home page of mlpy

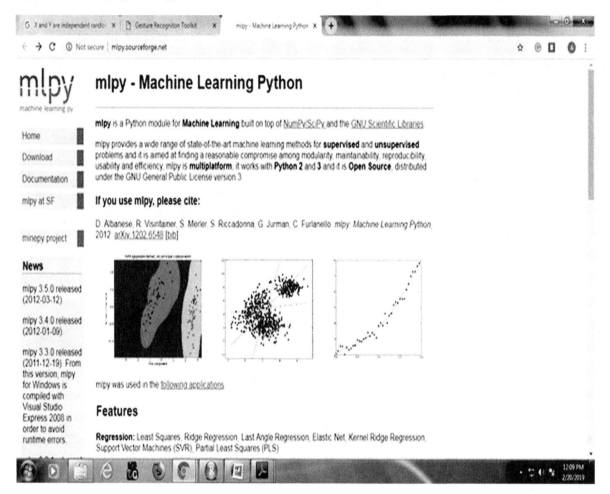

provides some of the best security out there, both in terms of software quality and built-in support for encryption, which is required by HIPAA. Java is logically robust, accommodating scalable APIs better than any other language.

Table 1. Support of machine learning algorithm by various toolkit

Algorithm	scikit-learn	mlpy	Orange	Dlib
Support Vector machine	Yes	yes	Yes	yes
k-Nearest Neighbors	Yes	Yes	Yes	No
PCA	Yes	Yes	Yes	No
k-Means	Yes	Yes	No	Yes
Hierarchical Clustering	Yes	Yes	Yes	No
Logistic Regression	Yes	Yes	Yes	No

It supports to create Cloud based EHR's and Java remains a critical technology that fascinates powerful interest and passion always. Java is a staple of enterprise computing world to solve several sensitive issues like healthcare. Java anchors Android apps development where Apps becomes the part and part of life.

Java EE (Enterprise Edition) 8 is also in the works and is expected to focus on supporting the latest Web standards, ease of development, and cloud support. Python is well-known among the most commonly used programming languages in the world. It lets you work more effective and productive and what's more, it is also considered to be one of the safest programming languages.

PYTHON

Python is widely used to produce web-applications for medical services. Software development using Python also allows the following capabilities:

- Web and Internet Development
- Database Access
- Desktop GUIs
- Scientific & Numeric
- Education
- Network Programming

Its main performance indicators in development process comprise ability to meet deadlines, quality and volume of code. In order to achieve these indicators during the development process one of the commonly used framework is Django. This framework is based on Python was developed in July 2005. Django promises a trustworthy list of built-in modules that are very useful and can be customized. Also it is provided with built-in security provisions against the three main sorts of web app attacks.

Being secure and having open-ended opportunities of modifying Django framework, it's been opted by many developers to realize requests and meet requirements for any business idea related to telemedicine and eHealth projects. There is a framework in Python for building API called Flask. It is often used for building prototypes which is very much helpful in delivering fruitful products. It guarantees stability and security features.

Advantages of using Python in Healthcare

1. Python, Django and other frameworks are enabled with quality principles agreeable with HIPAA checklist.
2. Supports healthcare projects in the Big data project domain too.
3. It is in line with the Database back-end assistance.
4. Perform platform independence with characteristics focused on iPods, iPhones and the web.

Python healthcare applications are used by many medical start-ups. Some of them are:

1. **Roam Analytics** is a platform that uses complete contextual data and machine learning to empower biopharmaceutical and medical device companies. The predictive insights are useful making knowledgeable decisions and provide better treatments. It could achieve the best possible treatments.

2. **AiCure** is an NIH and VC-founded healthcare start up. AiCure practices artificial intelligence to visually confirm medication absorption. The clinically-validated platform works on smartphones to reduce risk and optimize patient behaviour.

3. **Drchrono** is an American company that provides a software as a service patient care platform consisting of a Web- and cloud-based app for doctors and patients that makes electronic health records available digitally. It supports practice management and medical billing services.

CONCLUSION

Machine Learning is learning from data. Machine Learning Programs are hardware intensive as they include a number of intense mathematical computations like matrix multiplications and all. With the advent of GPU's, TPU's and faster processor computations are not that time consuming. Machine Learning is a product of statistics, mathematics, and computer science. As a practice, it has grown phenomenally in the last few years. It has empowered companies to build products like recommendation engines, self-driving cars etc. Libraries tend to be relatively stable and free of bugs. If we use appropriate libraries, it reduces the amount of code that is to be written. The fewer the lines of code, the better the functionality. Therefore, in most cases, it is better to use a library than to write our own code. An open source library consists of all the minute details that are dropped out of scientific literature. This chapter covers some of the case studies using python, java, R etc would motivate and use relevant tools for the implementation of machine learning algorithms. Based on the requirement the language for implementation can be selected and it should always ensures the quality.

REFERENCES

A Complete Tutorial on Tree Based Modeling from Scratch. (n.d.). Retrieved from https://www.analyticsvidhya.com/blog/2016/04/complete-tutorial-tree-based-modeling-scratch-in-python

Abadi, M., Barham, P., Chen, J., Chen, Z., Davis, A., & Dean, J. (2016). Tensorflow: a system for large-scale machine learning. *OSDI, 16*, 265-283.

Abeel, T., de Peer, Y. V., & Saeys, Y. (2009). Java-ML: A Machine Learning Library. *Journal of Machine Learning Research, 10*, 931–934.

Aksenova, S. (2004). *Machine Learning with WEKA WEKA Explorer Tutorial for WEKA Version 3.4. 3*. sabanciuniv.edu

Albanese, D., Visintainer, R., Merler, S., Riccadonna, S., Jurman, G., & Furlanello, C. (2012). *mlpy: Machine learning python*. arXiv preprint arXiv:1202.6548

Decision Tree. (2019, May 31). Retrieved from https://en.wikipedia.org/wiki/Decision_tree

Demšar, J., Curk, T., Erjavec, A., Gorup, Č., Hočevar, T., & Milutinovič, M. (2013). Orange: Data mining toolbox in Python. *Journal of Machine Learning Research, 14*(1), 2349–2353.

King, D. E. (2009). Dlib-ml: A machine learning toolkit. *Journal of Machine Learning Research*, *10*(Jul), 1755–1758.

Krill, P. (2014, September 30). *Four reasons to stick with Java, and four reasons to dump it*. Retrieved from https://www.javaworld.com/article/2689406/four-reasons-to-stick-with-java-and-four-reasons-to-dump-it.html

Pedregosa, F., Varoquaux, G., Gramfort, A., Michel, V., Thirion, B., & Grisel, O. (2011). Scikit-learn: Machine learning in Python. *Journal of Machine Learning Research*, *12*, 2825–2830.

Prabhakaran, S. (n.d.). *Eval(ez_write_tag([[728,90],'r_statistics_co-box-3','ezslot_2',109,'0']));Linear Regression*. Retrieved from http://r-statistics.co/Linear-Regression.html

Scikit-learn. (2019, May 30). Retrieved from https://en.wikipedia.org/wiki/Scikit-learn

Singh, H. (2018, June 26). *Machine Learning- What, Why, When and How?* Retrieved from https://towardsdatascience.com/machine-learning-what-why-when-and-how-9a2f244647a4

TensorFlow. (n.d.). Retrieved from https://www.tensorflow.org/tutorials

The R Project for Statistical Computing. (n.d.). Retrieved from https://www.r-project.org/

Weka 3: Machine Learning Software in Java. (n.d.). Retrieved from http://www.cs.waikato.ac.nz/ml/weka

Compilation of References

A Complete Tutorial on Tree Based Modeling from Scratch. (n.d.). Retrieved from https://www.analyticsvidhya.com/blog/2016/04/complete-tutorial-tree-based-modeling-scratch-in-python

Abadi, M., Barham, P., Chen, J., Chen, Z., Davis, A., & Dean, J. (2016). Tensorflow: a system for large-scale machine learning. OSDI, 16, 265-283.

Abadi, M., Chu, A., Goodfellow, I., McMahan, H. B., Mironov, I., Talwar, K., & Zhang, L. (2016). Deep learning with differential privacy. *Proceedings of the ACM SIGSAC Conference on Computer and Communications Security ACM*, 308–318.

Abdellaoui, J. E., & Berradi, H. (2018). Multipoint relay selection through estimated spatial relation in smart city environments. *2018 International Conference on Advanced Communication Technologies and Networking (CommNet)*, 1-10. 10.1109/COMMNET.2018.8360273

Abdi, H., & Williams, L. J. (2010). Principal component analysis. *Wiley Interdisciplinary Reviews: Computational Statistics, 2*(4), 433–459. doi:10.1002/wics.101

Abdurrazaq, I., Hati, S., & Eswaran, C. (2008, May). Morphology approach for features extraction in retinal images for diabetic retionopathy diagnosis. In *2008 International Conference on Computer and Communication Engineering* (pp. 1373-1377). IEEE. 10.1109/ICCCE.2008.4580830

Abeel, T., de Peer, Y. V., & Saeys, Y. (2009). Java-ML: A Machine Learning Library. *Journal of Machine Learning Research, 10*, 931–934.

Abhigna, B. S. (2018). Crowdsourcing– A Step Towards Advanced Machine Learning. *Procedia Computer Science, 132*, 632–642.

Abramov, R., & Herzberg, A. (2013). TCP Ack storm DoS attacks. *Computers & Security, 33*, 12–27. doi:10.1016/j.cose.2012.09.005

ADCIS. (n.d.). Retrieved from: http://www.adcis.net/en/third-party/messidor/

Adnane, A., Bidan, C., & de Sousa Júnior, R. T. (2013). Trust-based security for the OLSR routing proto-col. *Computer Communications, 36*(10), 1159–1171. doi:10.1016/j.comcom.2013.04.003

Agah, A., Basu, K., & Das, S. K. (2006). Security enforcement in wireless sensor networks: A framework based on non-cooperative games. *Pervasive and Mobile Computing, 2*(2), 137–158. doi:10.1016/j.pmcj.2005.12.001

Agarwal, A. B. X. I. V. (2014). Sentiment analysis of twitter feeds. *Lecture Notes in Computer Science, 8883*, 33–52. doi:10.1007/978-3-319-13820-6

Agarwal, N., Koti, S. R., Saran, S., & Kumar, A. S. (2018). Data mining techniques for predicting dengue outbreak in geospatial domain using weather parameters for New Delhi, India. *Current Science, 114*(11), 2281–2291.

Aggarwal, C. C. (2016). *Outlier analysis.* New York: Springer.

Agrawal, R., & Srikant, R. (1994). Fast Algorithms for Mining Association Rules. *Proc. 20th Int'l Conf. Very Large Data Bases (VLDB)*, 487-499.

Ahmad, A., & Dey, L. (2007). A k-mean clustering algorithm for mixed numeric and categorical data. *Data & Knowledge Engineering, 63*(2), 503–527. doi:10.1016/j.datak.2007.03.016

Ahmed, C. F., Tanbeer, S.-K., Jeong, B.-S., & Lee, Y.-K. (2009). Efficient Tree Structures for High Utility Pattern Mining in Incremental Databases. *IEEE Transactions on Knowledge and Data Engineering, 21*(12), 1708–1721. doi:10.1109/TKDE.2009.46

Aishwarya, R., Gayathri, P., & Jaisankar, N. (2013). A Method for Classification Using Machine Learning Technique for Diabetes. *IACSIT International Journal of Engineering and Technology, 5*(3), 2903–2908.

Aitalissdia, N., Hassan, M., Cherradi, M. B., Abbassi, A. E., & Bouattane, O. (2016). Parallel Implementation of Bias Field Correction Fuzzy C-Means Algorithm for Image Segmentation. *International Journal of Advanced Computer Science and Applications, 1*(3), 375–383.

Akbar, S., Sharif, M., Akram, M. U., Saba, T., Mahmood, T., & Kolivand, M. (2019). Automated techniques for blood vessels segmentation through fundus retinal images: A review. *Microscopy Research and Technique, 82*(2), 153–170. doi:10.1002/jemt.23172 PMID:30614150

Aksenova, S. (2004). *Machine Learning with WEKA WEKA Explorer Tutorial for WEKA Version 3.4. 3.* sabanciuniv.edu

Al-Ataby, A., & Al-Naima, F. (2010). A Modified High Capacity Image Steganography Technique Based on Wavelet Transform. *The International Arab Journal of Information Technology, 7*(4).

Albanese, D., Visintainer, R., Merler, S., Riccadonna, S., Jurman, G., & Furlanello, C. (2012). *mlpy: Machine learning python.* arXiv preprint arXiv:1202.6548

Albini, A., Pennesi, G., Donatelli, F., Cammarota, R., De Flora, S., & Noonan, D. M. (2010). Cardiotoxicity of anticancer drugs: The need for cardio-oncology and cardio-oncological prevention. *Journal of the National Cancer Institute, 102*(1), 14–25. doi:10.1093/jnci/djp440 PMID:20007921

Alessa, A., & Faezipour, M. (2018). *Preliminary Flu Outbreak Prediction Using Efficient Twitter Posts Classification and Linear Regression with Historical CDC Reports.* Preprint. doi:10.2196/12383

Alhadidi, B., Zubi, M. H., & Suleiman, H. N. (2007). Mammogram breast cancer image detection using image processing functions. *Information Technology Journal, 6*(2), 217–221. doi:10.3923/itj.2007.217.221

Ali, I., Cawkwell, F., Dwyer, E., & Green, S. (2017). Modeling Managed Grassland Biomass Estimation by Using Multitemporal Remote Sensing Data-A Machine Learning Approach. *IEEE Journal of Selected Topics in Applied Earth Observations and Remote Sensing, 10*(7), 3254–3264. doi:10.1109/JSTARS.2016.2561618

Al-Kofahi, Y., Lassoued, W., Lee, W., & Roysam, B. (2010). Improved automatic detection and segmentation of cell nuclei in histopathology images. *IEEE Transactions on Biomedical Engineering, 57*(4), 841–852. doi:10.1109/TBME.2009.2035102 PMID:19884070

Allyn. (2017). *A Comparison of a Machine Learning Model with EuroSCORE II in Predicting Mortality after Elective Cardiac Surgery: A Decision Curve Analysis.* PLOS.

Almomani, I., Al-Banna, E., & Al-Akhras, M. (2013). Logic-Based Security Architecture for Systems Providing Multihop Communication. *International Journal of Distributed Sensor Networks*, *2013*, 1–17.

Amara, J., Bouaziz, B., & Algergawy, A. (2017). *A deep learning-based approach for banana leaf diseases classification*. Lecture Notes in Informatics.

Amissah-Arthur, K. N., & Mensah, E. (2018). The past, present and future management of sickle cell retinopathy within an African context. *Eye (London, England)*, 1. PMID:29991740

Arafiyah, R., & Hermin, F. (2018, January). Data mining for dengue hemorrhagic fever (DHF) prediction with naive Bayes method. *Journal of Physics: Conference Series*, *948*(1), 012077. doi:10.1088/1742-6596/948/1/012077

Ardizzone, E., Pirrone, R., & Gambino, O. (2008). Bias Artifact Suppression on MR Volumes. *Computer Methods and Programs in Biomedicine*, *92*(1), 35–53. doi:10.1016/j.cmpb.2008.06.005 PMID:18644657

Ardizzone, E., Pirrone, R., & Gambino, O. (2014). Illumination correction in Biomedical Images. *Computer Information*, *33*, 175–196.

Asadi, H., Dowling, R., Yan, B., & Mitchell, P. (2014). Machine learning for outcome prediction of acute ischemic stroke post intra-arterial therapy. *PLoS One*, *9*(2), e88225. doi:10.1371/journal.pone.0088225 PMID:24520356

Asadi, H., Kok, H. K., Looby, S., Brennan, P., O'Hare, A., & Thornton, J. (2016). Outcomes and complications after endovascular treatment of Brain Arteriovenous Malformations: A Prognostication Attempt using artificial Intelligence. *World Neurosurgery*, *96*, 562–569. doi:10.1016/j.wneu.2016.09.086 PMID:27693769

Aswathy, M. A., & Jagannath, M. (2017). Detection of breast cancer on digital histopathology images: Present status and future possibilities. *Informatics in Medicine Unlocked*, *8*, 74–79. doi:10.1016/j.imu.2016.11.001

Axel, L., Costantini, J., & Listerud, J. (1987). Intensity Correction in Surface Coil MR Imaging. *AJR. American Journal of Roentgenology*, *148*(2), 418–420. doi:10.2214/ajr.148.2.418 PMID:3492123

Azzopardi, G., Strisciuglio, N., Vento, M., & Petkov, N. (2015). Trainable COSFIRE filters for vessel delineation with application to retinal images. *Medical Image Analysis*, *19*(1), 46–57. doi:10.1016/j.media.2014.08.002 PMID:25240643

Baldi, P., & Pollastri, G. (2004). The principled design of large-scale recursive neural network architectures-DAG-RNNs and the protein structure prediction problem. *Journal of Machine Learning Research*, *4*, 575–602.

Bankovic, Z., Fraga, D., Manuel Moya, J., Carlos Vallejo, J., Malagón, P., Araujo, Á., ... Nieto-Taladriz, O. (2011). Improving security in WMNs with reputation systems and self-organizing maps. *Journal of Network and Computer Applications*, *34*(2), 455–463. doi:10.1016/j.jnca.2010.03.023

Bansal & Rishiwal. (2014). Assessment of QoS based multicast routing protocols in MANET. *2014 5th International Conference - Confluence The Next Generation Information Technology Summit (Confluence)*, 421-426.

Barbosa, L., & Feng, J. (2010). Robust Sentiment Detection on Twitter from Biased and Noisy Data. Proceedings of the 23rd International Conference on Computational Linguistics: Posters. Association for Computational Linguistics, 36–44. 10.1016/j.sedgeo.2006.07.004

Barton, A. J. (2012). The regulation of mobile health applications. *BMC Medicine*, *10*(1), 46. doi:10.1186/1741-7015-10-46 PMID:22569114

Belgiu, M., & Drăguţ, L (2016). Random forest in remote sensing: A review of applications and future directions. *ISPRS Journal of Photogrammetry and Remote Sensing, 114*, 24-31.

Belsare, A. D., Mushrif, M. M., Pangarkar, M. A., & Meshram, N. (2016). Breast histopathology image segmentation using spatio-colour-texture based graph partition method. *Journal of Microscopy, 262*(3), 260–273. doi:10.1111/jmi.12361 PMID:26708167

Bengio, X. (2010). *Glorot, Understanding the difficulty of training deep feedforward neuralnetworks*. AISTATS.

Bengio, Y., Courville, A., & Vincent, P. (2013). Representation learning: A review and new perspectives. *IEEE Transactions on Pattern Analysis and Machine Intelligence, 35*(8), 1798–1828. doi:10.1109/TPAMI.2013.50 PMID:23787338

Bentley, P., Ganesalingam, J., Carlton Jones, A. L., Mahady, K., Epton, S., Rinne, P., ... Rueckert, D. (2014). Prediction of stroke thrombolysis outcome using CT brain machine learning. *NeuroImage. Clinical, 4*, 635–640. doi:10.1016/j.nicl.2014.02.003 PMID:24936414

Bholane, S., & Gore, D. (2016). Sentiment Analysis on Twitter Data Using Support Vector Machine. *International Journal of Computer Science Trends and Technology, 4*(3), 365–370. Retrieved from https://sivaanalytics.wordpress.com/2013/10/10/sentiment-analysis-on-twitter-data-using-r-part-i/%5Cnhttps://sivaanalytics.wordpress.com/2013/10/18/step-by-step-sentiment-analysis-on-twitter-data-using-r-with-airtel-tweets-part-ii/%5Cnhttps://sivaanalytic

Bifet, A., & Frank, E. (2010). Twitter-crc.pdf. Discovery Science - 13th International Conference Proceedings.

Binch, A., & Fox, C. W. (2017). Controlled comparison of machine vision algorithms for Rumex and Urtica detection in grassland. *Computers and Electronics in Agriculture, 140*, 123–138. doi:10.1016/j.compag.2017.05.018

Bodai, B. I., & Tuso, P. (2015). Breast cancer survivorship: A comprehensive review of long-term medical issues and lifestyle recommendations. *The Permanente Journal, 19*(2), 48–79. doi:10.7812/TPP/14-241 PMID:25902343

Boselli, R., Cesarini, M., Mercorio, F., & Mezzanzanica, M. (2018). Classifying online Job Advertisements through Machine Learning. *Future Generation Computer Systems, 86*, 319–328. doi:10.1016/j.future.2018.03.035

Boukerche, A., & Ren, Y. (2008). A trust-based security system for ubiquitous and pervasive computing environments. *Computer Communications, 31*(18), 4343–4351. doi:10.1016/j.comcom.2008.05.007

BrainWeb. (n.d.). *Brain web: Simulated Brain Database.* Retrieved from http://www. brainweb.bic.mni.mcgill.ca/brainweb

BRATS Challenge. (n.d.). Retrieved from https://www.smir.ch/BRATS

Brinkmann, B. H., Manduca, A., & Robb, R. A. (1998). Optimized Homomorphic Un-sharp Masking for MR Greyscale Inhomogeneity Correction. *IEEE Transactions on Medical Imaging, 17*(2), 161–171. doi:10.1109/42.700729 PMID:9688149

Buczak, A. L., Baugher, B., Moniz, L. J., Bagley, T., Babin, S. M., & Guven, E. (2018). Ensemble method for dengue prediction. *PLoS One, 13*(1), e0189988. doi:10.1371/journal.pone.0189988 PMID:29298320

Buczak, A. L., Koshute, P. T., Babin, S. M., Feighner, B. H., & Lewis, S. H. (2012). A data-driven epidemiological prediction method for dengue outbreaks using local and remote sensing data. *BMC Medical Informatics and Decision Making, 12*(1), 1. doi:10.1186/1472-6947-12-124 PMID:23126401

Bunn, P., & Ostrovsky, R. (2007). Secure two-party k-means clustering. In *Proceedings of the 14th ACM conference on Computer and communications security.* ACM.

Cachin, I. (1998). An information-theoretic model for steganography. *Proceedings of the 2nd International Workshop on Information Hiding, 15*, 68-88.

Canto, J. G., & Kiefe, C. I. (2014). Age-specific analysis of breast cancer versus heart disease mortality in women. *The American Journal of Cardiology, 113*(2), 410–411. doi:10.1016/j.amjcard.2013.08.055 PMID:24210676

Carrillo, J. F., Hoyos, M. H., Dávila, E. E., & Orkisz, M. (2007). Recursive tracking of vascular tree axes in 3D medical images. *International Journal of Computer Assisted Radiology and Surgery, 1*(6), 331–339. doi:10.100711548-007-0068-6

Carvajal, T. M., Viacrusis, K. M., Hernandez, L. F. T., Ho, H. T., Amalin, D. M., & Watanabe, K. (2018). Machine learning methods reveal the temporal pattern of dengue incidence using meteorological factors in metropolitan Manila, Philippines. *BMC Infectious Diseases, 18*(1), 183. doi:10.118612879-018-3066-0 PMID:29665781

Chadwick, D. W., & Fatema, K. (2012). A privacy preserving authorisation system for the cloud. *Journal of Computer and System Sciences, 78*(5), 1359–1373. doi:10.1016/j.jcss.2011.12.019

Chae, S., Kwon, S., & Lee, D. (2018). Predicting Infectious Disease Using Deep Learning and Big Data. *International Journal of Environmental Research and Public Health, 15*(8), 1596. doi:10.3390/ijerph15081596 PMID:30060525

Chakrabarti & Punera. (2011). Event Summarization Using Tweets. ICWSM, 66–73. doi:10.1016/j.clgc.2012.04.004

Chand, M., Armstrong, T., Britton, G., & Nash, G. F. (2007). How and why do we measure surgical risk. *Journal of the Royal Society of Medicine, 100*(11), 508–512. doi:10.1177/014107680710001113 PMID:18048708

Chang, D.-X., Zhang, X., & Zheng, C. (2009). A genetic algorithm with gene rearrangement for K-means clustering. *Pattern Recognition, 42*(7), 1210–1222. doi:10.1016/j.patcog.2008.11.006

Chan, T. F., & Vese, L. A. (2001). Active contours without edges. *IEEE Transactions on Image Processing, 10*(2), 266–277. doi:10.1109/83.902291 PMID:18249617

Chan, T.-C., Hu, T.-H., & Hwang, J.-S. (2015). Daily forecast of dengue fever incidents for urban villages in a city. *International Journal of Health Geographics, 14*(1), 9. doi:10.1186/1476-072X-14-9 PMID:25636965

Chatterjee, S., Dey, N., Shi, F., Ashour, A. S., Fong, S. J., & Sen, S. (2018). Clinical application of modified bag-of-features coupled with hybrid neural-based classifier in dengue fever classification using gene expression data. *Medical & Biological Engineering & Computing, 56*(4), 709–720. doi:10.100711517-017-1722-y PMID:28891000

Chaturvedi, S., Mishra, V., & Mishra, N. (2017). Sentiment analysis using machine learning for business intelligence. *IEEE International Conference on Power, Control, Signals and Instrumentation Engineering (ICPCSI)*, 2162-2166. 10.1109/ICPCSI.2017.8392100

Chatzis, & Sotirios, P. (2011). A fuzzy c-means-type algorithm for clustering of data with mixed numeric and categorical attributes employing a probabilistic dissimilarity functional. *Expert Systems With Applications, 38*(7), 8684-8689.

Chaudhuri, K., & Monteleoni, C. (2009). Privacy-preserving logistic regression. Advances in Neural Information Processing Systems, 289–296.

Chen, F. (2014). PRECISE: PRivacy-preserving cloud-assisted quality improvement service in healthcare. *Systems Biology (ISB), 2014 8th International Conference on.* 10.1109/ISB.2014.6990752

Chen, Li, Narayan, Subramanian, & Xie. (2016). Gene expression inference with deep learning. *Bioinfarmatics, 32,* 1832-1839.

Chen, T., & Guestrin, C. (2016, August). Xgboost: A scalable tree boosting system. In Proceedings of the 22nd *ACM SIGKDD* international conference on knowledge discovery and data mining (pp. 785-794). ACM.

Chen, Y., Qiu, L., Chen, W., Nguyen, L., & Katz, R.H. (2003). Efficient and adaptive web replication using content clustering. *Selected Areas in Communications, IEEE Journal on, 21*(6), 979-994.

Chen, J., Huang, H., Tian, S., & Qu, Y. (2009). Feature selection for text classification with Naïve Bayes. *Expert Systems with Applications, 36*(3), 5432–5435. doi:10.1016/j.eswa.2008.06.054

Chen, M.-S., Park, J.-S., & Yu, P. S. (1998). Efficient Data Mining for Path Traversal Patterns. *IEEE Transactions on Knowledge and Data Engineering, 10*(2), 209–221. doi:10.1109/69.683753

Chen, Z., He, N., Huang, Y., Qin, W. T., Liu, X., & Li, L. (2019). Integration of A Deep Learning Classifier with A Random Forest Approach for Predicting Malonylation Sites. *Genomics, Proteomics & Bioinformatics*. PMID:30639696

Clare, S., Alecci, M., & Jezzard, P. (2001). Compensating for B1 inhomge-neity using active transmit power modulation. *Magnetic Resonance Imaging, 19*(10), 1349–1352. doi:10.1016/S0730-725X(01)00467-2 PMID:11804763

Clemson. (n.d.). Structured analysis of the retina. *Clemson University.* Retrieved from: http://cecas.clemson.edu/~ahoover/stare/

Cohen, A., Nissim, N., & Elovici, Y. (2018). Novel set of general descriptive features for enhanced detection of malicious emails using machine learning methods. *Expert Systems with Applications, 110*, 143–169. doi:10.1016/j.eswa.2018.05.031

Cohen, L. D., & Kimmel, R. (1997). Global minimum for active contour models: A minimal path approach. *International Journal of Computer Vision, 24*(1), 57–78. doi:10.1023/A:1007922224810

Corey, K. M., Kashyap, S., Lorenzi, E., Lagoo-Deenadayalan, S. A., Heller, K., Whalen, K., ... Sendak, M. (2018). Development and validation of machine learning models to identify high-risk surgical patients using automatically curated electronic health record data (Pythia): A retrospective, single-site study'. *PLoS Medicine, 15*(11), e1002701–e1002701. doi:10.1371/journal.pmed.1002701 PMID:30481172

Creighton, C., & Hanash, S. (2003). Mining Gene Expression Databases for Association Rules. *Bioinformatics (Oxford, England), 19*(1), 79–86. doi:10.1093/bioinformatics/19.1.79 PMID:12499296

Créquit, P., Mansouri, G., Benchoufi, M., Vivot, A., & Ravaud, P. (2018). Mapping of Crowdsourcing in Health: Systematic Review. *Journal of Medical Internet Research, 20*(5). PMID:29764795

Cruz-Roa, A., Gilmore, H., Basavanhally, A., Feldman, M., Ganesan, S., Shih, N. N. C., ... Madabhushi, A. (2017). Accurate and reproducible invasive breast cancer detection in whole-slide images: A Deep Learning approach for quantifying tumor extent. *Scientific Reports, 7*(1), 46450. doi:10.1038rep46450 PMID:28418027

Cuizhi, L., & Yunkang, Y. (2011). A study on key technologies in the development of mobile e-commerce. *2011 International Conference on E-Business and E-Government (ICEE)*, 1-4. 10.1109/ICEBEG.2011.5886779

Cunningham, P., & Delany, S. J. (2007). K-Nearest neighbour classifiers. *Multiple Classifier Systems, 34*(8), 1–17.

Da Xu, L., He, W., & Li, S. (2014). Internet of things in industries: A survey. *IEEE Transactions on Industrial Informatics, 10*(4), 2233–2243. doi:10.1109/TII.2014.2300753

Davidov, D. (2010). Enhanced Sentiment Learning Using Twitter Hashtags and Smileys. Coling, 241–249.

Dawar, S., & Goyal, V. (2015). UP-Hist Tree: An Efficient Data Structure for Mining High Utility Patterns from Transaction Databases. *Proc. of the 19th International Database Engineering & Applications Symposium (IDEAS '15)*, 56-61.

De Caigny, A., Coussement, K., & De Bock, K. (2018). *A New Hybrid Classification Algorithm for Customer Churn Prediction Based on Logistic Regression and Decision Trees.* Academic Press.

Decision Tree. (2019, May 31). Retrieved from https://en.wikipedia.org/wiki/Decision_tree

Demšar, J., Curk, T., Erjavec, A., Gorup, Č., Hočevar, T., & Milutinovič, M. (2013). Orange: Data mining toolbox in Python. *Journal of Machine Learning Research, 14*(1), 2349–2353.

Deschamps, T., & Cohen, L. D. (2001). Fast extraction of minimal paths in 3D images and applications to virtual endoscopy. *Medical Image Analysis*, 5(4), 281–299. doi:10.1016/S1361-8415(01)00046-9 PMID:11731307

Devi, K.K.A., Matthew, Y., & Sandra, L.A. (2012). Advanced Neural Network in Artificial Intelligence Systems. *IEEE Trans on Artificial Intelligence Systems, 4*(9), 100 – 120.

Di Lena, P., Nagata, K., & Baldi, P. (2012). Deep architectures for protein contact map prediction. *Bioinformatics (Oxford, England)*, 28(19), 2449–2457. doi:10.1093/bioinformatics/bts475 PMID:22847931

Dogan, M., Beach, S., Simons, R., Lendasse, A., Penaluna, B., & Philibert, R. (2018). Blood-Based Biomarkers for Predicting the Risk for Five-Year Incident Coronary Heart Disease in the Framingham Heart Study via. *Machine Learning*. PMID:30567402

Dogantekin, E., Dogantekin, A., Avci, D., & Avci, L. (2010, July). An intelligent diagnosis system for diabetes on Linear Discriminant Analysis and Adaptive Network Based Fuzzy Inference System: LDA-ANFIS. *Digital Signal Processing*, 20(4), 1248–1255. doi:10.1016/j.dsp.2009.10.021

Dongxia, Z., Xiaoqing, H., & Chunyu, D. (2018). Review on the Research and Practice of Deep Learning and Reinforcement Learning in Smart Grids. *CSEE Journal of Power and Energy Systems, 4*(3).

Du, W., & Atallah, M. J. (2001). Privacy-preserving cooperative scientific computations. CSFW, 1, 273.

Du, W., Han, Y. S., & Chen, S. (2004). Privacy-preserving multivariate statistical analysis: Linear regression and classification. SDM, 4, 222–233.

Dumitrescu, S., Wu, X., & Wang, Z. (2003). *Detection of LSB Steganography via sample pair analysis. IEEE Trans*, 51, 128–136.

Dwork, C. (2006). Calibrating noise to sensitivity in private data analysis. In *Theory of cryptography*. Springer Berlin Heidelberg.

Ehlers, A. P. (2017). Improved Risk Prediction Following Surgery Using Machine Learning Algorithms. *EGEMS, 5*.

Eickholt, J., & Cheng, J. (2013). DNdisorder: Predicting protein disorder using boosting and deep networks. *BMC Bioinformatics*, 14(1), 88. doi:10.1186/1471-2105-14-88 PMID:23497251

Eifel, P., Axelson, J. A., & Costa, J. (2001). National institutes of health consensus development conference statement: Adjuvant therapy for breast cancer. *Journal of the National Cancer Institute*, 93(13), 979–989. doi:10.1093/jnci/93.13.979 PMID:11438563

Eltabakh, M. Y., Ouzzani, M., Khalil, M. A., Aref, W. G., & Elmagarmid, A. K. (2008). *Incremental Mining for Frequent Patterns in Evolving Time Series Databases. Technical Report CSD TR#08-02*. Purdue Univ.

Elter, M., & Held, C. (2008). Semi-automatic segmentation for the computer aided diagnosis of clustered microcalcifications. Proceedings of. SPIE 2008, 6915, 691524-691524.

Erwin, A., Gopalan, R. P., & Achuthan, N. R. (2008). Efficient Mining of High Utility Itemsets from Large Data Sets. *Proc. 12th Pacific-Asia Conf. Advances in Knowledge Discovery and Data Mining (PAKDD)*, 554-561. 10.1007/978-3-540-68125-0_50

Estapé T. (2018). Cancer in the elderly: Challenges and barriers. *Asia-Pacific Journal of Oncology Nursing*, 5(1), 40-42.

Fadlullah, Z. M., Tang, F., Mao, B., Kato, N., Akashi, O., Inoue, T., & Mizutani, K. (2017). State-of-the-art deep learning: Evolving machine intelligence toward tomorrow's intelligent network traffic control systems. *IEEE Commun. Surveys Tuts., 19*(4), 2432–2455. doi:10.1109/COMST.2017.2707140

Faouzi, E., Leung, H., & Kurian, A. (2011). Data fusion in intelligent transportation systems: Progress and challenges--A survey. *Information Fusion*, *12*(1), 4–10. doi:10.1016/j.inffus.2010.06.001

Fathima, A. S., Manimegalai, D., & Hundewale, N. (2011). A review of data mining classification techniques applied for diagnosis and prognosis of the arbovirus-dengue. *International Journal of Computer Science Issues*, *8*(6), 322.

Fatima, M., & Pasha, M. (2017). Survey of Machine Learning Algorithms for Disease Diagnostic. *Journal of Intelligent Learning Systems and Applications*, *9*(1), 1–16. doi:10.4236/jilsa.2017.91001

Fei, J., Yong, J., Hui, Z., Yi, D., Hao, L., Sufeng, M., ... Yongjun, W. (2017). Artificial intelligence in healthcare: Past, present and future. *Journal of Neurology, Neurosurgery, and Psychiatry*, *2*(4). Retrieved from https://emerj.com/ai-sector-overviews/machine-learning-medical-diagnostics-4-current-applications/

Feng, C., Wu, S., & Liu, N. (2017). A user-centric machine learning framework for cyber security operations center. *IEEE International Conference on Intelligence and Security Informatics (ISI)*, 173-175. 10.1109/ISI.2017.8004902

Fernández-Alemán, J. L., Señor, I. C., Lozoya, P. Á. O., & Toval, A. (2013). Security and privacy in electronic health records: A systematic literature review. *Journal of Biomedical Informatics*, *46*(3), 541–562. doi:10.1016/j.jbi.2012.12.003 PMID:23305810

Florian, J. (2010). *Normalization of Magnetic Resonance Images and its Application to the Diagnosis of the Scoliotic Spine* (Ph.D. thesis). University of Erlangen.

Foracchia, M., Grisan, E., & Ruggeri, A. (2004). Detection of optic disc in retinal images by means of a geometrical model of vessel structure. *IEEE Transactions on Medical Imaging*, *23*(10), 1189–1195. doi:10.1109/TMI.2004.829331 PMID:15493687

Fraz, M. M., Barman, S. A., Remagnino, P., Hoppe, A., Basit, A., Uyyanonvara, B., ... Owen, C. G. (2012). An approach to localize the retinal blood vessels using bit planes and centerline detection. *Computer Methods and Programs in Biomedicine*, *108*(2), 600–616. doi:10.1016/j.cmpb.2011.08.009 PMID:21963241

Fridrich, J., Goljan, M., & Du, R. (2001). Reliable Detection of LSB Steganography in Color and Grayscale Images. *Proc. of ACM Workshop on Multimedia and Security*, 32, 198-231. 10.1145/1232454.1232466

Friman, O., Hindennach, M., Kühnel, C., & Peitgen, H. O. (2010). Multiple hypothesis template tracking of small 3D vessel structures. *Medical Image Analysis*, *14*(2), 160–171. doi:10.1016/j.media.2009.12.003 PMID:20060770

Fuchs, B., Ritz, T., Halbach, B., & Hartl, F. (2011). Blended shopping: Interactivity and individualization. *Proceedings of the International Conference on e-Business*, 1-6.

Fuentes, A., Yoon, S., Kim, S. C., & Park, D. S. (2017). A robust deep-learning-based detector for real-time tomato plant diseases and pest recognition. *Sensors (Basel)*, *17*, 2022. doi:10.339017092022

Gambhir, S., Malik, S. K., & Kumar, Y. (2017). PSO-ANN based diagnostic model for the early detection of dengue disease. *New Horizons in Translational Medicine*, *4*(1-4), 1–8. doi:10.1016/j.nhtm.2017.10.001

Gambhir, S., Malik, S. K., & Kumar, Y. (2018). The Diagnosis of Dengue Disease: An Evaluation of Three Machine Learning Approaches. *International Journal of Healthcare Information Systems and Informatics*, *13*(3), 1–19. doi:10.4018/IJHISI.2018070101

Ganzetti, M., Wenderoth, N., & Mantini, D. (2016). Intensity Inhomogeneity Correction of Structural MR Images: A Data-Driven Approach to Define Input Algorithm Parameters. *Frontiers in Neuroinformatics*, *10*(10). PMID:27014050

Garcia-Ceja, E., Riegler, M., Nordgreen, T., Jakobsen, P., Oedegaard, K. J., & Tørresen, J. (2018). Mental health monitoring with multimodal sensing and machine learning: A survey. *Pervasive and Mobile Computing, 51*, 1–26. doi:10.1016/j.pmcj.2018.09.003

Garcıa-Tarifa, M. J., Martınez-Murcia, F. J., & Górriz, J. M. (2018, June). Retinal Blood Vessel Segmentation by Multichannel Deep Convolutional Autoencoder. In *International Joint Conference SOCO'18-CISIS'18-ICEUTE'18: San Sebastián, Spain, June 6-8, 2018 Proceedings* (Vol. 771, p. 37). Springer.

Gascon, A., Schoppmann, P., Balle, B., Raykova, M., Doerner, J., Zahur, S., & Evans, D. (n.d.). *Secure linear regression on vertically partitioned datasets*. Academic Press.

George, M. M., Kalaivani, S., & Sudhakar, M. S. (2017). A non-iterative multi-scale approach for intensity inhomogeneity correction in MRI. *Magnetic Resonance Imaging, 45*, 43–59. doi:10.1016/j.mri.2017.05.005 PMID:28549883

George, N., Chandrasekaran, K., & Binu, A. (2016). An objective study on improvement of task scheduling mechanism using computational intelligence in cloud computing. *2015 IEEE International Conference on Computational Intelligence and Computing Research, ICCIC 2015*. 10.1109/ICCIC.2015.7435660

Georgii, E., Richter, L., Ruckert, U., & Kramer, S. (2005). Analyzing Microarray Data Using Quantitative Association Rules. *Bioinformatics (Oxford, England), 21*(Suppl 2), 123–129. doi:10.1093/bioinformatics/bti1121 PMID:16204090

Ghaddar, B., & Naoum-Sawaya, J. (2017). *High Dimensional Data Classification and Feature Selection using Support Vector Machines*. Academic Press.

Gilad-Bachrach, R., Dowlin, N., Laine, K., Lauter, K., Naehrig, M., & Wernsing, J. (2016), Cryptonets: Applying neural networks to encrypted data with high throughput and accuracy. *Proceedings of The 33rd International Conference on Machine Learning*, 201–210.

Gilad-Bachrach, R., Laine, K., Lauter, K., Rindal, P., & Rosulek, M. (2016). *Secure data exchange: A marketplace in the cloud*. Cryptology ePrint Archive, Report 2016/620. Retrieved from http://eprint.iacr.org/ 2016/620

Gilad-Bachrach, R., Dowlin, N., & Laine, K. (2016). CryptoNets: applying neural networks to encrypted data with high throughput and accuracy. *International Conference on Machine Learning*, 201–10.

Gillies, R.J., Kinahan, P. E., Hricak, H. (2016). Radiomics: images are more than pictures, they are data. *Radiology, 278*(2), 563–77.

Go, A. S., Mozaffarian, D., & Roger, V. L. (2013). Heart disease and stroke statistics -- 2013 update: A report from the American Heart Association. *Circulation, 127*, e6–e245. PMID:23239837

Goel, S., Rana, A., & Kaur, M. (2013b). ADCT-based robust methodology for image steganography. *International Journal of Image, Graphics and Signal Processing, 5*(11).

Goel, S., Rana, A., & Kaur, M. (2013a). A review of comparison techniques of image steganography. *Global Journal of Computer Science and Technology Graphics & Vision, 13*(4), 9–14.

Gomes, A. L. V., Wee, L. J., Khan, A. M., Gil, L. H., Marques, E. T. Jr, Calzavara-Silva, C. E., & Tan, T. W. (2010). Classification of dengue fever patients based on gene expression data using support vector machines. *PLoS One, 5*(6), e11267. doi:10.1371/journal.pone.0011267 PMID:20585645

Gopinath, M. P., & Murali, S. (2017). Comparative study on Classification Algorithm for Diabetes Data set. *International Journal of Pure and Applied Mathematics, 117*(7), 47–52.

Grinblat, G. L., Uzal, L. C., Larese, M. G., & Granitto, P. M. (2016). Deep learning for plant identification using vein morphological patterns. *Computers and Electronics in Agriculture, 127*, 418–424. doi:10.1016/j.compag.2016.07.003

Grover, S., & Aujla, G. S. (2014). Prediction Model for Influenza Epidemic Based on Twitter Data. *International Journal of Advanced Research in Computer and Communication Engineering, 3*(7).

Guillemaud, R. (1998). Uniformity Correction with Homomorphic Filtering on Region of Interest. *IEEE International Conference on Image Processing, 2*, 872-875. 10.1109/ICIP.1998.723695

Guo, P., Liu, T., & Li, N. (2014). Design of automatic recognition of cucumber disease image. *Inf. Technol. J., 13*(13), 2129–2136.

Gupta, A., & Chhikara, R. (2018). Diabetic Retinopathy: Present and Past. *Procedia Computer Science, 132*, 1432–1440. doi:10.1016/j.procs.2018.05.074

Guyon, I., Dror, G., Lemaire, V., Taylor, G., & Silver, D. (2012). Unsupervised and Transfer Learning Challenge: a Deep Learning Approach. *Workshop and Conference Proceedings*, 97–111.

Guzmán-Cabrera, R., Guzmán-Sepúlveda, J. R., Torres-Cisneros, M. D., May-Arrioja, D. A., Ruiz-Pinales, J., Ibarra-Manzano, O. G., ... Parada, A. G. (2013). Digital image processing technique for breast cancer detection. *International Journal of Thermophysics, 34*(8-9), 1519–1531. doi:10.100710765-012-1328-4

Hall, L. D., & Llinas, J. (1997). An introduction to multisensor data fusion. *IEEE, 85*, 6-23.

Han, J., Kamber, M., & Pei, J. (2012). Data Preprocessing. *Data Mining*, 83-124. doi:10.1016/b978-0-12-381479-1.00003-4

Han, J., Dong, G., & Yin, Y. (1999). Efficient Mining of Partial Periodic Patterns in Time Series Database. *Proc. Int'l Conf. on Data Eng.*, 106-115.

Han, J., Pei, J., & Yin, Y. (2000). Mining Frequent Patterns without Candidate Generation. *Proc. ACM-SIGMOD Int'l Conf. Management of Data*, 1-12.

Harikumar, S., & Surya, P. (2015). K-Medoid Clustering for Heterogeneous DataSets. *Elsevier Procedia Computer Science, 70*, 226–237. doi:10.1016/j.procs.2015.10.077

Harmsen, J. J., & Pearlman, W. A. (2001). Steganalysis of LSB embedding using Image Metrics. *Proceedings of SPIE Security and Watermarking of Multimedia Contents V, 48*, 118–131.

Hatcher, W. G., & Yu, W. (2018). A Survey of Deep Learning: Platforms, Applications and Emerging Research Trends. *IEEE Access : Practical Innovations, Open Solutions, 6*, 24411–24432. doi:10.1109/ACCESS.2018.2830661

Hayashi, Y., & Yukita, S. (2016). Rule extraction using Recursive-Rule extraction algorithm with J48graft combined with sampling selection techniques for the diagnosis of type 2 diabetes mellitus in the Pima Indian dataset. *Informatics in Medicine Unlocked, 2*, 92–104. doi:10.1016/j.imu.2016.02.001

Hebb, D. O. (1949). The organization of behavior. *Journal of Applied Behavior Analysis, 25*, 575-577.

Henry, N. L., & Hayes, D. F. (2012). Cancer biomarkers. *Molecular Oncology, 6*(2), 140–146. doi:10.1016/j.molonc.2012.01.010 PMID:22356776

Hollon. (2018). A machine learning approach to predict early outcomes after pituitary adenoma surgery. *Neurosurgical Focus, 45*(5).

Honglak, L., Richard, L., Xiaoshi, W., Satinder, S., & Xiaoshi, W. (2017). *Deep Learning for Real-Time Atari Game Play Using Offline Monte-Carlo Tree Search Planning*. Academic Press.

Hoover, A., & Goldbaum, M. (2003). Locating the optic nerve in a retinal image using the fuzzy convergence of the blood vessels. *IEEE Transactions on Medical Imaging*, *22*(8), 951–958. doi:10.1109/TMI.2003.815900 PMID:12906249

Hopfield, J. J. (1982). Neural networks and physical systems with emergent collective computational abilities. *Proceedings of the National Academy of Sciences of the United States of America*, *79*(8), 2554–2558. doi:10.1073/pnas.79.8.2554 PMID:6953413

Hosmer, D. W., Jr., Lemeshow, S., & Sturdivant, R. X. (2013). *Applied logistic regression* (Vol. 398). John Wiley & Sons. doi:10.1109/SIU.2015.7130164

Huang & Zhexue. (1997). Clustering large data sets with mixed numeric and categorical values. In *Proceedings of the 1st Pacific-Asia conference on knowledge discovery and data mining (PAKDD)* (pp. 21-34). Academic Press.

Huang, Z. (1998). Extensions to the k-means algorithm for clustering large datasets with categorical values. *Data Mining and Knowledge Discovery*, *2*(3), 283–304. doi:10.1023/A:1009769707641

Hu, H., Wang, H., Wang, F., Langley, D., Avram, A., & Liu, M. (2018). Prediction of influenza-like illness based on the improved artificial tree algorithm and artificial neural network. *Scientific Reports*, *8*(4895). PMID:29559649

Huy, N. T., Thao, N. T. H., Ha, T. T. N., Lan, N. T. P., Nga, P. T. T., Thuy, T. T., ... Huong, V. T. Q. (2013). Development of clinical decision rules to predict recurrent shock in dengue. *Critical Care (London, England)*, *17*(6), R280. doi:10.1186/cc13135 PMID:24295509

Ikonomakis, M. (2005). Sotiris Kotsiantis, and V. Tampakas. "Text classification using machine learning techniques. *WSEAS Transactions on Computers*, *4*(8), 966–974.

Imageret. (n.d.) DIARETDB0-Standard diabetic retinopathy database calibration 1.0. *Imageret*. Retrieved from: http://www.it.lut.fi/project/imageret/diaretdb0/

Indumathi, M., & Vaithiyanathan, V. (2016). Reduced Overestimated Utility and Pruning Candidates using Incremental Mining. *Indian Journal of Science and Technology*, *9*(48). doi:10.17485/ijst/2016/v9i48/107990

ISI. (n.d.). DRIVE: Digital retinal images for vessel extraction. *ISI*. Retrieved from: https://www.isi.uu.nl/Research/Databases/DRIVE/

Islam, S. M. R., Kwak, D., Kabir, H., Hossain, M., & Kwak, K. S. (2015). The Internet of things for health care: A comprehensive survey. *IEEE Access: Practical Innovations, Open Solutions*, *3*, 678–708. doi:10.1109/ACCESS.2015.2437951

Jagannathan, G., & Wright, R. N. (2005). Privacy-preserving distributed k-means clus- tering over arbitrarily partitioned data. *Proceedings of the eleventh ACM SIGKDD international conference on Knowledge discovery in data mining ACM*, 593–599.

Jain, A. K. (2010). Data clustering: 50 years beyond K-means. *Pattern Recognition Letters*, *31*(8), 651–666. doi:10.1016/j.patrec.2009.09.011

Jati, D., Mantau, A. J., & Wasito, I. (2016). Dimensionality reduction using deep belief network in big data case study: Hyperspectral image classification. *Proc. Int.Workshop Big Data Inf. Secur. (IWBIS)*, 71-76.

Jiang, Z., Yepez, J., An, S., & Ko, S. (2017). Fast, accurate and robust retinal vessel segmentation system. *Biocybernetics and Biomedical Engineering*, *37*(3), 412–421. doi:10.1016/j.bbe.2017.04.001

Ji, J., Bai, T., Zhou, C., Ma, C., & Wang, Z. (2013). An improved k-prototypes clustering algorithm for mixed numeric and categorical data. *Neurocomputing*, *120*, 590–596. doi:10.1016/j.neucom.2013.04.011

Ji, J., Pang, W., Zhou, C., Han, X., & Wang, Z. (2012). A fuzzy k-prototype clustering algorithm for mixed numeric and categorical data. *Knowledge-Based Systems*, *30*, 129–135. doi:10.1016/j.knosys.2012.01.006

Joachims, T. (1998, April). Text categorization with support vector machines: Learning with many relevant features. In *European conference on machine learning* (pp. 137-142). Springer. 10.1007/BFb0026683

Joachims, T., & Kaufman, M. (2000). Estimating the Generalization Performance of a SVM Efficiently. *Proceedings of the International Conference on Machine Learning (ICML)*, 15, 28-54.

John, A., & Wang, F. (2015). *ET-LDA : Joint Topic Modeling for Aligning Events and their Twitter Feedback ET-LDA : Joint Topic Modeling for*. Academic Press.

Joseph & Grunwald. (n.d.). Pre-fetching Using Markov Predictors. *Journal of IEEE Transactions on Computers, 48*(2).

Jyoti, S., & Goel, A. (2009). A novel approach for clustering web user sessions using RST. *Advances in Computing, Control, & Telecommunication Technologies, 2*(1), 656-661.

Kannimuthua, S., & Vaithiyanathan, V. (2014). Discovery of High Utility Itemsets Using Genetic Algorithm with Ranked Mutation. Applied Artificial Intelligence: An International Journal, 337-359. doi:10.1080/08839514.2014.891839

Karim, M. N., Reid, C. M., Tran, L., Cochrane, A., & Billah, B. (2017). Missing Value Imputation Improves Mortality Risk Prediction Following Cardiac Surgery: An Investigation of an Australian Patient Cohort, Heart. *Lung and Circulation, 26*(3), 301–308. doi:10.1016/j.hlc.2016.06.1214 PMID:27546595

Kasamatsu, T., Hashimoto, J., Iyatomi, H., Nakahara, T., Bai, J., Kitamura, N., … Kubo, A. (2008). *Application of Support Vector Machine Classifiers to Preoperative Risk Stratification With Myocardial Perfusion Scintigraphy*. Academic Press.

Kavakiotis, I., Tsave, O., Salifoglou, A., Maglaveras, N., Vlahavas, I., & Chouvarda, I. (2017). Machine Learning and Data Mining Methods in Diabetes Research. *Computational and Structural Biotechnology Journal, 15*, 104–116. doi:10.1016/j.csbj.2016.12.005 PMID:28138367

Kawasaki, R., Kitano, S., Sato, Y., Yamashita, H., Nishimura, R., Tajima, N., & Japan Diabetes Complication and its Prevention prospective (JDCP) study Diabetic Retinopathy working group. (2018). Factors associated with non-proliferative diabetic retinopathy in patients with type 1 and type 2 diabetes: the Japan Diabetes Complication and its Prevention prospective study (JDCP study 4). *Diabetology International*, 1-9.

Kaymak, S., Helwan, A., & Uzun, D. (2017). Breast cancer image classification using artificial neural networks. *Procedia Computer Science, 120*, 126–131. doi:10.1016/j.procs.2017.11.219

Ker, J., Wang, L., Rao, J., & Lim, T. (2018). Deep learning applications in medical image analysis. *IEEE Access: Practical Innovations, Open Solutions, 6*, 9375–9389. doi:10.1109/ACCESS.2017.2788044

Kerri, W. (2018). Applications of crowdsourcing in health: An overview. *Journal of Global Health, 8*(1), 010502. doi:10.7189/jogh.08.010502 PMID:29564087

Khaleghi, B., Khamis, A., Karray, F. O., & Razavi, S. N. (2013). Multisensor data fusion: A review of the state-of-the-art. *Information Fusion, 14*(1), 28–44. doi:10.1016/j.inffus.2011.08.001

Khandare, P., Kambale, P., Narnavar, P., Galande, G., & Narnavar, J. (2014). Data hiding technique using steganography. *International Journal of Computer Science and Information Technologies, 5*(2), 1785–1787.

Khan, S., Ullah, R., Khan, A., Sohail, A., Wahab, N., Bilal, M., & Ahmed, M. (2017). Random forest-based evaluation of raman spectroscopy for dengue fever analysis. *Applied Spectroscopy, 71*(9), 2111–2117. doi:10.1177/0003702817695571 PMID:28862033

Khan, S., Ullah, R., Khan, A., Wahab, N., Bilal, M., & Ahmed, M. (2016). Analysis of dengue infection based on Raman spectroscopy and support vector machine (SVM). *Biomedical Optics Express*, 7(6), 2249–2256. doi:10.1364/BOE.7.002249 PMID:27375941

Kiefer, A. (2017). Using machine learning to forecast local epidemics of dengue fever in Latin America. *6th International Conference on Biostatistics and Bioinformatics*, Atlanta, GA.

Kim, Y. (2014). *Convolutional neural networks for sentence classification.* arXiv preprint arXiv:1408.5882

King, D. E. (2009). Dlib-ml: A machine learning toolkit. *Journal of Machine Learning Research*, 10(Jul), 1755–1758.

Krill, P. (2014, September 30). *Four reasons to stick with Java, and four reasons to dump it.* Retrieved from https://www.javaworld.com/article/2689406/four-reasons-to-stick-with-java-and-four-reasons-to-dump-it.html

Laureano-Rosario, A., Duncan, A., Mendez-Lazaro, P., Garcia-Rejon, J., Gomez-Carro, S., Farfan-Ale, J., ... Muller-Karger, F. (2018). Application of artificial neural networks for dengue fever outbreak predictions in the northwest coast of Yucatan, Mexico and San Juan, Puerto Rico. *Tropical Medicine and Infectious Disease, 3*(1), 5.

Lavanya & Valarmathie. (n.d.). *Big Data in Healthcare Using Cloud Database with Enhanced Privacy.* Academic Press.

Lee. (2018). Derivation and Validation of Machine Learning Approaches to Predict Acute Kidney Injury after Cardiac Surgery. *Journal of Clinical Medicine, 7.*

Lee, S. C., Paik, J., Ok, J., Song, I., & Kim, U. M. (2007). Efficient Mining of User Behaviors by Temporal Mobile Access Patterns. Int'l J. *Computer Science Security*, 7(2), 285–291.

Lena, P. D., Nagata, K., & Baldi, P. F. (2012). Deep spatio-temporal architectures and learning for protein structure prediction. *Advances in Neural Information Processing Systems*, 512–520.

Li, Rui, & Yanchao. (2016). PriExpress: Privacy-preserving express delivery with fine-grained attribute-based access control. *2016 IEEE Conference on Communications and Network Security (CNS)*, 333-341.

Liao, S., Gao, Y., Oto, A., & Shen, D. (2013). Representation learning: A unified deep learning framework for automatic prostate MR segmentation. *Med Image Comput Comput Assist Interv*, 16, 254–261. PMID:24579148

Li, C., John, C. G., & Davatzikos, C. (2014). Multiplicative intrinsic component optimization (MICO) for MRI bias field estimation and tissue segmentation. *Magnetic Resonance Imaging, 32*(32), 913–923. doi:10.1016/j.mri.2014.03.010 PMID:24928302

Li, H. F., Huang, H. Y., Chen, Y. C., Liu, Y. J., & Lee, S. Y. (2008). Fast and Memory Efficient Mining of High Utility Itemsets in Data Streams. *Proc. IEEE Eighth Int'l Conf. on Data Mining*, 881-886. 10.1109/ICDM.2008.107

Li, H., & Chutatape, O. (2001, October). Automatic location of optic disk in retinal images. In *Proceedings 2001 International Conference on Image Processing (Cat. No. 01CH37205)* (Vol. 2, pp. 837-840). IEEE. 10.1109/ICIP.2001.958624

Likar, B., Viergever, M. A., & Pernus, F. (2001). Retrospective correction of MR intensity inhomogeneity by information minimization. *IEEE Transactions on Medical Imaging, 20*(12), 1398–1410. doi:10.1109/42.974934 PMID:11811839

Lily, D., Chan, B., & Wang, T. G. (2013). A Simple Explanation of Neural Network in Artificial Intelligence. *IEEE Trans on Comtrol System, 247*, 1529–5651.

Lin, C.H., Chiu, D.Y., Wu, Y.H. & Chen, A.L.P. (2005). Mining Frequent Itemsets from Data Streams with a Time-Sensitive Sliding Window. *Proc. SIAM Int'l Conf. Data Mining (SDM '05).*

Lin, C.-W., Hong, T.-P., & Lu, W.-H. (2010). Effciently mining high average utility itemsets with a tree structure. *Proc. Int. Conf. Intell. Inf.Database Syst.*, 131-139.

Lin, C.-W., Yang, L., Fournier-Viger, P., Hong, T.-P., & Voznak, M. (2016). *A binary PSO approach to mine high-utility itemsets*. Methodologies And Application Springer.

Lin, J. C.-W., Ren, S., Fournier-Viger, P., & Hong, T.-P. (2017). EHAUPM: Efficient High Average-Utility Pattern Mining With Tighter Upper Bounds. *IEEE Access: Practical Innovations, Open Solutions, 5*, 12927–12940. doi:10.1109/ACCESS.2017.2717438

Lin, J. C.-W., Yang, L., Fournier-Viger, P., Wu, J. M.-T., Hong, T.-P., Wang, L. S.-L., & Zhan, J. (2016). Mining high-utility itemsets based on particle swarm optimization. *Engineering Applications of Artificial Intelligence, 55*, 320–330. doi:10.1016/j.engappai.2016.07.006

Lin, Z., Lanchantin, J., & Qi, Y. (2016). MUST-CNN: A multilayer shift-and-stitch deep convolutional architecture for sequence-based protein structure prediction. *Proceedings of the AAAI Conference on Artificial Intelligence, 8*.

Li, P., & Huang, H. (2016). *Clinical information extraction via convolutional neural network*. Academic Press.

Li, Q., Feng, B., Xie, L., Liang, P., Zhang, H., & Wang, T. (2016). A cross-modality learning approach for vessel segmentation in retinal images. *IEEE Transactions on Medical Imaging, 35*(1), 109–118. doi:10.1109/TMI.2015.2457891 PMID:26208306

Liu, Y., Liao, W., & Choudhary, A. (2005). A Fast High Utility Itemsets Mining Algorithm. *Proc. Utility-Based Data Mining Workshop*. 10.1145/1089827.1089839

Livingstone, M., & Hubel, D. (1988). Segregation of form, color, movement, and depth: Anatomy, physiology, and perception. *Science, 240*(4853), 740–749. doi:10.1126cience.3283936 PMID:3283936

Li, Y.-C., Yeh, J.-S., & Chang, C.-C. (2008). Isolated Items Discarding Strategy for Discovering High Utility Itemsets. *Data & Knowledge Engineering, 64*(1), 198–217. doi:10.1016/j.datak.2007.06.009

Li, Y., & Shibuya, T. (2015). Malphite: a convolutional neural network and ensemble learning based protein secondary structure predictor *Proc IEEE Int Conf Bioinformatics Biomed*, 1260-1266.

Lloyd, S., Mohseni, M., & Rebentrost, P. (2013). *Quantum algorithms for supervised and unsupervised machine learning*. arXiv preprint arXiv:1307.0411

Long, Z. A., Bakar, A. A., Hamdan, A. R., & Sahani, M. (2010, November). Multiple attribute frequent mining-based for dengue outbreak. In *International Conference on Advanced Data Mining and Applications* (pp. 489-496). Springer. 10.1007/978-3-642-17316-5_46

Luo, Z., Xu, H., & Chen, F. (2018). Utterance-Based Audio Sentiment Analysis Learned by a Parallel Combination of CNN and LSTM. Retrieved from http://arxiv.org/abs/1811.08065

Lv, X., Guan, Y., Yang, J., & Wu, J. (2016). Clinical relation extraction with deep learning. *Int J Hybrid Inf Technol, 9*, 237–248.

Lwin, M. O., Vijaykumar, S., Fernando, O. N. N., Cheong, S. A., Rathnayake, V. S., Lim, G., ... Foo, S. (2014). A 21st century approach to tackling dengue: Crowdsourced surveillance, predictive mapping and tailored communication. *Acta Tropica, 130*, 100–107. doi:10.1016/j.actatropica.2013.09.021 PMID:24161879

Lynch, B. (2017). *what-motivates-our-researchers*. Retrieved from https://nbcf.org.au/news/research-blog/what-motivates-our-researchers/

Ma, X., & Hovy, E. (2016). *End-to-end sequence labeling via bi-directional lstm-cnns-crf.* arXiv preprint arXiv:1603.01354

Madabhushi, A., & Udupa, J. K. (n.d.). New methods of MR Image Intensity Standardization Via Generalized Scale. *Proceedings of SPIE Medical Imaging, 5747*, 1143-1154.

Maghilnan, S. (2017). *Sentiment Analysis on Speaker Specific Speech Data.* Academic Press.

Malvia, S., Bagadi, S. A., Dubey, U. S., & Saxena, S. (2017). Epidemiology of breast cancer in Indian women. *Asia Pacific Journal of Clinical Oncology, 13*(4), 289–295. doi:10.1111/ajco.12661 PMID:28181405

Mannini, A., Trojaniello, D., Cereatti, A., & Sabatini, A. M. (2016). A machine Learning Framework for Gait classification using inertial sensors: Application to Elderly, Post-Stroke and Huntington's Disease Patients. *Sensors (Basel), 16*(1), 134. doi:10.339016010134 PMID:26805847

Maragos, P., Gros, P., Katsamanis, A., & Papandreou, G. (2008). Cross-modal integration for performance improving in multimedia: A review. *Multimodal Processing and Interaction*, 1-46.

Marín, D., Aquino, A., Gegúndez-Arias, M. E., & Bravo, J. M. (2011). A new supervised method for blood vessel segmentation in retinal images by using gray-level and moment invariants-based features. *IEEE Transactions on Medical Imaging, 30*(1), 146–158. doi:10.1109/TMI.2010.2064333 PMID:20699207

Martinez, R., Pasquier, N., & Pasquier, C. (2008). GenMiner: Mining nonredundant Association Rules from Integrated Gene Expression Data and Annotations. *Bioinformatics (Oxford, England), 24*(22), 2643–2644. doi:10.1093/bioinformatics/btn490 PMID:18799482

Mason, W., & Suri, S. (2012). Conducting behavioural research on Amazon's Mechanical Turk. *Behavior Research Methods, 44*(1), 1–23. doi:10.375813428-011-0124-6 PMID:21717266

Massat, M. B. (2018). A Promising future for AI in breast cancer screening. *Applied Radiology, 47*(9), 22–25.

McCulloch, W. S., & Pitts, W. (1943). A logical calculus of the ideas immanent in nervous activity. *The Bulletin of Mathematical Biophysics, 5*(4), 115–133. doi:10.1007/BF02478259

McGuire, K. P. (2016). Breast Anatomy and Physiology. In *Breast Disease*. Cham: Springer. doi:10.1007/978-3-319-22843-3_1

Mechelli, A. (2018). 202. Deep Learning Technology: Concepts and Applications in Biological Psychiatry. *Biological Psychiatry, 83*(9), S81–S82. doi:10.1016/j.biopsych.2018.02.221

Mendonca, A. M., & Campilho, A. (2006). Segmentation of retinal blood vessels by combining the detection of centerlines and morphological reconstruction. *IEEE Transactions on Medical Imaging, 25*(9), 1200–1213. doi:10.1109/TMI.2006.879955 PMID:16967805

Meurant & Gerard. (1992). *Data Fusion in Robotics and Machine Intelligence.* Academic Press.

Meyer, A., Zverinski, D., Pfahringer, B., Kempfert, J., Kuehne, T., Sündermann, S. H., ... Eickhoff, C. (2018). Machine learning for real-time prediction of complications in critical care: A retrospective study. *The Lancet. Respiratory Medicine, 6*(12), 905–914. doi:10.1016/S2213-2600(18)30300-X PMID:30274956

Meystre, S., & Haug, P. J. (2006). Natural language processing to extract medical problems from electronic clinical documents: Performance evaluation. *Journal of Biomedical Informatics, 39*(6), 589–599. doi:10.1016/j.jbi.2005.11.004 PMID:16359928

Michael, B., Tracy, K., & Samuel, D. G. (2011). Amazon's Mechanical Turk: A new source of inexpensive, yet high-quality, data. *Perspectives on Psychological Science, 6*(1), 3–5. doi:10.1177/1745691610393980 PMID:26162106

Ming, C., Ru, Z., Xinxin, N., & Yixian, Y. (2006). Analysis of Current Steganography Tools: Classifications & Features. *International Conference on Intelligent Information Hiding and Multimedia Signal Processing.*

Mitchell, T. (1997). *Machine Learning.* McGraw Hill.

Moccia, S., De Momi, E., El Hadji, S., & Mattos, L. S. (2018). Blood vessel segmentation algorithms—Review of methods, datasets and evaluation metrics. *Computer Methods and Programs in Biomedicine, 158*, 71–91. doi:10.1016/j.cmpb.2018.02.001 PMID:29544791

Mohamed, A.A. (2018). *Improving Deep Learning Performance Using Random Forest HTM Cortical Learning Algorithm.* Academic Press.

Mohammadzadeh, N., & Safdari, R. (2014). Patient monitoring in mobile health: Opportunities and challenges. *Medieval Archaeology, 68*(1), 57. PMID:24783916

Mohanty, S. P., Hughes, D. P., & Salathé, M. (2016). Using deep learning for image - based plant disease detection. *Frontiers in Plant Science, 01419*, 1419. doi:10.3389/fpls.2016.01419 PMID:27713752

Mohassel & Zhang. (2017). SecureML: A System for Scalable Privacy-Preserving Machine Learning. *IACR Cryptology ePrint Archive, 396.*

Mojahed, A., Bettencourt-Silva, H. J., & Wenjia, W. (2015). Applying clustering analysis to heterogeneous data using similarity matrix fusion (smf). In *International Workshop on Machine Learning and Data Mining in Pattern Recognition* (pp. 251-265). Springer. 10.1007/978-3-319-21024-7_17

Morellos, A., Pantazi, X. E., Moshou, D., Alexandridis, T., Whetton, R., Tziotzios, G., ... Mouazen, A. M. (2016). Machine learning based prediction of soil total nitrogen, organic carbon and moisture content by using VIS-NIR spectroscopy. *Biosystems Engineering, 152*, 104–116. doi:10.1016/j.biosystemseng.2016.04.018

Mountassir, A., Benbrahim, H., & Berrada, I. (2012). An empirical study to address the problem of unbalanced data sets in sentiment classification. Conference Proceedings - IEEE International Conference on Systems, Man and Cybernetics, 3298–3303. doi:10.1109/ICSMC.2012.6378300

Mutheneni, S. R., Mopuri, R., Naish, S., Gunti, D., &Upadhyayula, S. M. (2018). Spatial distribution and cluster analysis of dengue using self organizing maps in Andhra Pradesh, India, 2011–2013. *Parasite Epidemiology and Control, 3*(1), 52-61.

Nandini, V., Sriranjitha, R., & Yazhini, T. P. (2016). *Dengue detection and prediction system using data mining with frequency analysis. Computer Science & Information Technology.*

Nanthini, D., & Thangaraju, P. (2015, August). A Hybrid Classification Model For Diabetes Dataset Using Decision Tree. *International Journal of Emerging Technologies and Innovative Research, 2*(8), 3302–3308.

Narayanan, H. A. J., & Günes,, M. H. (2011). Ensuring access control in cloud provisioned healthcare systems. *Proc. IEEE Consum. Commun. Netw. Conf. (CCNC)*, 247–251. 10.1109/CCNC.2011.5766466

Naseer, T., & Burgard, W. (2017). Deep regression for monocular camera-based 6-DoF global localization in outdoor environments. *Proc. IEEE/RSJ Int. Conf. Intell. Robots Syst. (IROS)*, 1525-1530. 10.1109/IROS.2017.8205957

Nedzved, A., Ablameyko, S., & Pitas, I. (2006). Morphological segmentation of histology cell images. *Proceedings of IEEE International Special Topic Conference on Information Technology in Biomedicine, 1*, 500–503.

Neil, M., & Murthy, V. D. (2018). Machine learning, natural language programming, and electronic health records: The next step in the artificial intelligence journey? *The Journal of Allergy and Clinical Immunology, 141*(6), 2019–20121. doi:10.1016/j.jaci.2018.02.025 PMID:29518424

Nekovei, R., & Sun, Y. (1995). Back-propagation network and its configuration for blood vessel detection in angiograms. *IEEE Transactions on Neural Networks*, *6*(1), 64–72. doi:10.1109/72.363449 PMID:18263286

Niemeijer, M., Abràmoff, M. D., & Van Ginneken, B. (2009). Fast detection of the optic disc and fovea in color fundus photographs. *Medical Image Analysis*, *13*(6), 859–870. doi:10.1016/j.media.2009.08.003 PMID:19782633

Nikolaenko, V., Weinsberg, U., Ioannidis, S., Joye, M., Boneh, D., & Taft, N. (2013). Privacy-preserving ridge regression on hundreds of millions of records. In *Security and Privacy (SP), 2013 IEEE Symposium on*. IEEE.

Ordonez, C. (2003). Clustering binary data streams with K-means. In *Proceedings of the 8th ACM SIGMOD workshop on Research issues in data mining and knowledge discovery* (pp. 12-19). ACM.

Orhean, A. I., Pop, F., & Raicu, I. (2018). New scheduling approach using reinforcement learning for heterogeneous distributed systems. *Journal of Parallel and Distributed Computing*, *117*, 292–302. doi:10.1016/j.jpdc.2017.05.001

Otsu, N. (1979). A Threshold Selection Method from Gray-level Histograms. *IEEE Transactions on Systems, Man, and Cybernetics*, *9*(1), 62–66. doi:10.1109/TSMC.1979.4310076

Pallis, G., & Vakali, A., & Pokorny, J. (2008). A clustering-based pre-fetching scheme on a web cache environment. *Science Direct, Computer & Electrical Engineering*, *34*(4), 309–323.

Pang, B., & Lillian, L. S. V. (2002). Thumbs up? Sentiment Classification using Machine Learning Techniques. Proceedings of the Conference on Empirical Methods in Natural Language Processing (EMNLP), 57, 79–86. doi:10.3115/1118693.1118704

Pantanowitz, A., & Marwala, T. (2009). Missing Data Imputation Through the Use of the Random Forest Algorithm. *Proceedings of the Advances in Computational Intelligence*, 53-62. 10.1007/978-3-642-03156-4_6

Pantazi, X. E., Moshou, D., Oberti, R., West, J., Mouazen, A. M., & Bochtis, D. (2017). Detection of biotic and abiotic stresses in crops by using hierarchical self organizing classifiers. *Precision Agriculture*, *18*(3), 383–393. doi:10.1007/s11119-017-9507-8

Parikh, R., & Movassate, M. (2009). Sentiment analysis of user-generated twitter updates using various classification techniques. *Business Marketing*, 1–18. Retrieved from http://nlp.stanford.edu/courses/cs224n/2009/fp/19.pdf

Parlak, B., & Uysal, A. K. (2015, May). Classification of medical documents according to diseases. In *2015 23nd Signal Processing and Communications Applications Conference (SIU)* (pp. 1635-1638). IEEE.

Parvinen, P., Kaptein, M., Oinas-Kukkonen, H., & Cheung, C. (2015). Introduction to E-Commerce, Engagement, and Social Influence Minitrack. *2015 48th Hawaii International Conference on System Sciences*, 3257-3257. 10.1109/HICSS.2015.393

Patil, A. P., & Deka, P. C. (2016). An extreme learning machine approach for modeling evapotranspiration using extrinsic inputs. *Computers and Electronics in Agriculture*, *121*, 385–392. doi:10.1016/j.compag.2016.01.016

Patil, B. M., Joshi, R. C., & Toshniwal, D. (2010, December). Hybrid prediction model for Type-2 diabetic patients. *Expert Systems with Applications*, *37*(12), 8102–8108. doi:10.1016/j.eswa.2010.05.078

Patodkar, V. N., & I.R., S. (2017). Twitter as a Corpus for Sentiment Analysis and Opinion Mining. Ijarcce, 5(12), 320–322. doi:10.17148/IJARCCE.2016.51274

Pedregosa, F., Varoquaux, G., Gramfort, A., Michel, V., Thirion, B., & Grisel, O. (2011). Scikit-learn: Machine learning in Python. *Journal of Machine Learning Research*, *12*, 2825–2830.

Pei, J., Han, J., Lu, H., Nishio, S., Tang, S., & Yang, D. (2007). H-Mine: Fast and Space-Preserving Frequent Pattern Mining in Large Databases. *IIE Trans. Inst. of Industrial Engineers*, *39*(6), 593–605.

Perez Rosas, V., Mihalcea, R., & Morency, L. P. (2013). Multimodal sentiment analysis of spanish online videos. *IEEE Intelligent Systems, 28*(3), 38–45. doi:10.1109/MIS.2013.9

Pérez-Rosas, V., & Mihalcea, R. (2013). Sentiment analysis of online spoken reviews. Proceedings of the Annual Conference of the International Speech Communication Association, INTERSPEECH, 862–866.

Pizzuti, C., & Procopio, N. (2016). *A K-means Based Genetic Algorithm for Data Clustering.* SOCO-CISIS-ICEUTE.

Podlipnig, S., & Böszörmenyi, L. (2003). A survey of web cache replacement strategies. *ACM Computing Surveys, 35*(4), 374–398. doi:10.1145/954339.954341

Pollastri, G., & Baldi, P. (2002). Prediction of contact maps by GIOHMMs and recurrent neural networks using lateral propagation from all four cardinal corners. *Bioinformatics (Oxford, England),* 18. PMID:12169532

Pollastri, G., Przybylski, D., Rost, B., & Baldi, P. (2002). Improving the prediction of protein secondary structure in three and eight classes using recurrent neural networks and profiles. *Proteins, 47*(2), 228–235. doi:10.1002/prot.10082 PMID:11933069

Pons. (2006). Object Pre-fetching using Semantic Links. *Journal of ACM SIGMIS Database, 37*(1).

Poria, S., Cambria, E., Howard, N., Huang, G., & Hussain, A. (2016). Fusing audio, visual and textual clues for sentiment analysis from multimodal content. *Neurocomputing, 174,* 50–59. doi:10.1016/j.neucom.2015.01.095

Prabhakaran, S. (n.d.). *Eval(ez_write_tag([[728,90],'r_statistics_co-box-3','ezslot_2',109,'0']));Linear Regression.* Retrieved from http://r-statistics.co/Linear-Regression.html

Pradeep Kandhasamy, J., & Balamurali, S. (2015). Performance Analysis of Classifier Models to Predict Diabetes Mellitus. *Procedia Computer Science, 47,* 45–51. doi:10.1016/j.procs.2015.03.182

Pretorius, A., Bierman, S., & Steel, S. (2016). *A meta-analysis of research in random forests for classification.* Academic Press.

Privacy-Preserving Deep Learning via Additively Homomorphic Encryption. (2018). *IEEE Transactions on Information Forensics and Security, 13*(5), 1333-1345.

Qin, P., Chen, J., & Zeng, J. (2018). Large-scale tissue histopathology image segmentation based on feature pyramid. *EURASIP Journal on Image and Video Processing, 75,* 1–9.

Qisong, C., Yun, W., & Xiaowei, C. (2008) Research on Customers Demand Forecasting for E-business Web Site Based on LS-SVM. *Proc. International Symposium in Electronic Commerce and Security,* 66-70.

Rahaman, S. M., & Farhatullah, M. (2012). PccP: A Model for Preserving Cloud Computing Privacy. *International Conference on Data Science & Engineering (ICDSE),* 166–170. 10.1109/ICDSE.2012.6281900

Rahim, N. F., Taib, S. M., & Abidin, A. I. Z. (2017). Dengue fatality prediction using data mining. *Journal of Fundamental and Applied Sciences, 9*(6S), 671–683. doi:10.4314/jfas.v9i6s.52

Rahman, M. A., & Islam, M. (2014). A Hybrid Clustering Technique Combining a Novel Genetic Algorithm with K-Means. *Knowledge-Based Systems, 71,* 345–365. doi:10.1016/j.knosys.2014.08.011

Raja Sekhar Reddy, G., Manujunatha, S., & Sundeep Kumar, K. (2013). Evapotranpiration model using AI controller for automatic irrigation system. *International Journal of Computer Trends and Technology, 4*(7), 2311–2315.

Rajathi, N., Kanagaraj, S., Brahmanambika, R., & Manjubarkavi, K. (2018). Early Detection of Dengue Using Machine Learning Algorithms. *International Journal of Pure and Applied Mathematics, 118*(18), 3881–3887.

Rakhmetulayeva, S. B., Duisebekova, K. S., Mamyrbekov, A. M., Kozhamzharova, D. K., Astaubayeva, G. N., & Stamku-lova, K. (2018). Application of Classification Algorithm Based on SVM for Determining the Effectiveness of Treatment of Tuberculosis. Procedia Computer Science, 130, 231-238.

Ramezani, Maadi, & Khatami. (2018). Analysis of a Population of Diabetic Patients Databases in Weka Tool. *International Journal of Scientific and Engineering Research, 2*(5).

Ramos, P. J., Prieto, F. A., Montoya, E. C., & Oliveros, C. E. (2017). Automatic fruit count on coffee branches using computer vision. *Computers and Electronics in Agriculture, 137*, 9–22. doi:10.1016/j.compag.2017.03.010

Razzaghi, T., Safro, I., Ewing, J., Sadrfaridpour, E., & Scott, J. (2017). *Predictive models for bariatric surgery risks with imbalanced medical datasets.* Academic Press.

Razzak, M. I., Naz, S., & Zaib, A. (2018). Deep learning for medical image processing: Overview, challenges and the future. In *Classification in BioApps* (pp. 323–350). Cham: Springer. doi:10.1007/978-3-319-65981-7_12

Rehme, A. K., Volz, L. J., Feis, D. L., Bomilcar, F., Liebig, T., Eickhoff, S. B., ... Grefkes, C. (2015). Identifying neuro-imaging markers of Motor Disability in acute stroke by machine Learning Techniques. *Cereb Cortex, 25*(9), 3046–3056. doi:10.1093/cercor/bhu100 PMID:24836690

Reid, Thompson, Valdes, Fuller, Carpenter, Morin, ... Thomas, Jr. (n.d.). Artificial intelligence in radiation oncology: A specialty-wide disruptive transformation? In *Radiation and Oncology.* Elsevier.

Roh, Y., Heo, G., & Whang, S. E. (2018). *A survey on data collection for machine learning: a big data – AI integration perspective.* Retrieved from: https://arxiv.org/pdf/1811.03402.pdf

Rohit Rastogi, P., Agarwal, K., Gupta, R., & Jain, S. (2015). GA Based Clustering of Mixed Data Type of Attributes - Numeric, Categorical, Ordinal, Binary and Ratio Scaled. *BVICAM's International Journal of Information Technology, 7*(2), 861–865.

Rosenblatt, F. (1958). The perceptron: A probabilistic model for information storage and organization in the brain. *Psychological Review, 65*(6), 386–408. doi:10.1037/h0042519 PMID:13602029

Rouse, W. B. (2008). *Health care as a complex adaptive system: implications for design and management.* Bridge-Washington-National Academy of Engineering.

Sahi, M., Abbas, H., Saleem, K., Yang, X., Derhab, A., Orgun, M., ... Yaseen, A. (2018). Privacy Preservation in e-Healthcare Environments: State of the Art and Future Directions. *IEEE Access: Practical Innovations, Open Solutions, 6*, 464–478. doi:10.1109/ACCESS.2017.2767561

Sajana, Navya, Gayathri, & Reshma. (2018). Classification of Dengue using Machine Learning Techniques. *International Journal of Engineering & Technology, 7*(2), 212-218.

Salles, T., Gonçalves, M., Rodrigues, V., & Rocha, L. (2018). Improving random forests by neighborhood projection for effective text classification. Information Systems, 77, 1-21.

Samuel, A. L. (1959). Some Studies in Machine Learning Using the Game of Checkers. *IBM Journal of Research and Development, 44*(1), 210–229.

Sandeep, R. (2018). Use of Artificial Intelligence in Healthcare Delivery. In eHealth - Making Health Care Smarter. Intechopen.

Sanil, A. P., Karr, A. F., Lin, X., & Reiter, J. P. (2004). Privacy preserving regression modelling via distributed computation. In *Proceedings of the tenth ACM SIGKDD international conference on Knowledge discovery and data mining.* ACM.

Santos, C., Guimaraes, V., Niterói, R. J., & de Janeiro, R. (2015) Boosting named entity recognition with neural character embeddings. *Proceedings of NEWS 2015 the Fifth Named Entities Workshop.* 10.18653/v1/W15-3904

Santos, D. (2015). Categorical data clustering: What similarity measure to recommend? *Elsevier Expert Systems with Applications, 42*(3), 1247–1260. doi:10.1016/j.eswa.2014.09.012

Saravananathan & Velmurugan. (2016). Analyzing Diabetic Data using Classification Algorithms in Data Mining. *Indian Journal of Science and Technology, 9*(43).

Sathiyamoorthi & Baskaran. (2011). Data pre-processing techniques for pre-fetching and caching of web data through proxy server. *International Journal of Computer Science and Network Security, 11*(1), 92–98.

Sathiyamoorthi, V. (2017). *Improving the Performance of an Information Retrieval System through WEB Mining.* Doi:10.1515/itc-2017-0004

Sathiyamoorthi, V., & Murali Bhaskaran, V. (2011b). Data Pre-Processing Techniques for Pre-Fetching and Caching of Web Data through Proxy Server. *International Journal of Computer Science and Network Security, 11*(11), 92-98.

Sathiyamoorthi, V., & Ramya, P. (2014). Enhancing Proxy based Web Caching system using Clustering based Pre-fetching with Machine Learning Technique. *International Journal of Research in Engineering and Technology.*

Sathiyamoorthi, V. (2016). A Novel Cache Replacement Policy for Web Proxy Caching System Using Web Usage Mining. *International Journal of Information Technology and Web Engineering, 11*(2), 1–12. doi:10.4018/IJITWE.2016040101

Sathiyamoorthi, V., & Murali Bhaskaran, V. (2011a). Improving the Performance of Web Page Retrieval through Pre-Fetching and Caching. *European Journal of Scientific Research, 66*(2), 207–217.

Sathiyamoorthi, V., & Murali Bhaskaran, V. (2012). Optimizing the Web Cache performance by Clustering Based Pre-Fetching Technique Using Modified ART1. *International Journal of Computers and Applications, 44*(1), 51–60.

Sathiyamoorthi, V., & Murali Bhaskaran, V. (2013). Novel Approaches for Integrating MART1 Clustering Based Pre-Fetching Technique with Web Caching. *International Journal of Information Technology and Web Engineering, 8*(2), 18–32. doi:10.4018/jitwe.2013040102

Sathya, D., & Ganesh Kumar, P. (2017). Secured Remote Health Monitoring System. *IET Healthcare Technology Letters, 4*(6), 228–232. doi:10.1049/htl.2017.0033 PMID:29383257

Sayed, S. (2018). *Machine learning is the future of cancer prediction.* Retrieved from https://towardsdatascience.com/machine-learning-is-the-future-of-cancer-prediction-e4d28e7e6dfa

Sayi, T. J. V. R. K. M. K., & Krishna, R. K. N. S. (2012). Data Outsourcing in Cloud Environments: A Privacy Preserving Approach. *9th International Conference on Information Technology- New Generations,* 361–366.

Sazak, Ç., Nelson, C. J., & Obara, B. (2019). The multiscale bowler-hat transform for blood vessel enhancement in retinal images. *Pattern Recognition, 88,* 739–750. doi:10.1016/j.patcog.2018.10.011

Scikit-learn. (2019, May 30). Retrieved from https://en.wikipedia.org/wiki/Scikit-learn

Seth, E. (2014). Mobile Commerce: A Broader Perspective. *IT Professional, 16*(3), 61–65. doi:10.1109/MITP.2014.37

Shalaby, A., Mahmoud, A., Mesbah, S., El-Baz, M., Suri, J. S., & El-Baz, A. (2018). Accurate Unsupervised 3D Segmentation of Blood Vessels Using Magnetic Resonance Angiography. In Cardiovascular Imaging and Image Analysis (pp. 71-94). CRC Press.

Shankararaman, V., & Kit, L. E. (2014). Enterprise Systems Enabling Smart Commerce. *2014 IEEE 16th Conference on Business Informatics*, 50-53. 10.1109/CBI.2014.17

Shapiro, S. C. (1979). The SNePS Semantic Network Processing System. In N. V. Findler (Ed.), *Associative Networks* (pp. 179–203). New York: Academic Press. doi:10.1016/B978-0-12-256380-5.50011-6

Sharma, C. S. (2001). *India still has a low breast cancer survival rate of 66%: study*. Retrieved from https://www.livemint.com/Science/UaNco9nvoxQtxjneDS4LoO/India-still-has-a-low-breast-cancer-survival-rate-of-66-st.html

Shaukat, K., Masood, N., Mehreen, S., & Azmeen, U. (2015). Dengue fever prediction: A data mining problem. *Journal of Data Mining in Genomics & Proteomics*.

Sheshadri, H. S., & Kandaswany, A. (2006). Computer aided decision system for early detection of breast cancer. *The Indian Journal of Medical Research*, *124*(2), 149–154. PMID:17015928

Shie, B.-E., Hsiao, H.-F., Tseng, V.-S., & Yu, P.-S. (2011). Mining High Utility Mobile Sequential Patterns in Mobile Commerce Environments. *Proc. 16th Int'l Conf. DAtabase Systems for Advanced Applications (DASFAA '11), 6587*, 224-238. 10.1007/978-3-642-20149-3_18

Shin, Orton, Collins, Doran, & Leach. (n.d.). *Autoencoder in time-series analysis for unsupervised tissues characterisation in a large unlabelled medical image dataset.* Academic Press.

Shin, H., Kim, K. H., Song, C., Lee, I., Lee, K., Kang, J., & Kang, Y. K. (2010). Electrodiagnosis support system for localizing neural injury in an upper limb. *Journal of the American Medical Informatics Association*, *17*(3), 345–347. doi:10.1136/jamia.2009.001594 PMID:20442155

Shokri, R., & Shmatikov, V. (2015). Privacy-preserving deep learning. In *Proceedings of the 22nd ACM SIGSAC Conference on Computer and Communications Security*. ACM.

Shokri, R., & Shmatikov, V. (2015). Privacy-preserving deep learning. *Proceedings of the 22nd ACM SIGSAC Conference on Computer and Communications Security ACM*, 1310–1321.

Silver, D., Huang, A., Maddison, C. J., Guez, A., Sifre, L., van den Driessche, G., ... Hassabis, D. (2016). Mastering the game of Go with deep neural networks and tree search. *Nature*, *529*(7587), 484–489. doi:10.1038/nature16961 PMID:26819042

Singh, H. (2018, June 26). *Machine Learning- What, Why, When and How?* Retrieved from https://towardsdatascience.com/machine-learning-what-why-when-and-how-9a2f244647a4

Singh, N. P., & Srivastava, R. (2018). Extraction of retinal blood vessels by using an extended matched filter based on second derivative of gaussian. *Proceedings of the National Academy of Sciences, India Section A: Physical Sciences*, 1-9.

Singh, M., Sharma, S., Verma, A., & Sharma, N. (2017). Enhancement and Intensity Inhomogeneity Correction of Diffusion-Weighted MR Images of Neonatal and Infantile Brain Using Dynamic Stochastic Resonance. *Journal of Medical and Biological Engineering*, *37*(4), 508–518. doi:10.100740846-017-0270-0

Siriyasatien, P., Phumee, A., Ongruk, P., & Jampac, K. (2016). Analysis of significant factors for dengue fever incidence prediction. *International Journal of Pure and Applied Mathematics*, 3885. PMID:27083696

Sisodia, D., & Sisodia, D. S. (2018). Prediction of Diabetes using Classification Algorithms. *Procedia Computer Science*, *132*, 1578–1585. doi:10.1016/j.procs.2018.05.122

Skillicorn, D. (2007). *Understanding complex datasets: data mining with matrix decompositions.* Chapman and Hall/CRC.

Sladojevic, S., Arsenovic, M., Anderla, A., Culibrk, D., & Stefanovic, D. (2016). *Deep neural networks based recognition of plant diseases by leaf image classification.* Computat. Intelligence Neurosci; doi:10.1155/2016/3289801

Slavkovic, A. B., Nardi, Y., & Tibbits, M. M. (2007). Secure logistic regression of horizontally and vertically partitioned distributed databases. *Seventh IEEE International Conference on Data Mining Workshops (ICDMW)*, 723–728.

Soguero-Ruiz. (2016). Predicting colorectal surgical complications using heterogeneous clinical data and kernel methods. *Journal of Biomedical Informatics, 61*, 87-96.

Sønderby, S.K., & Winther, O. (n.d.). *Protein secondary structure prediction with long short term memory networks.* arXiv1412.7828

Song, S., Chaudhuri, K., & Sarwate, A. D. (2013). Stochastic gradient descent with dif- ferentially private updates. In *Global Conference on Signal and Information Processing (GlobalSIP)*. IEEE.

Song, W., & Huang, C. (2018). Mining High Utility Itemsets Using Bio-Inspired Algorithms: A Diverse Optimal Value Framework. *IEEE Access: Practical Innovations, Open Solutions, 6*, 19568–19582. doi:10.1109/ACCESS.2018.2819162

Soomro, T. A., Afifi, A. J., Gao, J., Hellwich, O., Khan, M. A., Paul, M., & Zheng, L. (2017, November). Boosting sensitivity of a retinal vessel segmentation algorithm with convolutional neural network. In *2017 International Conference on Digital Image Computing: Techniques and Applications (DICTA)* (pp. 1-8). IEEE. 10.1109/DICTA.2017.8227413

Stonelake, S., Thomson, P., & Suggett, N. (2015). Identification of the high risk emergency surgical patient: Which risk prediction model should be used. *Annals of Medicine and Surgery (London), 4*(3), 240–247. doi:10.1016/j.amsu.2015.07.004 PMID:26468369

Subramanian, K., & Kandhasamy, P. (2015). UP-GNIV: An expeditious high utility pattern mining algorithm for itemsets with negative utility values. *International Journal of Information Technology and Management, 14*(1), 26–42. doi:10.1504/IJITM.2015.066056

Sun, J., Fang, Y., & Zhu, X. (2010). Privacy and emergency response in e- healthcare leveraging wireless body sensor networks. *Wireless Communications, IEEE, 17*(1), 66–73. doi:10.1109/MWC.2010.5416352

Taber, J. K. A., Morisy, L. R., & Osbahr, A. J. III. (2010). Male breast cancer: Risk factors, diagnosis, and management. *Oncology Reports, 24*(5), 1115–1120. PMID:20878100

Tanbeer, S. K., Ahmed, C. F., Jeong, B.-S., & Lee, Y.-K. (2008). Efficient Frequent Pattern Mining over Data Streams. *Proc. ACM 17*th *Conf. Information and Knowledge Management.* 10.1145/1458082.1458326

Tang, D., Qin, B., & Liu, T. (2015). Document modelling with gated recurrent neural network for sentiment classification. In *Proceedings of the 2015 conference on empirical methods in natural language processing* (pp. 1422-1432). Academic Press. 10.18653/v1/D15-1167

Tang, F., & Ishwaran, H. (2017). *Random forest missing data algorithms.* Academic Press.

Tan, S., Li, Y., Sun, H., Guan, Z., Yan, X., Bu, J., ... He, X. (2014). Interpreting the public sentiment variations on Twitter. *IEEE Transactions on Knowledge and Data Engineering, 26*(5), 1158–1170. doi:10.1109/TKDE.2013.116

Tashk, A., Helfroush, M. S., & Danyali, H. (2014). A novel CAD system for mitosis detection using histopathology slide images. *Journal of Medical Signals and Sensors, 4*(2), 139–149. PMID:24761378

Temurtas, H., Yumusak, N., & Temurtas, F. (2009, May). A comparative study on diabetes disease diagnosis using neural networks. *Systems with Applications, 36*(4), 8610–8615. doi:10.1016/j.eswa.2008.10.032

Ten, W., Chang, C.Y., & Chen, M.S. (2005). Integrating web caching and web pre-fetching in client-side proxies. *Parallel and Distributed Systems, IEEE Transactions on, 16*(5), 444-455.

TensorFlow. (n.d.). Retrieved from https://www.tensorflow.org/tutorials

The Conversation. (2018). *Explainer: what is differential privacy and how can it protect your data?* Available at: http://theconversation.com/explainer-what-is-differential-privacy-and-how-can-it-protect-your-data-90686

The R Project for Statistical Computing. (n.d.). Retrieved from https://www.r-project.org/

Thitiprayoonwongse, D. A., Suriyaphol, P. R., & Soonthornphisaj, N. U. (2012). Data mining of Dengue Infection using Decision Tree. *Entropy (Basel, Switzerland)*.

Trilla, A., & Alias, F. (2013). Sentence-based sentiment analysis for expressive text-to-speech. *IEEE Transactions on Audio, Speech, and Language Processing, 21*(2), 223–233. doi:10.1109/TASL.2012.2217129

Troyanskaya, O. G. (2014). Deep supervised and convolutional generative stochastic network for protein secondary structure prediction. *Proc 31st Int Conf Mach Learn, 32*, 745–53.

Tseng, V. S., Chu, C. J., & Liang, T. (2006). Efficient Mining of Temporal High Utility Itemsets from Data Streams. *Proc. ACM KDD Workshop Utility-Based Data Mining Workshop (UBDM '06)*.

Tseng, V. S., Shie, B.-E., Wu, C. W., & Yu, P. S. (2013). Efficient Algorithms for Mining High Utility Itemsets from Transactional Databases. *IEEE Transactions on Knowledge and Data Engineering, 25*(8), 1772–1786. doi:10.1109/TKDE.2012.59

Tseng, V. S., Wu, C.-W., Shie, B.-E., & Yu, P. S. (2010). UP-Growth: An Efficient Algorithm for High Utility Itemsets Mining. *Proc. 16th ACM SIGKDD Conf. Knowledge Discovery and Data Mining (KDD '10)*, 253-262. 10.1145/1835804.1835839

Tustison, N. J., Avants, B. B., Cook, P. A., Zheng, Y., Egan, A., Yushkevich, P. A., & James, C. (2010). N4ITK: Improved N3 Bias Correction. *IEEE Transactions on Medical Imaging, 29*(6), 1310–1320. doi:10.1109/TMI.2010.2046908 PMID:20378467

University of Lincoln. (n.d.). Review: Retinal Vessel Image set for estimation widths. *University of Lincoln.* Retrieved from: http://www.aldiri.info/REVIEWDB/REVIEWDB.aspx

Utomo, C. P., Kardiana, A., & Yuliwulandri, R. (2014). Breast cancer diagnosis using artificial neural networks with extreme learning techniques. *International Journal of Advanced Research in Artificial Intelligence, 3*(7), 10–14.

Vaidya, J., Yu, H., & Jiang, X. (2008). Privacy-preserving svm classification. *Knowledge and Information Systems, 14*(2), 161–178. doi:10.100710115-007-0073-7

Vengerov, D. (2009). A reinforcement learning framework for utility-based scheduling in resource-constrained systems. *Future Generation Computer Systems, 25*(7), 728–736. doi:10.1016/j.future.2008.02.006

Vianna, G.K., Oliveira, G.S., & Cunha, G.V. (2017). A neuro-automata decision support system for the control of late blight in tomato crops. *World Acad. Sci., Eng. Technol., Int. J. Comput., Electr., Autom., Control Inform. Eng., 11*(4), 455–462.

Vijeta, S. (2015). Malaria Outbreak Prediction Model Using Machine Learning. *International Journal of Advanced Research in Computer Engineering & Technology, 4*(12), 4415–4419.

Villar, J. R., González, S., Sedano, J., Chira, C., & Trejo-Gabriel-Galan, J. M. (2015). Improving human activity recognition and its application in early stroke diagnosis. *International Journal of Neural Systems, 25*(4), 1450036. doi:10.1142/S0129065714500361 PMID:25684369

Vovk, U., Pernus, F., & Likar, B. (2007). A Review of Methods for Correction of Intensity Inhomogeneity in MRI. *IEEE Transactions on Medical Imaging, 26*(3), 405–421. doi:10.1109/TMI.2006.891486 PMID:17354645

Wagh, V. M., Panaskar, D. B., Muley, A. A., Mukate, S. V., Logale, Y. P., & Aamalawar, M. L. (2016). Prediction of groundwater suitability for irrigation using artificial neural network model: A case study of Nanded tehsil, Maharashtra, India. *Modeling Earth Systems and Environment, Springer, 2*(4), 1–10. doi:10.100740808-016-0250-3

Walter, T., & Klein, J. C. (2001, October). Segmentation of color fundus images of the human retina: Detection of the optic disc and the vascular tree using morphological techniques. In *International Symposium on Medical Data Analysis* (pp. 282-287). Springer. 10.1007/3-540-45497-7_43

Wang, S., Li, W., Liu, S., & Xu, J. (2016). RaptorX-Property: A web server for protein structure property prediction. *Nucleic Acids Research, 44*. PMID:27112573

Wang, S., Weng, S., Ma, J., & Tang, Q. (2015). DeepCNF-D: Predicting protein order/disorder regions by weighted deep convolutional neural fields. *International Journal of Molecular Sciences, 16*(8), 17315–17330. doi:10.3390/ijms160817315 PMID:26230689

Wang, S., Yin, Y., Cao, G., Wei, B., Zheng, Y., & Yang, G. (2015). Hierarchical retinal blood vessel segmentation based on feature and ensemble learning. *Neurocomputing, 149*, 708–717. doi:10.1016/j.neucom.2014.07.059

Wang, X., Jiang, X., & Ren, J. (2019). Blood vessel segmentation from fundus image by a cascade classification framework. *Pattern Recognition, 88*, 331–341. doi:10.1016/j.patcog.2018.11.030

Wang, X., Zhu, F., Jiang, J., & Li, S. (2013). Earthquake Shakes Twitter Users: Real-time Event Detection by Social Sensors. *Lecture Notes in Computer Science, 7923*, 502–513. doi:10.1007/978-3-642-38562-9-51

Wan, Y., & Wu, C. (2009). Fitting and Prediction for Crack Propagation Rate Based on Machine Learning Optimal Algorithm. *International Conference on E-Learning, E-Business, Enterprise Information Systems, and E-Government*, 93-96. 10.1109/EEEE.2009.31

Weka 3: Machine Learning Software in Java. (n.d.). Retrieved from http://www.cs.waikato.ac.nz/ml/weka

Wernick, M. N., Yang, Y., Brankov, J. G., Yourganov, G., & Strother, S. C. (2010). Medical imaging and machine learning. IEEE Signal Processing Magazine, 25–38. doi:10.1109/MSP.2010.936730 PubMed

Widrow, B., & Michael, L. A. (1990). 30 years of adaptive neural networks: Perceptron, madaline, and backpropagation. *Proceedings of the IEEE, 78*(9), 1415–1442. doi:10.1109/5.58323

Willcock, S., Martínez-López, J., Hooftman, D. A. P., Bagstad, K. J., Balbi, S., Marzo, A., ... Athanasiadis, I. N. (2018). Machine learning for ecosystem services. *Ecosystem Services, 33*, 165–174. doi:10.1016/j.ecoser.2018.04.004

Wöllmer, M., Weninger, F., Knaup, T., Schuller, B., Sun, C., Sagae, K., & Morency, L.-P. (2013). YouTube Movie Reviews: Sentiment Analysis in an Audio-Visual Context. *IEEE Intelligent Systems, 28*(3), 46–53. doi:10.1109/MIS.2013.34

Wong, A., Young, A. T., Liang, A. S., Gonzales, R., Douglas, V. C., & Hadley, D. (2018). Development and validation of an electronic health record–based machine learning model to estimate delirium risk in newly hospitalized patients without known cognitive impairment. *JAMA Network Open, 1*(4), e181018. doi:10.1001/jamanetworkopen.2018.1018 PMID:30646095

Wongkhamdi, T., Cooharojananone, N., & Khlaisang, J. (2017). The study of mobile learning readiness in rural area: Case of North-Eastern of Thailand. *2017 International Symposium on Computers in Education (SIIE)*, 1-6. 10.1109/SIIE.2017.8259665

Woochul K., & Daeyeon K. (2018). *DeepRT: A Predictable Deep Learning Inference Framework for IoT Devices.* Academic Press.

Wrzesień, M., Treder, W., Klamkowski, K., & Rudnicki, W. R. (2018). Prediction of the apple scab using machine learning and simple weather stations. *Computers and Electronics in Agriculture.* doi:10.1016/j.compag.2018.09.026

Wu, S., Teruya, T., Kawamoto, J., Sakuma, J., & Kikuchi, H. (2013). Privacy- preservation for stochastic gradient descent application to secure logistic regression. *The 27th Annual Conference of the Japanese Society for Artificial Intelligence*, 1–4.

Wu, H., Yang, S., Huang, Z., He, J., & Wang, X. (2018). Type 2 diabetes mellitus prediction model based on data mining. *Informatics in Medicine Unlocked*, *10*, 100–107. doi:10.1016/j.imu.2017.12.006

Xiao, R., Ding, H., Zhai, F., Zhou, W., & Wang, G. (2018). Cerebrovascular segmentation of TOF-MRA based on seed point detection and multiple-feature fusion. *Computerized Medical Imaging and Graphics*, *69*, 1–8. doi:10.1016/j.compmedimag.2018.07.002 PMID:30142578

Xia, R., Xu, F., Zong, C., Li, Q., Qi, Y., & Li, T. (2015). Dual Sentiment Analysis: Considering Two Sides of One Review. *IEEE Transactions on Knowledge and Data Engineering*, *27*(8), 2120–2133. doi:10.1109/TKDE.2015.2407371

Xin, X., Haibo, H., Dongbin, Z., Shiliang, S., Lucian, B., & Simon, X. Y. (2016). *Machine Learning with Applications to Autonomous Systems.* Hindawi Publishing Corporation.

Xu, & Ibrahim. (n.d.). Towards Semantics-Based Pre-fetching to Reduce Web Access Latency. *Proceedings IEEE Computer Society Symposium, SAINT'03.*

Xu, C., Pham, D. L., & Prince, J. L. (2000). Image segmentation using deformable models. Handbook of Medical Imaging, 2, 129-174.

Xu, J., Xiang, L., Wang, G., Ganesan, S., Feldman, M., Shih, N. N. C., ... Madabhushi, A. (2015). Sparse non-negative matrix factorization (SNMF) based color unmixing for breast histopathological image analysis. *Computerized Medical Imaging and Graphics*, *46*, 20–29. doi:10.1016/j.compmedimag.2015.04.002 PMID:25958195

Xu, Y., Mou, L., Li, G., Chen, Y., & Peng, H. (2015). Classifying relations via long short term memory networks along shortest dependency path. *Proceedings of Conference on Empirical Methods in Natural Language Processing.* 10.18653/v1/D15-1206

Yang, L., Meer, P., & Foran, D. (2005). Unsupervised segmentation based on robust estimation and color active contour models. *IEEE Transactions on Information Technology in Biomedicine*, *9*(3), 475–486. doi:10.1109/TITB.2005.847515 PMID:16167702

Yang, X., Zhao, P., Zhang, X., Lin, J., & Yu, W. (2017). Toward a Gaussian mixture model-based detection scheme against data integrity attacks in the smart grid. *IEEE Internet Things J.*, *4*(1), 147–161.

Yao, H., Hamilton, H. J., & Butz, C. J. (2004). A foundational approach to mining itemset utilities from databases. *Proc. SIAM Int. Conf. Data Mining*, 482-486. 10.1137/1.9781611972740.51

Yasodha & Kannan. (2011). A novel hybrid intelligent system with missing value imputation for diabetes diagnosis. *Alexandria Engineering Journal, 57*(3).

Ye, H., Shen, H., & Dong, Y. (2017). *Using Evidence-Based medicine through Advanced Data Analytics to work toward a National Standard for Hospital-based acute ischemic Stroke treatment.* Mainland China.

Yi & Chen. (n.d.). Prediction of Web Page Accesses by Proxy Server Log. *ACM Journal of World Wide Web, 5*(1).

Ying, W., Lu, C., & Zuo, C. (2015). Coal mine safety production forewarning based on improved BP neural network. *International Journal of Mining Science and Technology*, *25*(2), 319–324. doi:10.1016/j.ijmst.2015.02.023

Youssif, A. A. H. A. R., Ghalwash, A. Z., & Ghoneim, A. A. S. A. R. (2008). Optic disc detection from normalized digital fundus images by means of a vessels' direction matched filter. *IEEE Transactions on Medical Imaging*, *27*(1), 11–18. doi:10.1109/TMI.2007.900326 PMID:18270057

Yu, H., Vaidya, J., & Jiang, X. (2006). Privacy-preserving svm classification on vertically partitioned data. In *Pacific-Asia Conference on Knowledge Discovery and Data Mining*. Springer.

Yu, S., Moor, B., & Moreau, Y. (2009). Clustering by heterogeneous data fusion: framework and applications. *NIPS Workshop*.

Yuan, J. (2013). *Sentribute: Image Sentiment Analysis from a Mid-level Perspective Categories and Subject Descriptors*. Academic Press.

Yun, C.-H., & Chen, M.-S. (2000). Using Pattern-Join and Purchase-Combination for Mining Web Transaction Patterns in an Electronic Commerce Environment. *Proc. IEEE 24th Ann. Int'l Computer Software and Application Conf.*, 99-104.

Yun, C.-H., & Chen, M. S. (2007). Mining Mobile Sequential Patterns in a Mobile Commerce Environment. IEEE Trans. Systems, Man, and Cybernetics-Part C. *Applications and Rev.*, *37*(2), 278–295.

Yusof, Y., & Mustaffa, Z. (2011). Dengue Outbreak Prediction: A Least Squares Support Vector Machines Approach. *International Journal of Computer Theory and Engineering*, *3*(4).

Zhang, J., Dashtbozorg, B., Bekkers, E., Pluim, J. P., Duits, R., & ter Haar Romeny, B. M. (2016). Robust retinal vessel segmentation via locally adaptive derivative frames in orientation scores. *IEEE Transactions on Medical Imaging*, *35*(12), 2631–2644. doi:10.1109/TMI.2016.2587062 PMID:27514039

Zhang, Q., Xie, Y., & Ye, P. (2013). Acute ischaemic stroke prediction from physiological time series patterns. *The Australasian Medical Journal*, *6*(5), 280–286. doi:10.4066/AMJ.2013.1650 PMID:23745149

Zhang, S.-H., Gu, N., Lian, J.-X., & Li, S.-H. (2003). Workflow process mining based on machine learning. *Proceedings of the 2003 International Conference on Machine Learning and Cybernetics (IEEE Cat. No.03EX693)*, 2319-2323. 10.1109/ICMLC.2003.1259895

Zhang, S., Wu, X., You, Z., & Zhang, L. (2017). Leaf image based cucumber disease recognition using sparse representation classification. *Computers and Electronics in Agriculture*, *134*, 135–141. doi:10.1016/j.compag.2017.01.014

Zhao, S., Yao, H., Gao, Y., Ding, G., & Chua, T. S. (2018). Predicting Personalized Image Emotion Perceptions in Social Networks. IEEE Transactions on Affective Computing, 9(4), 526–540. doi:10.1109/TAFFC.2016.2628787

Zhao, L., & Li, F. (2008). Statistical Machine Learning in Natural Language Understanding: Object Constraint Language Translator for Business Process. *IEEE International Symposium on Knowledge Acquisition and Modeling Workshop*, 1056-1059. 10.1109/KAMW.2008.4810674

Zhao, S., Yao, H., Gao, Y., Ji, R., & Ding, G. (2017). Continuous Probability Distribution Prediction of Image Emotions via Multitask Shared Sparse Regression. *IEEE Transactions on Multimedia*, *19*(3), 632–645. doi:10.1109/TMM.2016.2617741

Zhao, Y., Rada, L., Chen, K., Harding, S. P., & Zheng, Y. (2015). Automated vessel segmentation using infinite perimeter active contour model with hybrid region information with application to retinal images. *IEEE Transactions on Medical Imaging*, *34*(9), 1797–1807. doi:10.1109/TMI.2015.2409024 PMID:25769147

Zhou, M., & Mu, Y. (2011). Privacy-Preserved Access Control for Cloud Computing. *International Joint Conference of IEEE TrustCom-11/IEEE ICESS-11/FCST-11*, 83–90. 10.1109/TrustCom.2011.14

Zhou, J., Lin, X., Dong, X., & Cao, Z. (2015). PSMPA: Patient Self-Controllable and Multi-Level Privacy-Preserving Cooperative Authentication in Distributedm-Healthcare Cloud Computing System. *Parallel and Distributed Systems, IEEE Transactions on, 26*(6), 1693–1703. doi:10.1109/TPDS.2014.2314119

Zhu, Fu, & Han. (2015). Online anomaly detection on e-commerce based on variable-length behavior sequence. *11th International Conference on Wireless Communications, Networking and Mobile Computing (WiCOM 2015)*, 1-8.

Zöllner, J., & Federrath, H. (1998). Modeling the security of steganographic systems. *Proceedings of the 2nd Workshop on Information Hiding*, 17, 228-256.

About the Contributors

Sathiyamoorthi Velayutham is currently working as an Associate Professor in Computer Science and Engineering Department at Sona College of Technology, Salem, Tamil Nadu, India. He was born on June 21, 1983, at Omalur in Salem District, Tamil Nadu, India. He received his Bachelor of Engineering degree in Information Technology from Periyar University, Salem with First Class. He obtained his Master of Engineering degree in Computer Science and Engineering from Anna University, Chennai with Distinction and secured 30th University Rank.He received his Ph.D degree from Anna University, Chennai in Web Mining. His areas of specialization include Web Usage Mining, Data Structures, Design and Analysis of Algorithm and Operating System. He has published five papers in International Journals and eight papers in various National and International conferences. He has also participated in various National level Workshops and Seminars conducted by various reputed institutions.

* * *

Aswathy M. A received B.Tech. degree in Electronics and Communication Engineering from Vidya Academy of Science and Technology, Kerala and M.E. degree in Applied Electronics from K.S.R. College of Technology, Tamilnadu, India, in 2011 and 2013 respectively. She has been with the Department of Electronics Engineering as Lecturer at SETCEM, Kerala, India. Currently, she is working as Ph.D. Scholar at Vellore Institute of Technology (VIT) Chennai, Tamilnadu, India. Her fields of interest are biomedical engineering, digital image processing and signal processing.

Divya A is Assistant Professor in Department of Computer Science, Jaya Engineering College. She completed her Bachelor of Engineering in 2012 and Master of Engineering in Computer Science in 2014 and started working towards her doctoral research by 2015. Her research areas include privacy preservation, machine learning and cloud computing.

Vadivel A. is an Associate Professor in the Department of Computer Science and Engineering of School of Engineering & Applied Sciences at SRM University-AP, Amaravati, India. He holds M.Sc in Applied Electronics from the National Institute of Technology- Trichy (1992), M.Tech. in Computer Science and Data Processing from Indian Institute of Technology, Kharagpur (2000), and a Ph.D. in Computer Science and Engineering from Indian Institute of Technology, Kharagpur (2006). Prior to joining the SRM in 2017, Dr. A Vadivel worked in various technical and scientific positions in the Indian Institute of Technology Kharagpur (1994-2006) and held faculty positions at the Bharathidasan University Trichy (2006-2007) and the National Institute of Technology Trichy (2007-2017). Dr. A Vadivel is the recipient of Young Scientist Award (Fast Track Scheme), DST Govt. of India in 2007, Indo-US Research Fellow Award by Indo-US Science and Technology Forum, Govt. of India in 2008. Obama-Singh (Indo-US) Knowledge Initiative Award by Govt. of India in 2013.Dr. A Vadivel has carried out research at University of Nevada Las Vegas, USA under Indo-US research Fellow award in 2008 and Obama-Singh (Indo-US) knowledge initiative award in 2013. Dr. A Vadivel's current research interests include Object Tracking in Video Sequence, Visual Sensor Networks, Multimedia Information Retrieval and Mammogram Analysis and Interpretation. He has supervised five PhD dissertations and 60 Masters thesis. He has published 107 publications, which include 35 journal publications, 2 books, 2 book chapters and 67 conference publications. Dr. A Vadivel has carried out 4 funded projects from DST Govt. of India, 3 funded project from MHRD Govt. of India, 1 funded project from UGC Govt. of India, 1 funded project from Rajiv Gandhi National Institute of Youth Development, Govt. of India. Dr. A Vadivel has taught courses such as Data Structures and Algorithms, Software Project Management, Artificial Intelligence, Soft Computing, Computer Graphics and Multimedia, Computer Networks, Information Retrieval, Visual Programming, Programming using C, C++, JAVA and Python and Data Science. Dr. A Vadivel is a Member of ISTE, member of Computer Society of Indian (CSI) and member of Indian Science Congress. He has visited China, Singapore, Dubai, Thailand, Japan and USA for research purpose.

Usha B. Ajay is working as Associate Professor and Head of the Department in Information Science & Engineering, BMSIT&M, Bengaluru. She received her Ph.D in Computer Science from Visvesvaraya Technological University, Belagavi in the Year 2016. Her research interests include Information security, Image Processing, Compiler Design and Cognitive Science. She has published nearly 25 papers in reputed International Journal & Conferences. She serves as a reviewer of various renowned International Journals and Conferences.

Krishnakumar B. is pursuing Ph.D., in Machine Learning under Anna University. Currently he is a Assistant Professor in the department of Computer Science & Engineering in Kongu Engineering College, Tamilnadu, India. He has completed 11 years of teaching service. He has published 5 articles in International &National Journals. He has published 9 articles in International & National Conference. He has organized 2 funded seminars and workshops.

Bhagyashree Bagwe is a B. Tech. Information Technology student in the Vellore Institute of Technology. Being a meritorious student in her college, she is interested in machine learning and generic coding. She has interned for RBS, Bangalore (2019) and WebEngage, Mumbai (2018).

Astha Baranwal is a B.Tech (Bachelor of Technology), Information Technology student in the Vellore Institute of Technology, India. She is an avid data science enthusiast and loves to explore new technologies involved in this field. She is currently interning in the R&D department of CNSI, Chennai.

Gunavathi C. is currently working as an Associate Professor in the School of Information Technology and Engineering at Vellore Institute of Technology, Vellore, Tamil Nadu, India. She received her Ph.D from Anna University, Chennai, India. She received her B.E (CSE) and M.E (CSE) from Bharathidasan University and Anna University, India, respectively. She has around 12 years of teaching experience. Her research interest includes data mining in Bioinformatics and Soft computing techniques.

Jagadeesan D working as Associate Professor in the Department of Commerce and Management, Cherraan's Arts Science College, Kangayam. He received his Bachelor of Science in Electronics at SNR Sons College, Bharathiar University, Coimbatore, in the year 1994. He completed his Master of Business Administration at RVS College, Bharathiar University, Coimbatore, in the year 2000. He completed his Master of Philosophy in Management at SNR Sons College, Bharathiar University, Coimbatore, in the year 2011.

Sathya D. works as Assistant Professor II in Department Computer Science & Engineering at Kumaraguru College of Technology, Coimbatore, Tamilnadu, India. She is pursuing PhD on Data Security in Wireless Sensor Networks at Anna University, Chennai. She has published about 40 papers in both conferences and journals.

Pon Harshavardhanan is an Experienced Professor with long demonstrated experience of working in the higher education industry. Skilled in developing projects and carrying out research in the area of Distributed systems, Cloud computing, Big data and Data Science with the programming skill in Java, Python, R and C. Passionate in teaching in Higher Education, research and development and innovative technological advancements. Strong education professional with doctoral, master and bachelor degree in Computer Science and Engineering.

Akilandeswari J. is the Professor, Head of Department of Information Technology, Sona College of Technology, Salem. She has experience of over 20 years in Teaching and Research. She is a Gold Medalist from Bharathidasan University in Bachelor's of Computer Science and Engineering. She had completed M.E and Ph.D. in Computer Science and Engineering from NIT, Tiruchirappalli. She has published papers in various international journals and conferences. Her areas of interests include Data mining, Web Mining, Data Analytics and Cloud Computing. She is a member of the IEEE Computer Society.

Dhayanithi J. is the Assistant Professor, Department of Computer Science and Engineering, Sona College of Technology, Salem. He has experience of over 8 years in Teaching and Research. His research interest includes Data mining, Mining on heterogeneous data.

Jayanthi J is working as an associate professor in the department of Computer Science and Engineering, Sona College of Technology(SCT),Salem, Tamilnadu, India. She is having three years of Industrial experience as a software engineer and 17 years of teaching experience in SCT. Her area of interest includes web technologies, software engineering, Software Testing, Artificial Intelligence, Internet of Things, Data mining and Big Data Analytics. She has published more than fifty papers in the national and international journals and conferences. She is one of the co-investigator of the DST funded project on CDSS for Breast Cancer for rural women community. She has received many appreciation awards for the teaching and learning and Research and Development activities.

Logeswaran K. received the ME degree in computer science and engineering from Anna university, Chennai, India, in 2011 and B.Tech degree in information technology from Anna university, Chennai, India in 2009. He is presently pursuing his Ph.D. (Part time) in Information and Communication Engineering under Anna University Chennai. He is currently working as Assistant Professor in the department of Information Technology at Kongu Engineering College, Perundurai, India. His research interests are in the areas of data mining, knowledge discovery and networking. He has authored over 15 research papers in refereed journals and international conferences.

Venu K. is currently working as a Assistant Professor in the Department of Computer Science & Engineering in Kongu Engineering College, Tamilnadu, India. She is pursuing Ph.D., in Machine Learning under Anna University. She has completed 2 years of teaching service. She has published 3 articles in International/ National Conference.

Prasanna Kumar K. R. received his BE (2008) in Computer Science and Engineering from Anna University, Chennai and the ME (2010) in Computer Science and Engineering from Anna University, Coimbatore. He is presently pursuing his Ph.D. (Part time) in Computer Science and Engineering under Anna University Chennai. He is currently working as Assistant Professor in Department of Information Technology at Kongu Engineering College, Perundurai, Tamilnadu. His research interests include Grid computing, Cloud Computing and Nature inspired algorithms. He has published more than 16 technical papers in international journals and conferences.

V. Jeyakrishnan received his Bachelor of Technology (B.Tech.) in Information Technology from Anna University, Chennai, Tamil Nadu, India in 2006 and Master of Technology (M.Tech.) in Information Technology from Anna University, Coimbatore, India in 2010 .He also received his PhD from Anna University in 2017, has served in the field of education for over 12 years and he has served in the IT industry for nearly 2 years. Currently he is working as Associate Professor in the Department of Computer Science and Engineering, SAINTGITS College of Engineering, Kottayam, Kerala, India. He has published 16 International Journals, 8 International Conferences and 3 National level conference papers. His Area of research in Machine Learning, Deep Learning, Cloud Computing, Optimization Technology, and Big Data.

Bharathiraja M is PhD scholar in Department of Civil Engineering, IIT Madras. He completed his Master of Science in Intelligent Transportation System at University of Applied Science, Vienna in 2016. He is working on Image Processing and Data-driven Modeling for traffic forecasting.

Jagannath M. is an Associate Professor in the School of Electronics Engineering at VIT University, Chennai, India. Prior to joining VIT University, he was heading the Department of Biomedical Engineering at SMK Fomra Institute of Technology, Chennai, India. He obtained his Ph.D. from IIT Madras, Chennai in the year 2012. He has served the position of Senior Project Officer at Indian Institute of Technology Madras, Chennai, India. He has taught at Sri Sai Ram Engineering College, Chennai; Madras Medical Mission, Chennai; Vellore Institute of Technology, Vellore. He received IndiraGandhi Sadbhavna Gold Medal Award for Individual Achievement and Service to the Nation from Global Economic Progress and Research Association, India, 2014. He received Technical Icon of the Year 2012 from the Institution of Engineering and Technology, Young Professional Society (Chennai Network), UK. He also received Half Time Research Associate (HTRA) Fellowship from IIT Madras during July 2007-December 2011. He has more than 50 research articles published in various reputed conferences and journals.

Senbagavalli M. has a doctoral degree from Anna University on the topic, 'Opinion Mining of Health Data for Cardiovascular Disease Diagnosis Using Unsupervised Feature Selection Algorithm'. She also holds an M.E. in Computer Science and Engineering from Jayam College of Engineering and Technology and a B.E. in Information Technology degree from the Sona College of Technology. now she is working as Associate Professor in the department of Information technology in Alliance University,Bangalore. Her areas of teaching and research include: Data Mining, Big Data Analytics, IoT, Computer Networks, Object Oriented Programming (C++ and Java), Object Oriented Analysis and Design, Visual Programming, C# and .Net, Software Testing, Software Engineering and Quality Assurance, Design and Analysis of Algorithms. She has presented and published papers in national and international conferences/ journals focusing on Data Mining, Big Data Analytics, Cloud Computing and Opinion Mining.

Vanitha M. holds PhD in computer science from VIT University. Presently she is working as Associate Professor in VIT University, Vellore. Her current research includes High speed architecture for cryptography, Machine Learning.

Aswathy M. A. received B.Tech. degree in Electronics and Communication Engineering from Vidya Academy of Science and Technology, Kerala and M.E. degree in Applied Electronics from K.S.R. College of Technology, Tamil Nadu, India, in 2011 and 2013 respectively. She has been with the Department of Electronics Engineering as Lecturer at SET College of Engineering and Management, Kerala, India. Currently, she is pursuing her Ph.D. degree at Vellore Institute of Technology (VIT) Chennai, Tamil Nadu, India. Her fields of interest are biomedical engineering, digital image processing and signal processing.

R. Murugan was received the B.E. degree in Electronics and Communication Engineering, the M.E. degree in Embedded System Technologies from Anna University, Chennai, Tamilnadu and the Ph.D. degree from Information and Communication Engineering, Centre for Research, Anna University, Chennai, Tamilnadu, India. He worked as Assistant Professor, in the Department of Electronics and Communication Engineering, Aalim Muhammed Salegh College of Engineering, Chennai from 01st August 2010 to 15th December 2017. He worked as Assistant Professor, in the Department of Electronics and Communication Engineering, St.peter's Engineering College, Hyderabad from 08th January 2018 to 30th May 2018. He is working as Assistant Professor, in the Department of Electronics and Communication Engineering, National Institute of Technology (NIT), Silchar since 15th June 2018. He published 42 research articles in various international, national journals and conferences as on date. He is the active member of the Institute of Electrical and Electronics Engineers (IEEE) the USA and the life member of Indian Society for Technical Education (ISTE), India. His research interest includes embedded systems, image processing and machine learning.

Sasipriyaa N. is currently working as a Assistant Professor in the department of Computer Science & Engineering in Kongu Engineering College, Tamilnadu, India. She has completed 11 years of teaching service. She has published 4 articles in International & National Journals. She has published 8 articles in International & National Conference. She has organized 1 funded workshop.

Sangeetha K. Nanjundaswamy is working as Assistant Professor in the Department of Electronics & Communication Engineering, JSSATE, Bengaluru. She received her M.Tech from Visvesvaraya Technological University, Belagavi. She is pursuing her research in the area of Information Security. She has published nearly 9 papers in reputed International Journal & Conferences. She serves as a reviewer of various renowned International Journals and Conferences.

Anitha Natarajan is an Assistant Professor in the Department of Information Technology, Kongu Engineering College. She is pursuing PhD from Anna University, Chennai. She has published 10 papers in national and international conferences and journals. Her research interests are machine learning techniques, data science, prescriptive analytics and nature inspired optimization techniques.

Chitra P is Professor in Department of Computer Science & Engineering, Thiagarajar College of Engineering. She completed her B.E from Madurai Kamaraj University during 1995; subsequently she worked as lecturer and completed her M.E and Ph.D in CSE during 2004 and 2011, respectively. She is a reviewer for many national and international peer reviewed journals and member of technical program committee for many IEEE national and international conferences. She has under her credits many publications in reputed international conferences and journals in the areas of distributed systems, cloud computing, Multicore architectures.

Karthikeyan P. obtained his the Bachelor of Engineering (B.E.,) in Computer Science and Engineering from Anna University, Chennai, and Tamil nadu, India in 2005 and received his Master of Engineering (M.E,) in Computer Science and Engineering from Anna University, Coimbatore India in 2009. He is currently working as Assistant Professor in CSE Department of Karunya Institute of Technology and Sciences. He has completed Ph.D. degree in Anna University, Chennai in 2018. His research area includes cloud computing and machine learning.

Suresh P. is currently working as Associate Professor in the Department of Information Technology, Kongu Engineering College, Perundurai, Erode. He has a work experience of 13 years in teaching. He has completed his Ph.D in Anna University, Chennai. He is contributing towards research in the area of Grid and Cloud Computing for the past 9 years. He has published 24 research papers in reputed journals indexed by Scopus and SCI and presented 25 papers in National and International Conferences. His areas of interest are Networks, Cloud Computing and Big data. Currently he is working in the areas of Machine Learning and IoT. He is one of the recognized Supervisors in the Faculty of Information and Communication Engineering under Anna University, Chennai. He is currently guiding Ph.D scholars in the areas of Machine Learning and Cloud. He has received grants from various funding agencies like DRDO, ICMR, and CSIR towards the conduct of seminars and workshops. He has received Best Faculty Award from Kongu Engineering College. He is currently acting as Reviewer and Editorial Board member in reputed journals.

Swathypriyadharsini P. is working as a Assistant Professor at Bannari Amman Institute of Technology, Erode, Tamil Nadu. She completed her Master of Engineering in Computer Science Engineering (CSE) at Bannari Amman Institute of Technology, Erode, Tamil Nadu, India and Bachelor of Engineering in CSE at Avinashilingam University, Coimbatore, Tamil Nadu, India. Her research interests include data mining, soft computing, machine learning and artificial intelligence.

Natesan Palanisamy has completed his Ph.D., degree in Network security in 2013 in Anna University. Currently he is a Professor in the department of Computer Science & Engineering in Kongu Engineering

College, Tamilnadu, India. He has completed 22 years of teaching service. He has published 17 articles in International /National Journals. He has authored 1 book chapter with reputed publishers. He is serving as a Editorial/Advisory board member for many Journals. He has completed 4 funded projects and organized 7 funded seminars and workshops.

Bhushan Patil has done Master of Engineering in Electronics and Telecommunication. He has worked as an Automation engineer. He has various International Conference Paper Publications published under his name. He is an active Research Scholar. He is currently writing various chapters for different publication houses and along with it he is also a Reviewer and Editorial Review Board Member of more than 30 International Journals. He is also currently editing a book which shall be published next year.

K. Premalatha is currently working as a Professor in the Department of Computer Science and Engineering at Bannari Amman Institute of Technology, Erode, Tamil Nadu, India. She completed her Ph. D. in Computer Science and Engineering (CSE) at Anna University, Chennai, India. She did her Master of Engineering in CSE and Bachelor of Engineering in CSE at Bharathiar University, Coimbatore, Tamil Nadu, India. She has 24 years of teaching experience in academic field. She published 92 papers in national and international journals and presented more than 20 papers in international and national conferences. Her research interests include data mining and soft computing.

Arul Murugan R. is currently working as an Assistant Professor in Computer Science and Engineering Department at Sona College of Technology, Salem, Tamil Nadu, India. He received his Bachelor degree in Information Technology from K.S.R College of Engineering, Namakkal with First Class. He obtained his Master degree in Information Technology from K.S.R College of Engineering, Namakkal with distinction. He has worked in web application development, Big Data and Machine Learning projects in the industry. His areas of specialization include Internet of Things, Cloud Computing and Machine Learning. He has published three papers in International Journals. He has also participated in various National-level Workshops and Seminars conducted by various reputed organization.

R. Rajagopal was born in Salem district of Tamilnadu, India. He completed PhD in Anna University, Chennai, India. He received ME-CSE degree from Anna University of Technology, Coimbatore in 2009 and B.E-CSE degree from Anna University, Chennai, India in 2005. His area of Research is Cloud Computing, Operating System, Software Engineering, High Performance Computing. Currently he is working as a Associate Professor in Department of CSE, Vel Tech Multi Tech Dr. Rangarajan Dr. Sakunthala Engineering College, Avadi, India.

Devi Priya Rangasamy is an Associate Professor in the Department of Information Technology, Kongu Engineering College. She has received her PhD from Anna University, Chennai in 2013. She has published about 75 papers in national and international conferences and journals. Her research interests are data warehousing and mining and nature inspired algorithms.

Mamata Rath, M.Tech, Ph.D (Comp.Sc), has twelve years of experience in teaching as well as in research and her research interests include Mobile Adhoc Networks, Internet of Things, Ubiquitous Computing, VANET, Social Network, IoT, Big Data, and Computer Security.

Anitha Elavarasi S received the B.E. and M.E degree in Computer Science and Engineering from Anna University, India, in 2003 and 2007 respectively. She completed her Ph.D. degrees in ICE from Anna University, India, in 2016. She worked as a lecturer and later become an Assistant professor in the Department of Computer Science and Engineering, at Sona College of Technology, Salem, Tamilnadu, India.. Her area of research includes data mining, clustering techniques and machine learning. She has published nine papers in International Journals. She has also participated in various National-level Workshops and Seminars conducted by various reputed organization. She has more than 12 years of teaching experiences.

Indumathi S. obtained her B.E degree in Electronics and Communication Engineering from than-gavelu engineering college, Chennai and Master's degree from Anna University with first class in 2009. She is currently working as Assistant Professor in Jerusalem College of Engineering in the department of Information Technology, Chennai. She has 10 years of teaching experience. She is passionate towards innovative projects and has guided many students in the field of Networks, Artificial intelligence, etc.

Kannimuthu S. is currently working as Associate Professor in the Department of CSE at Karpagam College of Engineering, Coimbatore, Tamil Nadu, India. He is also an In-Charge for the Center of Excellence in Algorithms. He did PhD in Computer Science and Engineering at Anna University, Chennai. He did his M.E (CSE) and B.Tech (IT) at Anna University, Chennai. He has more than 12 years of teaching and industrial experience. He is the recognized supervisor of Anna University, Chennai. One PhD candidate is completed her research under his guidance. He is now guiding 7 PhD Research Scholars. He has published 34 research articles in various International Journals. He published 1 book on "Artificial Intelligence" and 2 Book Chapters (Web of Science). He has presented a number of papers in various National and International conferences. He has visited more than 45 Engineering colleges and delivered more than 80 Guest Lectures on various topics. He is the reviewer for 6 Journals and 3 Books. He has successfully completed the consultancy project through Industry-Institute Interaction for ZF Wind Power Antwerpen Ltd., Belgium. He has received fund Rs. 70,000 from DRDO and ISRO to conduct two workshops and one seminar. He has guided a number of research-oriented as well as application oriented projects organized by well known companies like IBM. He is actively involving in setting up lab for Cloud Computing, Big Data Analytics, Open Source Software, Internet Technologies etc., His research interests include Artificial Intelligence, Data Structures and Algorithms, Machine Learning, Big Data Analytics, Component Based Enterprise Software Development, Web Technologies, Web Services and Open Source Software.

Rajkumar S. is currently working as a Senior Technical Lead in Engineering and R&D Services, HCL Technologies Ltd., India. He has done his Big Data Analytics (BDA) from Indian Institute of Management, Bangalore (IIMB) and he is pursuing an M. Tech in Data Analytics specialization from BITS Pilani. He has over 15 years of rich industry experience in Automating the complex jobs using NLP / Machine Learning / RPA with Python/Java/Hive/Spark/.net/MSSQL/MYSQL in the field of Data Mining /Text processing.

Savitha S. is an Assistant Professor in the Department of Computer Science and Engineering, K.S.R. College of Engineering (Autonomous), India. She received her Master of Engineering degree in Computer Science and Engineering in 2012 from Anna University, Chennai, India. She is a Research scholar in

Anna University, Chennai. She has published more than 15 papers in referred journals and conference proceedings. Her research interest includes Data Mining, Big Data, Cloud computing, Databases and Artificial Intelligence. She is a professional member of ISTE.

Sumathi S. obtained her B.E degree in Computer science and Engineering from GCE, Tirunelveli in 2000, and Master's degree from Sathyabama University with distinction in 2009. She received her Doctorate from Anna University in January 2017. She is currently working as Associate Professor in St.Joseph's College of Engineering in the department of Information Technology, Chennai. She has 15 years of teaching experience. She has published 12 papers in journal and International conferences. From 2000 to 2002, she worked as an embedded software engineer and completed several projects for NIOT-Chennai. She is passionate towards innovative projects and has guided many students in the field of Networks, Artificial intelligence etc. She has also mentored students in competitions such as Smart India Hackathon and Nokia Technology Day. She has been invited as session chair for many international conferences. Her student's project has been nominated for CTS best project and also for INAE award. She is an active Doctoral Committee member through which she has provided guidance to those carrying out research.

Velliangiri S. obtained his Bachelor's in Computer Science and Engineering from Anna University, Chennai. Master's in Computer Science and Engineering from karpagam University, Coimbatore and Doctor of Philosophy in Information and Communication Engineering from Anna University, Chennai. Currently he is working as a Associate Professor in CMR Institute of Technology, Hyderabad, Telangana. He was a member of Institute of Electrical and Electronics Engineers (IEEE) and International Association of Engineers (IAENG). He is specialized in Network security and Optimization techniques. He published ten International journals and presented five International conferences. He was the reviewer of Springer, Inderscience and reputed scopus indexed journals.

Praylin Selva Blessy S. A. received her B.E. degree in Electronics and Communication Engineering from C.S.I. Institute of Engineering, Thovalai in 2006 .She received her M.E. degree from Noorul Islam College of Engineering, Kumaracoil in 2008. She received her PhD degree in Information and Communication Engineering at Anna University, Chennai in 2018.Her research interests include image processing, medical imaging and pattern recognition. She has published papers in International Journals.

Shaila S. G. is an Associate Professor in the Department of Computer Science & Engineering in Dayananda Sagar University. She did her Ph. D. from National Institute of Technology, Tiruchirapalli, Tamil Nadu in the area of Multimedia Information Retrieval in Distributed System. She has totally 14 years of teaching and research experience. She has also worked for Central Power Research Institute as a Trainee Engineer for one year and later she worked as a Junior Research Fellow for DST project for the period of 2 year 8 months. She has also worked as a member of Student Exchange program for the "Obama-Singh Knowledge Initiative Program UNLV, Las Vegas, US ", an Indo-US collaborated Project. Her areas of interest are Information Retrieval, Image Processing, Cognitive Science and Pattern Recognition.

D. Sudaroli conducts cross functional knowledge training with well renowned corporates and believes the power of teaching is one exclusive sign of knowledge. She has taught operating systems, computer networks, computer organization, testing and various programming languages. She is a Cisco Certified Professional and her roots in the corporate sector is with Tata Consultancy Services with some noteworthy awards like fast tracker and 'let's clone you'. Her corporate training experience includes many corporates including Wipro Technologies, Tata Tele Services etc. She has got the creditability from the Photonic University-Sweden. Her research interests are in the areas of machine learning, digital forensics, network security, wireless networks.

C. Helen Sulochana is Professor in the Department of Electronics and Communication Engineering at St.Xaviers Catholic College of Engineering, Nagercoil, India. She received her B.E. degree from Madurai Kamaraj University, India, M.Tech. degree from University of Kerala, India and Ph.D degree from Anna University Chennai, India. She has published papers in International Journals and conference proceedings. She is reviewer of several International journals and books. She has organized conferences and workshops. Her area of interest includes Digital image processing, cellular networks and computer vision.

Rajkumari Sunanda is pusuing her Mtech degree in Computer Science and Engineering in Dayananda Sagar University. She has main interest domain is deep learning, cloud computing, IOT and robotics. She has attended a conference on the topic "Cloud based File Sharing" on International Conference on Recent Trends in Technology ICRTT – 2018 in Collaboration with IJCA. She had published a paper on the same topic on "Cloud based File Sharing" Novateur Publications International Journal Of Innovations In Engineering Research And Technology [IJIERT].

Jeyakrishnan V received his Bachelor of Technology (B.Tech.) in Information Technology from Anna University, Chennai, Tamilnadu, India in 2006 and Master of Technology (M.Tech.) in Information Technology from Anna University, Coimbatore, India in 2010 .He also received his PhD from Anna University in 2017, has served in the field of education for over 12 years and he has served in the IT industry for nearly 2 years. Currently he is working as Associate Professor in the Department of Computer Science and Engineering, SAINTGITS College of Engineering, Kottayam, Kerala, India. He has published 16 International Journals, 8 International Conferences and 3 National level conference papers. His Area of research in Machine Learning, Deep Learning, Cloud Computing, Optimization Technology and Big data.

Naksha V is an MTECH student in the Department of Computer Science & Engineering in Dayananda Sagar University. She did her Bachelor of Engineering from Tjhon Institute of Technology,Banglore, karnataka in the feild of Computer Science and Engineering. She is currently pursuing mtech under the guidance of Dr. S.G Shaila. Her areas of interest are Machine learning,IOT,Data analytics.

Karunakaran V. received B.E.degree from Mahendra Engineering College and M.E. degree from National Engineering College. He is pursuing Ph.D. degree from anna University, Chennai, India. Currently working as an Assistant Professor in the department of Computer Science and Engineering, Karunya Institute of Technology and Sciences. His area of interest is in the field of Data Mining, Machine Learning and Big Data Analytics.

Sudha V is working as Assistant Professor II in Department Computer Science & Engineering at Kumaraguru College of Technology, Coimbatore, Tamilnadu, India. She received her BE degree in Computer Science and Engineering from VMKV Engineering College, Salem and ME degree in Computer Science and Engineering from CEG Campus, Anna University. She is currently pursuing her Ph.D at Anna University in the area of Theoretical Computer Science.

Manisha Vohra has done Master of Engineering in Electronics and Telecommunication. She has various International Conference Paper Publications published under her name. She is an active Research Scholar. She is currently writing various chapters for different publication houses and along with it she is also a Reviewer and Editorial Review Board Member of more than 25 International journals. She is also currently editing a book which shall be published next year.

Index

Ensure Quality Research is Introduced to the Academic Community

Become an IGI Global Reviewer for Authored Book Projects

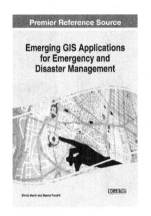 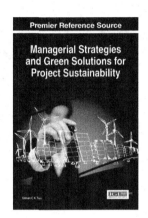  

The overall success of an authored book project is dependent on quality and timely reviews.

In this competitive age of scholarly publishing, constructive and timely feedback significantly expedites the turnaround time of manuscripts from submission to acceptance, allowing the publication and discovery of forward-thinking research at a much more expeditious rate. Several IGI Global authored book projects are currently seeking highly-qualified experts in the field to fill vacancies on their respective editorial review boards:

Applications and Inquiries may be sent to:
development@igi-global.com

Applicants must have a doctorate (or an equivalent degree) as well as publishing and reviewing experience. Reviewers are asked to complete the open-ended evaluation questions with as much detail as possible in a timely, collegial, and constructive manner. All reviewers' tenures run for one-year terms on the editorial review boards and are expected to complete at least three reviews per term. Upon successful completion of this term, reviewers can be considered for an additional term.

If you have a colleague that may be interested in this opportunity,
we encourage you to share this information with them.

Printed in the United States
By Bookmasters